Van Helsing
vs. Frankenstein

Writer **PAT SHAND**

Artwork **LEONARDO COLAPIETRO**

Colors **SLAMET MUJIONO**

Flashback Illustrations **ROBERTA INGRANATA**

Letters **JIM CAMPBELL**

Editor **PAT SHAND**

Art Direction & Design **CHRISTOPHER COTE**

Cover Art **RICHARD ORTIZ**
VLENIA DI NAPOLI

Grimm Universe created by **JOE BRUSHA**
RALPH TEDESCO

This volume reprints Van Helsing vs. Frankenstein 1-5 published by Zenescope Entertainment.
First Edition, August 2017 • ISBN: 978-1942275510

WWW.ZENESCOPE.COM

Joe Brusha President & Chief Creative Officer
Christopher Cote Art Director
Dave Franchini Assistant Editor
Jessica Rossana Assistant Editor
Ashley Vanacore Graphic Designer

Jennifer Bermel Director of Business Development
Jason Condeelis Direct Market Sales & Customer Service
Adam Kelly Marketing & Social Media Manager
Kirby Kistler VIP & Consumer Sales Manager
Stu Kropnick Operations Manager
Ralph Tedesco VP Film & Television

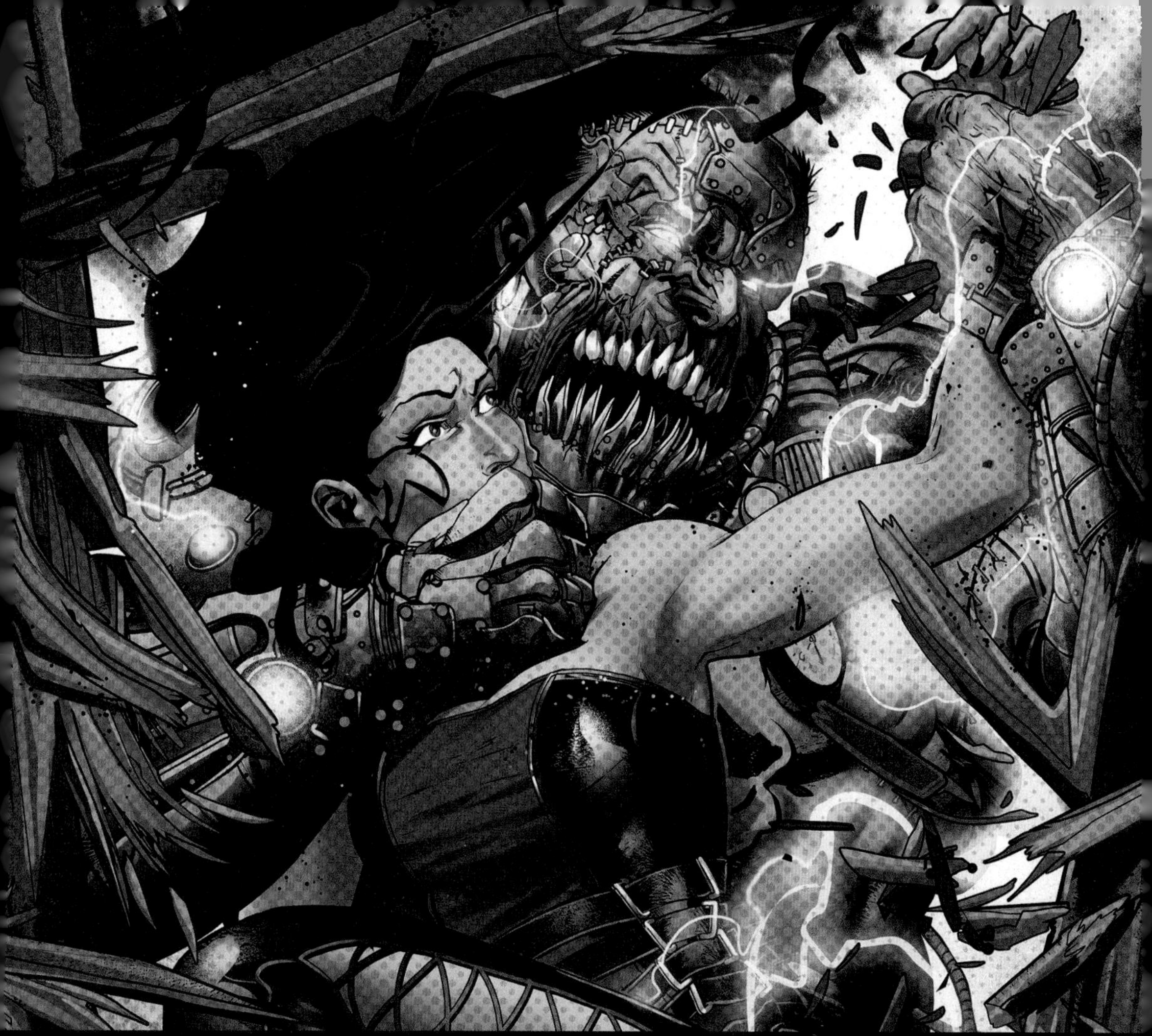

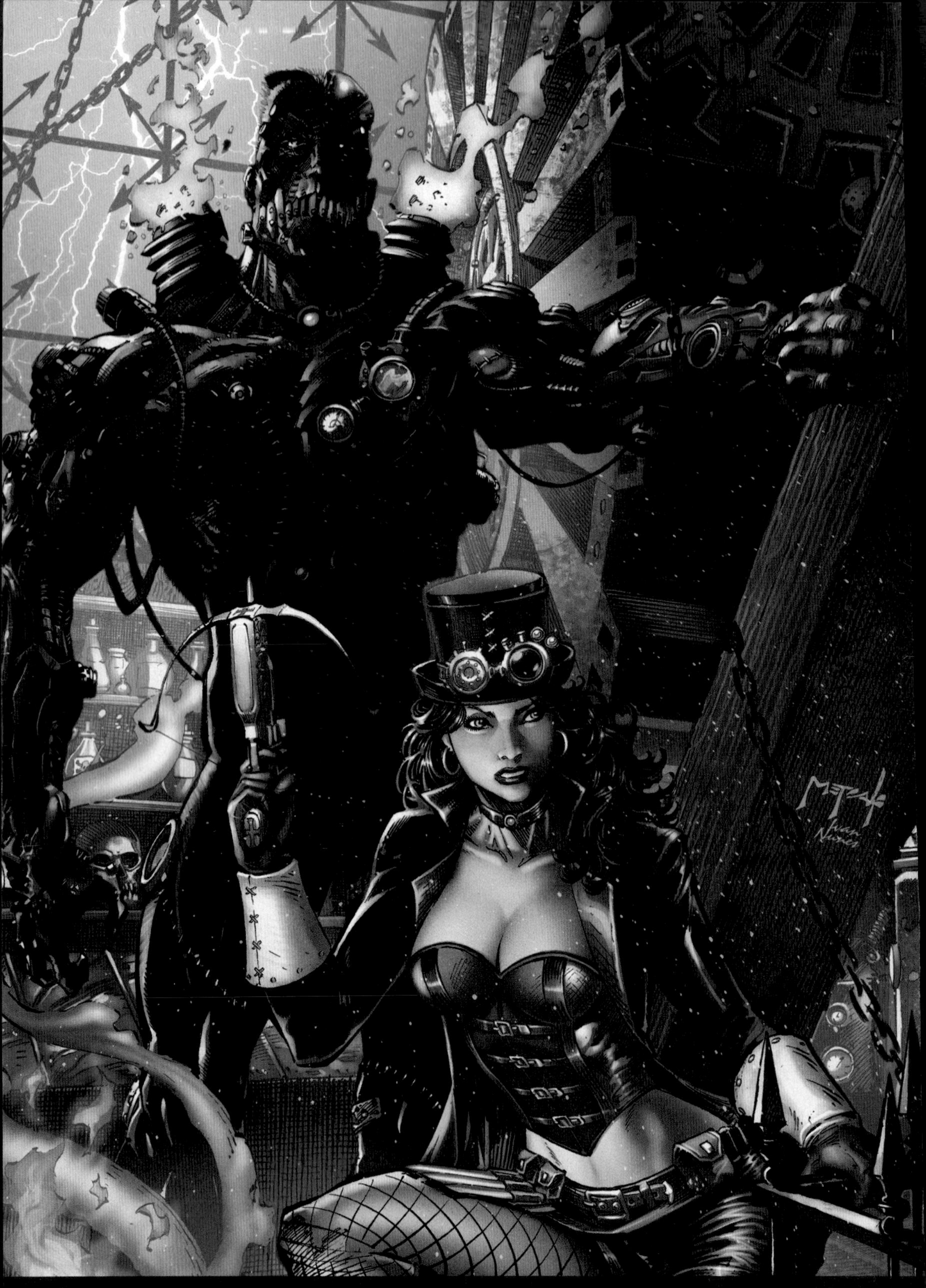

CHAPTER ONE

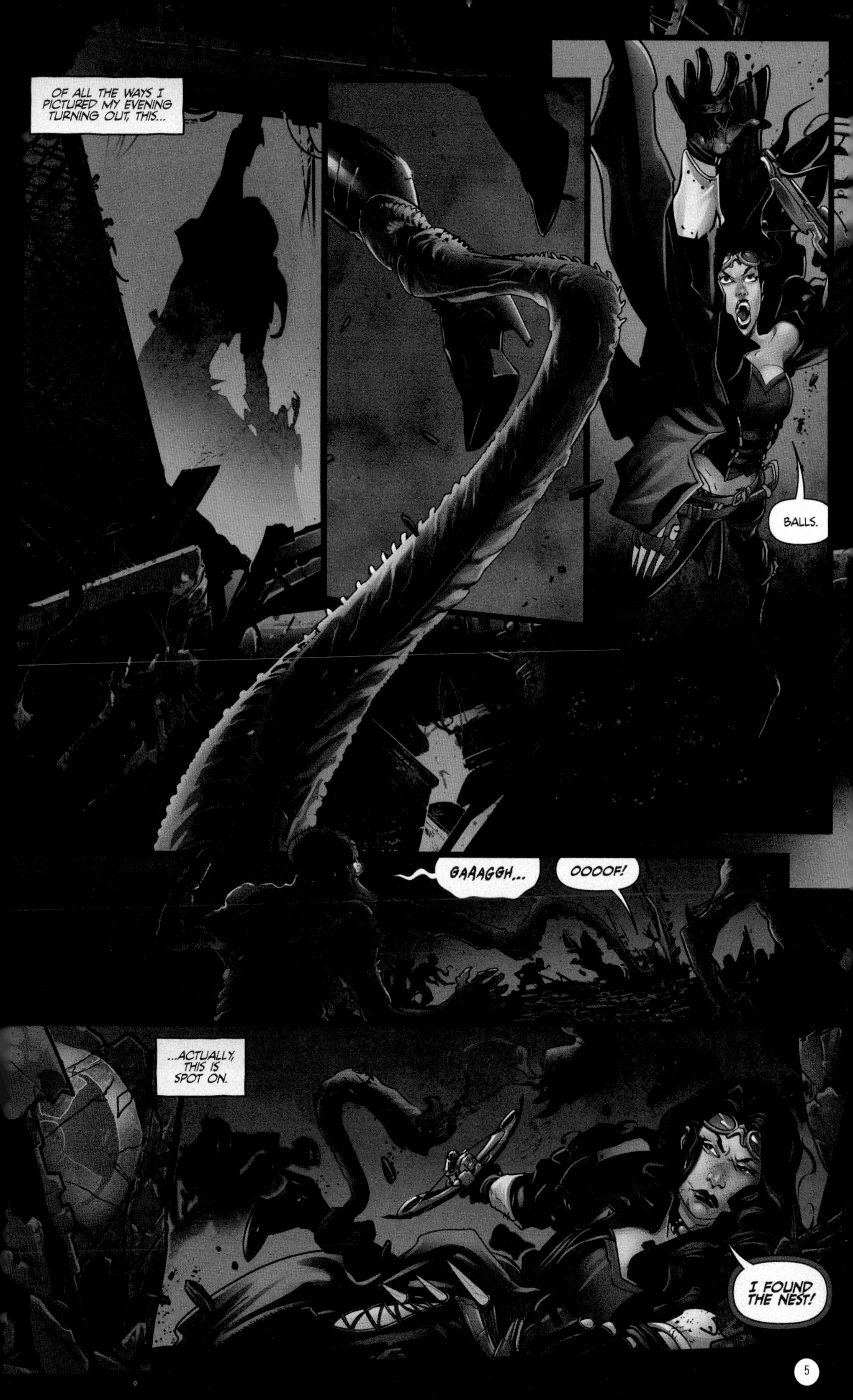
OF ALL THE WAYS I PICTURED MY EVENING TURNING OUT, THIS...
BALLS.
GAAAGGH...
OOOOF!
...ACTUALLY, THIS IS SPOT ON.
I FOUND THE NEST!

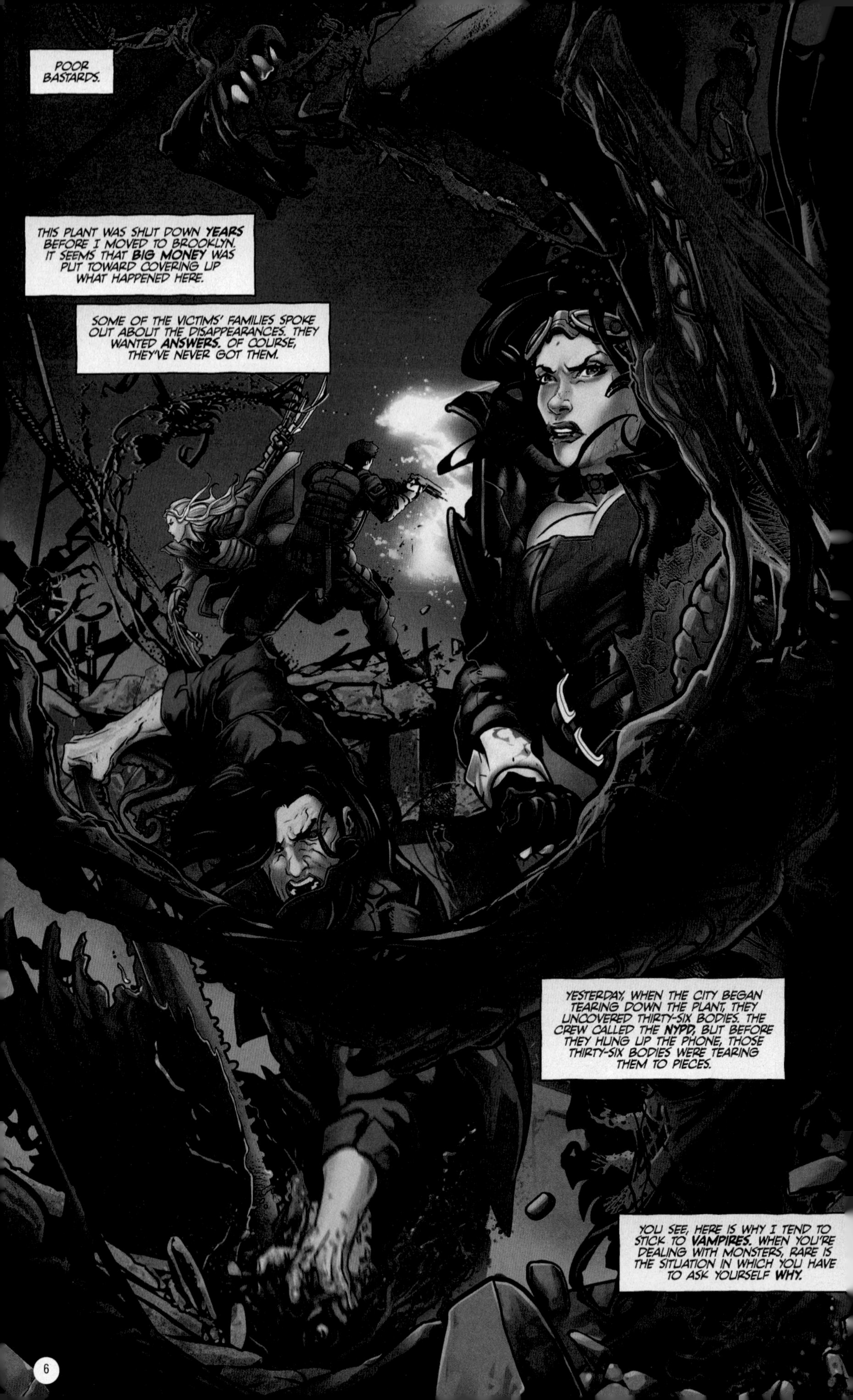

POOR BASTARDS.
THIS PLANT WAS SHUT DOWN **YEARS** BEFORE I MOVED TO BROOKLYN. IT SEEMS THAT **BIG MONEY** WAS PUT TOWARD COVERING UP WHAT HAPPENED HERE.
SOME OF THE VICTIMS' FAMILIES SPOKE OUT ABOUT THE DISAPPEARANCES. THEY WANTED **ANSWERS.** OF COURSE, THEY'VE NEVER GOT THEM.
YESTERDAY, WHEN THE CITY BEGAN TEARING DOWN THE PLANT, THEY UNCOVERED THIRTY-SIX BODIES. THE CREW CALLED THE **NYPD,** BUT BEFORE THEY HUNG UP THE PHONE, THOSE THIRTY-SIX BODIES WERE TEARING THEM TO PIECES.
YOU SEE, HERE IS WHY I TEND TO STICK TO **VAMPIRES.** WHEN YOU'RE DEALING WITH MONSTERS, RARE IS THE SITUATION IN WHICH YOU HAVE TO ASK YOURSELF **WHY.**

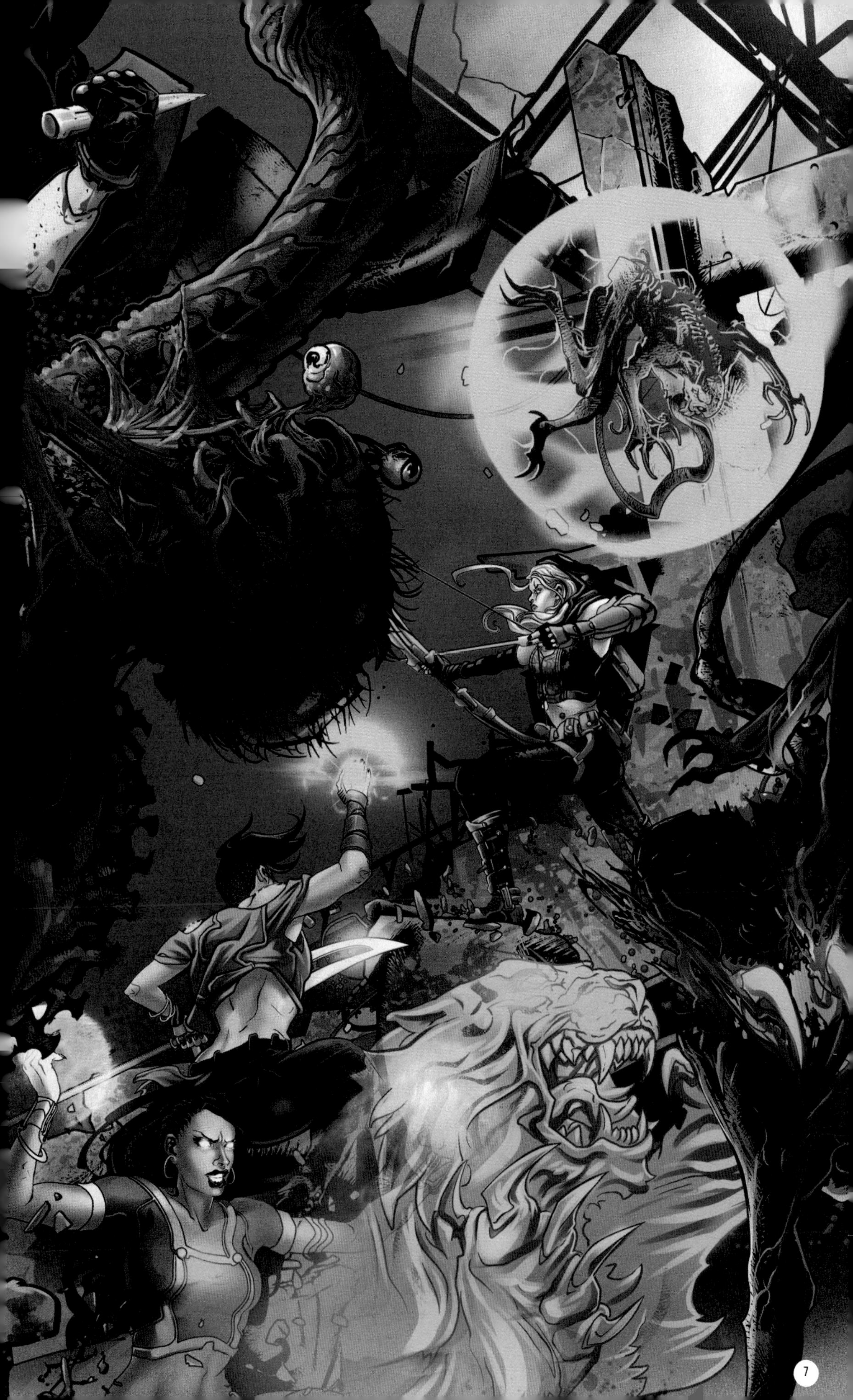

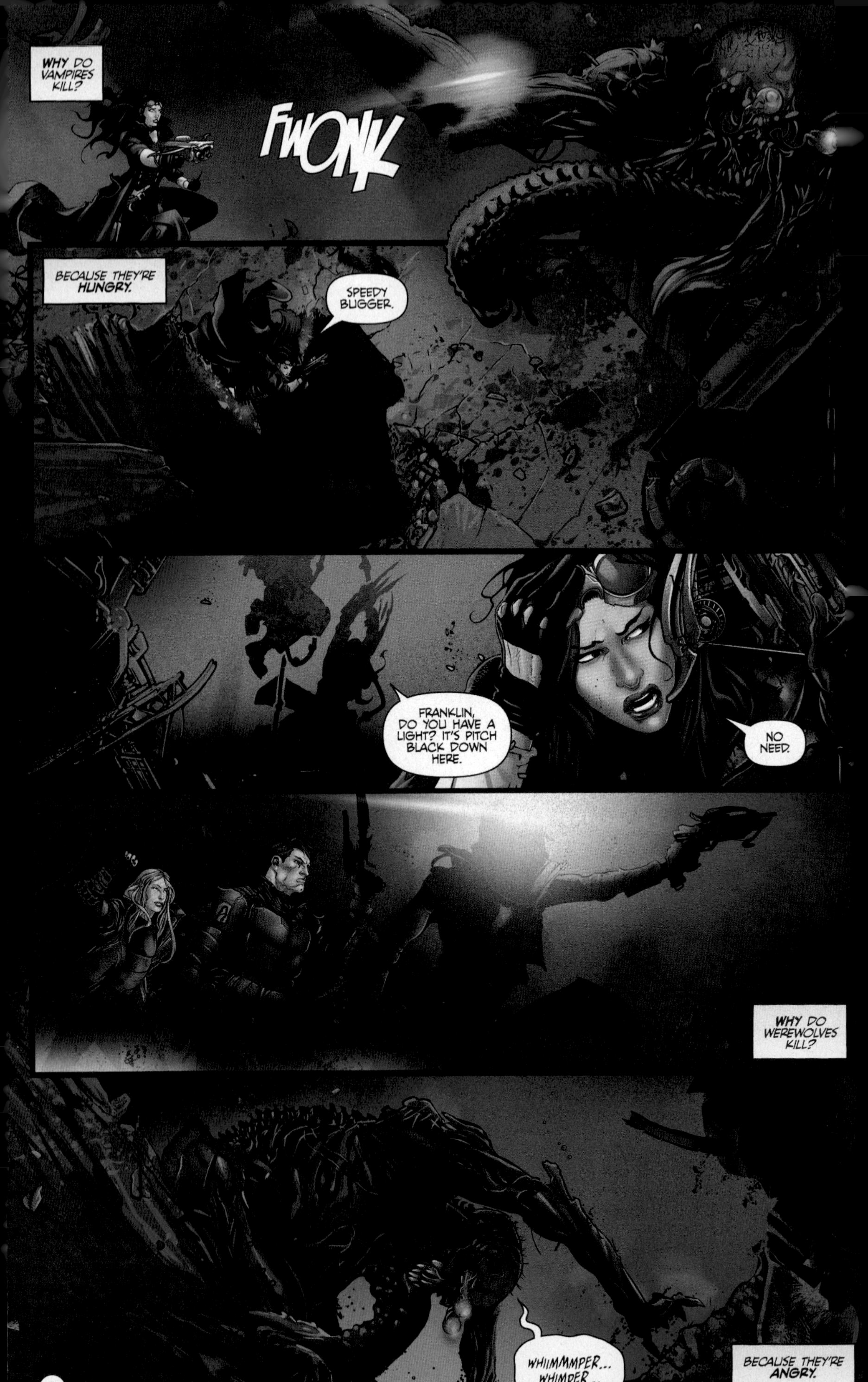
WHY DO VAMPIRES KILL?
FWONK
BECAUSE THEY'RE HUNGRY.
SPEEDY BUGGER.
FRANKLIN, DO YOU HAVE A LIGHT? IT'S PITCH BLACK DOWN HERE.
NO NEED.
WHY DO WEREWOLVES KILL?
WHIIMMMPER... WHIMPER...
BECAUSE THEY'RE ANGRY.

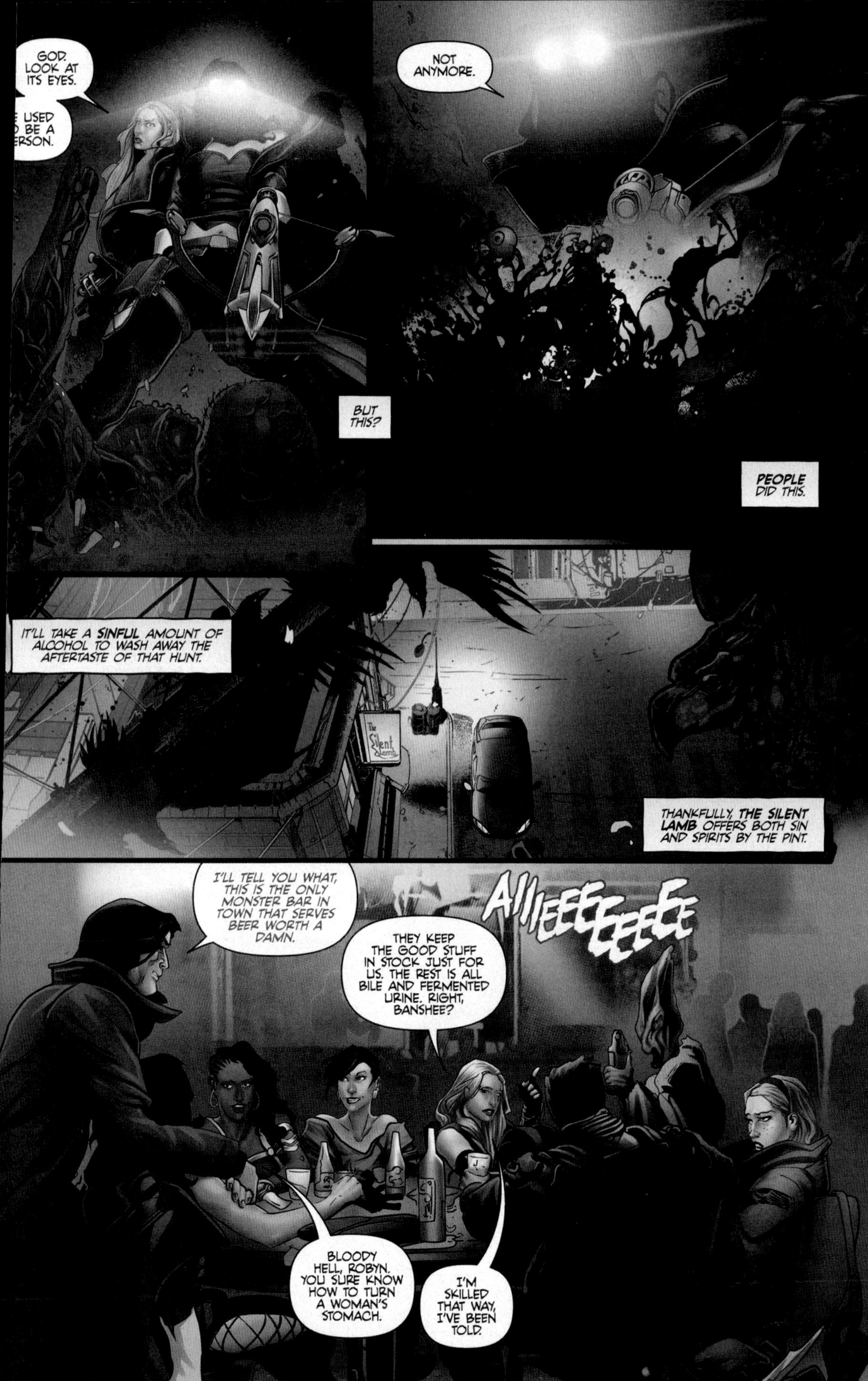
GOD. LOOK AT ITS EYES.
E USED D BE A ERSON.
NOT ANYMORE.
BUT THIS?
PEOPLE DID THIS.
IT'LL TAKE A SINFUL AMOUNT OF ALCOHOL TO WASH AWAY THE AFTERTASTE OF THAT HUNT.
The Silent Lamb
THANKFULLY, THE SILENT LAMB OFFERS BOTH SIN AND SPIRITS BY THE PINT.
I'LL TELL YOU WHAT, THIS IS THE ONLY MONSTER BAR IN TOWN THAT SERVES BEER WORTH A DAMN.
AIIIEEEEEEEEEE
THEY KEEP THE GOOD STUFF IN STOCK JUST FOR US. THE REST IS ALL BILE AND FERMENTED URINE. RIGHT, BANSHEE?
BLOODY HELL, ROBYN. YOU SURE KNOW HOW TO TURN A WOMAN'S STOMACH.
I'M SKILLED THAT WAY, I'VE BEEN TOLD.

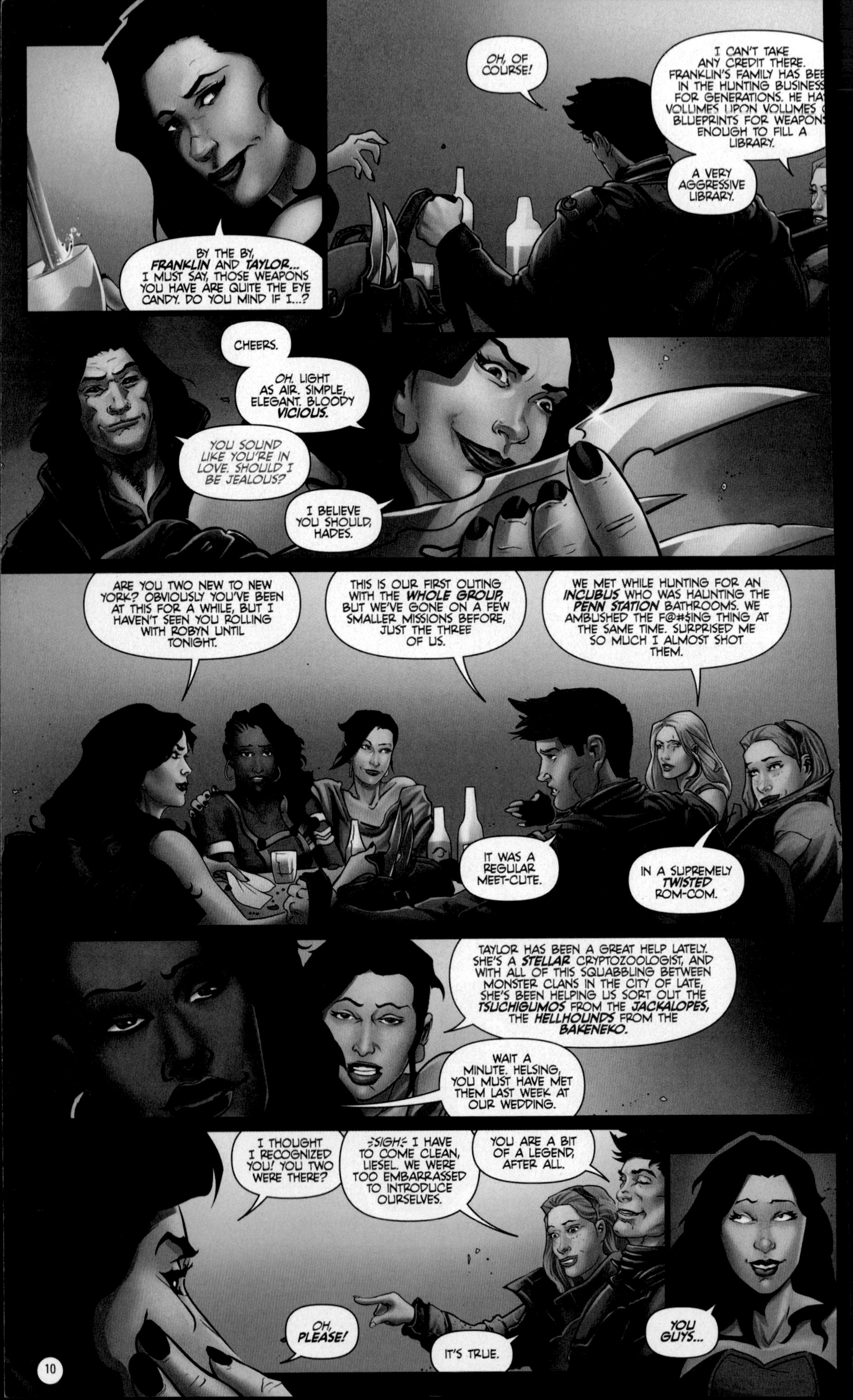

BY THE BY, FRANKLIN AND TAYLOR... I MUST SAY, THOSE WEAPONS YOU HAVE ARE QUITE THE EYE CANDY. DO YOU MIND IF I...?
OH, OF COURSE!
I CAN'T TAKE ANY CREDIT THERE. FRANKLIN'S FAMILY HAS BEE IN THE HUNTING BUSINES FOR GENERATIONS. HE HA VOLUMES UPON VOLUMES O BLUEPRINTS FOR WEAPON ENOUGH TO FILL A LIBRARY.
A VERY AGGRESSIVE LIBRARY.
CHEERS.
OH. LIGHT AS AIR. SIMPLE, ELEGANT. BLOODY VICIOUS.
YOU SOUND LIKE YOU'RE IN LOVE. SHOULD I BE JEALOUS?
I BELIEVE YOU SHOULD, HADES.
ARE YOU TWO NEW TO NEW YORK? OBVIOUSLY YOU'VE BEEN AT THIS FOR A WHILE, BUT I HAVEN'T SEEN YOU ROLLING WITH ROBYN UNTIL TONIGHT.
THIS IS OUR FIRST OUTING WITH THE WHOLE GROUP, BUT WE'VE GONE ON A FEW SMALLER MISSIONS BEFORE, JUST THE THREE OF US.
WE MET WHILE HUNTING FOR AN INCUBUS WHO WAS HAUNTING THE PENN STATION BATHROOMS. WE AMBUSHED THE F@#$ING THING AT THE SAME TIME. SURPRISED ME SO MUCH I ALMOST SHOT THEM.
IT WAS A REGULAR MEET-CUTE.
IN A SUPREMELY TWISTED ROM-COM.
TAYLOR HAS BEEN A GREAT HELP LATELY. SHE'S A STELLAR CRYPTOZOOLOGIST, AND WITH ALL OF THIS SQUABBLING BETWEEN MONSTER CLANS IN THE CITY OF LATE, SHE'S BEEN HELPING US SORT OUT THE TSUCHIGUMOS FROM THE JACKALOPES, THE HELLHOUNDS FROM THE BAKENEKO.
WAIT A MINUTE. HELSING, YOU MUST HAVE MET THEM LAST WEEK AT OUR WEDDING.
I THOUGHT I RECOGNIZED YOU! YOU TWO WERE THERE?
SIGH I HAVE TO COME CLEAN, LIESEL. WE WERE TOO EMBARRASSED TO INTRODUCE OURSELVES.
YOU ARE A BIT OF A LEGEND, AFTER ALL.
OH, PLEASE!
IT'S TRUE.
YOU GUYS...

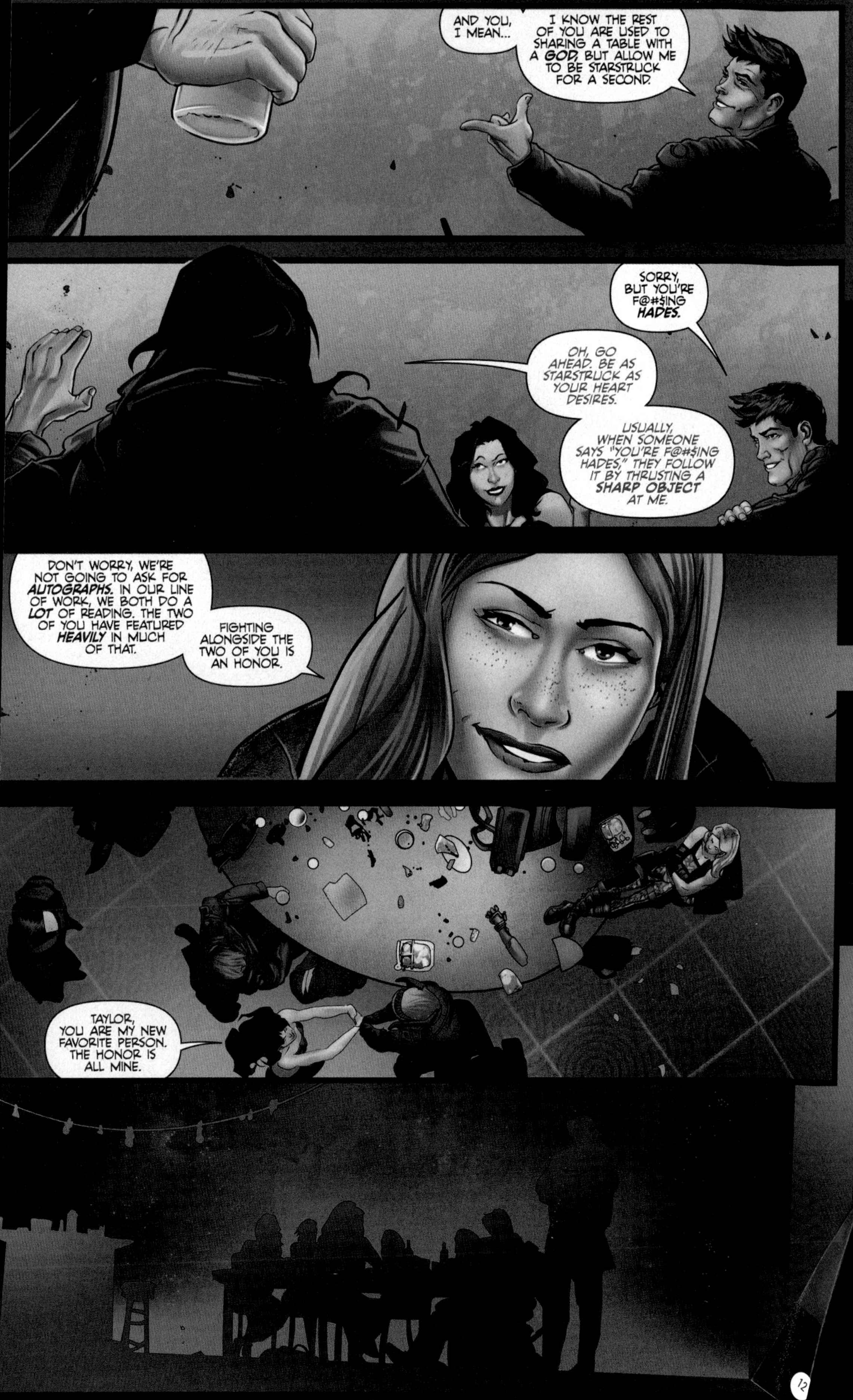

AND YOU, I MEAN...
I KNOW THE REST OF YOU ARE USED TO SHARING A TABLE WITH A GOD, BUT ALLOW ME TO BE STARSTRUCK FOR A SECOND.
SORRY, BUT YOU'RE F@#$ING HADES.
OH, GO AHEAD. BE AS STARSTRUCK AS YOUR HEART DESIRES.
USUALLY, WHEN SOMEONE SAYS "YOU'RE F@#$ING HADES," THEY FOLLOW IT BY THRUSTING A SHARP OBJECT AT ME.
DON'T WORRY, WE'RE NOT GOING TO ASK FOR AUTOGRAPHS. IN OUR LINE OF WORK, WE BOTH DO A LOT OF READING. THE TWO OF YOU HAVE FEATURED HEAVILY IN MUCH OF THAT.
FIGHTING ALONGSIDE THE TWO OF YOU IS AN HONOR.
TAYLOR, YOU ARE MY NEW FAVORITE PERSON. THE HONOR IS ALL MINE.

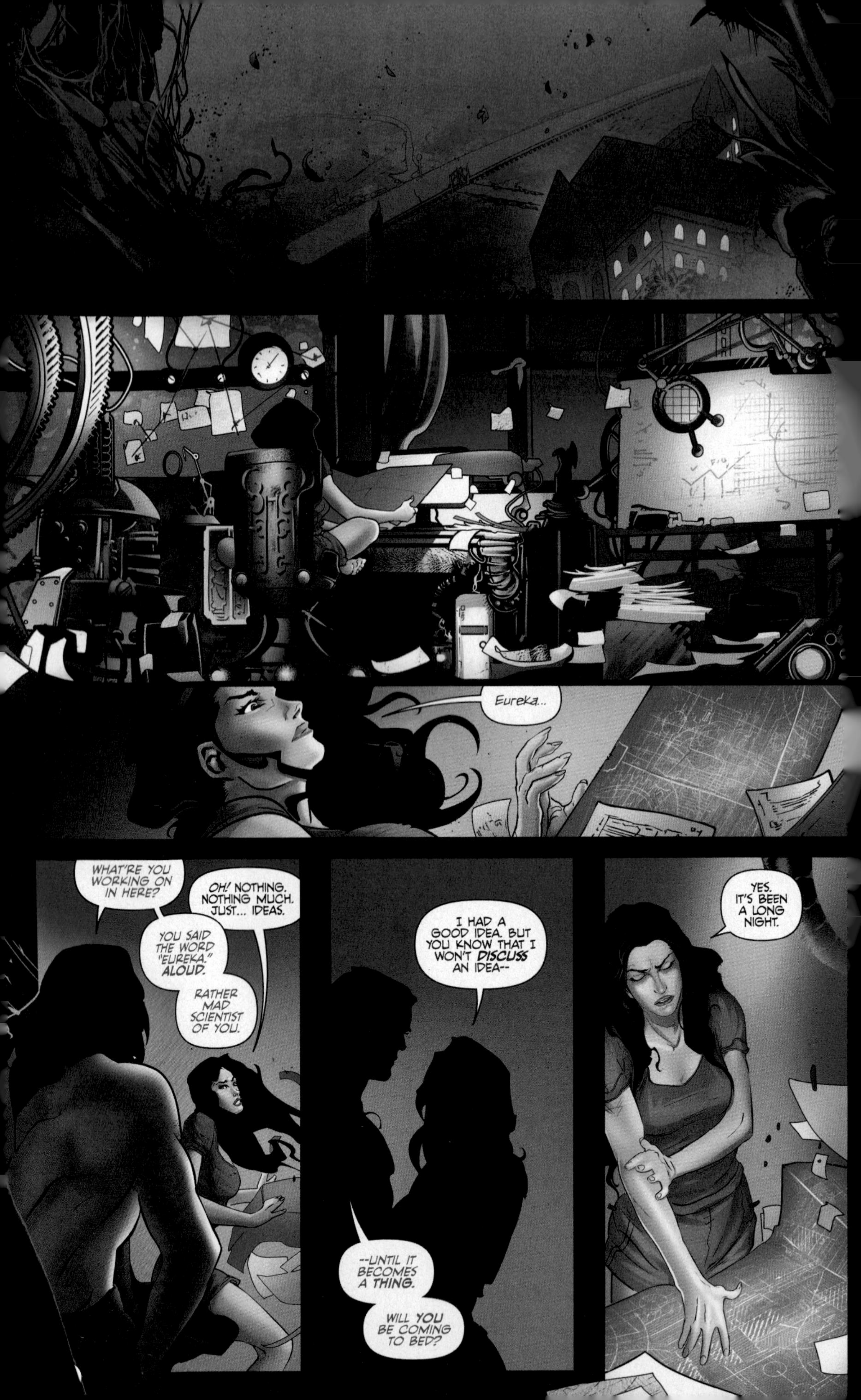
Eureka...
WHAT'RE YOU WORKING ON IN HERE?
OH! NOTHING. NOTHING MUCH. JUST... IDEAS.
YOU SAID THE WORD "EUREKA." ALOUD.
RATHER MAD SCIENTIST OF YOU.
I HAD A GOOD IDEA. BUT YOU KNOW THAT I WON'T DISCUSS AN IDEA--
--UNTIL IT BECOMES A THING.
WILL YOU BE COMING TO BED?
YES. IT'S BEEN A LONG NIGHT.

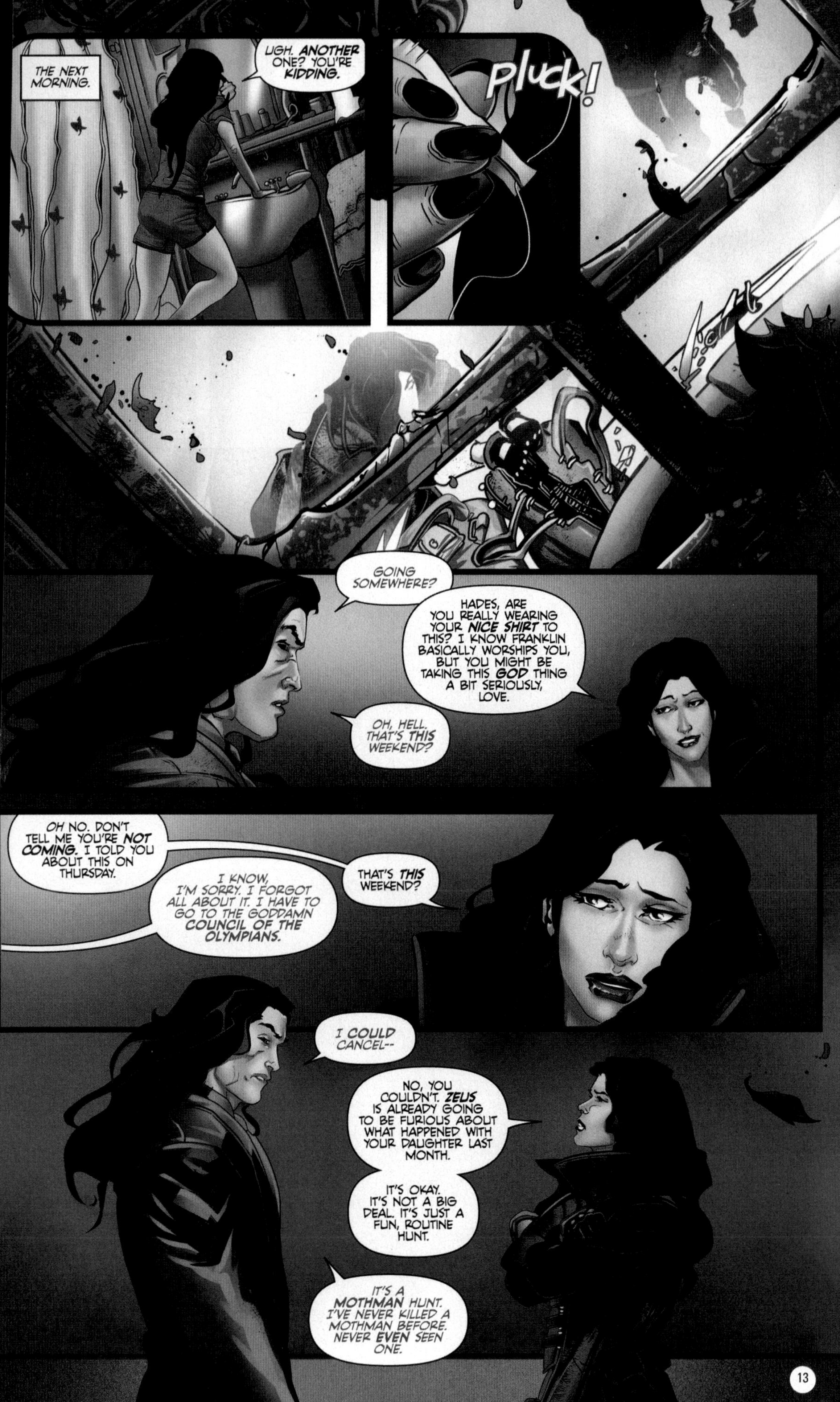
THE NEXT MORNING.
UGH. **ANOTHER** ONE? YOU'RE **KIDDING.**
PLUCK!
GOING SOMEWHERE?
HADES, ARE YOU REALLY WEARING YOUR **NICE SHIRT** TO THIS? I KNOW FRANKLIN BASICALLY WORSHIPS YOU, BUT YOU MIGHT BE TAKING THIS **GOD** THING A BIT SERIOUSLY, LOVE.
OH, HELL. THAT'S **THIS** WEEKEND?
OH NO. DON'T TELL ME YOU'RE **NOT COMING.** I TOLD YOU ABOUT THIS ON THURSDAY.
THAT'S **THIS** WEEKEND?
I KNOW, I'M SORRY. I FORGOT ALL ABOUT IT. I HAVE TO GO TO THE GODDAMN **COUNCIL OF THE OLYMPIANS.**
I **COULD** CANCEL--
NO, YOU COULDN'T. **ZEUS** IS ALREADY GOING TO BE FURIOUS ABOUT WHAT HAPPENED WITH YOUR DAUGHTER LAST MONTH.
IT'S OKAY. IT'S NOT A BIG DEAL. IT'S JUST A FUN, ROUTINE HUNT.
IT'S A **MOTHMAN** HUNT. I'VE NEVER KILLED A MOTHMAN BEFORE. NEVER **EVEN** SEEN ONE.

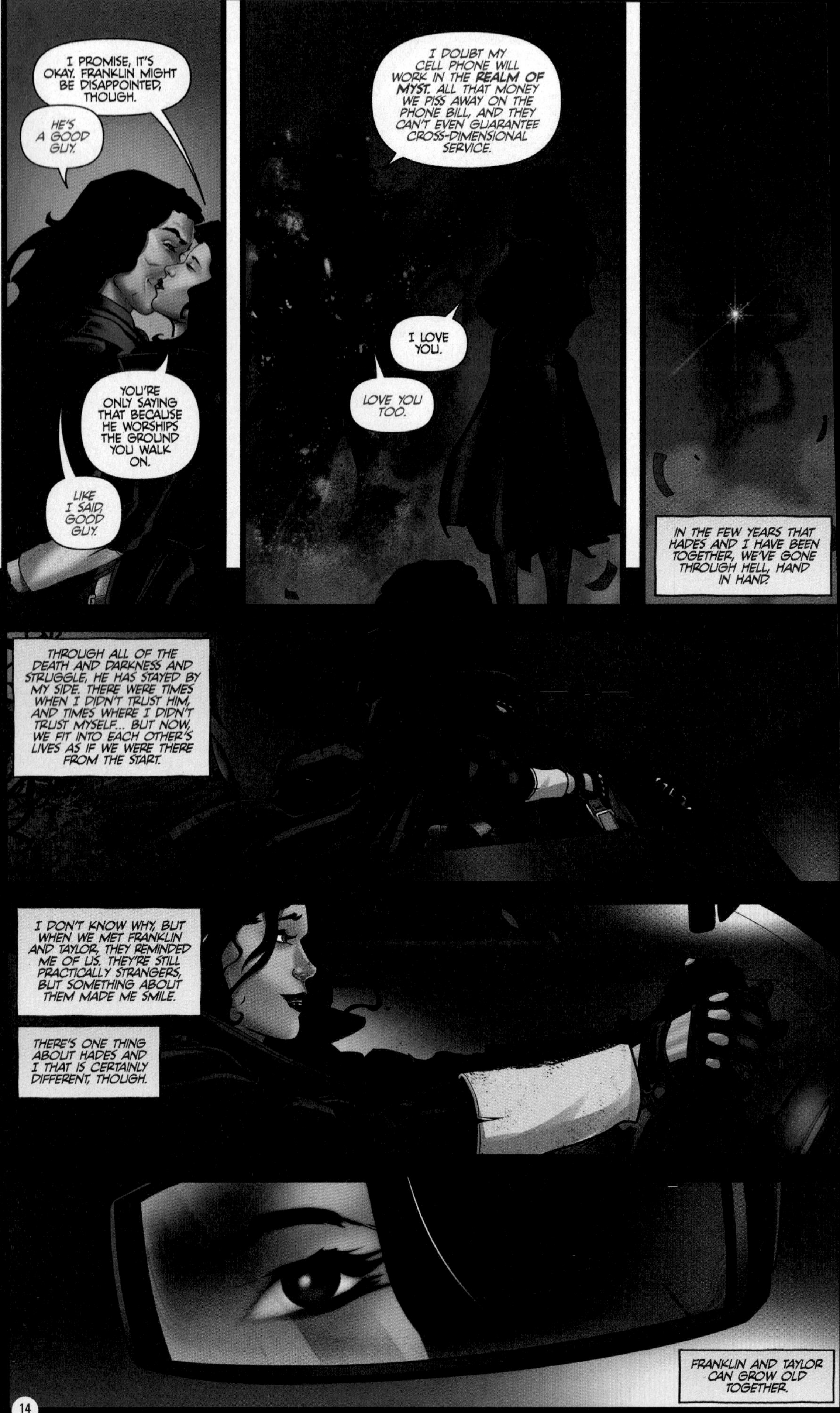

I PROMISE, IT'S OKAY. FRANKLIN MIGHT BE DISAPPOINTED, THOUGH.
HE'S A GOOD GUY.
YOU'RE ONLY SAYING THAT BECAUSE HE WORSHIPS THE GROUND YOU WALK ON.
LIKE I SAID, GOOD GUY.
I DOUBT MY CELL PHONE WILL WORK IN THE REALM OF MYST. ALL THAT MONEY WE PISS AWAY ON THE PHONE BILL, AND THEY CAN'T EVEN GUARANTEE CROSS-DIMENSIONAL SERVICE.
I LOVE YOU.
LOVE YOU TOO.
IN THE FEW YEARS THAT HADES AND I HAVE BEEN TOGETHER, WE'VE GONE THROUGH HELL, HAND IN HAND.
THROUGH ALL OF THE DEATH AND DARKNESS AND STRUGGLE, HE HAS STAYED BY MY SIDE. THERE WERE TIMES WHEN I DIDN'T TRUST HIM, AND TIMES WHERE I DIDN'T TRUST MYSELF... BUT NOW, WE FIT INTO EACH OTHER'S LIVES AS IF WE WERE THERE FROM THE START.
I DON'T KNOW WHY, BUT WHEN WE MET FRANKLIN AND TAYLOR, THEY REMINDED ME OF US. THEY'RE STILL PRACTICALLY STRANGERS, BUT SOMETHING ABOUT THEM MADE ME SMILE.
THERE'S ONE THING ABOUT HADES AND I THAT IS CERTAINLY DIFFERENT, THOUGH.
FRANKLIN AND TAYLOR CAN GROW OLD TOGETHER.

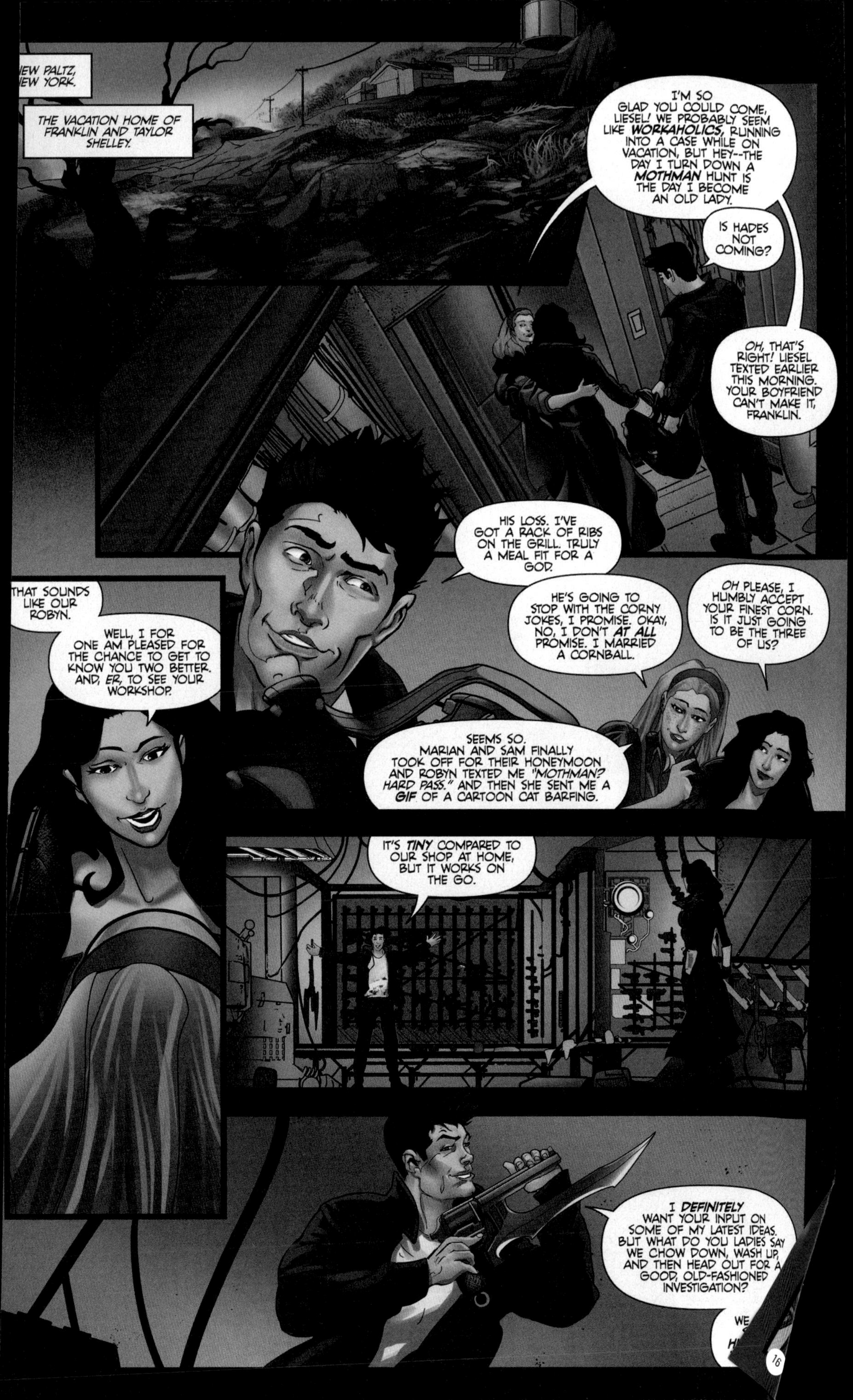

NEW PALTZ, NEW YORK.
THE VACATION HOME OF FRANKLIN AND TAYLOR SHELLEY.
I'M SO GLAD YOU COULD COME, LIESEL! WE PROBABLY SEEM LIKE WORKAHOLICS, RUNNING INTO A CASE WHILE ON VACATION, BUT HEY--THE DAY I TURN DOWN A MOTHMAN HUNT IS THE DAY I BECOME AN OLD LADY.
IS HADES NOT COMING?
OH, THAT'S RIGHT! LIESEL TEXTED EARLIER THIS MORNING. YOUR BOYFRIEND CAN'T MAKE IT, FRANKLIN.
HIS LOSS. I'VE GOT A RACK OF RIBS ON THE GRILL. TRULY A MEAL FIT FOR A GOD.
OH PLEASE, I HUMBLY ACCEPT YOUR FINEST CORN. IS IT JUST GOING TO BE THE THREE OF US?
HE'S GOING TO STOP WITH THE CORNY JOKES, I PROMISE. OKAY, NO, I DON'T AT ALL PROMISE. I MARRIED A CORNBALL.
SEEMS SO. MARIAN AND SAM FINALLY TOOK OFF FOR THEIR HONEYMOON AND ROBYN TEXTED ME "MOTHMAN? HARD PASS." AND THEN SHE SENT ME A GIF OF A CARTOON CAT BARFING.
THAT SOUNDS LIKE OUR ROBYN.
WELL, I FOR ONE AM PLEASED FOR THE CHANCE TO GET TO KNOW YOU TWO BETTER. AND, ER, TO SEE YOUR WORKSHOP.
IT'S TINY COMPARED TO OUR SHOP AT HOME, BUT IT WORKS ON THE GO.
I DEFINITELY WANT YOUR INPUT ON SOME OF MY LATEST IDEAS. BUT WHAT DO YOU LADIES SAY WE CHOW DOWN, WASH UP, AND THEN HEAD OUT FOR A GOOD, OLD-FASHIONED INVESTIGATION?

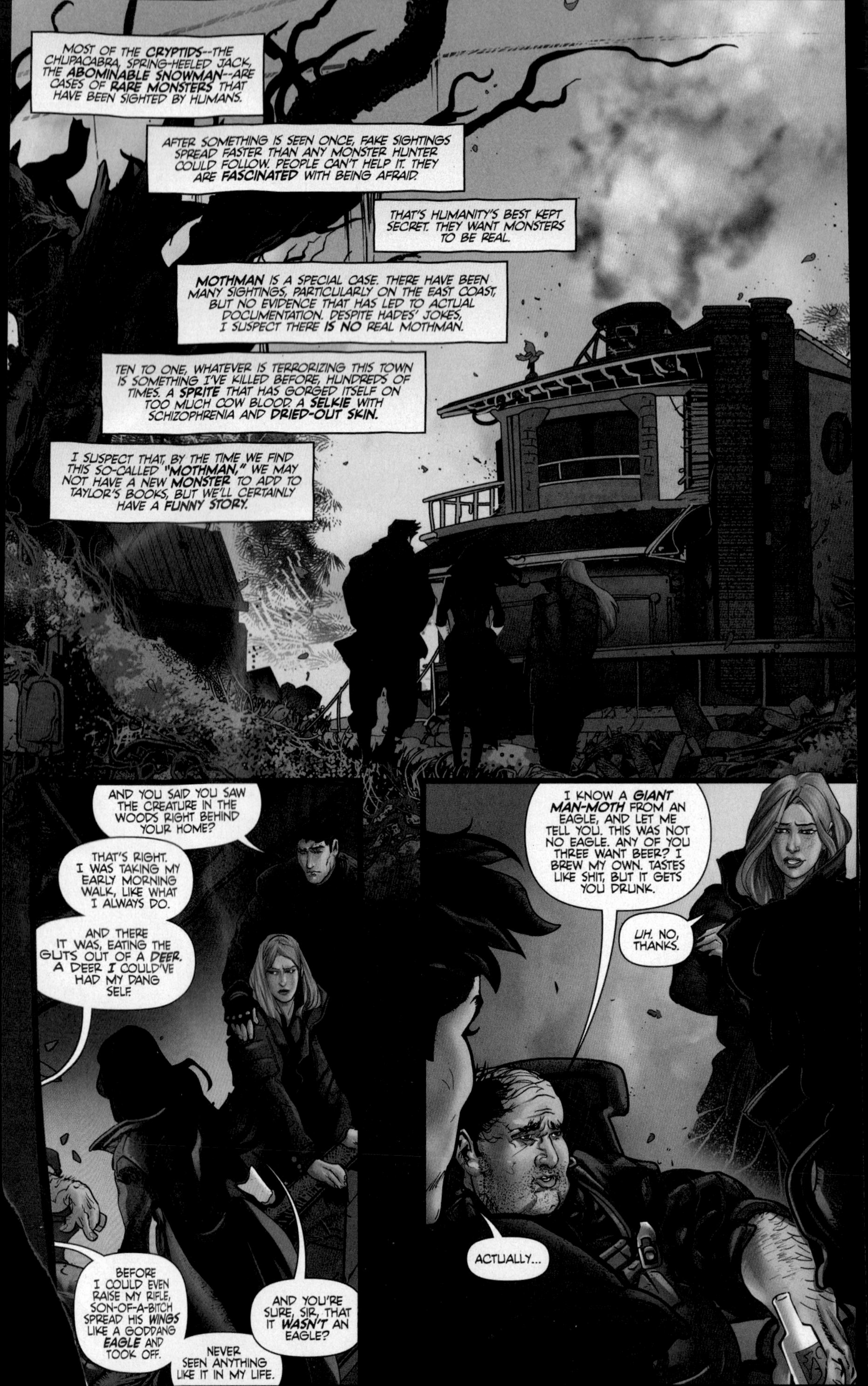
MOST OF THE CRYPTIDS--THE CHUPACABRA, SPRING-HEELED JACK, THE ABOMINABLE SNOWMAN--ARE CASES OF RARE MONSTERS THAT HAVE BEEN SIGHTED BY HUMANS.
AFTER SOMETHING IS SEEN ONCE, FAKE SIGHTINGS SPREAD FASTER THAN ANY MONSTER HUNTER COULD FOLLOW. PEOPLE CAN'T HELP IT. THEY ARE FASCINATED WITH BEING AFRAID.
THAT'S HUMANITY'S BEST KEPT SECRET. THEY WANT MONSTERS TO BE REAL.
MOTHMAN IS A SPECIAL CASE. THERE HAVE BEEN MANY SIGHTINGS, PARTICULARLY ON THE EAST COAST, BUT NO EVIDENCE THAT HAS LED TO ACTUAL DOCUMENTATION. DESPITE HADES' JOKES, I SUSPECT THERE IS NO REAL MOTHMAN.
TEN TO ONE, WHATEVER IS TERRORIZING THIS TOWN IS SOMETHING I'VE KILLED BEFORE, HUNDREDS OF TIMES. A SPRITE THAT HAS GORGED ITSELF ON TOO MUCH COW BLOOD. A SELKIE WITH SCHIZOPHRENIA AND DRIED-OUT SKIN.
I SUSPECT THAT, BY THE TIME WE FIND THIS SO-CALLED "MOTHMAN," WE MAY NOT HAVE A NEW MONSTER TO ADD TO TAYLOR'S BOOKS, BUT WE'LL CERTAINLY HAVE A FUNNY STORY.
AND YOU SAID YOU SAW THE CREATURE IN THE WOODS RIGHT BEHIND YOUR HOME?
THAT'S RIGHT. I WAS TAKING MY EARLY MORNING WALK, LIKE WHAT I ALWAYS DO.
AND THERE IT WAS, EATING THE GUTS OUT OF A DEER. A DEER I COULD'VE HAD MY DANG SELF.
BEFORE I COULD EVEN RAISE MY RIFLE, SON-OF-A-BITCH SPREAD HIS WINGS LIKE A GODDANG EAGLE AND TOOK OFF.
NEVER SEEN ANYTHING LIKE IT IN MY LIFE.
AND YOU'RE SURE, SIR, THAT IT WASN'T AN EAGLE?
I KNOW A GIANT MAN-MOTH FROM AN EAGLE, AND LET ME TELL YOU. THIS WAS NOT NO EAGLE. ANY OF YOU THREE WANT BEER? I BREW MY OWN. TASTES LIKE SHIT, BUT IT GETS YOU DRUNK.
UH. NO, THANKS.
ACTUALLY...

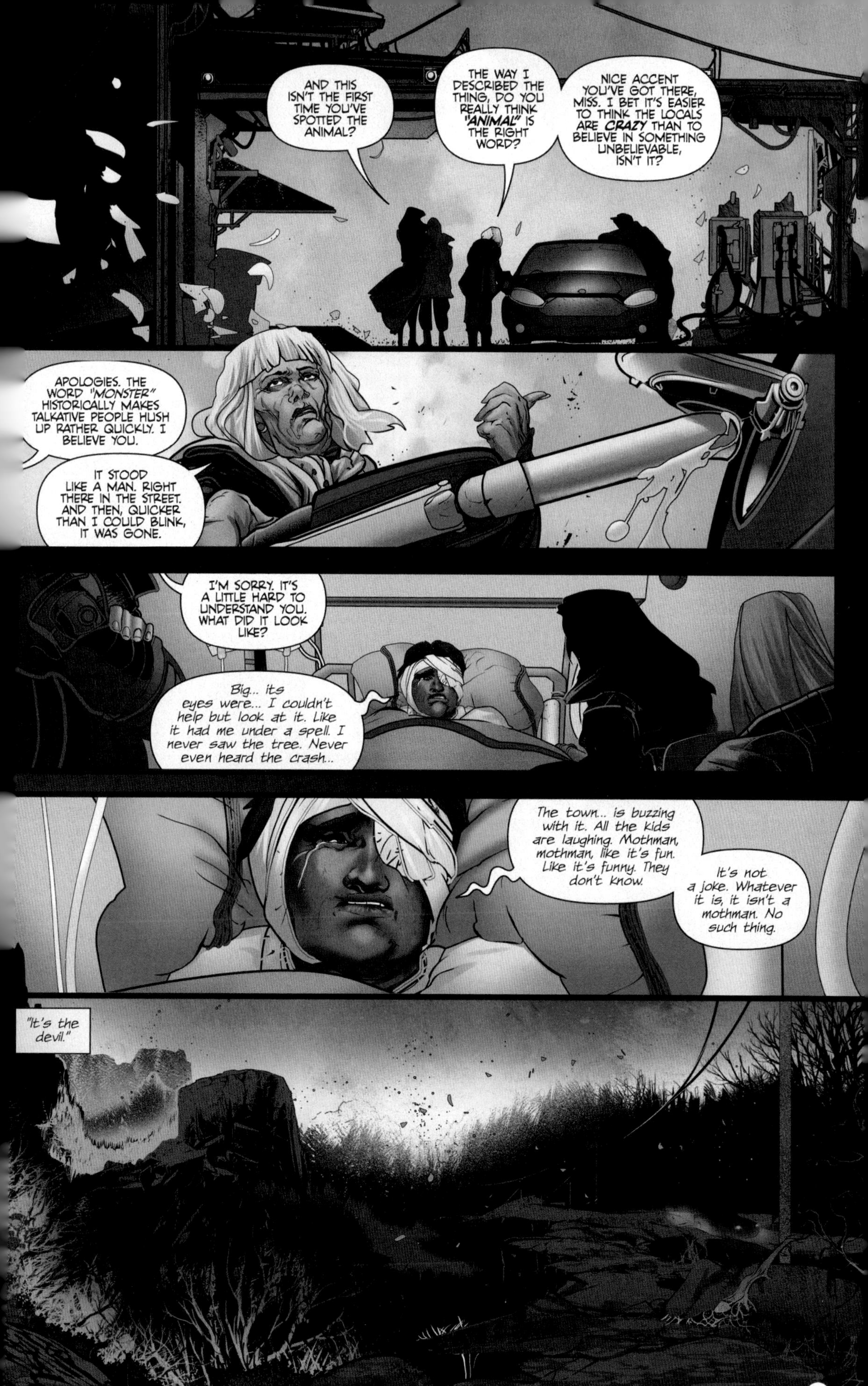
AND THIS ISN'T THE FIRST TIME YOU'VE SPOTTED THE ANIMAL?
THE WAY I DESCRIBED THE THING, DO YOU REALLY THINK "ANIMAL" IS THE RIGHT WORD?
NICE ACCENT YOU'VE GOT THERE, MISS. I BET IT'S EASIER TO THINK THE LOCALS ARE CRAZY THAN TO BELIEVE IN SOMETHING UNBELIEVABLE, ISN'T IT?
APOLOGIES. THE WORD "MONSTER" HISTORICALLY MAKES TALKATIVE PEOPLE HUSH UP RATHER QUICKLY. I BELIEVE YOU.
IT STOOD LIKE A MAN. RIGHT THERE IN THE STREET. AND THEN, QUICKER THAN I COULD BLINK, IT WAS GONE.
I'M SORRY. IT'S A LITTLE HARD TO UNDERSTAND YOU. WHAT DID IT LOOK LIKE?
Big... its eyes were... I couldn't help but look at it. Like it had me under a spell. I never saw the tree. Never even heard the crash...
The town... is buzzing with it. All the kids are laughing. Mothman, mothman, like it's fun. Like it's funny. They don't know.
It's not a joke. Whatever it is, it isn't a mothman. No such thing.
"It's the devil."

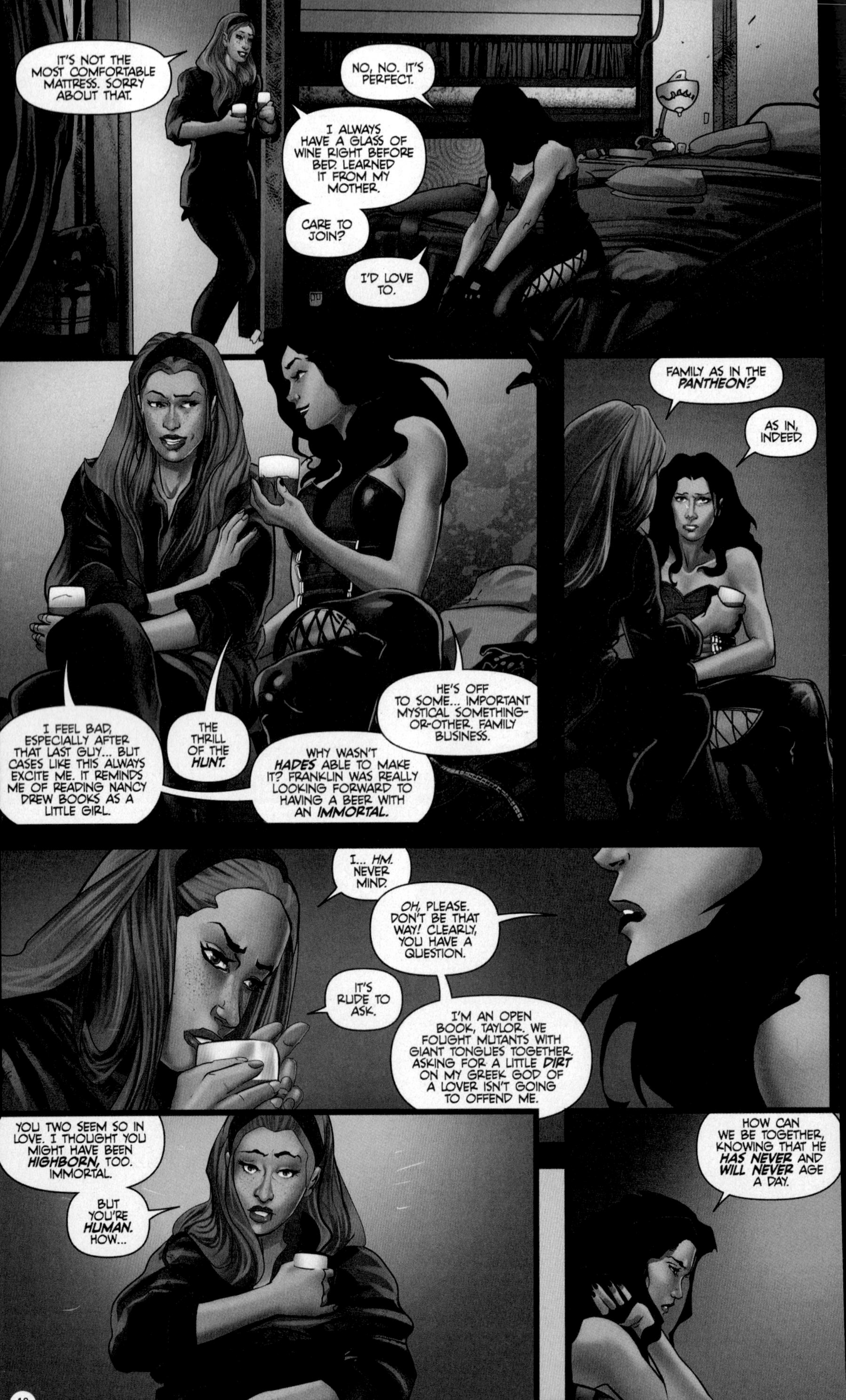
IT'S NOT THE MOST COMFORTABLE MATTRESS. SORRY ABOUT THAT.
NO, NO. IT'S PERFECT.
I ALWAYS HAVE A GLASS OF WINE RIGHT BEFORE BED. LEARNED IT FROM MY MOTHER.
CARE TO JOIN?
I'D LOVE TO.
I FEEL BAD, ESPECIALLY AFTER THAT LAST GUY... BUT CASES LIKE THIS ALWAYS EXCITE ME. IT REMINDS ME OF READING NANCY DREW BOOKS AS A LITTLE GIRL.
THE THRILL OF THE *HUNT.*
WHY WASN'T ***HADES*** ABLE TO MAKE IT? FRANKLIN WAS REALLY LOOKING FORWARD TO HAVING A BEER WITH AN ***IMMORTAL.***
HE'S OFF TO SOME... IMPORTANT MYSTICAL SOMETHING-OR-OTHER. FAMILY BUSINESS.
FAMILY AS IN THE ***PANTHEON?***
AS IN, INDEED.
I... *HM.* NEVER MIND.
OH, PLEASE. DON'T BE THAT WAY! CLEARLY, YOU HAVE A QUESTION.
IT'S RUDE TO ASK.
I'M AN OPEN BOOK, TAYLOR. WE FOUGHT MUTANTS WITH GIANT TONGUES TOGETHER. ASKING FOR A LITTLE ***DIRT*** ON MY GREEK GOD OF A LOVER ISN'T GOING TO OFFEND ME.
YOU TWO SEEM SO IN LOVE. I THOUGHT YOU MIGHT HAVE BEEN ***HIGHBORN,*** TOO. IMMORTAL.
BUT YOU'RE ***HUMAN.*** HOW...
HOW CAN WE BE TOGETHER, KNOWING THAT HE ***HAS NEVER*** AND ***WILL NEVER*** AGE A DAY.

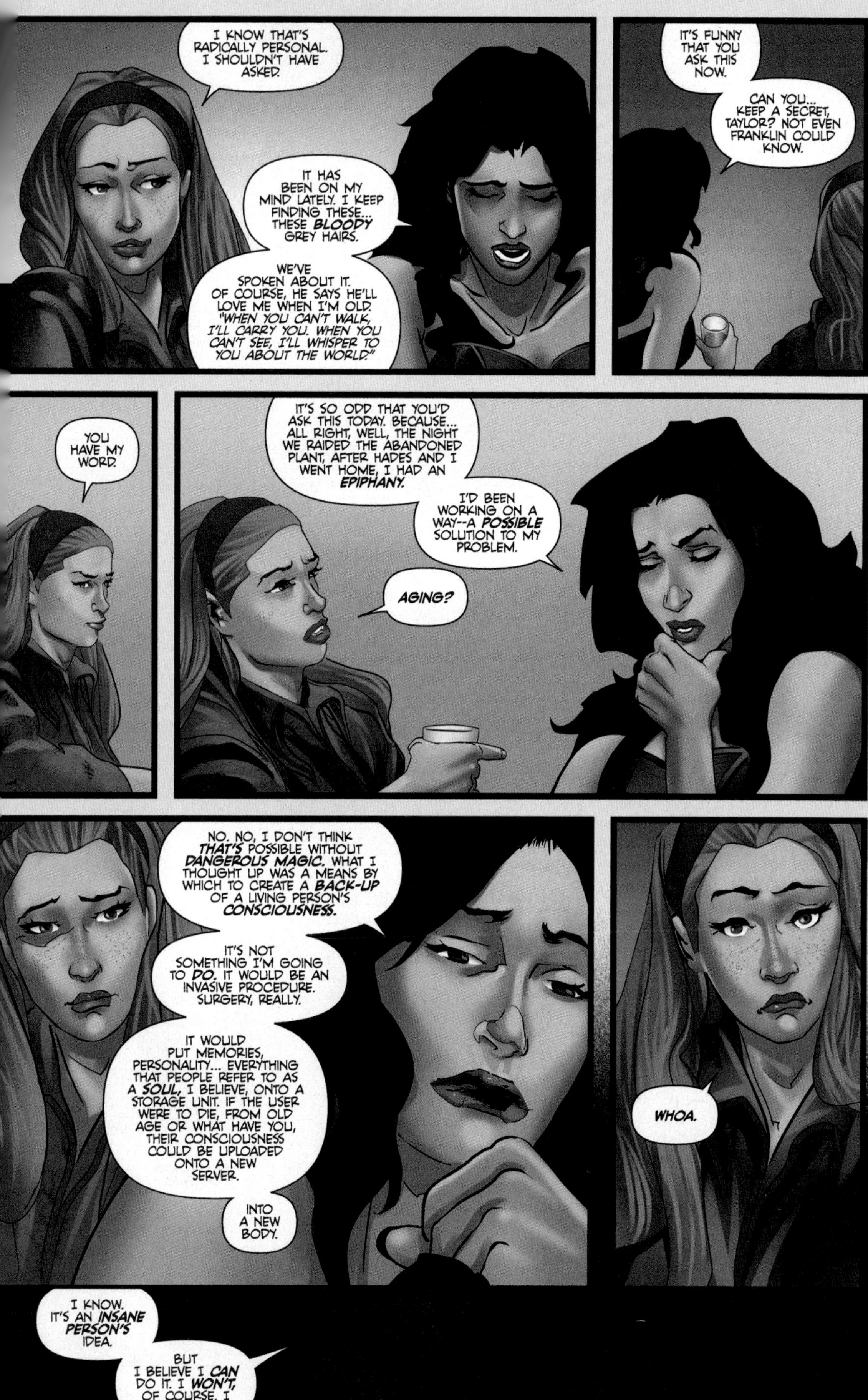
I KNOW THAT'S RADICALLY PERSONAL. I SHOULDN'T HAVE ASKED.
IT HAS BEEN ON MY MIND LATELY. I KEEP FINDING THESE... THESE BLOODY GREY HAIRS.
WE'VE SPOKEN ABOUT IT. OF COURSE, HE SAYS HE'LL LOVE ME WHEN I'M OLD. "WHEN YOU CAN'T WALK, I'LL CARRY YOU. WHEN YOU CAN'T SEE, I'LL WHISPER TO YOU ABOUT THE WORLD."
IT'S FUNNY THAT YOU ASK THIS NOW.
CAN YOU... KEEP A SECRET, TAYLOR? NOT EVEN FRANKLIN COULD KNOW.
YOU HAVE MY WORD.
IT'S SO ODD THAT YOU'D ASK THIS TODAY. BECAUSE... ALL RIGHT, WELL, THE NIGHT WE RAIDED THE ABANDONED PLANT, AFTER HADES AND I WENT HOME, I HAD AN EPIPHANY.
I'D BEEN WORKING ON A WAY--A POSSIBLE SOLUTION TO MY PROBLEM.
AGING?
NO. NO, I DON'T THINK THAT'S POSSIBLE WITHOUT DANGEROUS MAGIC. WHAT I THOUGHT UP WAS A MEANS BY WHICH TO CREATE A BACK-UP OF A LIVING PERSON'S CONSCIOUSNESS.
IT'S NOT SOMETHING I'M GOING TO DO. IT WOULD BE AN INVASIVE PROCEDURE. SURGERY, REALLY.
IT WOULD PUT MEMORIES, PERSONALITY... EVERYTHING THAT PEOPLE REFER TO AS A SOUL, I BELIEVE, ONTO A STORAGE UNIT. IF THE USER WERE TO DIE, FROM OLD AGE OR WHAT HAVE YOU, THEIR CONSCIOUSNESS COULD BE UPLOADED ONTO A NEW SERVER.
INTO A NEW BODY.
WHOA.
I KNOW. IT'S AN INSANE PERSON'S IDEA.
BUT I BELIEVE I CAN DO IT. I WON'T, OF COURSE. I WON'T.

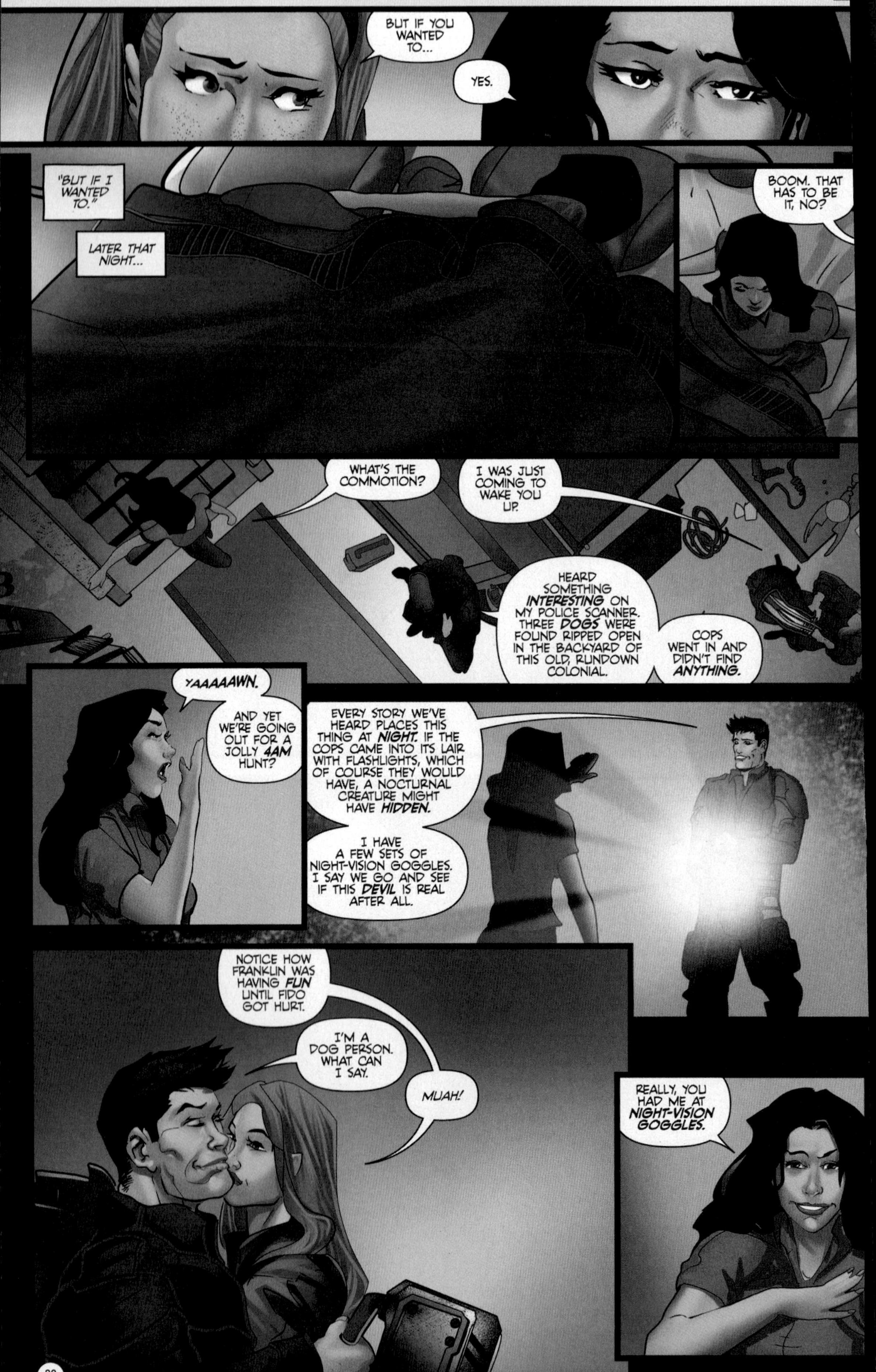

BUT IF YOU WANTED TO...
YES.
"BUT IF I WANTED TO."
LATER THAT NIGHT...
BOOM. THAT HAS TO BE IT, NO?
WHAT'S THE COMMOTION?
I WAS JUST COMING TO WAKE YOU UP.
HEARD SOMETHING INTERESTING ON MY POLICE SCANNER. THREE DOGS WERE FOUND RIPPED OPEN IN THE BACKYARD OF THIS OLD, RUNDOWN COLONIAL.
COPS WENT IN AND DIDN'T FIND ANYTHING.
YAAAAAWN.
AND YET WE'RE GOING OUT FOR A JOLLY 4AM HUNT?
EVERY STORY WE'VE HEARD PLACES THIS THING AT NIGHT. IF THE COPS CAME INTO ITS LAIR WITH FLASHLIGHTS, WHICH OF COURSE THEY WOULD HAVE, A NOCTURNAL CREATURE MIGHT HAVE HIDDEN.
I HAVE A FEW SETS OF NIGHT-VISION GOGGLES. I SAY WE GO AND SEE IF THIS DEVIL IS REAL AFTER ALL.
NOTICE HOW FRANKLIN WAS HAVING FUN UNTIL FIDO GOT HURT.
I'M A DOG PERSON. WHAT CAN I SAY.
MUAH!
REALLY, YOU HAD ME AT NIGHT-VISION GOGGLES.

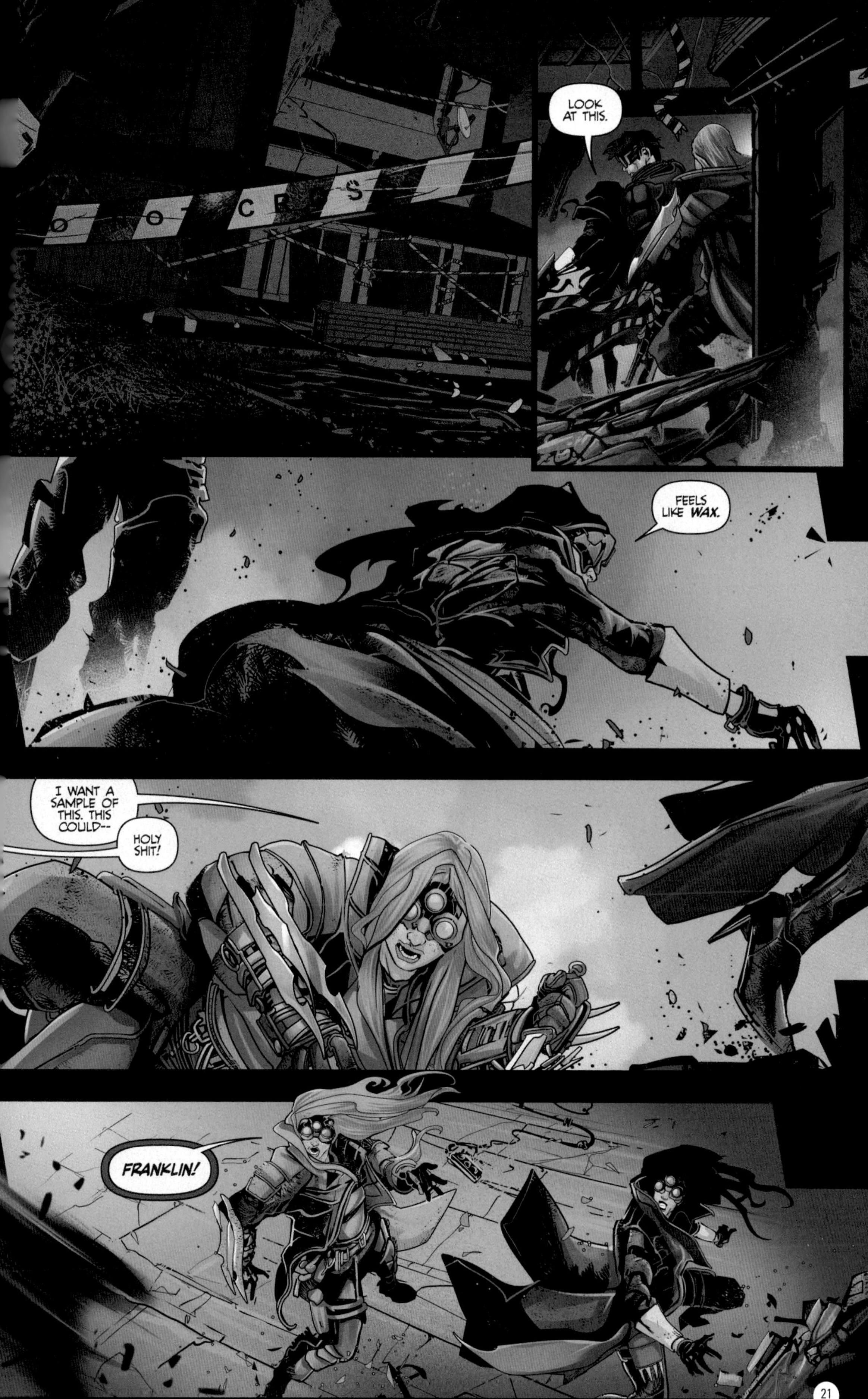
LOOK AT THIS.
FEELS LIKE WAX.
I WANT A SAMPLE OF THIS. THIS COULD--
HOLY SHIT!
FRANKLIN!

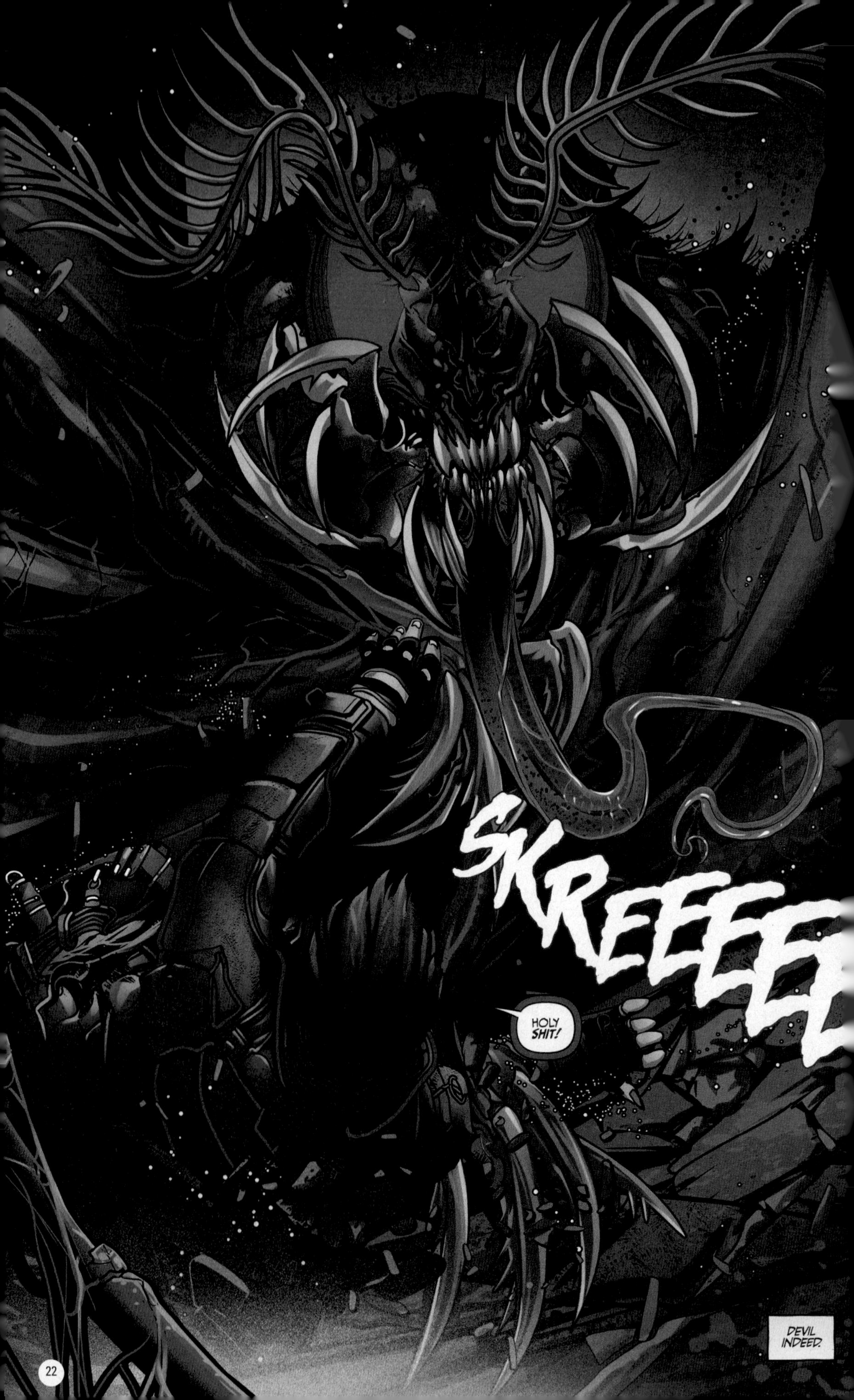
SKREEEEE
HOLY SHIT!
DEVIL INDEED.

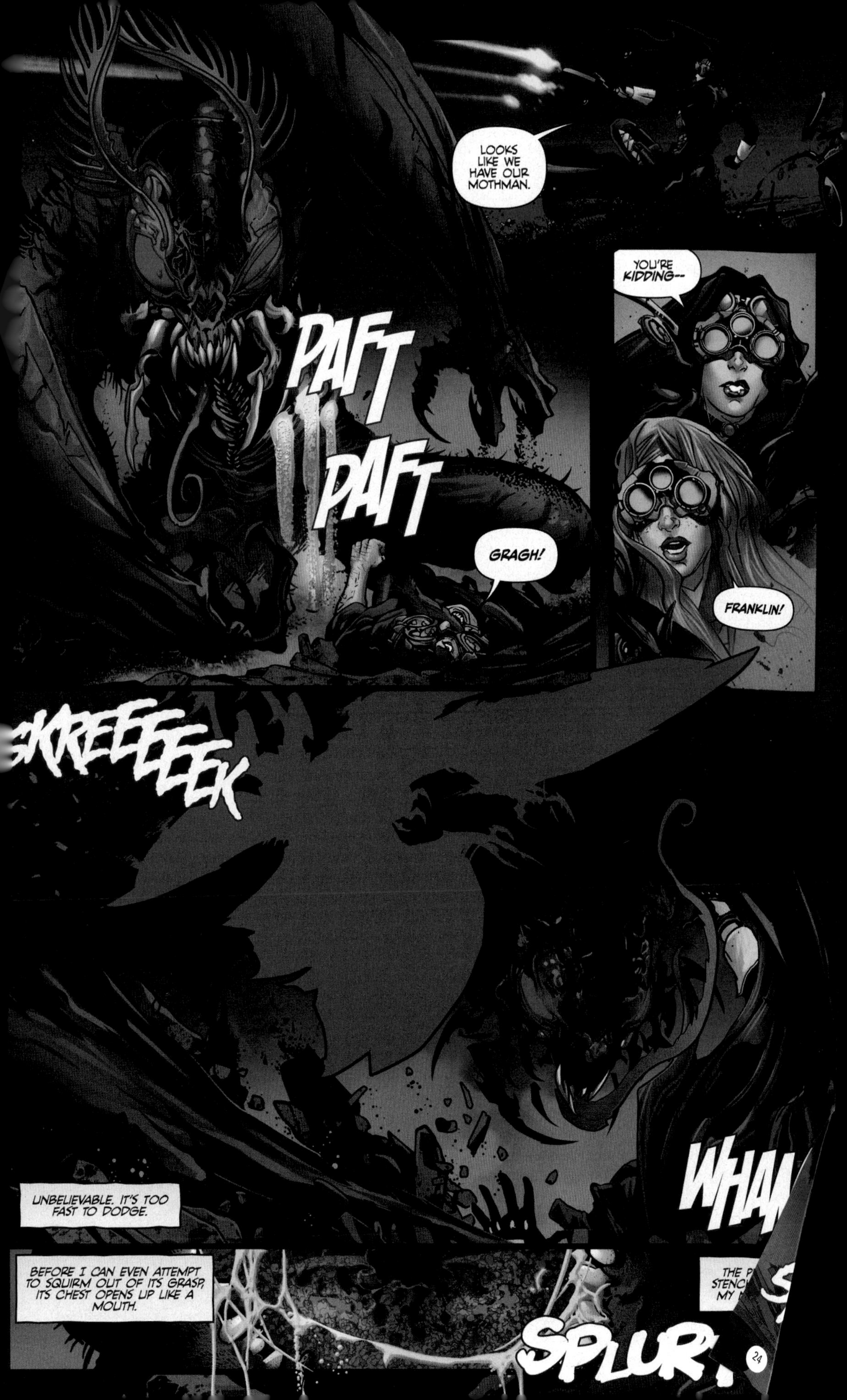
LOOKS LIKE WE HAVE OUR MOTHMAN.
YOU'RE KIDDING--
PAFT
PAFT
GRAGH!
FRANKLIN!
SKREEEEEEEK
UNBELIEVABLE. IT'S TOO FAST TO DODGE.
WHAM
BEFORE I CAN EVEN ATTEMPT TO SQUIRM OUT OF ITS GRASP, ITS CHEST OPENS UP LIKE A MOUTH.
SPLUR

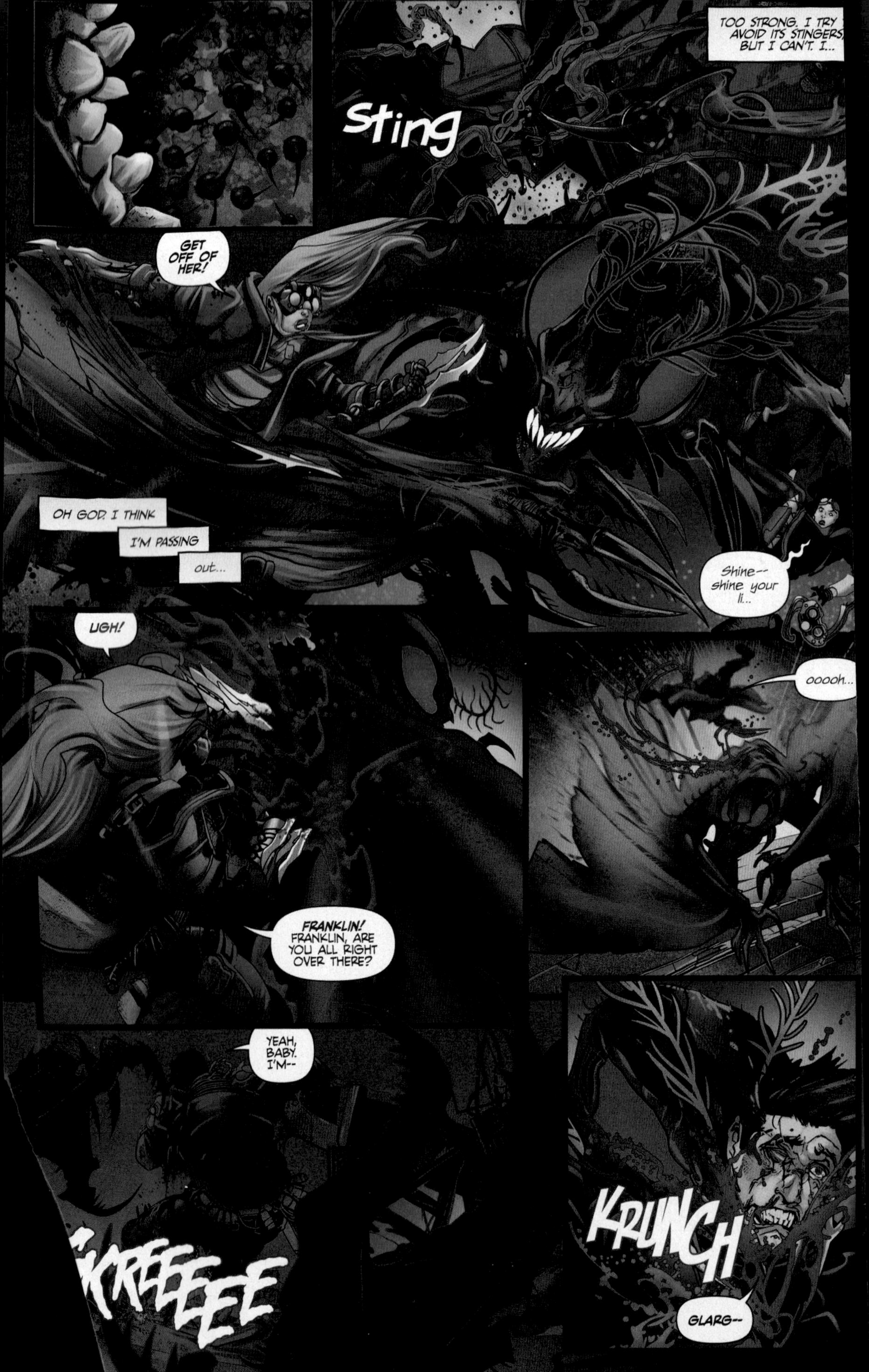
TOO STRONG. I TRY TO AVOID ITS STINGERS, BUT I CAN'T. I...
Sting
GET OFF OF HER!
OH GOD. I THINK
I'M PASSING
out...
Shine-- shine your li...
UGH!
ooooh...
FRANKLIN! FRANKLIN, ARE YOU ALL RIGHT OVER THERE?
YEAH, BABY. I'M--
KRUNCH
SKREEEEEE
GLARG--

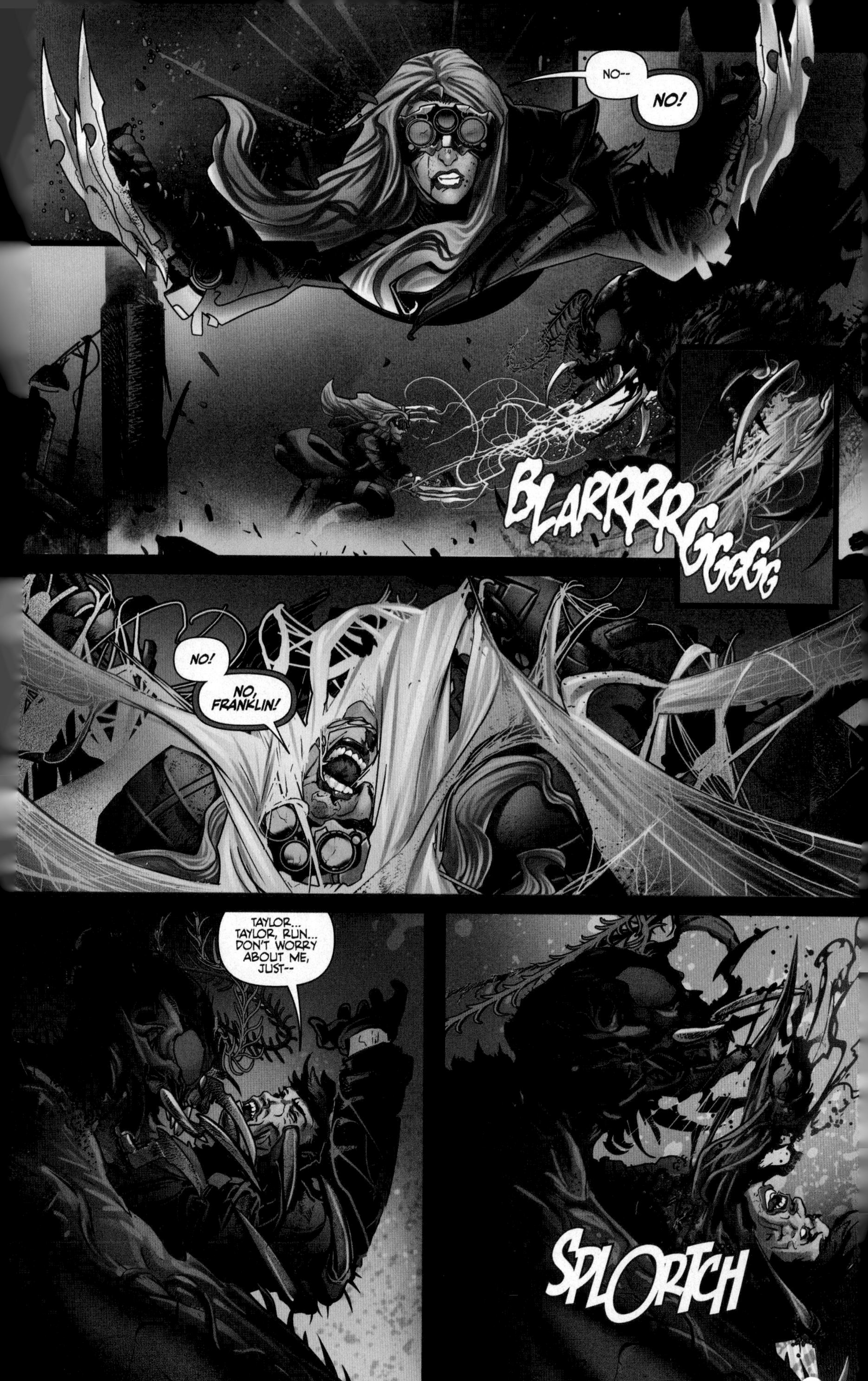

NO--
NO!
BLARRRRGGGGG
NO!
NO, FRANKLIN!
TAYLOR... TAYLOR, RUN... DON'T WORRY ABOUT ME, JUST--
SPLORTCH

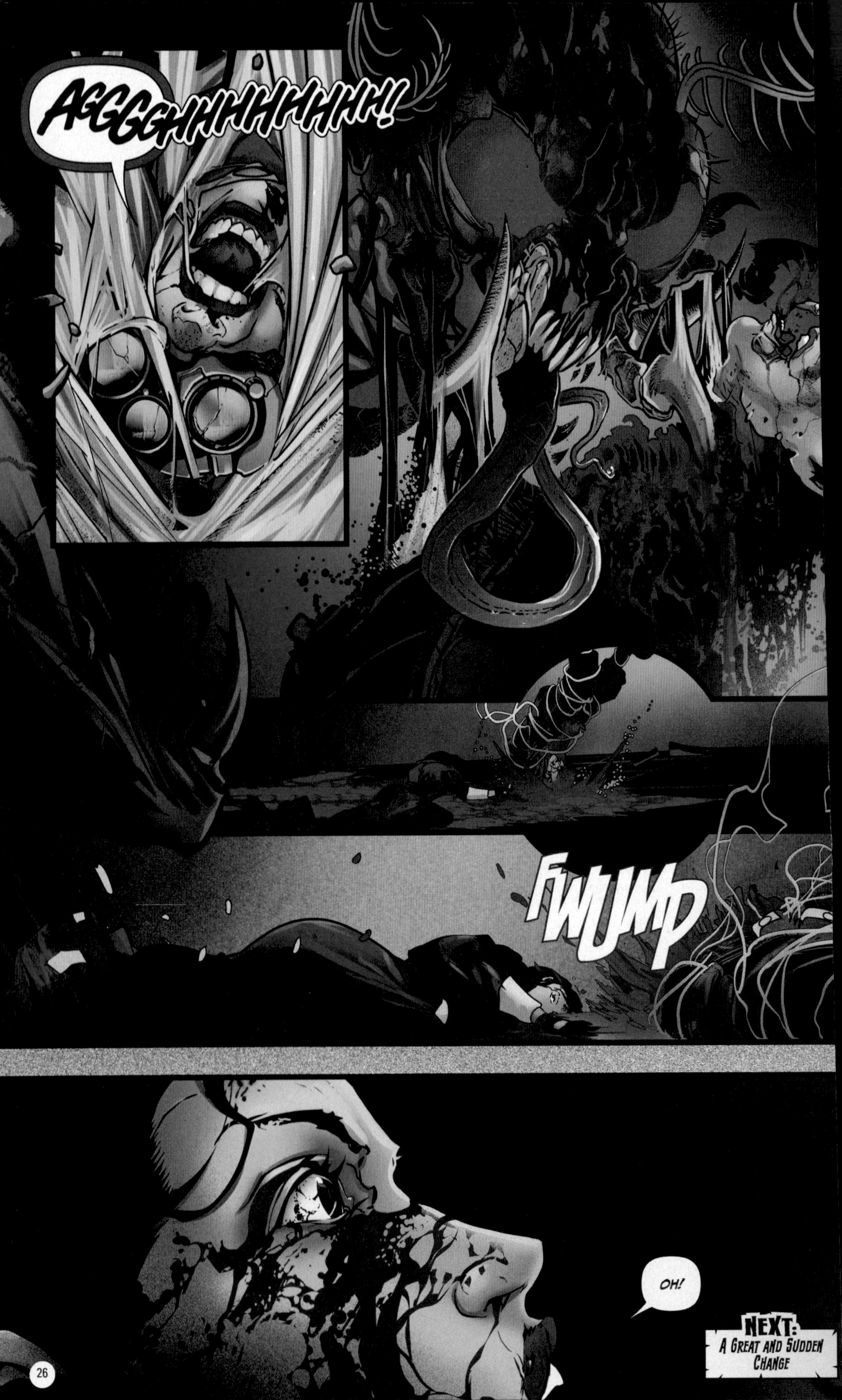
AGGGGHHHHHHHHH!
FWUMP
OH!
NEXT: A GREAT AND SUDDEN CHANGE

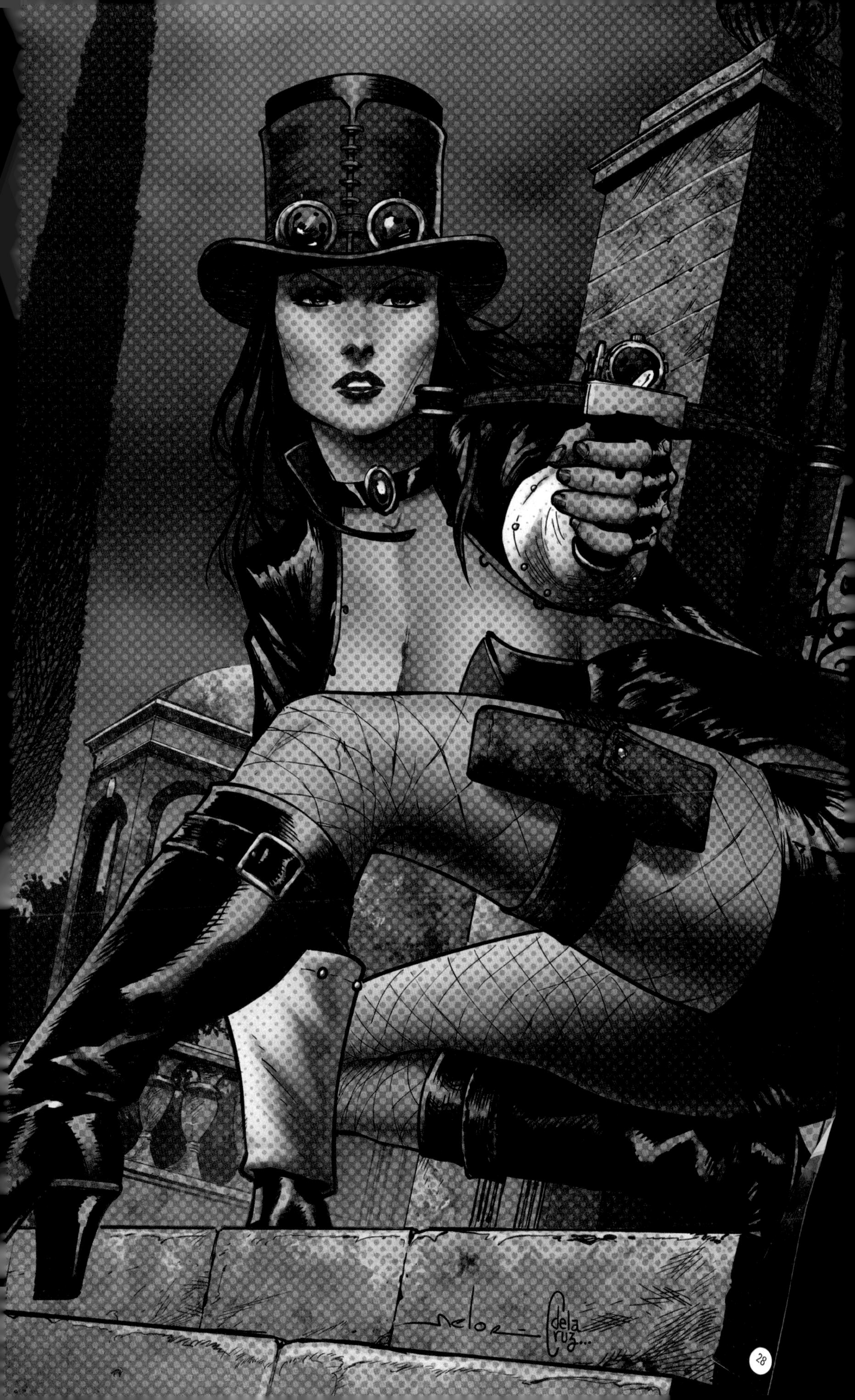

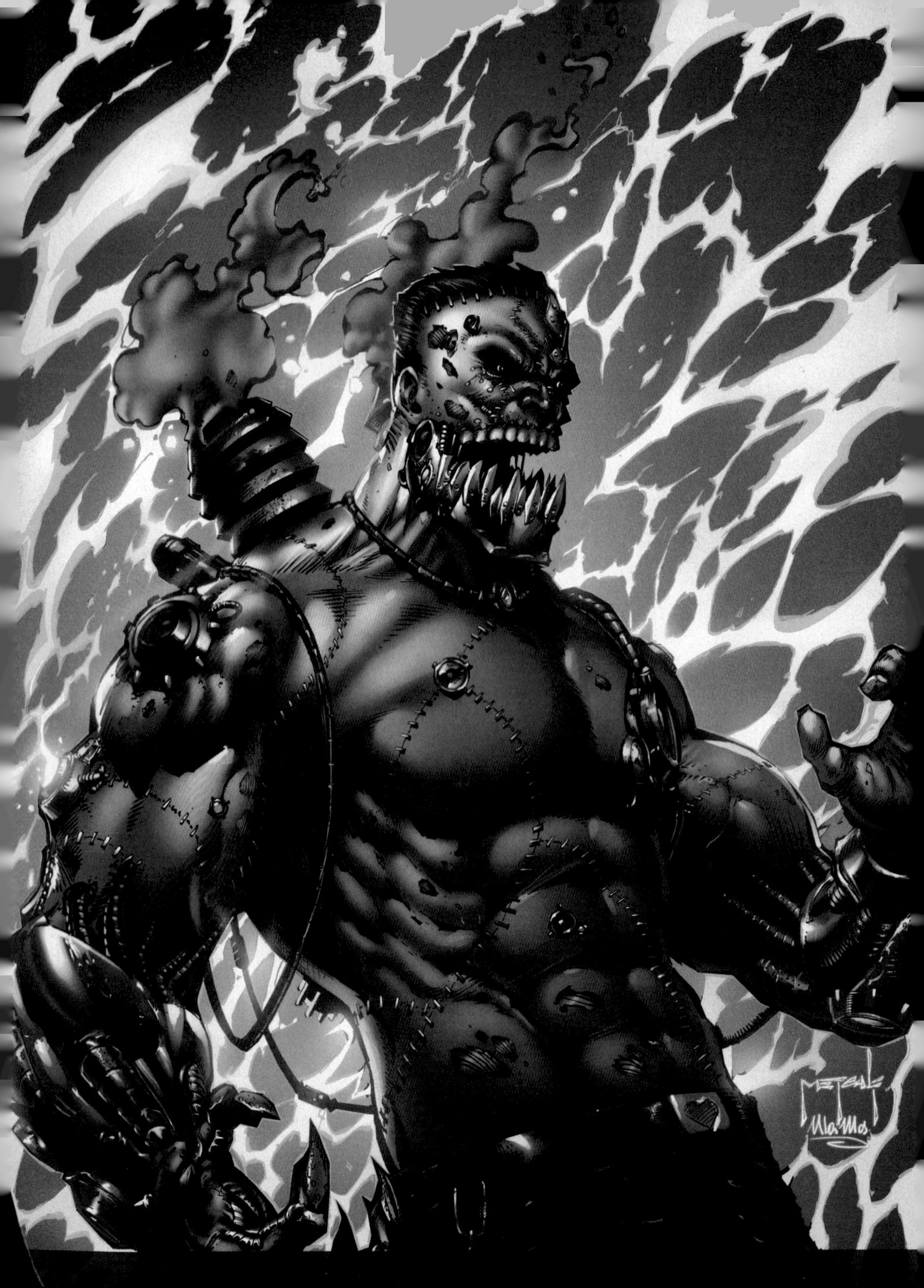

CHAPTER TWO

A GREAT AND SUDDEN CHANGE

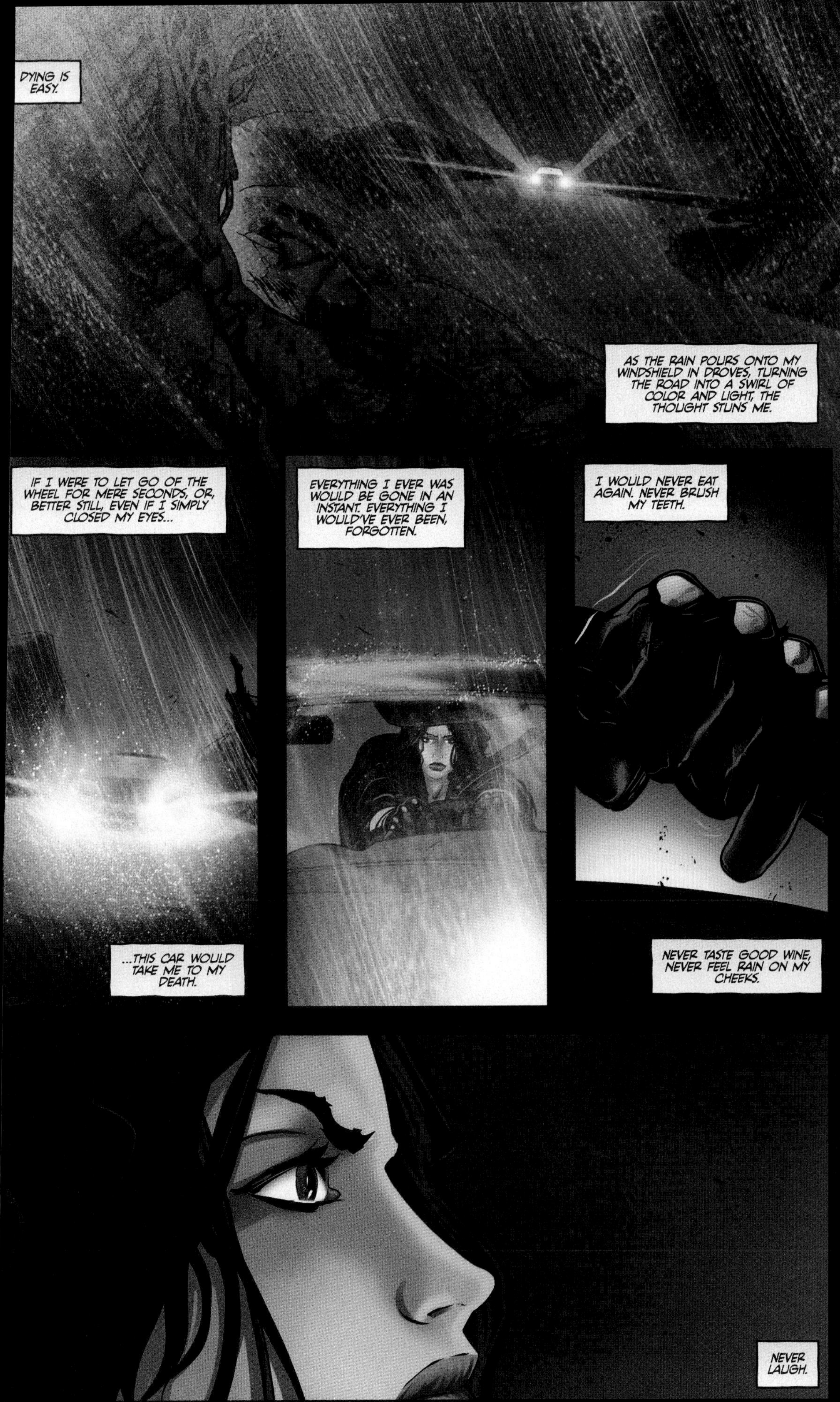
DYING IS EASY.
AS THE RAIN POURS ONTO MY WINDSHIELD IN DROVES, TURNING THE ROAD INTO A SWIRL OF COLOR AND LIGHT, THE THOUGHT STUNS ME.
IF I WERE TO LET GO OF THE WHEEL FOR MERE SECONDS, OR, BETTER STILL, EVEN IF I SIMPLY CLOSED MY EYES...
...THIS CAR WOULD TAKE ME TO MY DEATH.
EVERYTHING I EVER WAS WOULD BE GONE IN AN INSTANT. EVERYTHING I WOULD'VE EVER BEEN, FORGOTTEN.
I WOULD NEVER EAT AGAIN. NEVER BRUSH MY TEETH.
NEVER TASTE GOOD WINE, NEVER FEEL RAIN ON MY CHEEKS.
NEVER LAUGH.

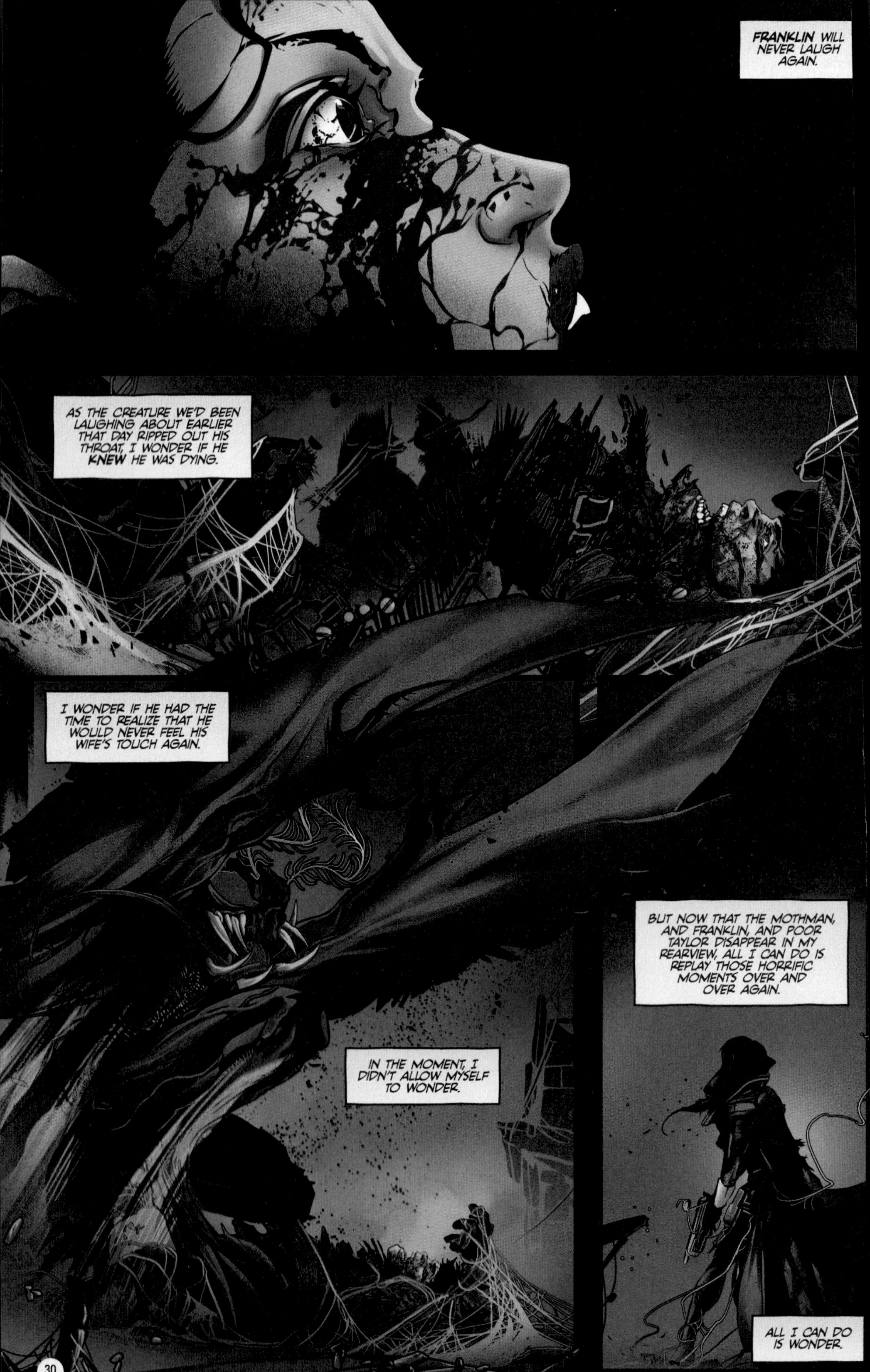
FRANKLIN WILL NEVER LAUGH AGAIN.
AS THE CREATURE WE'D BEEN LAUGHING ABOUT EARLIER THAT DAY RIPPED OUT HIS THROAT, I WONDER IF HE KNEW HE WAS DYING.
I WONDER IF HE HAD THE TIME TO REALIZE THAT HE WOULD NEVER FEEL HIS WIFE'S TOUCH AGAIN.
BUT NOW THAT THE MOTHMAN, AND FRANKLIN, AND POOR TAYLOR DISAPPEAR IN MY REARVIEW, ALL I CAN DO IS REPLAY THOSE HORRIFIC MOMENTS OVER AND OVER AGAIN.
IN THE MOMENT, I DIDN'T ALLOW MYSELF TO WONDER.
ALL I CAN DO IS WONDER.

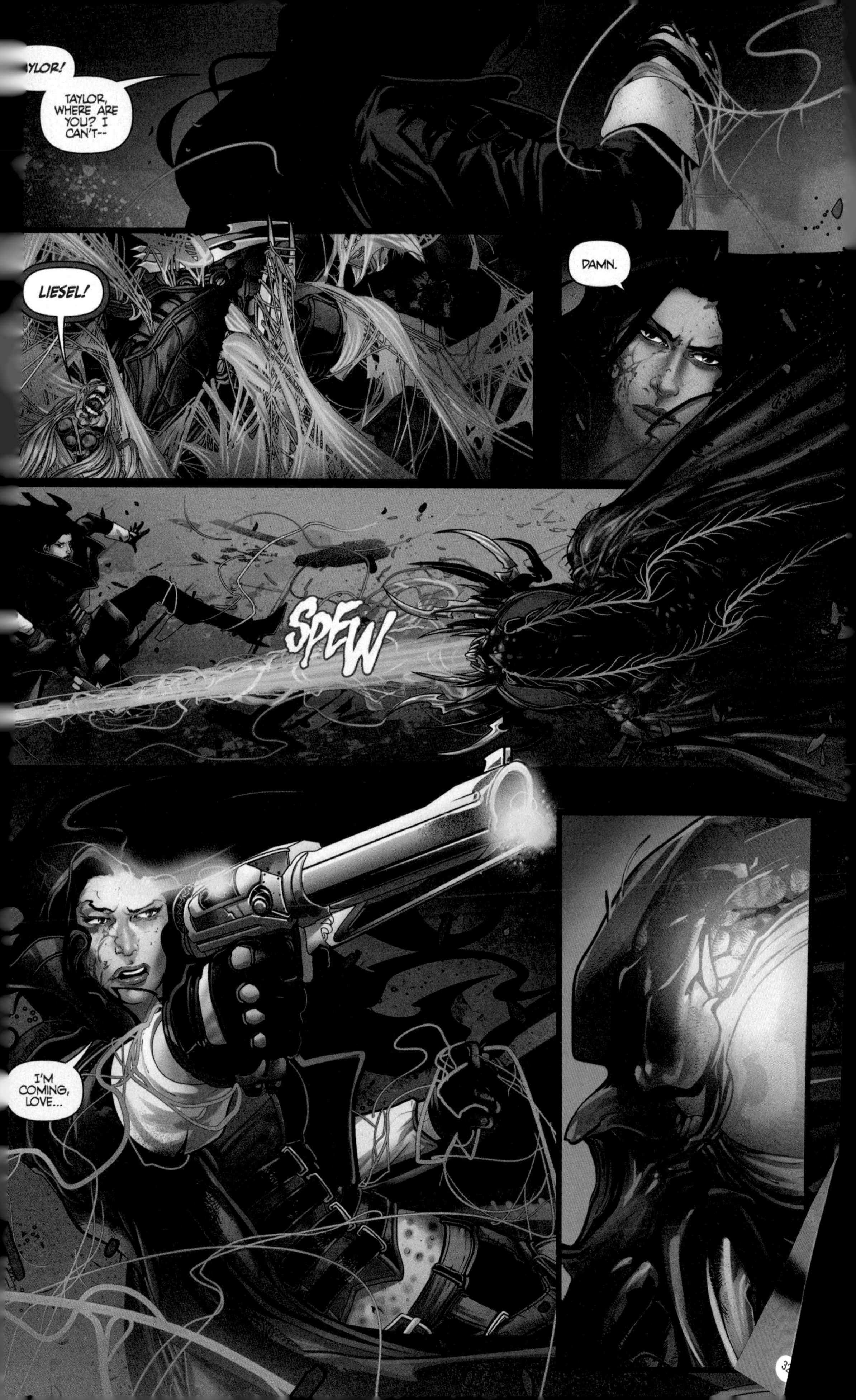
AYLOR!
TAYLOR, WHERE ARE YOU? I CAN'T--
LIESEL!
DAMN.
SPEW
I'M COMING, LOVE...

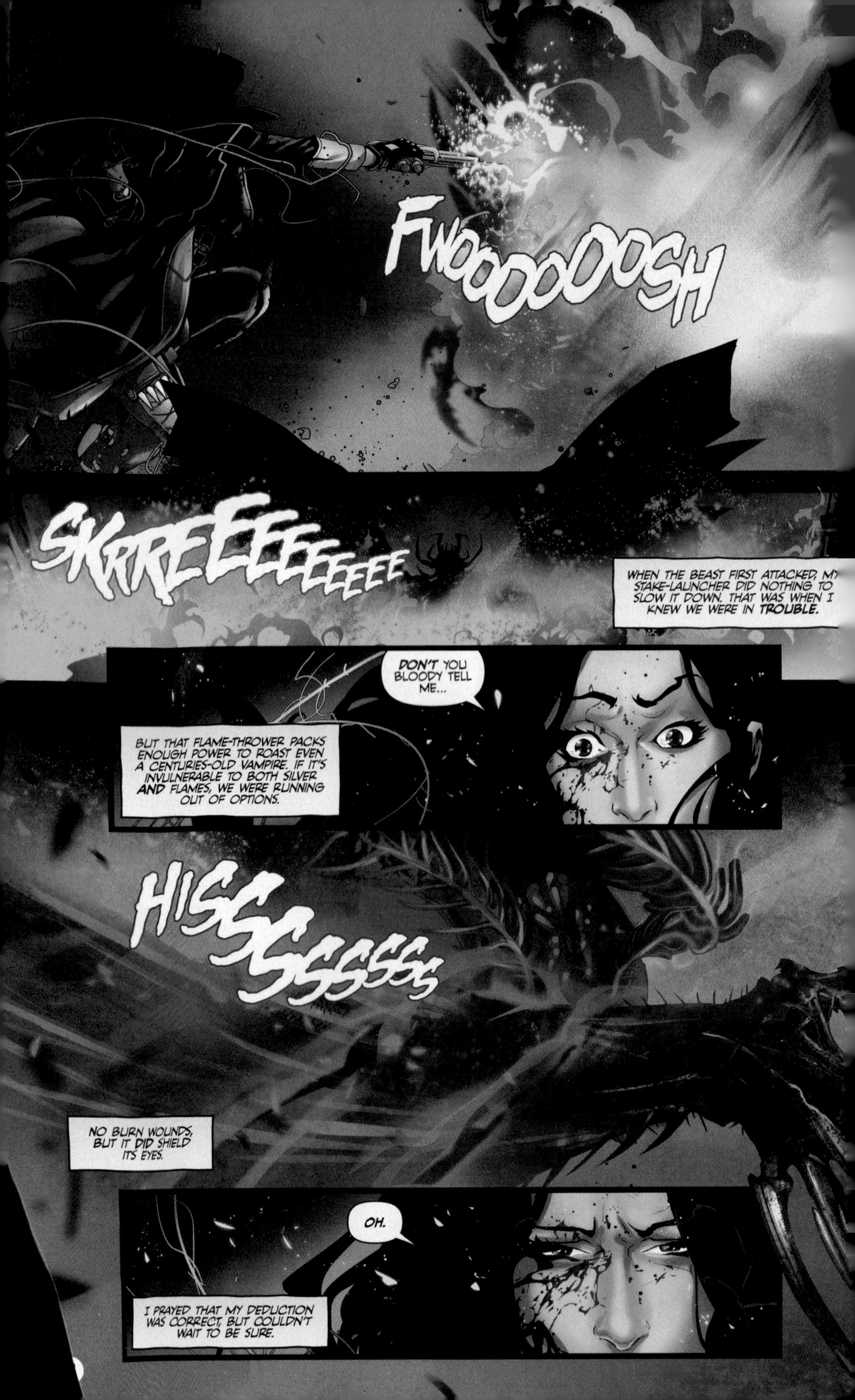
FWOOOOOOOSH
SKRREEEEEEEEEE
WHEN THE BEAST FIRST ATTACKED, MY STAKE-LAUNCHER DID NOTHING TO SLOW IT DOWN. THAT WAS WHEN I KNEW WE WERE IN TROUBLE.
DON'T YOU BLOODY TELL ME...
BUT THAT FLAME-THROWER PACKS ENOUGH POWER TO ROAST EVEN A CENTURIES-OLD VAMPIRE. IF IT'S INVULNERABLE TO BOTH SILVER AND FLAMES, WE WERE RUNNING OUT OF OPTIONS.
HISSSSSSSS
NO BURN WOUNDS, BUT IT DID SHIELD ITS EYES.
OH.
I PRAYED THAT MY DEDUCTION WAS CORRECT, BUT COULDN'T WAIT TO BE SURE.

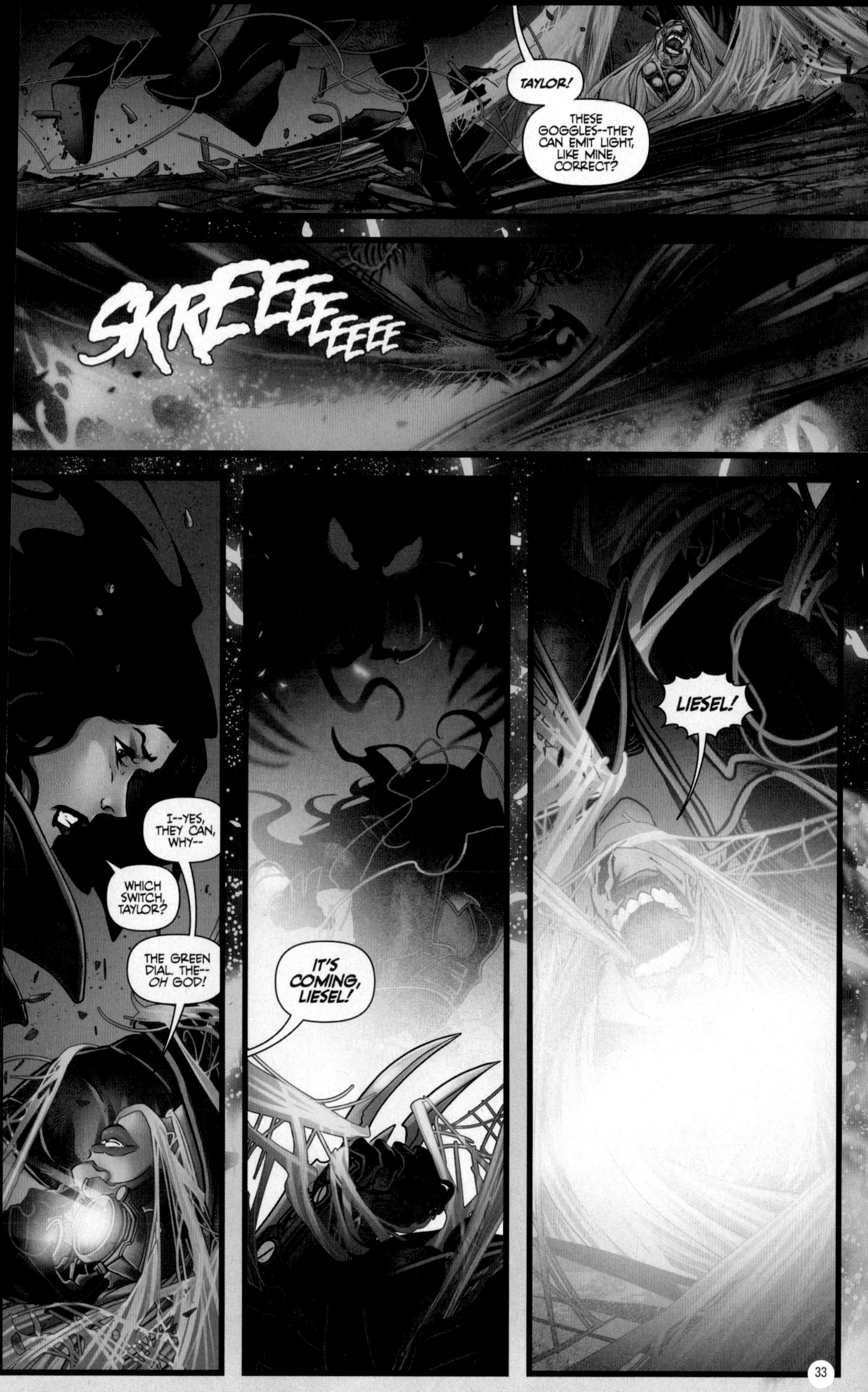
TAYLOR!
THESE GOGGLES--THEY CAN EMIT LIGHT, LIKE MINE, CORRECT?
SKREEEEEEEEE
I--YES, THEY CAN, WHY--
WHICH SWITCH, TAYLOR?
THE GREEN DIAL. THE-- OH GOD!
IT'S COMING, LIESEL!
LIESEL!

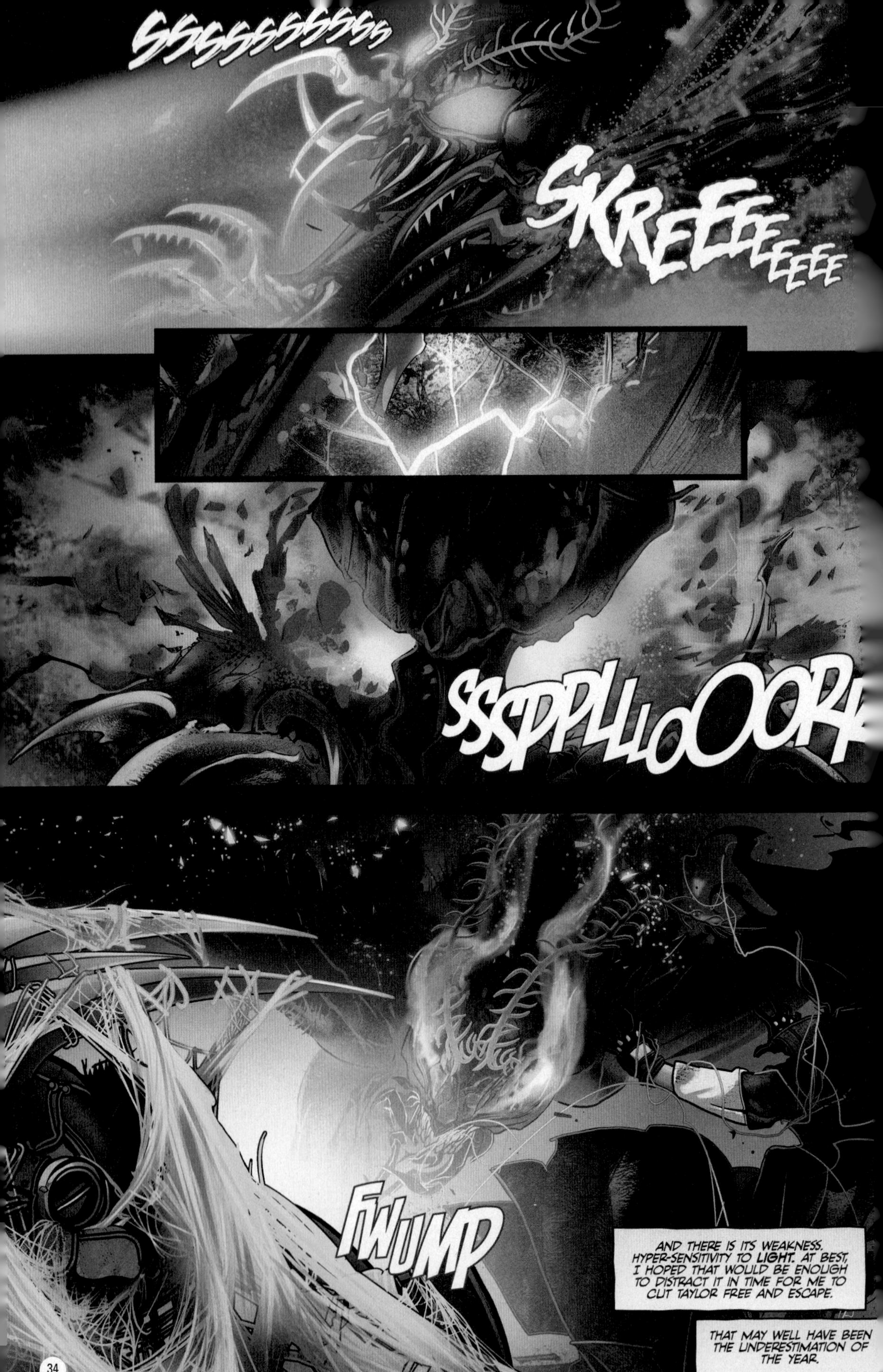
SSSSSSSSSSS
SKREEEEEEEE
SSSPPLLLOOORH
FWUMP
AND THERE IS ITS WEAKNESS. HYPER-SENSITIVITY TO **LIGHT**. AT BEST, I HOPED THAT WOULD BE ENOUGH TO DISTRACT IT IN TIME FOR ME TO CUT TAYLOR FREE AND ESCAPE.
THAT MAY WELL HAVE BEEN THE UNDERESTIMATION OF THE YEAR.

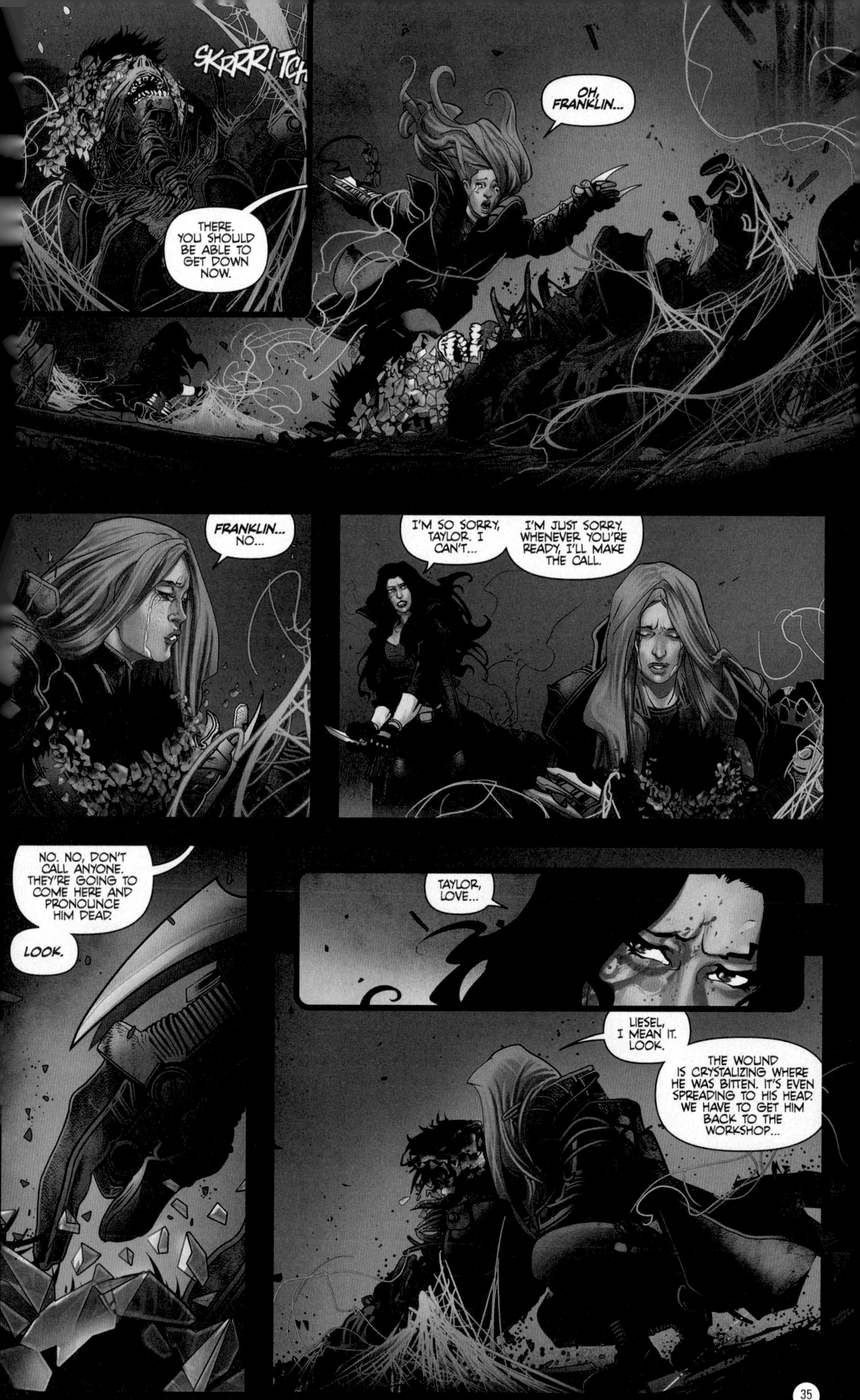
SKRRRITCH
THERE. YOU SHOULD BE ABLE TO GET DOWN NOW.
OH, FRANKLIN...
FRANKLIN... NO...
I'M SO SORRY, TAYLOR. I CAN'T...
I'M JUST SORRY. WHENEVER YOU'RE READY, I'LL MAKE THE CALL.
NO. NO, DON'T CALL ANYONE. THEY'RE GOING TO COME HERE AND PRONOUNCE HIM DEAD.
LOOK.
TAYLOR, LOVE...
LIESEL, I MEAN IT. LOOK.
THE WOUND IS CRYSTALIZING WHERE HE WAS BITTEN. IT'S EVEN SPREADING TO HIS HEAD. WE HAVE TO GET HIM BACK TO THE WORKSHOP...

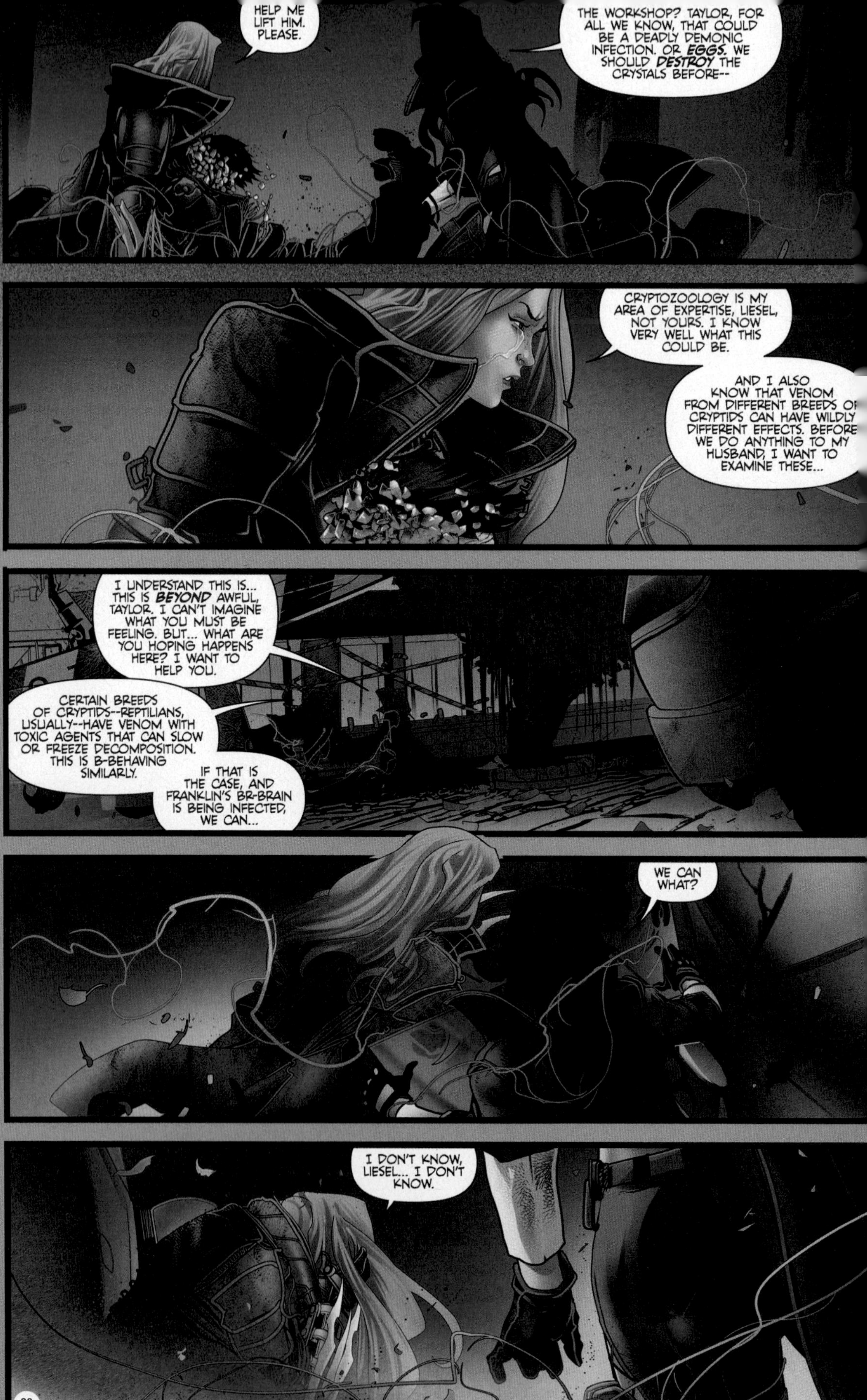
HELP ME LIFT HIM. PLEASE.
THE WORKSHOP? TAYLOR, FOR ALL WE KNOW, THAT COULD BE A DEADLY DEMONIC INFECTION. OR *EGGS.* WE SHOULD *DESTROY* THE CRYSTALS BEFORE--
CRYPTOZOOLOGY IS MY AREA OF EXPERTISE, LIESEL, NOT YOURS. I KNOW VERY WELL WHAT THIS COULD BE.
AND I ALSO KNOW THAT VENOM FROM DIFFERENT BREEDS OF CRYPTIDS CAN HAVE WILDLY DIFFERENT EFFECTS. BEFORE WE DO ANYTHING TO MY HUSBAND, I WANT TO EXAMINE THESE...
I UNDERSTAND THIS IS... THIS IS *BEYOND* AWFUL, TAYLOR. I CAN'T IMAGINE WHAT YOU MUST BE FEELING. BUT... WHAT ARE YOU HOPING HAPPENS HERE? I WANT TO HELP YOU.
CERTAIN BREEDS OF CRYPTIDS--REPTILIANS, USUALLY--HAVE VENOM WITH TOXIC AGENTS THAT CAN SLOW OR FREEZE DECOMPOSITION. THIS IS B-BEHAVING SIMILARLY.
IF THAT IS THE CASE, AND FRANKLIN'S BR-BRAIN IS BEING INFECTED, WE CAN...
WE CAN WHAT?
I DON'T KNOW, LIESEL... I DON'T KNOW.

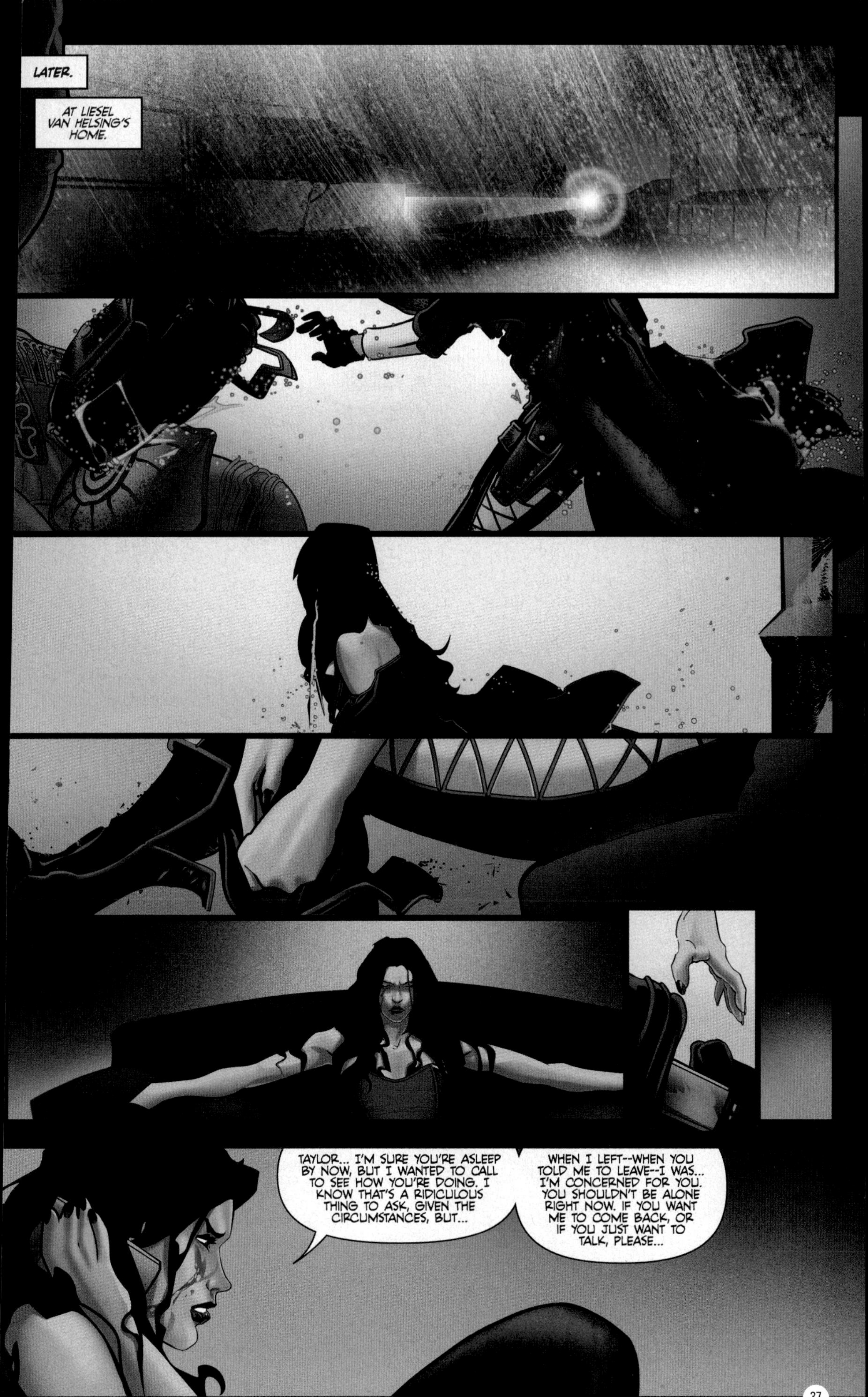
LATER.
AT LIESEL VAN HELSING'S HOME.
TAYLOR... I'M SURE YOU'RE ASLEEP BY NOW, BUT I WANTED TO CALL TO SEE HOW YOU'RE DOING. I KNOW THAT'S A RIDICULOUS THING TO ASK, GIVEN THE CIRCUMSTANCES, BUT...
WHEN I LEFT--WHEN YOU TOLD ME TO LEAVE--I WAS... I'M CONCERNED FOR YOU. YOU SHOULDN'T BE ALONE RIGHT NOW. IF YOU WANT ME TO COME BACK, OR IF YOU JUST WANT TO TALK, PLEASE...

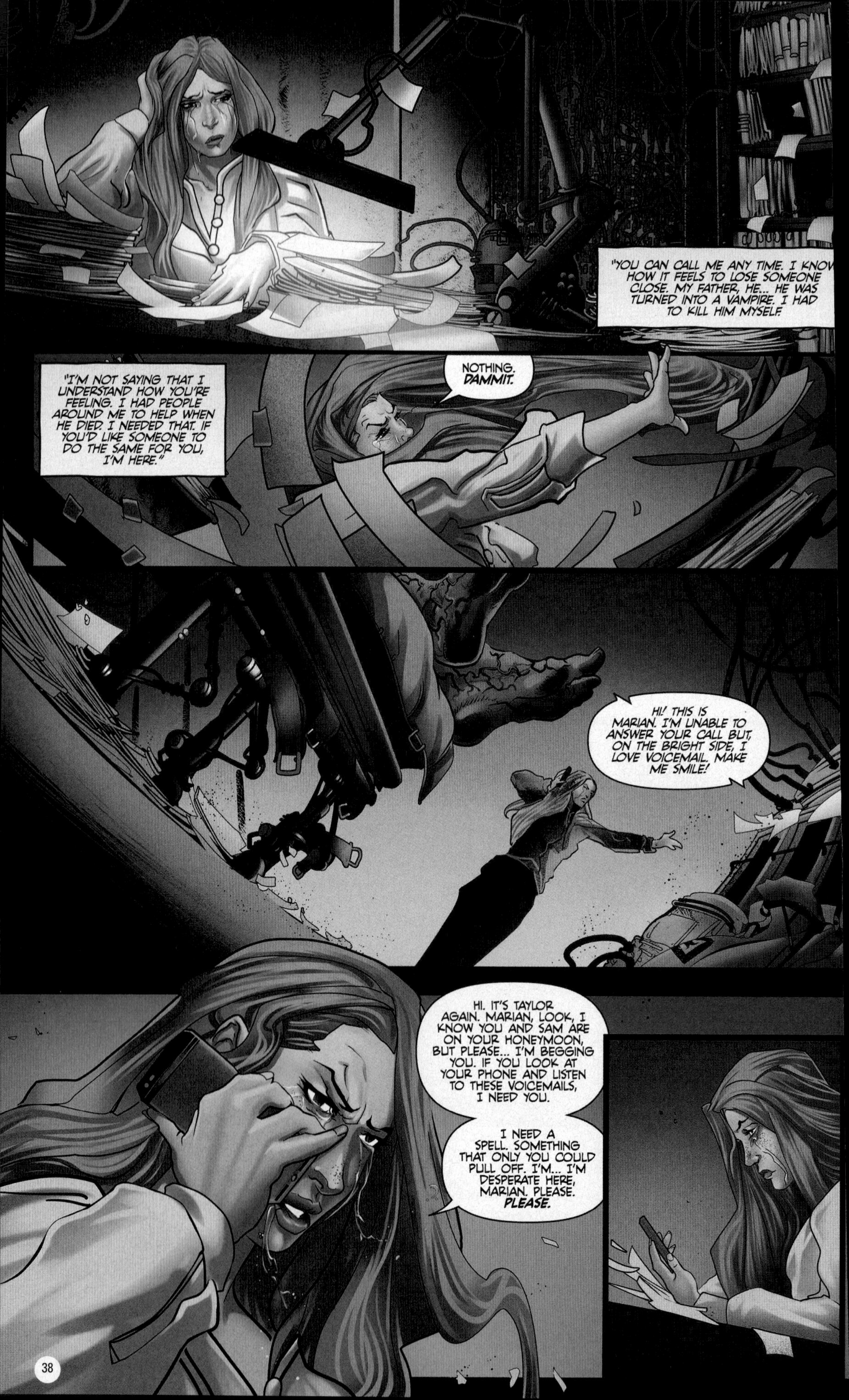
"YOU CAN CALL ME ANY TIME. I KNOW HOW IT FEELS TO LOSE SOMEONE CLOSE. MY FATHER, HE... HE WAS TURNED INTO A VAMPIRE. I HAD TO KILL HIM MYSELF.
"I'M NOT SAYING THAT I UNDERSTAND HOW YOU'RE FEELING. I HAD PEOPLE AROUND ME TO HELP WHEN HE DIED. I NEEDED THAT. IF YOU'D LIKE SOMEONE TO DO THE SAME FOR YOU, I'M HERE."
NOTHING. DAMMIT.
HI! THIS IS MARIAN. I'M UNABLE TO ANSWER YOUR CALL BUT, ON THE BRIGHT SIDE, I LOVE VOICEMAIL. MAKE ME SMILE!
HI. IT'S TAYLOR AGAIN. MARIAN, LOOK, I KNOW YOU AND SAM ARE ON YOUR HONEYMOON, BUT PLEASE... I'M BEGGING YOU. IF YOU LOOK AT YOUR PHONE AND LISTEN TO THESE VOICEMAILS, I NEED YOU.
I NEED A SPELL. SOMETHING THAT ONLY YOU COULD PULL OFF. I'M... I'M DESPERATE HERE, MARIAN. PLEASE. PLEASE.

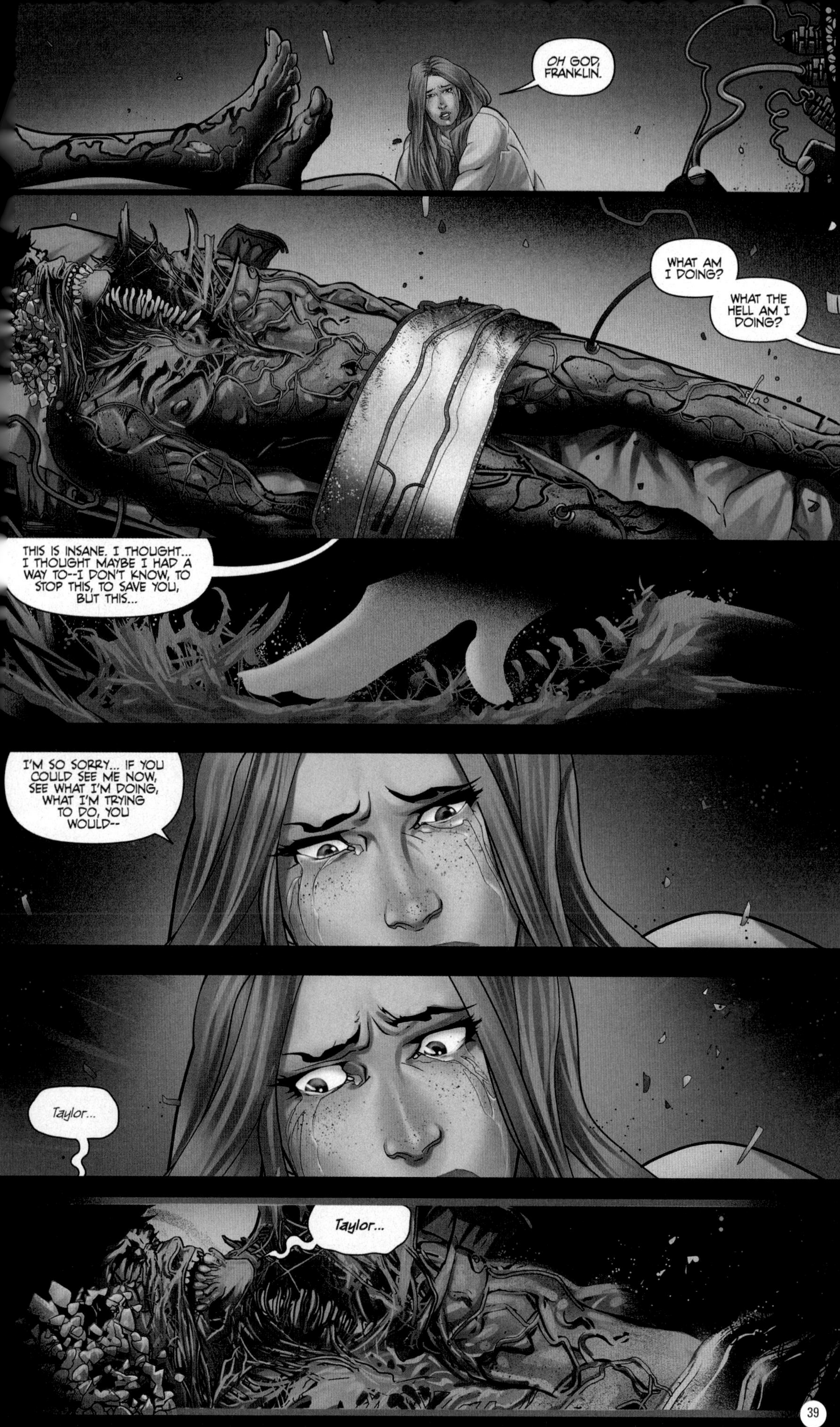
OH GOD, FRANKLIN.
WHAT AM I DOING?
WHAT THE HELL AM I DOING?
THIS IS INSANE. I THOUGHT... I THOUGHT MAYBE I HAD A WAY TO--I DON'T KNOW, TO STOP THIS, TO SAVE YOU, BUT THIS...
I'M SO SORRY... IF YOU COULD SEE ME NOW, SEE WHAT I'M DOING, WHAT I'M TRYING TO DO, YOU WOULD--
Taylor...
Taylor...

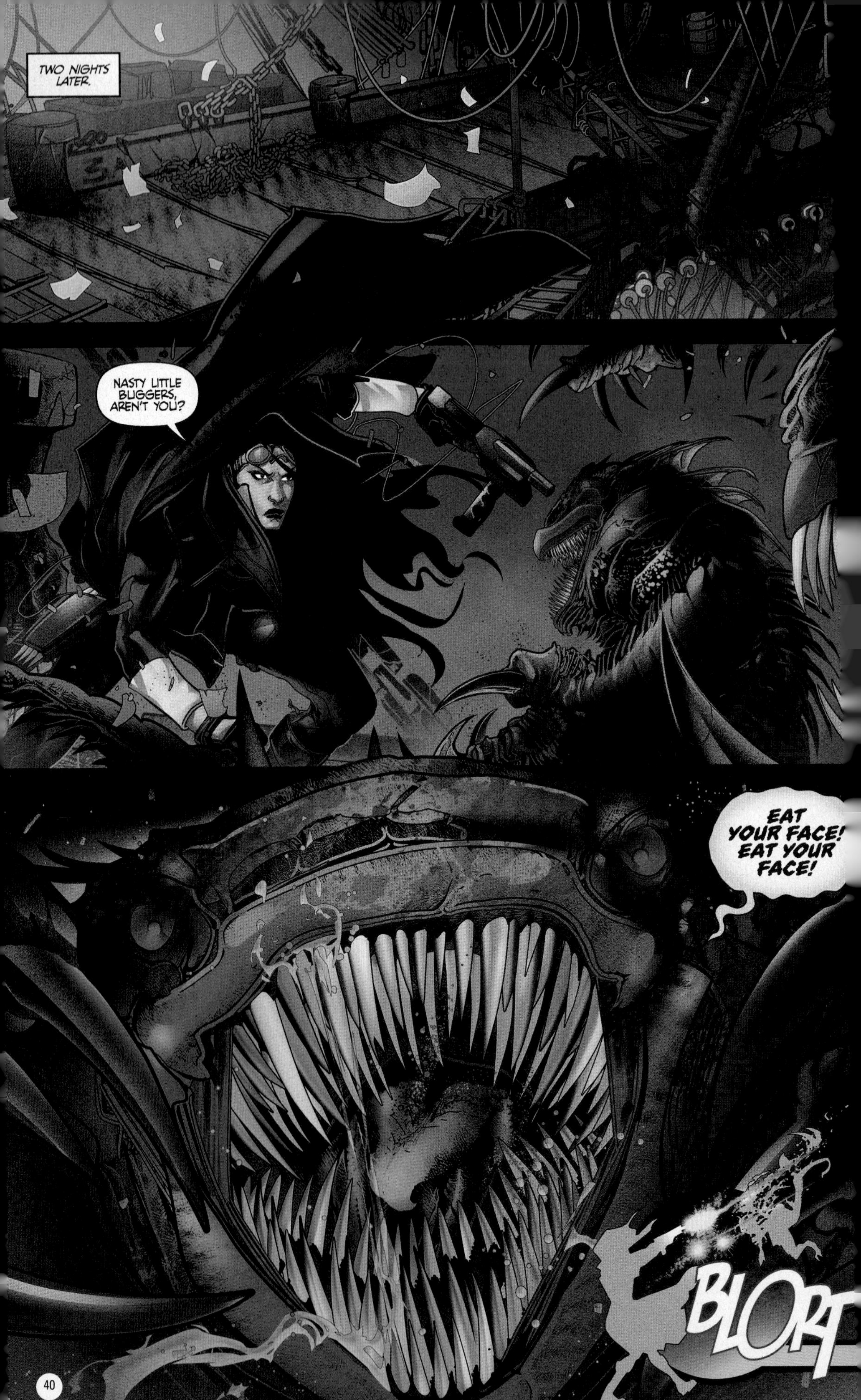
TWO NIGHTS LATER.
NASTY LITTLE BUGGERS, AREN'T YOU?
EAT YOUR FACE! EAT YOUR FACE!
BLORT

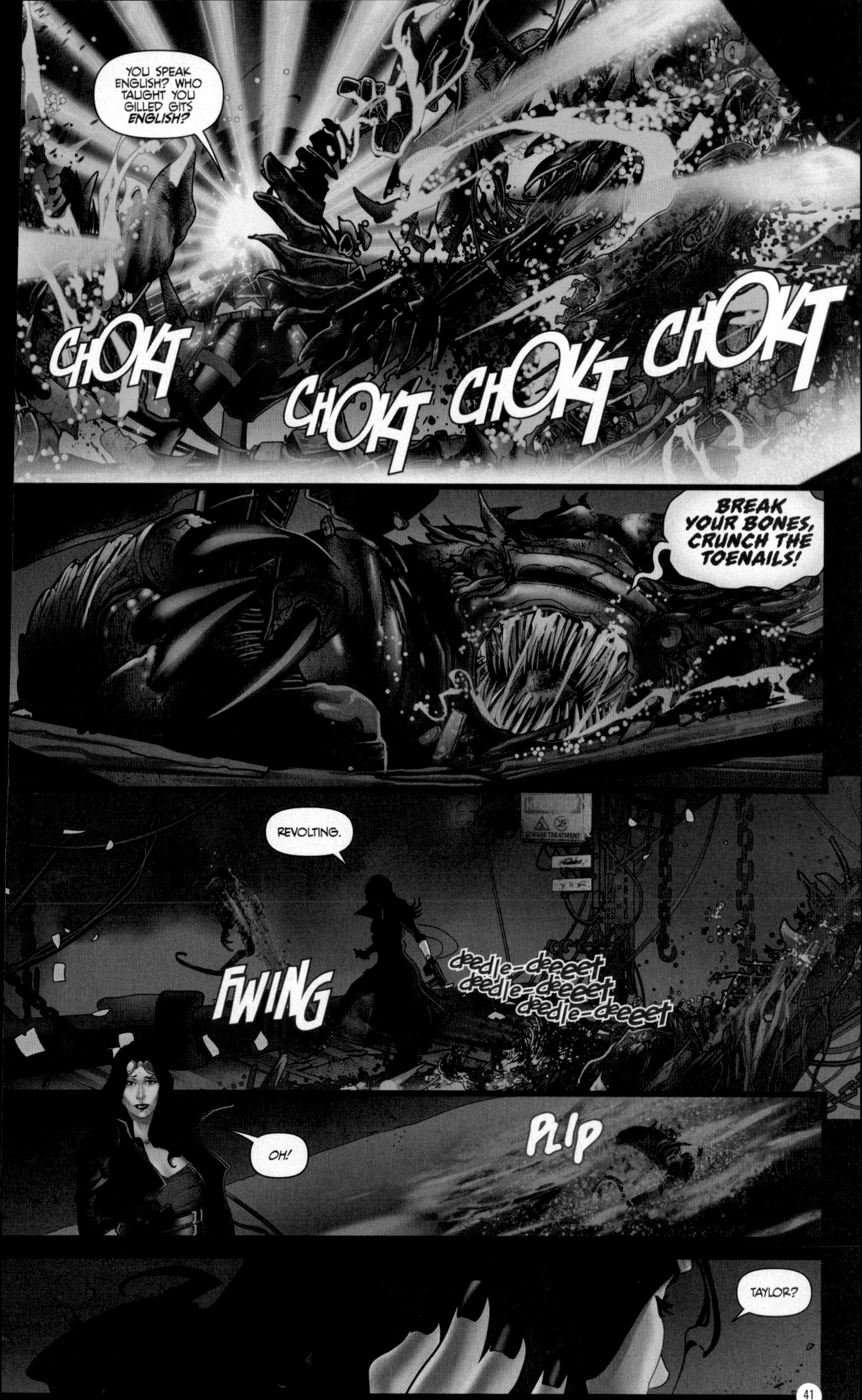

YOU SPEAK ENGLISH? WHO TAUGHT YOU GILLED GITS *ENGLISH?*
CHOKT
CHOKT
CHOKT
CHOKT
BREAK YOUR BONES, CRUNCH THE TOENAILS!
REVOLTING.
SEWAGE TREATMENT
FWING
deedle-deeeet
deedle-deeeet
deedle-deeeet
OH!
PLIP
TAYLOR?

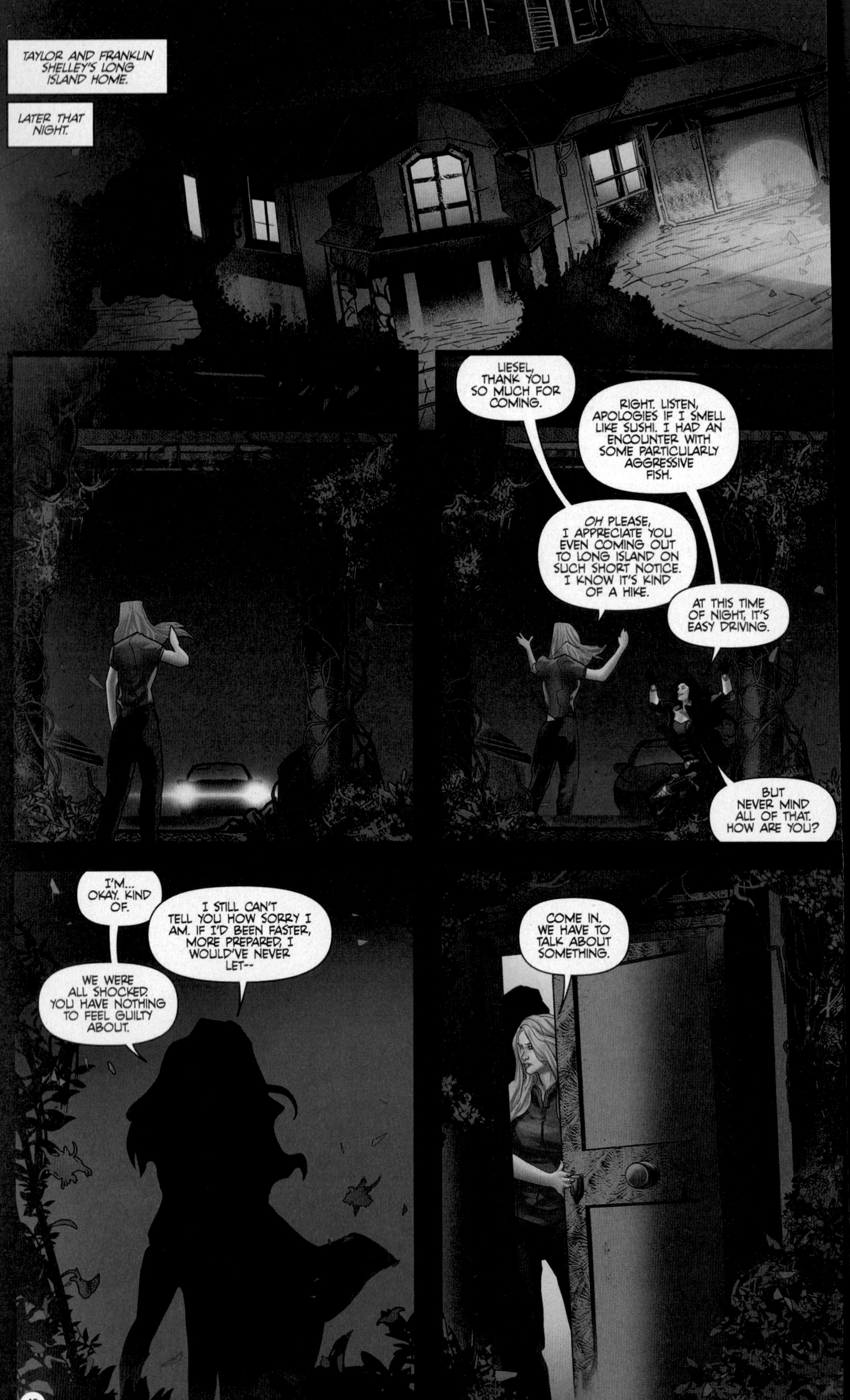

TAYLOR AND FRANKLIN SHELLEY'S LONG ISLAND HOME.
LATER THAT NIGHT.
LIESEL, THANK YOU SO MUCH FOR COMING.
RIGHT. LISTEN, APOLOGIES IF I SMELL LIKE SUSHI. I HAD AN ENCOUNTER WITH SOME PARTICULARLY AGGRESSIVE FISH.
OH PLEASE, I APPRECIATE YOU EVEN COMING OUT TO LONG ISLAND ON SUCH SHORT NOTICE. I KNOW IT'S KIND OF A HIKE.
AT THIS TIME OF NIGHT, IT'S EASY DRIVING.
BUT NEVER MIND ALL OF THAT. HOW ARE YOU?
I'M... OKAY. KIND OF.
I STILL CAN'T TELL YOU HOW SORRY I AM. IF I'D BEEN FASTER, MORE PREPARED, I WOULD'VE NEVER LET--
WE WERE ALL SHOCKED. YOU HAVE NOTHING TO FEEL GUILTY ABOUT.
COME IN. WE HAVE TO TALK ABOUT SOMETHING.

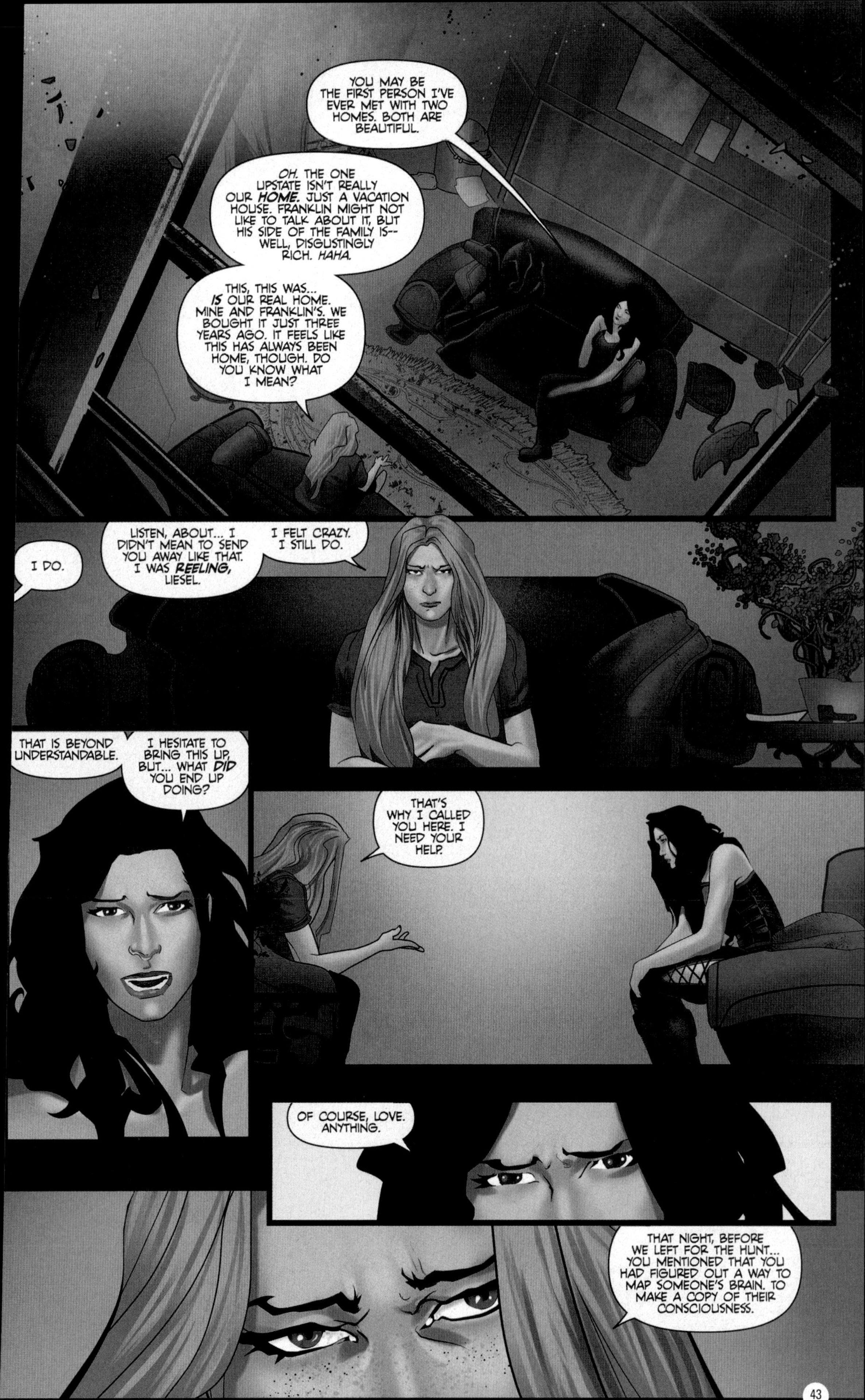
YOU MAY BE THE FIRST PERSON I'VE EVER MET WITH TWO HOMES. BOTH ARE BEAUTIFUL.
OH. THE ONE UPSTATE ISN'T REALLY OUR HOME. JUST A VACATION HOUSE. FRANKLIN MIGHT NOT LIKE TO TALK ABOUT IT, BUT HIS SIDE OF THE FAMILY IS-- WELL, DISGUSTINGLY RICH. HAHA.
THIS, THIS WAS... IS OUR REAL HOME. MINE AND FRANKLIN'S. WE BOUGHT IT JUST THREE YEARS AGO. IT FEELS LIKE THIS HAS ALWAYS BEEN HOME, THOUGH. DO YOU KNOW WHAT I MEAN?
I DO.
LISTEN, ABOUT... I DIDN'T MEAN TO SEND YOU AWAY LIKE THAT. I WAS REELING, LIESEL.
I FELT CRAZY. I STILL DO.
THAT IS BEYOND UNDERSTANDABLE.
I HESITATE TO BRING THIS UP, BUT... WHAT DID YOU END UP DOING?
THAT'S WHY I CALLED YOU HERE. I NEED YOUR HELP.
OF COURSE, LOVE. ANYTHING.
THAT NIGHT, BEFORE WE LEFT FOR THE HUNT... YOU MENTIONED THAT YOU HAD FIGURED OUT A WAY TO MAP SOMEONE'S BRAIN. TO MAKE A COPY OF THEIR CONSCIOUSNESS.

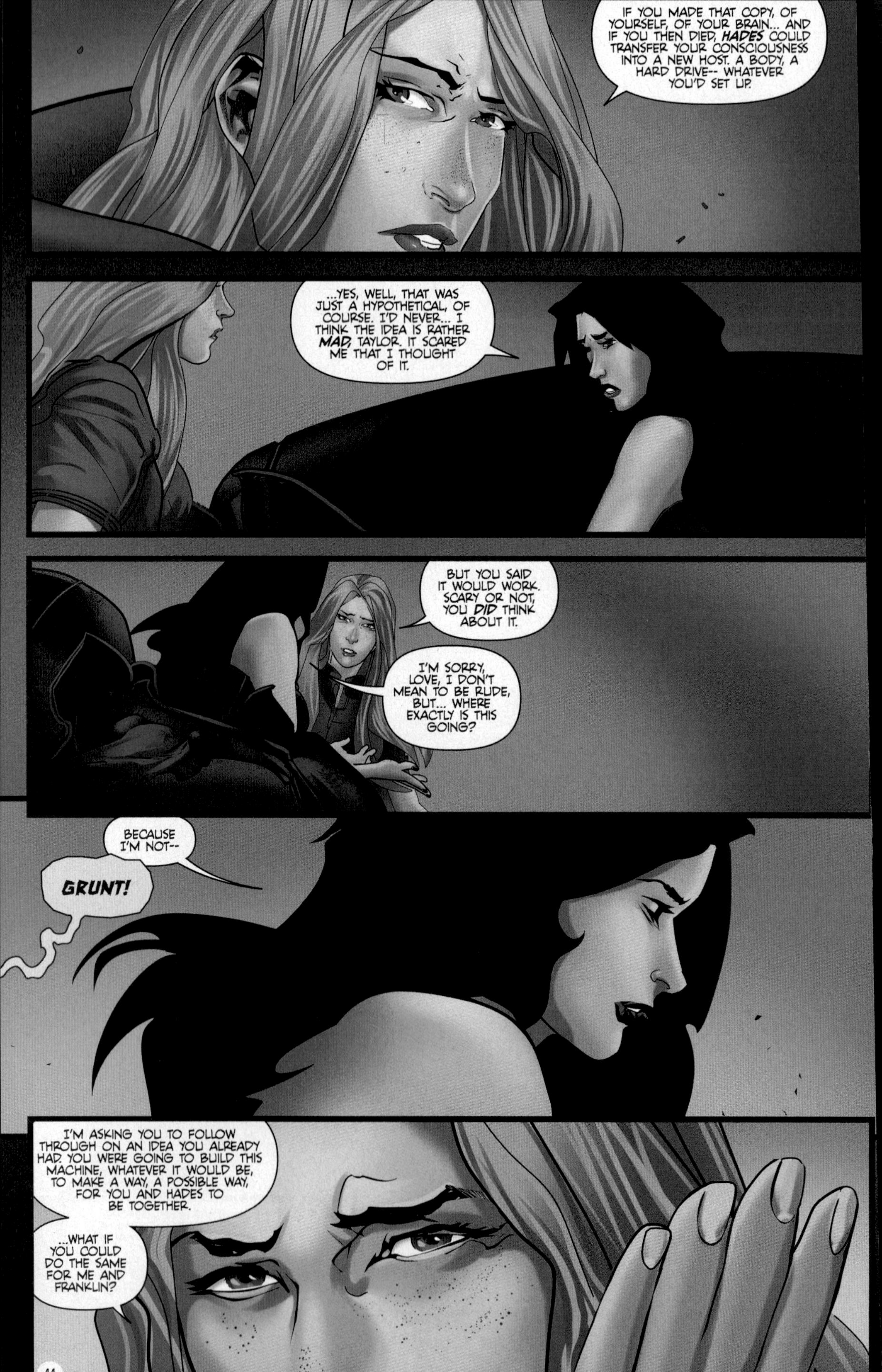
IF YOU MADE THAT COPY, OF YOURSELF, OF YOUR BRAIN... AND IF YOU THEN DIED, HADES COULD TRANSFER YOUR CONSCIOUSNESS INTO A NEW HOST. A BODY, A HARD DRIVE-- WHATEVER YOU'D SET UP.
...YES, WELL, THAT WAS JUST A HYPOTHETICAL, OF COURSE. I'D NEVER... I THINK THE IDEA IS RATHER MAD, TAYLOR. IT SCARED ME THAT I THOUGHT OF IT.
BUT YOU SAID IT WOULD WORK. SCARY OR NOT, YOU DID THINK ABOUT IT.
I'M SORRY, LOVE, I DON'T MEAN TO BE RUDE, BUT... WHERE EXACTLY IS THIS GOING?
BECAUSE I'M NOT--
GRUNT!
I'M ASKING YOU TO FOLLOW THROUGH ON AN IDEA YOU ALREADY HAD. YOU WERE GOING TO BUILD THIS MACHINE, WHATEVER IT WOULD BE, TO MAKE A WAY, A POSSIBLE WAY, FOR YOU AND HADES TO BE TOGETHER.
...WHAT IF YOU COULD DO THE SAME FOR ME AND FRANKLIN?

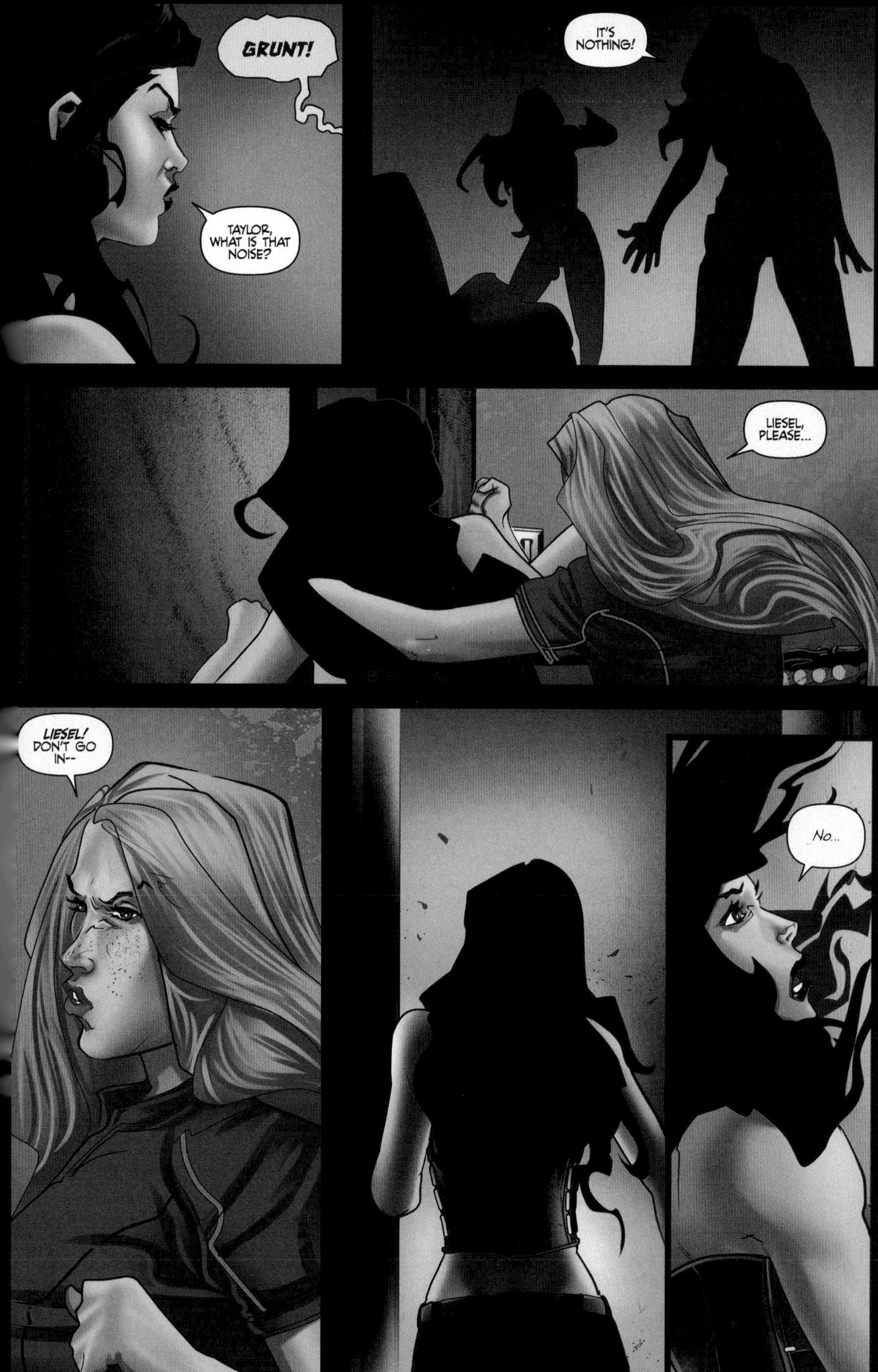
GRUNT!
TAYLOR, WHAT IS THAT NOISE?
IT'S NOTHING!
LIESEL, PLEASE...
LIESEL! DON'T GO IN--
No...

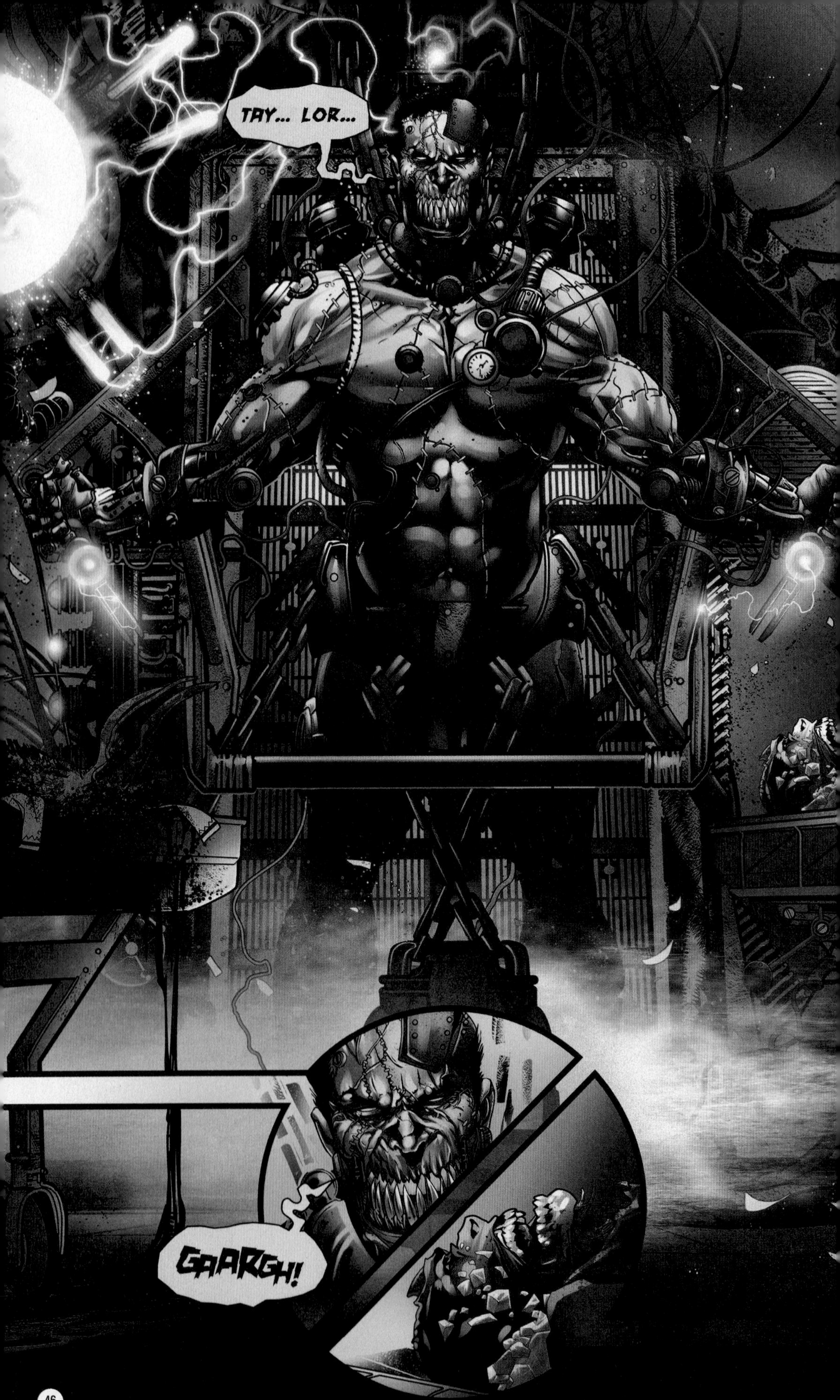
TAY... LOR...
GAARGH!

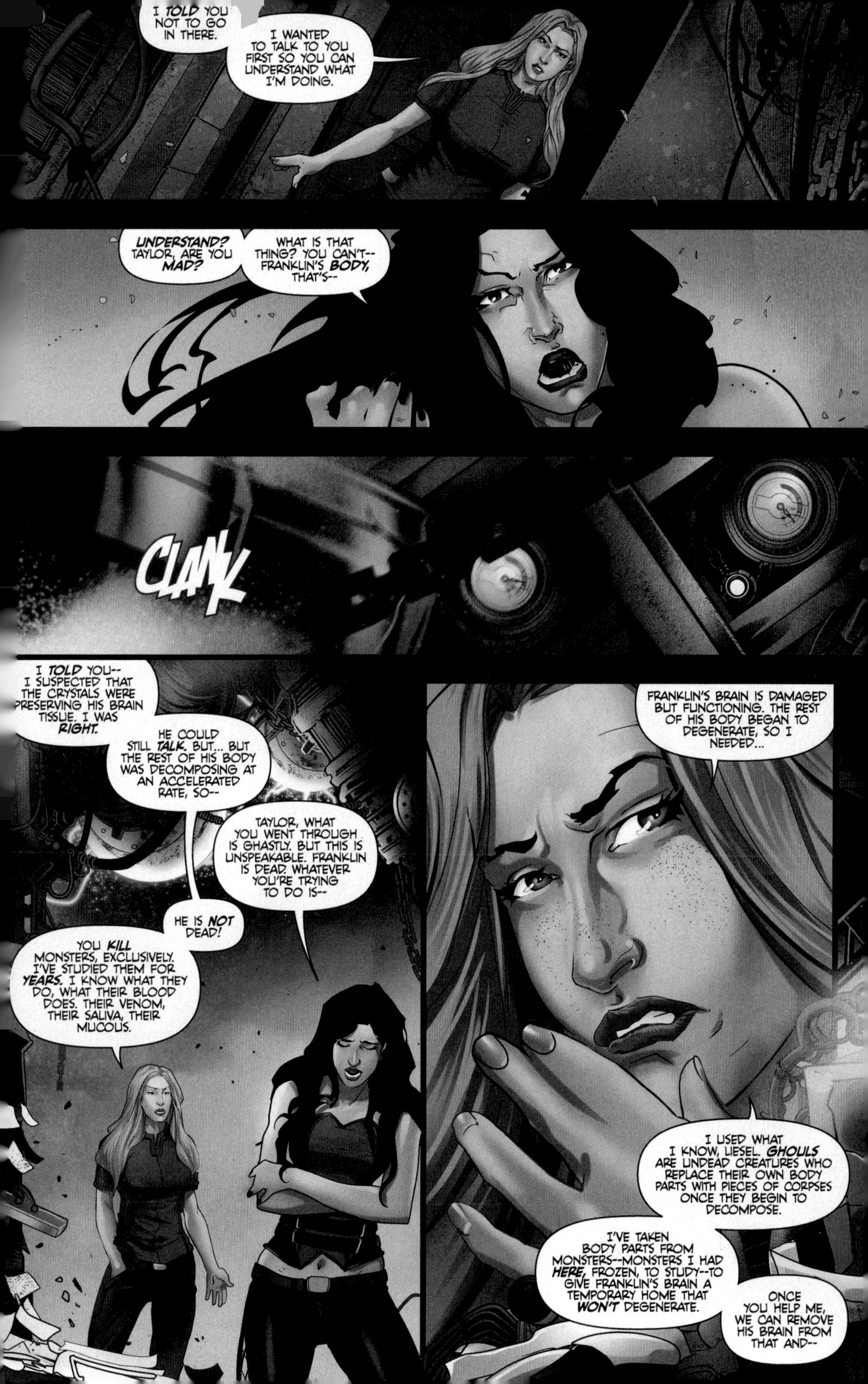
I TOLD YOU NOT TO GO IN THERE.
I WANTED TO TALK TO YOU FIRST SO YOU CAN UNDERSTAND WHAT I'M DOING.
UNDERSTAND? TAYLOR, ARE YOU MAD?
WHAT IS THAT THING? YOU CAN'T-- FRANKLIN'S BODY, THAT'S--
CLANK
I TOLD YOU-- I SUSPECTED THAT THE CRYSTALS WERE PRESERVING HIS BRAIN TISSUE. I WAS RIGHT.
HE COULD STILL TALK. BUT... BUT THE REST OF HIS BODY WAS DECOMPOSING AT AN ACCELERATED RATE, SO--
TAYLOR, WHAT YOU WENT THROUGH IS GHASTLY. BUT THIS IS UNSPEAKABLE. FRANKLIN IS DEAD. WHATEVER YOU'RE TRYING TO DO IS--
HE IS NOT DEAD!
YOU KILL MONSTERS, EXCLUSIVELY. I'VE STUDIED THEM FOR YEARS. I KNOW WHAT THEY DO, WHAT THEIR BLOOD DOES. THEIR VENOM, THEIR SALIVA, THEIR MUCOUS.
FRANKLIN'S BRAIN IS DAMAGED BUT FUNCTIONING. THE REST OF HIS BODY BEGAN TO DEGENERATE, SO I NEEDED...
I USED WHAT I KNOW, LIESEL. GHOULS ARE UNDEAD CREATURES WHO REPLACE THEIR OWN BODY PARTS WITH PIECES OF CORPSES ONCE THEY BEGIN TO DECOMPOSE.
I'VE TAKEN BODY PARTS FROM MONSTERS--MONSTERS I HAD HERE, FROZEN, TO STUDY--TO GIVE FRANKLIN'S BRAIN A TEMPORARY HOME THAT WON'T DEGENERATE.
ONCE YOU HELP ME, WE CAN REMOVE HIS BRAIN FROM THAT AND--

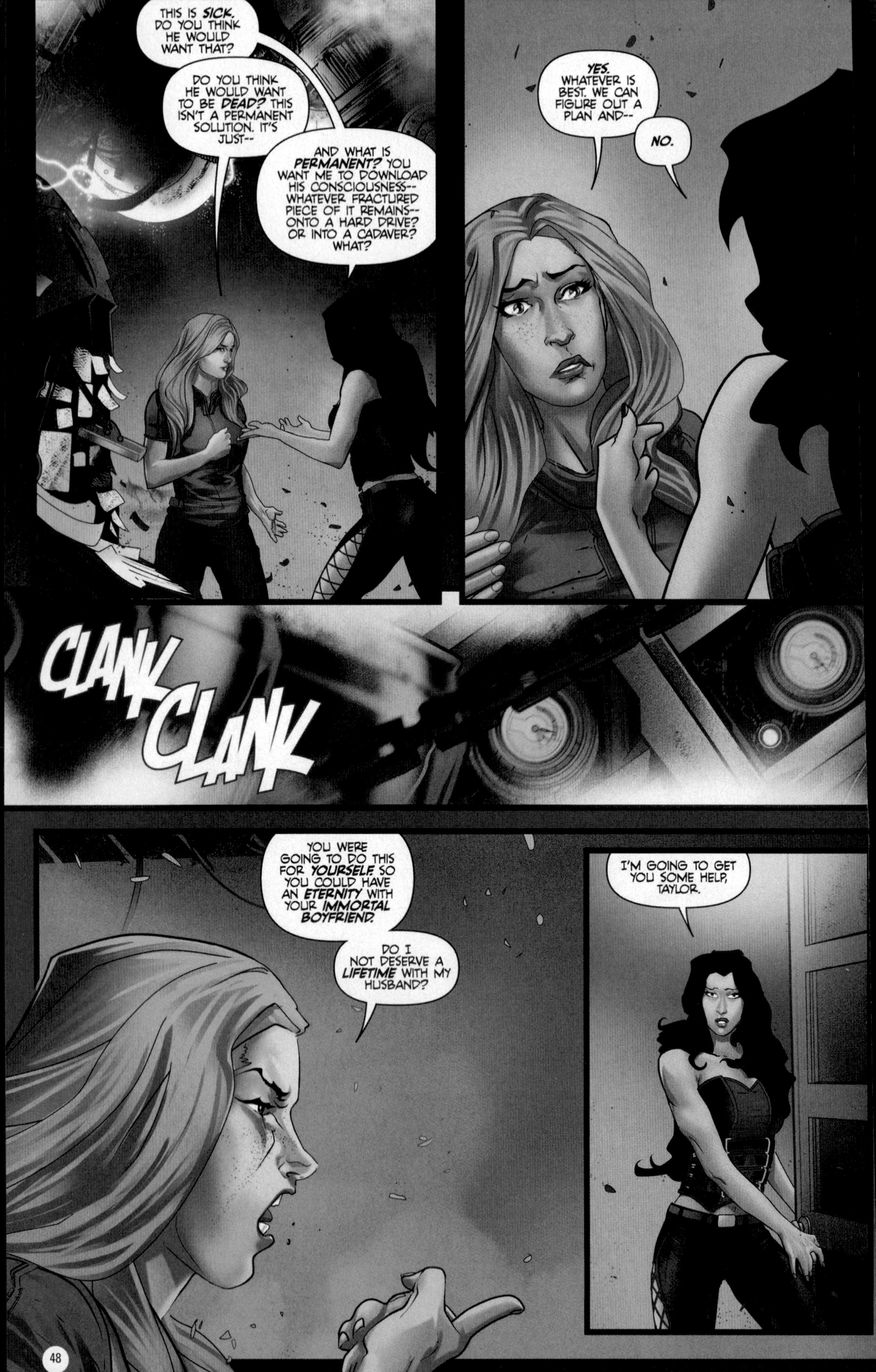
THIS IS SICK. DO YOU THINK HE WOULD WANT THAT?
DO YOU THINK HE WOULD WANT TO BE DEAD? THIS ISN'T A PERMANENT SOLUTION. IT'S JUST--
AND WHAT IS PERMANENT? YOU WANT ME TO DOWNLOAD HIS CONSCIOUSNESS-- WHATEVER FRACTURED PIECE OF IT REMAINS-- ONTO A HARD DRIVE? OR INTO A CADAVER? WHAT?
YES. WHATEVER IS BEST. WE CAN FIGURE OUT A PLAN AND--
NO.
CLANK
CLANK
YOU WERE GOING TO DO THIS FOR YOURSELF. SO YOU COULD HAVE AN ETERNITY WITH YOUR IMMORTAL BOYFRIEND.
DO I NOT DESERVE A LIFETIME WITH MY HUSBAND?
I'M GOING TO GET YOU SOME HELP, TAYLOR.

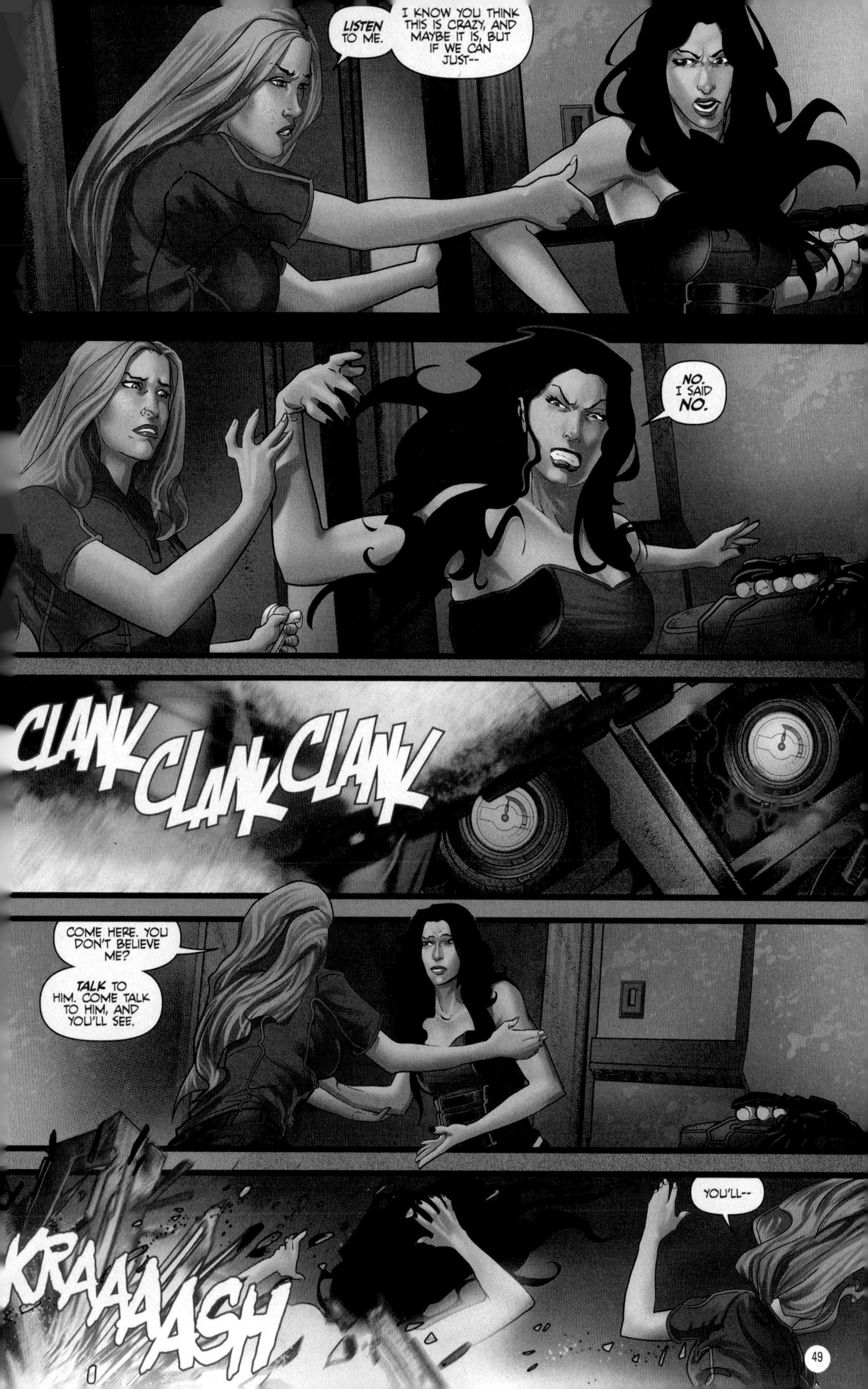
LISTEN TO ME.
I KNOW YOU THINK THIS IS CRAZY, AND MAYBE IT IS, BUT IF WE CAN JUST--
NO. I SAID NO.
CLANK CLANK CLANK
COME HERE. YOU DON'T BELIEVE ME?
TALK TO HIM. COME TALK TO HIM, AND YOU'LL SEE.
KRAAAAASH
YOU'LL--

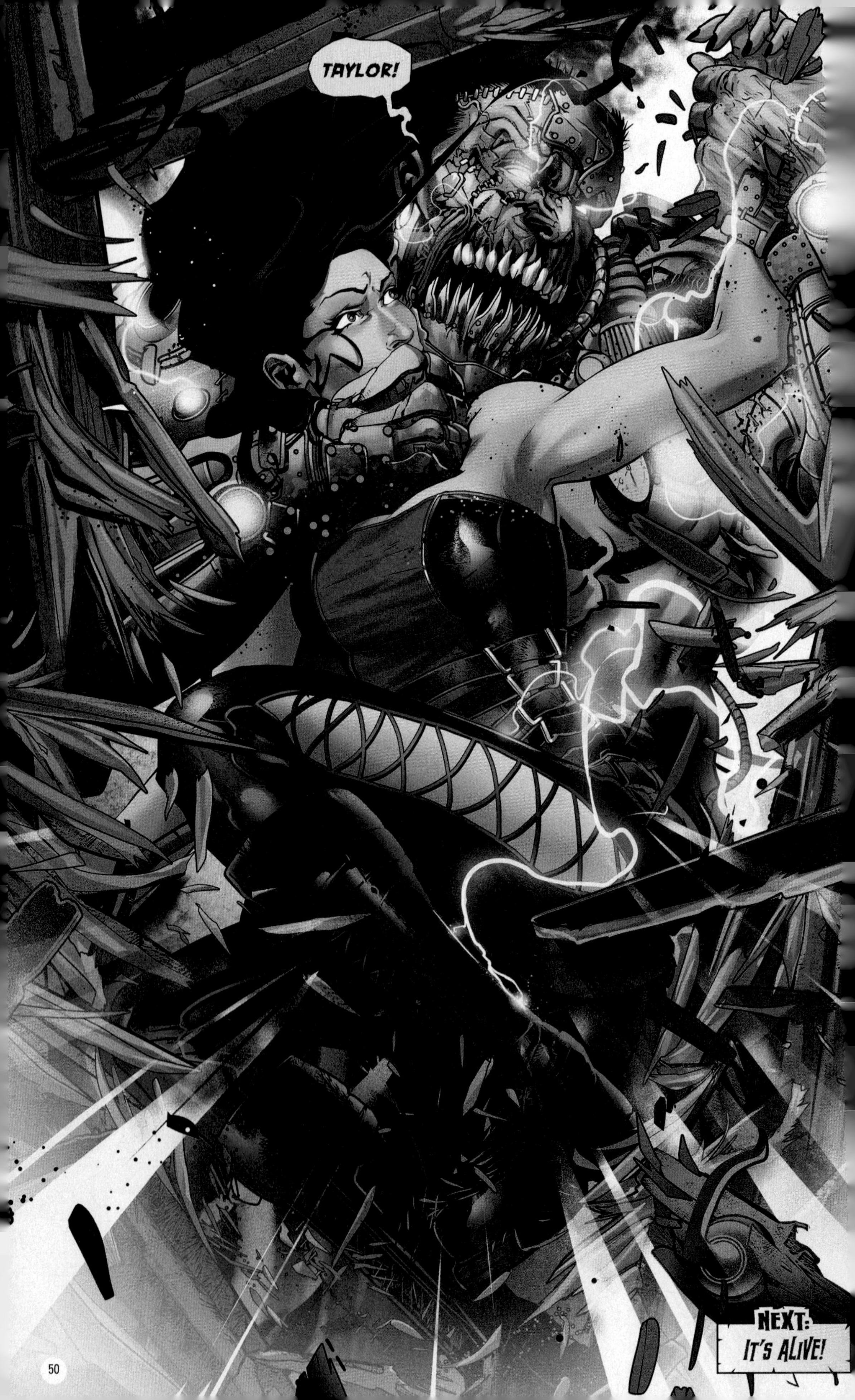
TAYLOR!
NEXT:
IT'S ALIVE!

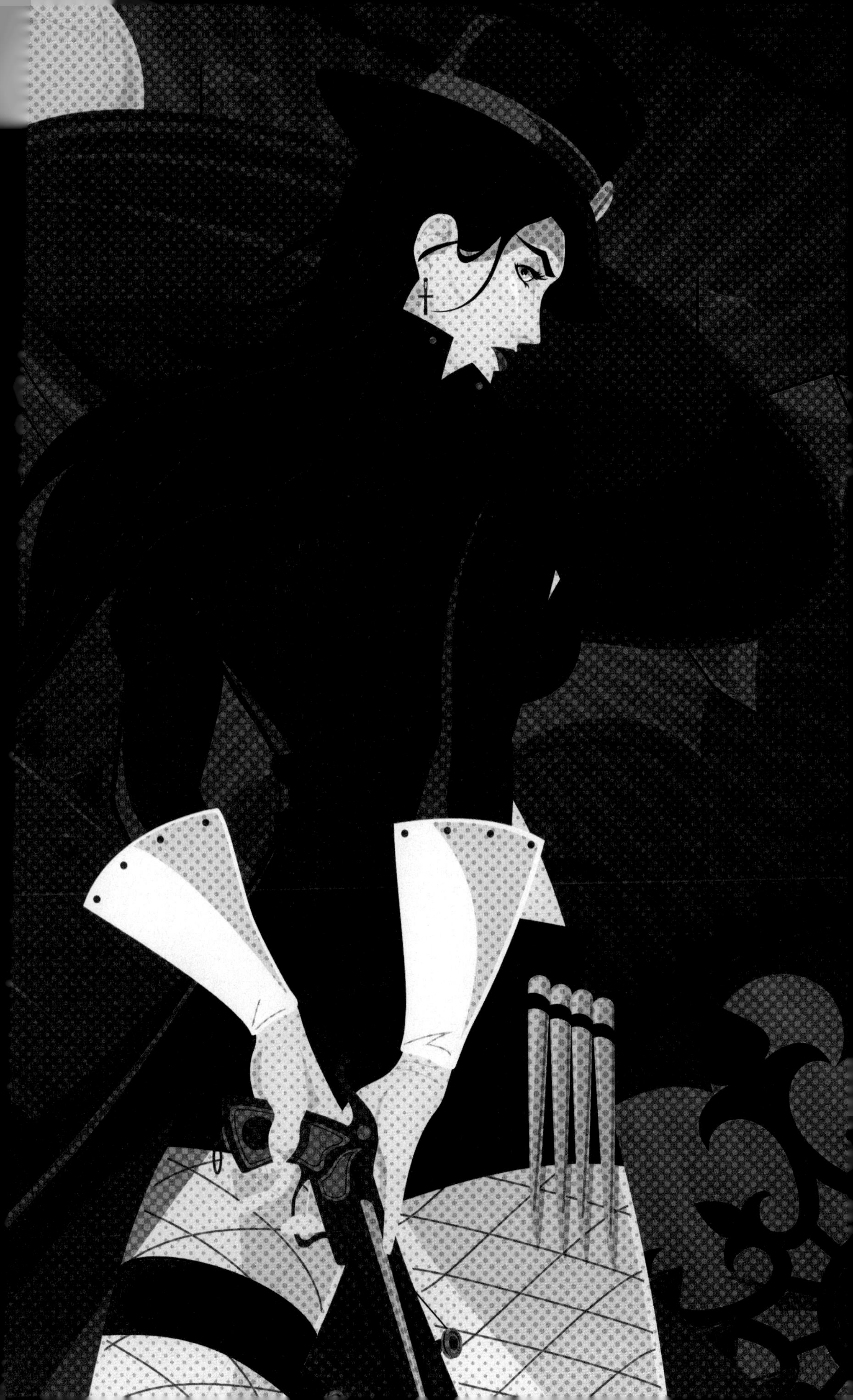

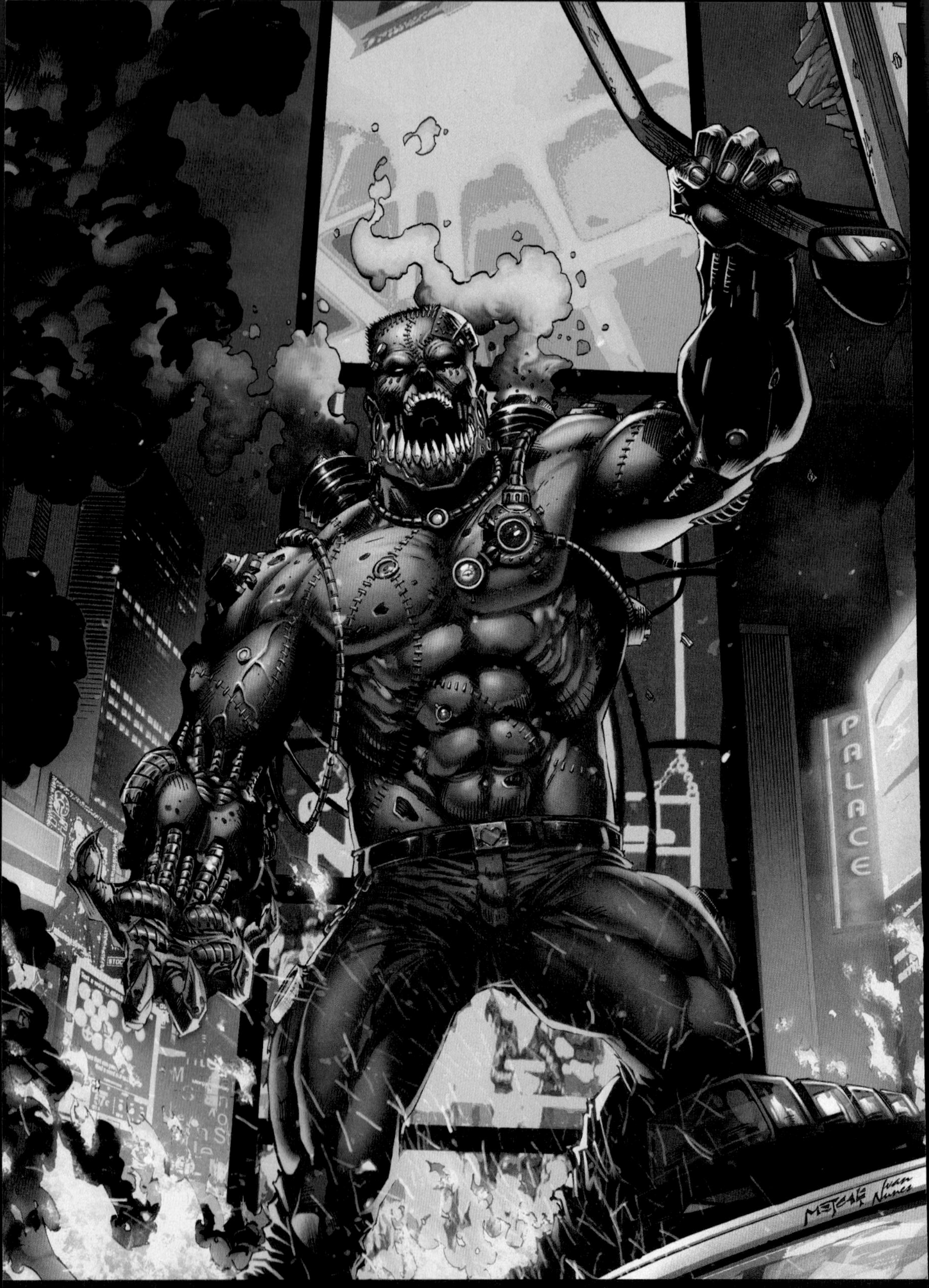
PALACE

CHAPTER THREE

IT'S ALIVE

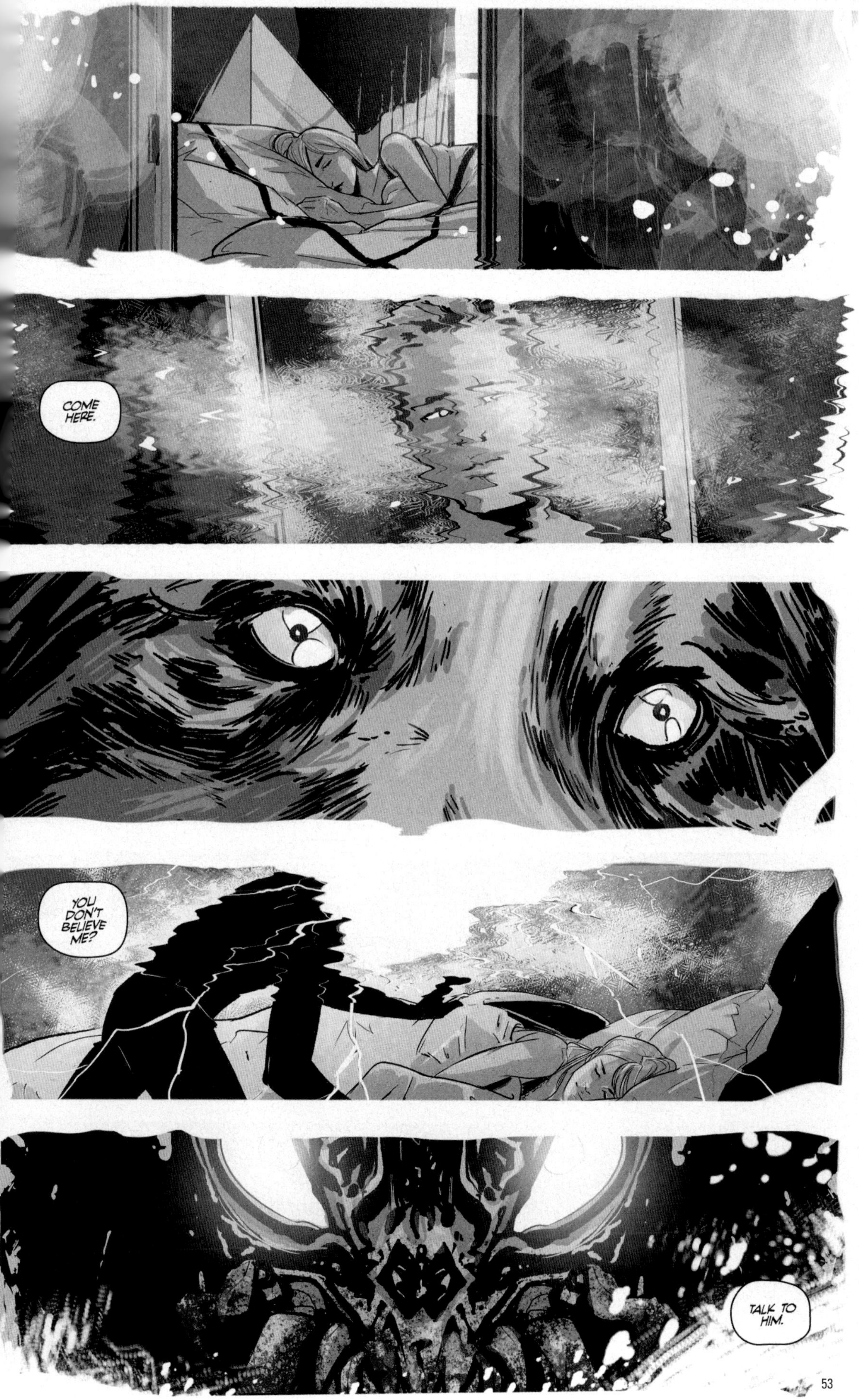
COME HERE.
YOU DON'T BELIEVE ME?
TALK TO HIM.

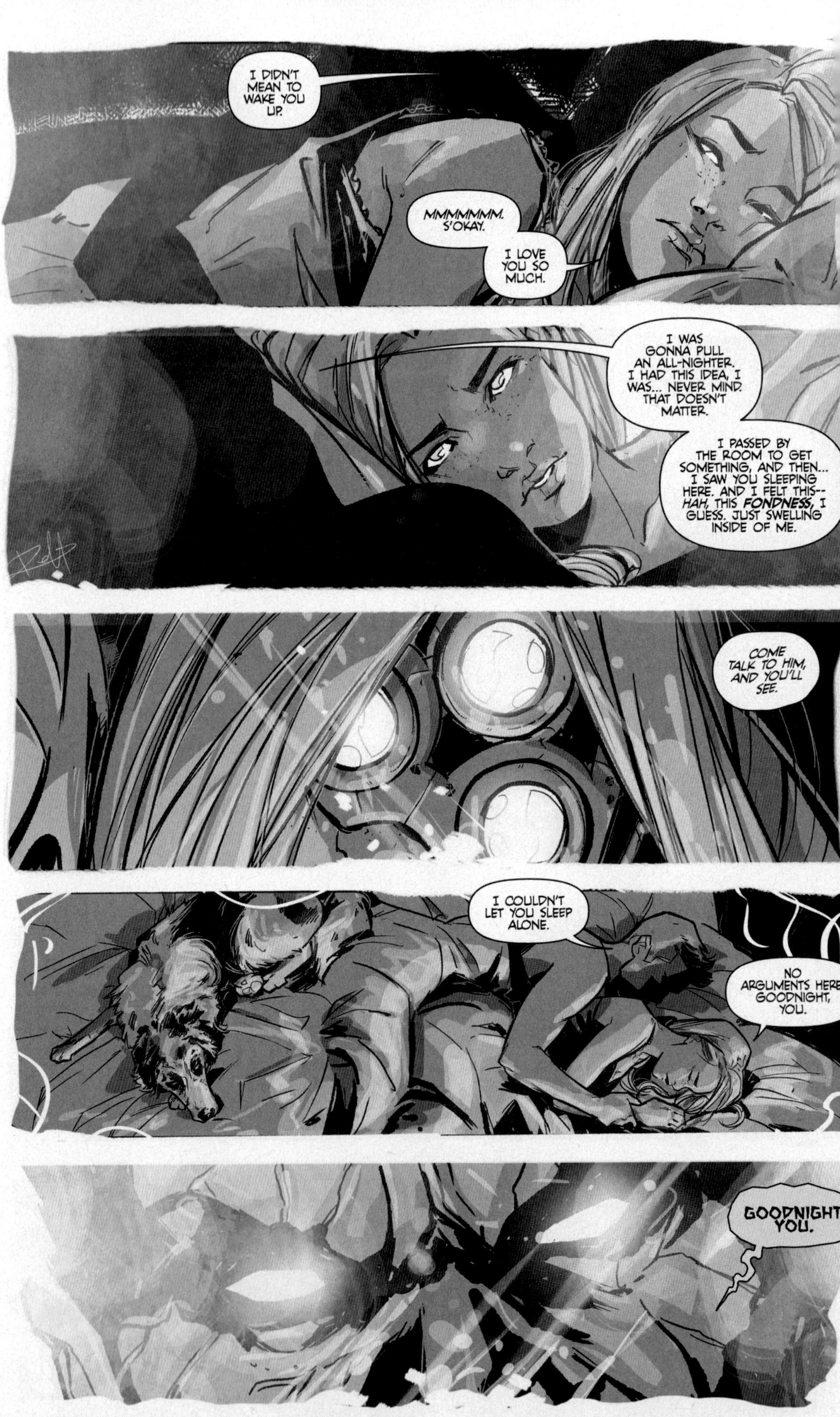
I DIDN'T MEAN TO WAKE YOU UP.
MMMMMMM. S'OKAY.
I LOVE YOU SO MUCH.
I WAS GONNA PULL AN ALL-NIGHTER. I HAD THIS IDEA, I WAS... NEVER MIND. THAT DOESN'T MATTER.
I PASSED BY THE ROOM TO GET SOMETHING, AND THEN... I SAW YOU SLEEPING HERE. AND I FELT THIS-- HAH, THIS FONDNESS, I GUESS. JUST SWELLING INSIDE OF ME.
COME TALK TO HIM, AND YOU'LL SEE.
I COULDN'T LET YOU SLEEP ALONE.
NO ARGUMENTS HERE. GOODNIGHT, YOU.
GOODNIGHT, YOU.

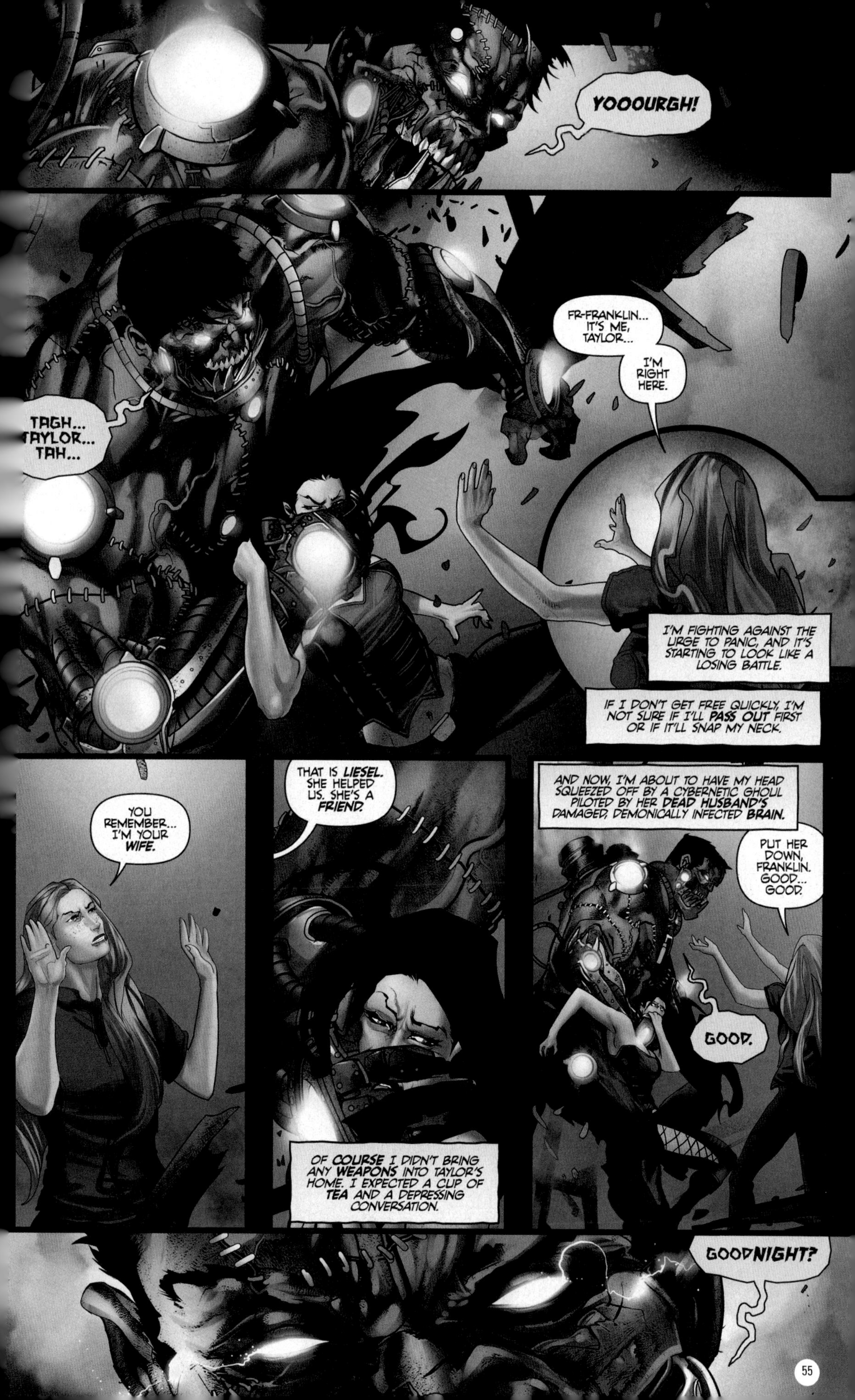

YOOOURGH!
FR-FRANKLIN... IT'S ME, TAYLOR...
I'M RIGHT HERE.
TAGH... TAYLOR... TAH...
I'M FIGHTING AGAINST THE URGE TO PANIC, AND IT'S STARTING TO LOOK LIKE A LOSING BATTLE.
IF I DON'T GET FREE QUICKLY, I'M NOT SURE IF I'LL PASS OUT FIRST OR IF IT'LL SNAP MY NECK.
YOU REMEMBER... I'M YOUR WIFE.
THAT IS LIESEL. SHE HELPED US. SHE'S A FRIEND.
OF COURSE I DIDN'T BRING ANY WEAPONS INTO TAYLOR'S HOME. I EXPECTED A CUP OF TEA AND A DEPRESSING CONVERSATION.
AND NOW, I'M ABOUT TO HAVE MY HEAD SQUEEZED OFF BY A CYBERNETIC GHOUL PILOTED BY HER DEAD HUSBAND'S DAMAGED, DEMONICALLY INFECTED BRAIN.
PUT HER DOWN, FRANKLIN. GOOD... GOOD.
GOOD.
GOODNIGHT?

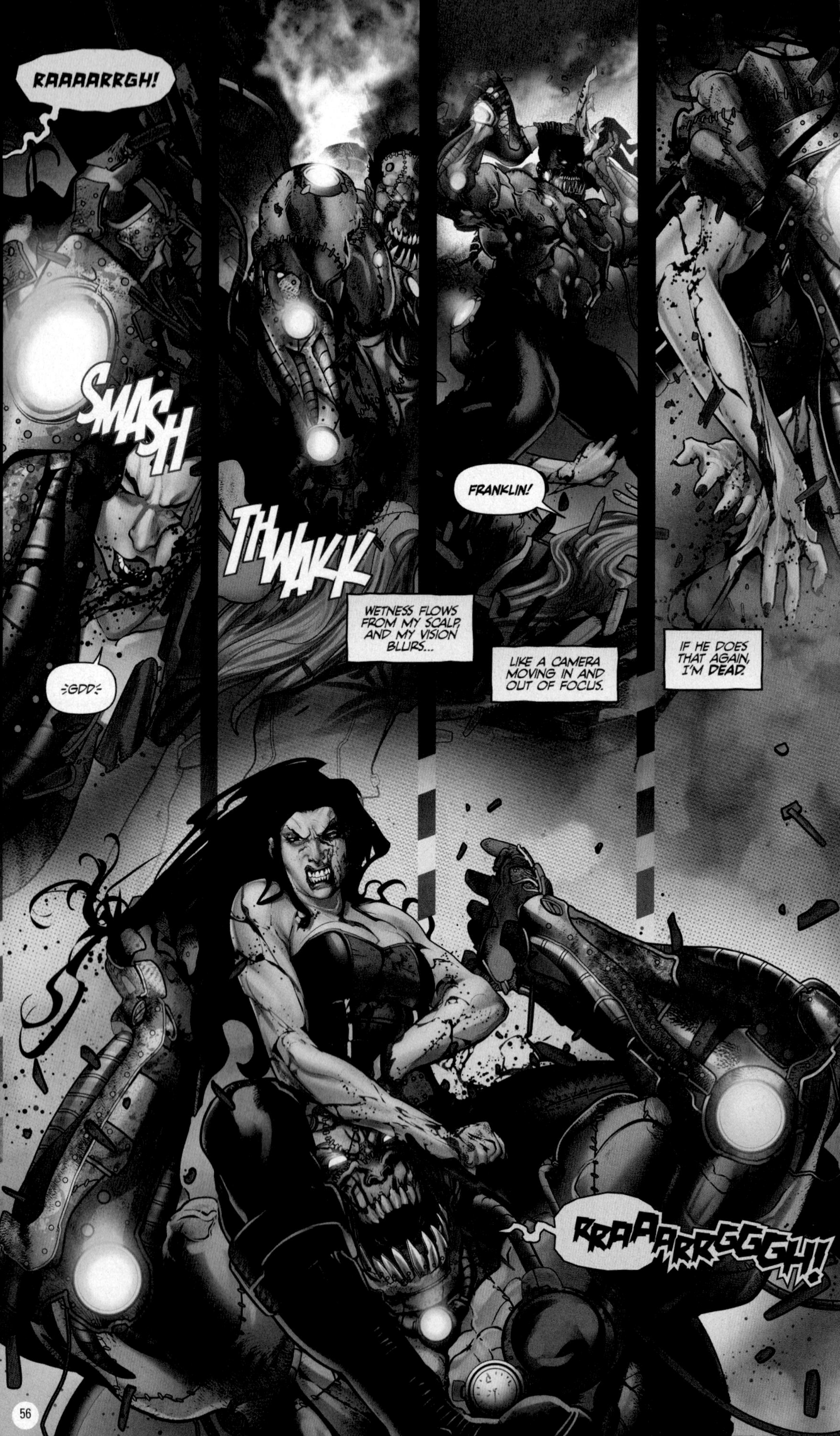
RAAAARRGH!
SMASH
GDD
THWAKK
WETNESS FLOWS FROM MY SCALP, AND MY VISION BLURS...
FRANKLIN!
LIKE A CAMERA MOVING IN AND OUT OF FOCUS.
IF HE DOES THAT AGAIN, I'M DEAD.
RRAAAARRGGGH!!

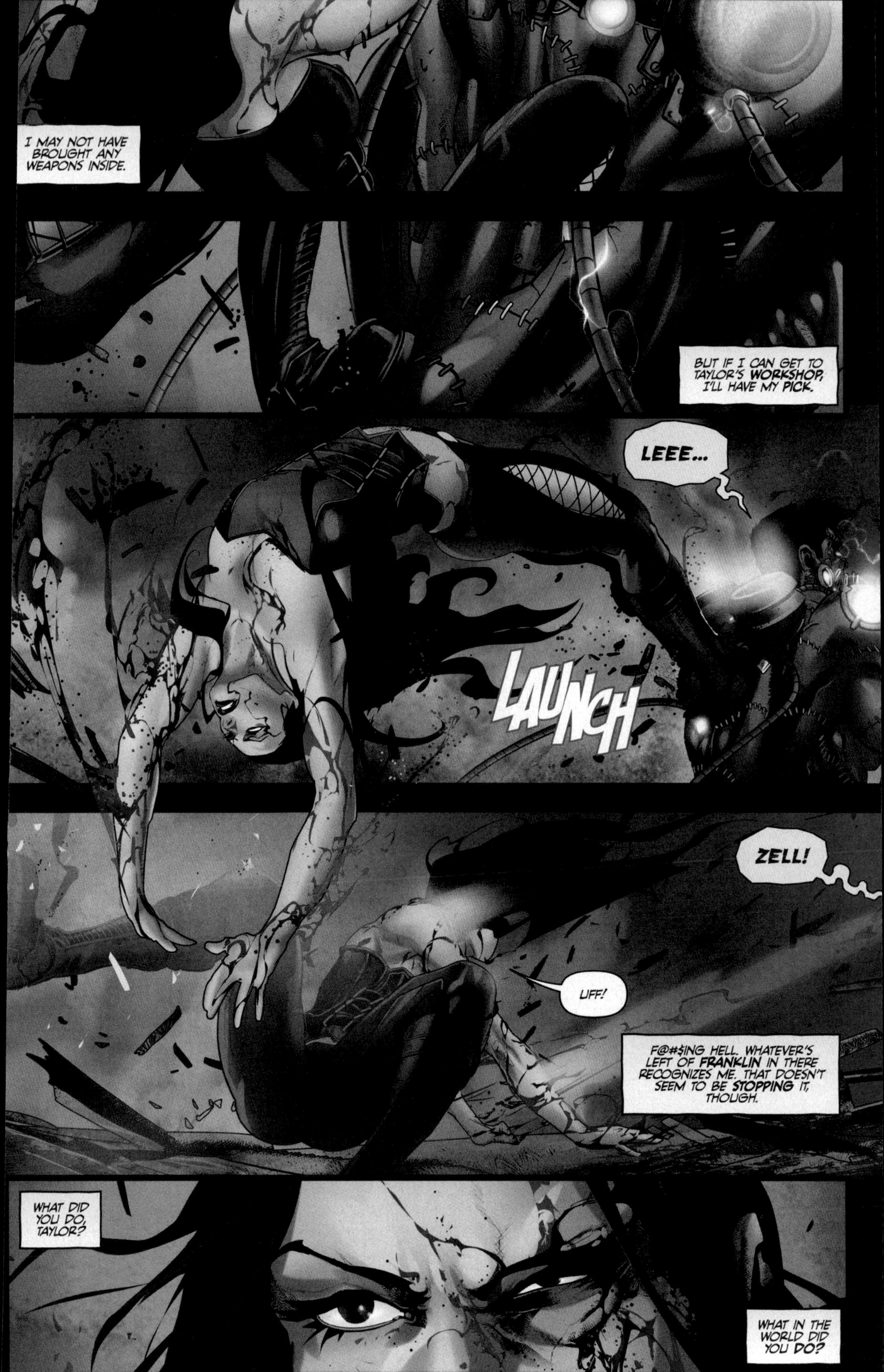
I MAY NOT HAVE BROUGHT ANY WEAPONS INSIDE.
BUT IF I CAN GET TO TAYLOR'S **WORKSHOP**, I'LL HAVE MY **PICK**.
LEEE...
LAUNCH
ZELL!
UFF!
F@#$ING HELL. WHATEVER'S LEFT OF **FRANKLIN** IN THERE RECOGNIZES ME. THAT DOESN'T SEEM TO BE **STOPPING** IT, THOUGH.
WHAT DID YOU DO, TAYLOR?
WHAT IN THE WORLD DID YOU **DO**?

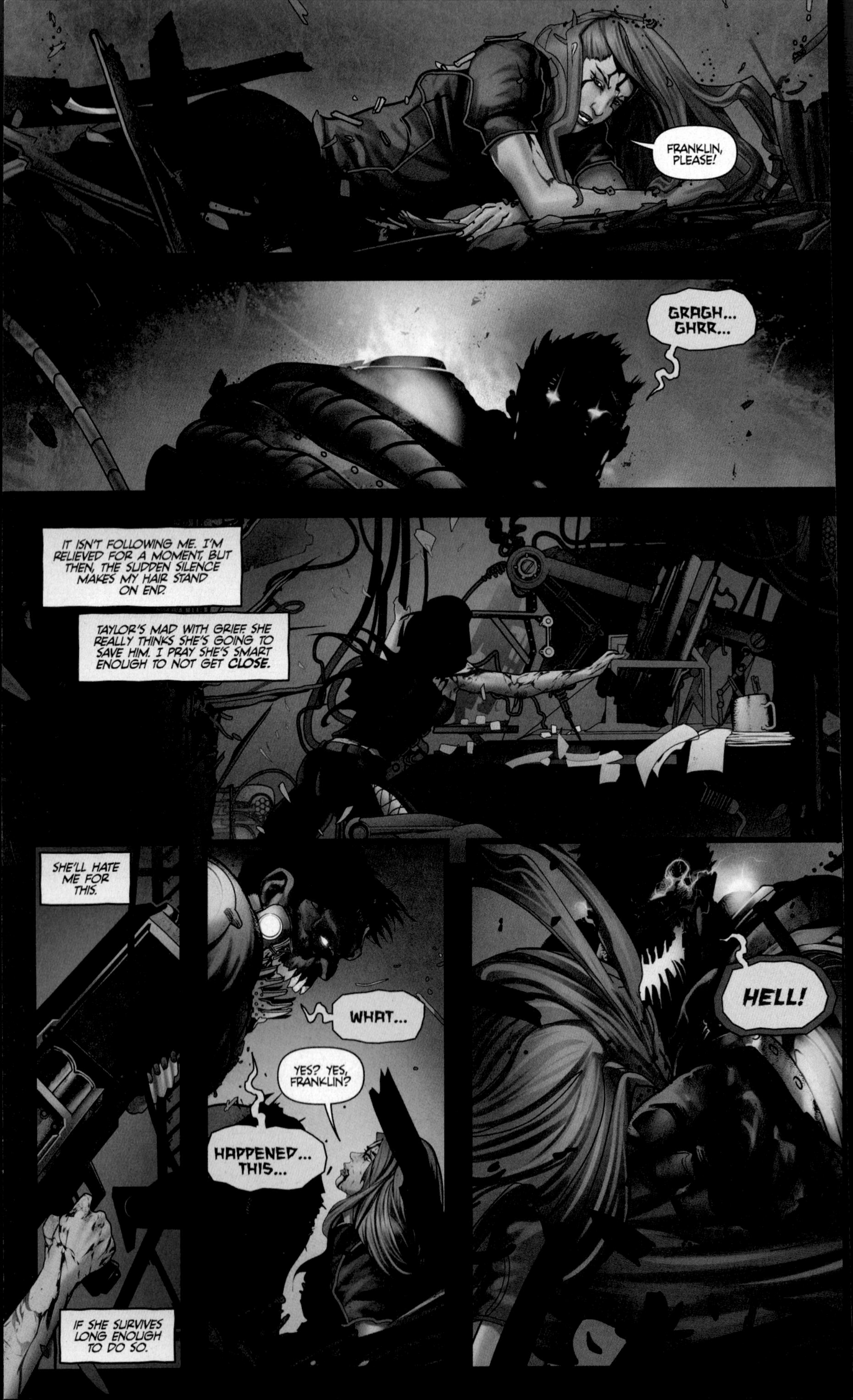
FRANKLIN, PLEASE!
GRAGH... GHRR...
IT ISN'T FOLLOWING ME. I'M RELIEVED FOR A MOMENT, BUT THEN, THE SUDDEN SILENCE MAKES MY HAIR STAND ON END.
TAYLOR'S MAD WITH GRIEF. SHE REALLY THINKS SHE'S GOING TO SAVE HIM. I PRAY SHE'S SMART ENOUGH TO NOT GET **CLOSE.**
SHE'LL HATE ME FOR THIS.
IF SHE SURVIVES LONG ENOUGH TO DO SO.
WHAT...
YES? YES, FRANKLIN?
HAPPENED... THIS...
HELL!

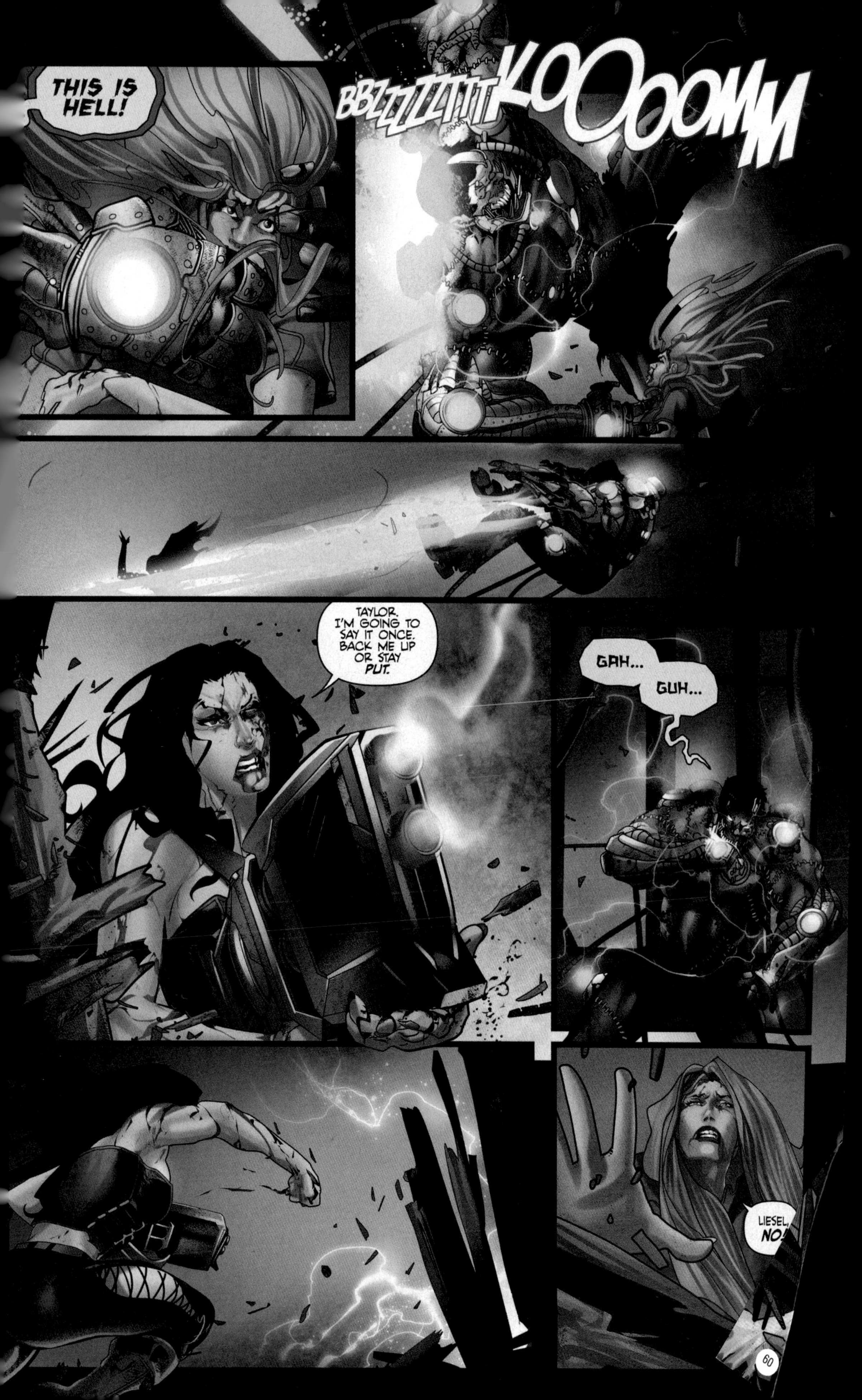
THIS IS HELL!
BBZZZZZTTTTKOOOOOOMM
TAYLOR. I'M GOING TO SAY IT ONCE. BACK ME UP OR STAY PUT.
GAH...
GUH...
LIESEL, NO!

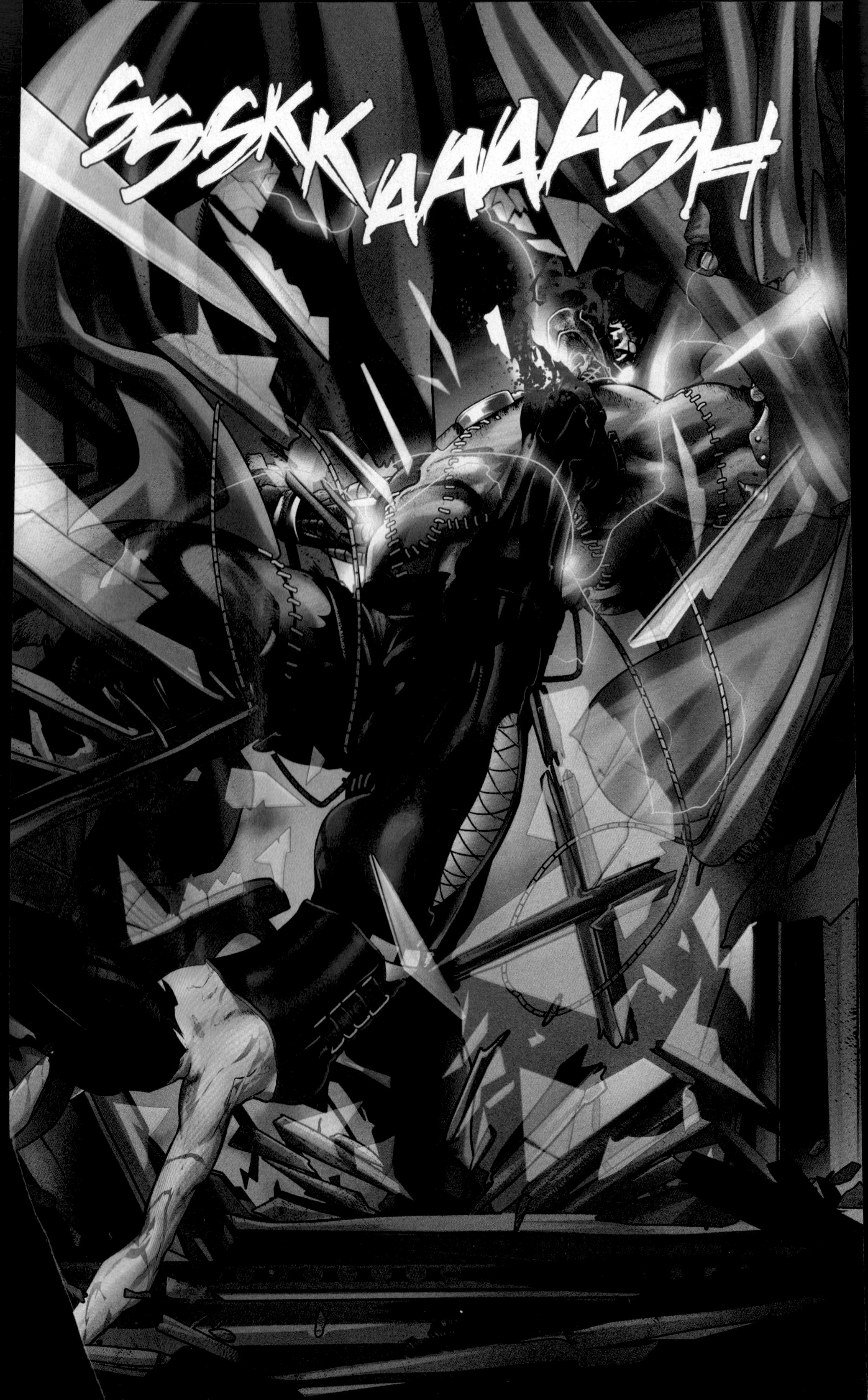
SSSKKAAAAASH

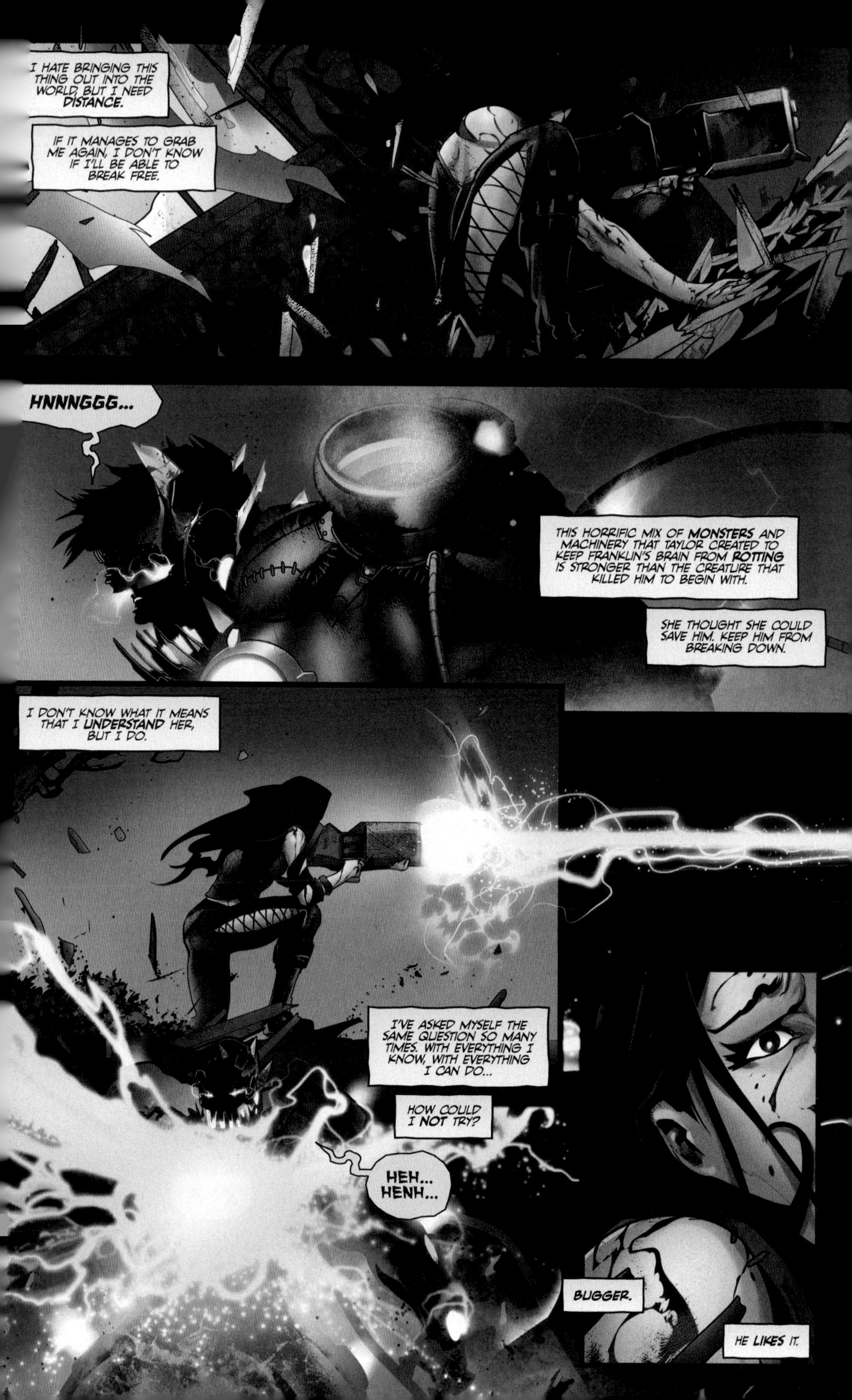
I HATE BRINGING THIS THING OUT INTO THE WORLD, BUT I NEED DISTANCE.
IF IT MANAGES TO GRAB ME AGAIN, I DON'T KNOW IF I'LL BE ABLE TO BREAK FREE.
HNNNGGG...
THIS HORRIFIC MIX OF MONSTERS AND MACHINERY THAT TAYLOR CREATED TO KEEP FRANKLIN'S BRAIN FROM ROTTING IS STRONGER THAN THE CREATURE THAT KILLED HIM TO BEGIN WITH.
SHE THOUGHT SHE COULD SAVE HIM. KEEP HIM FROM BREAKING DOWN.
I DON'T KNOW WHAT IT MEANS THAT I UNDERSTAND HER, BUT I DO.
I'VE ASKED MYSELF THE SAME QUESTION SO MANY TIMES. WITH EVERYTHING I KNOW, WITH EVERYTHING I CAN DO...
HOW COULD I NOT TRY?
HEH... HENH...
BUGGER.
HE LIKES IT.

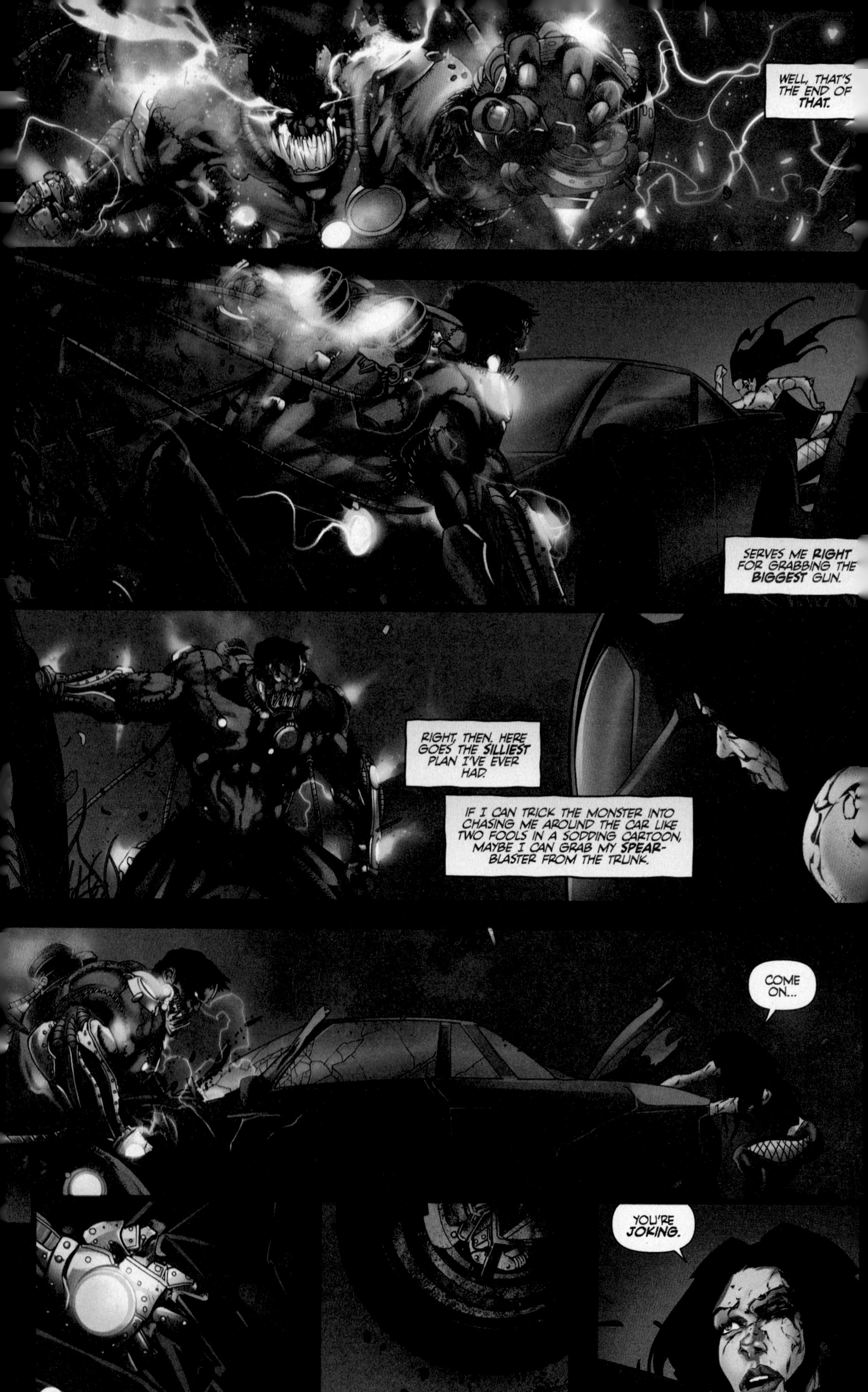
WELL, THAT'S THE END OF THAT.
SERVES ME RIGHT FOR GRABBING THE BIGGEST GUN.
RIGHT, THEN. HERE GOES THE SILLIEST PLAN I'VE EVER HAD.
IF I CAN TRICK THE MONSTER INTO CHASING ME AROUND THE CAR LIKE TWO FOOLS IN A SODDING CARTOON, MAYBE I CAN GRAB MY SPEAR-BLASTER FROM THE TRUNK.
COME ON...
YOU'RE JOKING.

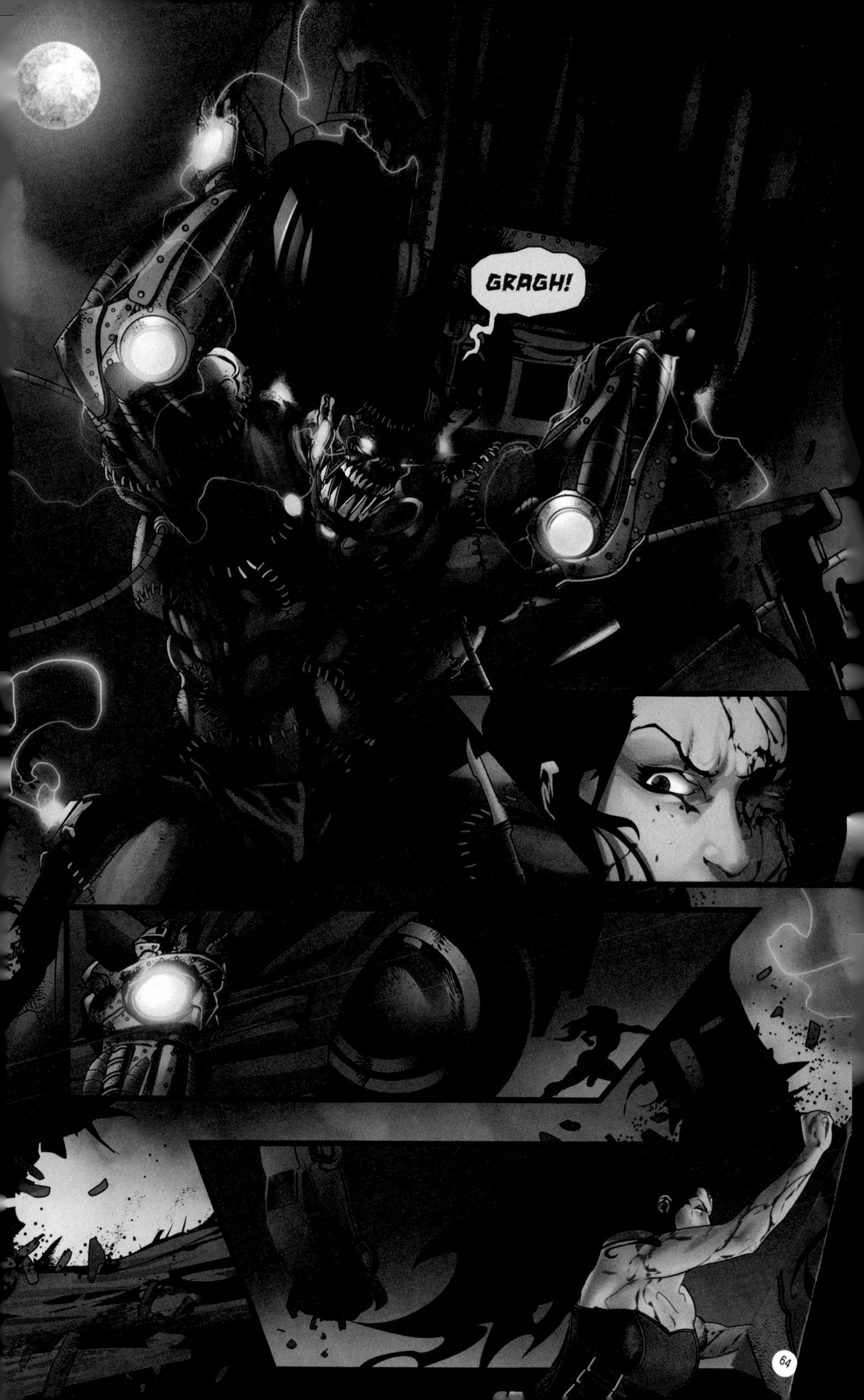
GRAGH!

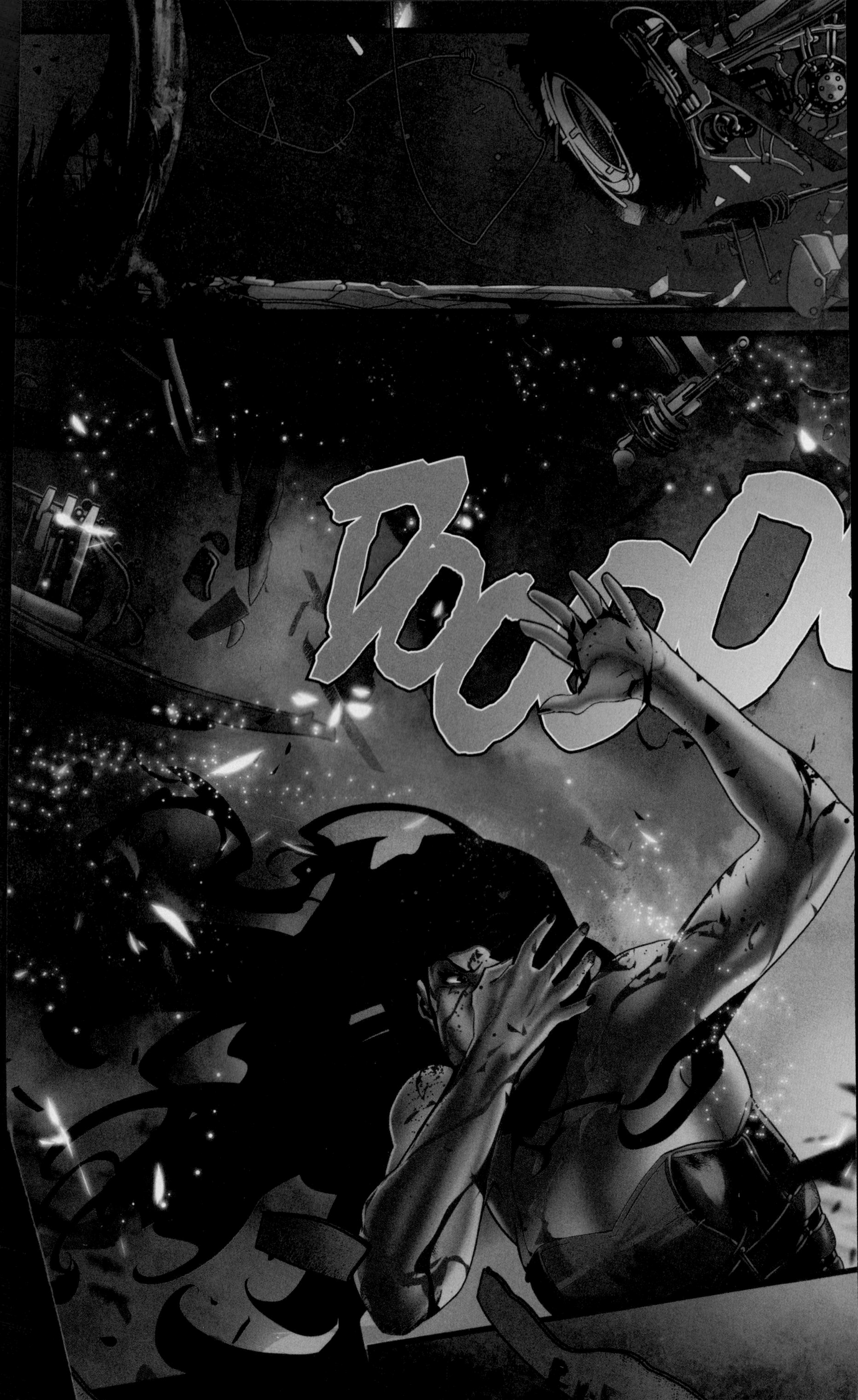

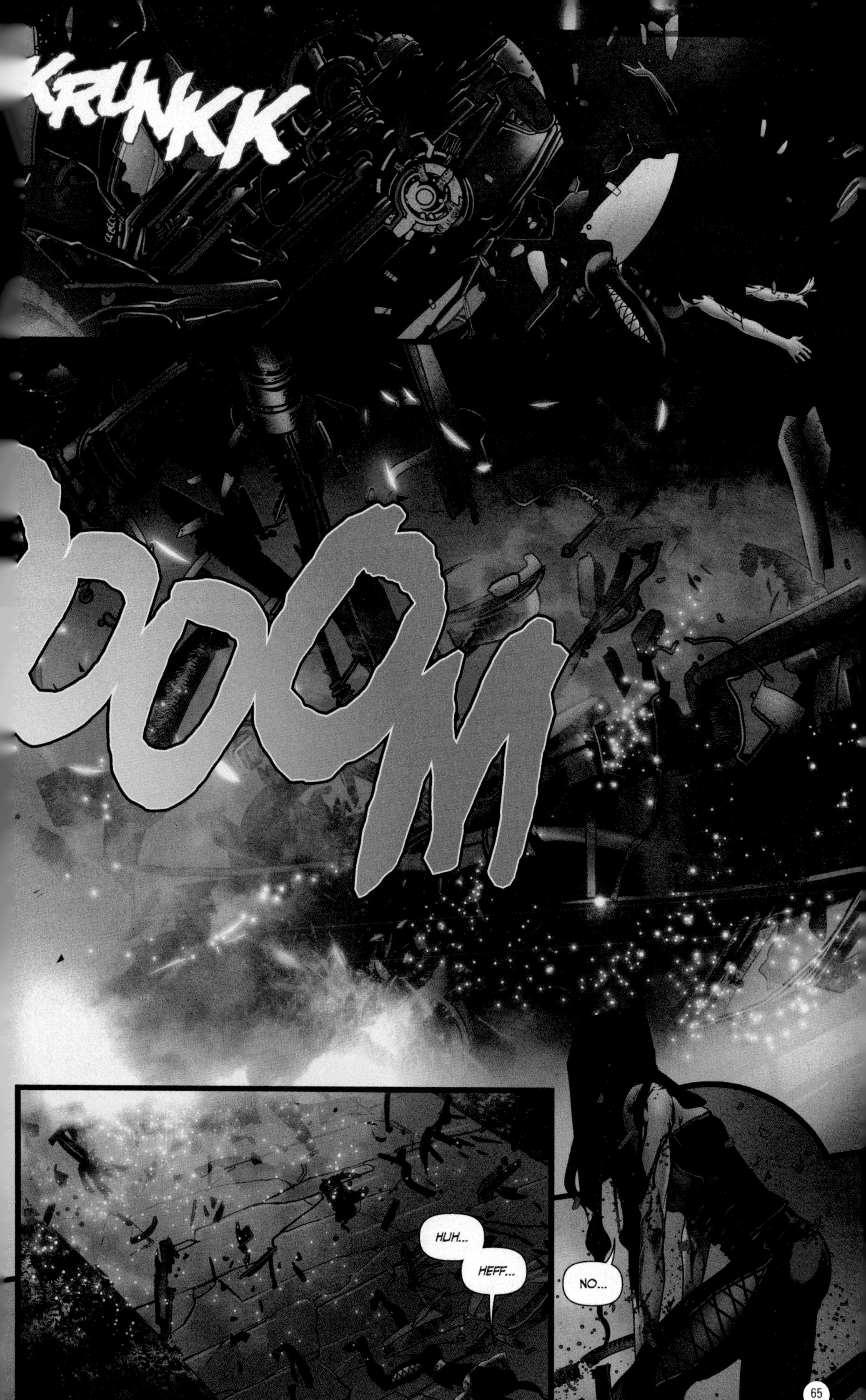
KRUNKK
OOOM
HUH...
HEFF...
NO...

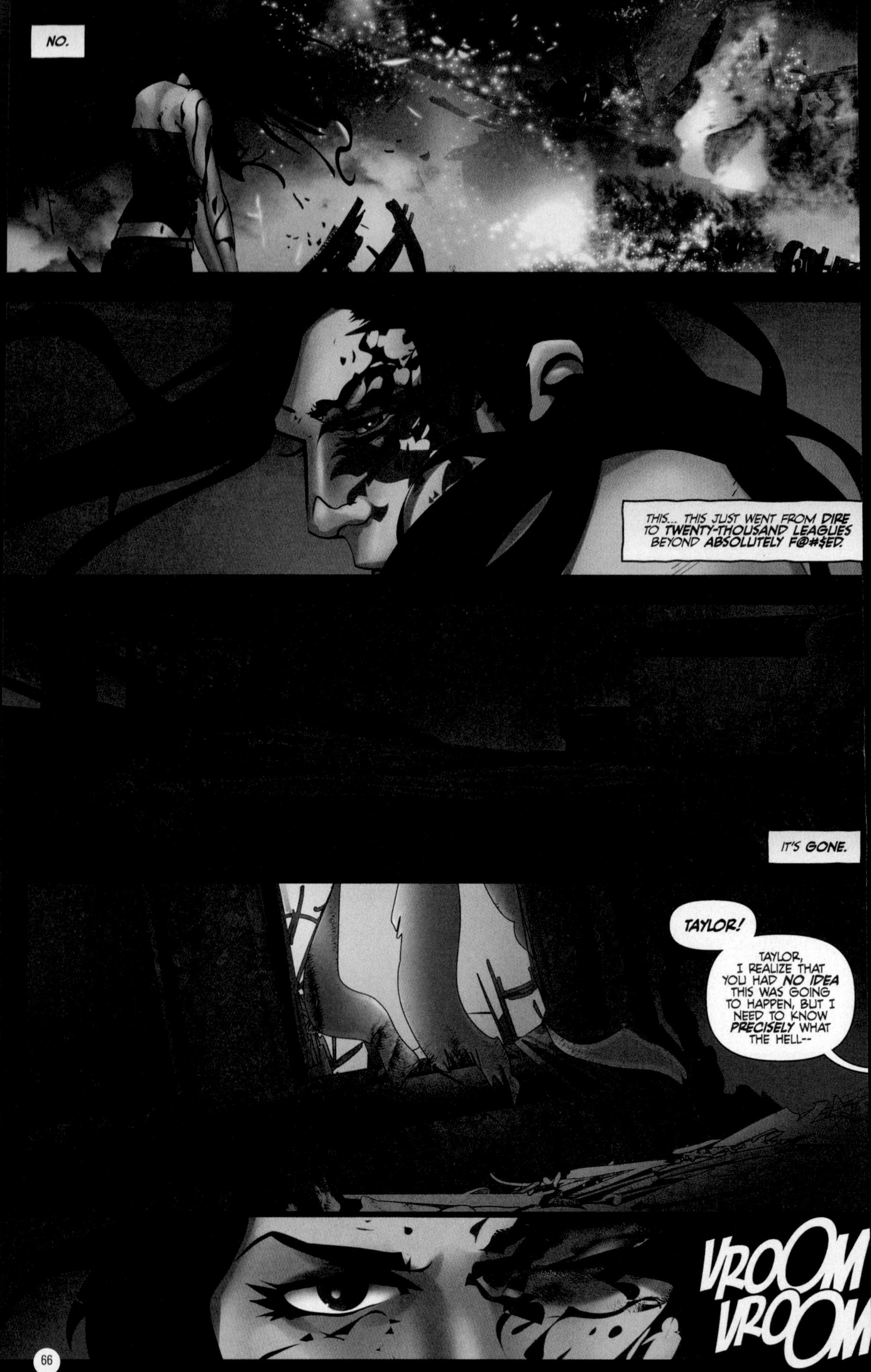
NO.
THIS... THIS JUST WENT FROM DIRE TO TWENTY-THOUSAND LEAGUES BEYOND ABSOLUTELY F@#$ED.
IT'S GONE.
TAYLOR!
TAYLOR, I REALIZE THAT YOU HAD NO IDEA THIS WAS GOING TO HAPPEN, BUT I NEED TO KNOW PRECISELY WHAT THE HELL--
VROOM VROOM

VrrRRRRRRoOM

NO!
YOU AREN'T GOING ANYWHERE!
TAYLOR!

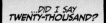

...DID I SAY TWENTY-THOUSAND?

TAYLOR!

I FEAR THAT MAY HAVE BEEN A CONSERVATIVE ESTIMATION.

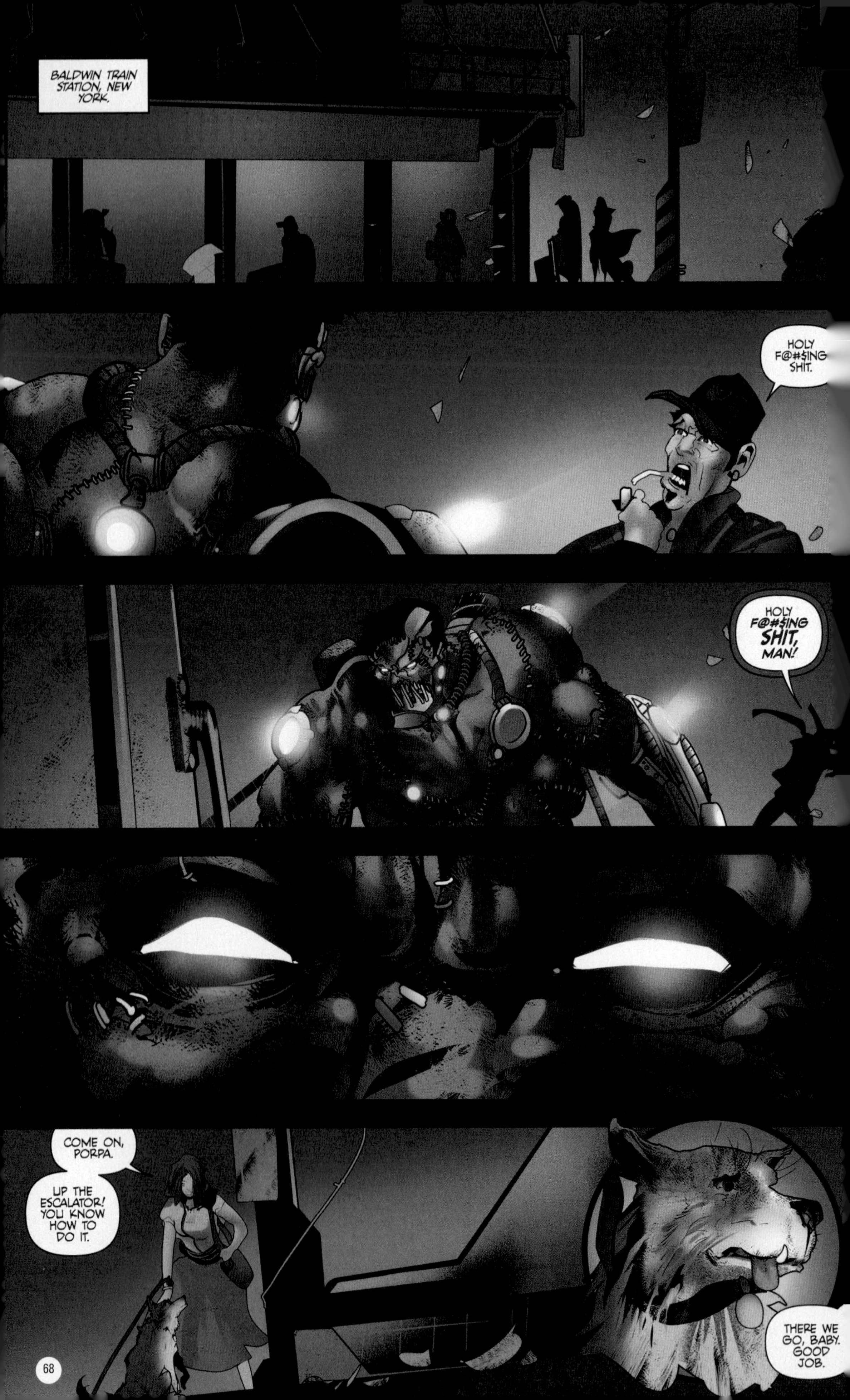
BALDWIN TRAIN STATION, NEW YORK.
HOLY F@#$ING SHIT.
HOLY F@#$ING SHIT, MAN!
COME ON, PORPA.
UP THE ESCALATOR! YOU KNOW HOW TO DO IT.
THERE WE GO, BABY. GOOD JOB.

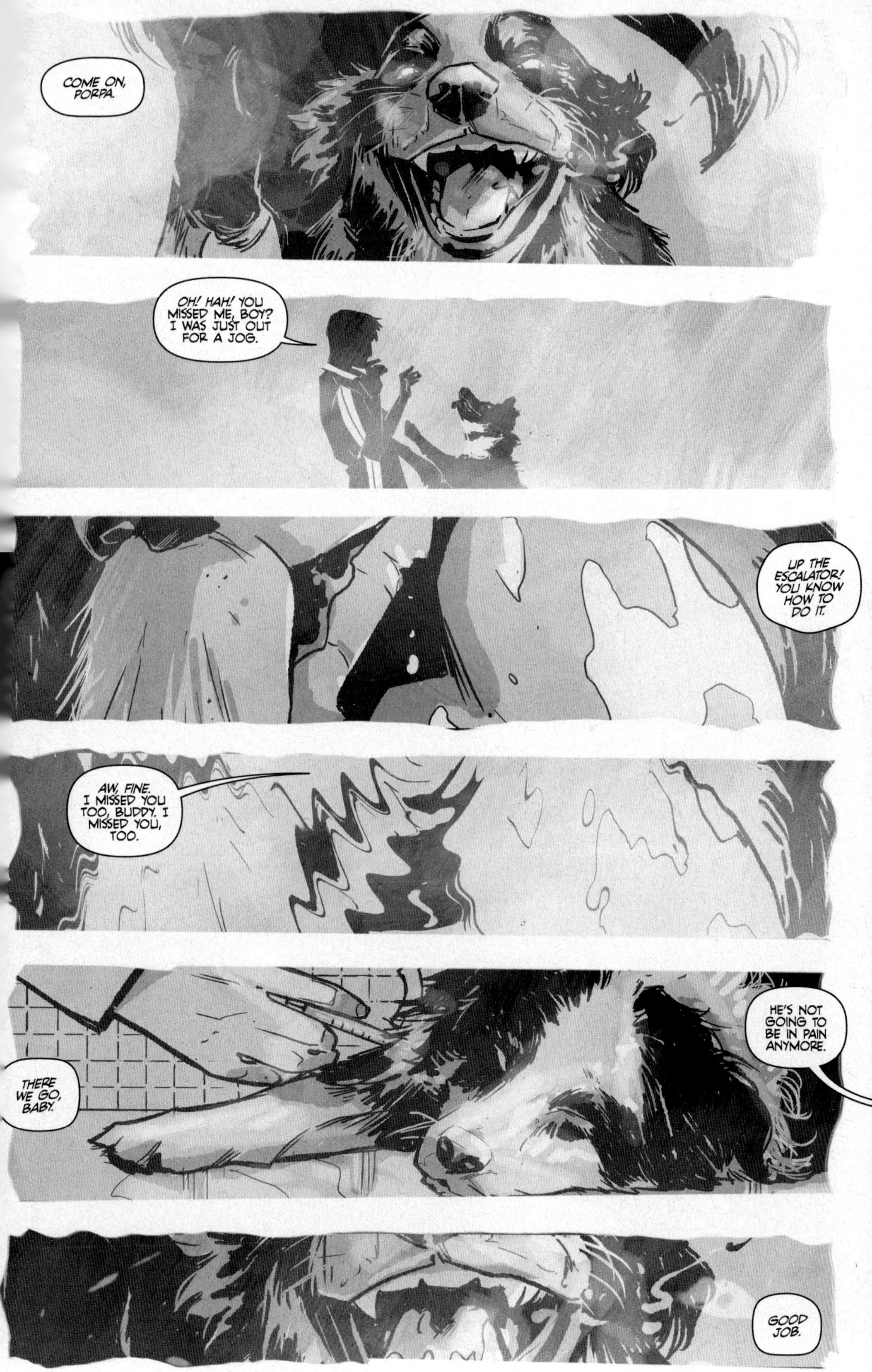
COME ON, PORPA.
OH! HAH! YOU MISSED ME, BOY? I WAS JUST OUT FOR A JOG.
UP THE ESCALATOR! YOU KNOW HOW TO DO IT.
AW, FINE. I MISSED YOU TOO, BUDDY. I MISSED YOU, TOO.
HE'S NOT GOING TO BE IN PAIN ANYMORE.
THERE WE GO, BABY.
GOOD JOB.

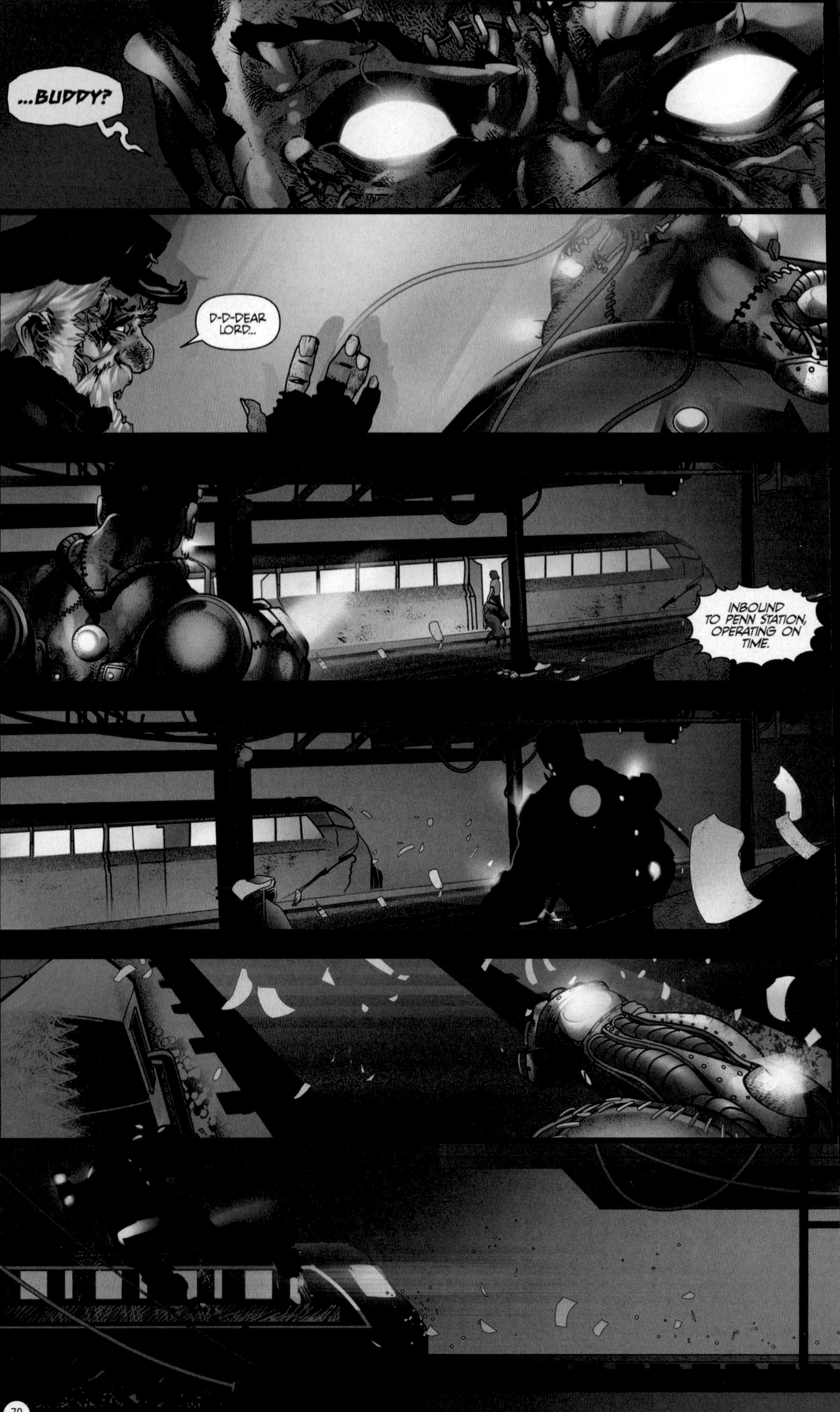
...BUDDY?
D-D-DEAR LORD...
INBOUND TO PENN STATION, OPERATING ON TIME.

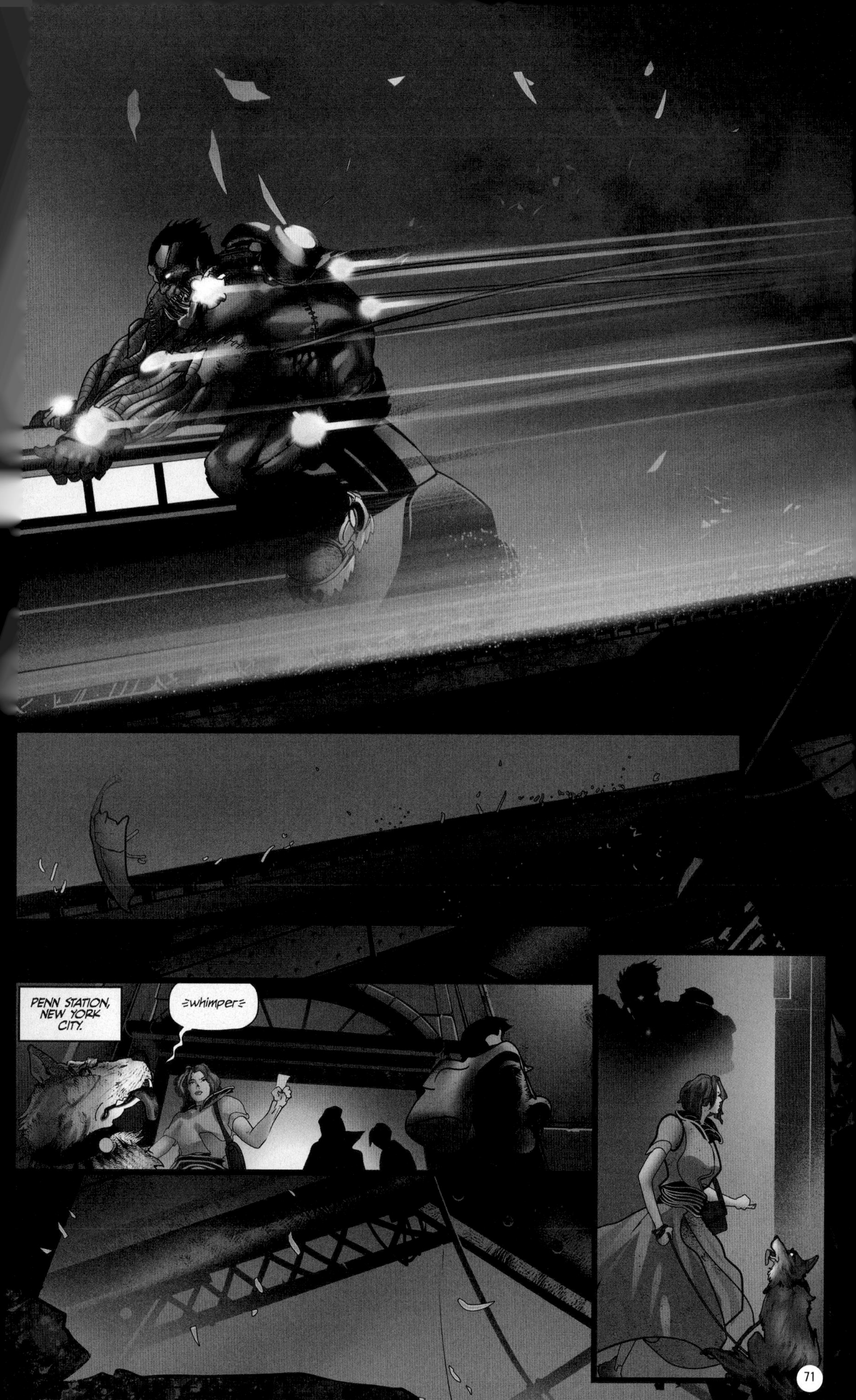

PENN STATION, NEW YORK CITY.
=whimper=

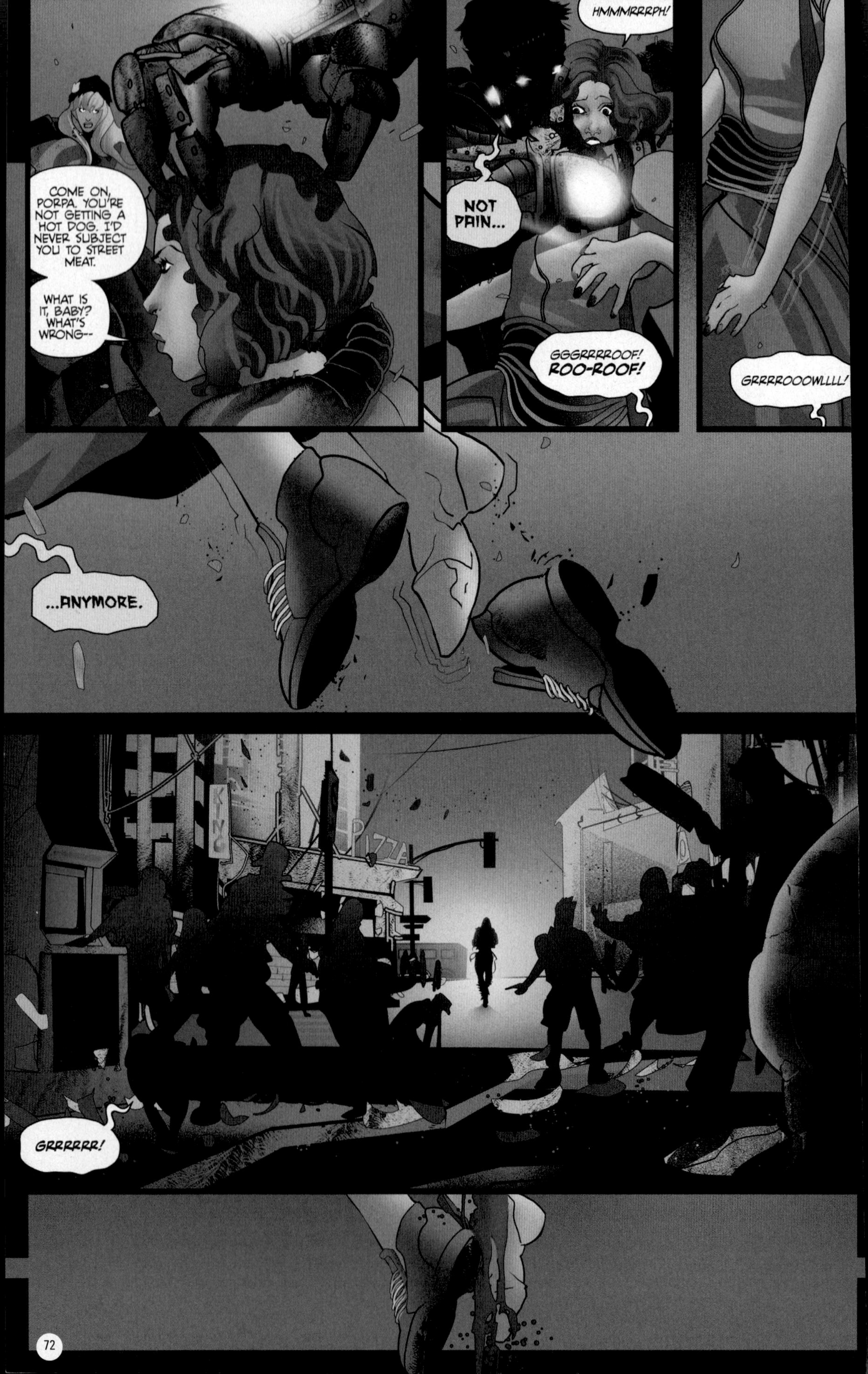
HMMMRRRPH!
COME ON, PORPA. YOU'RE NOT GETTING A HOT DOG. I'D NEVER SUBJECT YOU TO STREET MEAT.
WHAT IS IT, BABY? WHAT'S WRONG--
NOT PAIN...
GGGRRRROOF! ROO-ROOF!
GRRRROOOWLLLL!
...ANYMORE.
KING
PIZZA
GRRRRRR!

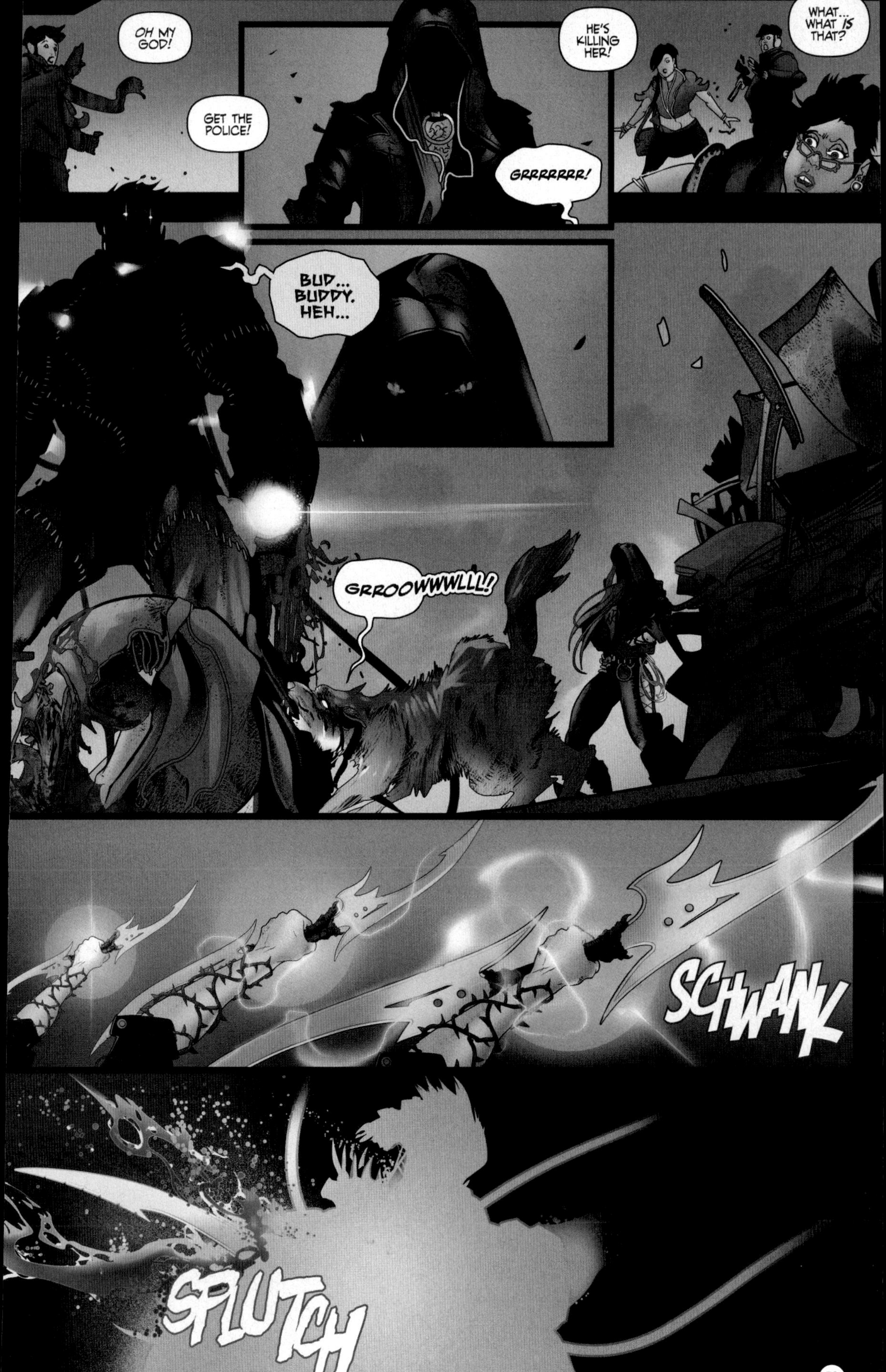
OH MY GOD!
GET THE POLICE!
HE'S KILLING HER!
GRRRRRRR!
WHAT... WHAT IS THAT?
BUD... BUDDY. HEH...
GRROOWWWLLL!
SCHWANK
SPLUTCH

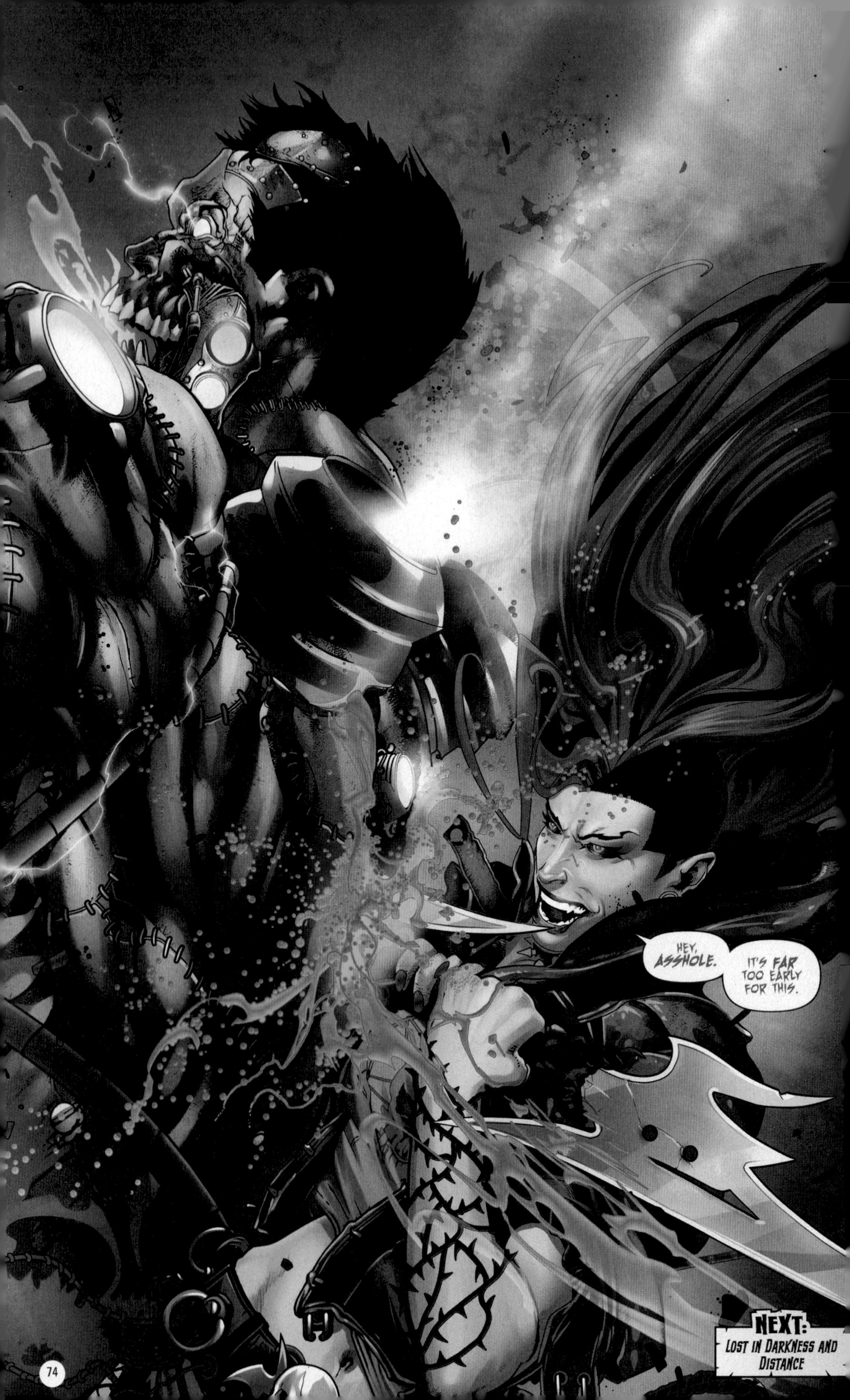
HEY, ASSHOLE.
IT'S FAR TOO EARLY FOR THIS.
NEXT:
LOST IN DARKNESS AND DISTANCE

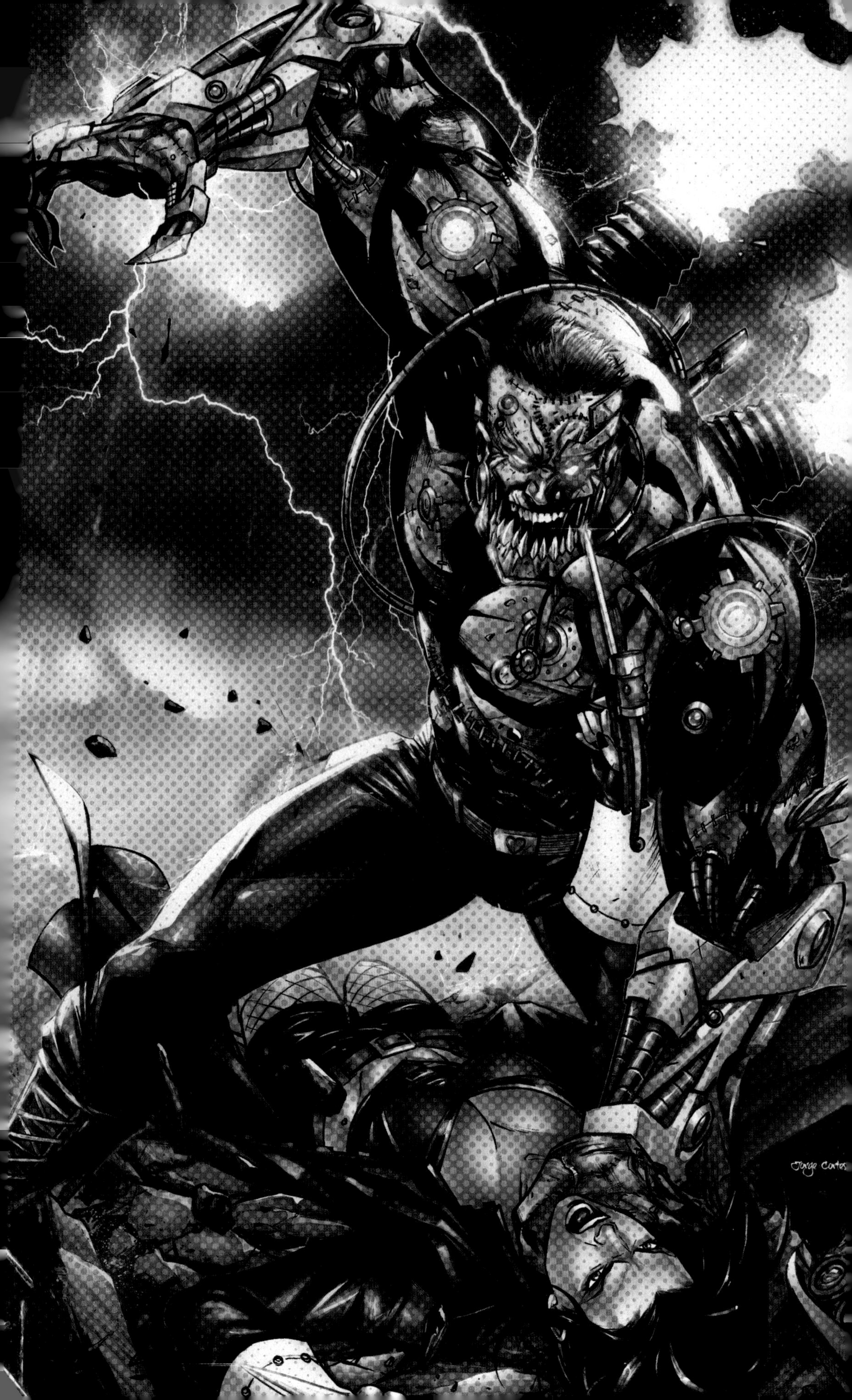
Jorge Cortes

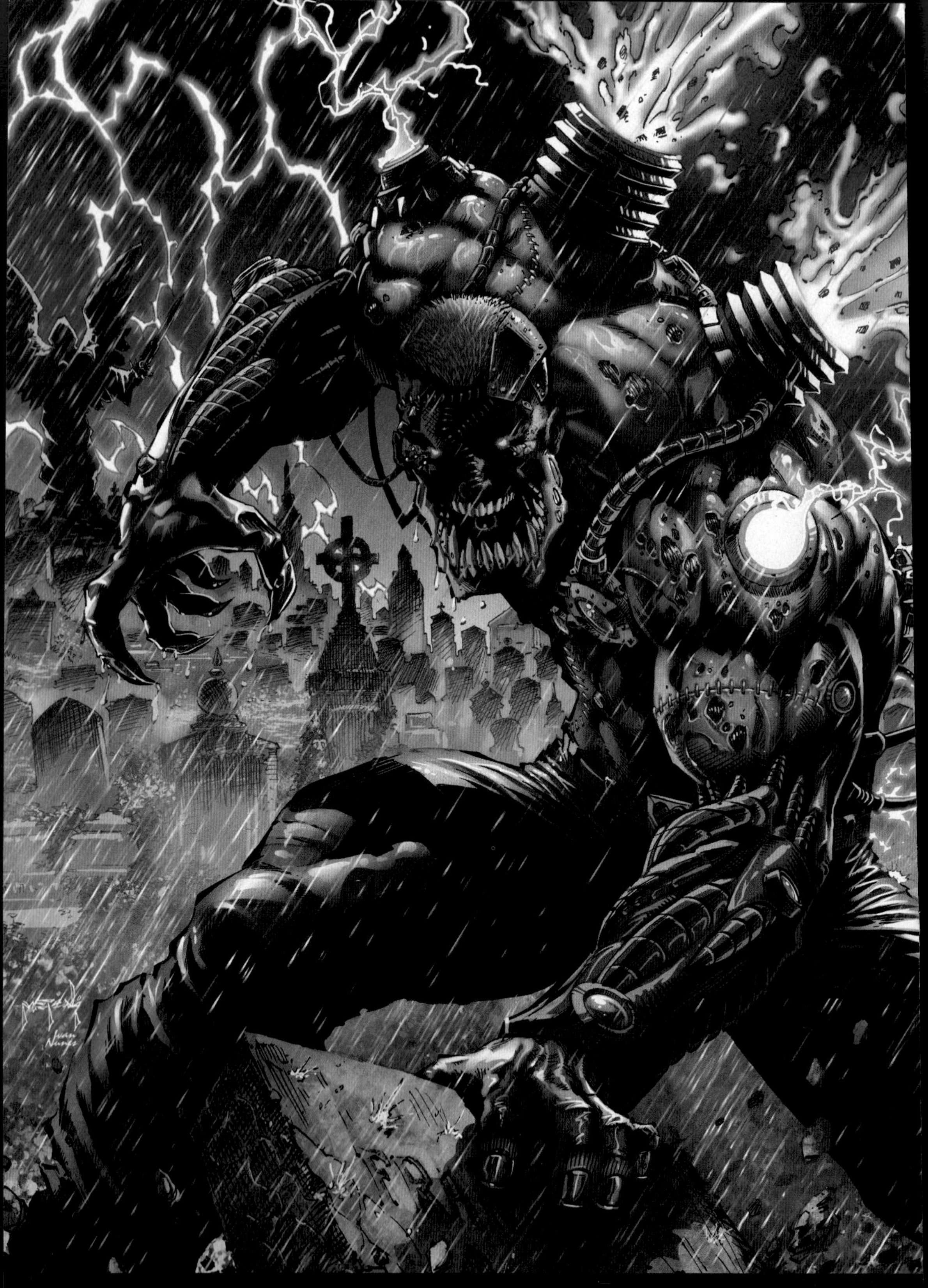

CHAPTER FOUR

LOST IN DARKNESS AND DISTANCE

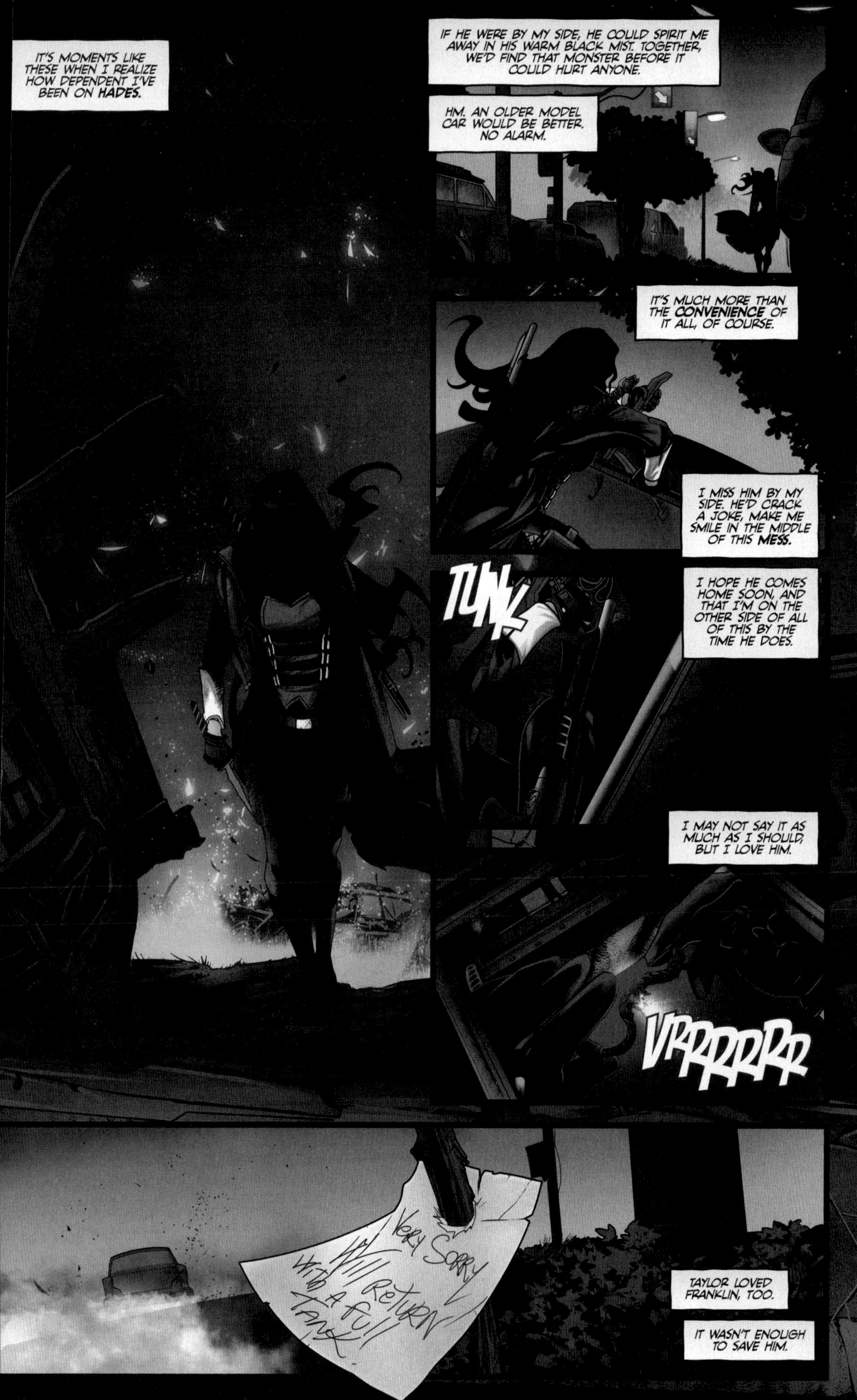

IT'S MOMENTS LIKE THESE WHEN I REALIZE HOW DEPENDENT I'VE BEEN ON HADES.
IF HE WERE BY MY SIDE, HE COULD SPIRIT ME AWAY IN HIS WARM BLACK MIST. TOGETHER, WE'D FIND THAT MONSTER BEFORE IT COULD HURT ANYONE.
HM. AN OLDER MODEL CAR WOULD BE BETTER. NO ALARM.
IT'S MUCH MORE THAN THE CONVENIENCE OF IT ALL, OF COURSE.
I MISS HIM BY MY SIDE. HE'D CRACK A JOKE, MAKE ME SMILE IN THE MIDDLE OF THIS MESS.
TUNK
I HOPE HE COMES HOME SOON, AND THAT I'M ON THE OTHER SIDE OF ALL OF THIS BY THE TIME HE DOES.
I MAY NOT SAY IT AS MUCH AS I SHOULD, BUT I LOVE HIM.
VRRRRRRR
Very Sorry
Will Return
with a full
Tank
TAYLOR LOVED FRANKLIN, TOO.
IT WASN'T ENOUGH TO SAVE HIM.

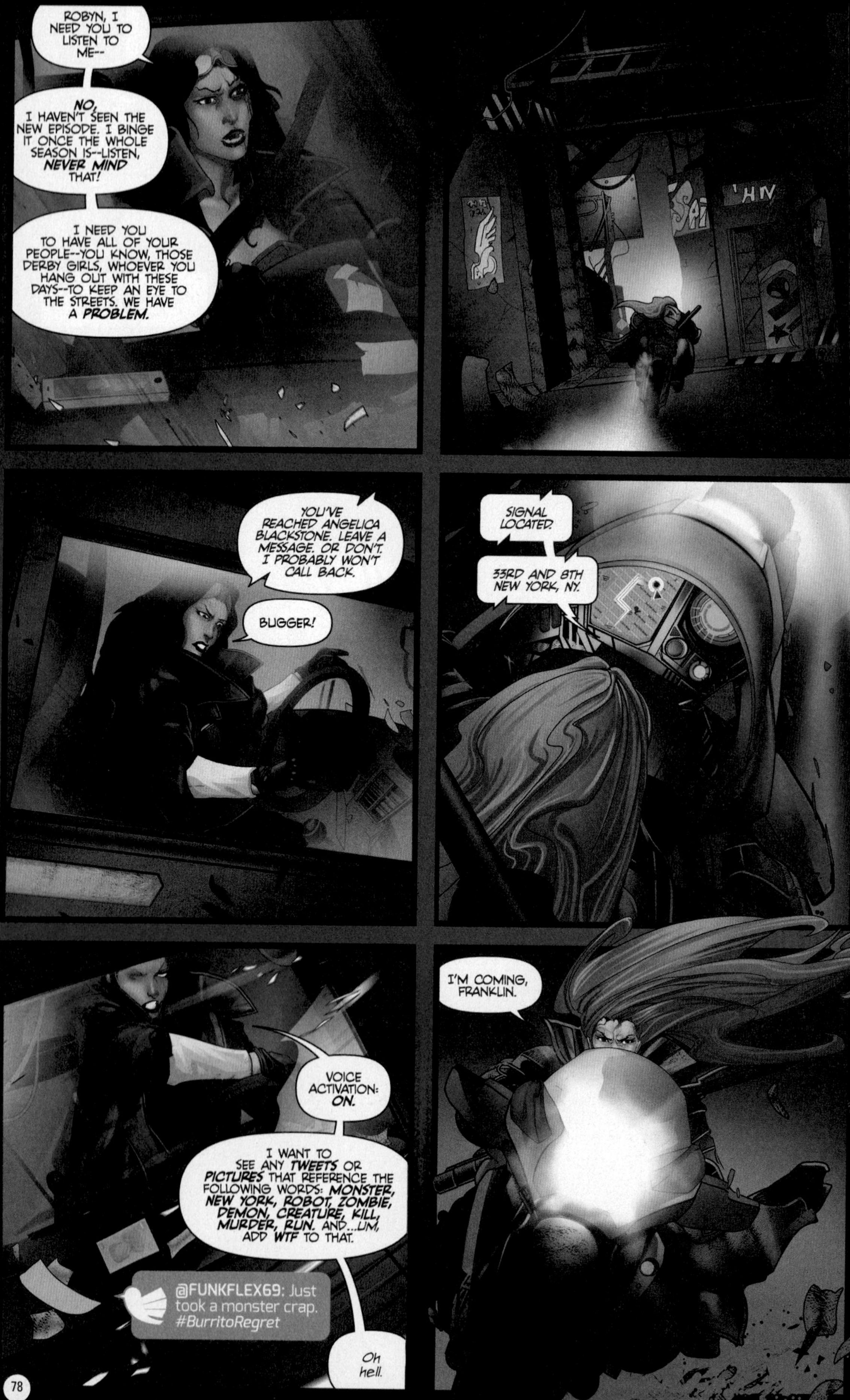
ROBYN, I NEED YOU TO LISTEN TO ME--
NO, I HAVEN'T SEEN THE NEW EPISODE. I BINGE IT ONCE THE WHOLE SEASON IS--LISTEN, NEVER MIND THAT!
I NEED YOU TO HAVE ALL OF YOUR PEOPLE--YOU KNOW, THOSE DERBY GIRLS, WHOEVER YOU HANG OUT WITH THESE DAYS--TO KEEP AN EYE TO THE STREETS. WE HAVE A PROBLEM.
YOU'VE REACHED ANGELICA BLACKSTONE. LEAVE A MESSAGE. OR DON'T. I PROBABLY WON'T CALL BACK.
BUGGER!
SIGNAL LOCATED.
33RD AND 8TH NEW YORK, NY.
VOICE ACTIVATION: ON.
I WANT TO SEE ANY TWEETS OR PICTURES THAT REFERENCE THE FOLLOWING WORDS: MONSTER, NEW YORK, ROBOT, ZOMBIE, DEMON, CREATURE, KILL, MURDER, RUN. AND...UM, ADD WTF TO THAT.
@FUNKFLEX69: Just took a monster crap. #BurritoRegret
Oh hell.
I'M COMING, FRANKLIN.

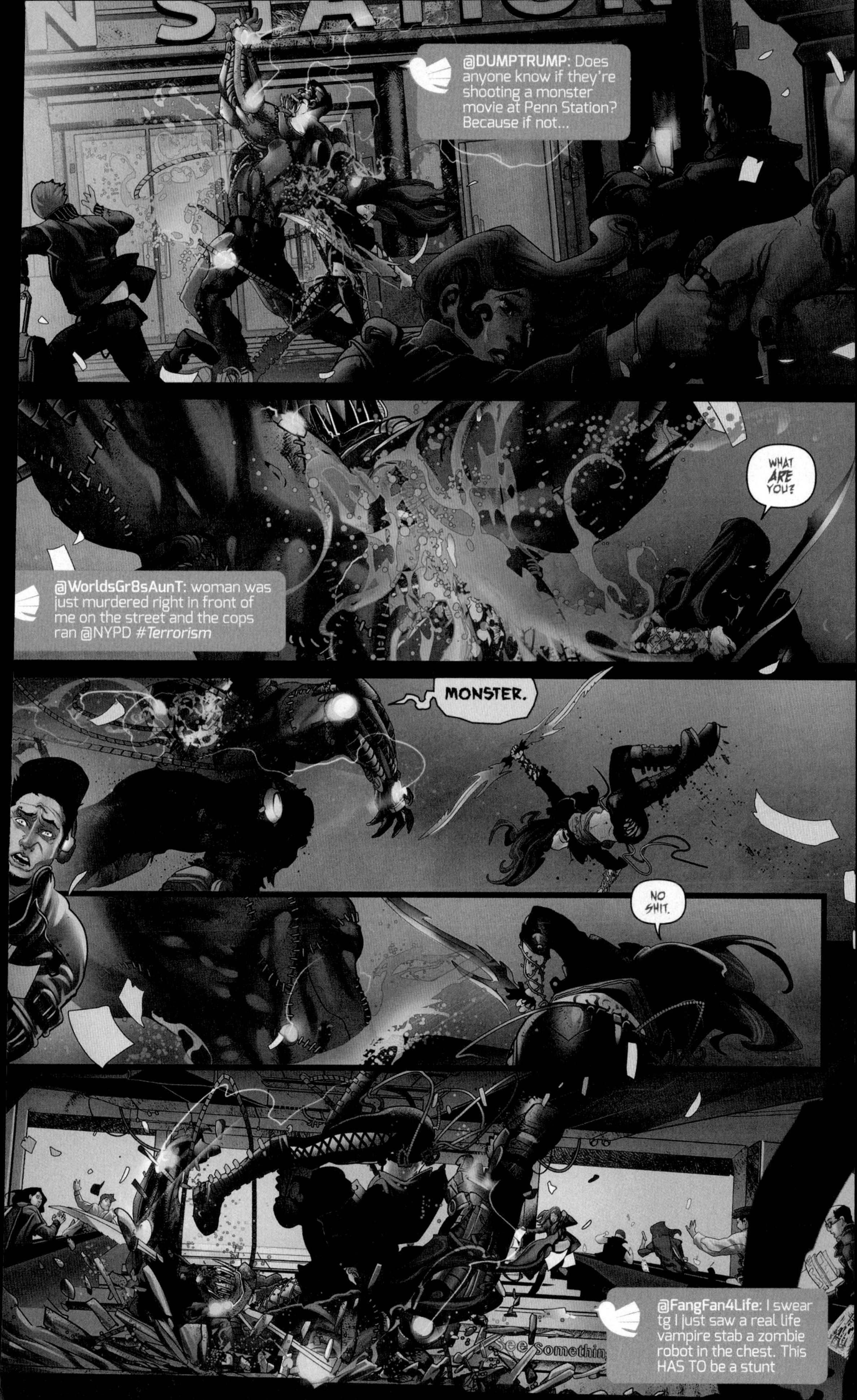

@DUMPTRUMP: Does anyone know if they're shooting a monster movie at Penn Station? Because if not...
WHAT ARE YOU?
@WorldsGr8sAunT: woman was just murdered right in front of me on the street and the cops ran @NYPD #Terrorism
MONSTER.
NO SHIT.
@FangFan4Life: I swear tg I just saw a real life vampire stab a zombie robot in the chest. This HAS TO be a stunt

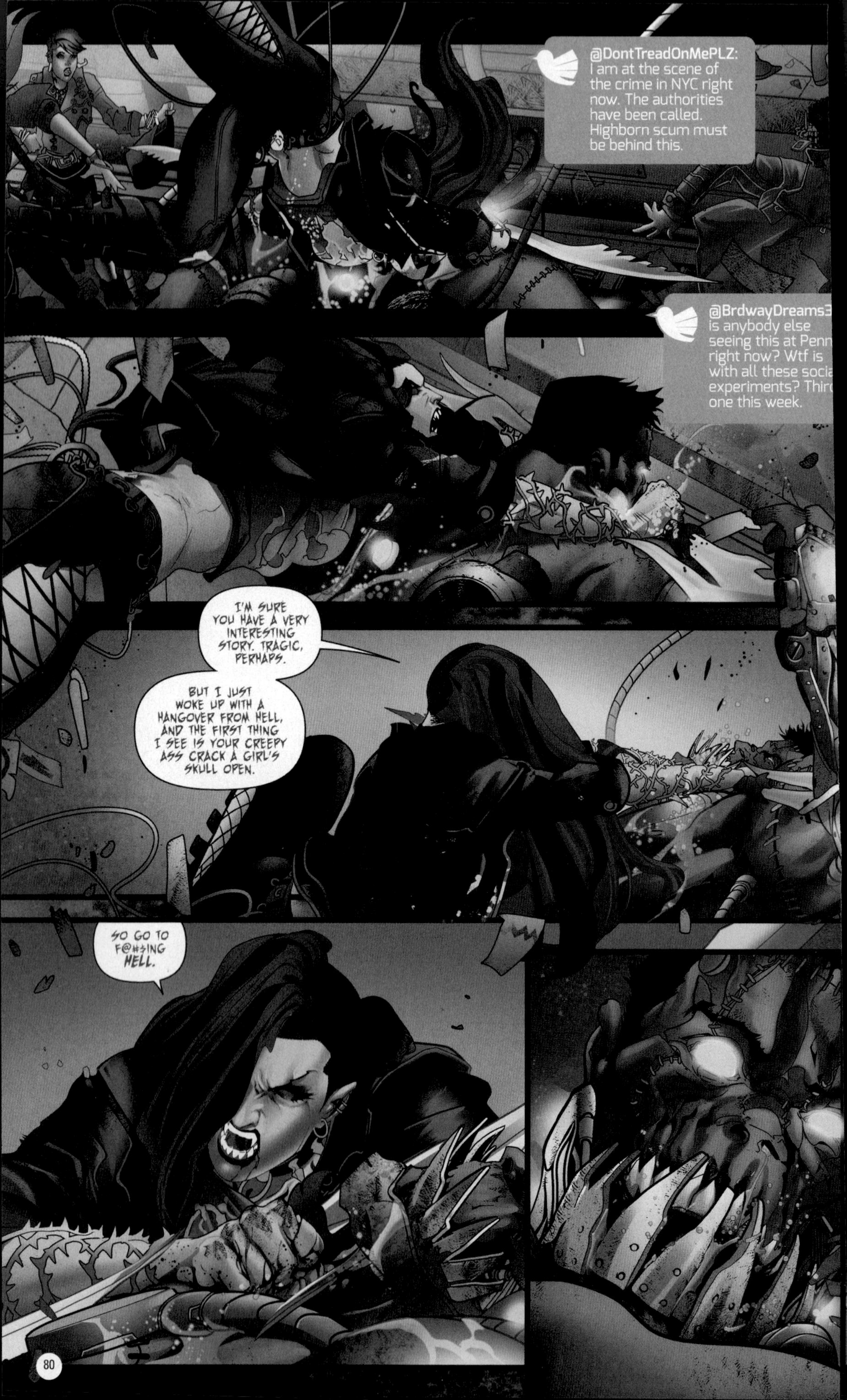
@DontTreadOnMePLZ: I am at the scene of the crime in NYC right now. The authorities have been called. Highborn scum must be behind this.
@BrdwayDreams3 is anybody else seeing this at Penn right now? Wtf is with all these socia experiments? Third one this week.
I'M SURE YOU HAVE A VERY INTERESTING STORY. TRAGIC, PERHAPS.
BUT I JUST WOKE UP WITH A HANGOVER FROM HELL, AND THE FIRST THING I SEE IS YOUR CREEPY ASS CRACK A GIRL'S SKULL OPEN.
SO GO TO F@#$ING HELL.

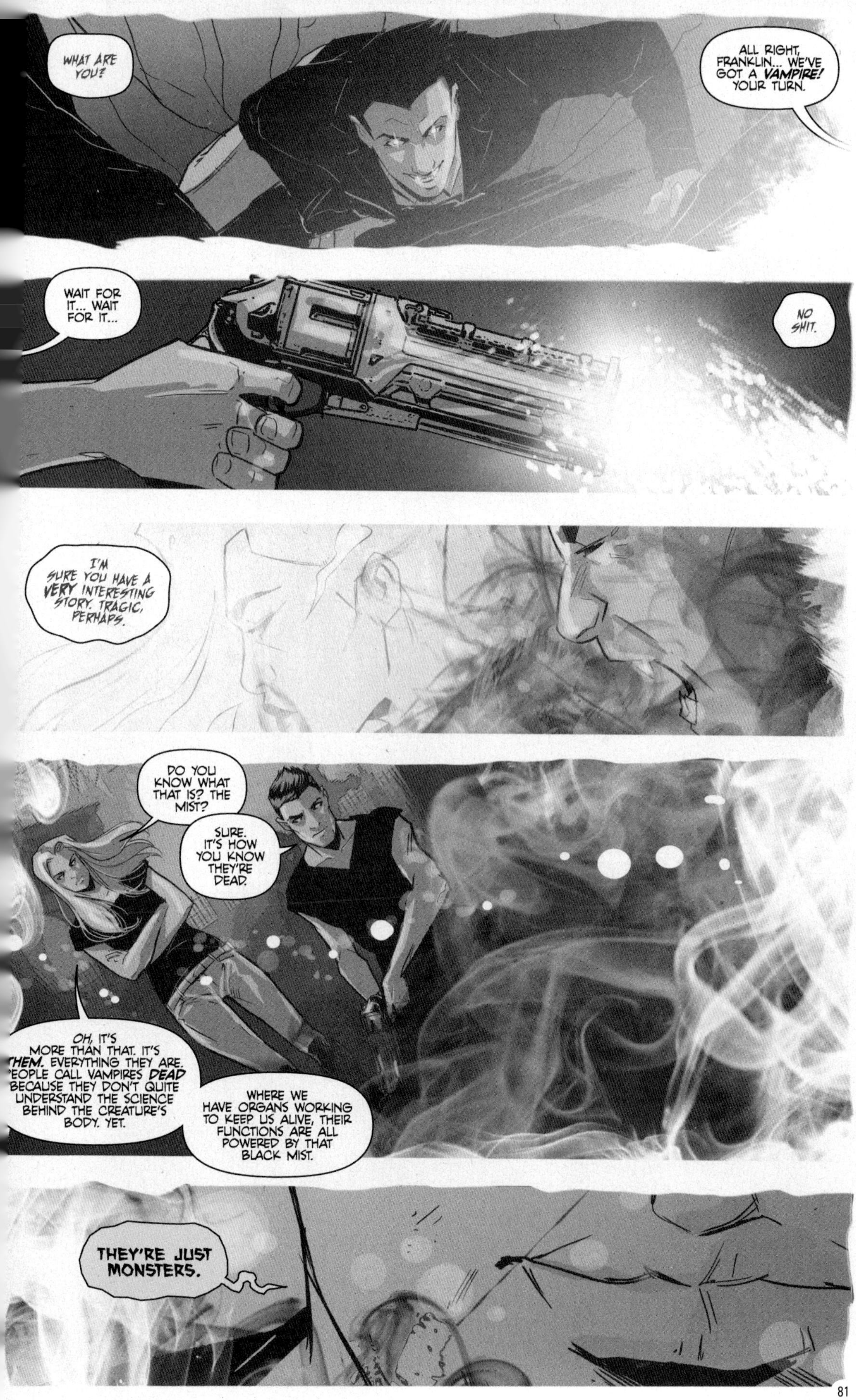
WHAT ARE YOU?
ALL RIGHT, FRANKLIN... WE'VE GOT A VAMPIRE! YOUR TURN.
WAIT FOR IT... WAIT FOR IT...
NO SHIT.
I'M SURE YOU HAVE A VERY INTERESTING STORY. TRAGIC, PERHAPS.
DO YOU KNOW WHAT THAT IS? THE MIST?
SURE. IT'S HOW YOU KNOW THEY'RE DEAD.
OH, IT'S MORE THAN THAT. IT'S THEM. EVERYTHING THEY ARE. PEOPLE CALL VAMPIRES DEAD BECAUSE THEY DON'T QUITE UNDERSTAND THE SCIENCE BEHIND THE CREATURE'S BODY. YET.
WHERE WE HAVE ORGANS WORKING TO KEEP US ALIVE, THEIR FUNCTIONS ARE ALL POWERED BY THAT BLACK MIST.
THEY'RE JUST MONSTERS.

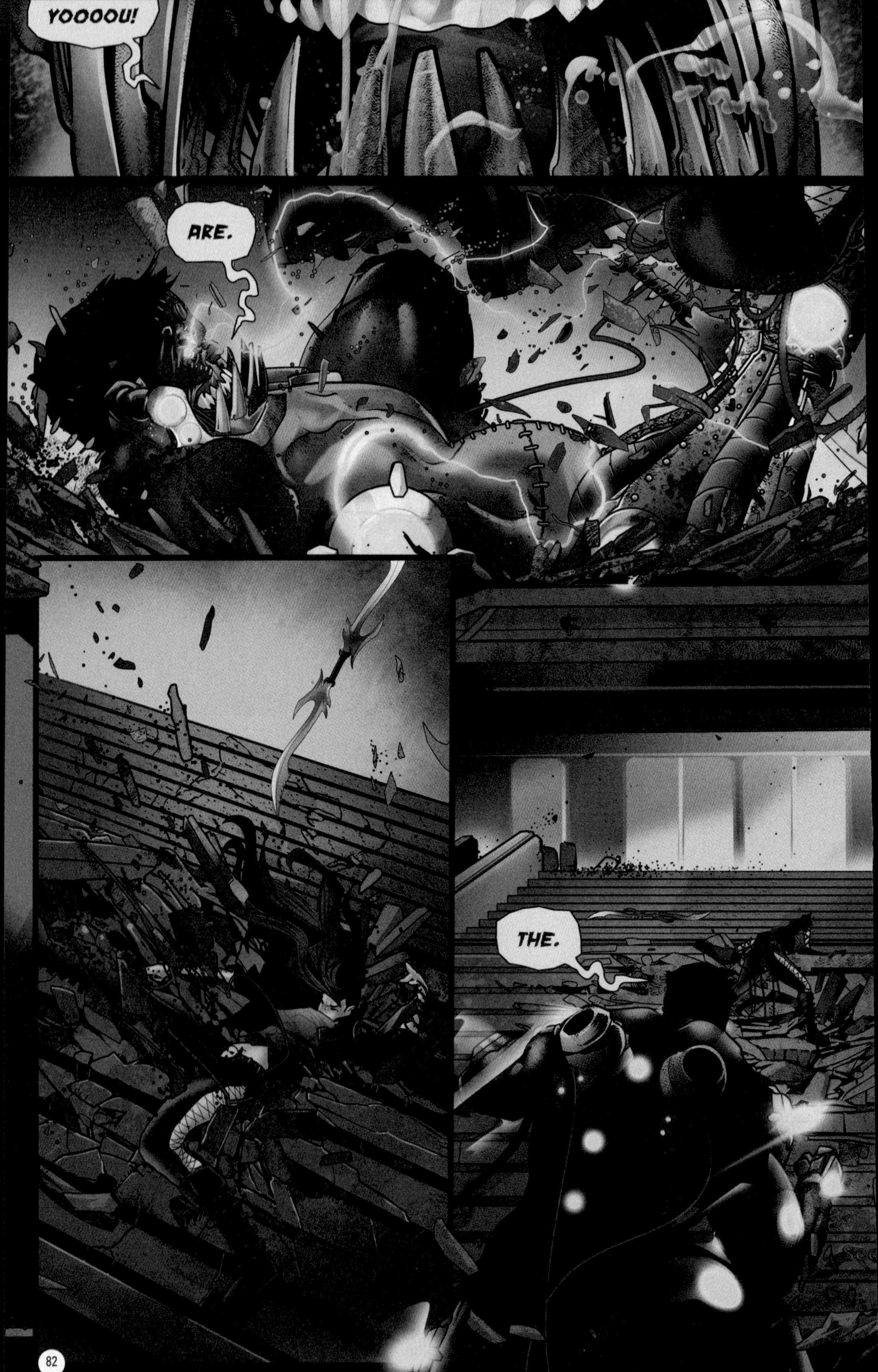
YOOOOU!
ARE.
THE.

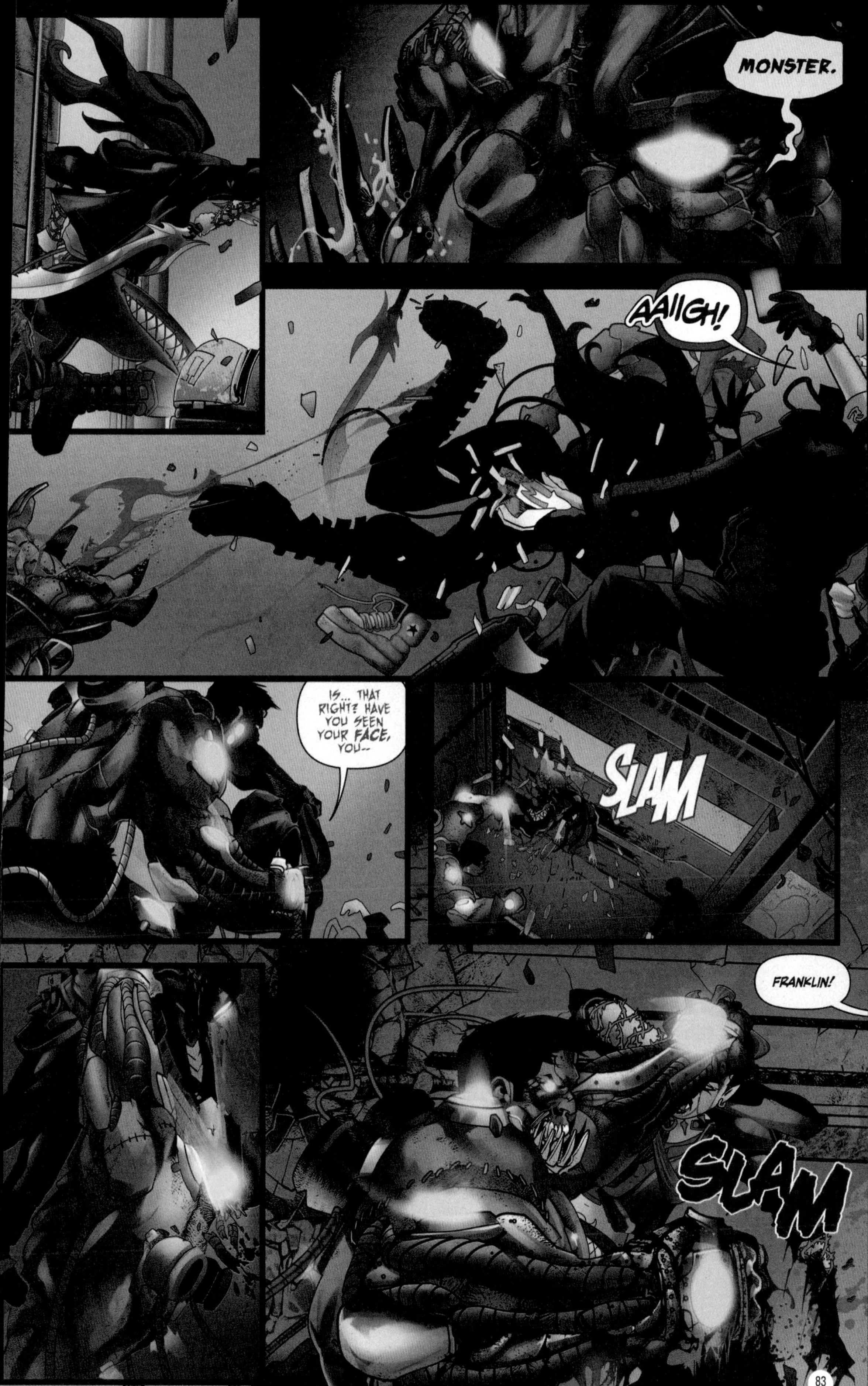
MONSTER.
AAIIGH!
IS... THAT RIGHT? HAVE YOU SEEN YOUR FACE, YOU--
SLAM
FRANKLIN!
SLAM

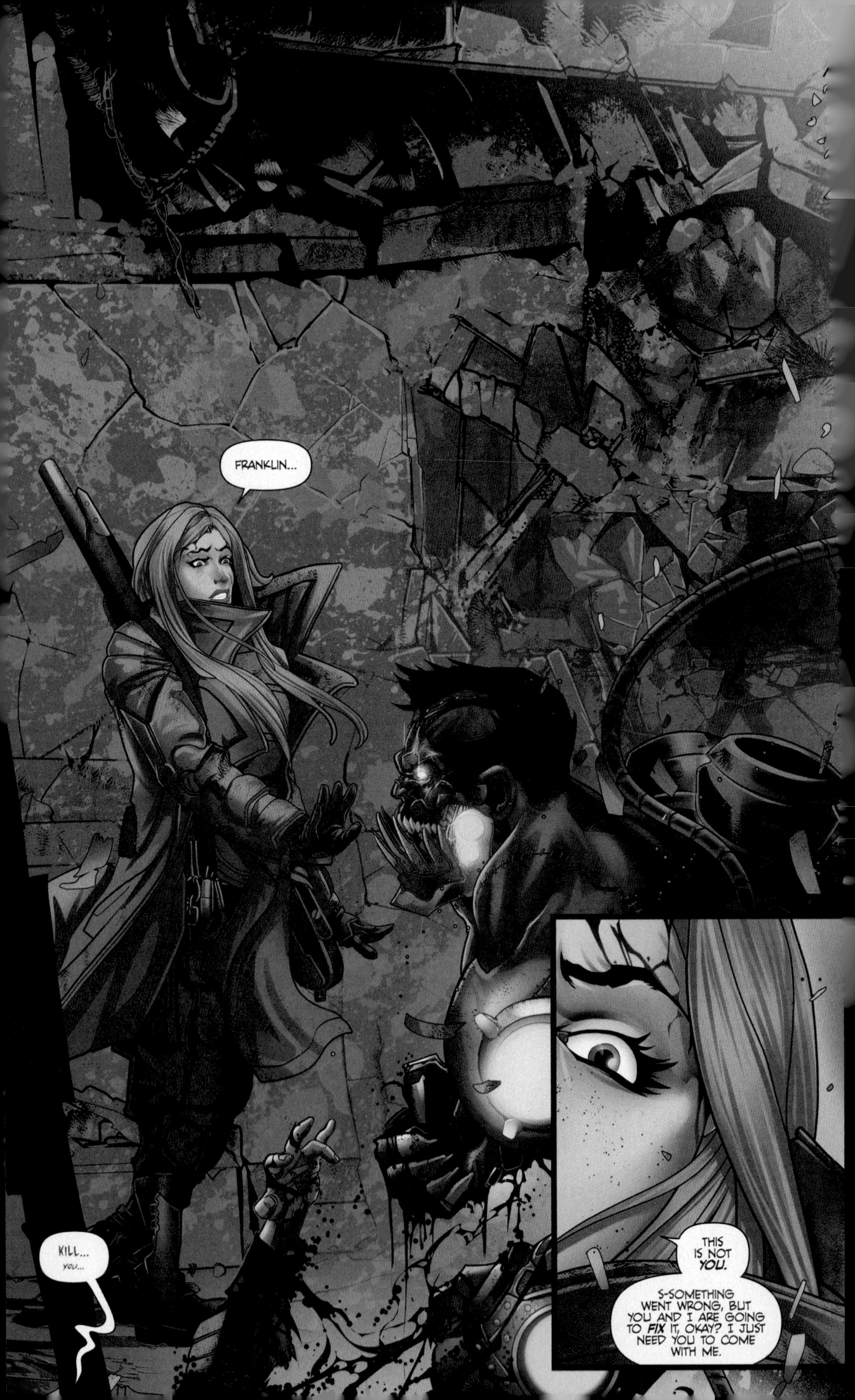
FRANKLIN...
KILL... YOU...
THIS IS NOT *YOU.*
S-SOMETHING WENT WRONG, BUT YOU AND I ARE GOING TO *FIX* IT, OKAY? I JUST NEED YOU TO COME WITH ME.

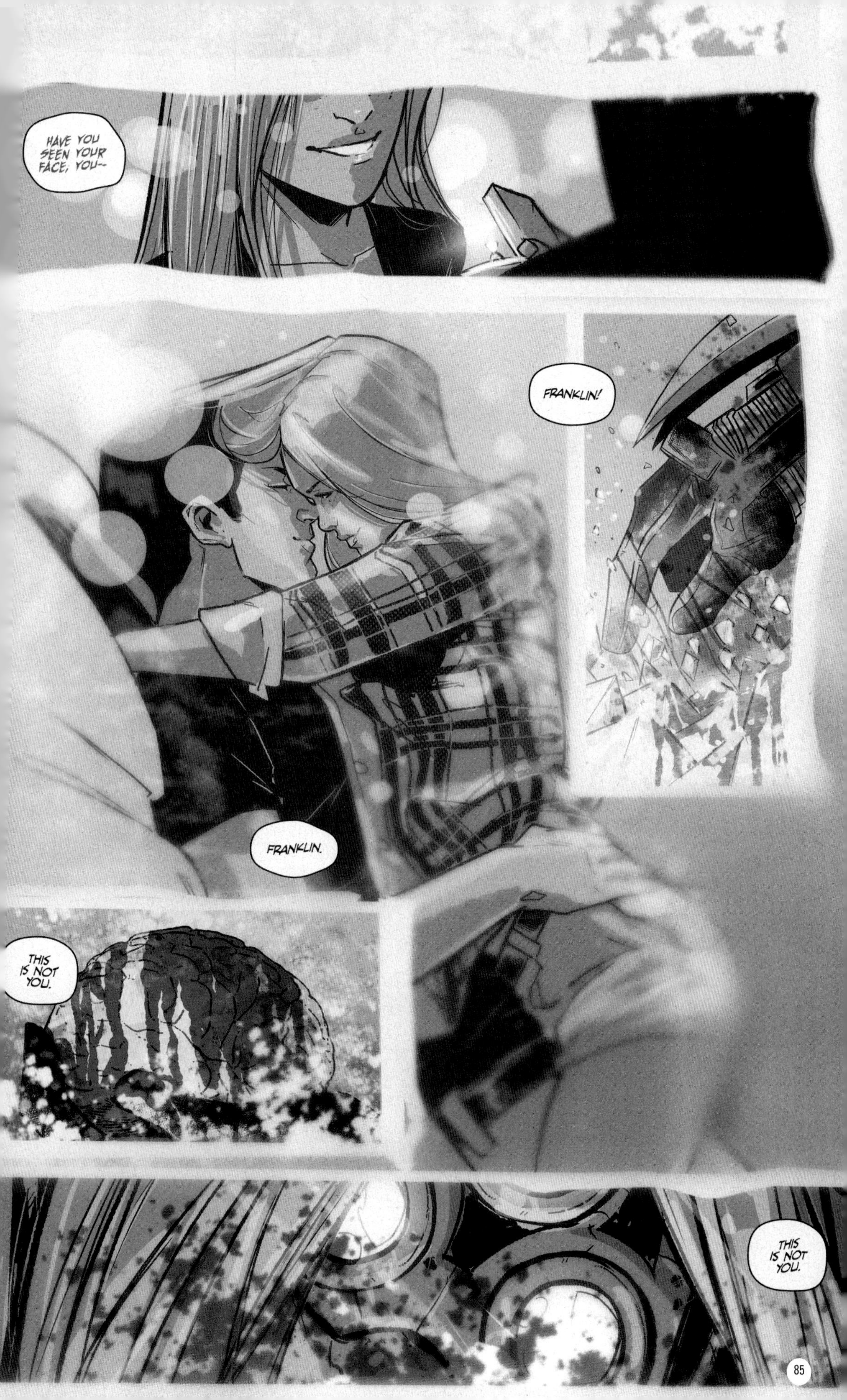

HAVE YOU SEEN YOUR FACE, YOU--
FRANKLIN!
FRANKLIN.
THIS IS NOT YOU.
THIS IS NOT YOU.

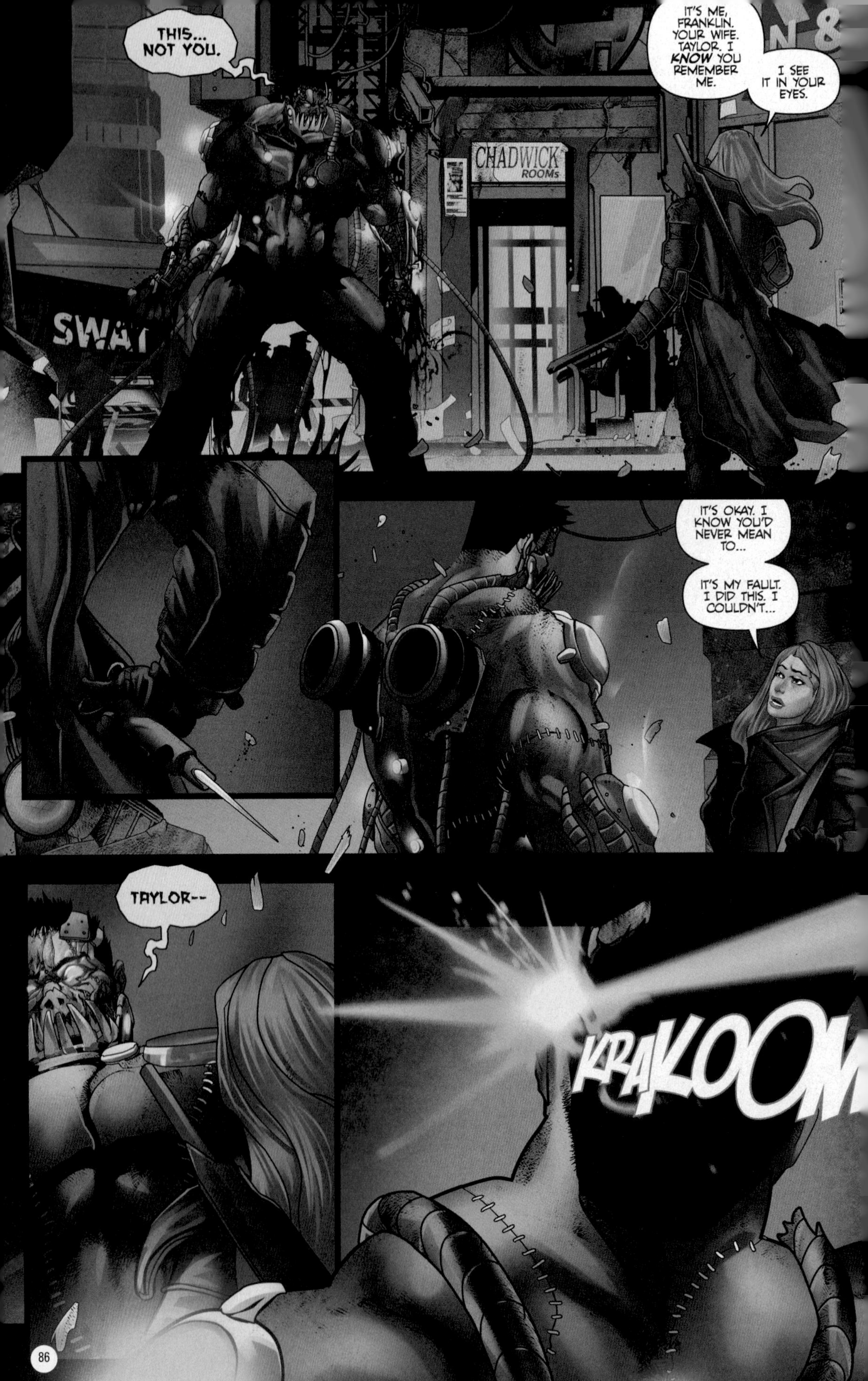
THIS... NOT YOU.
IT'S ME, FRANKLIN. YOUR WIFE. TAYLOR. I KNOW YOU REMEMBER ME.
I SEE IT IN YOUR EYES.
CHADWICK ROOMS
SWAY
IT'S OKAY. I KNOW YOU'D NEVER MEAN TO...
IT'S MY FAULT. I DID THIS. I COULDN'T...
TAYLOR--
KRAKOOM

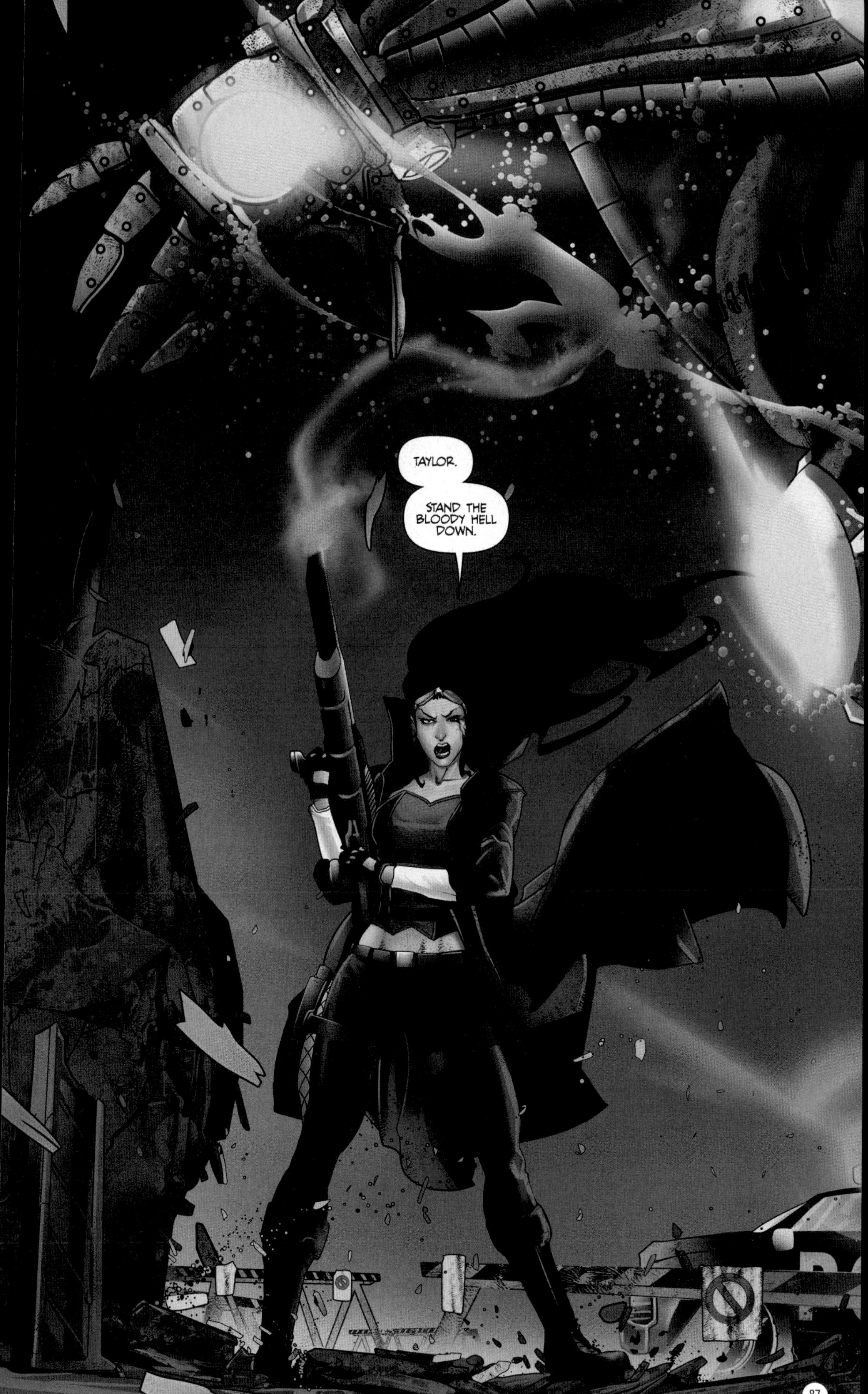
TAYLOR.
STAND THE BLOODY HELL DOWN.

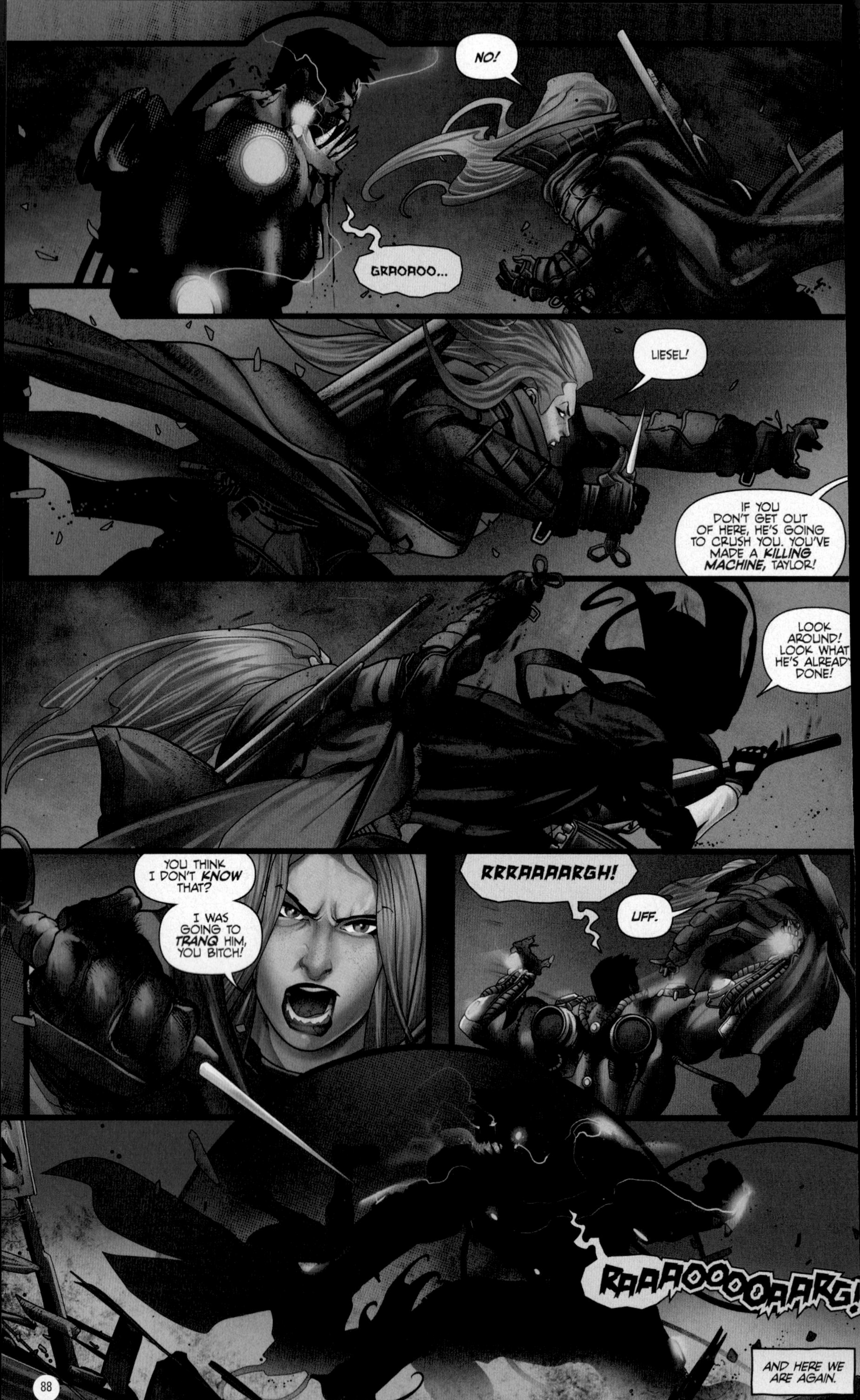
NO!
GRAORRR...
LIESEL!
IF YOU DON'T GET OUT OF HERE, HE'S GOING TO CRUSH YOU. YOU'VE MADE A KILLING MACHINE, TAYLOR!
LOOK AROUND! LOOK WHAT HE'S ALREADY DONE!
YOU THINK I DON'T KNOW THAT?
I WAS GOING TO TRANQ HIM, YOU BITCH!
RRRAAAARGH!
UFF.
RAAAOOOOOAARG!
AND HERE WE ARE AGAIN.

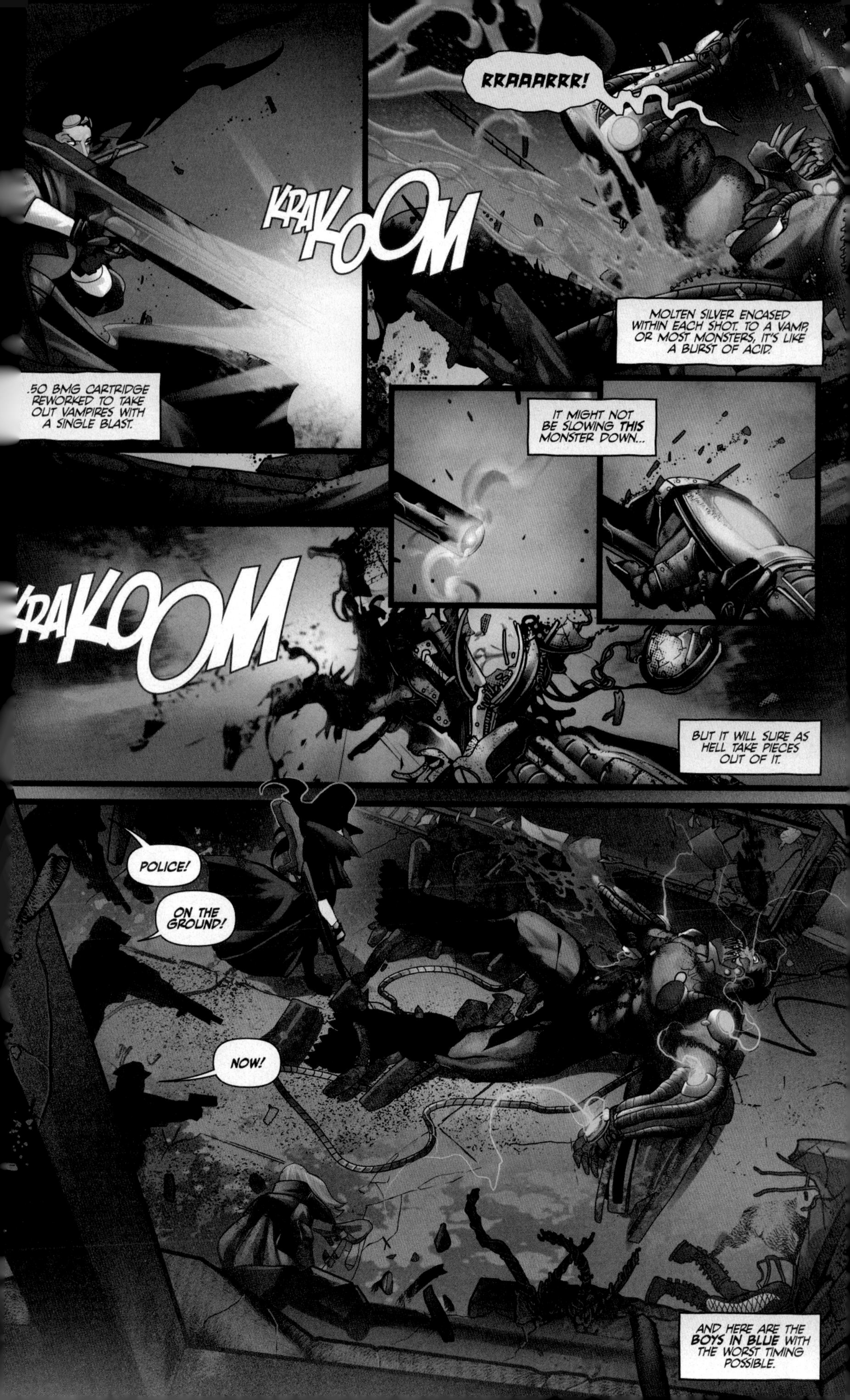
RRAAARRR!
KRAKOOM
.50 BMG CARTRIDGE REWORKED TO TAKE OUT VAMPIRES WITH A SINGLE BLAST.
MOLTEN SILVER ENCASED WITHIN EACH SHOT. TO A VAMP, OR MOST MONSTERS, IT'S LIKE A BURST OF ACID.
IT MIGHT NOT BE SLOWING THIS MONSTER DOWN...
KRAKOOM
BUT IT WILL SURE AS HELL TAKE PIECES OUT OF IT.
POLICE!
ON THE GROUND!
NOW!
AND HERE ARE THE BOYS IN BLUE WITH THE WORST TIMING POSSIBLE.

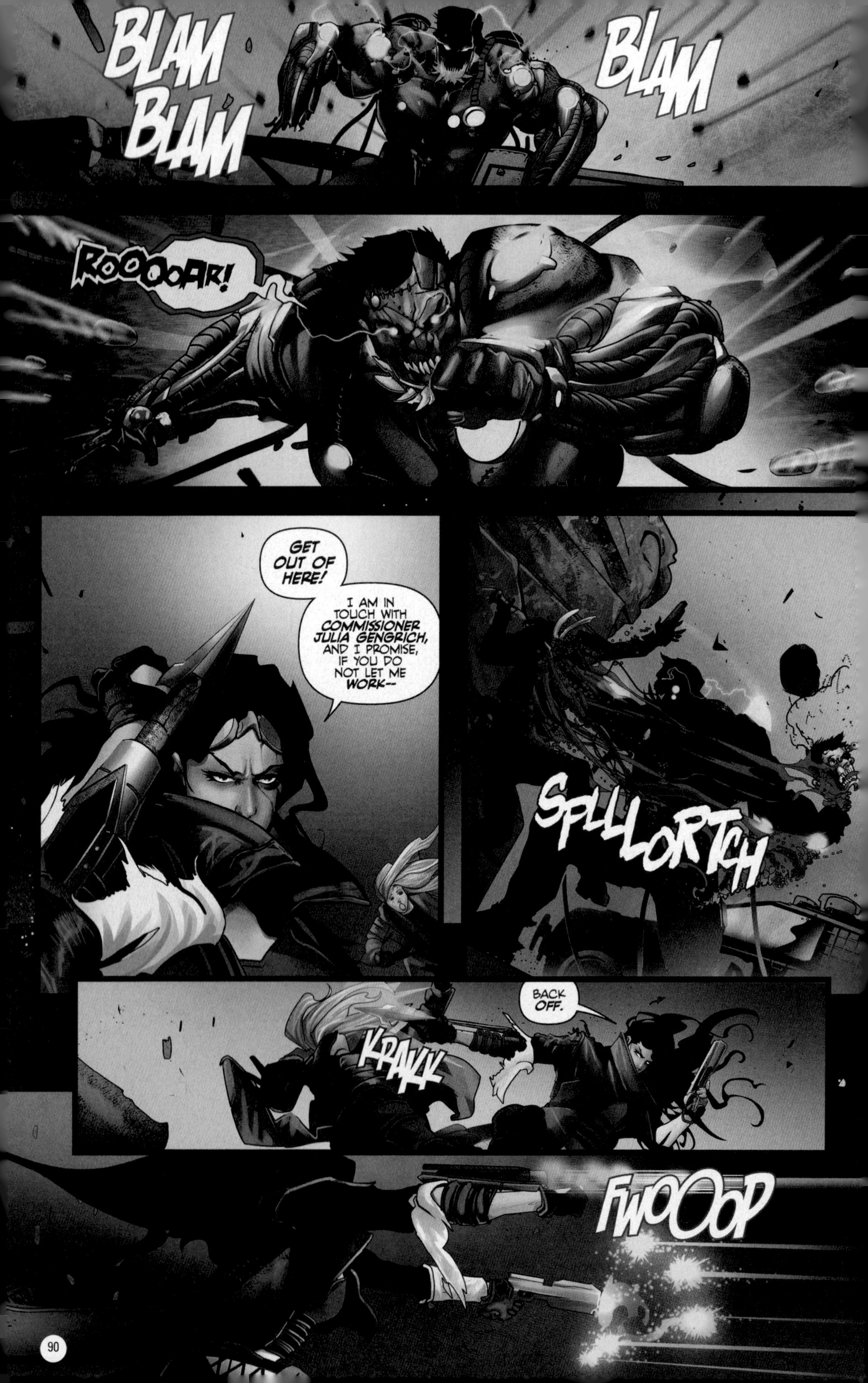
BLAM
BLAM
BLAM
ROOOOAR!
GET OUT OF HERE!
I AM IN TOUCH WITH COMMISSIONER JULIA GENGRICH, AND I PROMISE, IF YOU DO NOT LET ME WORK--
SPLLLORTCH
BACK OFF.
KRAKK
FWOOOP

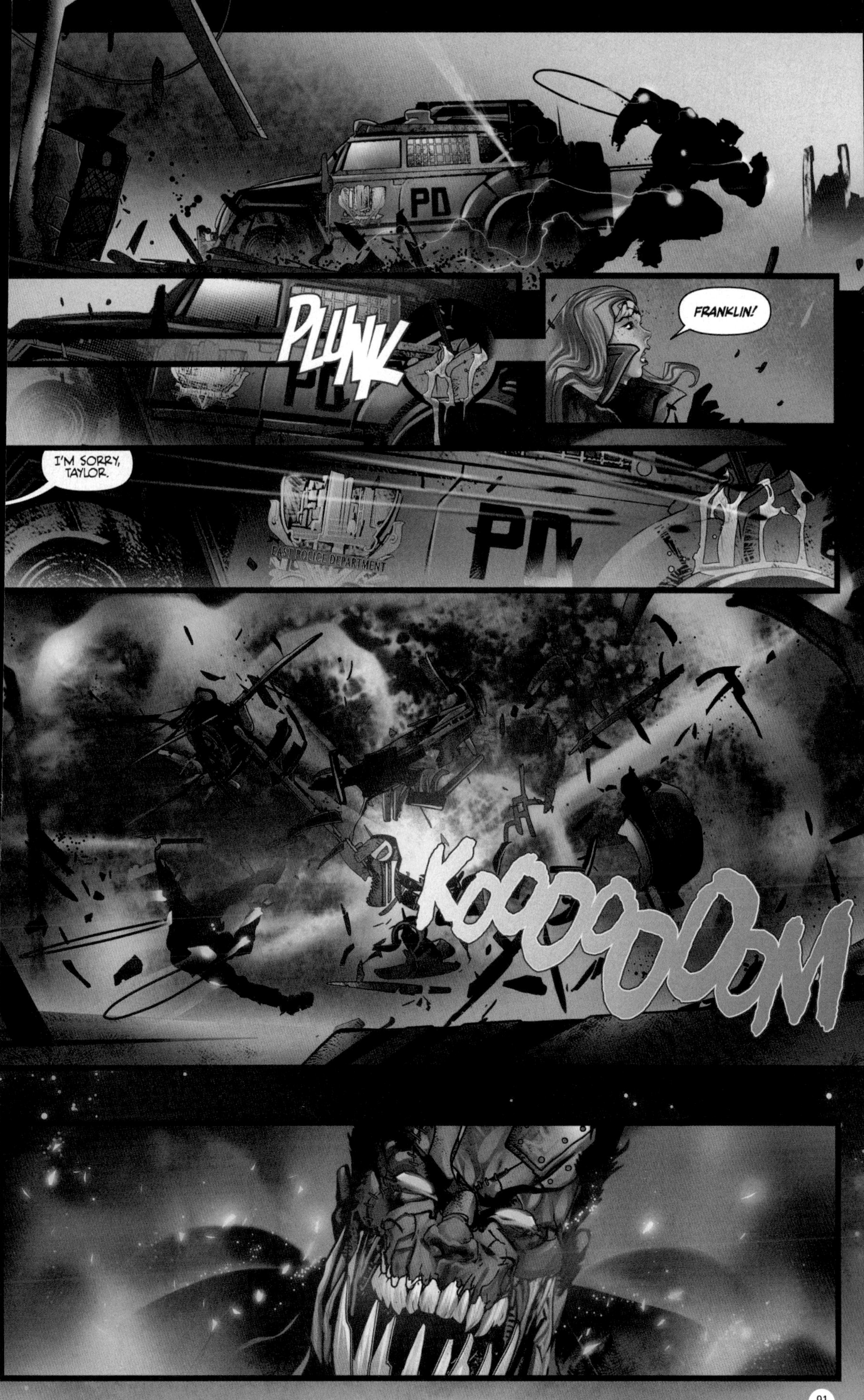
PD
PLUNK
FRANKLIN!
I'M SORRY, TAYLOR.
PD
EAST POLICE DEPARTMENT
KOOOOOOOM

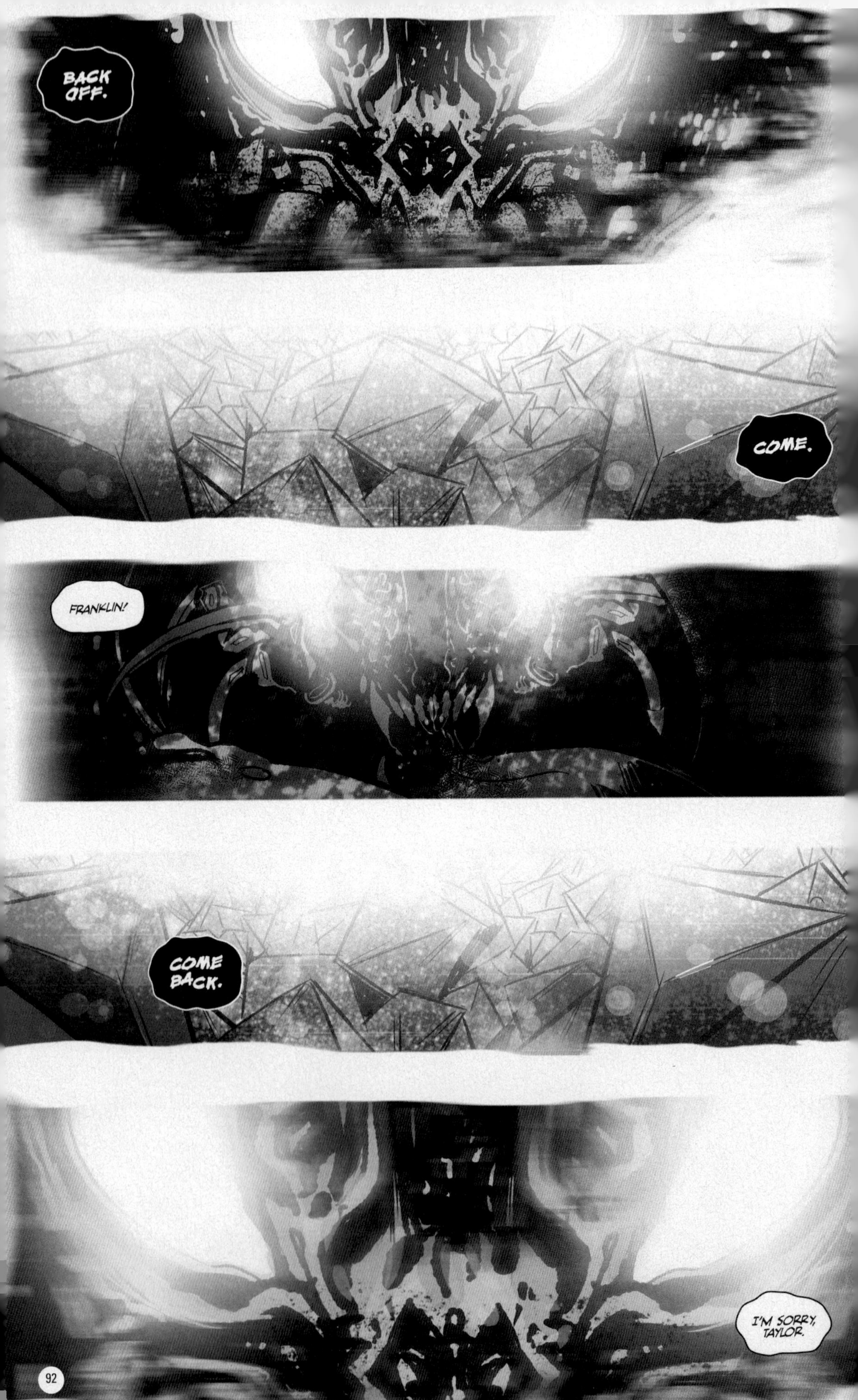
BACK OFF.
COME.
FRANKLIN!
COME BACK.
I'M SORRY, TAYLOR.

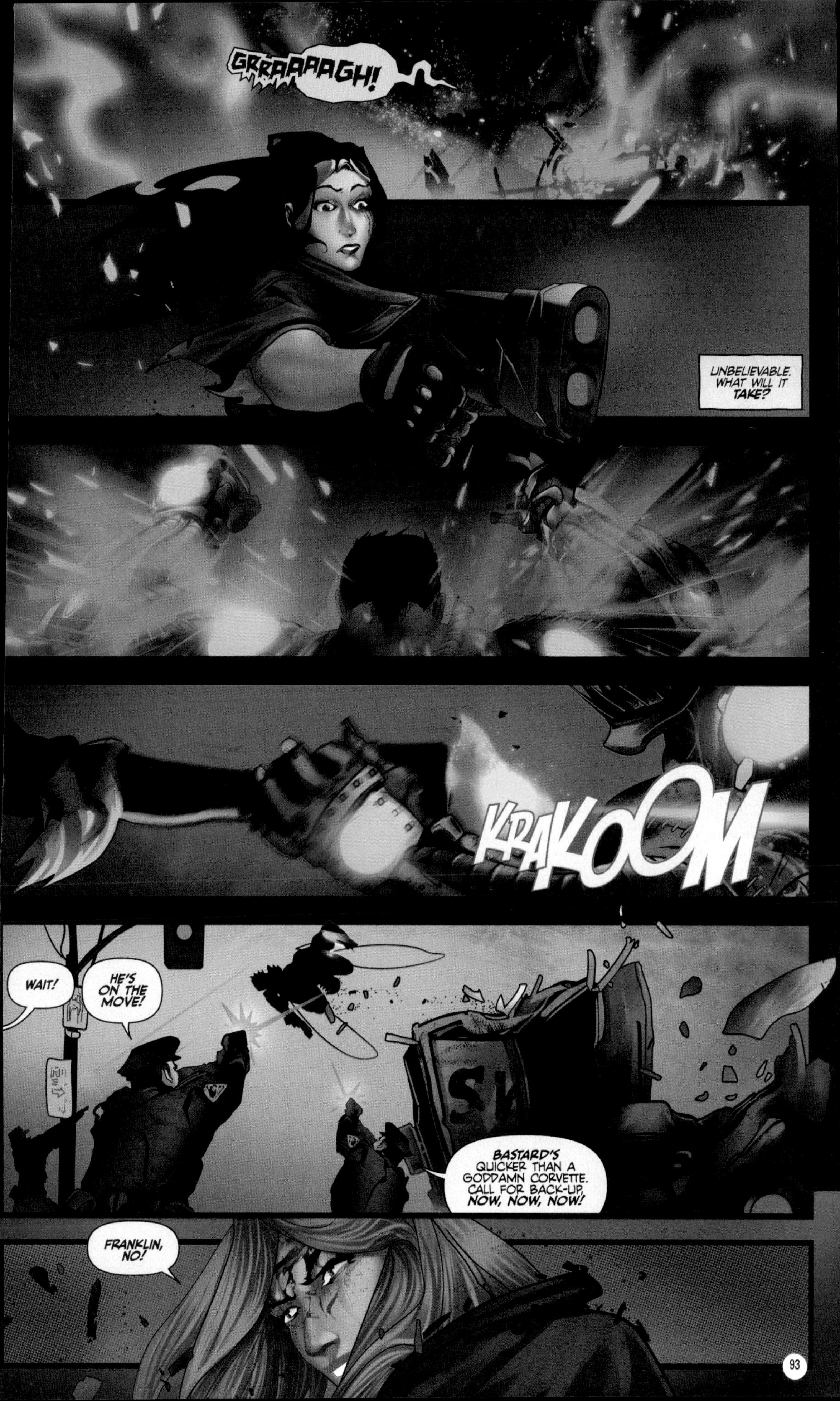
GRRAAAAGH!
UNBELIEVABLE. WHAT WILL IT TAKE?
KRAKOOM
WAIT!
HE'S ON THE MOVE!
BASTARD'S QUICKER THAN A GODDAMN CORVETTE. CALL FOR BACK-UP, NOW, NOW, NOW!
FRANKLIN, NO!

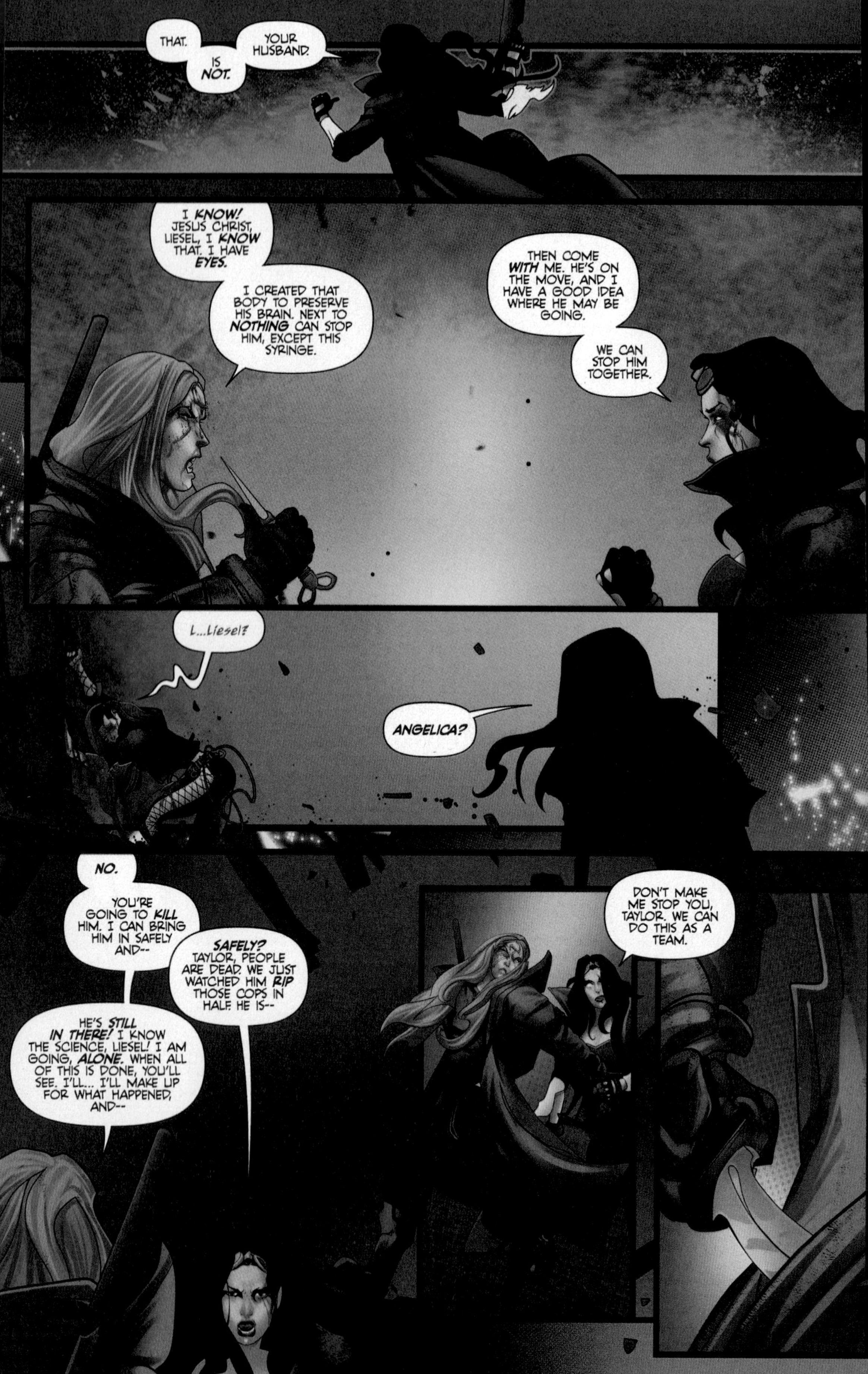

THAT.
IS NOT.
YOUR HUSBAND.
I KNOW! JESUS CHRIST, LIESEL, I KNOW THAT. I HAVE EYES.
I CREATED THAT BODY TO PRESERVE HIS BRAIN. NEXT TO NOTHING CAN STOP HIM, EXCEPT THIS SYRINGE.
THEN COME WITH ME. HE'S ON THE MOVE, AND I HAVE A GOOD IDEA WHERE HE MAY BE GOING.
WE CAN STOP HIM TOGETHER.
L...Liesel?
ANGELICA?
NO.
YOU'RE GOING TO KILL HIM. I CAN BRING HIM IN SAFELY AND--
SAFELY? TAYLOR, PEOPLE ARE DEAD. WE JUST WATCHED HIM RIP THOSE COPS IN HALF. HE IS--
HE'S STILL IN THERE! I KNOW THE SCIENCE, LIESEL! I AM GOING, ALONE. WHEN ALL OF THIS IS DONE, YOU'LL SEE. I'LL... I'LL MAKE UP FOR WHAT HAPPENED, AND--
DON'T MAKE ME STOP YOU, TAYLOR. WE CAN DO THIS AS A TEAM.

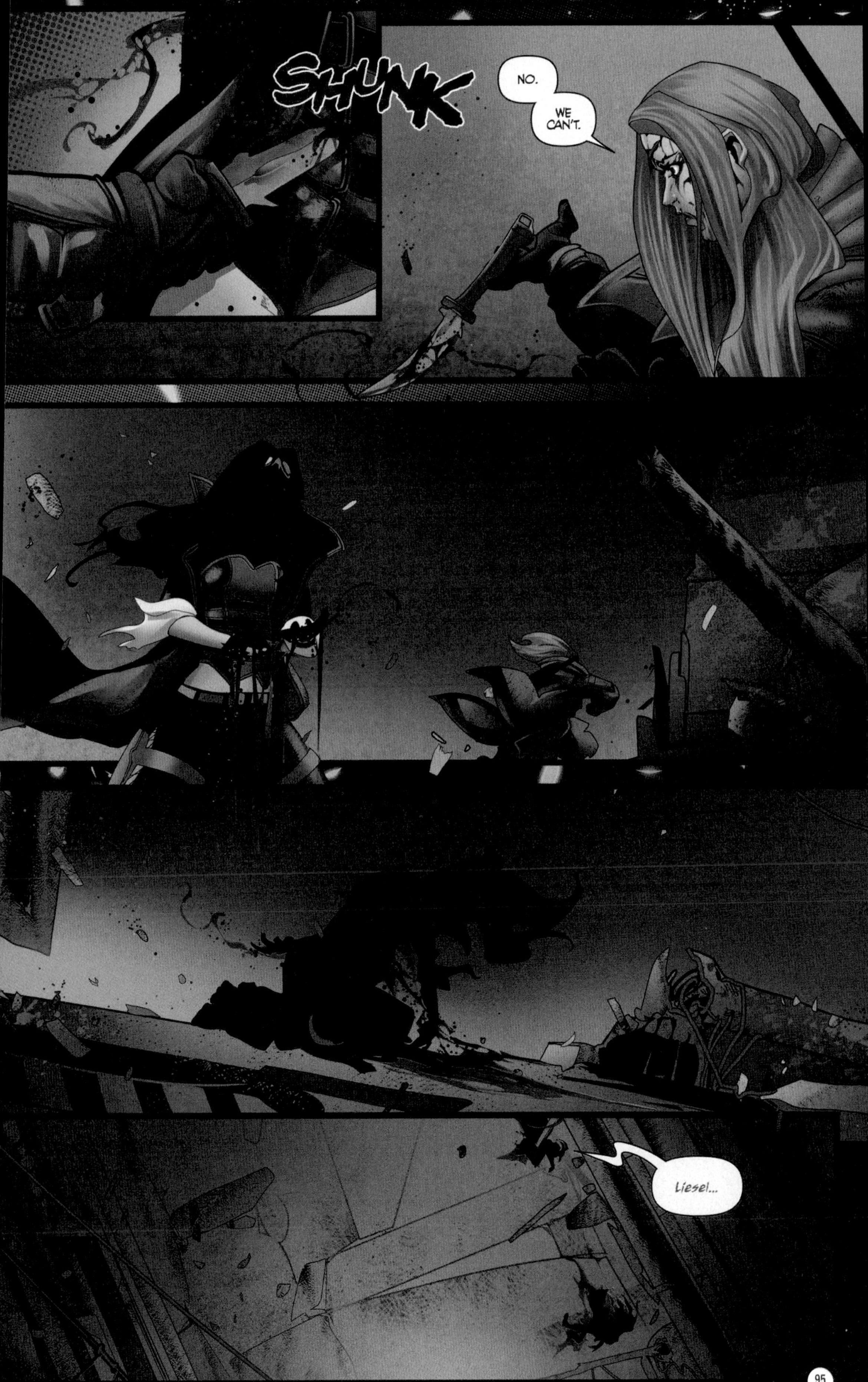
SHUNK
NO.
WE CAN'T.
Liesel...

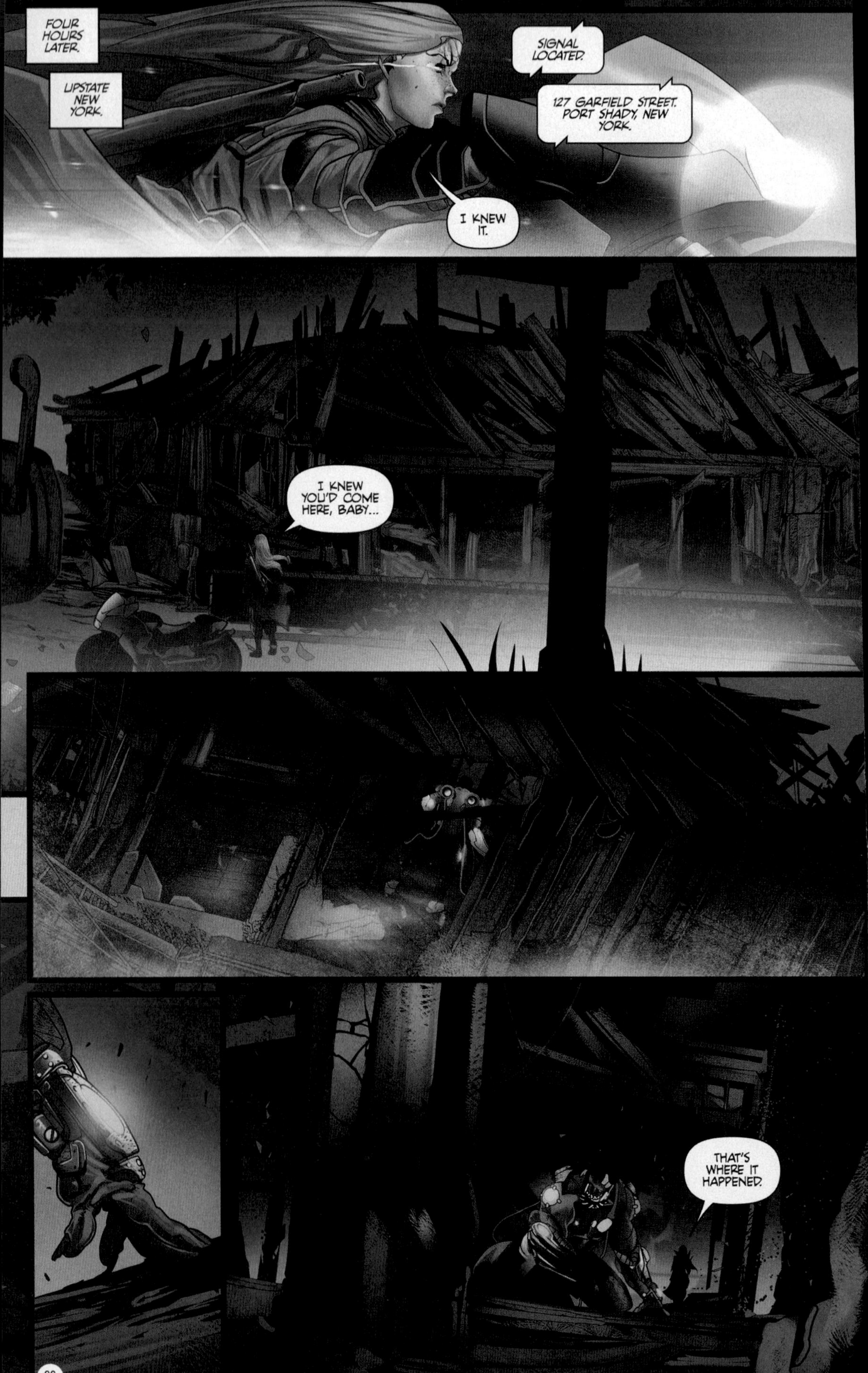
FOUR HOURS LATER.
UPSTATE NEW YORK.
SIGNAL LOCATED.
127 GARFIELD STREET. PORT SHADY, NEW YORK.
I KNEW IT.
I KNEW YOU'D COME HERE, BABY...
THAT'S WHERE IT HAPPENED.

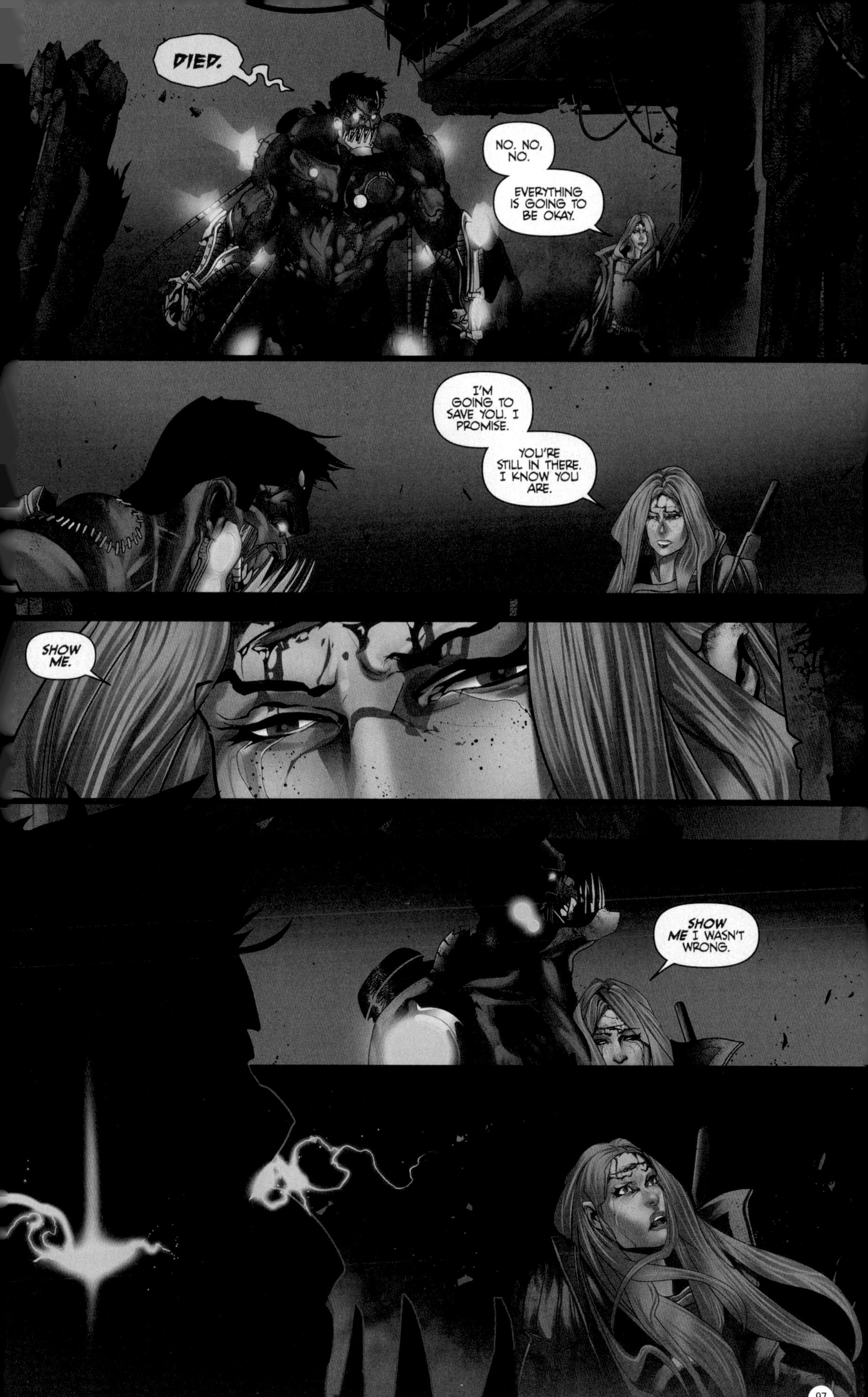
DIED.
NO. NO, NO.
EVERYTHING IS GOING TO BE OKAY.
I'M GOING TO SAVE YOU. I PROMISE.
YOU'RE STILL IN THERE. I KNOW YOU ARE.
SHOW ME.
SHOW ME I WASN'T WRONG.

WRONG.
NEXT:
NO GRIEF

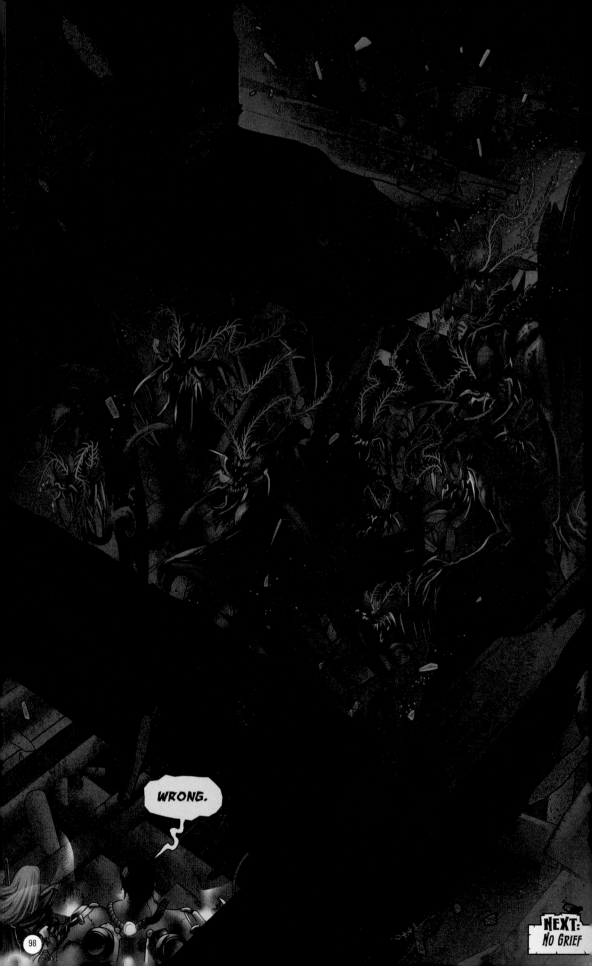

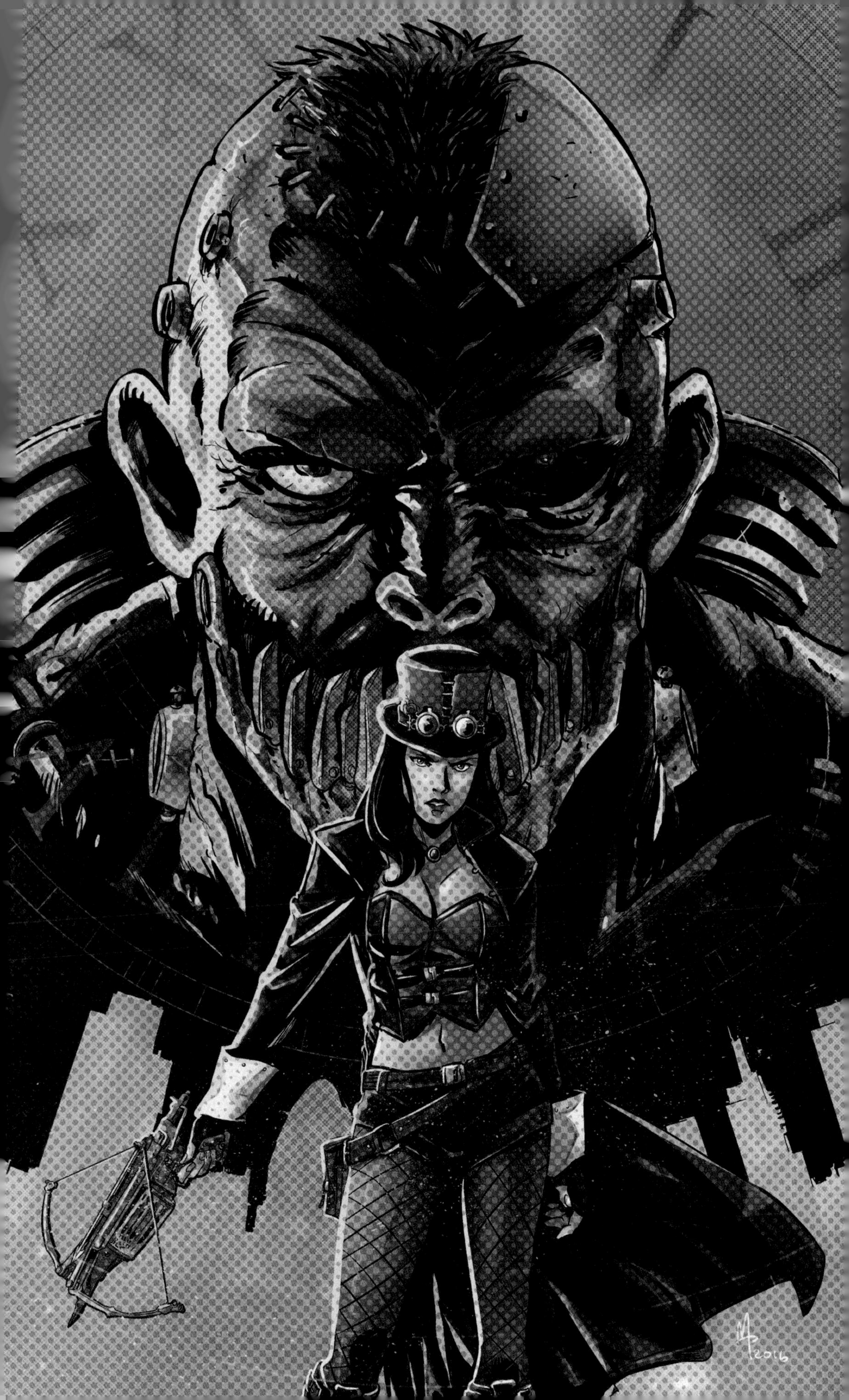

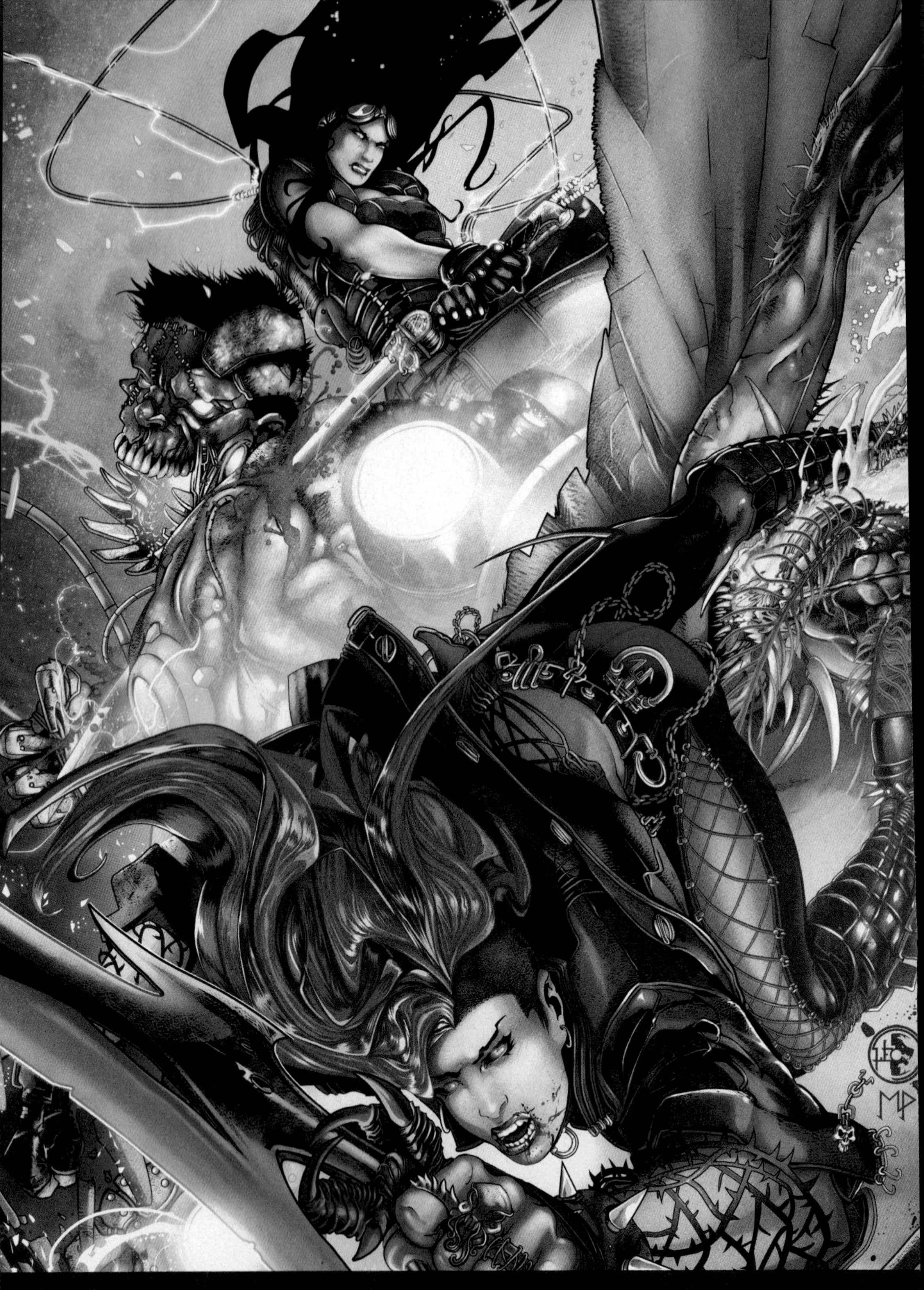

CHAPTER FIVE
NO GRIEF

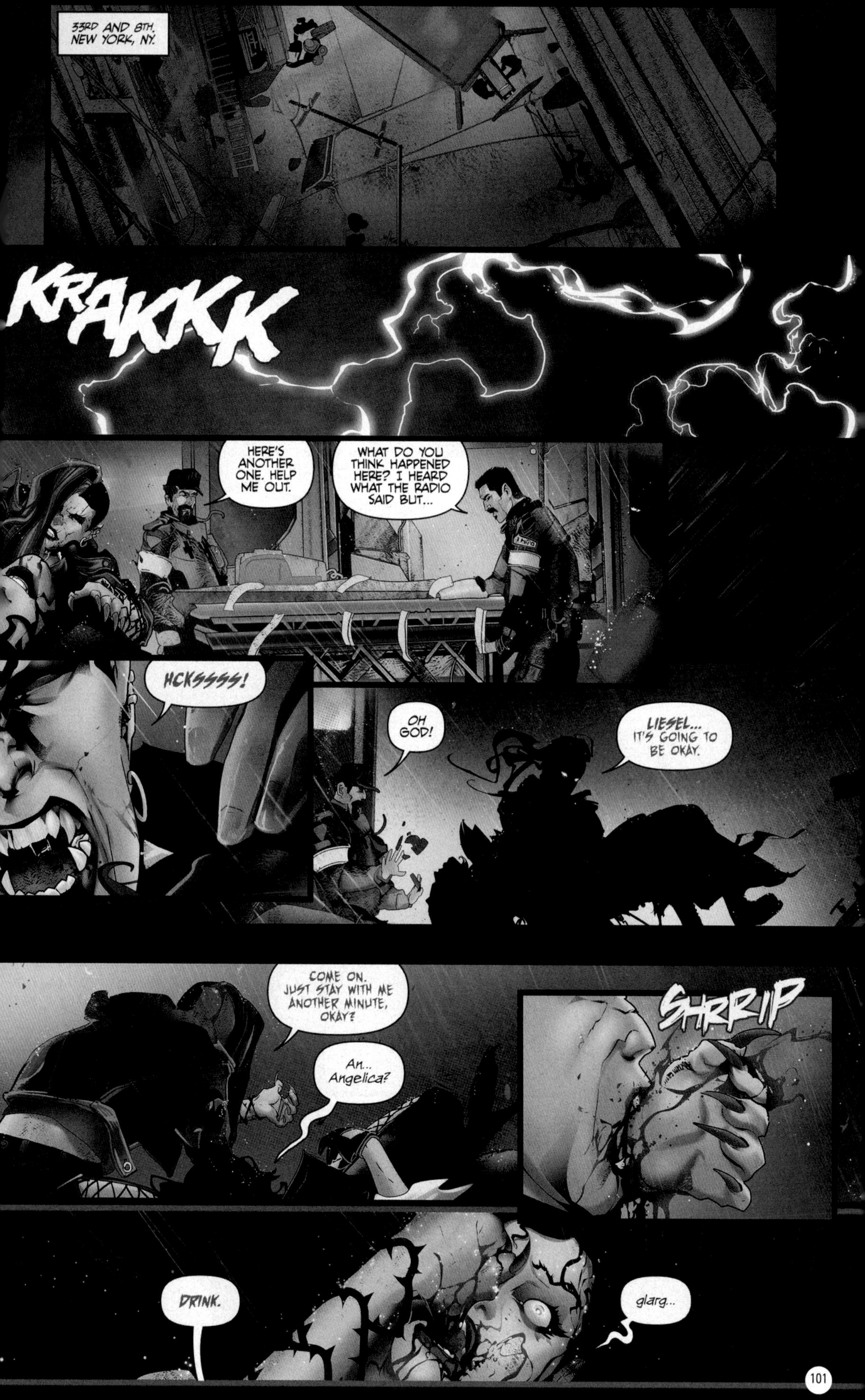

33RD AND 8TH, NEW YORK, NY.
KRAKKK
HERE'S ANOTHER ONE. HELP ME OUT.
WHAT DO YOU THINK HAPPENED HERE? I HEARD WHAT THE RADIO SAID BUT...
HCKSSSSS!
OH GOD!
LIESEL... IT'S GOING TO BE OKAY.
COME ON. JUST STAY WITH ME ANOTHER MINUTE, OKAY?
An... Angelica?
SHRRIP
DRINK.
glarg...

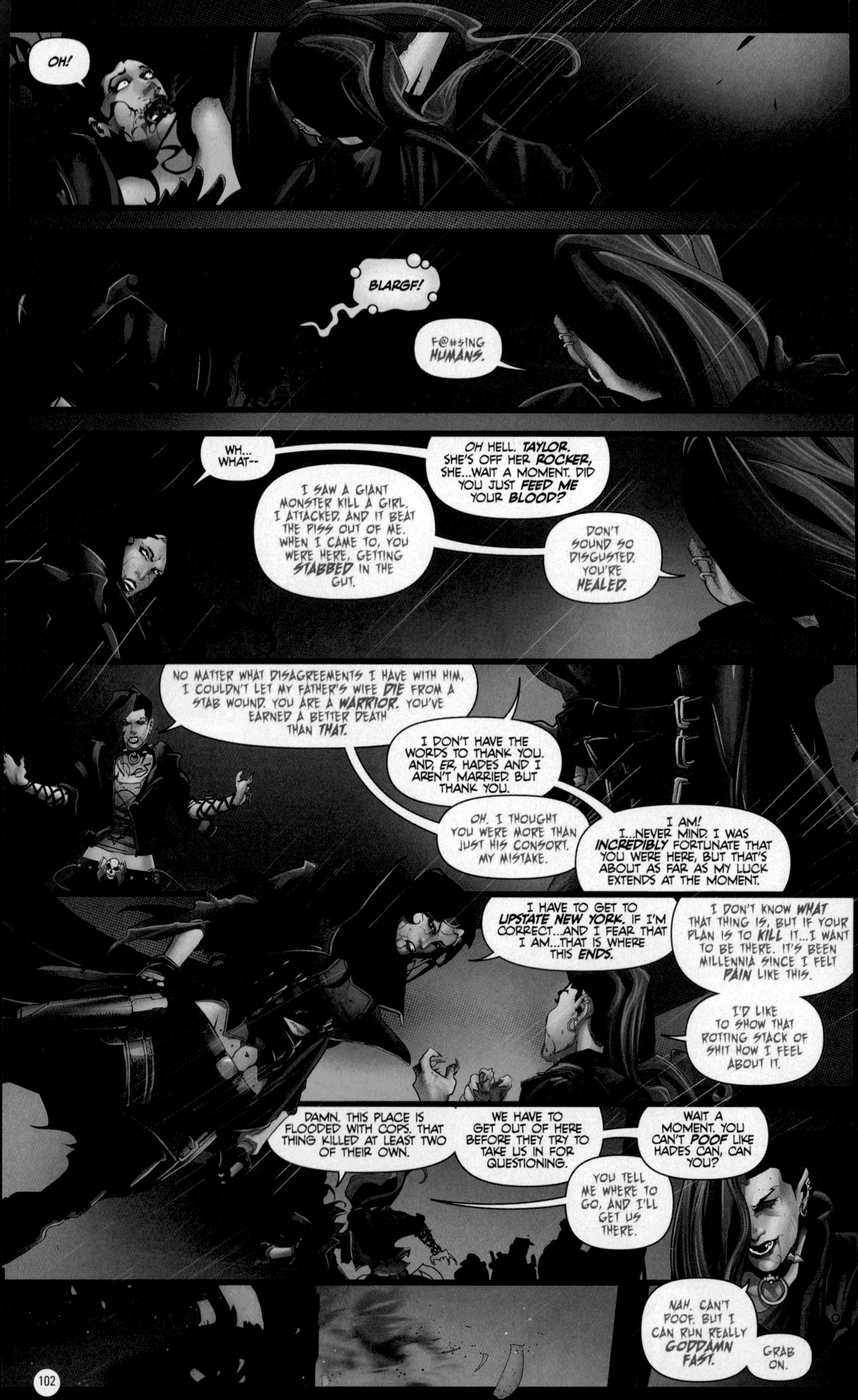
OH!
BLARGF!
F@#$ING HUMANS.
WH... WHAT--
OH HELL. TAYLOR. SHE'S OFF HER ROCKER, SHE...WAIT A MOMENT. DID YOU JUST FEED ME YOUR BLOOD?
I SAW A GIANT MONSTER KILL A GIRL. I ATTACKED, AND IT BEAT THE PISS OUT OF ME. WHEN I CAME TO, YOU WERE HERE, GETTING STABBED IN THE GUT.
DON'T SOUND SO DISGUSTED. YOU'RE HEALED.
NO MATTER WHAT DISAGREEMENTS I HAVE WITH HIM, I COULDN'T LET MY FATHER'S WIFE DIE FROM A STAB WOUND. YOU ARE A WARRIOR. YOU'VE EARNED A BETTER DEATH THAN THAT.
I DON'T HAVE THE WORDS TO THANK YOU. AND, ER, HADES AND I AREN'T MARRIED. BUT THANK YOU.
OH. I THOUGHT YOU WERE MORE THAN JUST HIS CONSORT. MY MISTAKE.
I AM! I...NEVER MIND. I WAS INCREDIBLY FORTUNATE THAT YOU WERE HERE, BUT THAT'S ABOUT AS FAR AS MY LUCK EXTENDS AT THE MOMENT.
I HAVE TO GET TO UPSTATE NEW YORK. IF I'M CORRECT...AND I FEAR THAT I AM...THAT IS WHERE THIS ENDS.
I DON'T KNOW WHAT THAT THING IS, BUT IF YOUR PLAN IS TO KILL IT...I WANT TO BE THERE. IT'S BEEN MILLENNIA SINCE I FELT PAIN LIKE THIS.
I'D LIKE TO SHOW THAT ROTTING STACK OF SHIT HOW I FEEL ABOUT IT.
DAMN. THIS PLACE IS FLOODED WITH COPS. THAT THING KILLED AT LEAST TWO OF THEIR OWN.
WE HAVE TO GET OUT OF HERE BEFORE THEY TRY TO TAKE US IN FOR QUESTIONING.
WAIT A MOMENT. YOU CAN'T POOF LIKE HADES CAN, CAN YOU?
YOU TELL ME WHERE TO GO, AND I'LL GET US THERE.
NAH. CAN'T POOF. BUT I CAN RUN REALLY GODDAMN FAST.
GRAB ON.

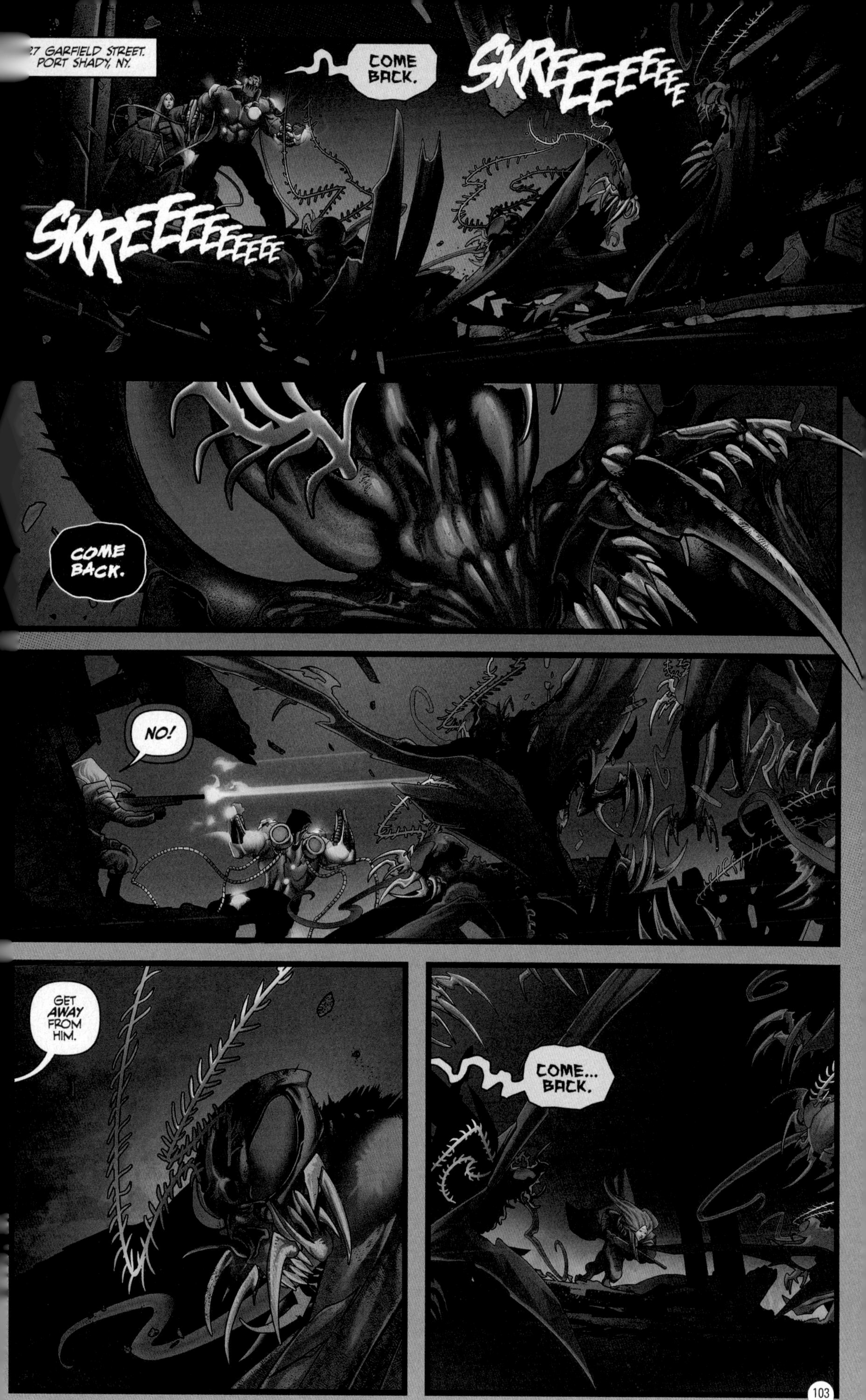
27 GARFIELD STREET. PORT SHADY, NY.
COME BACK.
SKREEEEEEEEE
SKREEEEEEEEEE
COME BACK.
NO!
GET AWAY FROM HIM.
COME... BACK.

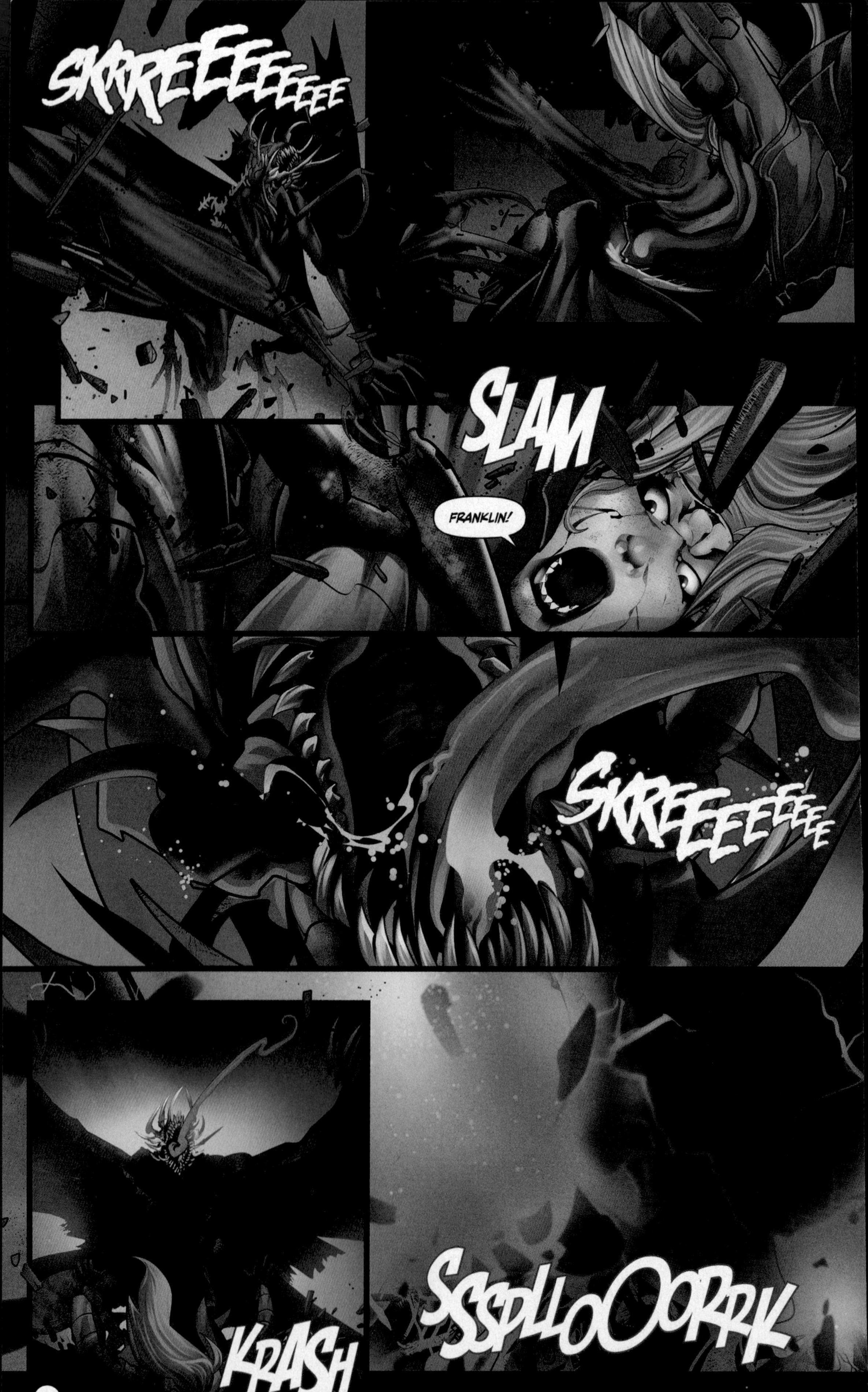
SKRREEEEEEEEE
SLAM
FRANKLIN!
SKREEEEEEEEE
KRASH
SSSPLLOOORRK

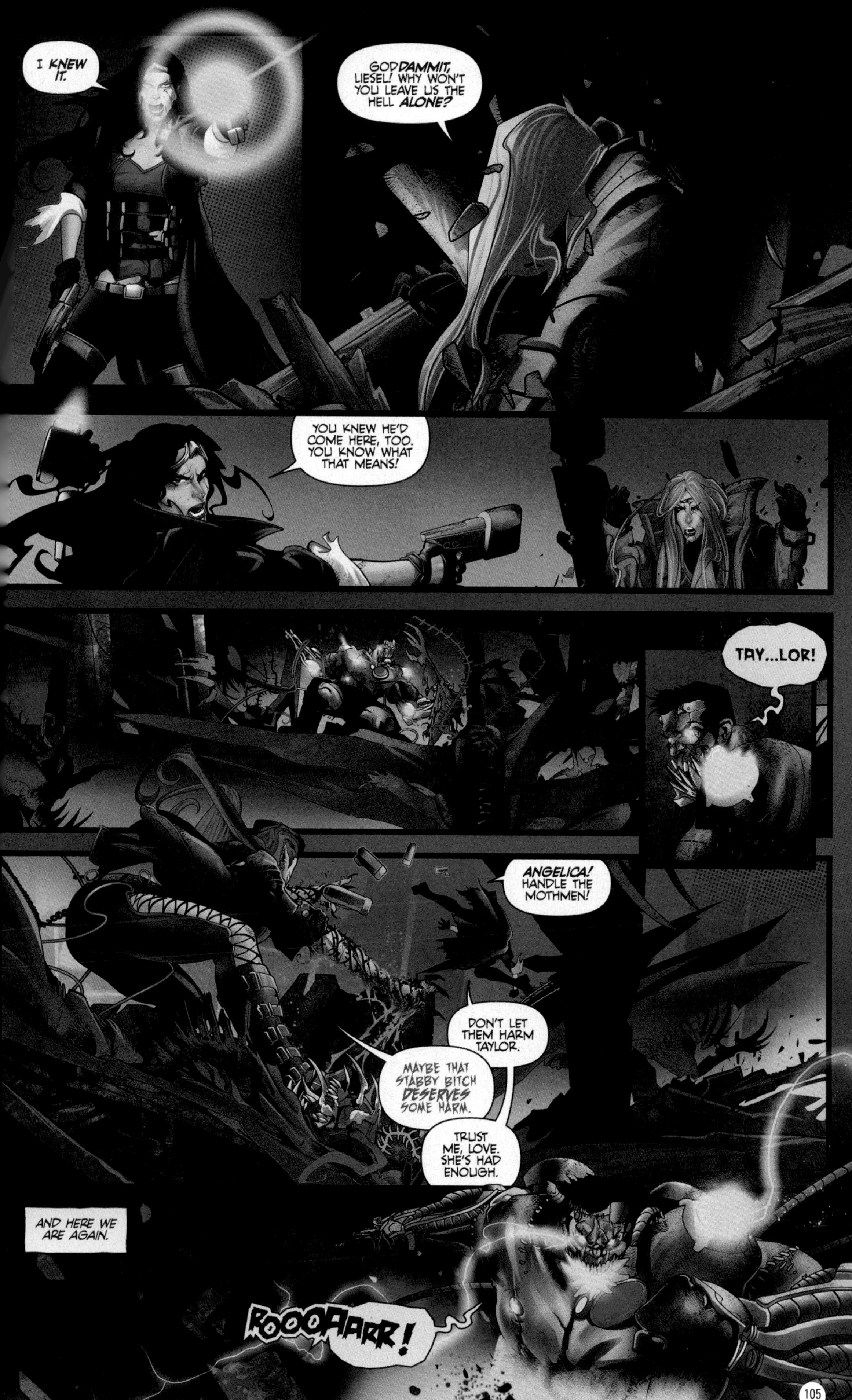

I KNEW IT.
GODDAMMIT, LIESEL! WHY WON'T YOU LEAVE US THE HELL ALONE?
YOU KNEW HE'D COME HERE, TOO. YOU KNOW WHAT THAT MEANS!
TAY...LOR!
ANGELICA! HANDLE THE MOTHMEN!
DON'T LET THEM HARM TAYLOR.
MAYBE THAT STABBY BITCH DESERVES SOME HARM.
TRUST ME, LOVE. SHE'S HAD ENOUGH.
AND HERE WE ARE AGAIN.
ROOOAARR!

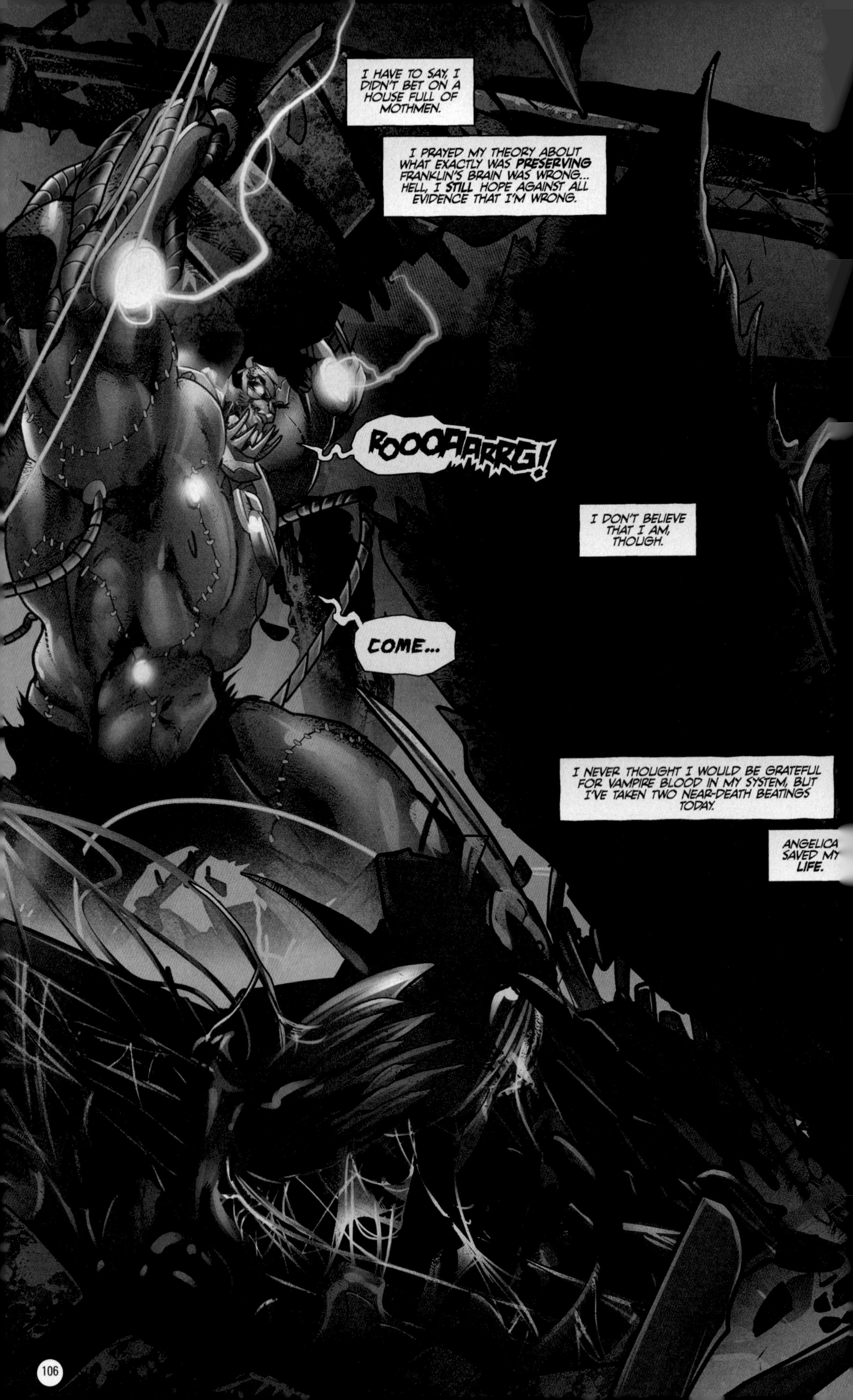

I HAVE TO SAY, I DIDN'T BET ON A HOUSE FULL OF MOTHMEN.
I PRAYED MY THEORY ABOUT WHAT EXACTLY WAS **PRESERVING** FRANKLIN'S BRAIN WAS WRONG... HELL, I **STILL** HOPE AGAINST ALL EVIDENCE THAT I'M WRONG.
ROOOAARRG!
I DON'T BELIEVE THAT I AM, THOUGH.
COME...
I NEVER THOUGHT I WOULD BE GRATEFUL FOR VAMPIRE BLOOD IN MY SYSTEM, BUT I'VE TAKEN TWO NEAR-DEATH BEATINGS TODAY.
ANGELICA SAVED MY **LIFE.**

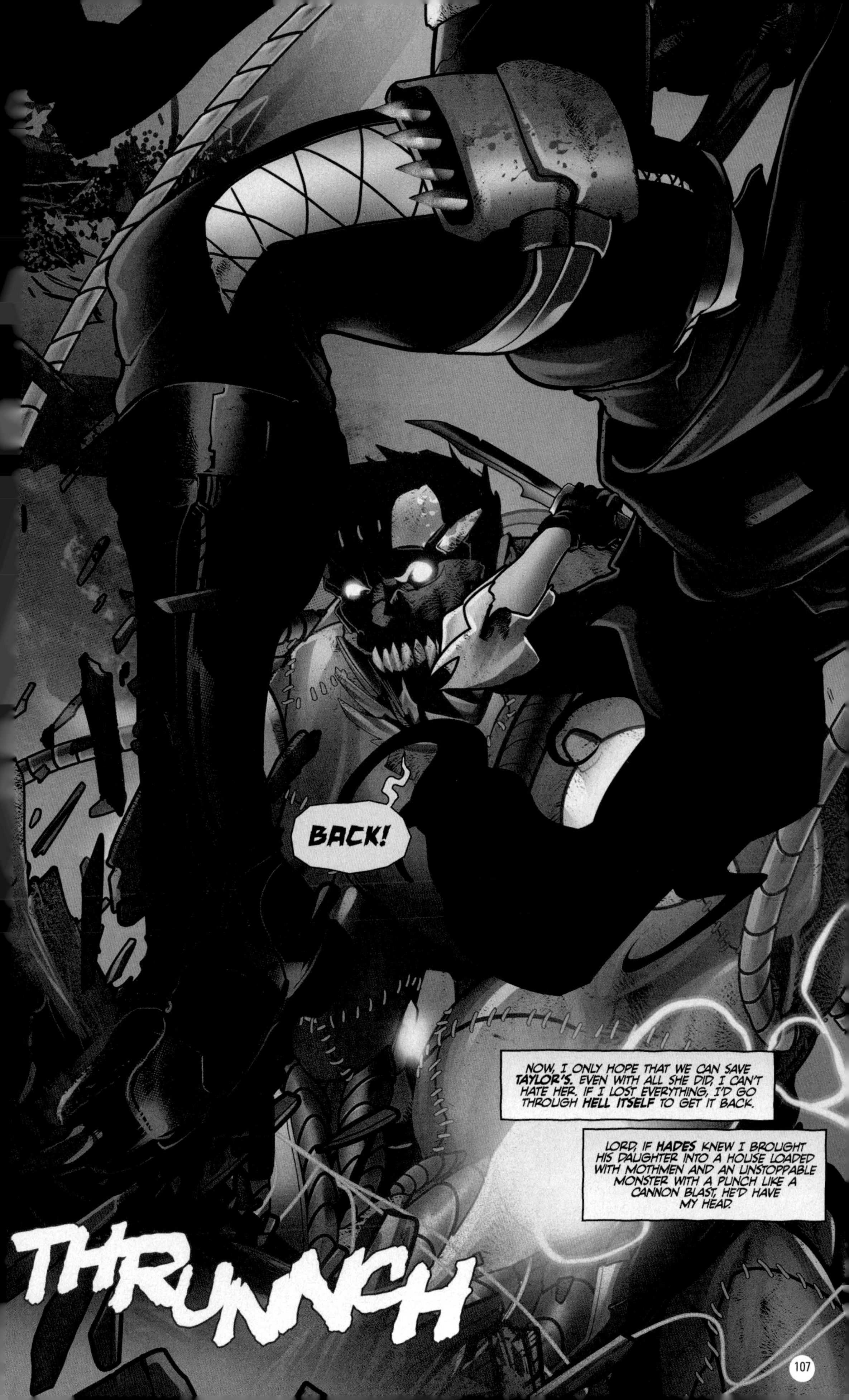
BACK!
NOW, I ONLY HOPE THAT WE CAN SAVE TAYLOR'S. EVEN WITH ALL SHE DID, I CAN'T HATE HER. IF I LOST EVERYTHING, I'D GO THROUGH HELL ITSELF TO GET IT BACK.
LORD, IF HADES KNEW I BROUGHT HIS DAUGHTER INTO A HOUSE LOADED WITH MOTHMEN AND AN UNSTOPPABLE MONSTER WITH A PUNCH LIKE A CANNON BLAST, HE'D HAVE MY HEAD.
THRUNNCH

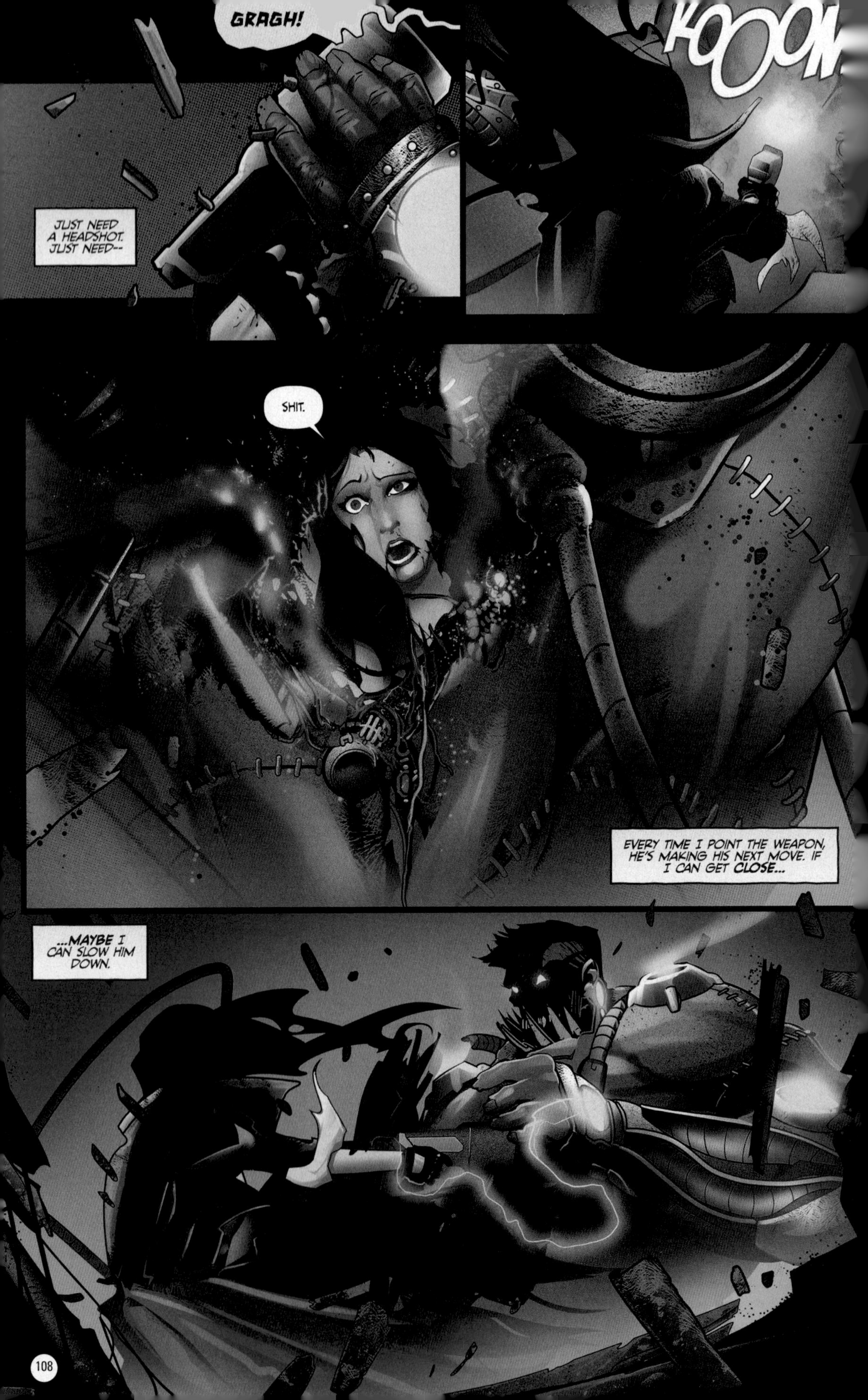
GRAGH!
KOOOM
JUST NEED A HEADSHOT. JUST NEED--
SHIT.
EVERY TIME I POINT THE WEAPON, HE'S MAKING HIS NEXT MOVE. IF I CAN GET CLOSE...
...MAYBE I CAN SLOW HIM DOWN.

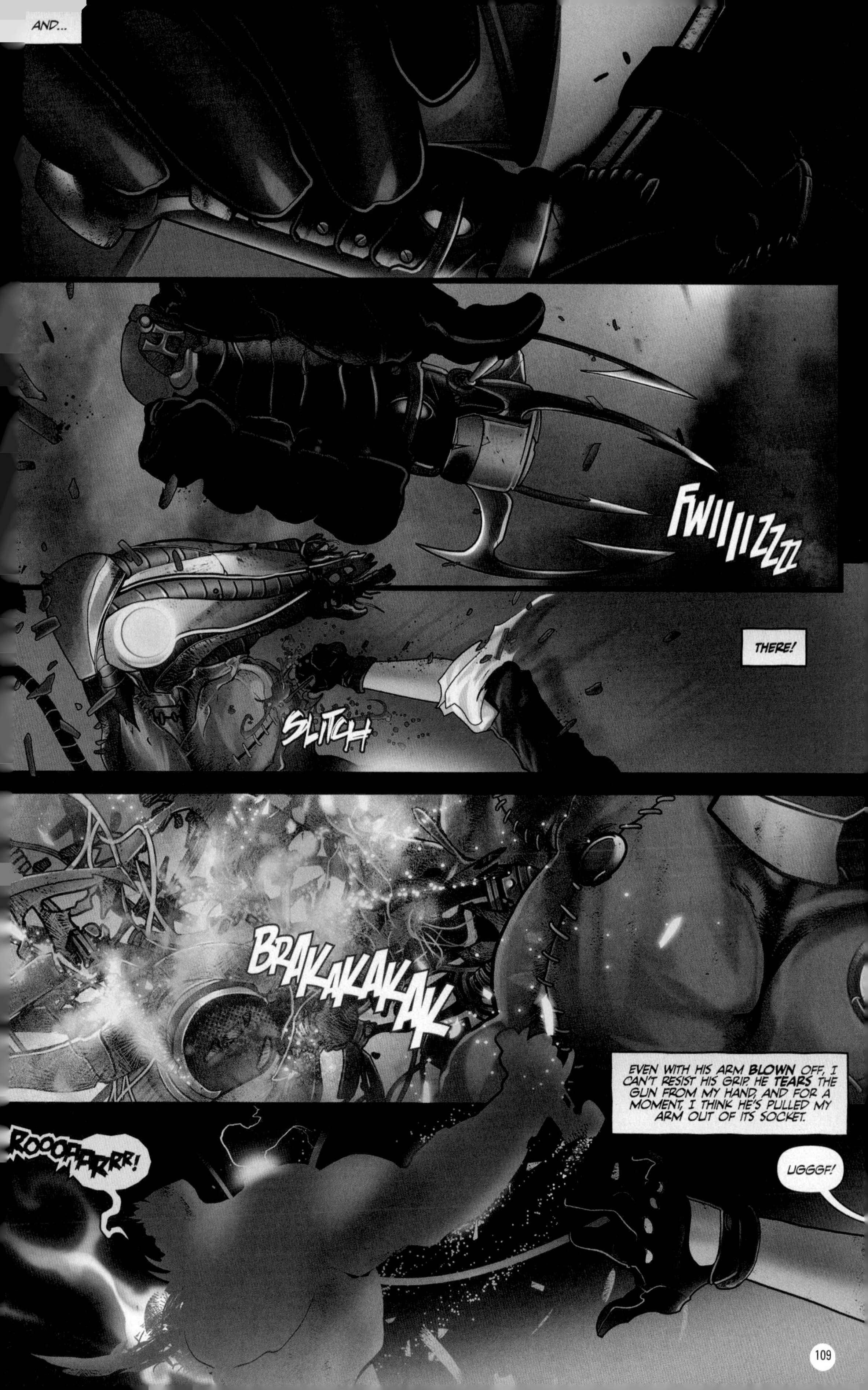
AND...
FWIIIIIZZZZ
SLITCH
THERE!
BRAKAKAKAKAK
EVEN WITH HIS ARM BLOWN OFF, I CAN'T RESIST HIS GRIP. HE TEARS THE GUN FROM MY HAND, AND FOR A MOMENT, I THINK HE'S PULLED MY ARM OUT OF ITS SOCKET.
ROOOARRRR!
UGGGF!

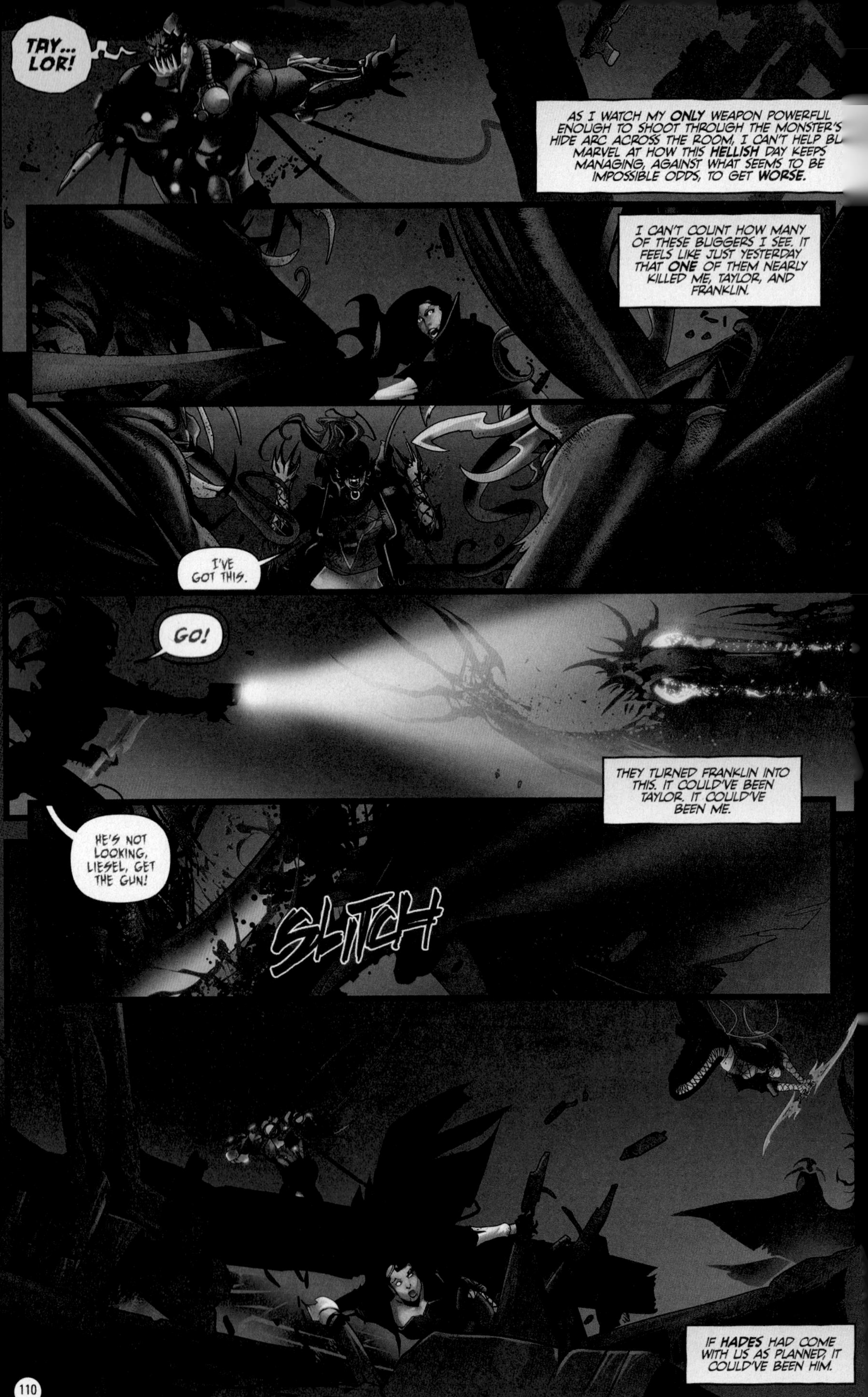
TAY... LOR!
AS I WATCH MY ONLY WEAPON POWERFUL ENOUGH TO SHOOT THROUGH THE MONSTER'S HIDE ARC ACROSS THE ROOM, I CAN'T HELP BU MARVEL AT HOW THIS HELLISH DAY KEEPS MANAGING, AGAINST WHAT SEEMS TO BE IMPOSSIBLE ODDS, TO GET WORSE.
I CAN'T COUNT HOW MANY OF THESE BUGGERS I SEE. IT FEELS LIKE JUST YESTERDAY THAT ONE OF THEM NEARLY KILLED ME, TAYLOR, AND FRANKLIN.
I'VE GOT THIS.
GO!
THEY TURNED FRANKLIN INTO THIS. IT COULD'VE BEEN TAYLOR. IT COULD'VE BEEN ME.
HE'S NOT LOOKING, LIESEL, GET THE GUN!
SLITCH
IF HADES HAD COME WITH US AS PLANNED, IT COULD'VE BEEN HIM.

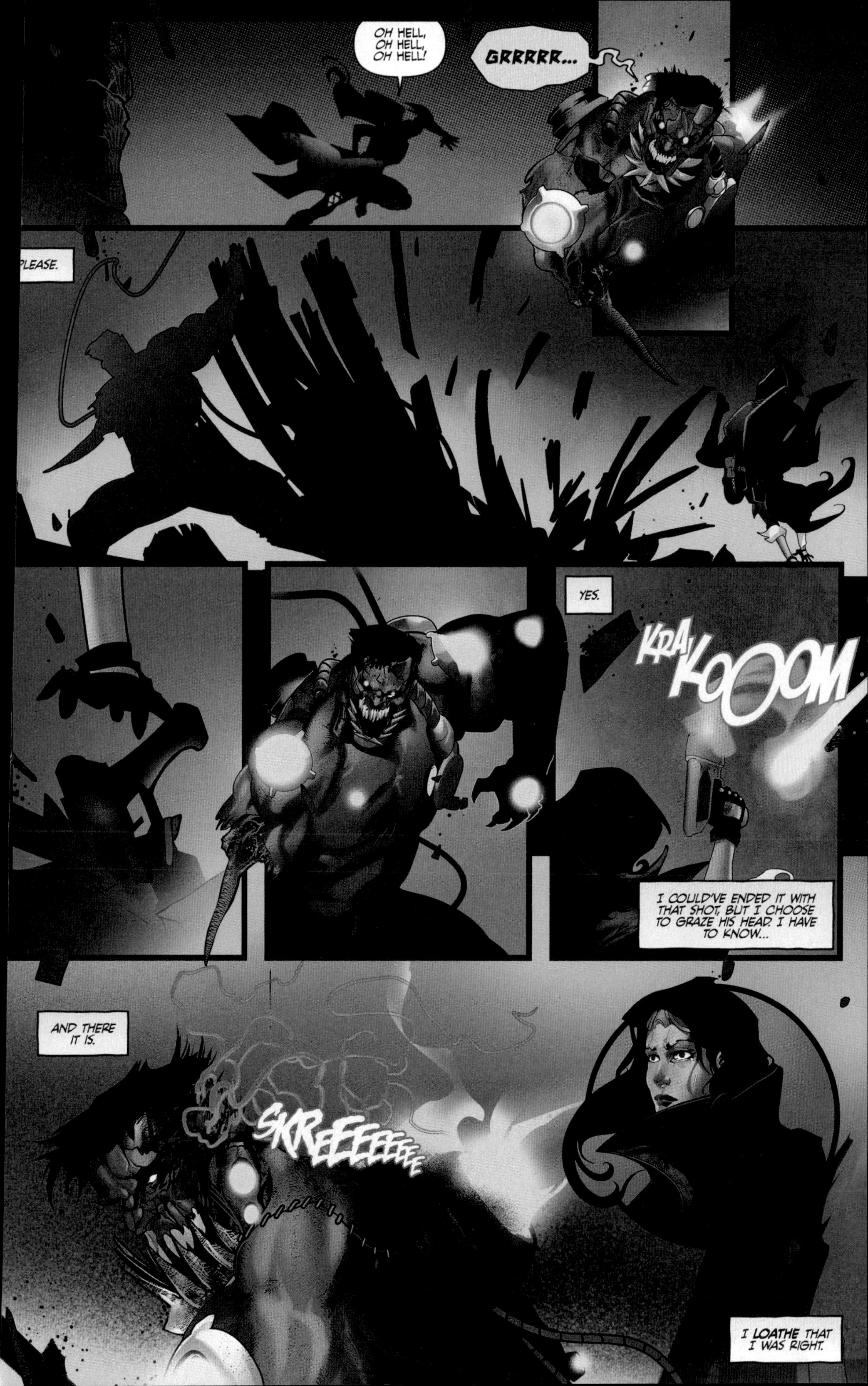
OH HELL, OH HELL, OH HELL!
GRRRRR...
PLEASE.
YES.
KRA KOOOM
I COULD'VE ENDED IT WITH THAT SHOT, BUT I CHOOSE TO GRAZE HIS HEAD. I HAVE TO KNOW...
AND THERE IT IS.
SKREEEEEEEE
I LOATHE THAT I WAS RIGHT.

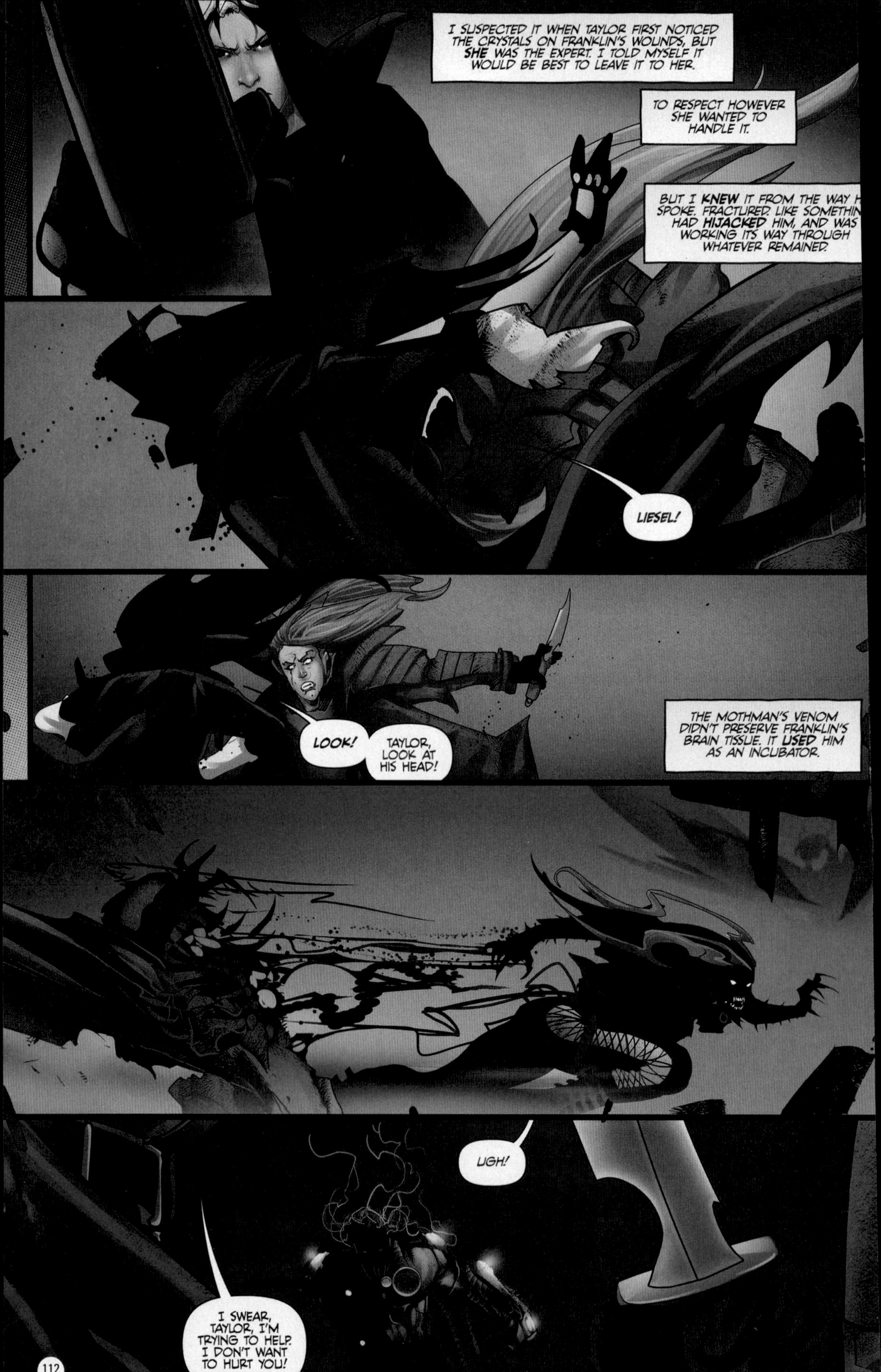
I SUSPECTED IT WHEN TAYLOR FIRST NOTICED THE CRYSTALS ON FRANKLIN'S WOUNDS, BUT SHE WAS THE EXPERT. I TOLD MYSELF IT WOULD BE BEST TO LEAVE IT TO HER.
TO RESPECT HOWEVER SHE WANTED TO HANDLE IT.
BUT I KNEW IT FROM THE WAY H SPOKE. FRACTURED. LIKE SOMETHIN HAD HIJACKED HIM, AND WAS WORKING ITS WAY THROUGH WHATEVER REMAINED.
LIESEL!
LOOK!
TAYLOR, LOOK AT HIS HEAD!
THE MOTHMAN'S VENOM DIDN'T PRESERVE FRANKLIN'S BRAIN TISSUE. IT USED HIM AS AN INCUBATOR.
UGH!
I SWEAR, TAYLOR, I'M TRYING TO HELP. I DON'T WANT TO HURT YOU!

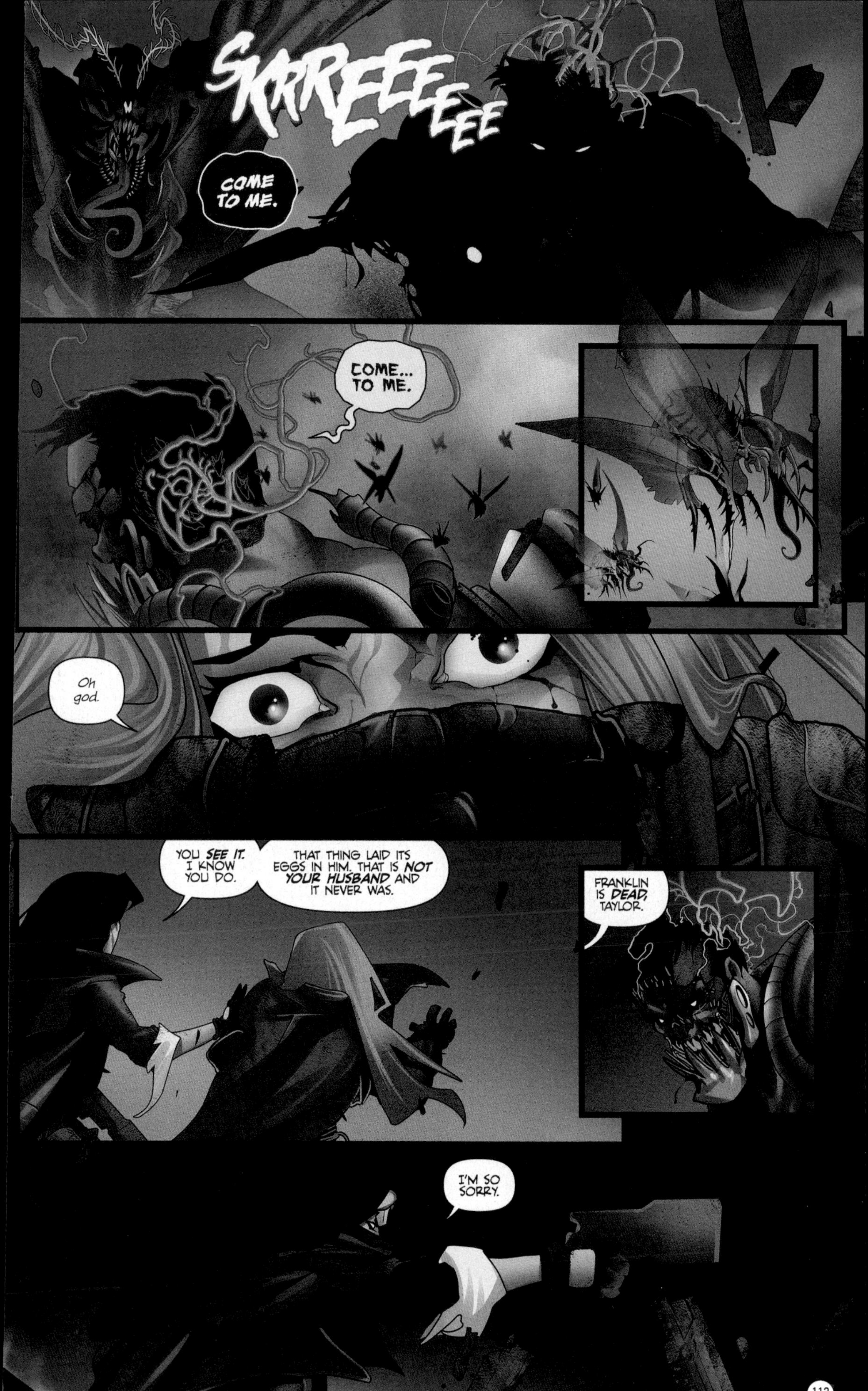
SKRREEEEEEE
COME TO ME.
COME... TO ME.
Oh god.
YOU SEE IT. I KNOW YOU DO.
THAT THING LAID ITS EGGS IN HIM. THAT IS NOT YOUR HUSBAND AND IT NEVER WAS.
FRANKLIN IS DEAD, TAYLOR.
I'M SO SORRY.

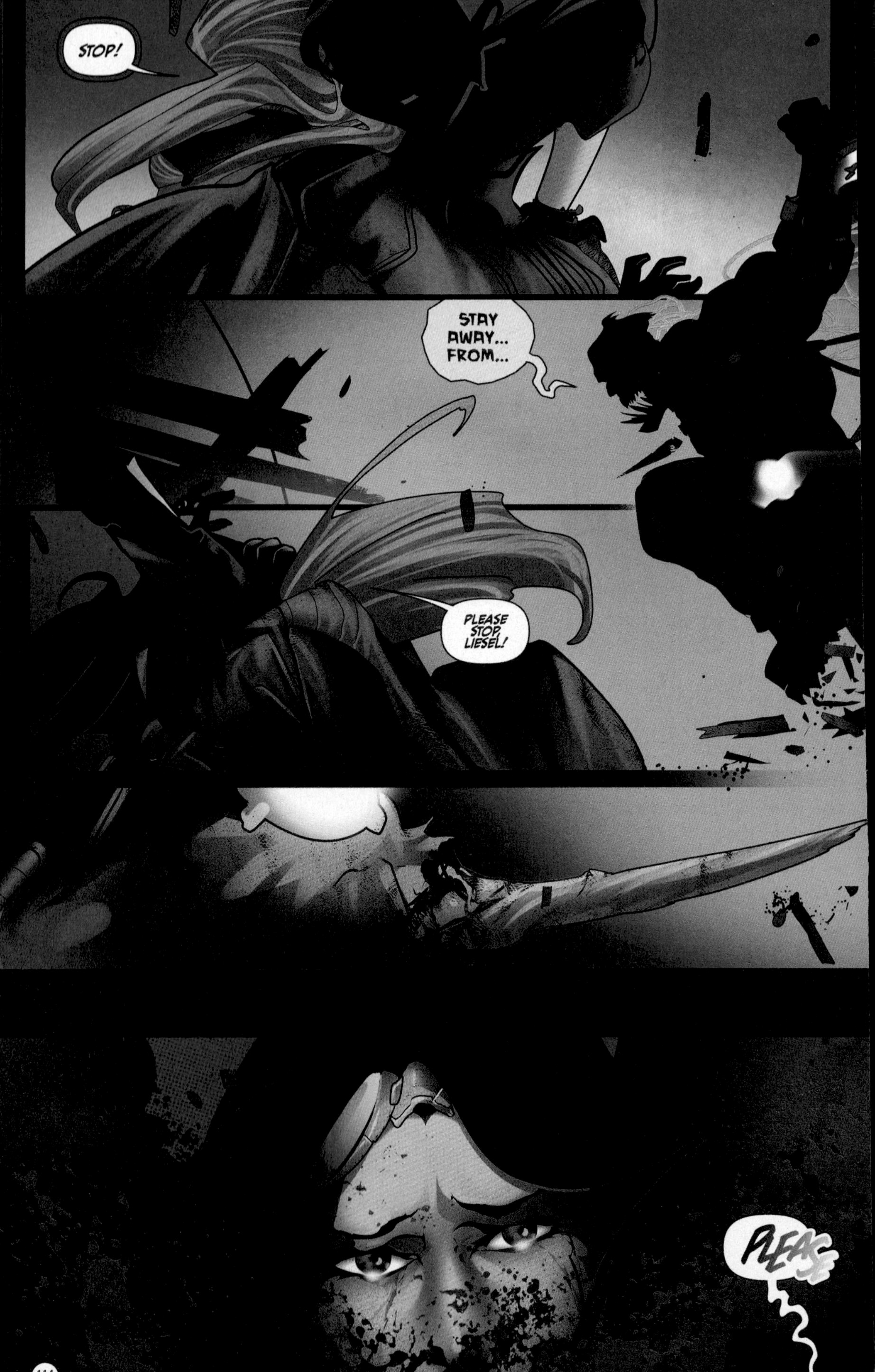
STOP!
STAY AWAY... FROM...
PLEASE STOP, LIESEL!
PLEASE

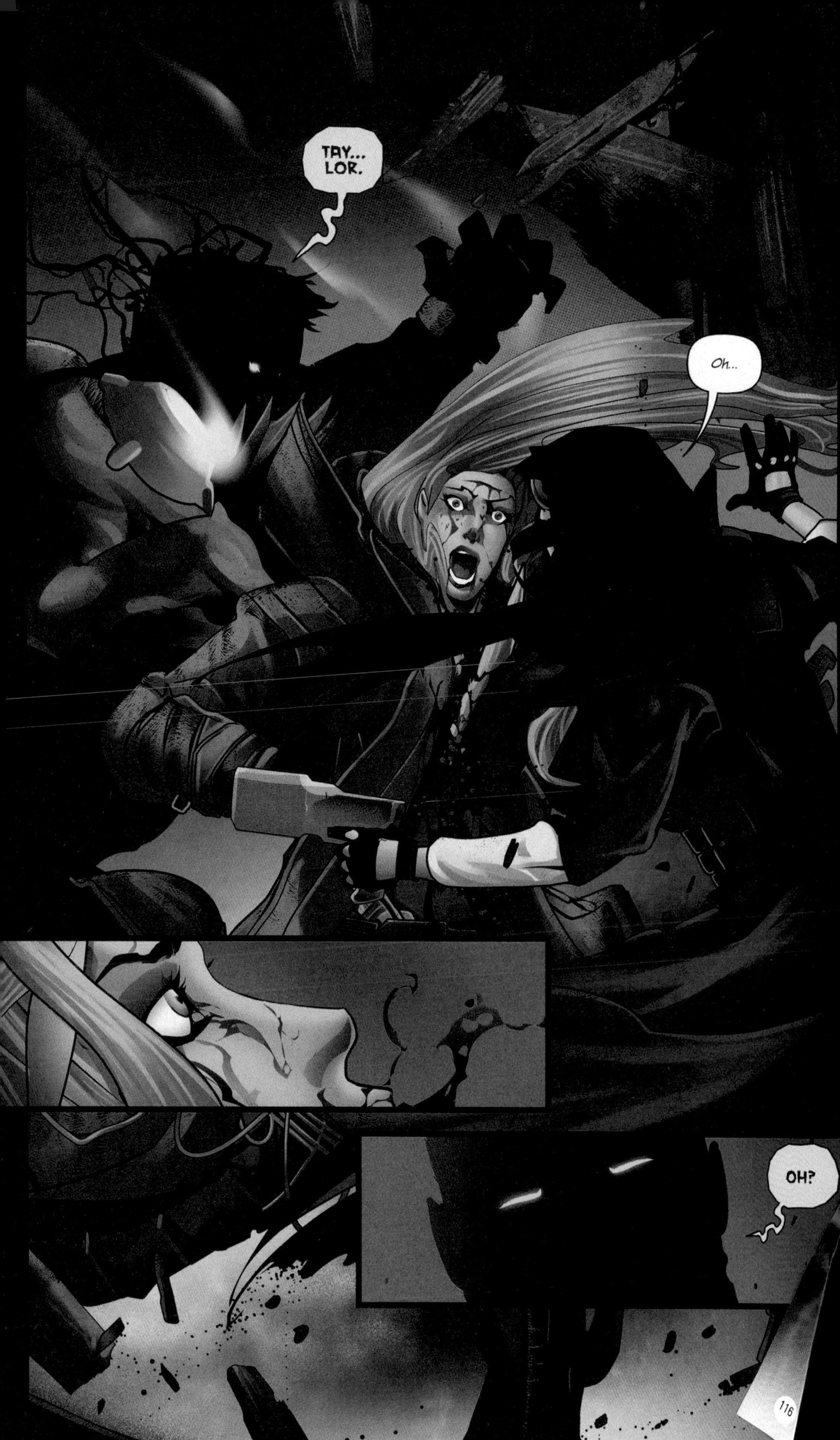
TAY... LOR.
Oh..
OH?

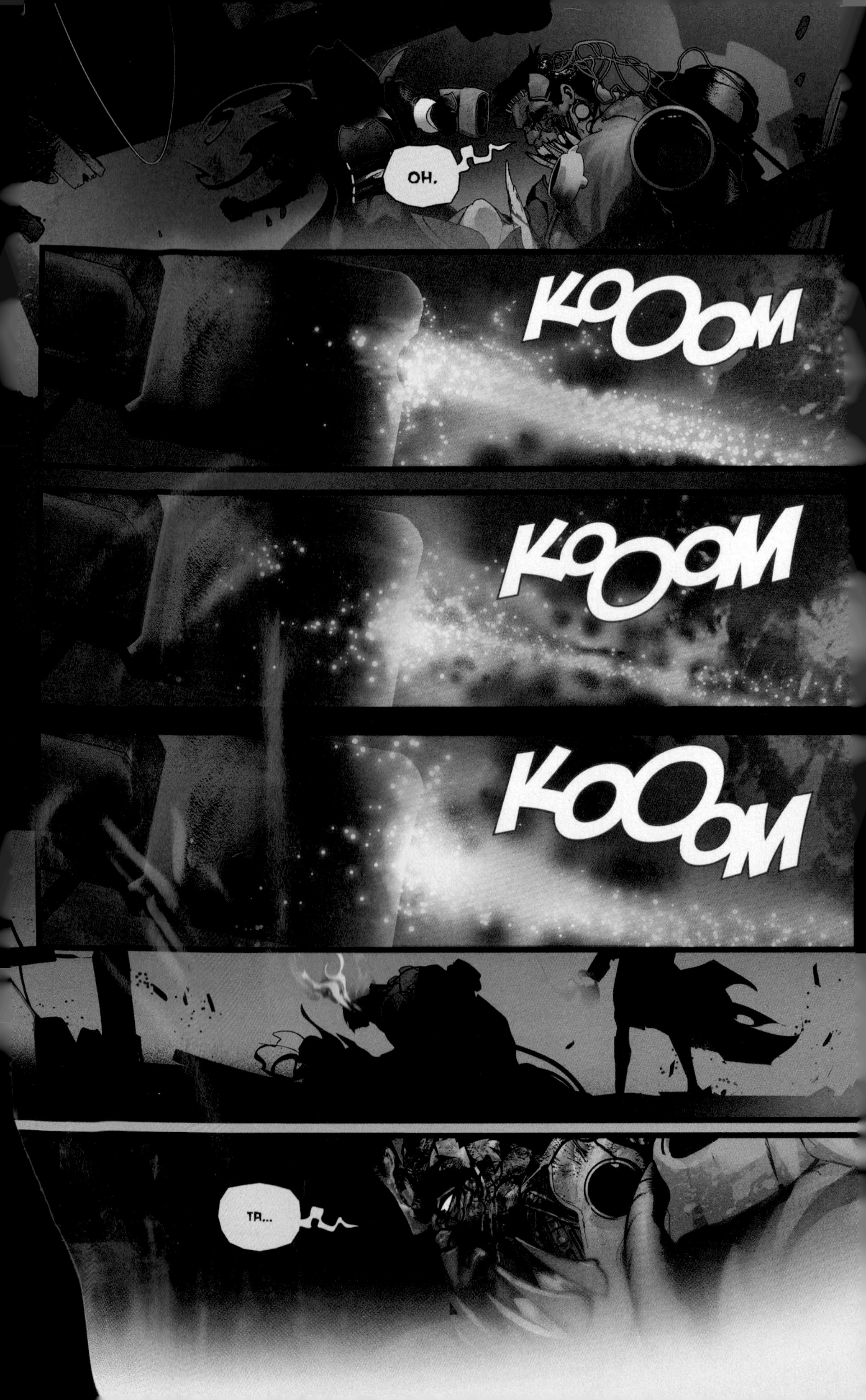
OH.
KOOOM
KOOOM
KOOOM
TA...

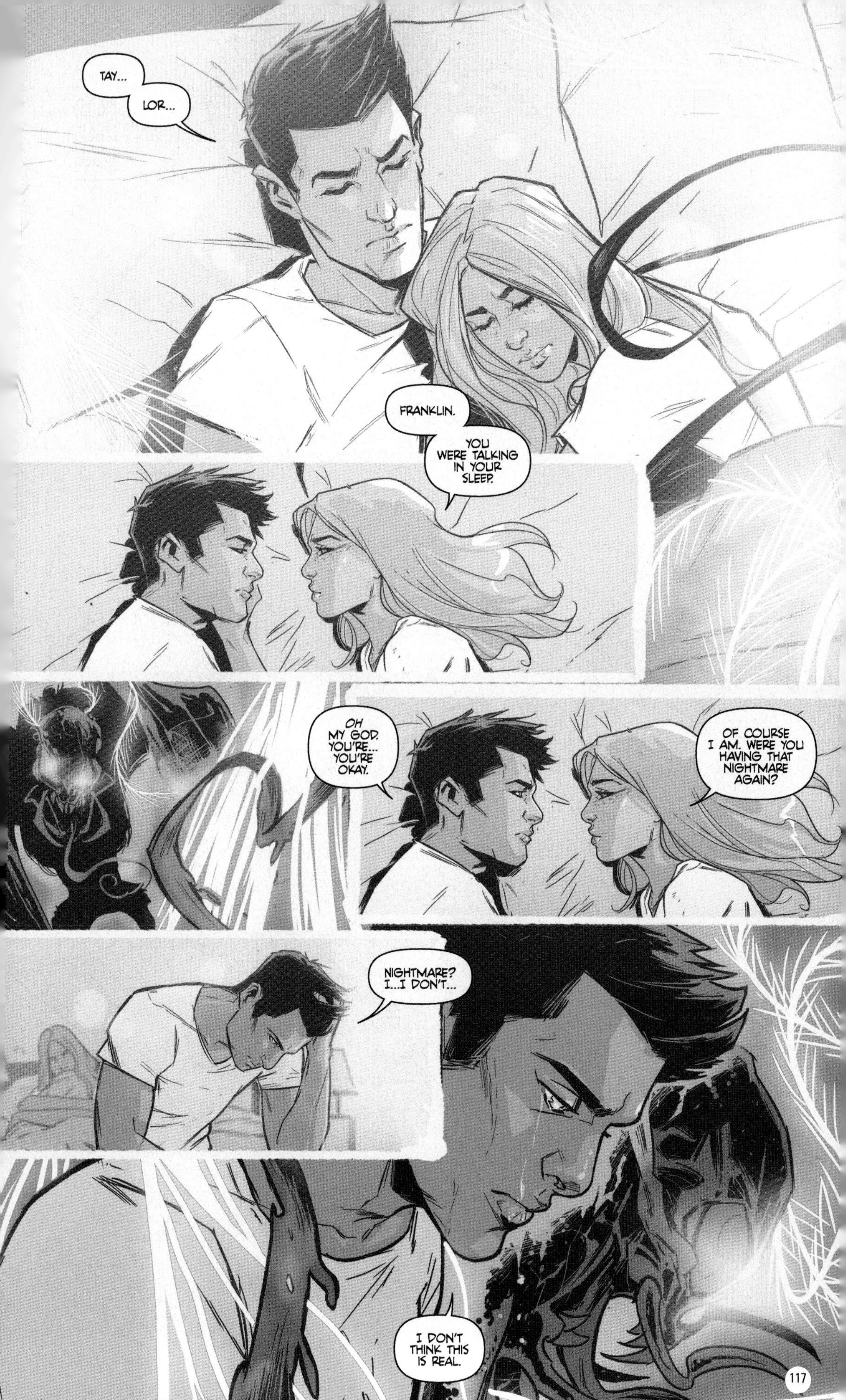
TAY...
LOR...
FRANKLIN.
YOU WERE TALKING IN YOUR SLEEP.
OH MY GOD. YOU'RE... YOU'RE OKAY.
OF COURSE I AM. WERE YOU HAVING THAT NIGHTMARE AGAIN?
NIGHTMARE? I...I DON'T...
I DON'T THINK THIS IS REAL.

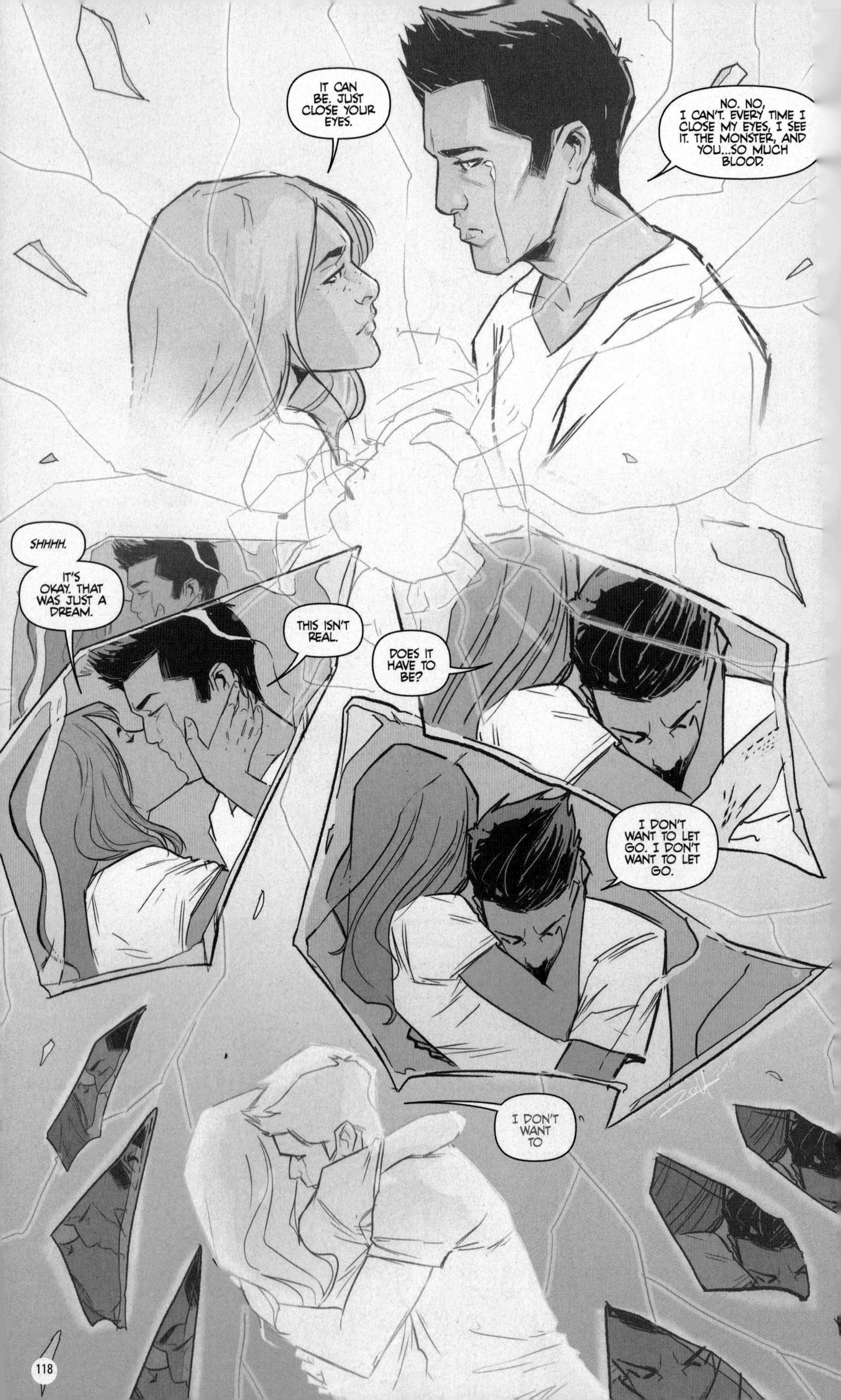
IT CAN BE. JUST CLOSE YOUR EYES.
NO. NO, I CAN'T. EVERY TIME I CLOSE MY EYES, I SEE IT. THE MONSTER, AND YOU...SO MUCH BLOOD.
SHHHH.
IT'S OKAY. THAT WAS JUST A DREAM.
THIS ISN'T REAL.
DOES IT HAVE TO BE?
I DON'T WANT TO LET GO. I DON'T WANT TO LET GO.
I DON'T WANT TO

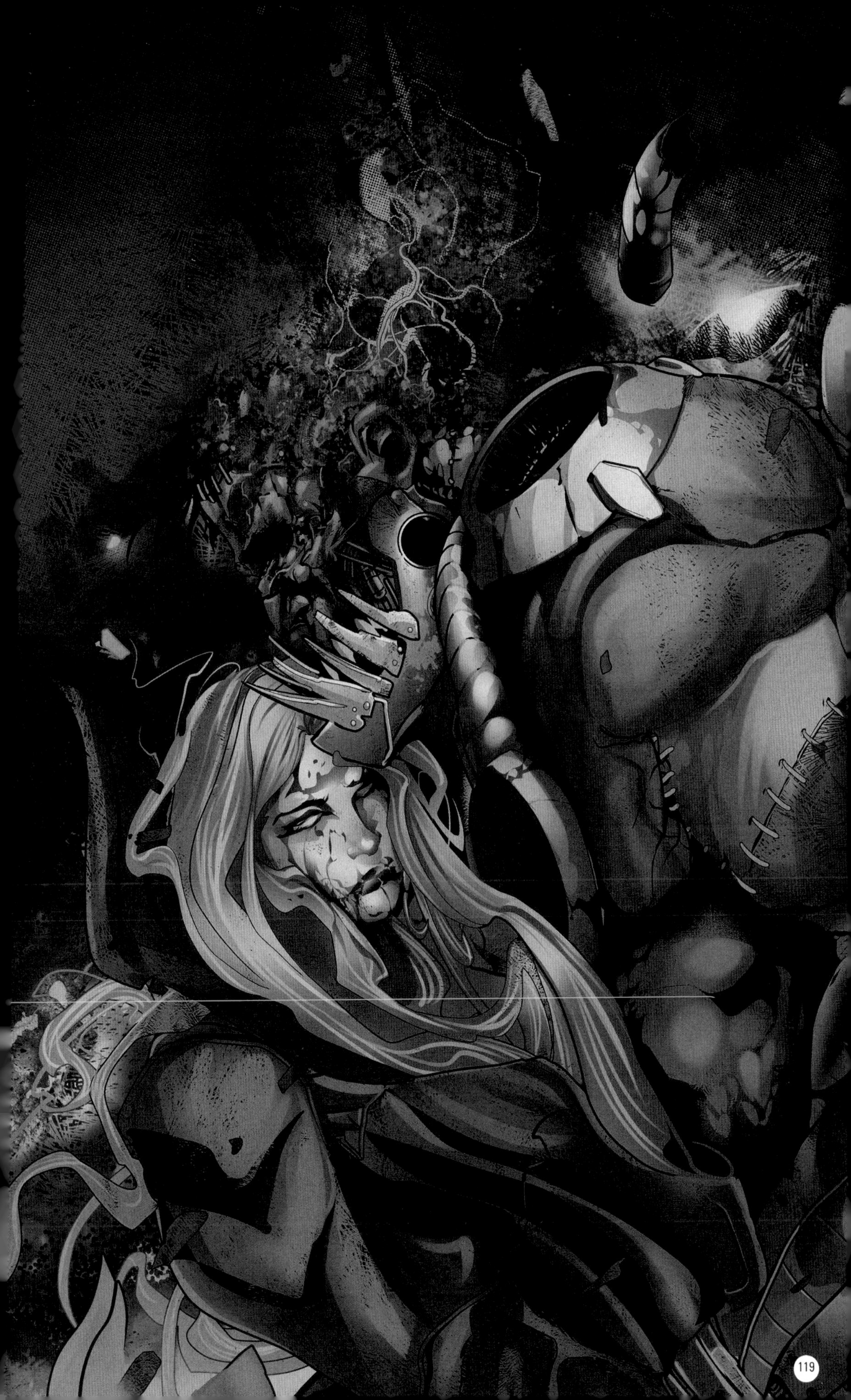

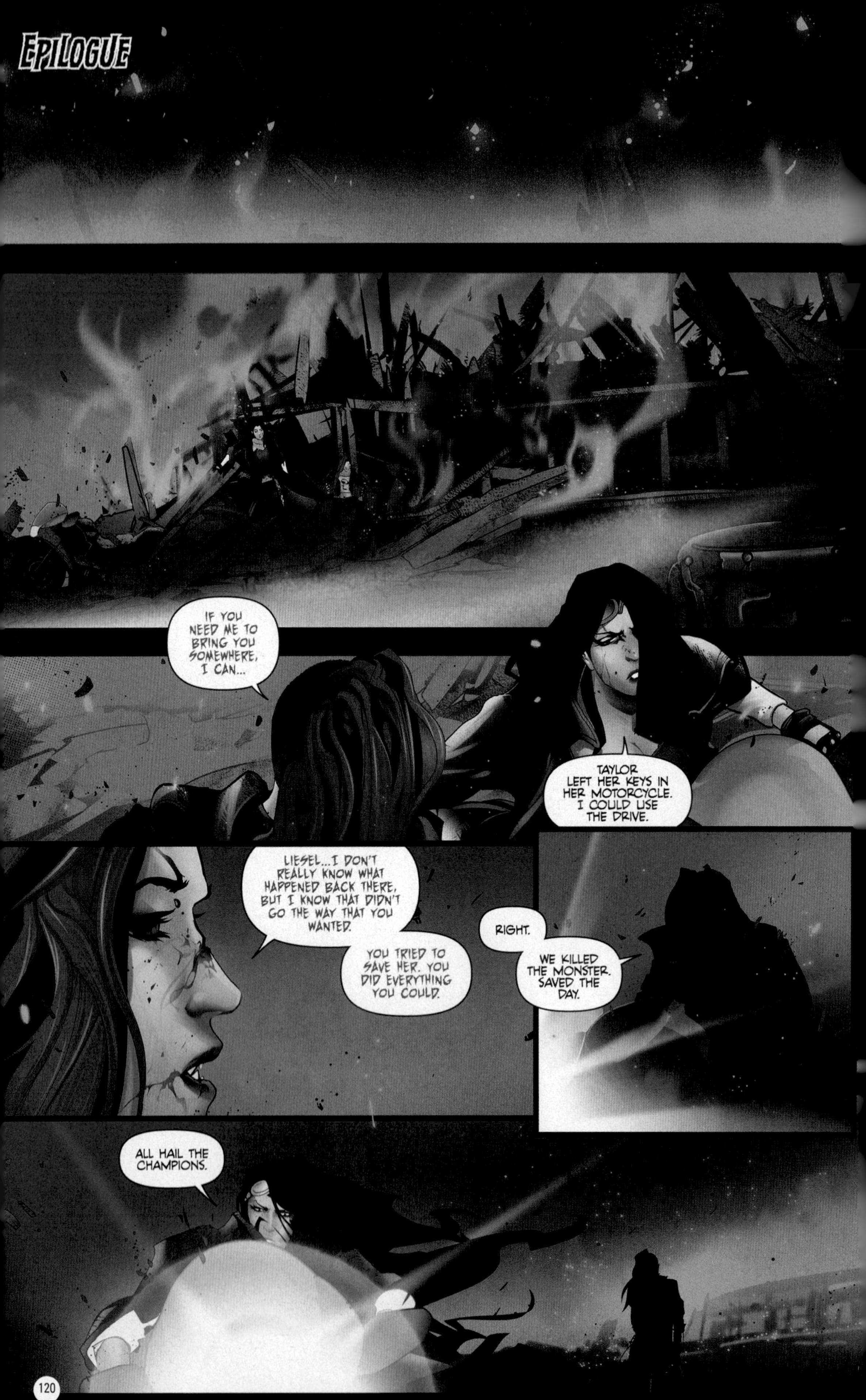
EPILOGUE
IF YOU NEED ME TO BRING YOU SOMEWHERE, I CAN...
TAYLOR LEFT HER KEYS IN HER MOTORCYCLE. I COULD USE THE DRIVE.
LIESEL...I DON'T REALLY KNOW WHAT HAPPENED BACK THERE, BUT I KNOW THAT DIDN'T GO THE WAY THAT YOU WANTED.
YOU TRIED TO SAVE HER. YOU DID EVERYTHING YOU COULD.
RIGHT.
WE KILLED THE MONSTER. SAVED THE DAY.
ALL HAIL THE CHAMPIONS.

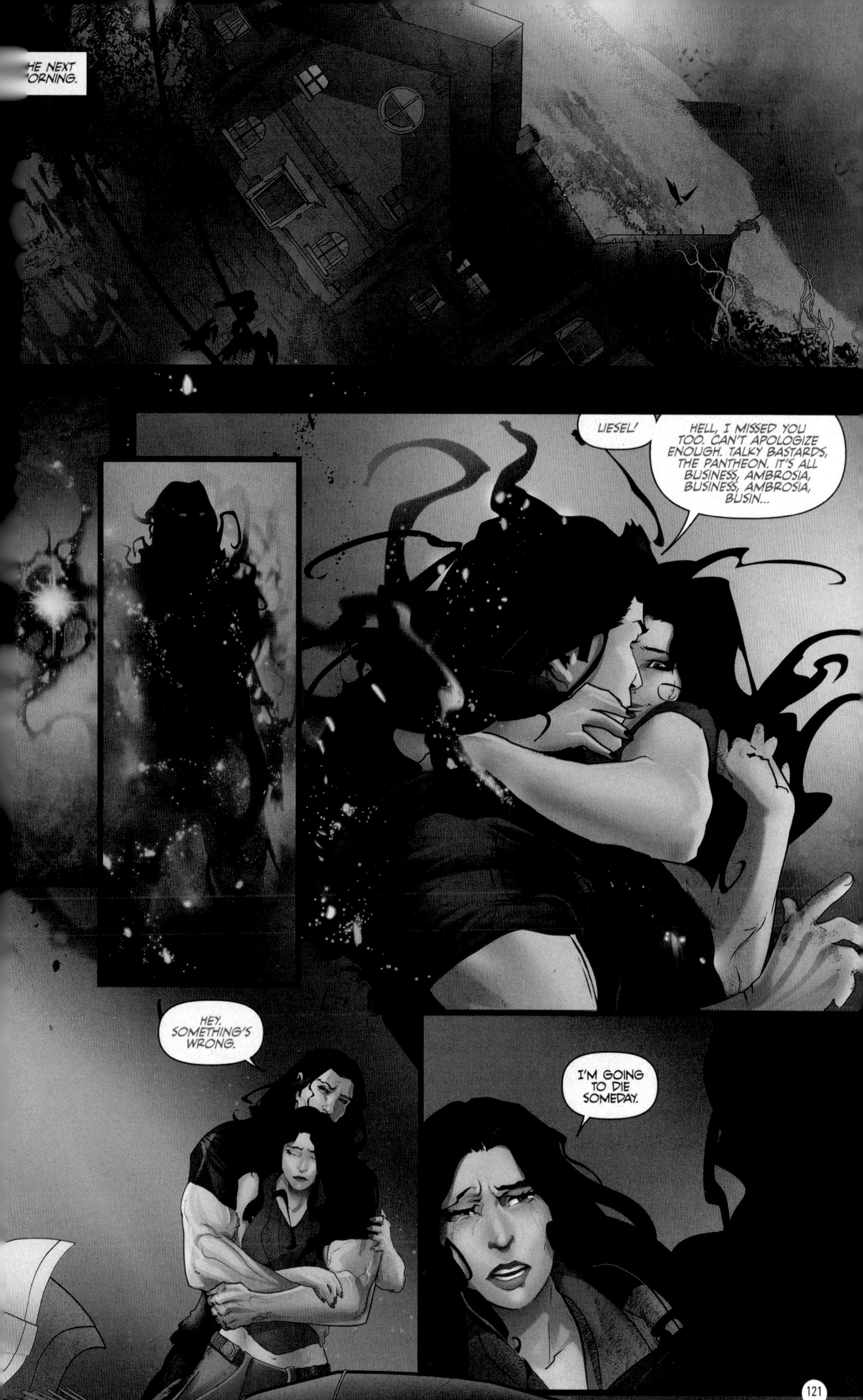
HE NEXT ORNING.
LIESEL!
HELL, I MISSED YOU TOO. CAN'T APOLOGIZE ENOUGH. TALKY BASTARDS, THE PANTHEON. IT'S ALL BUSINESS, AMBROSIA, BUSINESS, AMBROSIA, BUSIN...
HEY. SOMETHING'S WRONG.
I'M GOING TO DIE SOMEDAY.

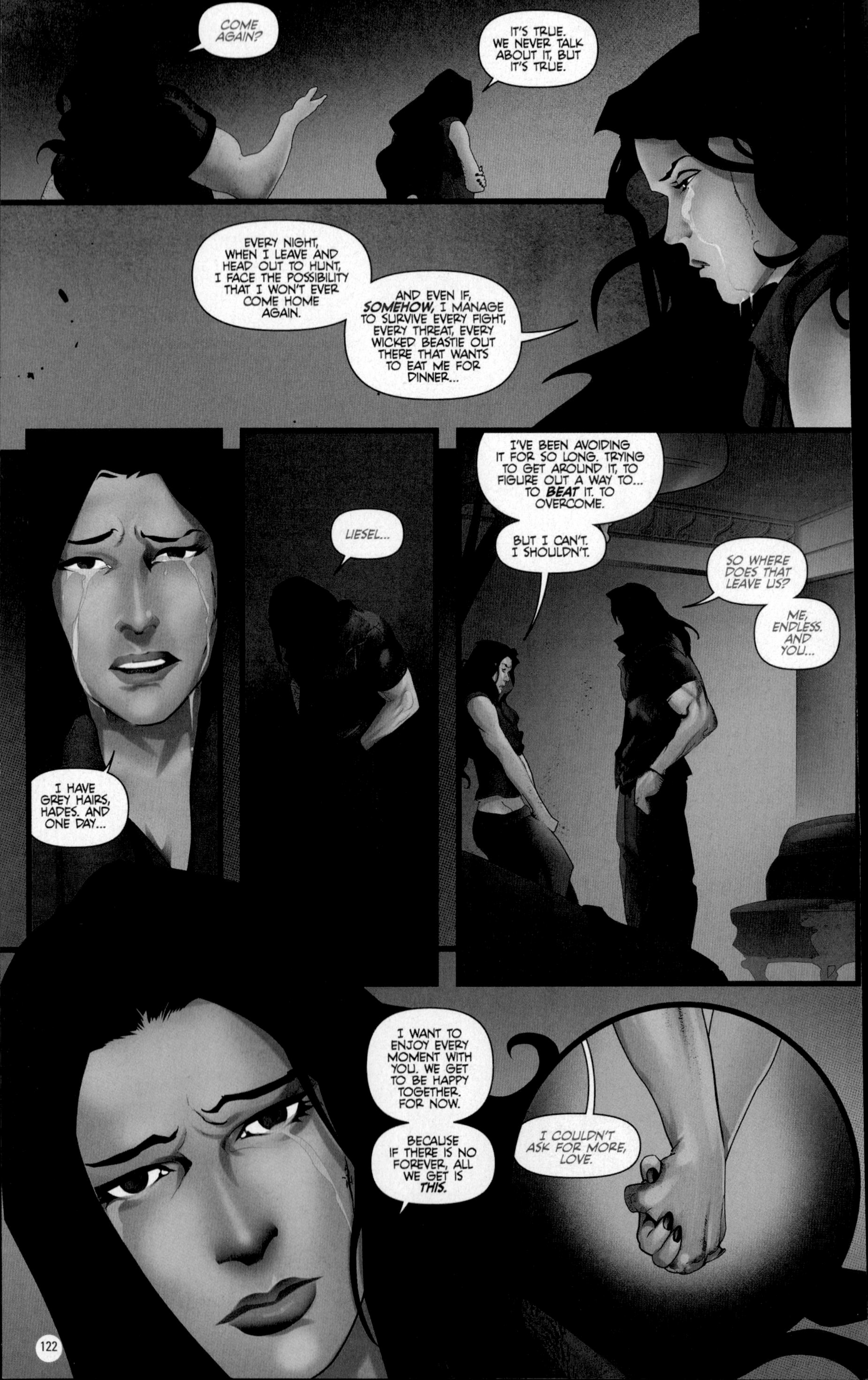
COME AGAIN?
IT'S TRUE. WE NEVER TALK ABOUT IT, BUT IT'S TRUE.
EVERY NIGHT, WHEN I LEAVE AND HEAD OUT TO HUNT, I FACE THE POSSIBILITY THAT I WON'T EVER COME HOME AGAIN.
AND EVEN IF, SOMEHOW, I MANAGE TO SURVIVE EVERY FIGHT, EVERY THREAT, EVERY WICKED BEASTIE OUT THERE THAT WANTS TO EAT ME FOR DINNER...
I HAVE GREY HAIRS, HADES. AND ONE DAY...
LIESEL...
I'VE BEEN AVOIDING IT FOR SO LONG. TRYING TO GET AROUND IT, TO FIGURE OUT A WAY TO... TO BEAT IT. TO OVERCOME.
BUT I CAN'T. I SHOULDN'T.
SO WHERE DOES THAT LEAVE US?
ME, ENDLESS. AND YOU...
I WANT TO ENJOY EVERY MOMENT WITH YOU. WE GET TO BE HAPPY TOGETHER. FOR NOW.
BECAUSE IF THERE IS NO FOREVER, ALL WE GET IS THIS.
I COULDN'T ASK FOR MORE, LOVE.

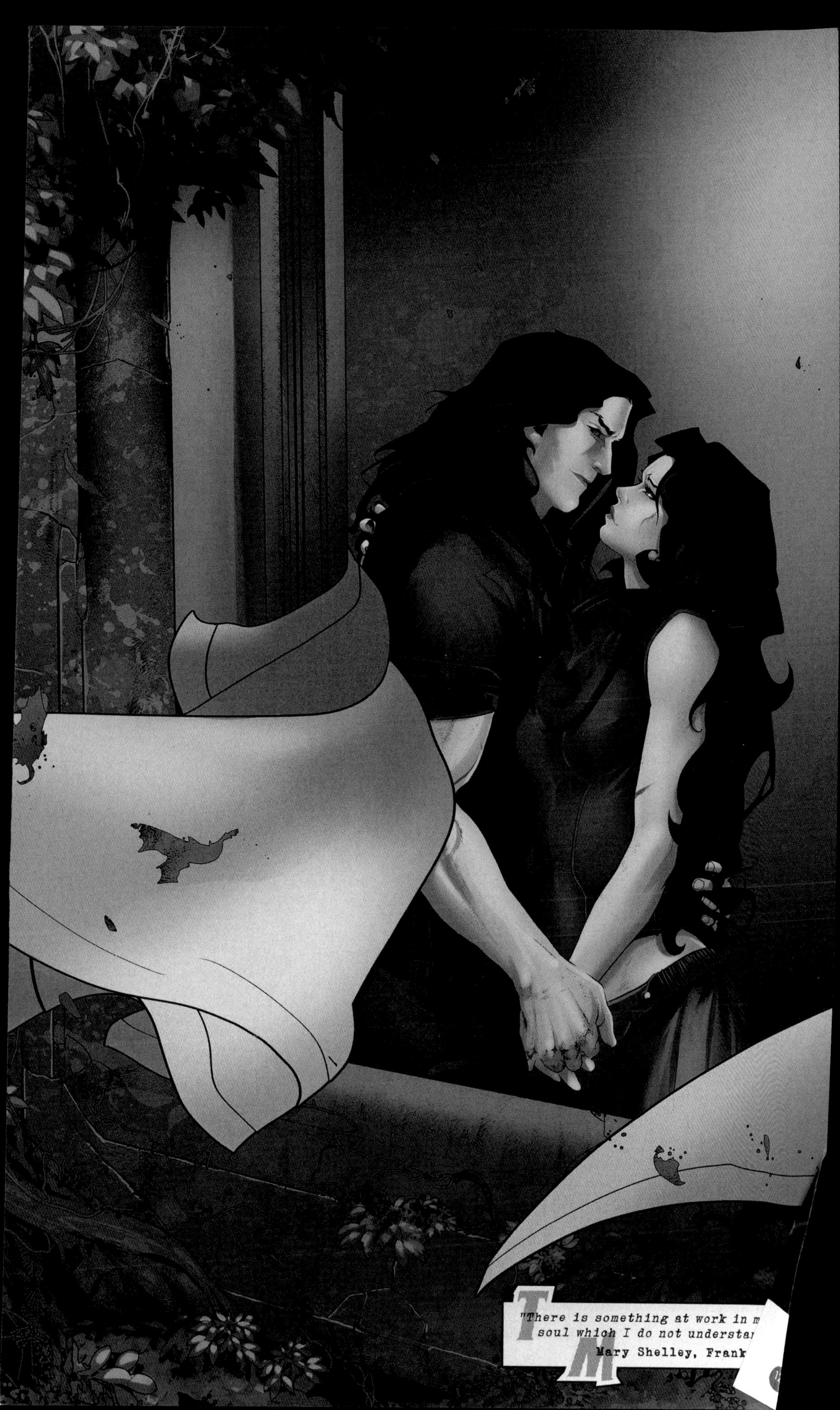
T M
"There is something at work in m
soul which I do not understa
Mary Shelley, Frank

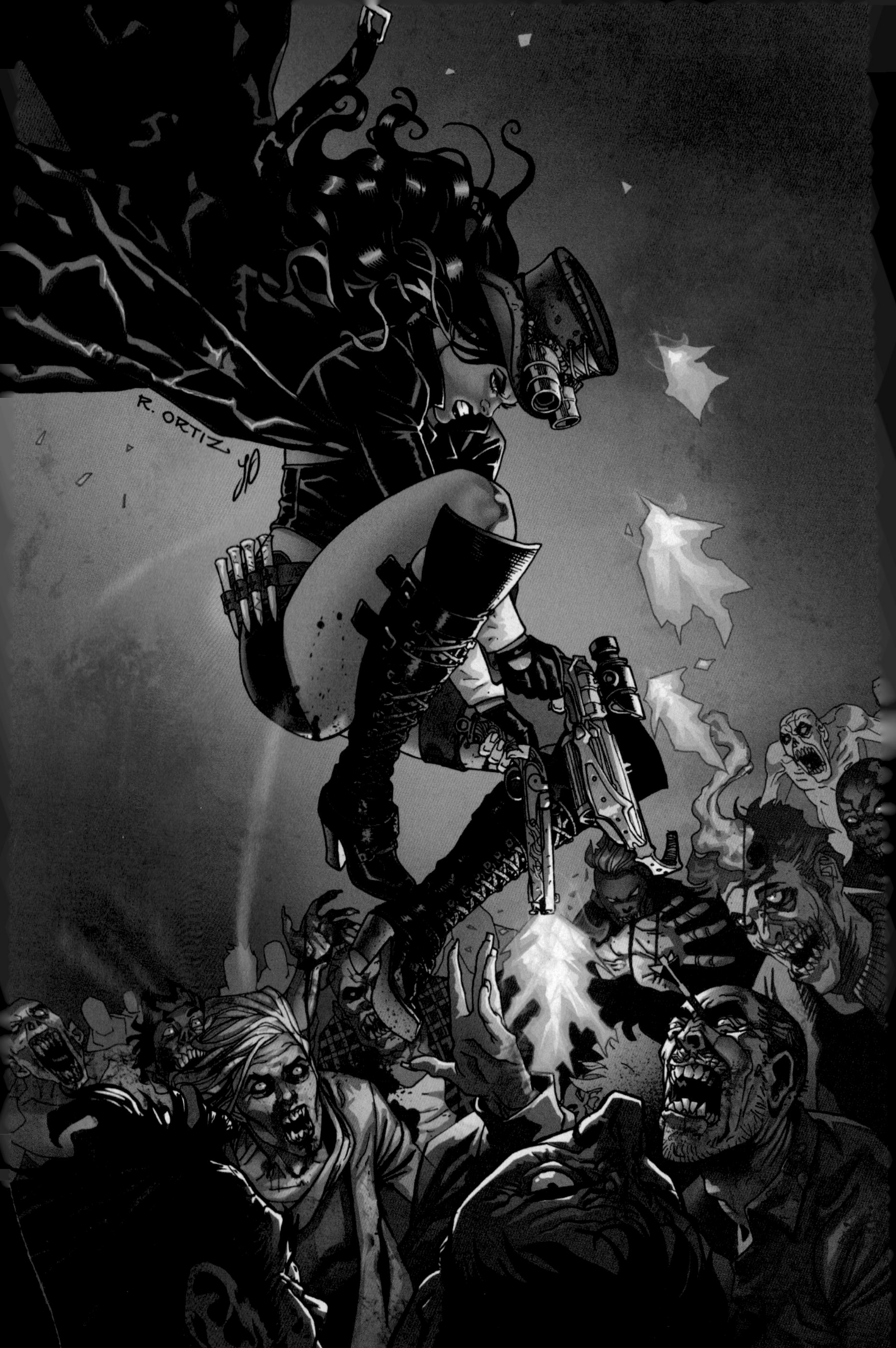
R. ORTIZ

Van Helsing vs. Frankenstein #1 • Cover A
Artwork by Richard Ortiz • Colors by Ylenia Di Napoli

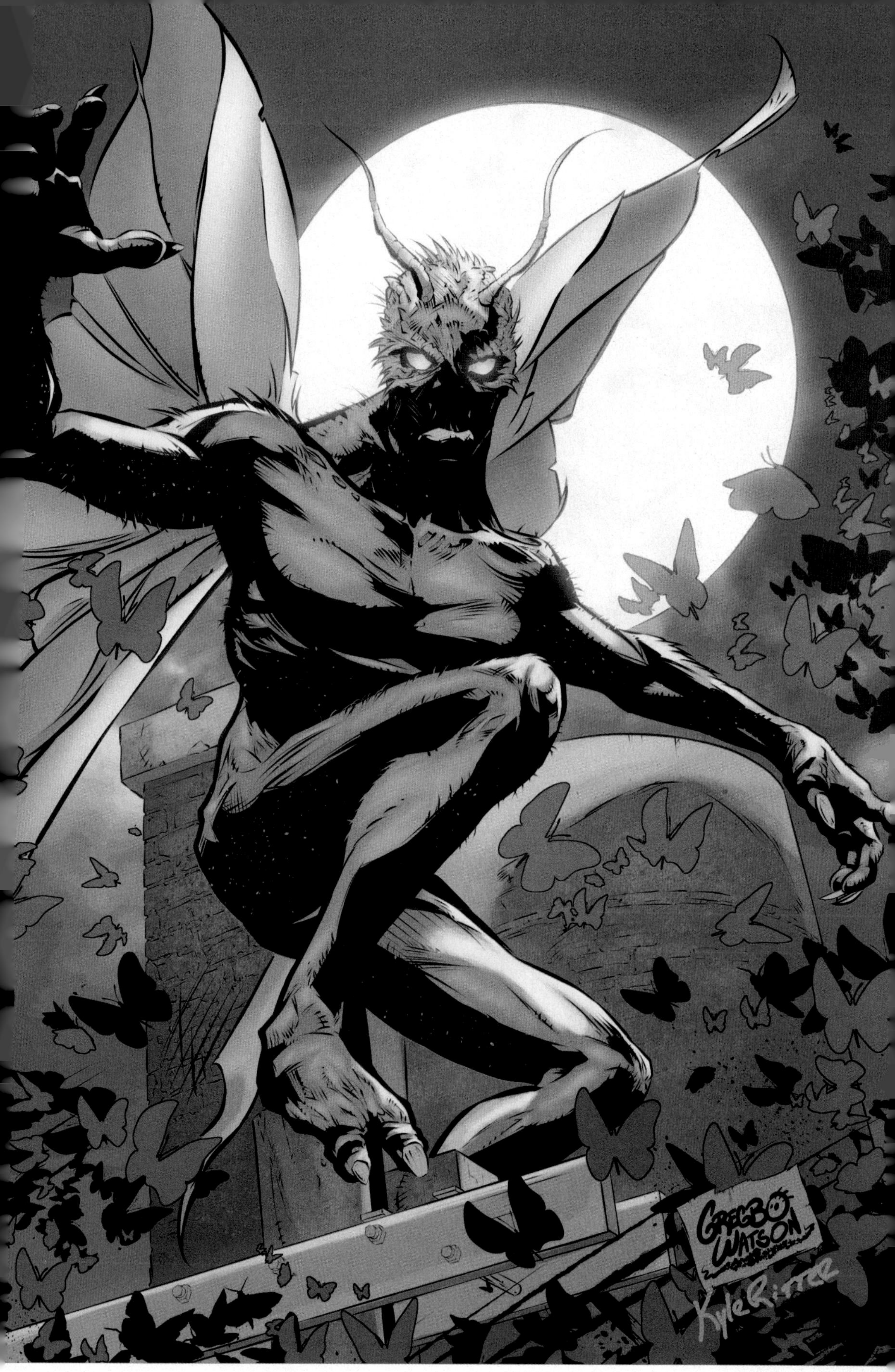
GREGBO WATSON

Van Helsing vs. Frankenstein #1 • Cover B
Artwork by Gregbo Watson • Colors by Kyle Ritter

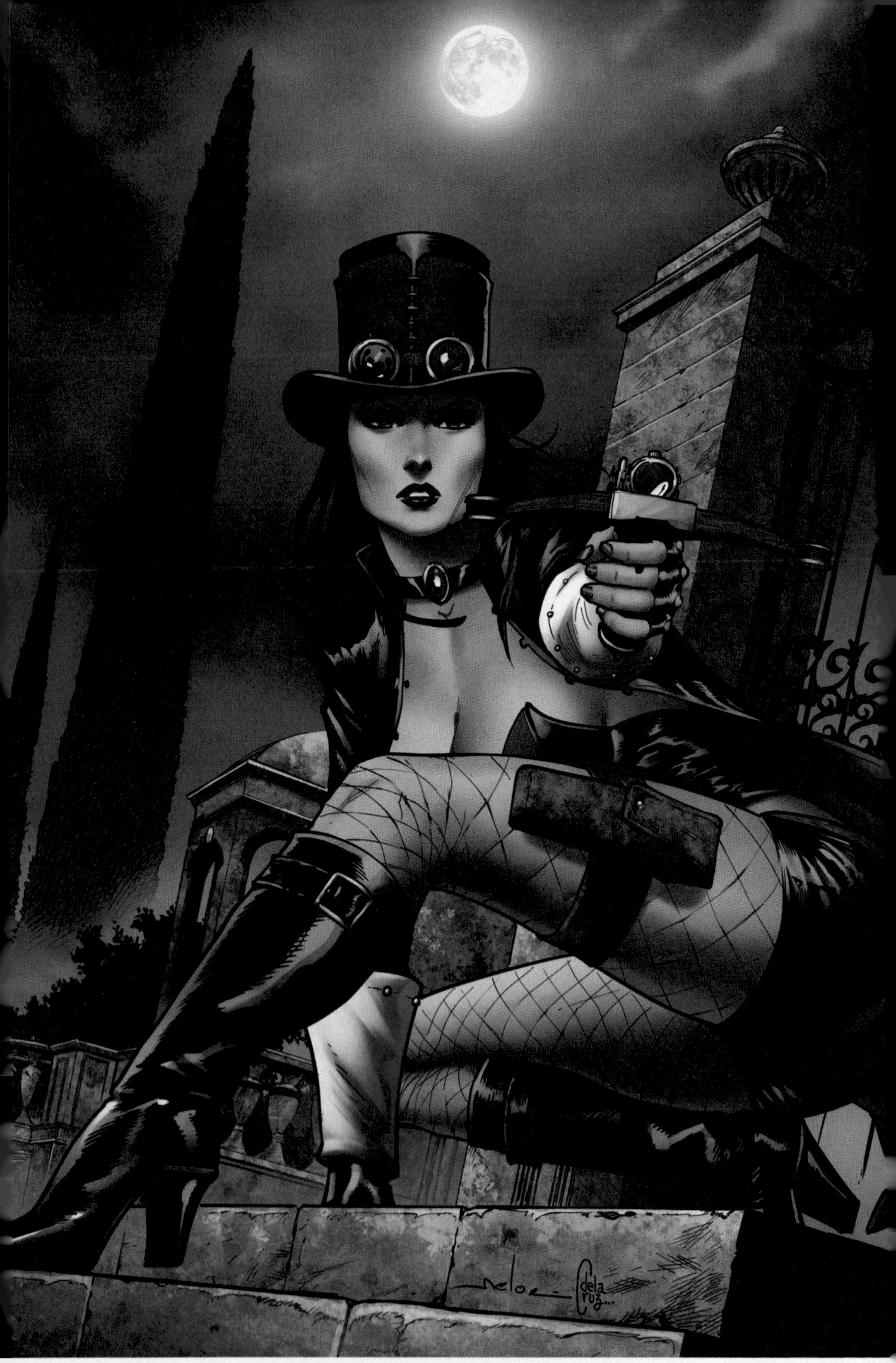

Van Helsing vs. Frankenstein #1 • Cover C
Artwork by Andrea Meloni • Colors by Ceci de la Cruz

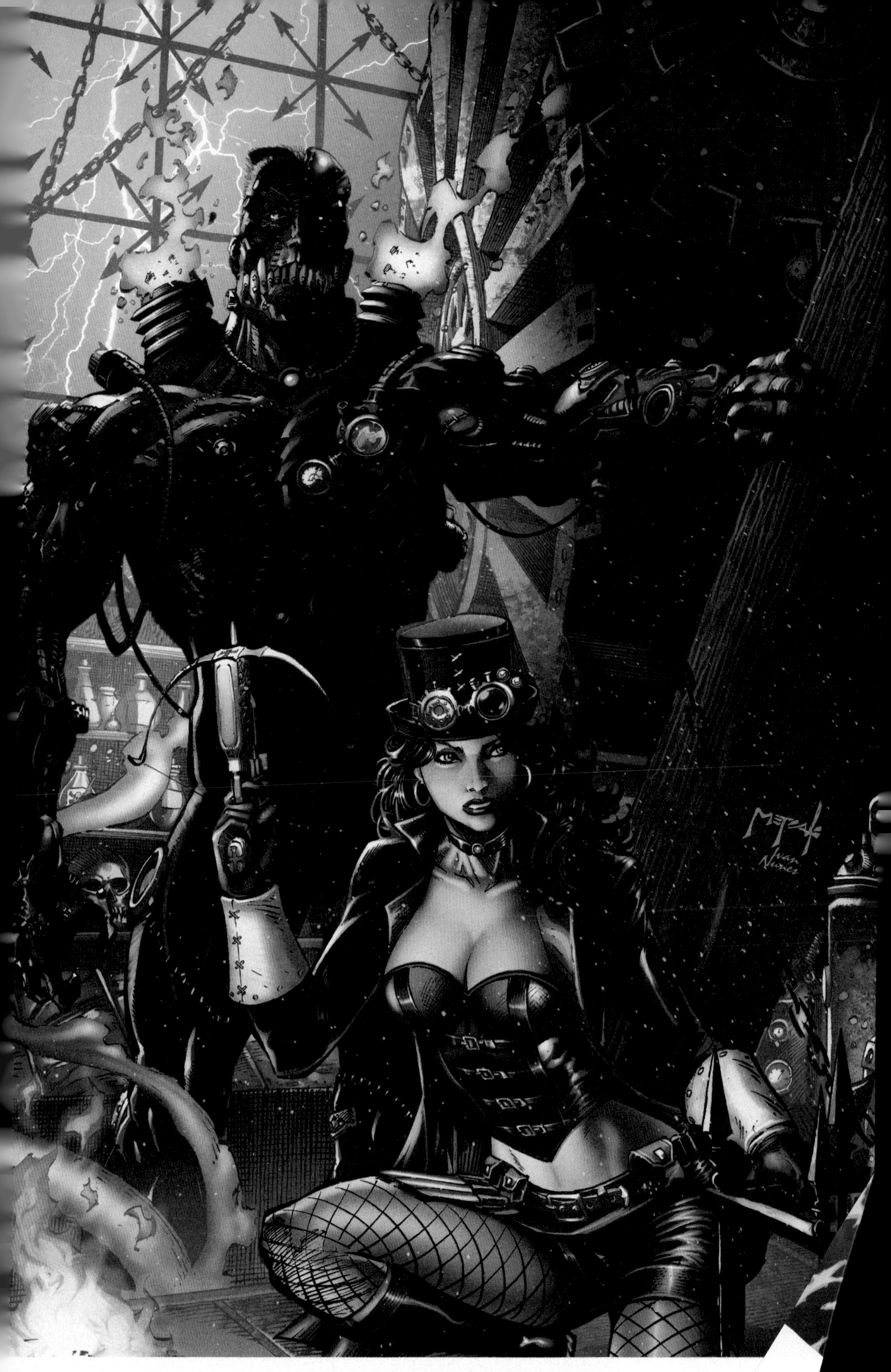

Van Helsing vs. Frankenstein #1 • Cover D
Artwork by Jason Metcalf • Colors by Ivan Nunes

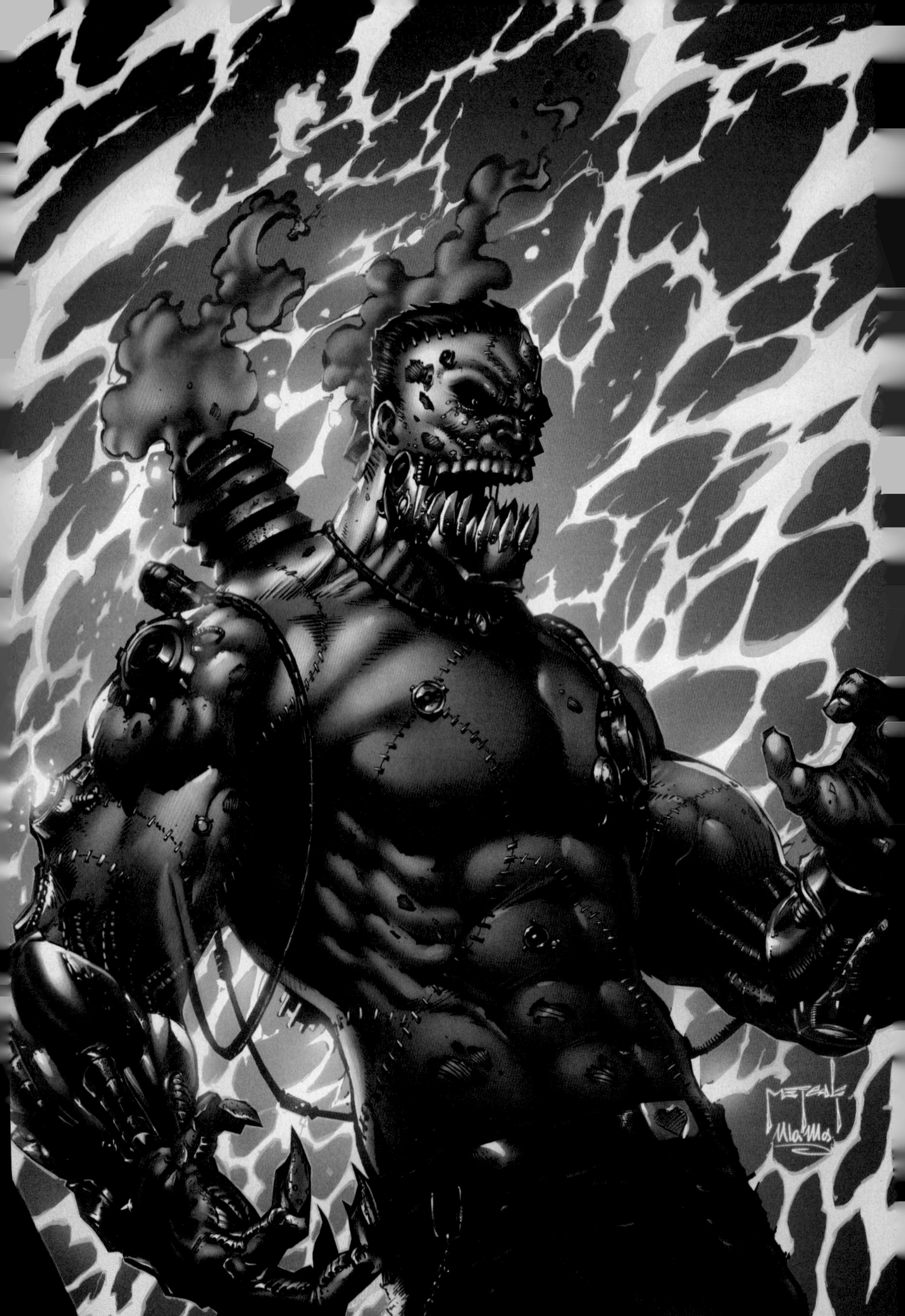

Van Helsing vs. Frankenstein #2 • Cover A
Artwork by Jason Metcalf • Colors by Ula Mos

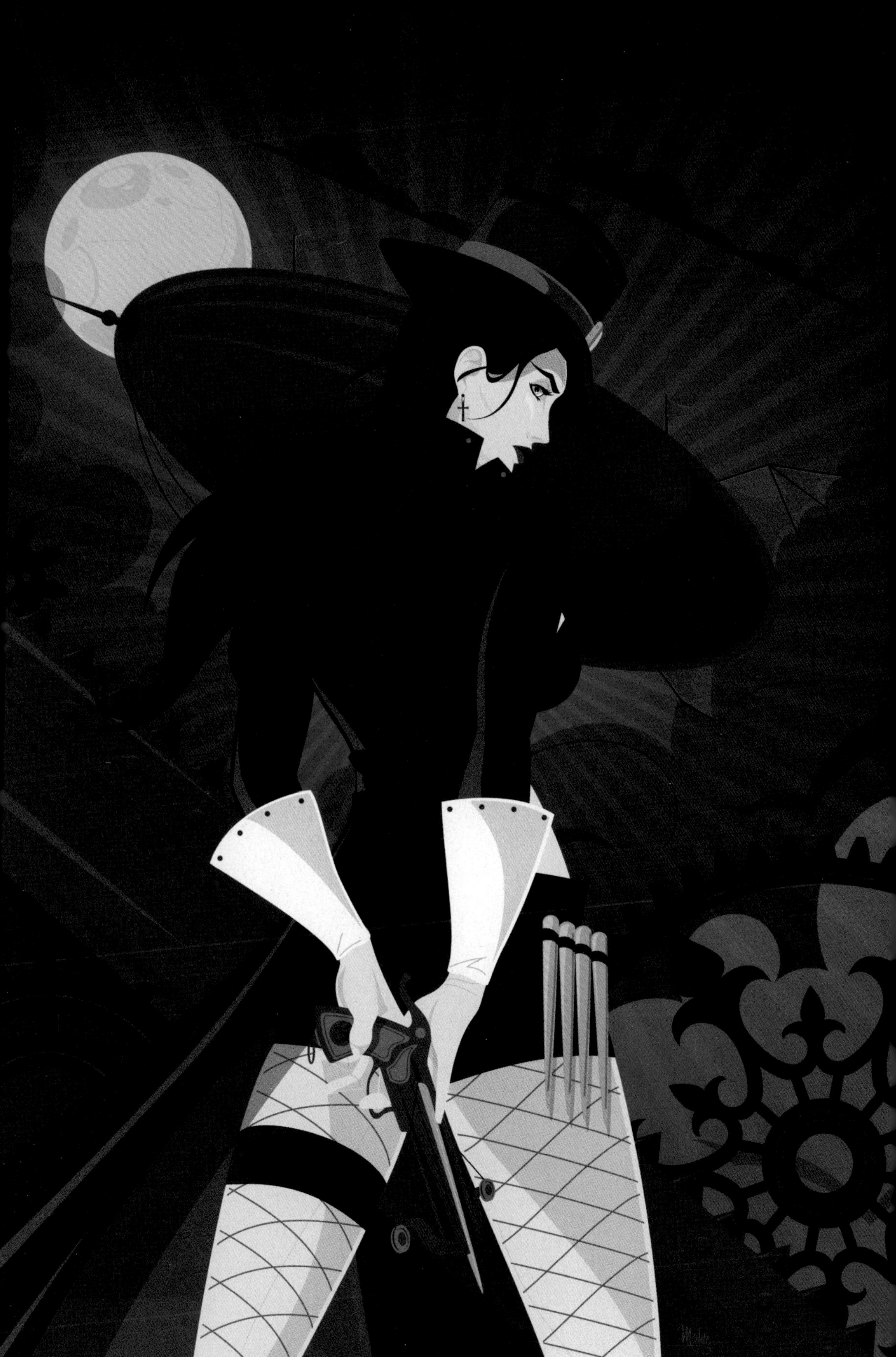

Van Helsing vs. Frankenstein #2 • Cover B
Artwork by Mike Mahle

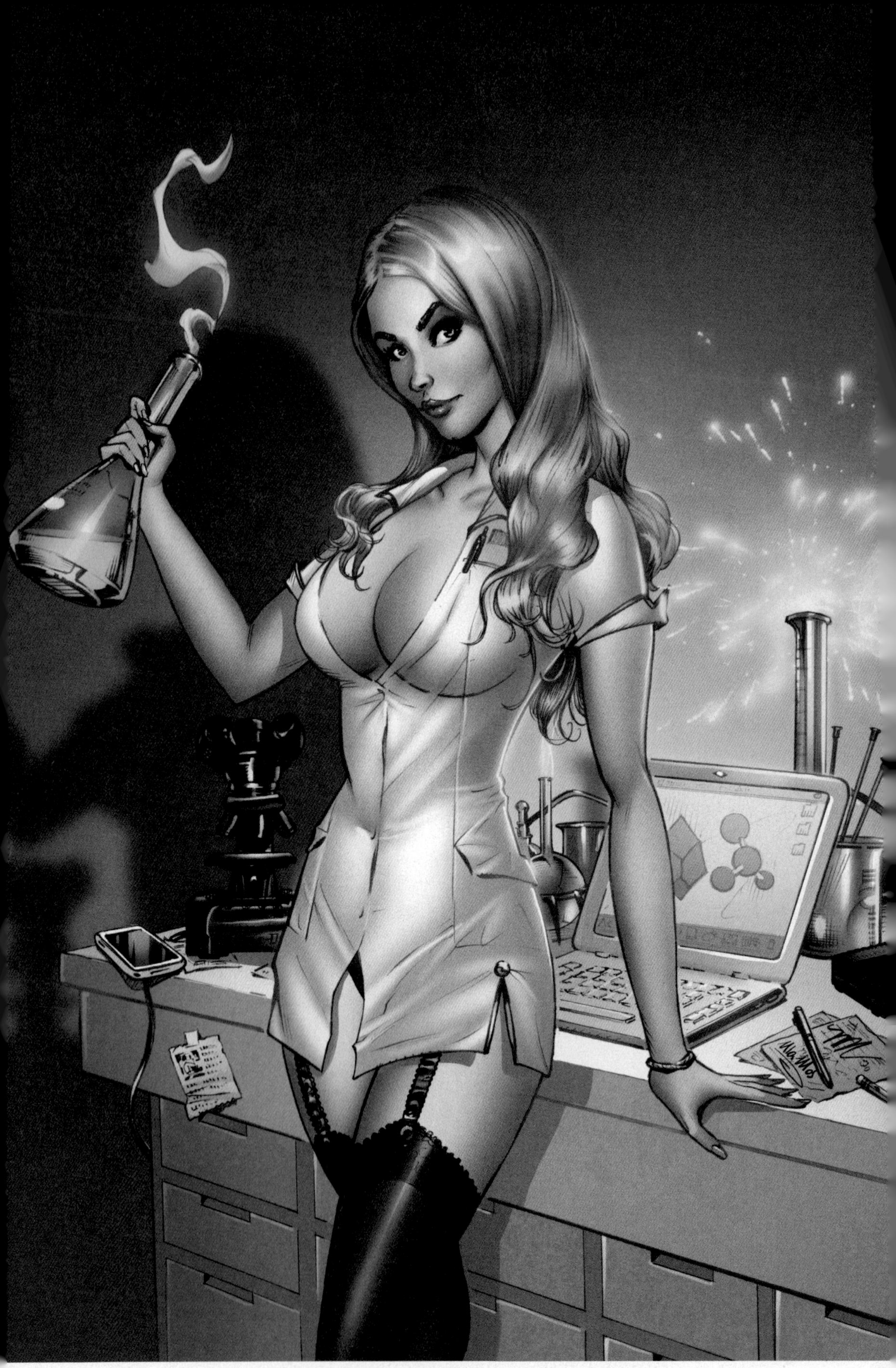

Van Helsing vs. Frankenstein #2 • Cover C
Artwork by Michael Dooney • Colors by Ula Mos

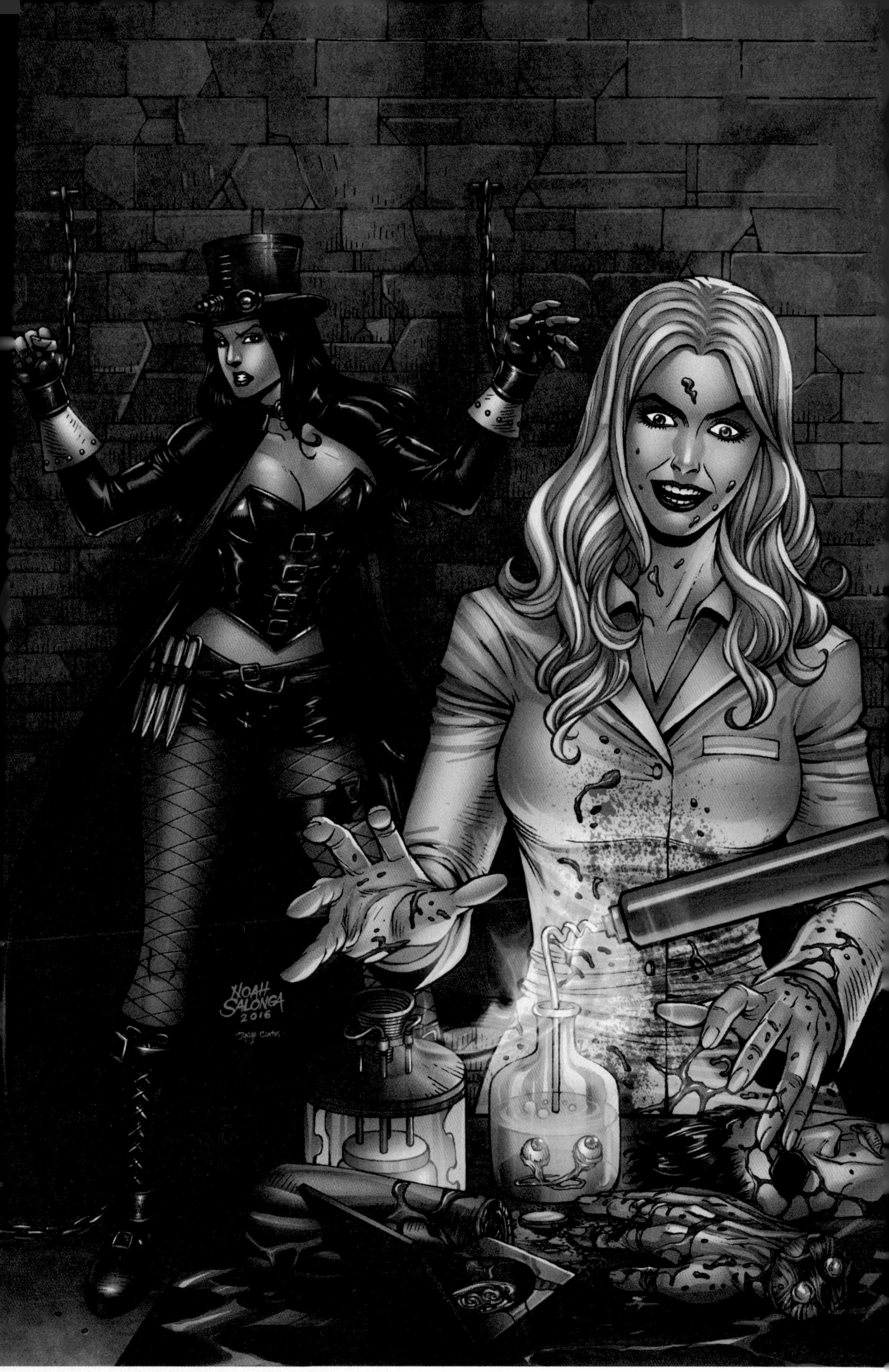
NOAH SALONGA 2016

Van Helsing vs. Frankenstein #2 • Cover D
Artwork by Noah Salonga • Colors by Jorge Cortes

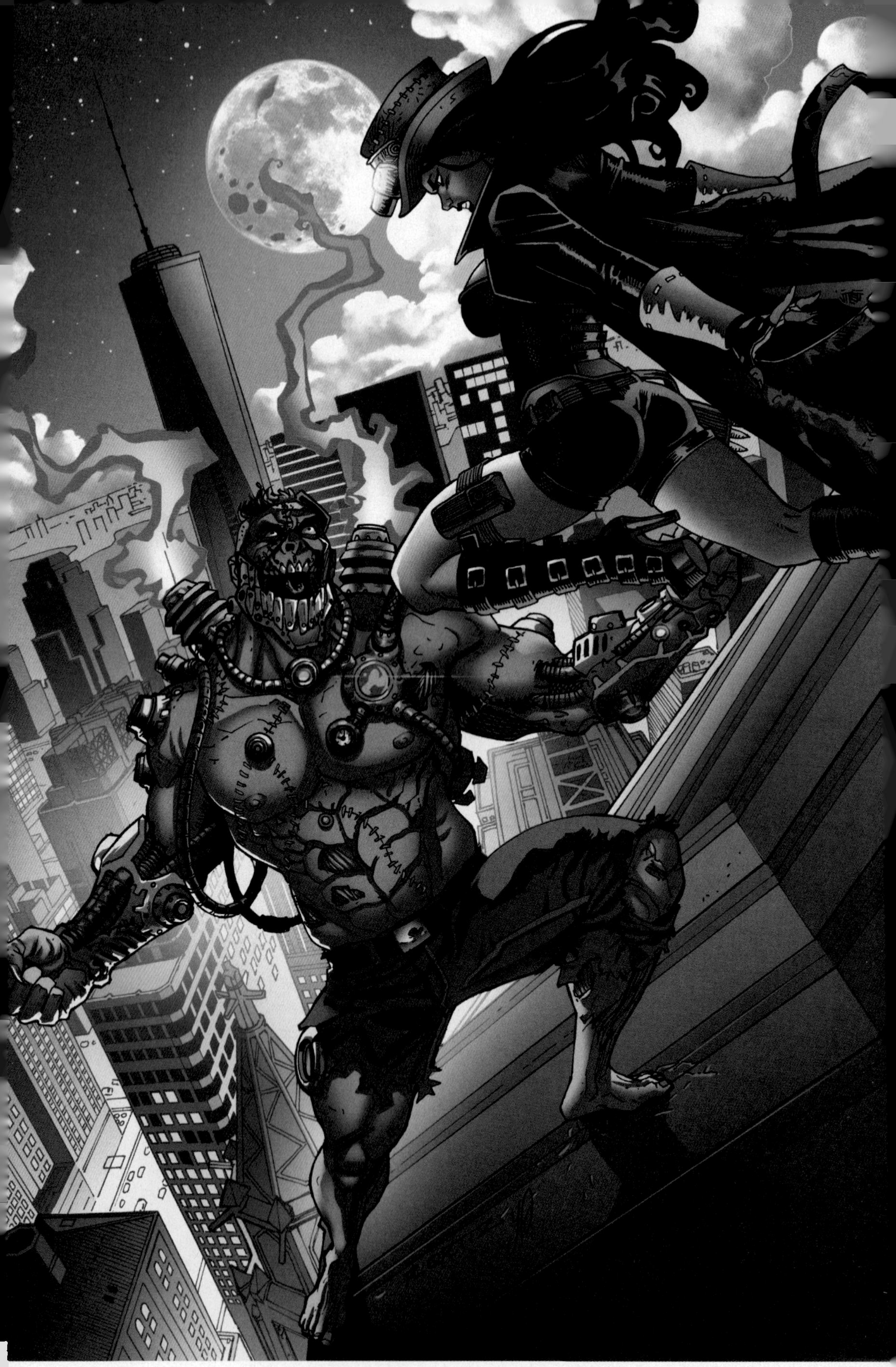

Van Helsing vs. Frankenstein #3 • Cover A
Artwork by Richard Ortiz • Colors by Ylenia Di Napoli

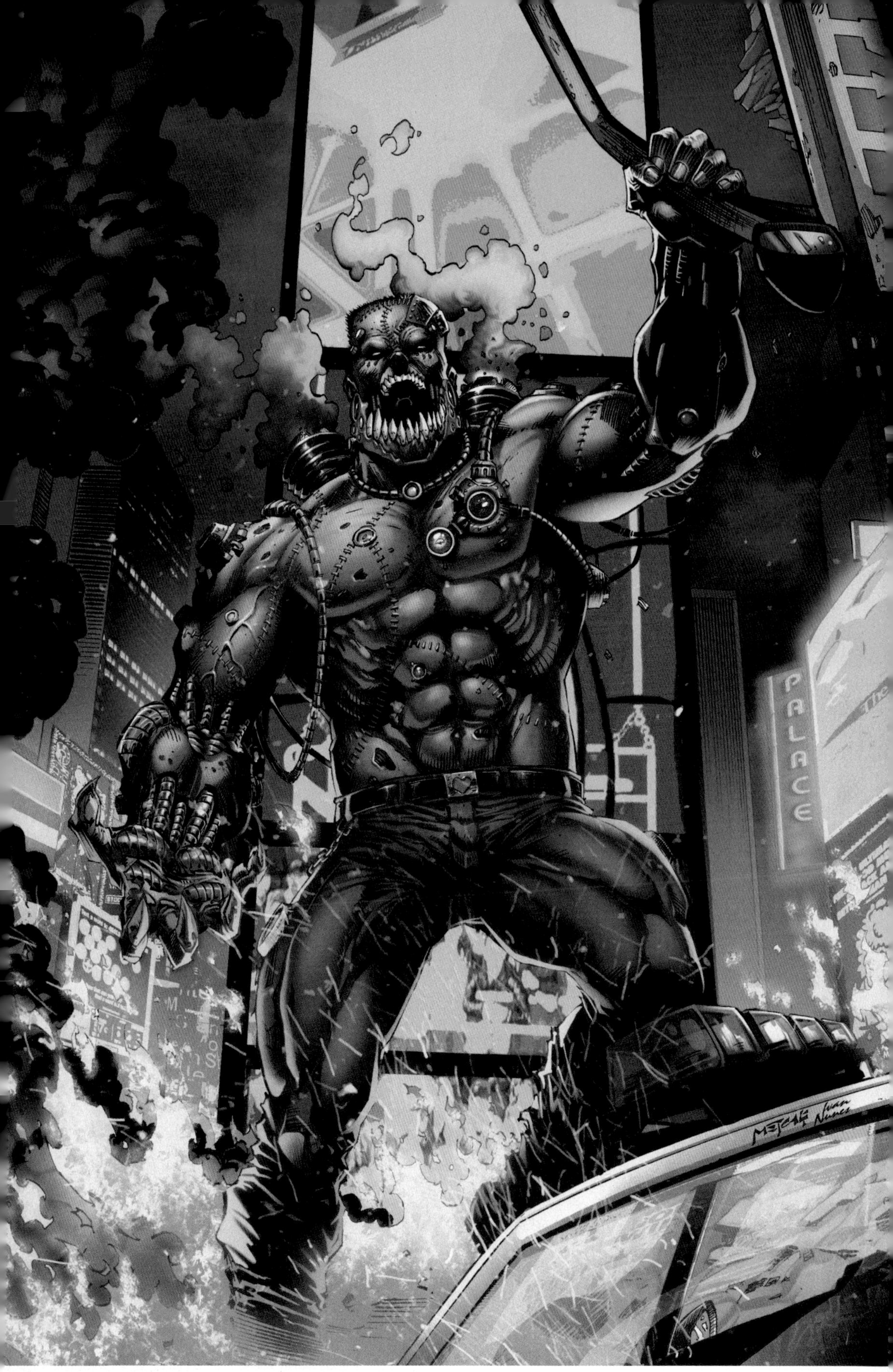
PALACE

Van Helsing vs. Frankenstein #3 • Cover B
Artwork by Jason Metcalf • Colors by Ivan Nunes

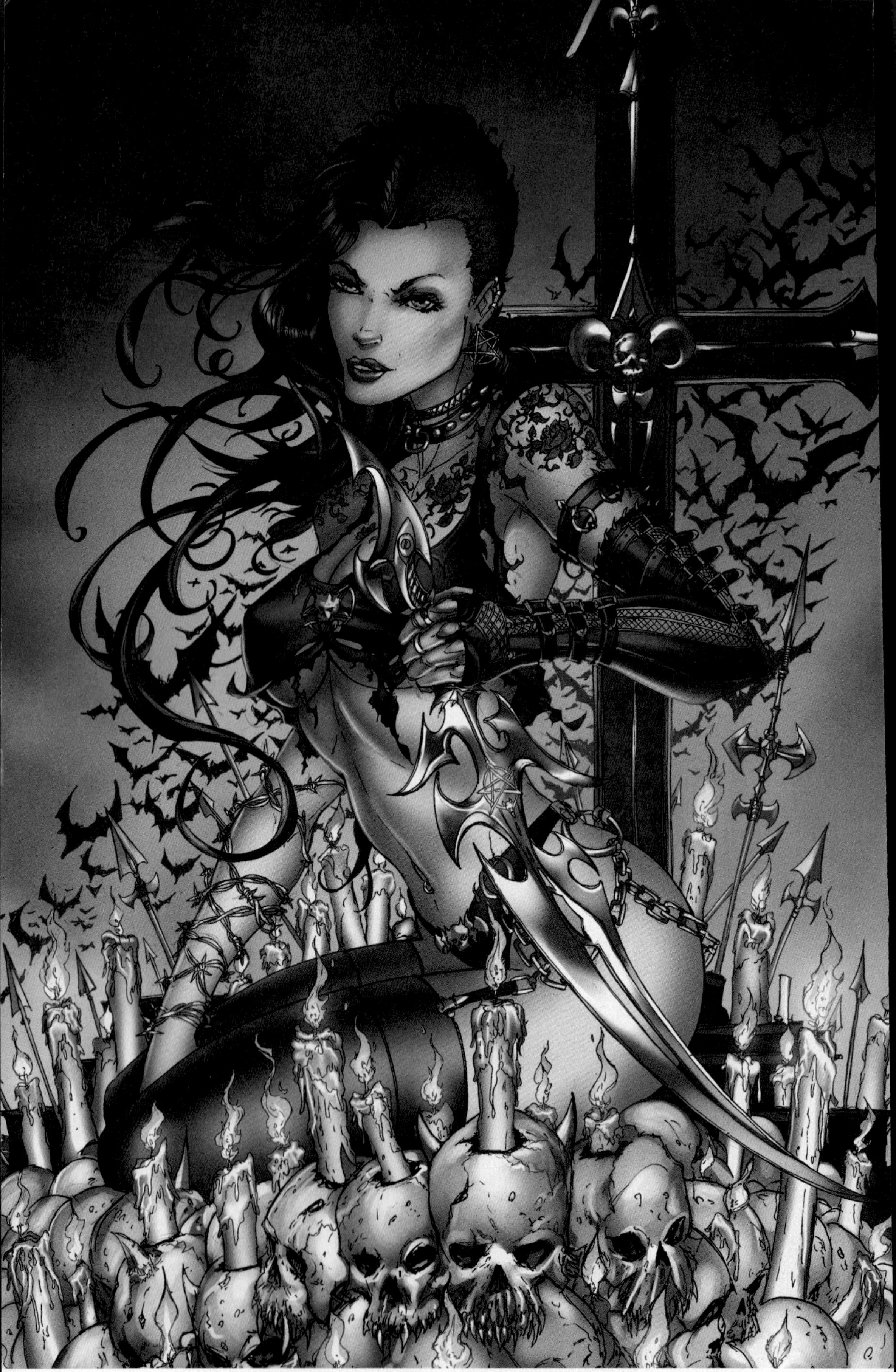

Van Helsing vs. Frankenstein #3 • Cover C
Artwork by Jamie Tyndall • Colors by Ula Mos

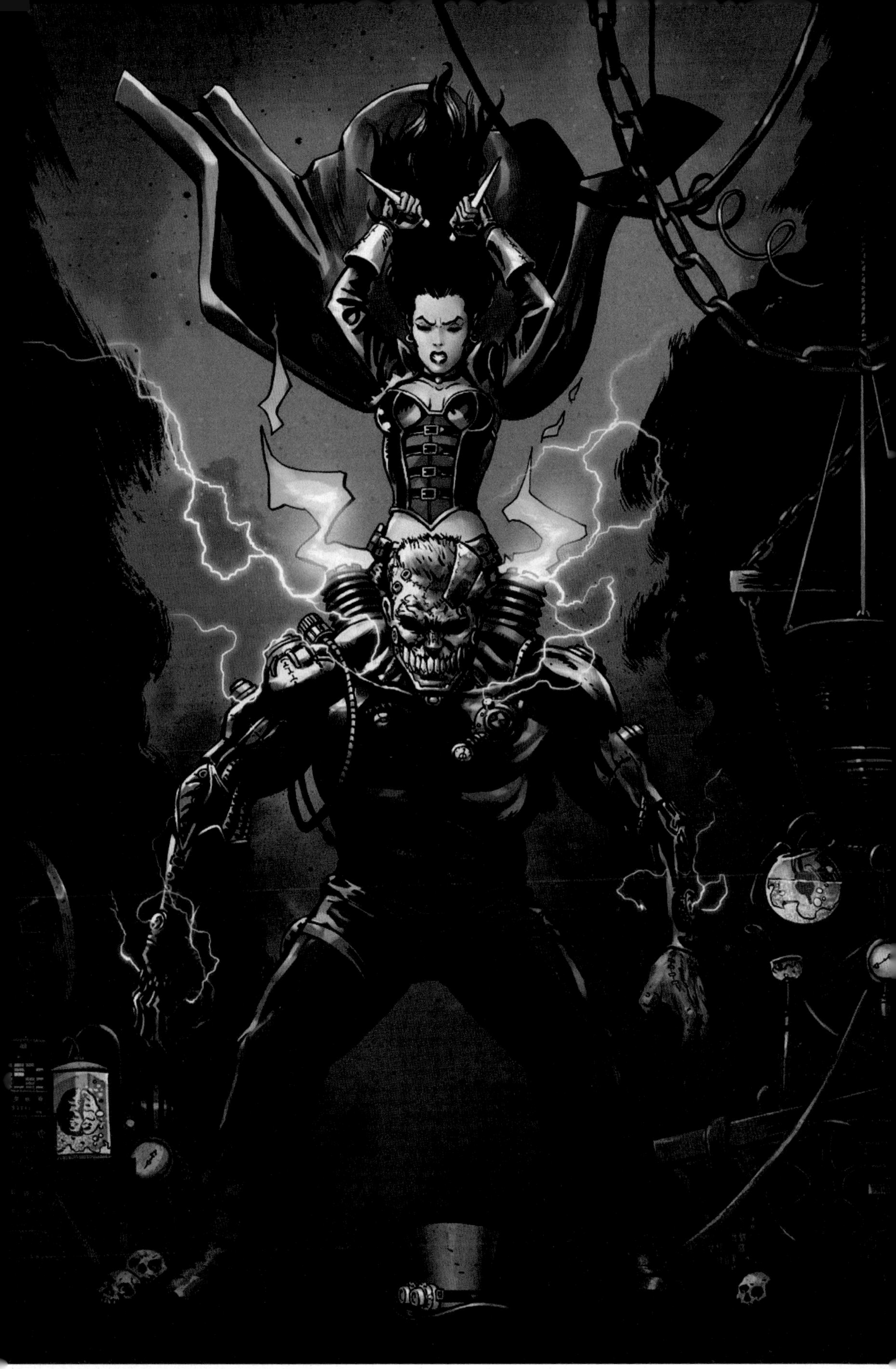

Van Helsing vs. Frankenstein #3 • Cover D
Artwork by Sami Kivela • Colors by Mohan Sivakami

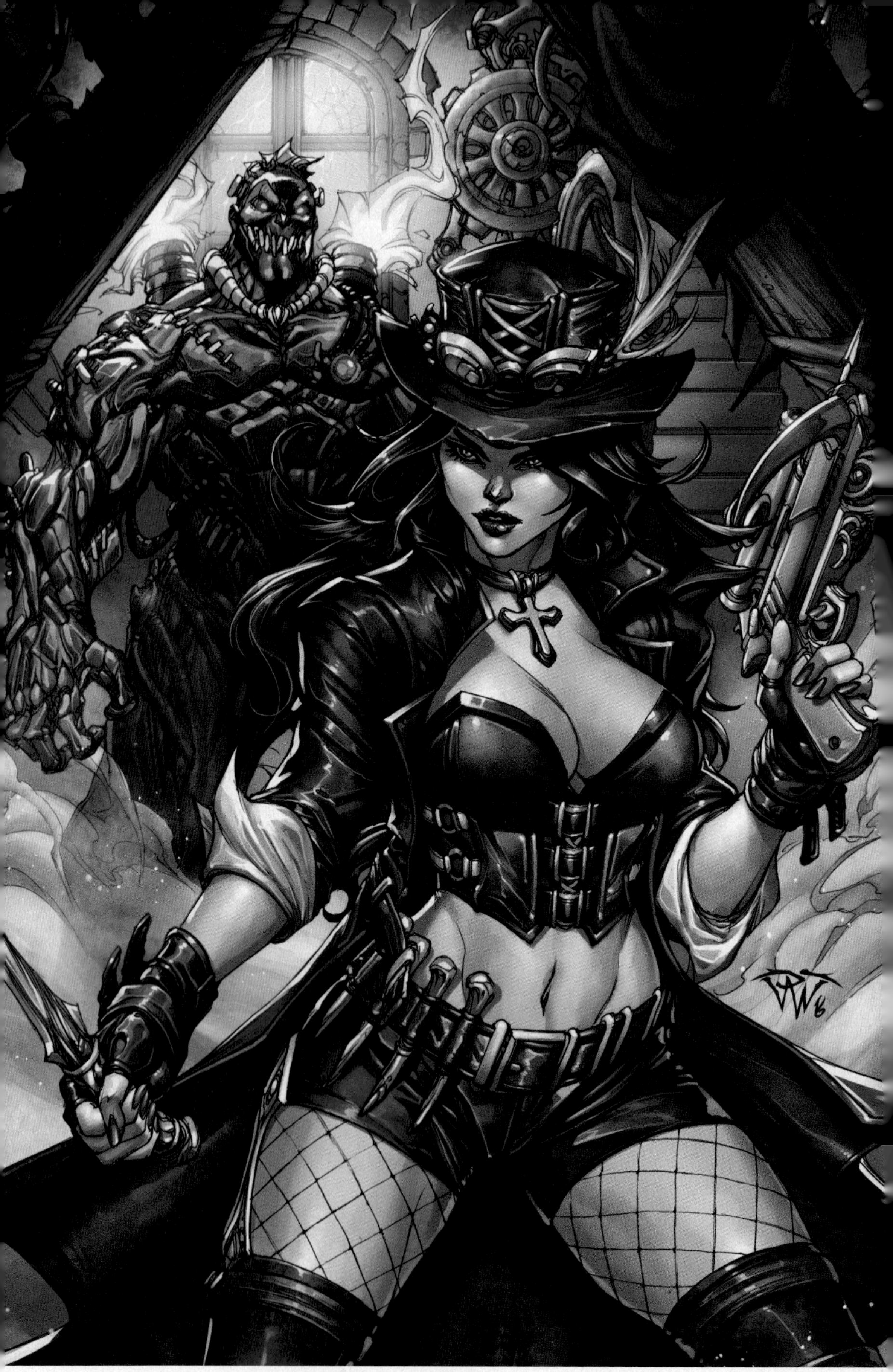

Van Helsing vs. Frankenstein #4 • Cover A
Artwork by Paolo Pantalena • Colors by Arif Prianto

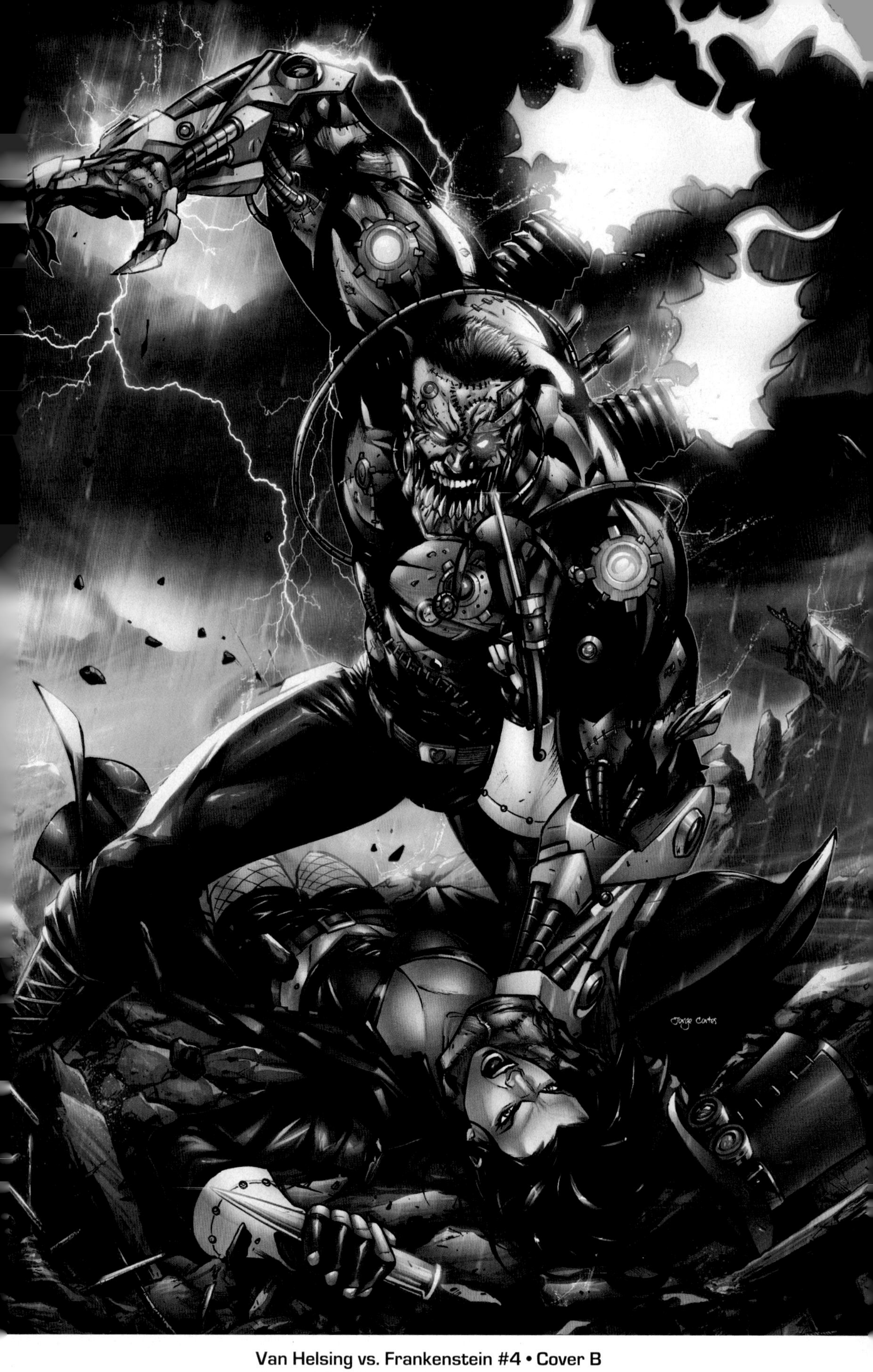

Van Helsing vs. Frankenstein #4 • Cover B
Artwork by Riveiro • Colors by Jorge Cortes

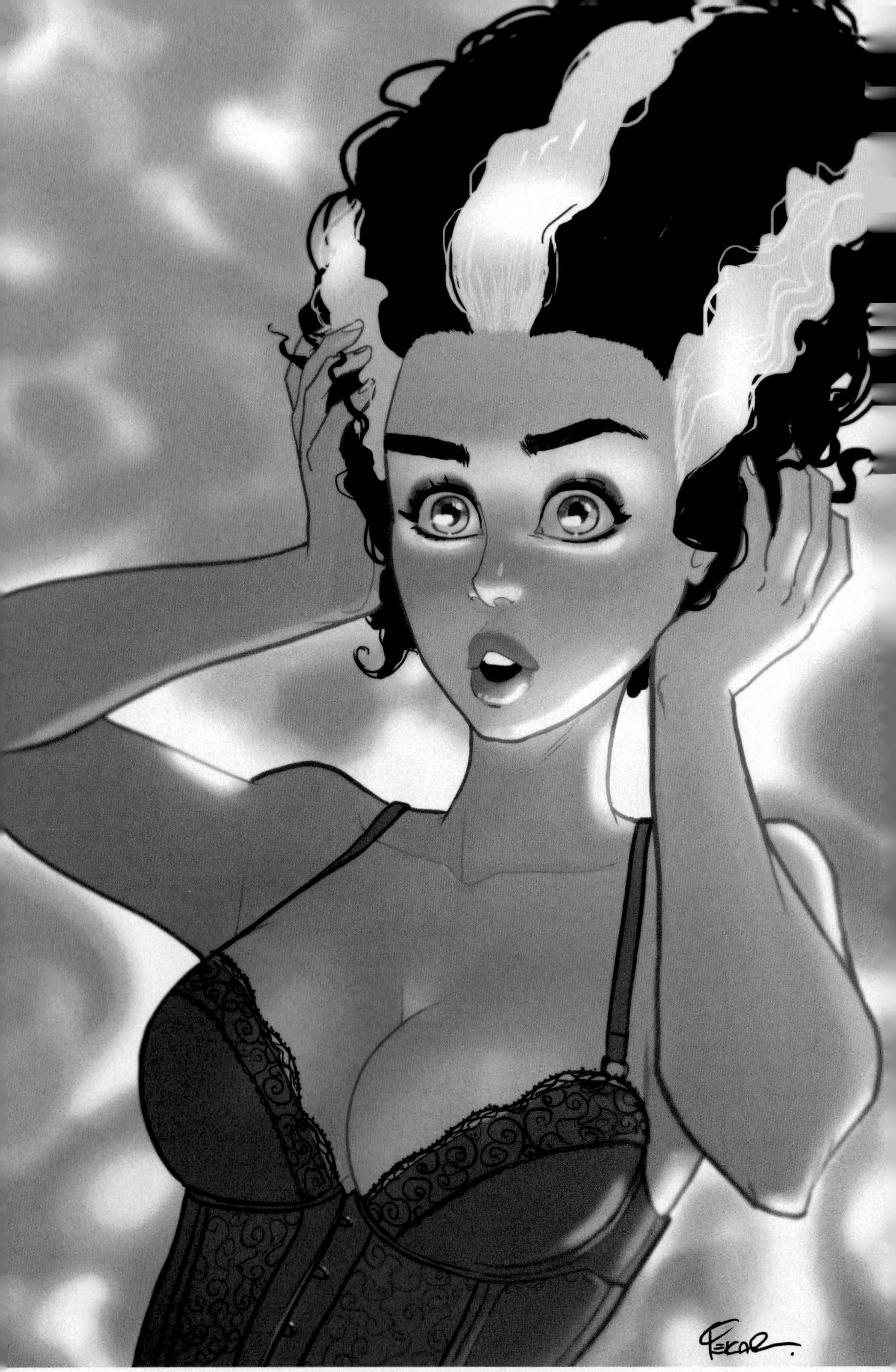
Pekar

Van Helsing vs. Frankenstein #4 • Cover C
Artwork by Joe Pekar

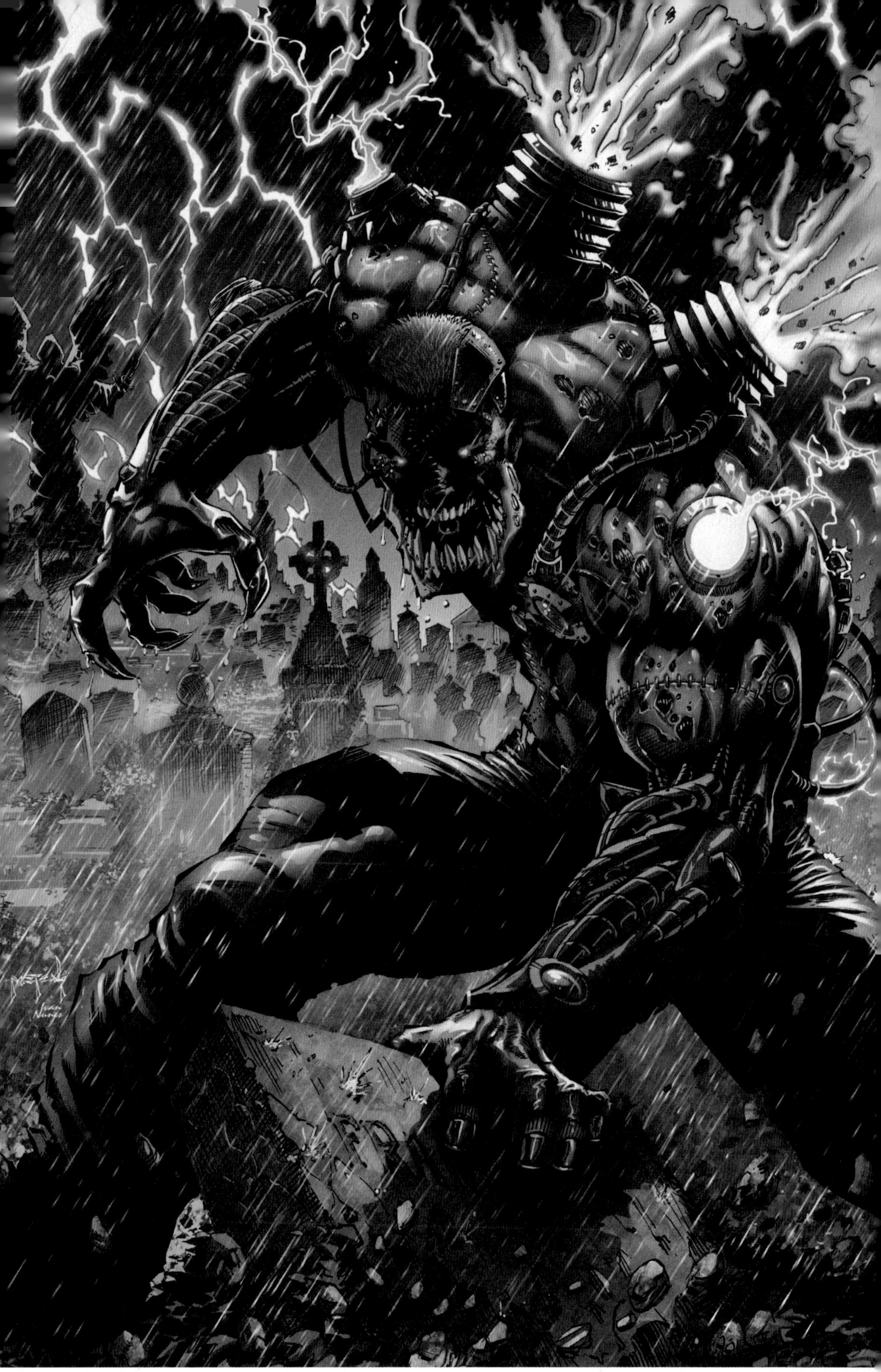

Van Helsing vs. Frankenstein #4 • Cover D
Artwork by Jason Metcalf • Colors by Ivan Nunes

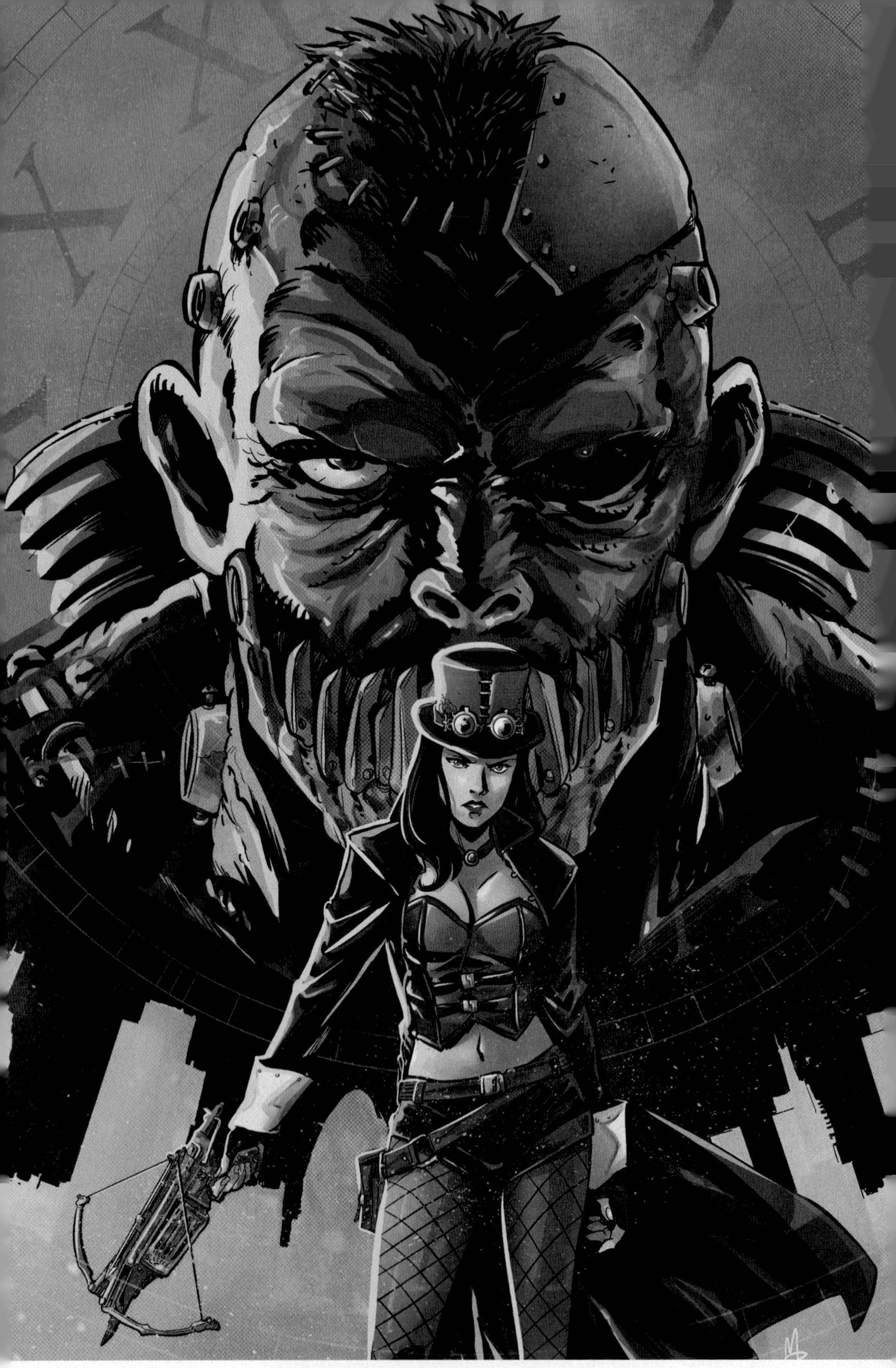

Van Helsing vs. Frankenstein #5 • Cover A
Artwork by Manuel Preitano

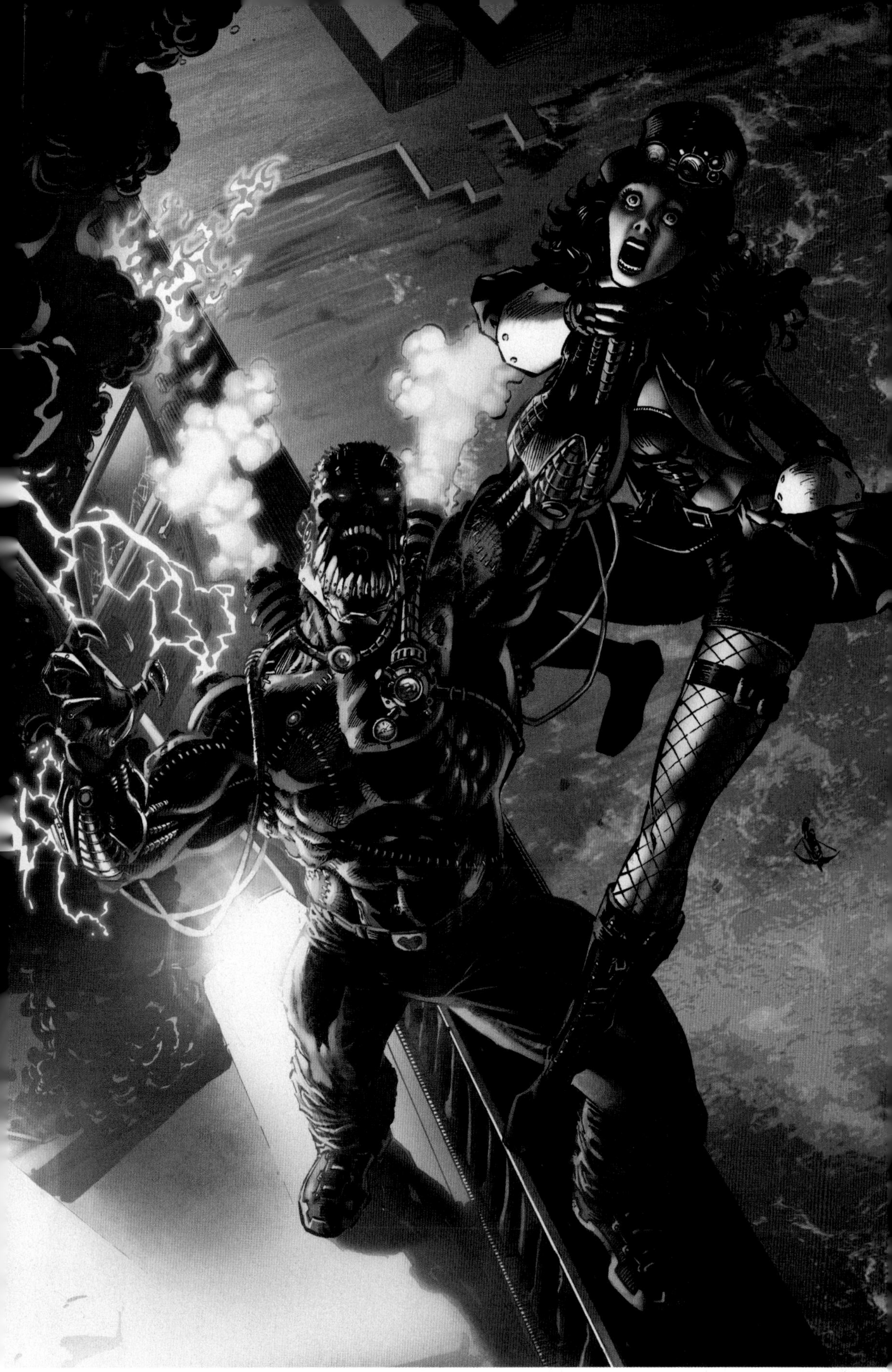

Van Helsing vs. Frankenstein #5 • Cover B
Artwork by Jason Metcalf • Colors by Ivan Nunes

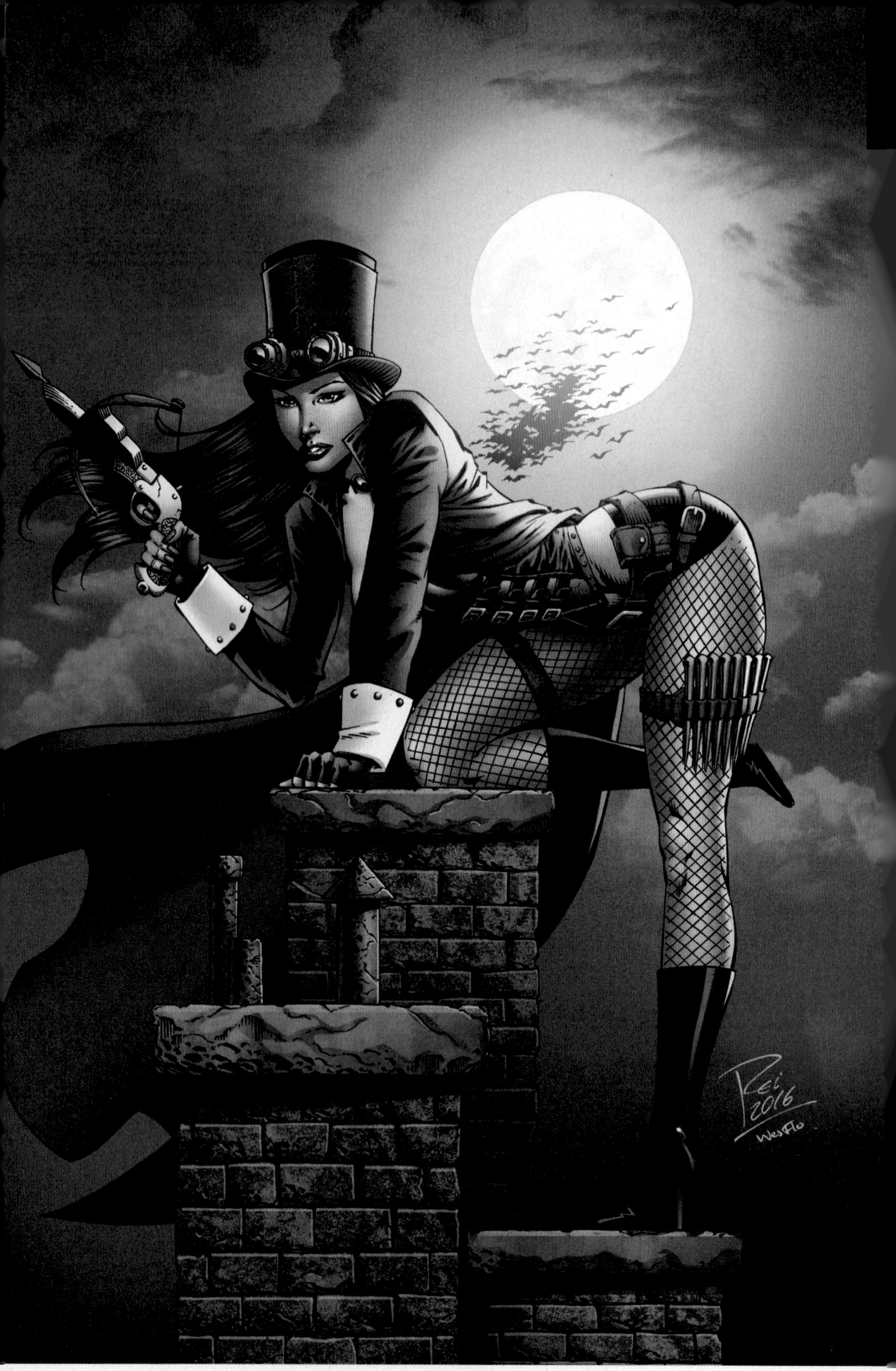
Rei 2016
WesFlo

Van Helsing vs. Frankenstein #5 • Cover C
Artwork by Renato Rei • Colors by Wes Hartman

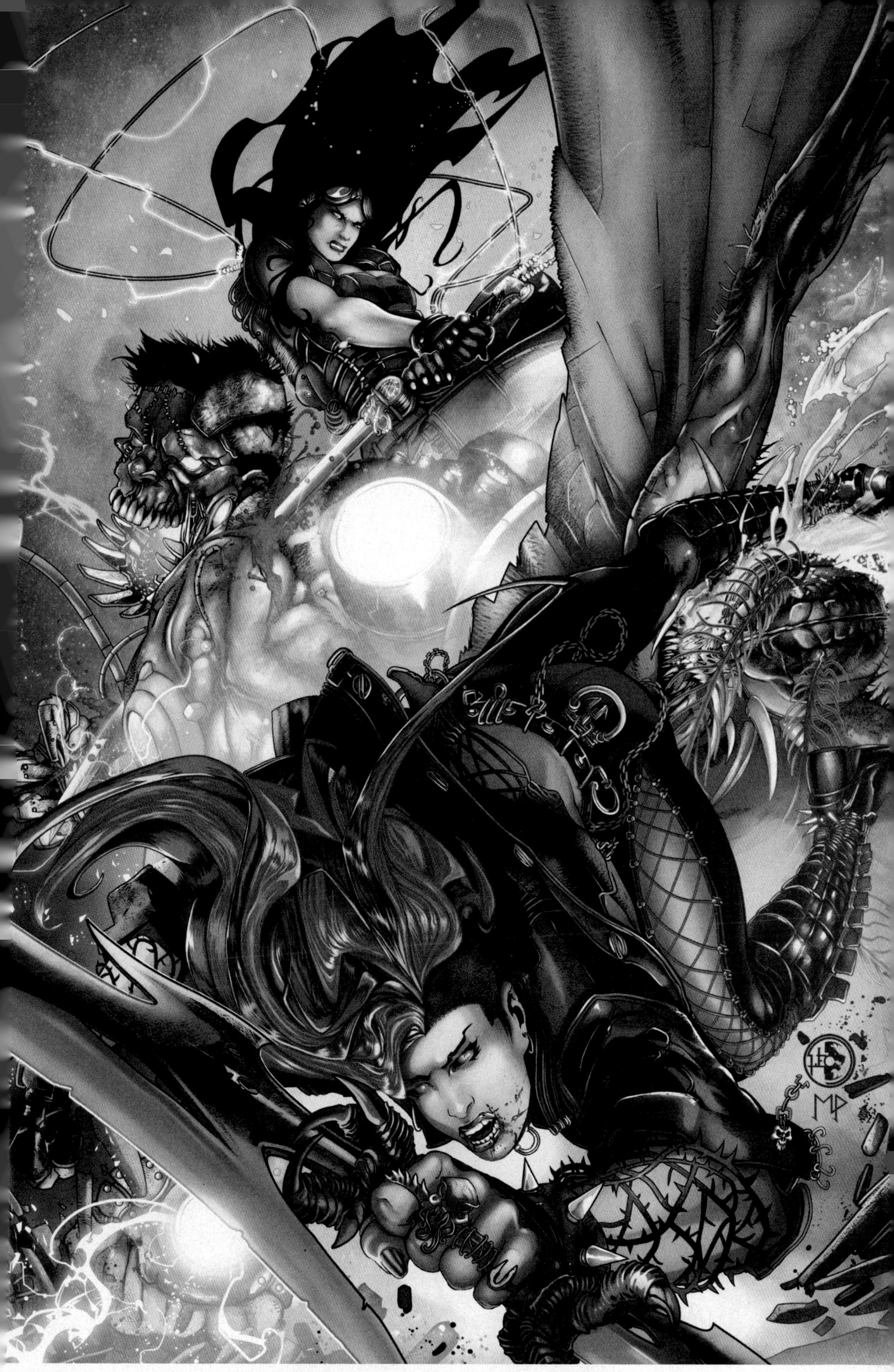

Van Helsing vs. Frankenstein #5 • Cover D
Artwork by Leonardo Colapietro • Colors by Marco Pagnotta

COLLECT ALL THE VAN HELSING BOOKS

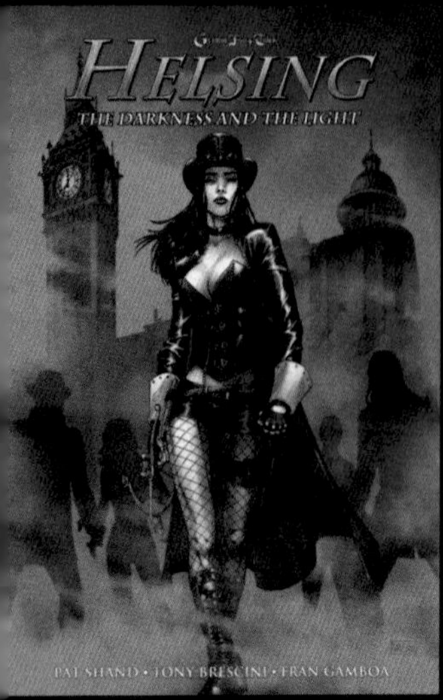
HELSING
THE DARKNESS AND THE LIGHT
PAT SHAND • TONY BRESCINI • FRAN GAMBOA

Helsing: The Darkness and the Light

Pat Shand (W) Tony Brescini (A)
Fran Gamboa (C)

Helsing is a brilliant inventor and expert vampire killer, two skills she picked up from her legendary father, Abraham Van Helsing. However, the normally unflappable Helsing has her world shaken up when Abraham's journal is anonymously mailed to her home in New York. She discovers a clue that leads her on a cross-continental journey to find out what happened to him. But what Helsing doesn't know is that her travels will bring her face to face with her father's most dangerous nemesis.

Diamond: JUN141617
ISBN: 978-1-939683-77-9

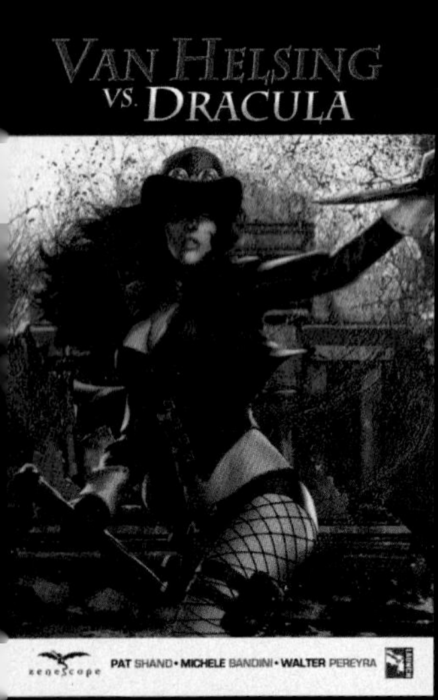
VAN HELSING
VS. DRACULA
zenescope
PAT SHAND • MICHELE BANDINI • WALTER PEREYRA

Van Helsing vs. Dracula

Pat Shand (W) Michele Bandini (A)
Walter Pereyra (C)

Last year, Liesel Van Helsing was attacked by an evil from her father's past... but she survived, and has moved on with her life. Besides becoming the name that vampires in the tri-state area fear, she's also found love in the strangest of places. However, when old friends come calling on her for help, she will find herself pulled into a final conflict with the deadliest vampire of all time!

Diamond: NOV151835
ISBN: 978-1942275268

> "A singular achievement. Visceral excellence. A++"
> **—Fandom Post**

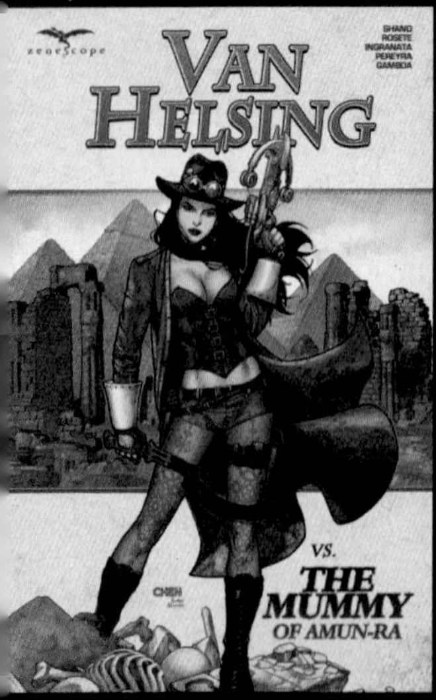
zenescope
VAN HELSING
SHAND ROSETE INGRANATA PEREYRA GAMBOA
VS.
THE MUMMY OF AMUN-RA

Van Helsing vs. The Mummy of Amun-Ra

Pat Shand (W) Marc Rosete & Roberta Ingranata (A)
Walter Pereyra & Fran Gamboa (C)

After facing a devastating personal loss, Liesel Van Helsing wages war against the supernatural threat in New York City with a new level of fury. However, an enemy from Liesel's past is back with power unlike any enemy the vampire hunter has ever faced. To defeat this new foe, Liesel must grapple both with her horrific past and her dismal future if she hopes to emerge from this battle alive.

COMING SOON
Diamond: JUN172244
ISBN: 978-1942275541

Van Helsing trade paperbacks are currently available at your local comic retailer and zenescope.com

Origins
VOLUME 1

published by
Top Cow Productions, Inc.
Los Angeles

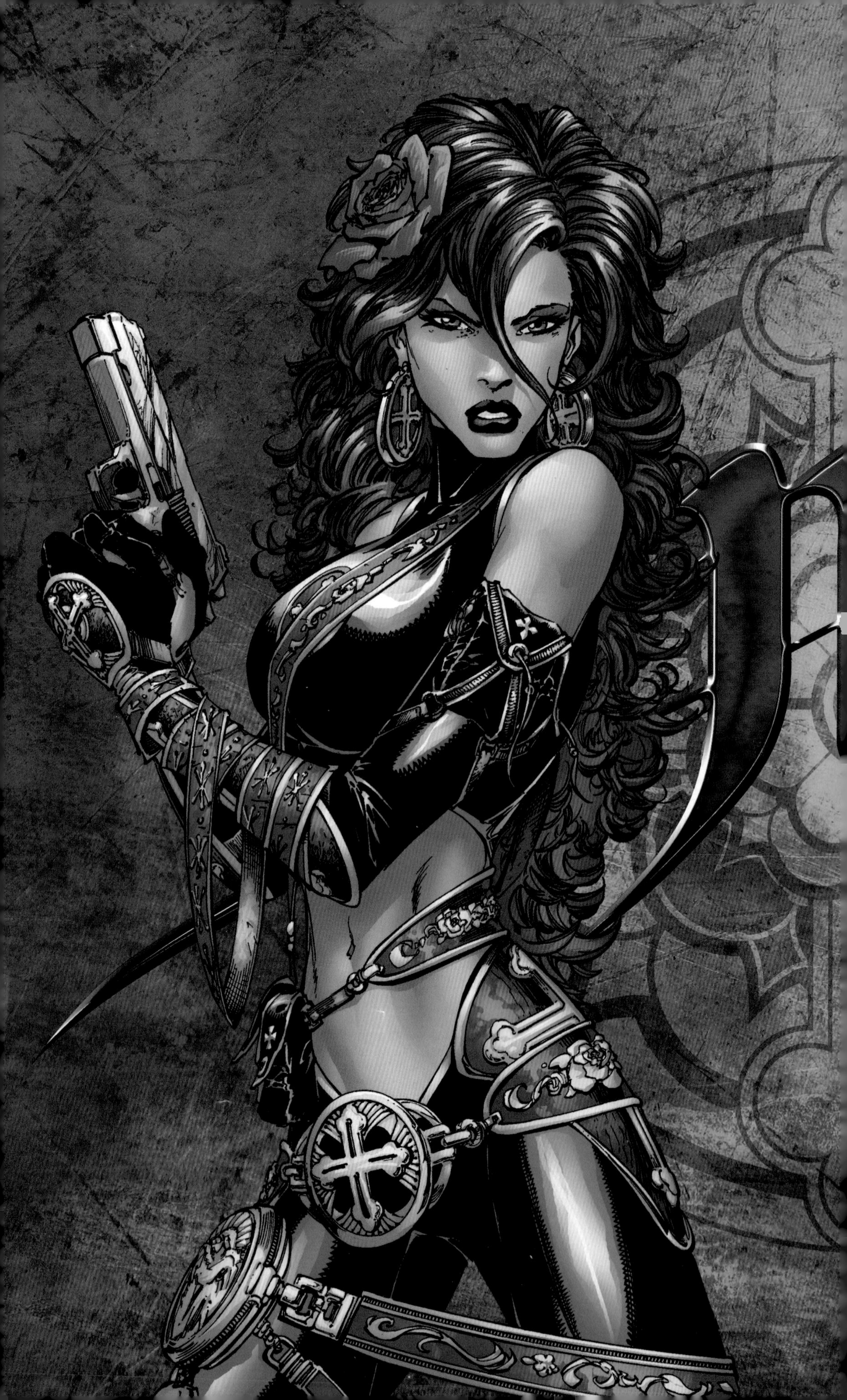

the Magdalena

Origins

VOLUME 1

For Top Cow Productions, Inc.:
Marc Silvestri - Chief Executive Officer
Matt Hawkins - President and Chief Operating Officer
Filip Sablik - Publisher
Phil Smith - Managing Editor
Atom Freeman - Director of Sales & Marketing
Bryan Rountree - Assistant to the Publisher
Christine Dinh - Marketing Assistant
Mark Haynes - Webmaster
Kyle Economou - Intern

Original Editions edited by:
David Wohl, Sonia Im,
Renae Geerlings & Matt Hawkins

For this edition
Cover art by:
Joe Benitez, Joe Weems V
and Peter Steigerwald

For this edition
Book Design and Layout by:
Phil Smith

 for **image** comics
publisher:
Eric Stephenson

888-COMIC-BOOK

to find the comic shop
nearest you call:
1-888-COMICBOOK

Want more info? check out:
www.topcow.com and **www.topcowstore.com**
for news and exclusive Top Cow merchandise!

Magdalena: Origins volume 1 Trade Paperback
Decmeber 2010. FIRST PRINTING. ISBN: 978-1-60706-205-9
Published by Image Comics Inc. Office of Publication: 2134 Allston Way, Second Floor
Berkeley, CA 94704. $14.99 U.S.D. Originally published in single magazine form as
The Darkness issues 15-19 and Magdalena volume 1 issues 1-3. The Darkness and
Magdalena © 2010 Top Cow Productions, Inc. All rights reserved. "The Darkness,"
"Magdalena", the The Darkness and Magdalena logos, and the likeness of all
characters (human or otherwise) featured herein are registered trademarks of Top Cow
Productions, Inc. Image Comics and the Image Comics logo are trademarks of Image
Comics, Inc. The characters, events, and stories in this publication are entirely fictional.
Any resemblance to actual persons (living or dead), events, institutions, or locales,
without satiric intent, is coincidental. No portion of this publication may be reproduced
or transmitted, in any form or by any means, without the express written permission of
Top Cow Productions, Inc. **PRINTED IN KOREA.**

ORIGINS
VOLUME 1

TABLE OF CONTENTS

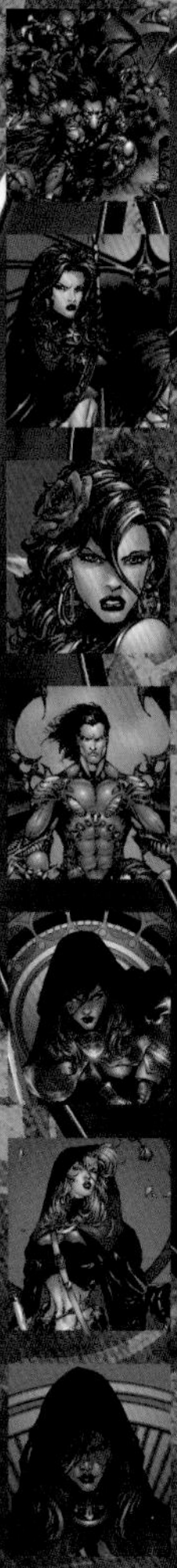

The Darkness

#15

ISSUE

story by: Malachy Coney
pencils by: Joe Benitez
inks by: Joe Weems V, Victor Llamas,
Marlo Alquiza
colors by: Matt Nelson, Richard Isanove,
Tyson Wengler
letters by: Dennis Heisler

inks assists by: Marco "Madman" Galli

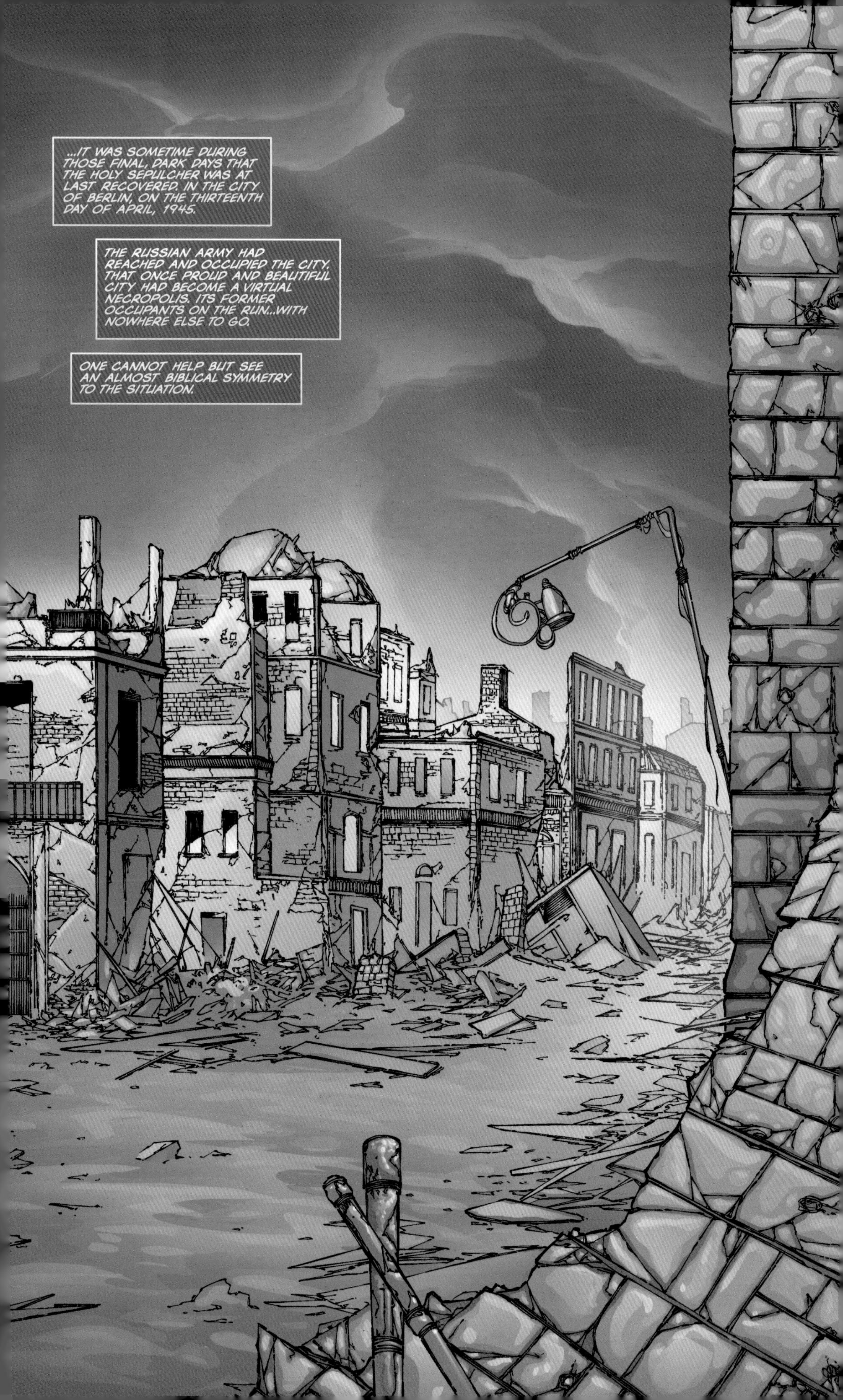
...IT WAS SOMETIME DURING THOSE FINAL, DARK DAYS THAT THE HOLY SEPULCHER WAS AT LAST RECOVERED. IN THE CITY OF BERLIN, ON THE THIRTEENTH DAY OF APRIL, 1945.
THE RUSSIAN ARMY HAD REACHED AND OCCUPIED THE CITY. THAT ONCE PROUD AND BEAUTIFUL CITY HAD BECOME A VIRTUAL NECROPOLIS. ITS FORMER OCCUPANTS ON THE RUN...WITH NOWHERE ELSE TO GO.
ONE CANNOT HELP BUT SEE AN ALMOST BIBLICAL SYMMETRY TO THE SITUATION.

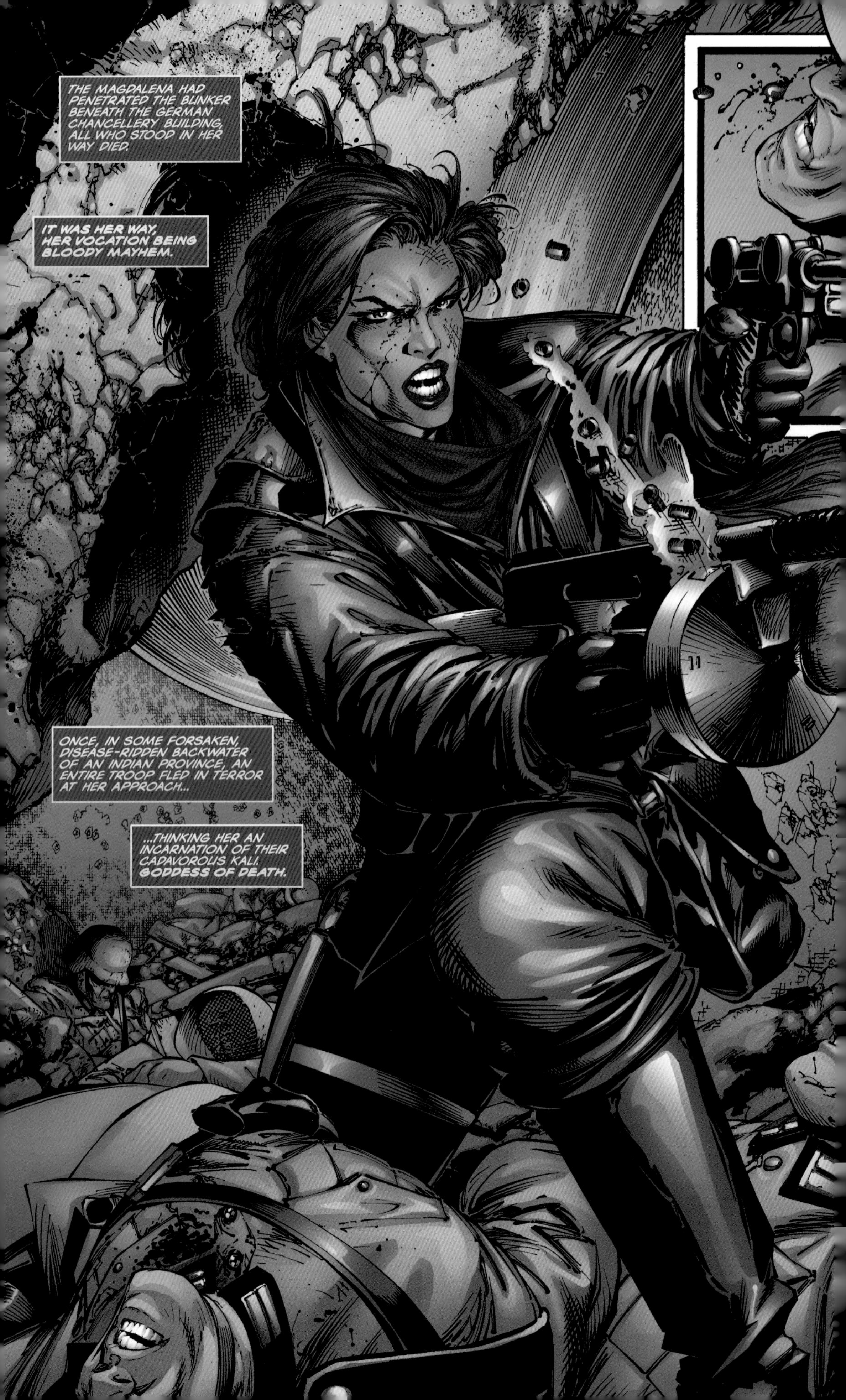
THE MAGDALENA HAD PENETRATED THE BUNKER BENEATH THE GERMAN CHANCELLERY BUILDING. ALL WHO STOOD IN HER WAY DIED.
IT WAS HER WAY, HER VOCATION BEING BLOODY MAYHEM.
ONCE, IN SOME FORSAKEN, DISEASE-RIDDEN BACKWATER OF AN INDIAN PROVINCE, AN ENTIRE TROOP FLED IN TERROR AT HER APPROACH...
...THINKING HER AN INCARNATION OF THEIR CADAVOROUS KALI. GODDESS OF DEATH.

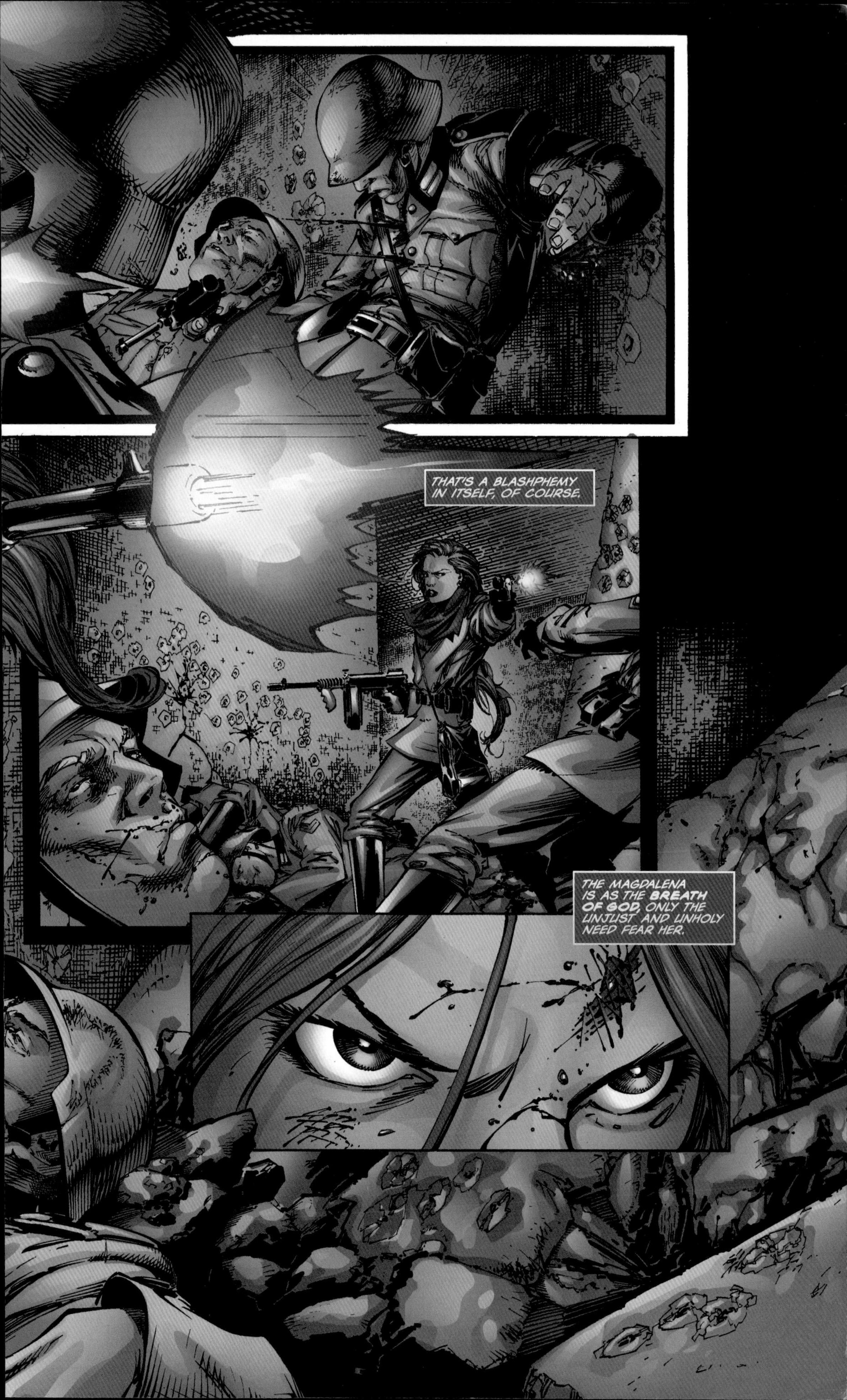
THAT'S A BLASHPHEMY IN ITSELF, OF COURSE.
THE MAGDALENA IS AS THE **BREATH OF GOD**, ONLY THE UNJUST AND UNHOLY NEED FEAR HER.

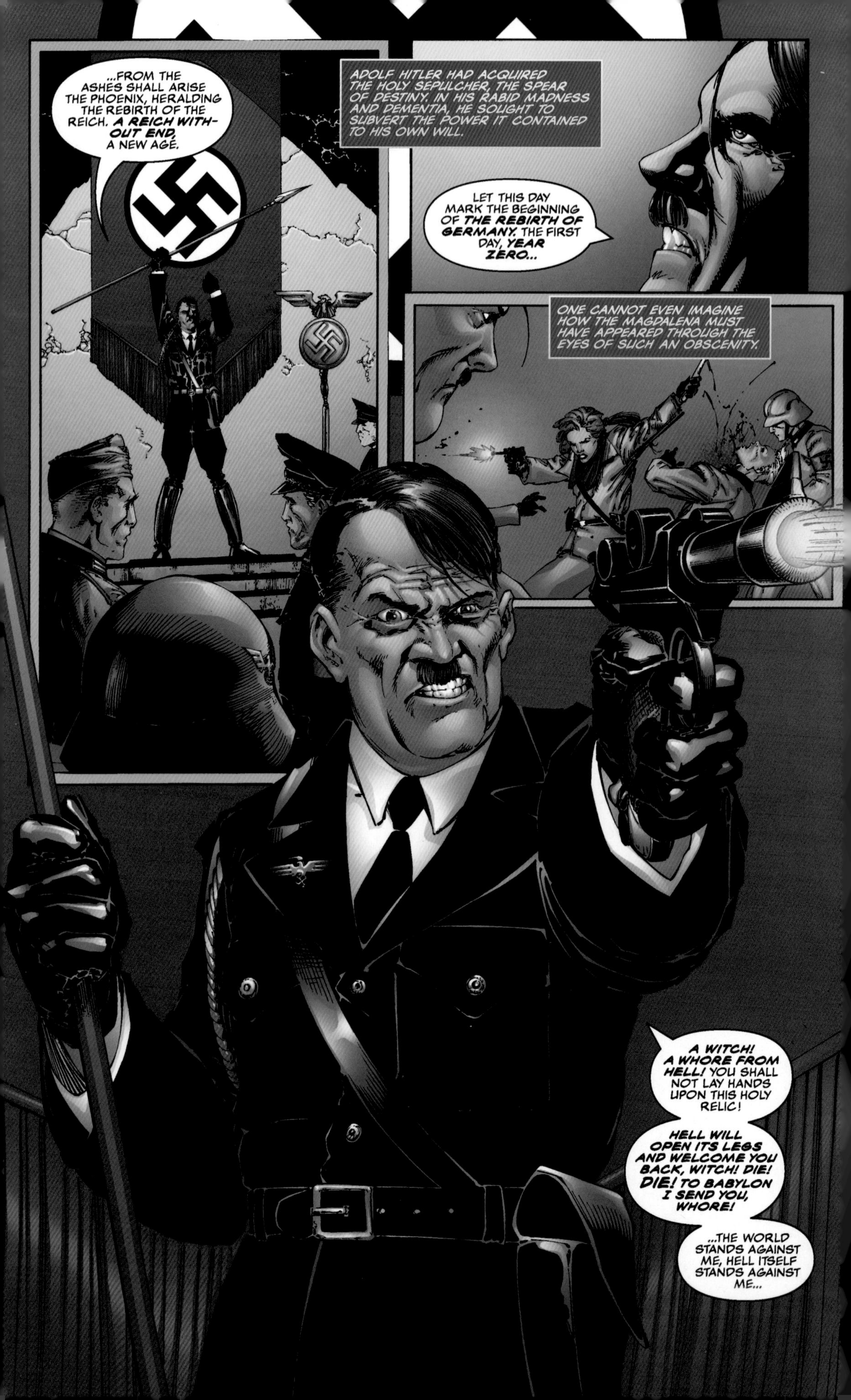
...FROM THE ASHES SHALL ARISE THE PHOENIX, HERALDING THE REBIRTH OF THE REICH. A REICH WITH-OUT END, A NEW AGE.
ADOLF HITLER HAD ACQUIRED THE HOLY SEPULCHER, THE SPEAR OF DESTINY. IN HIS RABID MADNESS AND DEMENTIA, HE SOUGHT TO SUBVERT THE POWER IT CONTAINED TO HIS OWN WILL.
LET THIS DAY MARK THE BEGINNING OF THE REBIRTH OF GERMANY. THE FIRST DAY, YEAR ZERO...
ONE CANNOT EVEN IMAGINE HOW THE MAGDALENA MUST HAVE APPEARED THROUGH THE EYES OF SUCH AN OBSCENITY.
A WITCH! A WHORE FROM HELL! YOU SHALL NOT LAY HANDS UPON THIS HOLY RELIC!
HELL WILL OPEN ITS LEGS AND WELCOME YOU BACK, WITCH! DIE! DIE! TO BABYLON I SEND YOU, WHORE!
...THE WORLD STANDS AGAINST ME, HELL ITSELF STANDS AGAINST ME...

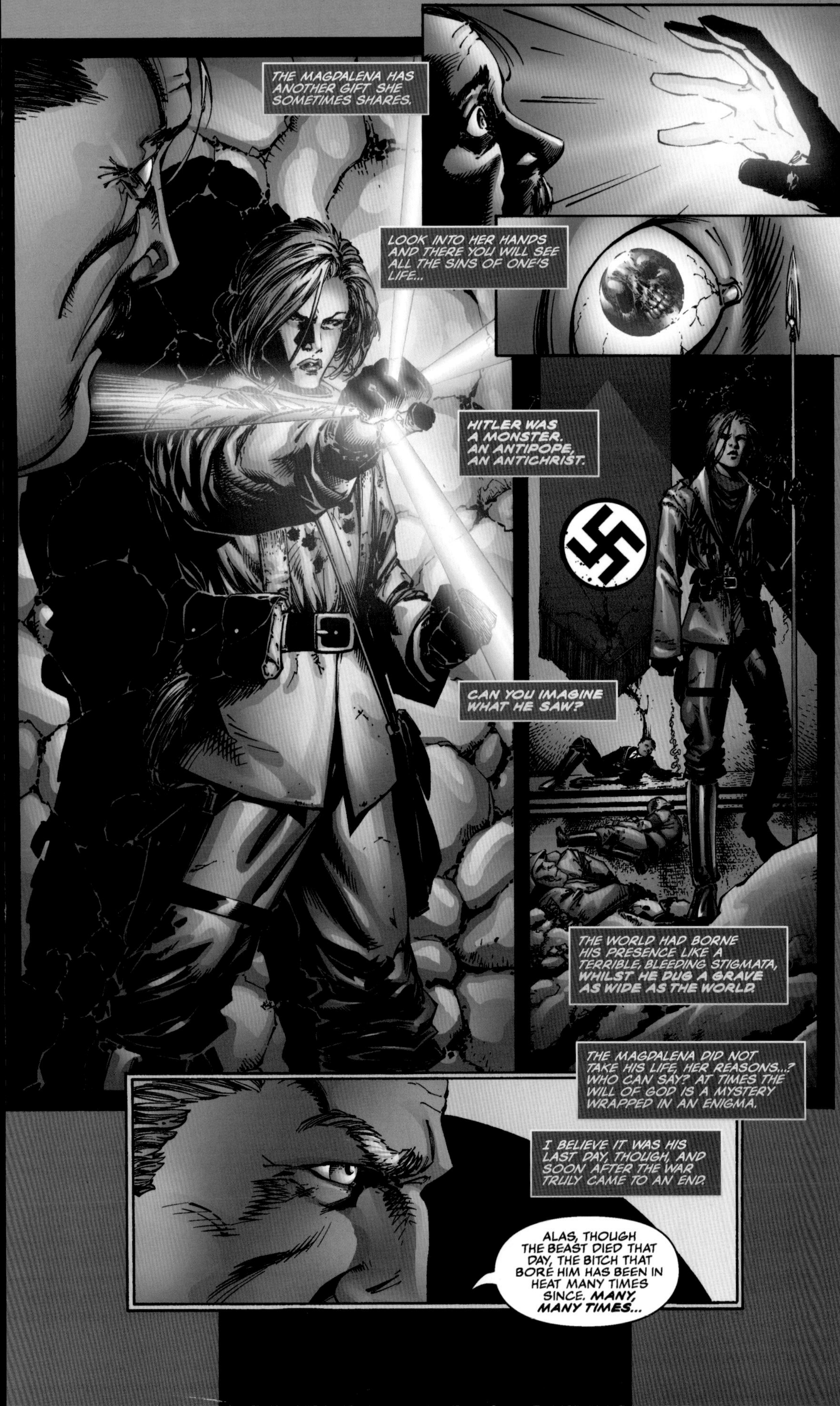
THE MAGDALENA HAS ANOTHER GIFT SHE SOMETIMES SHARES.
LOOK INTO HER HANDS AND THERE YOU WILL SEE ALL THE SINS OF ONE'S LIFE...
HITLER WAS A MONSTER. AN ANTIPOPE, AN ANTICHRIST.
CAN YOU IMAGINE WHAT HE SAW?
THE WORLD HAD BORNE HIS PRESENCE LIKE A TERRIBLE, BLEEDING STIGMATA, WHILST HE DUG A GRAVE AS WIDE AS THE WORLD.
THE MAGDALENA DID NOT TAKE HIS LIFE, HER REASONS...? WHO CAN SAY? AT TIMES THE WILL OF GOD IS A MYSTERY WRAPPED IN AN ENIGMA.
I BELIEVE IT WAS HIS LAST DAY, THOUGH, AND SOON AFTER THE WAR TRULY CAME TO AN END.
ALAS, THOUGH THE BEAST DIED THAT DAY, THE BITCH THAT BORE HIM HAS BEEN IN HEAT MANY TIMES SINCE. MANY, MANY TIMES...

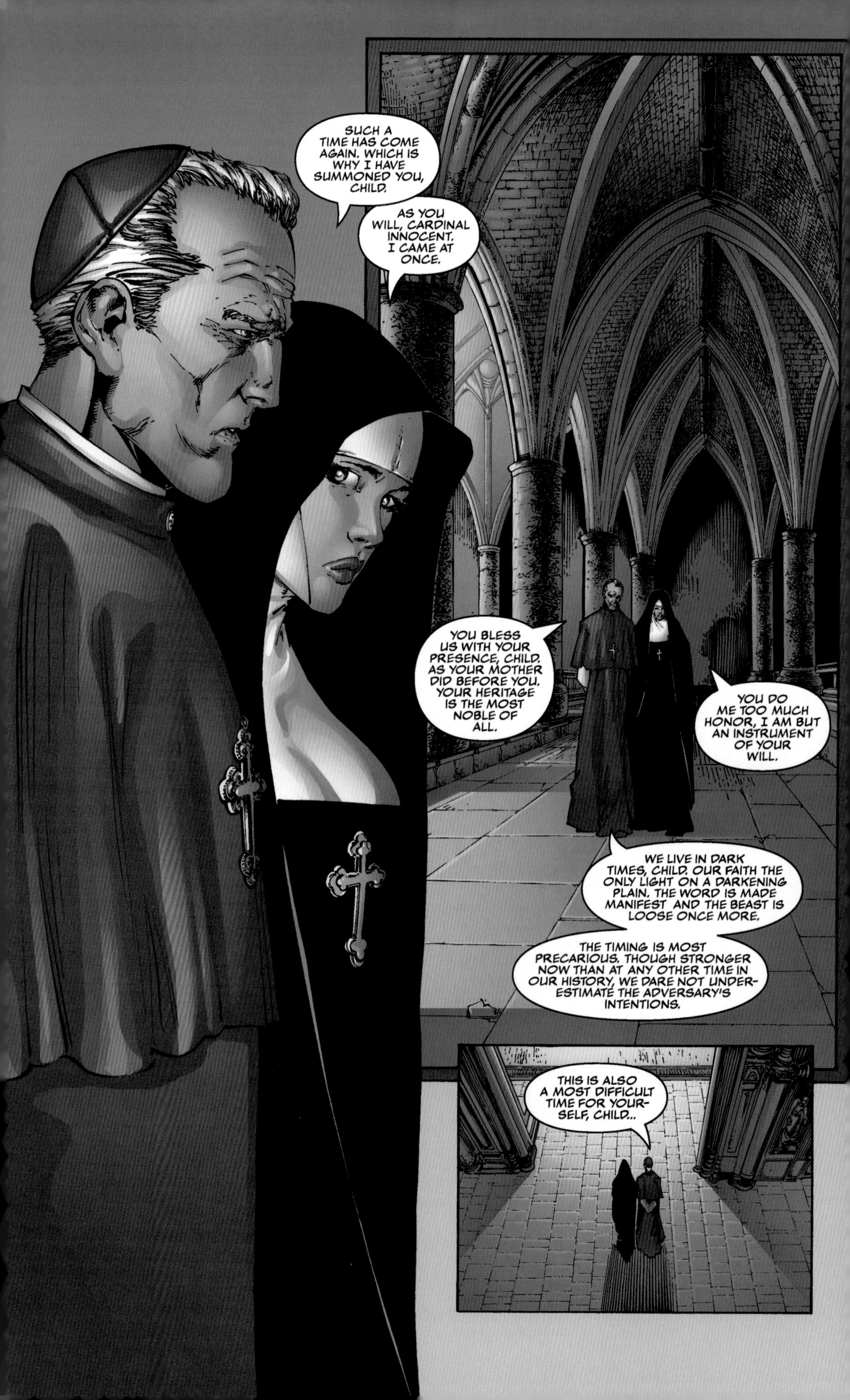
SUCH A TIME HAS COME AGAIN. WHICH IS WHY I HAVE SUMMONED YOU, CHILD.
AS YOU WILL, CARDINAL INNOCENT. I CAME AT ONCE.
YOU BLESS US WITH YOUR PRESENCE, CHILD. AS YOUR MOTHER DID BEFORE YOU. YOUR HERITAGE IS THE MOST NOBLE OF ALL.
YOU DO ME TOO MUCH HONOR, I AM BUT AN INSTRUMENT OF YOUR WILL.
WE LIVE IN DARK TIMES, CHILD. OUR FAITH THE ONLY LIGHT ON A DARKENING PLAIN. THE WORD IS MADE MANIFEST AND THE BEAST IS LOOSE ONCE MORE.
THE TIMING IS MOST PRECARIOUS. THOUGH STRONGER NOW THAN AT ANY OTHER TIME IN OUR HISTORY, WE DARE NOT UNDER-ESTIMATE THE ADVERSARY'S INTENTIONS.
THIS IS ALSO A MOST DIFFICULT TIME FOR YOUR-SELF, CHILD...

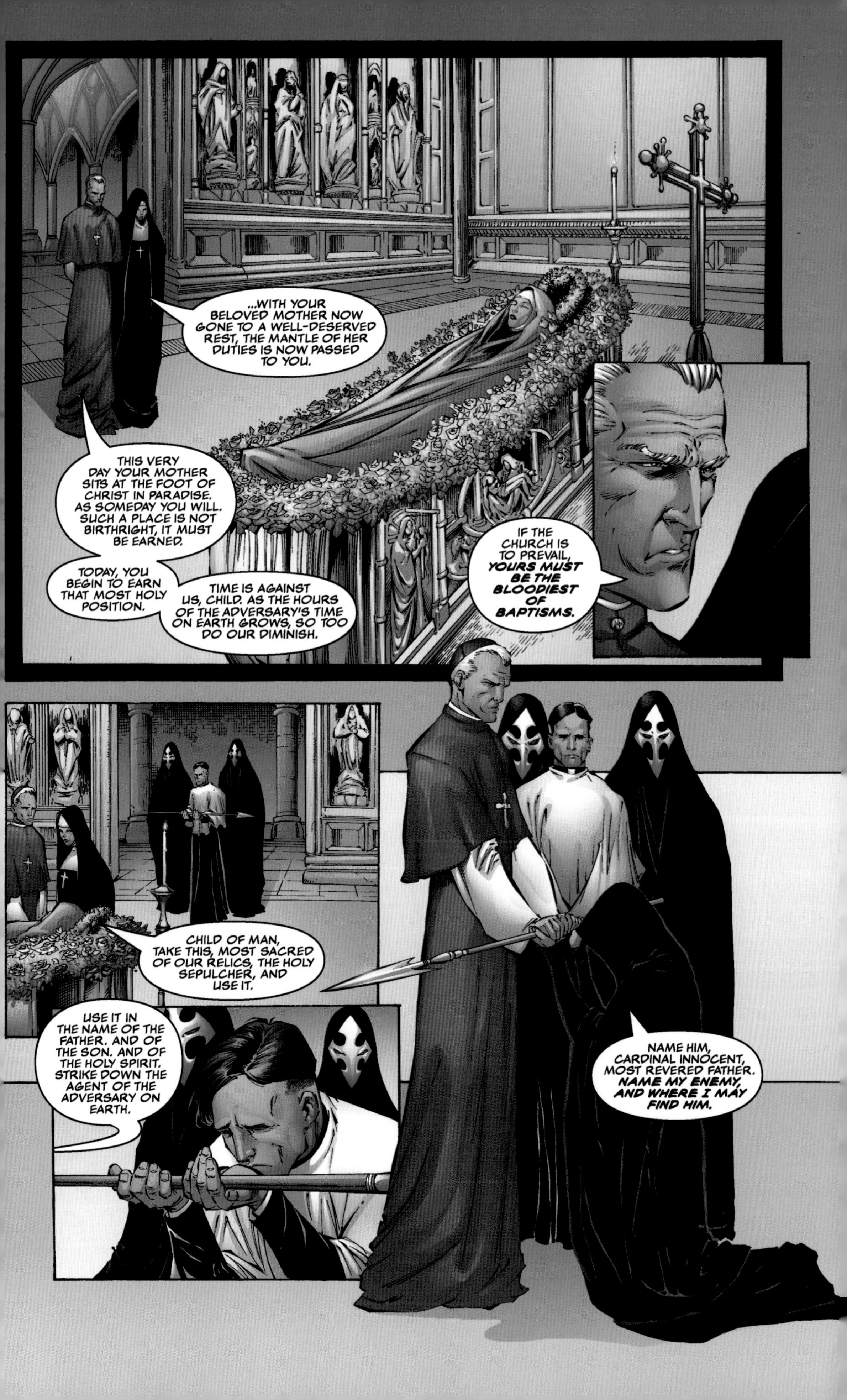
...WITH YOUR BELOVED MOTHER NOW GONE TO A WELL-DESERVED REST, THE MANTLE OF HER DUTIES IS NOW PASSED TO YOU.
THIS VERY DAY YOUR MOTHER SITS AT THE FOOT OF CHRIST IN PARADISE. AS SOMEDAY YOU WILL. SUCH A PLACE IS NOT BIRTHRIGHT, IT MUST BE EARNED.
TODAY, YOU BEGIN TO EARN THAT MOST HOLY POSITION.
TIME IS AGAINST US, CHILD. AS THE HOURS OF THE ADVERSARY'S TIME ON EARTH GROWS, SO TOO DO OUR DIMINISH.
IF THE CHURCH IS TO PREVAIL, YOURS MUST BE THE BLOODIEST OF BAPTISMS.
CHILD OF MAN, TAKE THIS, MOST SACRED OF OUR RELICS, THE HOLY SEPULCHER, AND USE IT.
USE IT IN THE NAME OF THE FATHER. AND OF THE SON. AND OF THE HOLY SPIRIT. STRIKE DOWN THE AGENT OF THE ADVERSARY ON EARTH.
NAME HIM, CARDINAL INNOCENT, MOST REVERED FATHER. NAME MY ENEMY, AND WHERE I MAY FIND HIM.

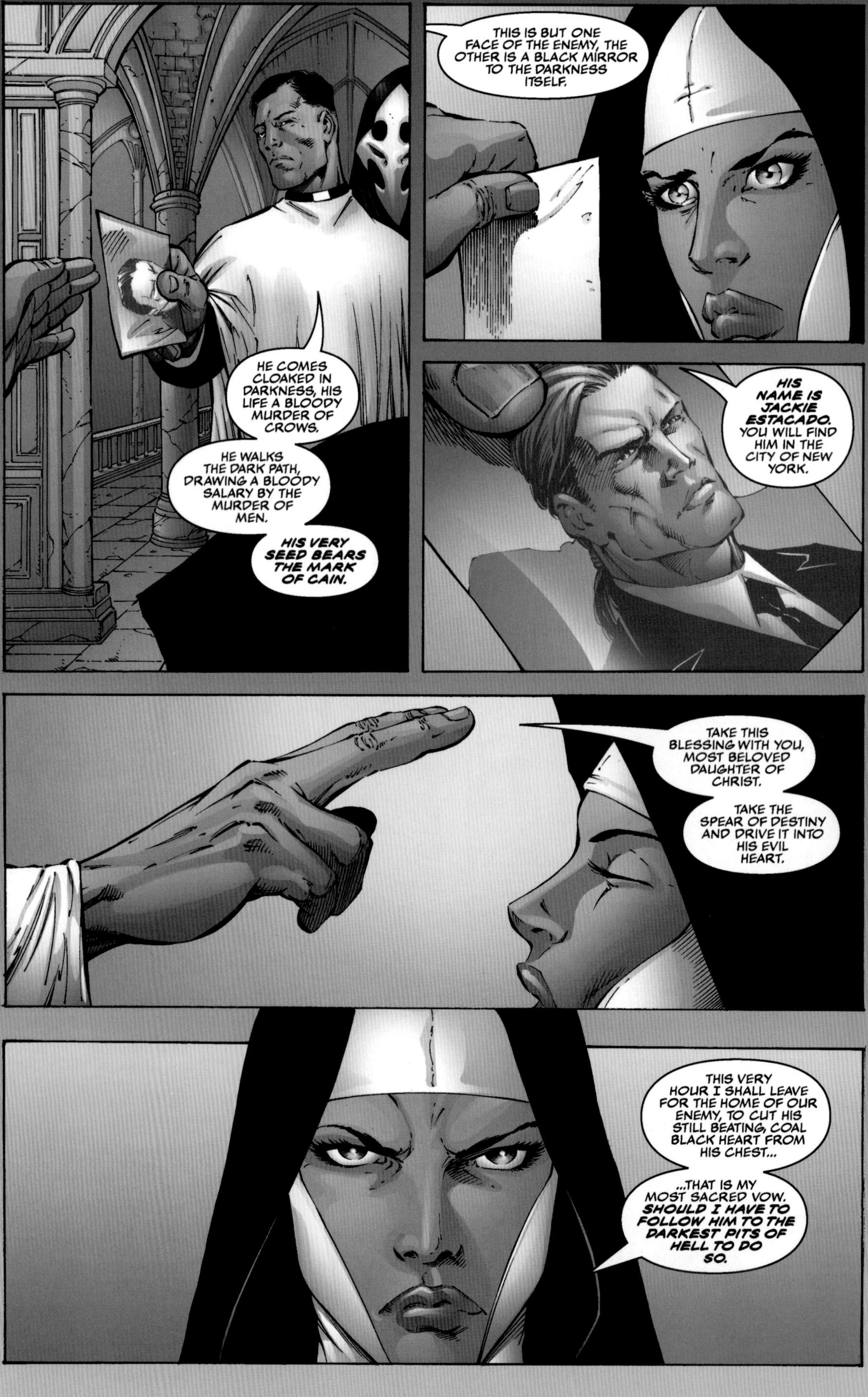
HE COMES CLOAKED IN DARKNESS, HIS LIFE A BLOODY MURDER OF CROWS.
HE WALKS THE DARK PATH, DRAWING A BLOODY SALARY BY THE MURDER OF MEN.
HIS VERY SEED BEARS THE MARK OF CAIN.
THIS IS BUT ONE FACE OF THE ENEMY, THE OTHER IS A BLACK MIRROR TO THE DARKNESS ITSELF.
HIS NAME IS JACKIE ESTACADO. YOU WILL FIND HIM IN THE CITY OF NEW YORK.
TAKE THIS BLESSING WITH YOU, MOST BELOVED DAUGHTER OF CHRIST.
TAKE THE SPEAR OF DESTINY AND DRIVE IT INTO HIS EVIL HEART.
THIS VERY HOUR I SHALL LEAVE FOR THE HOME OF OUR ENEMY, TO CUT HIS STILL BEATING, COAL BLACK HEART FROM HIS CHEST...
...THAT IS MY MOST SACRED VOW. SHOULD I HAVE TO FOLLOW HIM TO THE DARKEST PITS OF HELL TO DO SO.

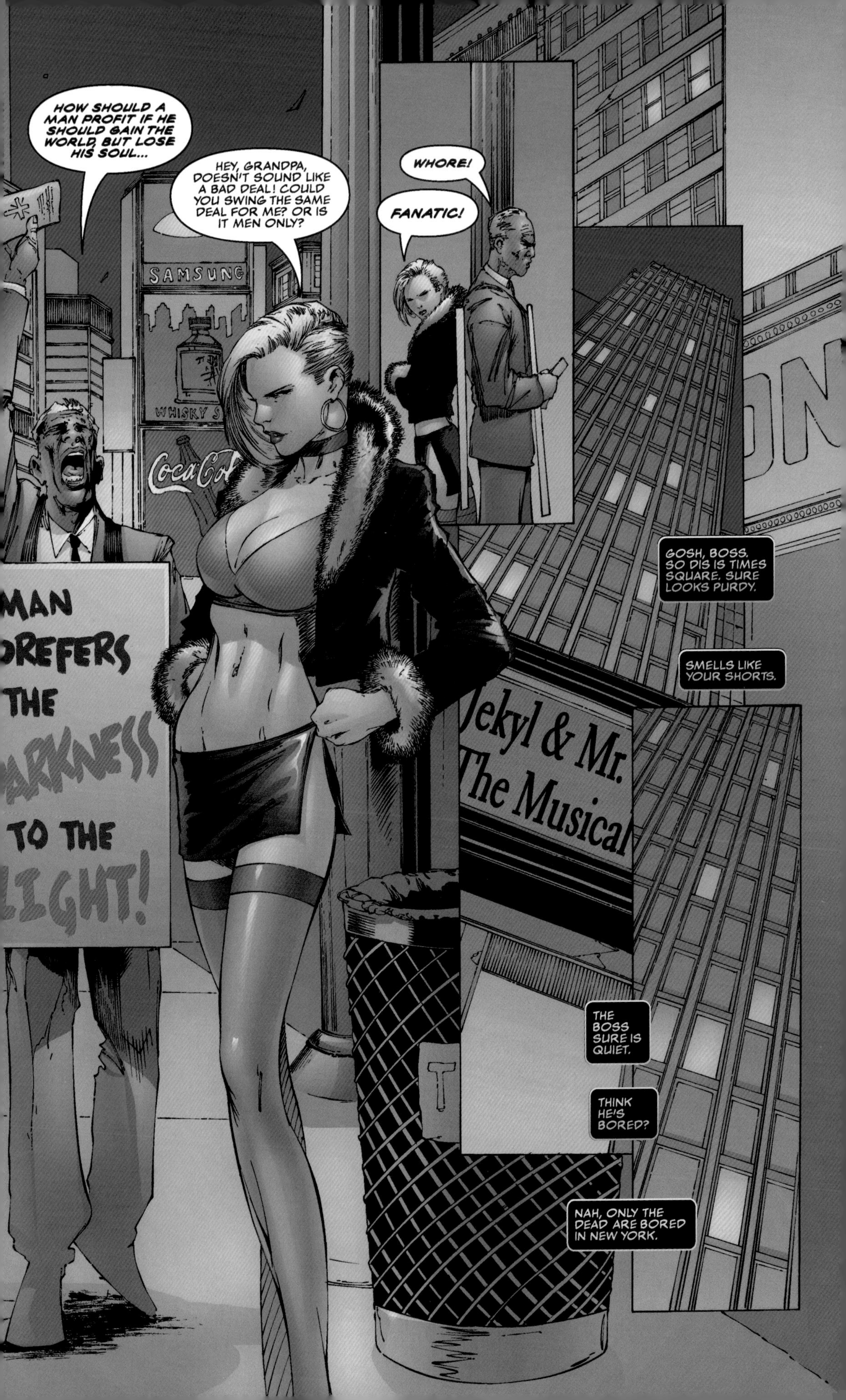
HOW SHOULD A MAN PROFIT IF HE SHOULD GAIN THE WORLD, BUT LOSE HIS SOUL...
HEY, GRANDPA, DOESN'T SOUND LIKE A BAD DEAL! COULD YOU SWING THE SAME DEAL FOR ME? OR IS IT MEN ONLY?
WHORE!
FANATIC!
SAMSUNG
Coca-Cola
MAN PREFERS THE DARKNESS TO THE LIGHT!
GOSH, BOSS. SO DIS IS TIMES SQUARE. SURE LOOKS PURDY.
SMELLS LIKE YOUR SHORTS.
Jekyl & Mr.
The Musical
THE BOSS SURE IS QUIET.
THINK HE'S BORED?
NAH, ONLY THE DEAD ARE BORED IN NEW YORK.

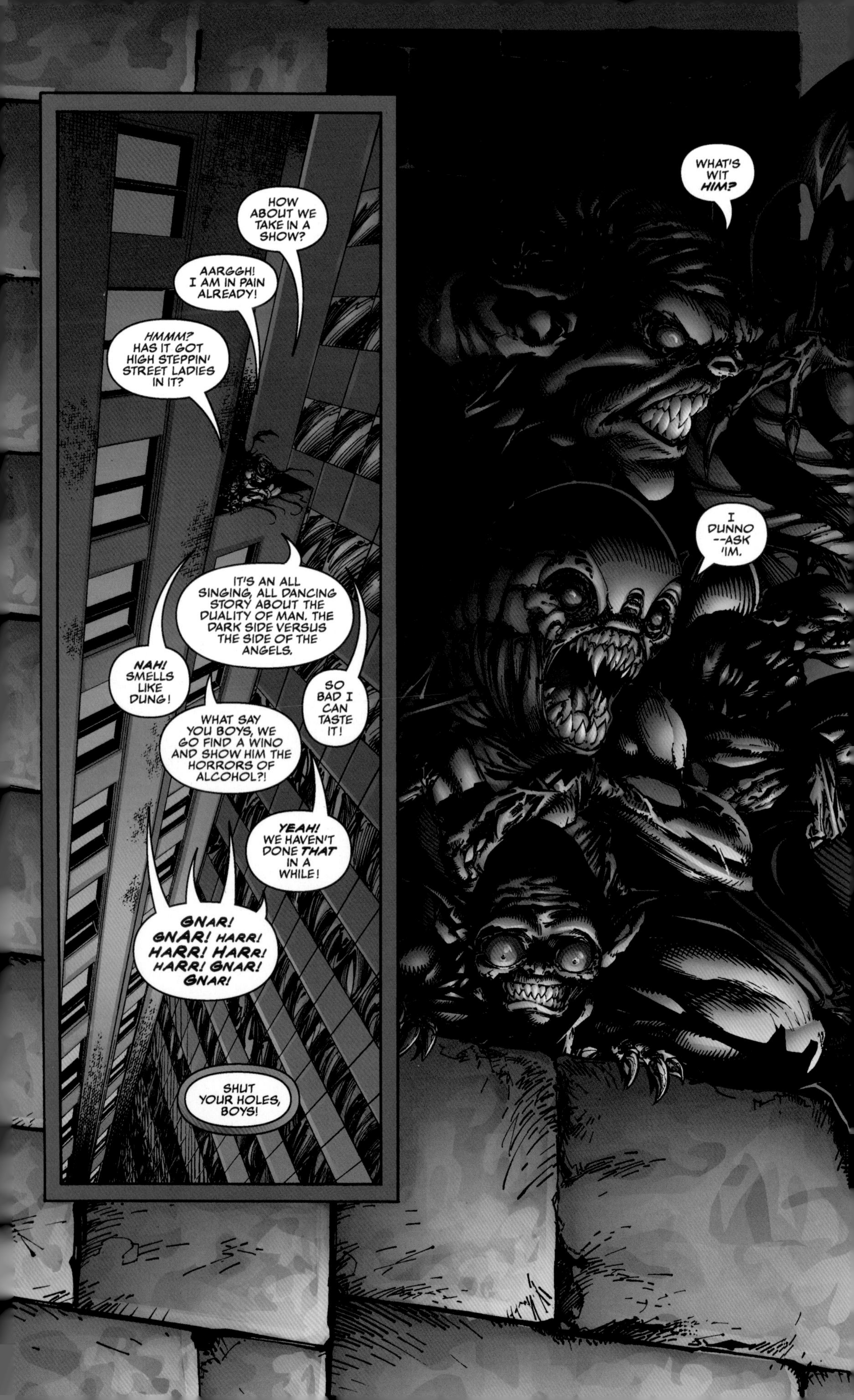
HOW ABOUT WE TAKE IN A SHOW?
AARGGH! I AM IN PAIN ALREADY!
HMMM? HAS IT GOT HIGH STEPPIN' STREET LADIES IN IT?
IT'S AN ALL SINGING, ALL DANCING STORY ABOUT THE DUALITY OF MAN. THE DARK SIDE VERSUS THE SIDE OF THE ANGELS.
NAH! SMELLS LIKE DUNG!
SO BAD I CAN TASTE IT!
WHAT SAY YOU BOYS, WE GO FIND A WINO AND SHOW HIM THE HORRORS OF ALCOHOL?!
YEAH! WE HAVEN'T DONE THAT IN A WHILE!
GNAR! GNAR! HARR! HARR! HARR! HARR! GNAR! GNAR!
SHUT YOUR HOLES, BOYS!
WHAT'S WIT HIM?
I DUNNO --ASK 'IM.

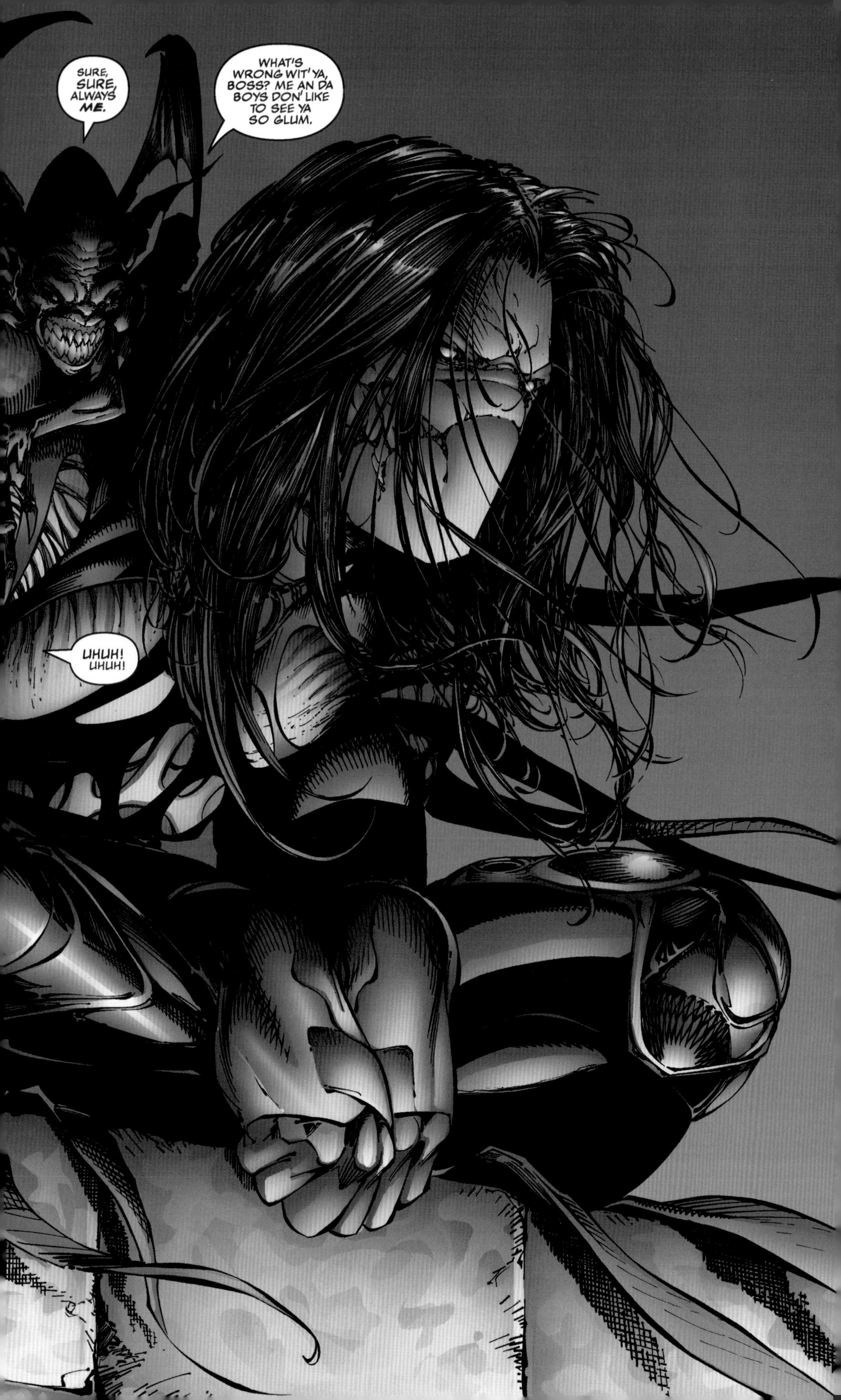
SURE, SURE, ALWAYS ME.
WHAT'S WRONG WIT' YA, BOSS? ME AN DA BOYS DON' LIKE TO SEE YA SO GLUM.
UHUH! UHUH!

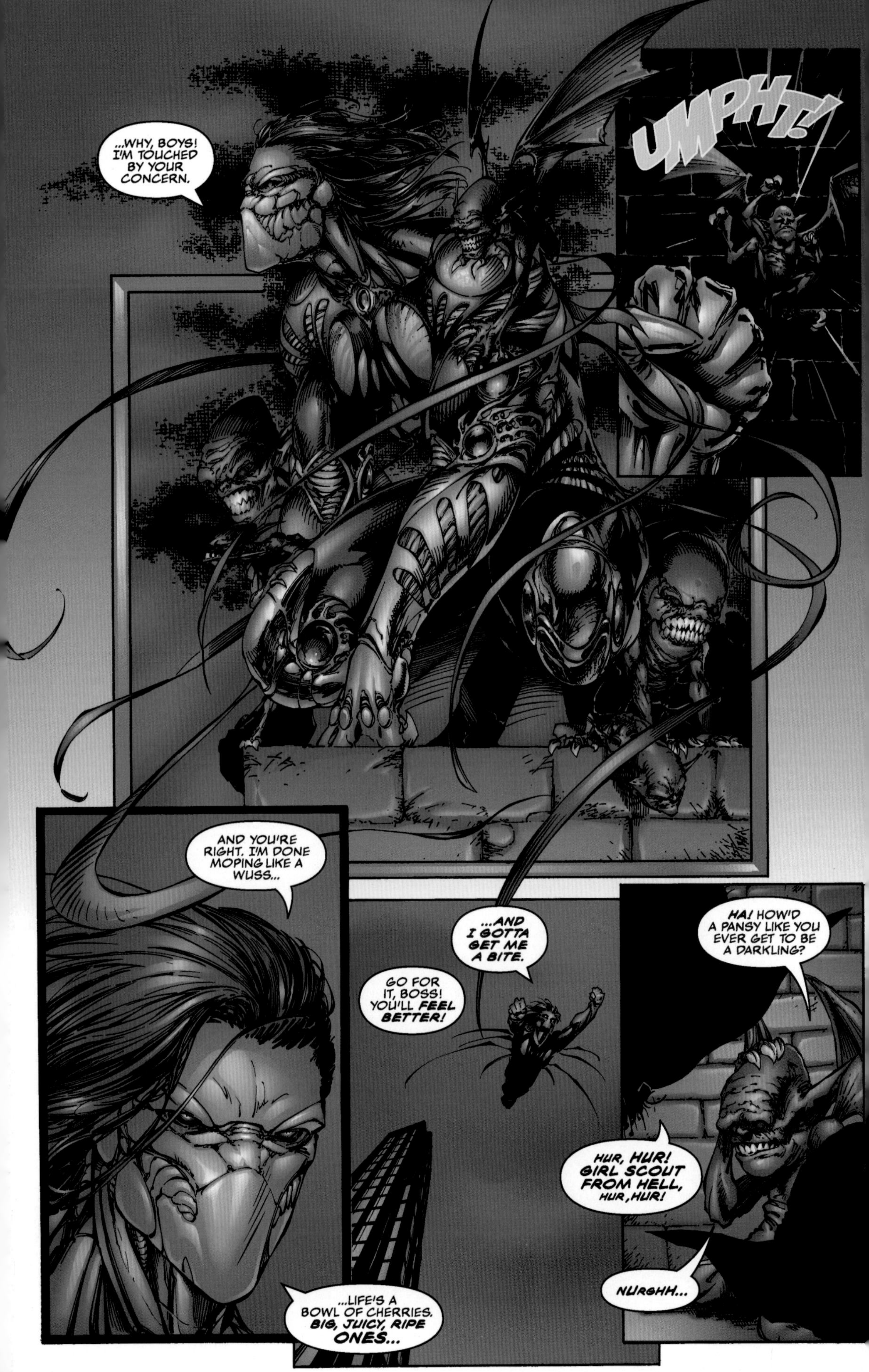
...WHY, BOYS! I'M TOUCHED BY YOUR CONCERN.
UMPHT!
AND YOU'RE RIGHT. I'M DONE MOPING LIKE A WUSS...
...LIFE'S A BOWL OF CHERRIES. BIG, JUICY, RIPE ONES...
GO FOR IT, BOSS! YOU'LL FEEL BETTER!
...AND I GOTTA GET ME A BITE.
HA! HOW'D A PANSY LIKE YOU EVER GET TO BE A DARKLING?
HUR, HUR! GIRL SCOUT FROM HELL, HUR, HUR!
NURGHH...

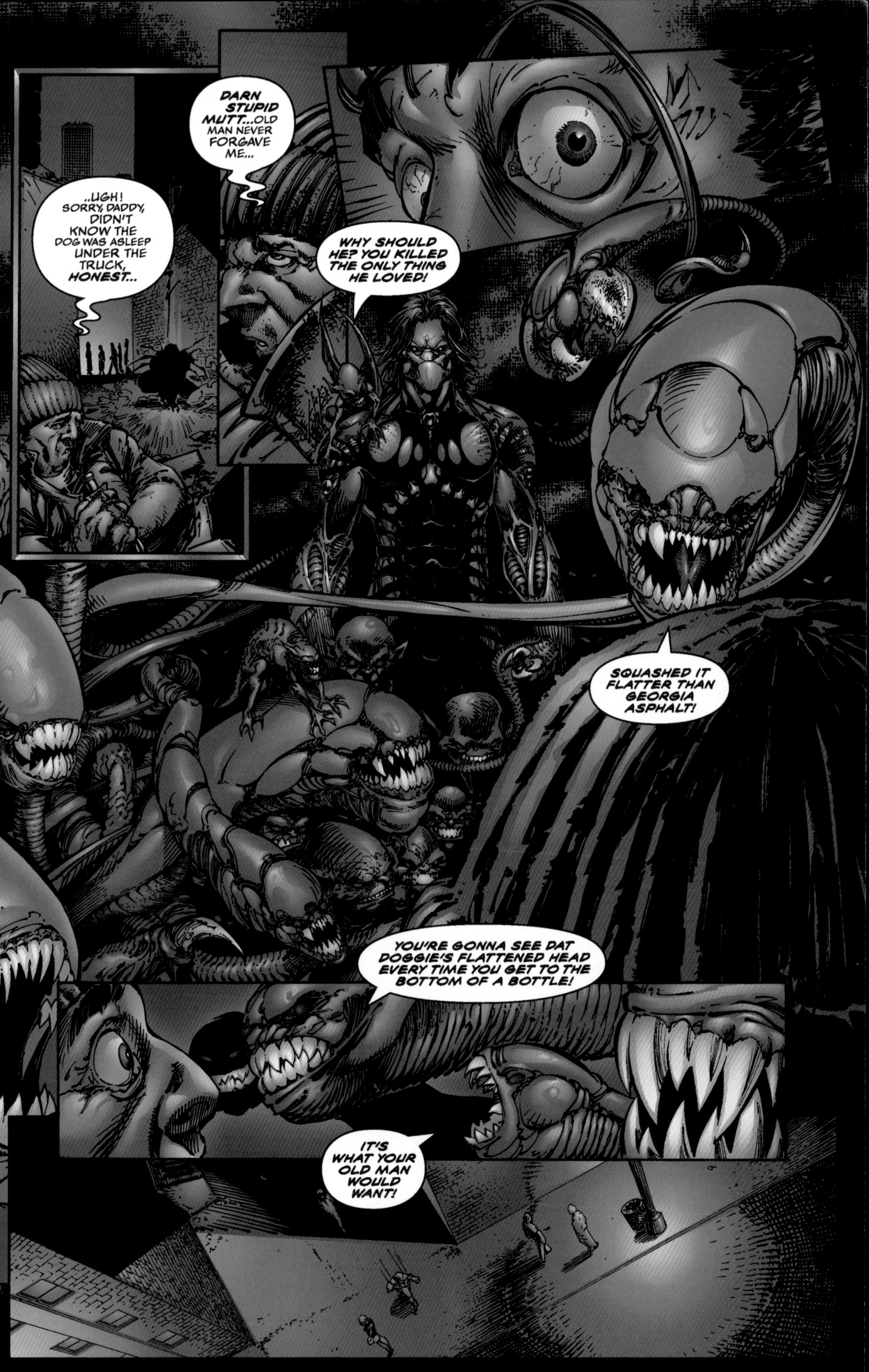
..UGH! SORRY, DADDY, DIDN'T KNOW THE DOG WAS ASLEEP UNDER THE TRUCK, HONEST...
DARN STUPID MUTT...OLD MAN NEVER FORGAVE ME...
WHY SHOULD HE? YOU KILLED THE ONLY THING HE LOVED!
SQUASHED IT FLATTER THAN GEORGIA ASPHALT!
YOU'RE GONNA SEE DAT DOGGIE'S FLATTENED HEAD EVERY TIME YOU GET TO THE BOTTOM OF A BOTTLE!
IT'S WHAT YOUR OLD MAN WOULD WANT!

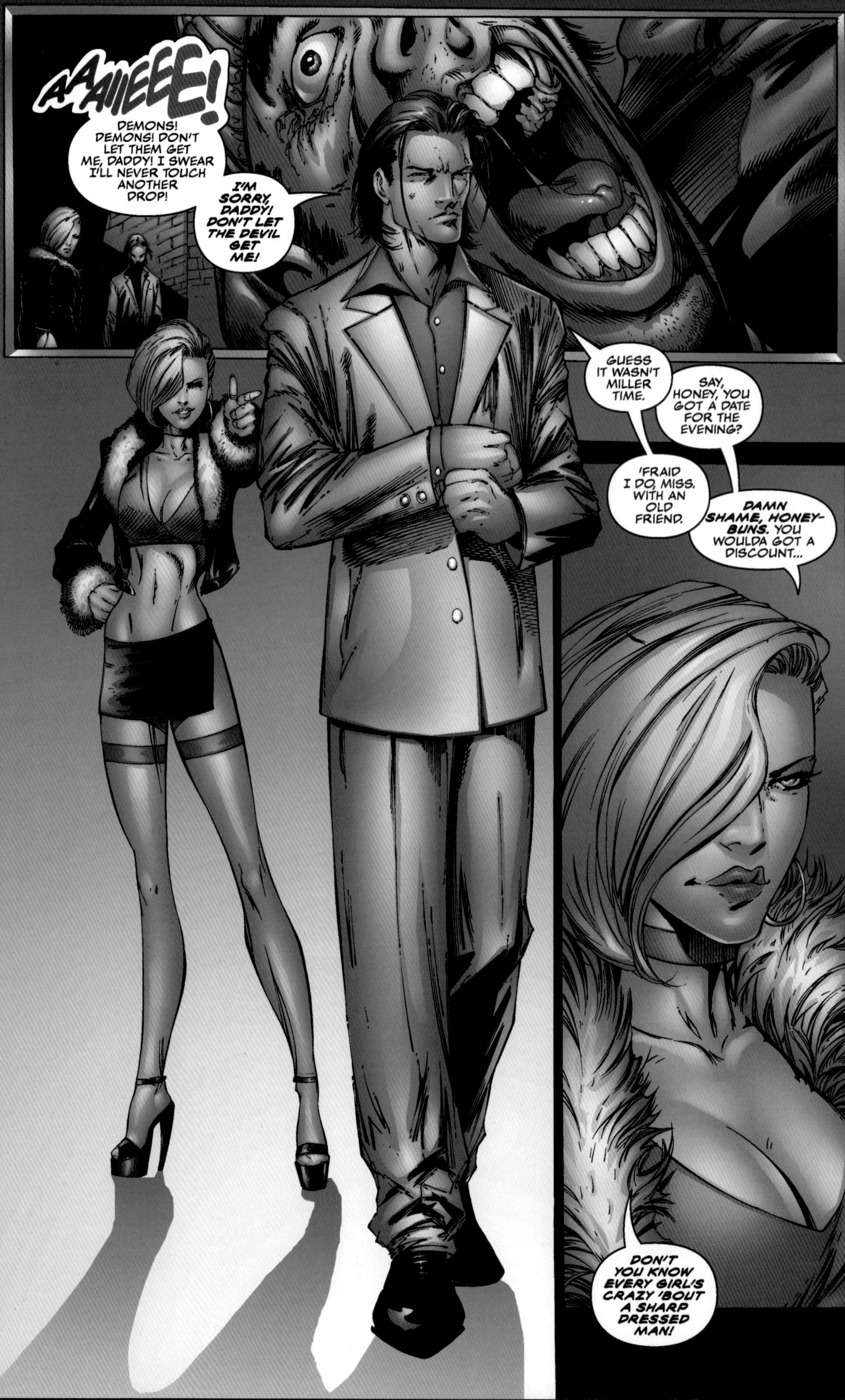
AAAIIEEEE!
DEMONS! DEMONS! DON'T LET THEM GET ME, DADDY! I SWEAR I'LL NEVER TOUCH ANOTHER DROP!
I'M SORRY, DADDY! DON'T LET THE DEVIL GET ME!
GUESS IT WASN'T MILLER TIME.
SAY, HONEY, YOU GOT A DATE FOR THE EVENING?
'FRAID I DO, MISS. WITH AN OLD FRIEND.
DAMN SHAME, HONEY-BUNS. YOU WOULDA GOT A DISCOUNT...
DON'T YOU KNOW EVERY GIRL'S CRAZY 'BOUT A SHARP DRESSED MAN!

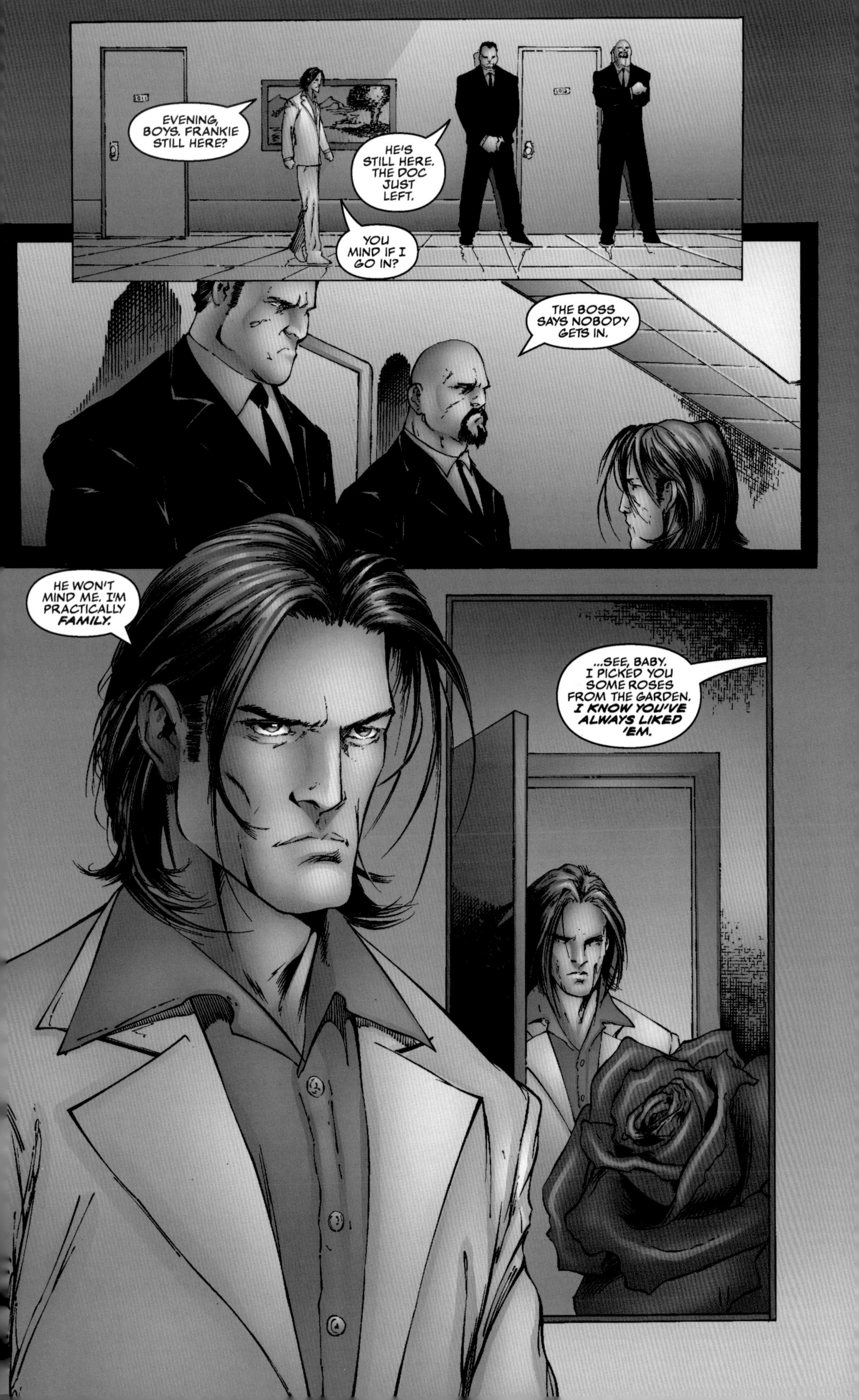

EVENING, BOYS. FRANKIE STILL HERE?
HE'S STILL HERE. THE DOC JUST LEFT.
YOU MIND IF I GO IN?
THE BOSS SAYS NOBODY GETS IN.
HE WON'T MIND ME. I'M PRACTICALLY *FAMILY.*
...SEE, BABY. I PICKED YOU SOME ROSES FROM THE GARDEN. ***I KNOW YOU'VE ALWAYS LIKED 'EM.***

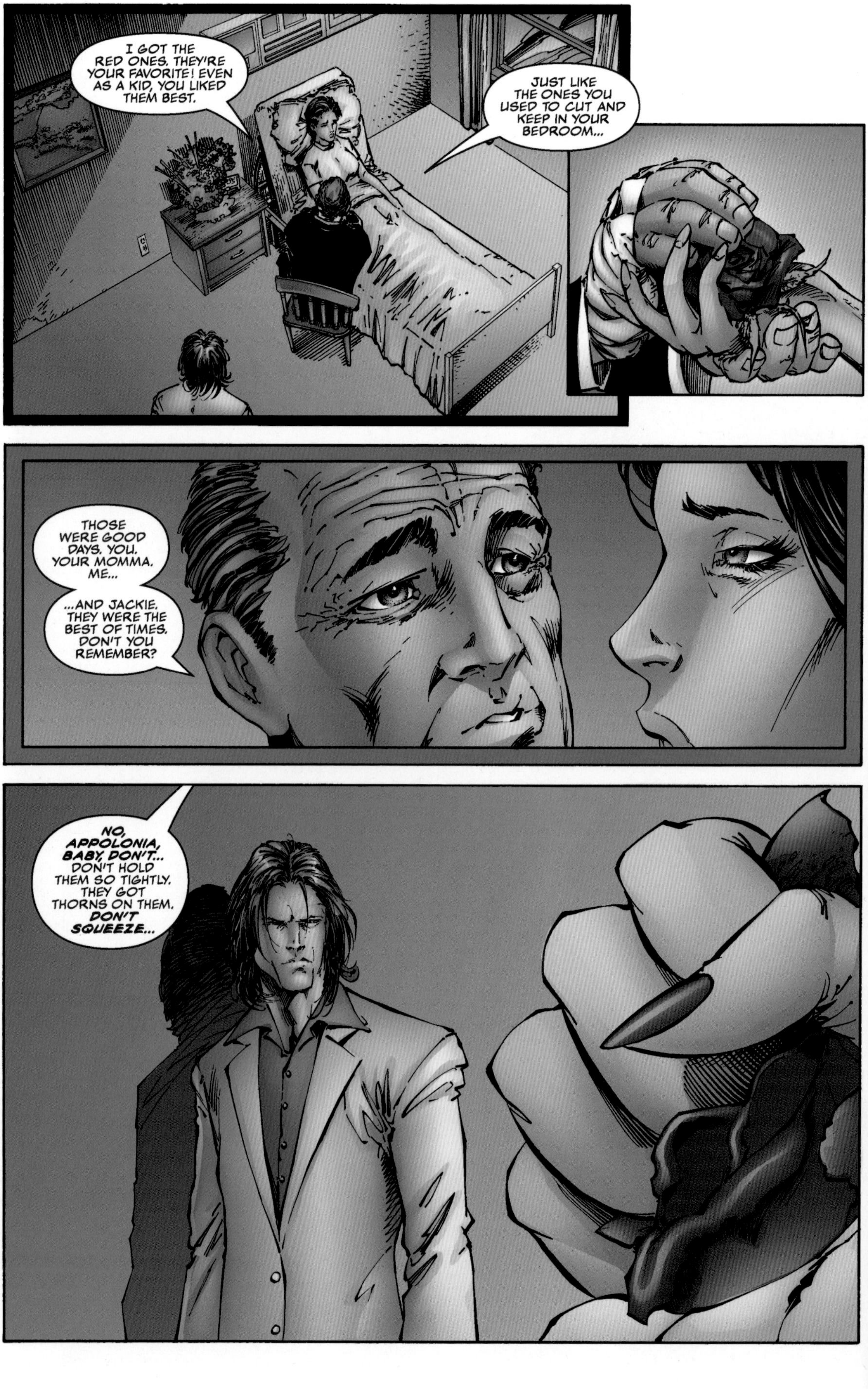
I GOT THE RED ONES. THEY'RE YOUR FAVORITE! EVEN AS A KID, YOU LIKED THEM BEST.
JUST LIKE THE ONES YOU USED TO CUT AND KEEP IN YOUR BEDROOM...
THOSE WERE GOOD DAYS. YOU. YOUR MOMMA. ME...
...AND JACKIE. THEY WERE THE BEST OF TIMES. DON'T YOU REMEMBER?
NO, APPOLONIA, BABY, DON'T... DON'T HOLD THEM SO TIGHTLY. THEY GOT THORNS ON THEM. DON'T SQUEEZE...

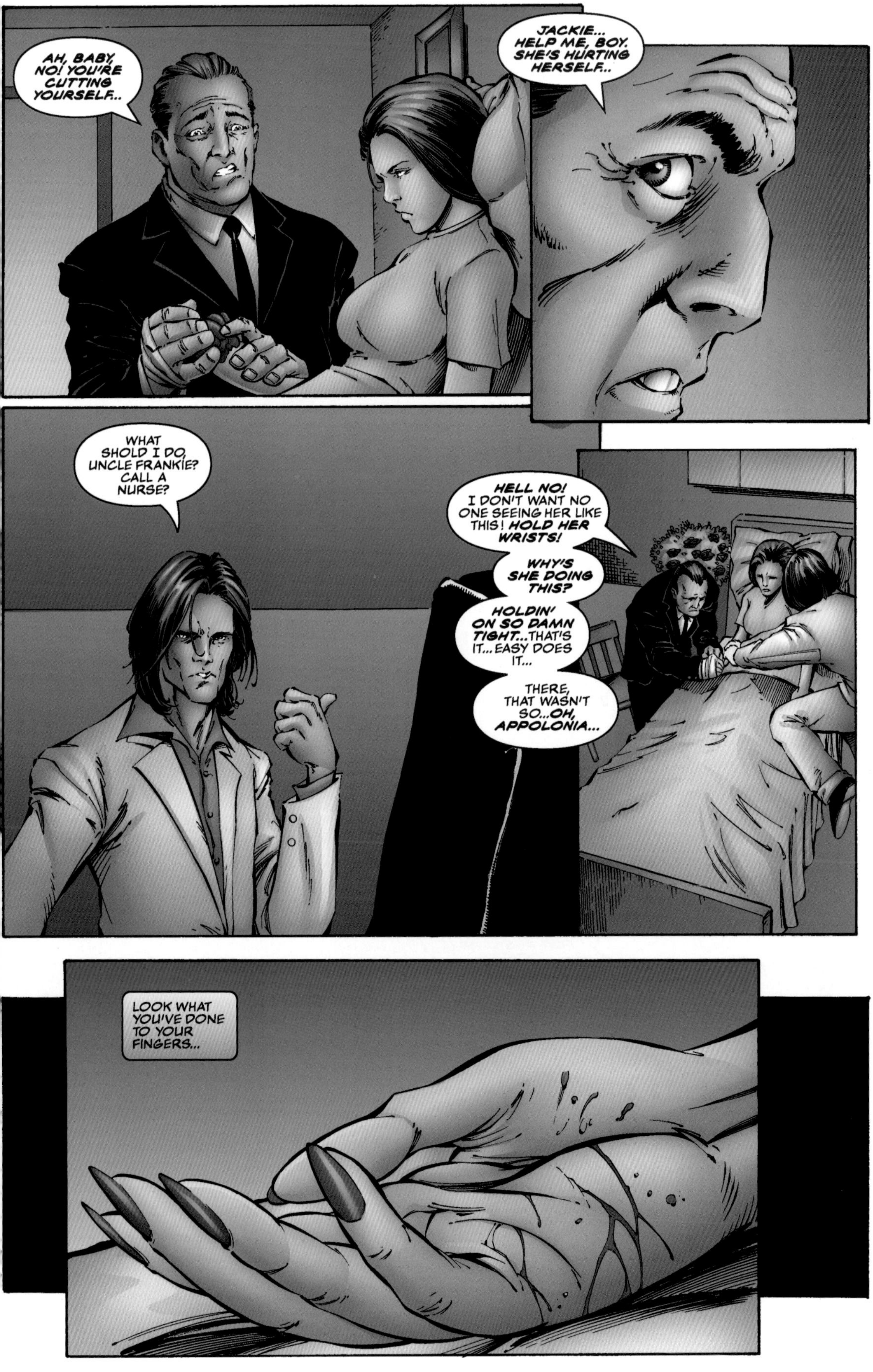
AH, BABY, NO! YOU'RE CUTTING YOURSELF..
JACKIE... HELP ME, BOY. SHE'S HURTING HERSELF..
WHAT SHOLD I DO, UNCLE FRANKIE? CALL A NURSE?
HELL NO! I DON'T WANT NO ONE SEEING HER LIKE THIS! HOLD HER WRISTS!
WHY'S SHE DOING THIS?
HOLDIN' ON SO DAMN TIGHT...THAT'S IT...EASY DOES IT...
THERE, THAT WASN'T SO...OH, APPOLONIA...
LOOK WHAT YOU'VE DONE TO YOUR FINGERS...

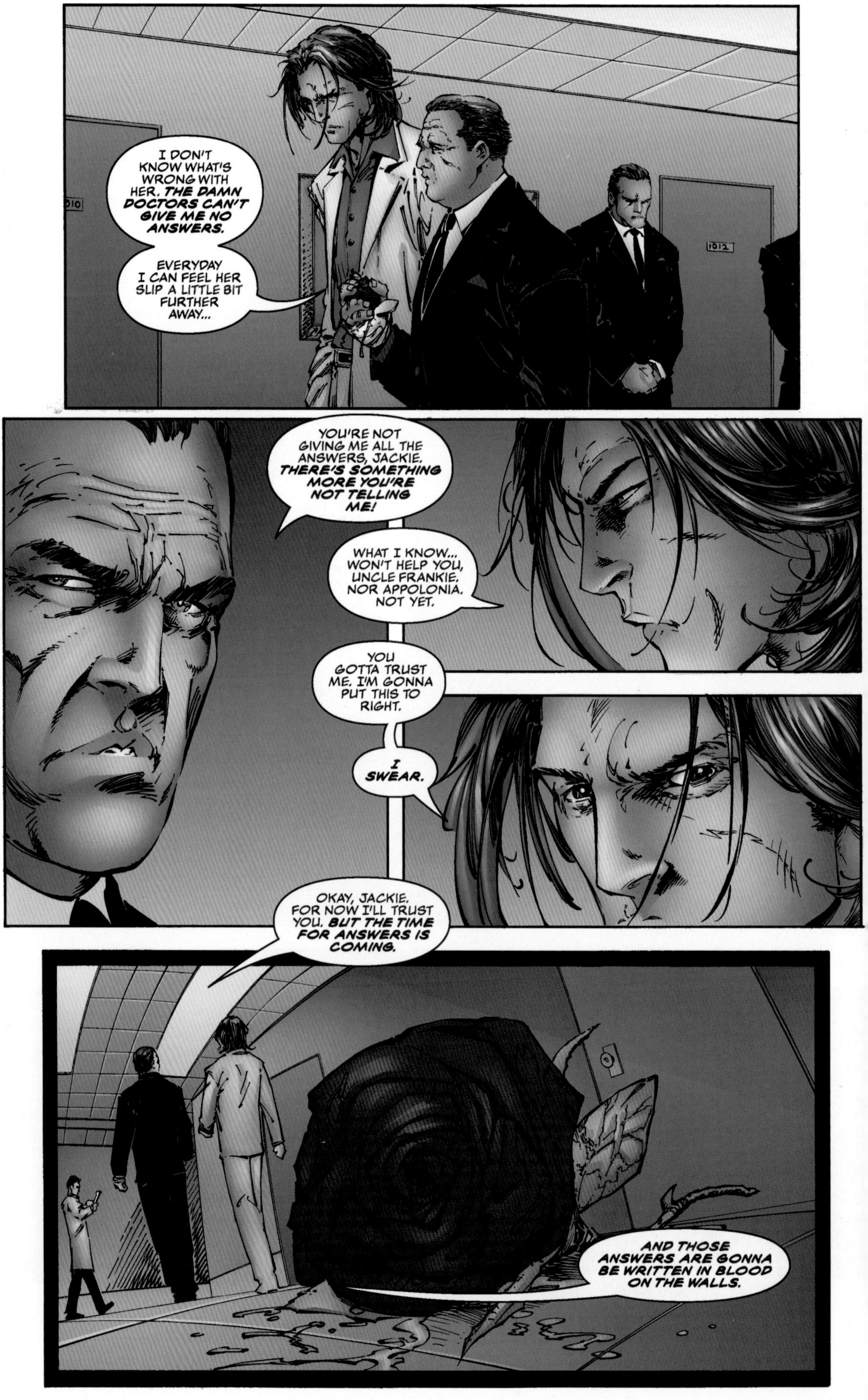
I DON'T KNOW WHAT'S WRONG WITH HER. THE DAMN DOCTORS CAN'T GIVE ME NO ANSWERS.
EVERYDAY I CAN FEEL HER SLIP A LITTLE BIT FURTHER AWAY...
YOU'RE NOT GIVING ME ALL THE ANSWERS, JACKIE. THERE'S SOMETHING MORE YOU'RE NOT TELLING ME!
WHAT I KNOW... WON'T HELP YOU, UNCLE FRANKIE. NOR APPOLONIA. NOT YET.
YOU GOTTA TRUST ME. I'M GONNA PUT THIS TO RIGHT.
I SWEAR.
OKAY, JACKIE. FOR NOW I'LL TRUST YOU. BUT THE TIME FOR ANSWERS IS COMING.
AND THOSE ANSWERS ARE GONNA BE WRITTEN IN BLOOD ON THE WALLS.

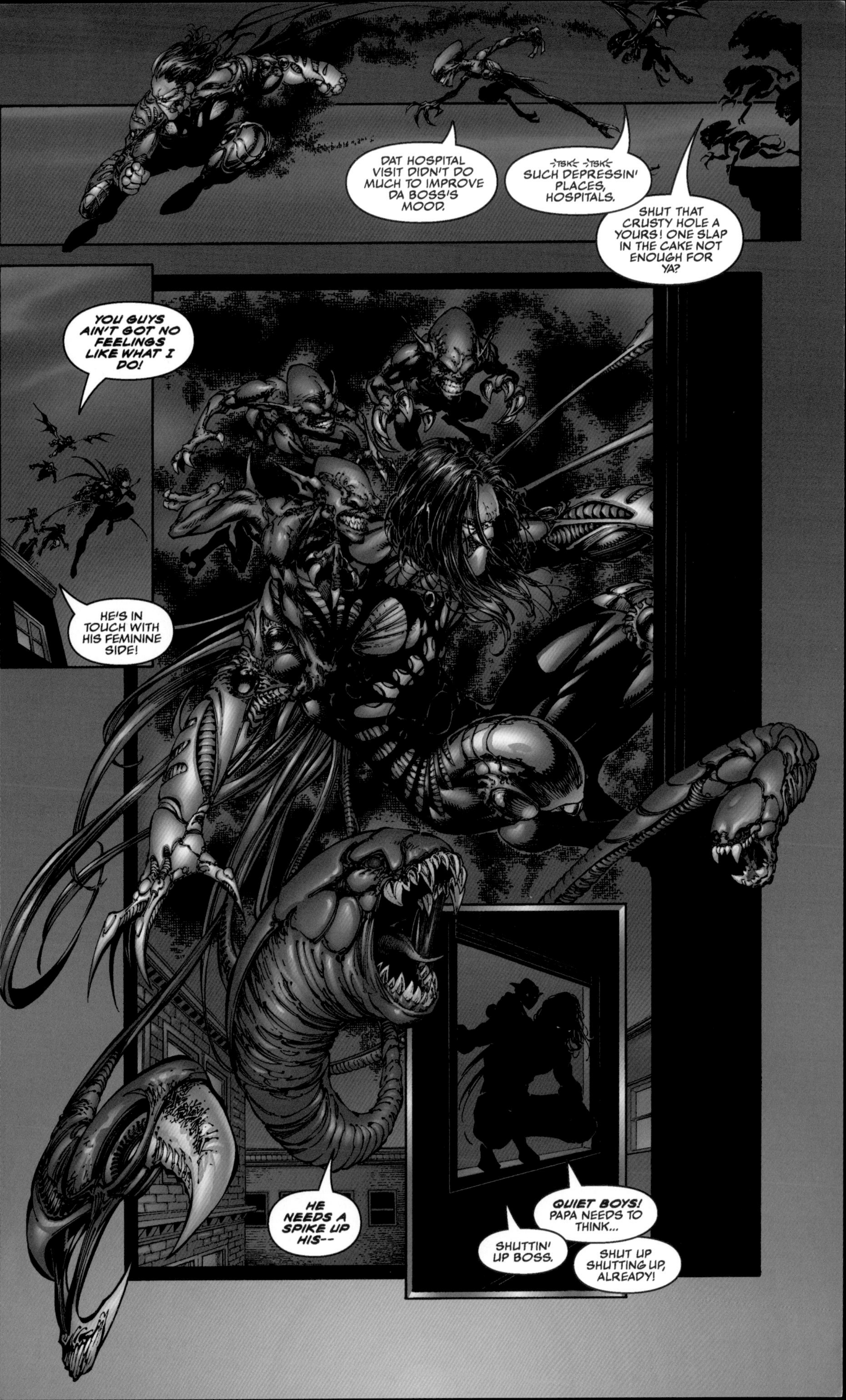
DAT HOSPITAL VISIT DIDN'T DO MUCH TO IMPROVE DA BOSS'S MOOD.
TSK TSK SUCH DEPRESSIN' PLACES, HOSPITALS.
SHUT THAT CRUSTY HOLE A YOURS! ONE SLAP IN THE CAKE NOT ENOUGH FOR YA?
YOU GUYS AIN'T GOT NO FEELINGS LIKE WHAT I DO!
HE'S IN TOUCH WITH HIS FEMININE SIDE!
HE NEEDS A SPIKE UP HIS--
QUIET BOYS! PAPA NEEDS TO THINK...
SHUTTIN' UP BOSS.
SHUT UP SHUTTING UP, ALREADY!

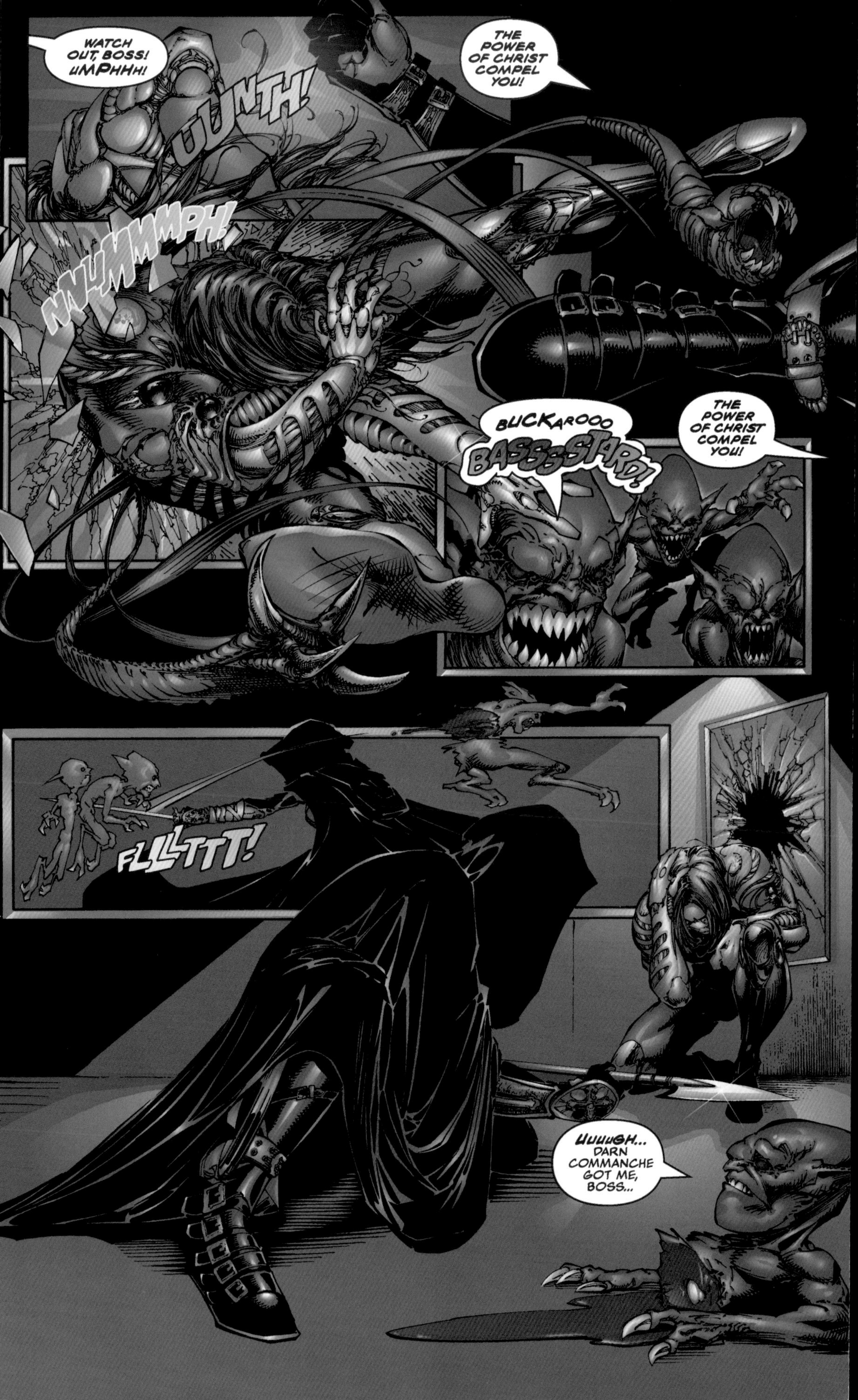

WATCH OUT, BOSS! uMPhhh!
THE POWER OF CHRIST COMPEL YOU!
UUNTH!
NNUMMMPH!
BUCKarooo BASSsSTARD!
THE POWER OF CHRIST COMPEL YOU!
FLLLTTT!
UuuuGH... DARN COMMANCHE GOT ME, BOSS...

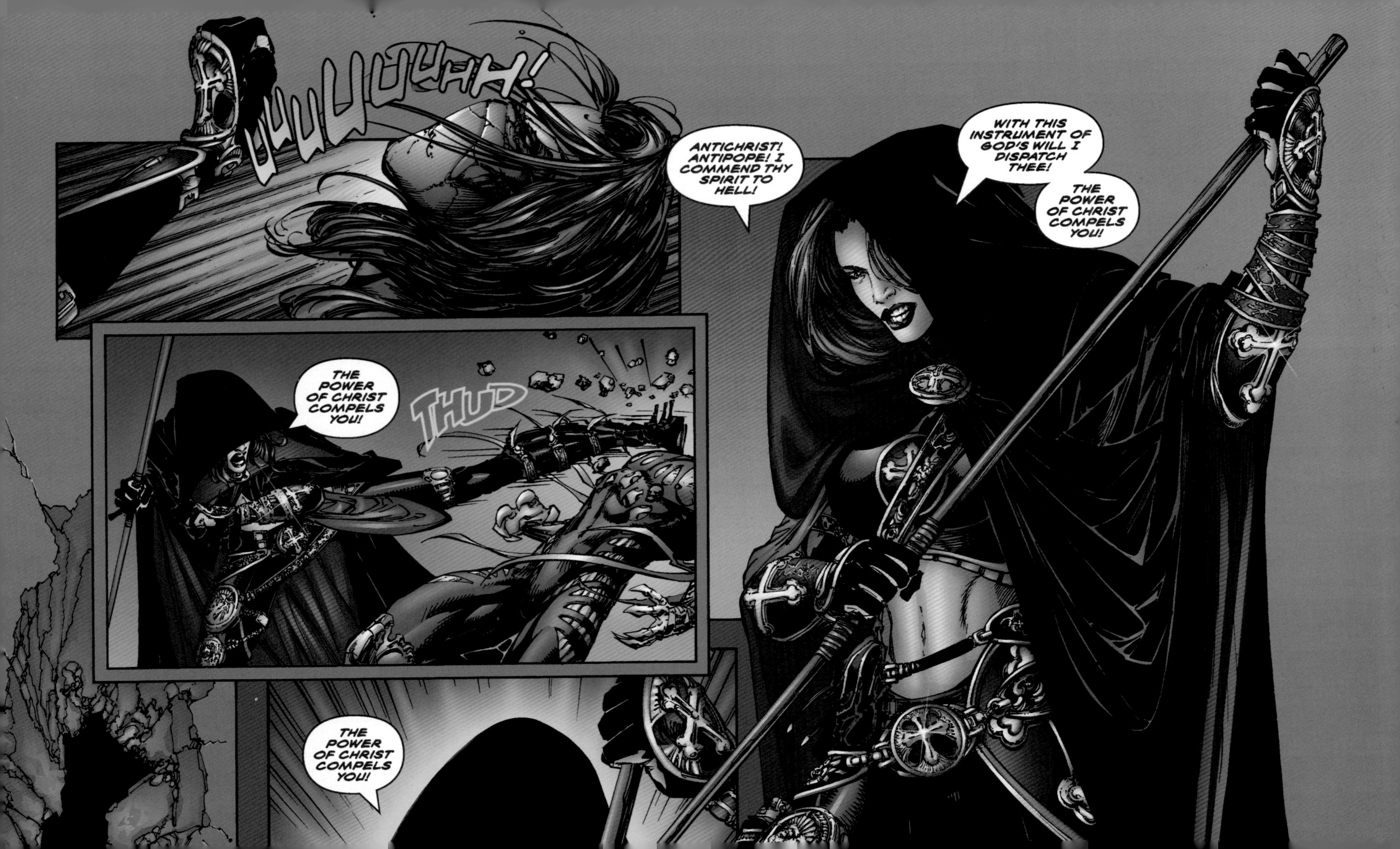
UUUUUUUHH!
THE POWER OF CHRIST COMPELS YOU!
THUD
THE POWER OF CHRIST COMPELS YOU!
ANTICHRIST! ANTIPOPE! I COMMEND THY SPIRIT TO HELL!
WITH THIS INSTRUMENT OF GOD'S WILL I DISPATCH THEE!
THE POWER OF CHRIST COMPELS YOU!

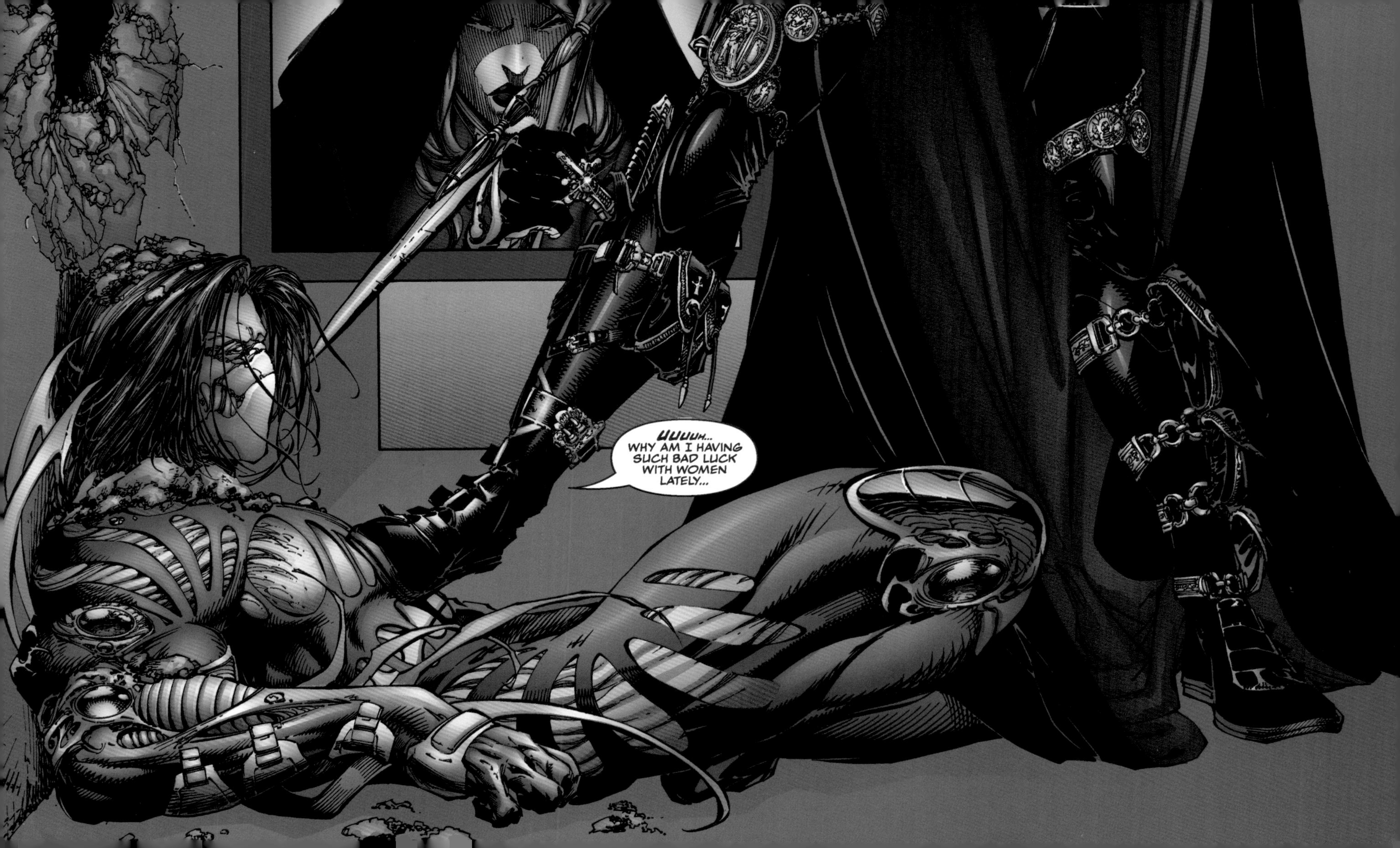
UUUUH... WHY AM I HAVING SUCH BAD LUCK WITH WOMEN LATELY...

The Darkness
ISSUE #16

story by: Malachy Coney
pencils by: Joe Benitez
inks by: Joe Weems V, Victor Llamas,
Marlo Alquiza, Jonathan Sibal
colors by: Matt Nelson, Richard Isanove,
Tyson Wengler, Haberlin Studios
letters by: Dennis Heisler

inks assists by: Marco "Madman" Galli

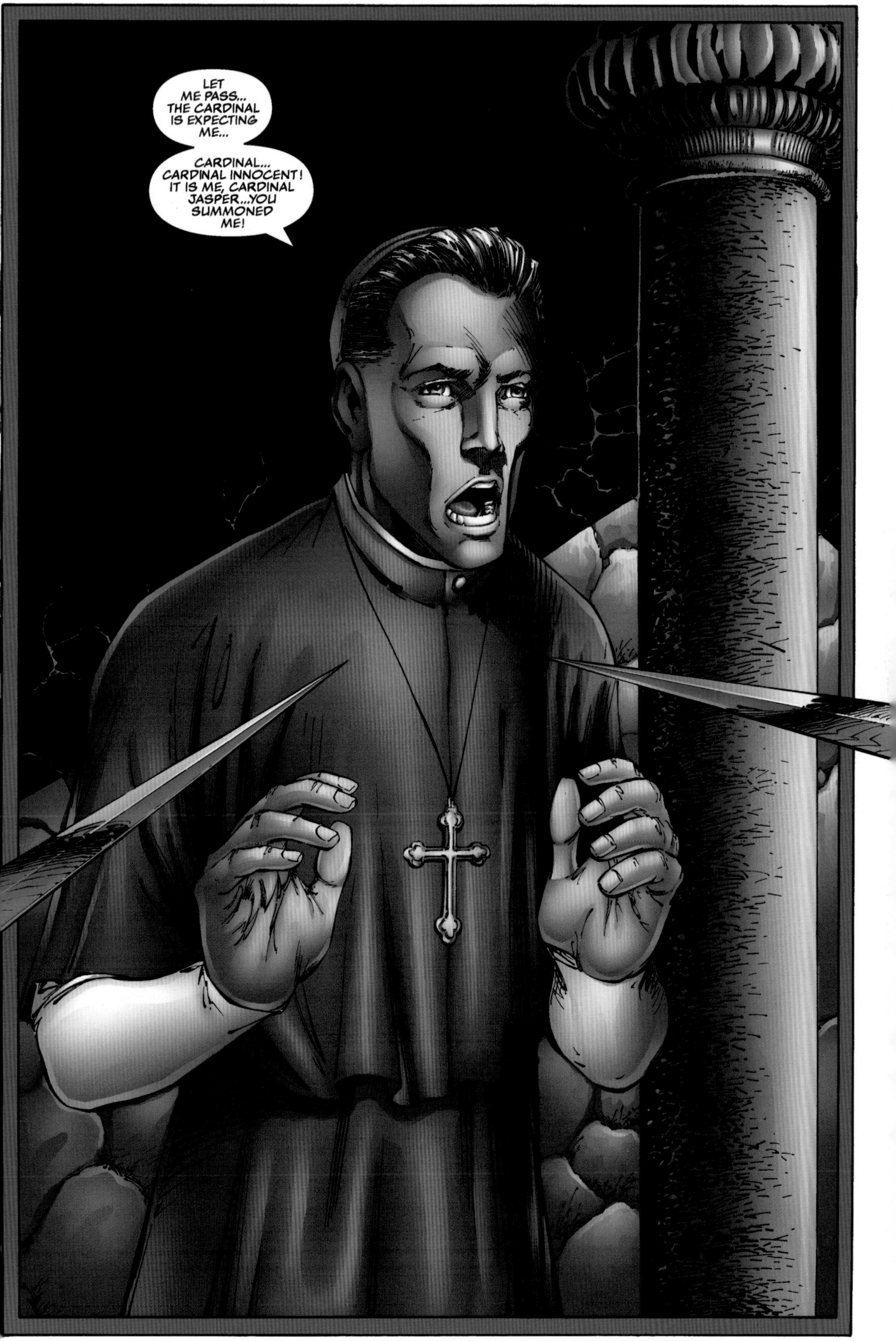
LET ME PASS... THE CARDINAL IS EXPECTING ME...
CARDINAL... CARDINAL INNOCENT! IT IS ME, CARDINAL JASPER...YOU SUMMONED ME!

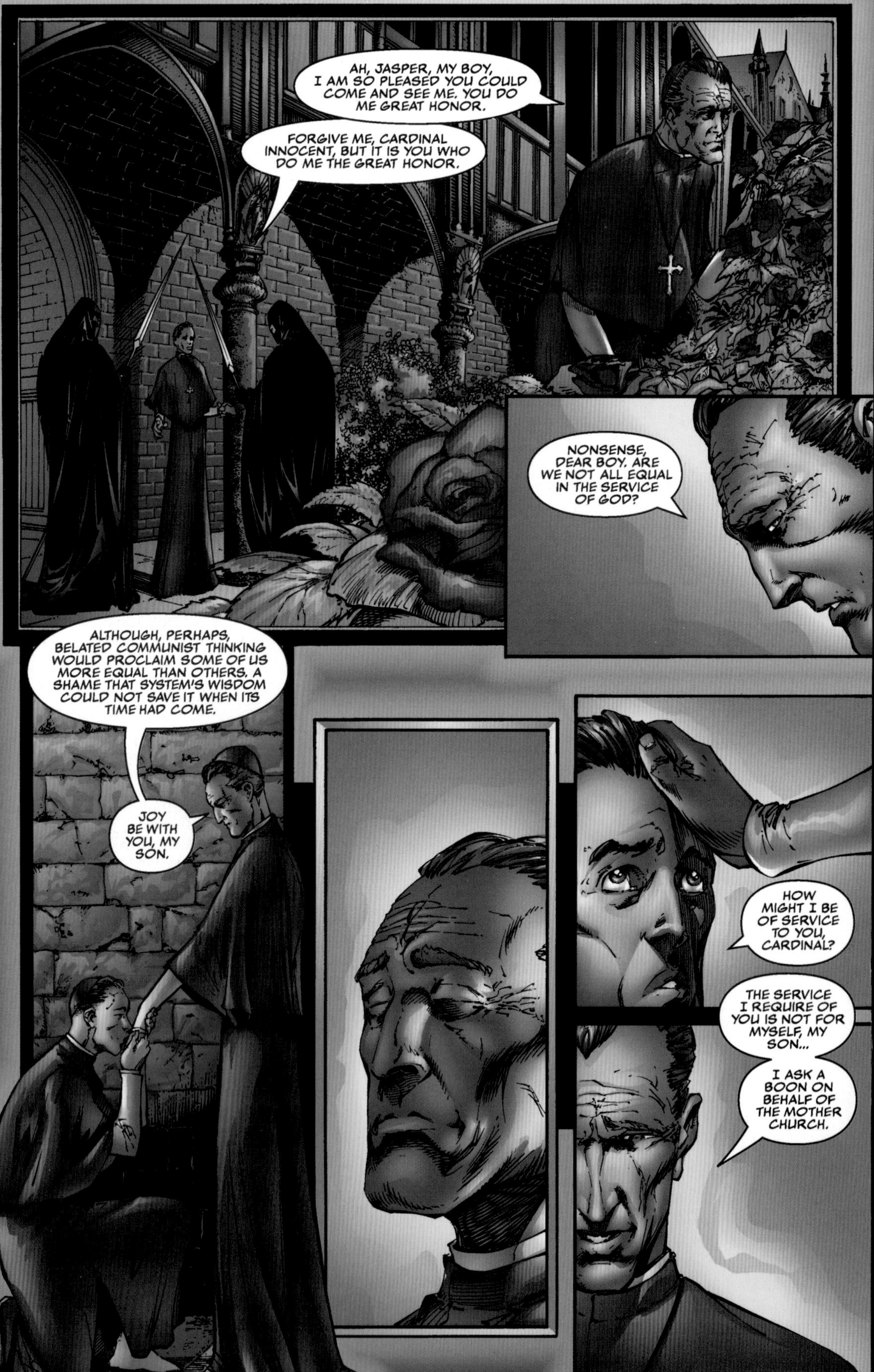
AH, JASPER, MY BOY, I AM SO PLEASED YOU COULD COME AND SEE ME. YOU DO ME GREAT HONOR.
FORGIVE ME, CARDINAL INNOCENT, BUT IT IS YOU WHO DO ME THE GREAT HONOR.
NONSENSE, DEAR BOY. ARE WE NOT ALL EQUAL IN THE SERVICE OF GOD?
ALTHOUGH, PERHAPS, BELATED COMMUNIST THINKING WOULD PROCLAIM SOME OF US MORE EQUAL THAN OTHERS. A SHAME THAT SYSTEM'S WISDOM COULD NOT SAVE IT WHEN ITS TIME HAD COME.
JOY BE WITH YOU, MY SON.
HOW MIGHT I BE OF SERVICE TO YOU, CARDINAL?
THE SERVICE I REQUIRE OF YOU IS NOT FOR MYSELF, MY SON...
I ASK A BOON ON BEHALF OF THE MOTHER CHURCH.

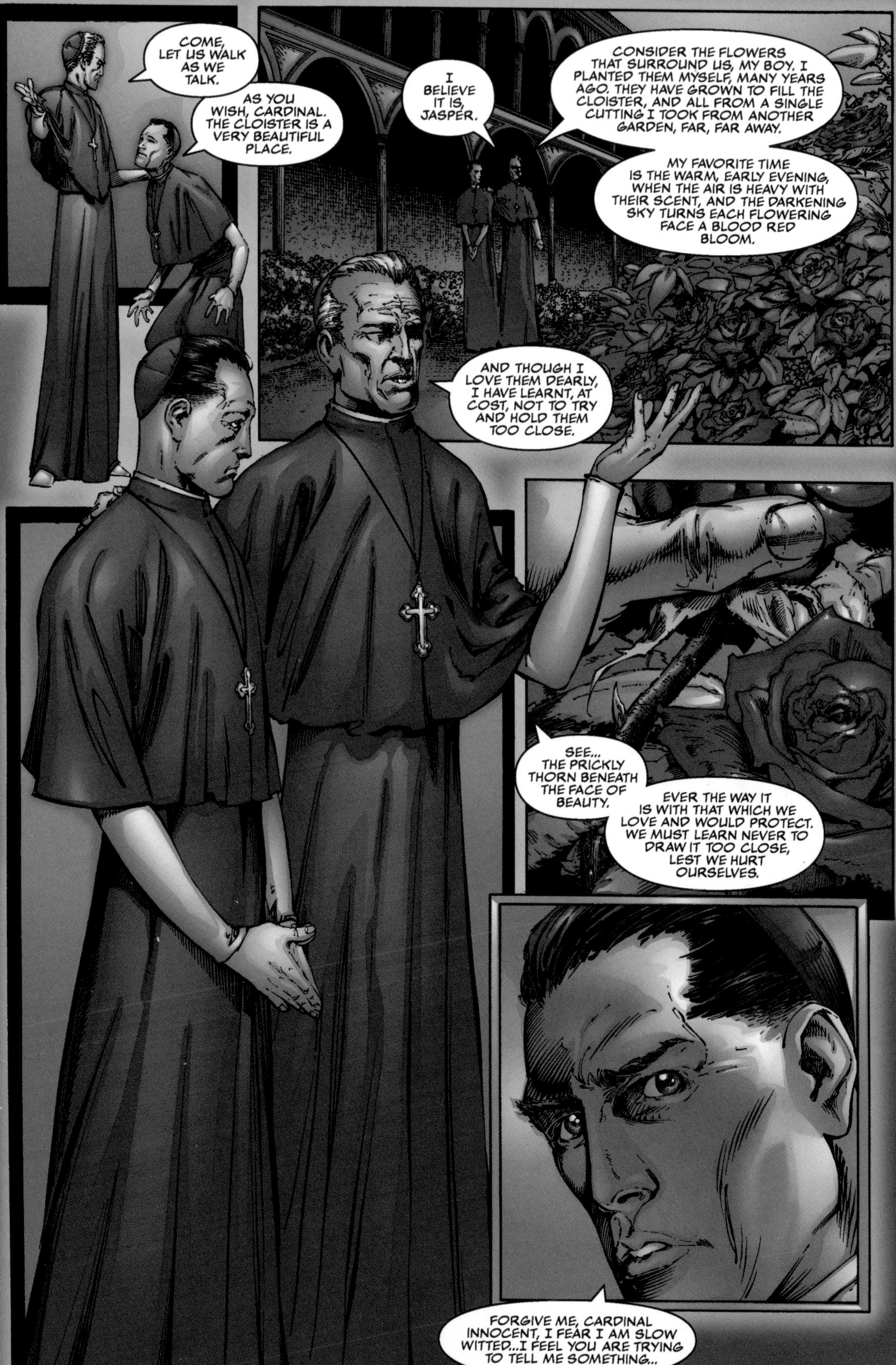
COME, LET US WALK AS WE TALK.
AS YOU WISH, CARDINAL. THE CLOISTER IS A VERY BEAUTIFUL PLACE.
I BELIEVE IT IS, JASPER.
CONSIDER THE FLOWERS THAT SURROUND US, MY BOY. I PLANTED THEM MYSELF, MANY YEARS AGO. THEY HAVE GROWN TO FILL THE CLOISTER, AND ALL FROM A SINGLE CUTTING I TOOK FROM ANOTHER GARDEN, FAR, FAR AWAY.
MY FAVORITE TIME IS THE WARM, EARLY EVENING, WHEN THE AIR IS HEAVY WITH THEIR SCENT, AND THE DARKENING SKY TURNS EACH FLOWERING FACE A BLOOD RED BLOOM.
AND THOUGH I LOVE THEM DEARLY, I HAVE LEARNT, AT COST, NOT TO TRY AND HOLD THEM TOO CLOSE.
SEE... THE PRICKLY THORN BENEATH THE FACE OF BEAUTY.
EVER THE WAY IT IS WITH THAT WHICH WE LOVE AND WOULD PROTECT. WE MUST LEARN NEVER TO DRAW IT TOO CLOSE, LEST WE HURT OURSELVES.
FORGIVE ME, CARDINAL INNOCENT, I FEAR I AM SLOW WITTED...I FEEL YOU ARE TRYING TO TELL ME SOMETHING...

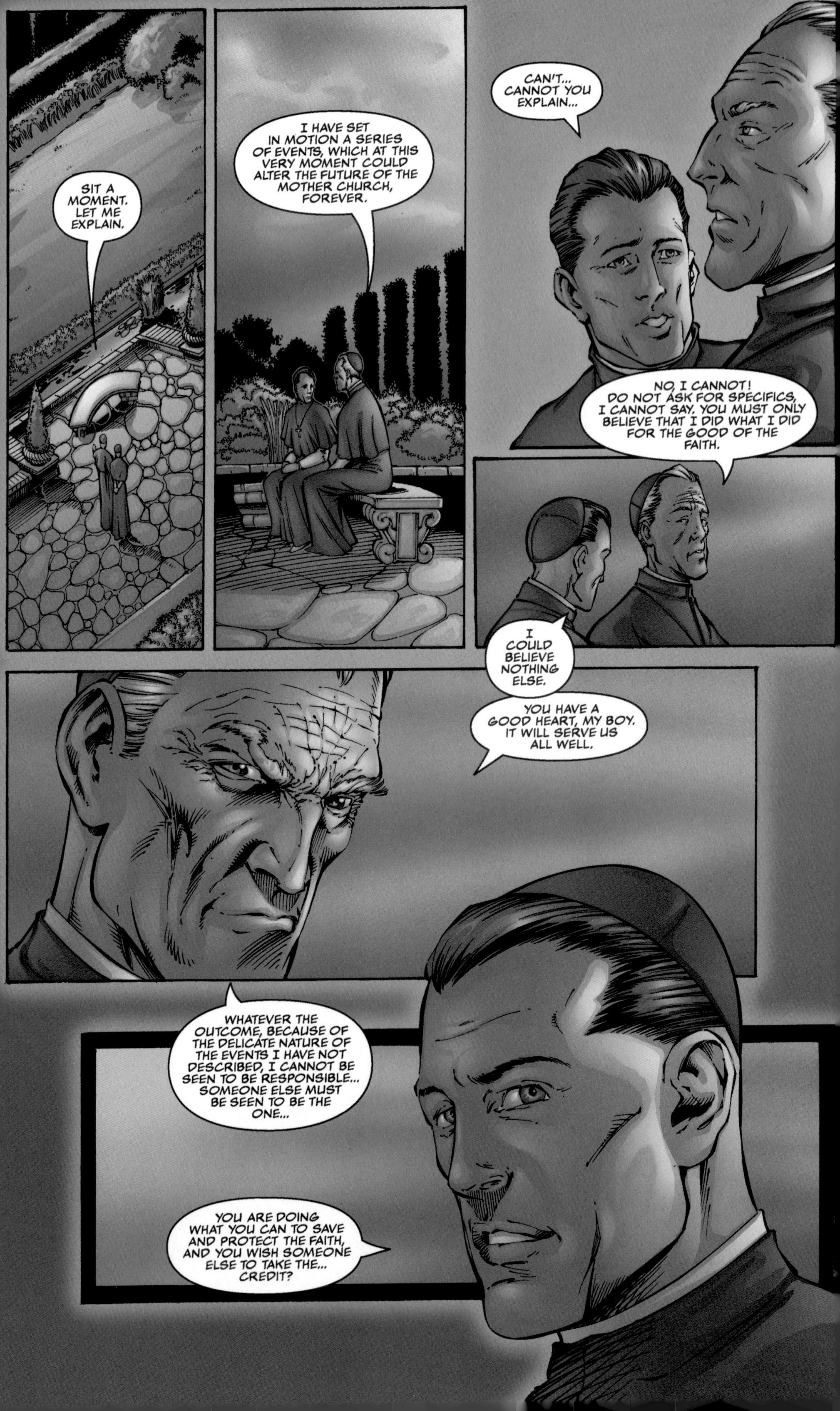
SIT A MOMENT. LET ME EXPLAIN.
I HAVE SET IN MOTION A SERIES OF EVENTS, WHICH AT THIS VERY MOMENT COULD ALTER THE FUTURE OF THE MOTHER CHURCH, FOREVER.
CAN'T... CANNOT YOU EXPLAIN...
NO, I CANNOT! DO NOT ASK FOR SPECIFICS, I CANNOT SAY. YOU MUST ONLY BELIEVE THAT I DID WHAT I DID FOR THE GOOD OF THE FAITH.
I COULD BELIEVE NOTHING ELSE.
YOU HAVE A GOOD HEART, MY BOY. IT WILL SERVE US ALL WELL.
WHATEVER THE OUTCOME, BECAUSE OF THE DELICATE NATURE OF THE EVENTS I HAVE NOT DESCRIBED, I CANNOT BE SEEN TO BE RESPONSIBLE... SOMEONE ELSE MUST BE SEEN TO BE THE ONE...
YOU ARE DOING WHAT YOU CAN TO SAVE AND PROTECT THE FAITH, AND YOU WISH SOMEONE ELSE TO TAKE THE... CREDIT?

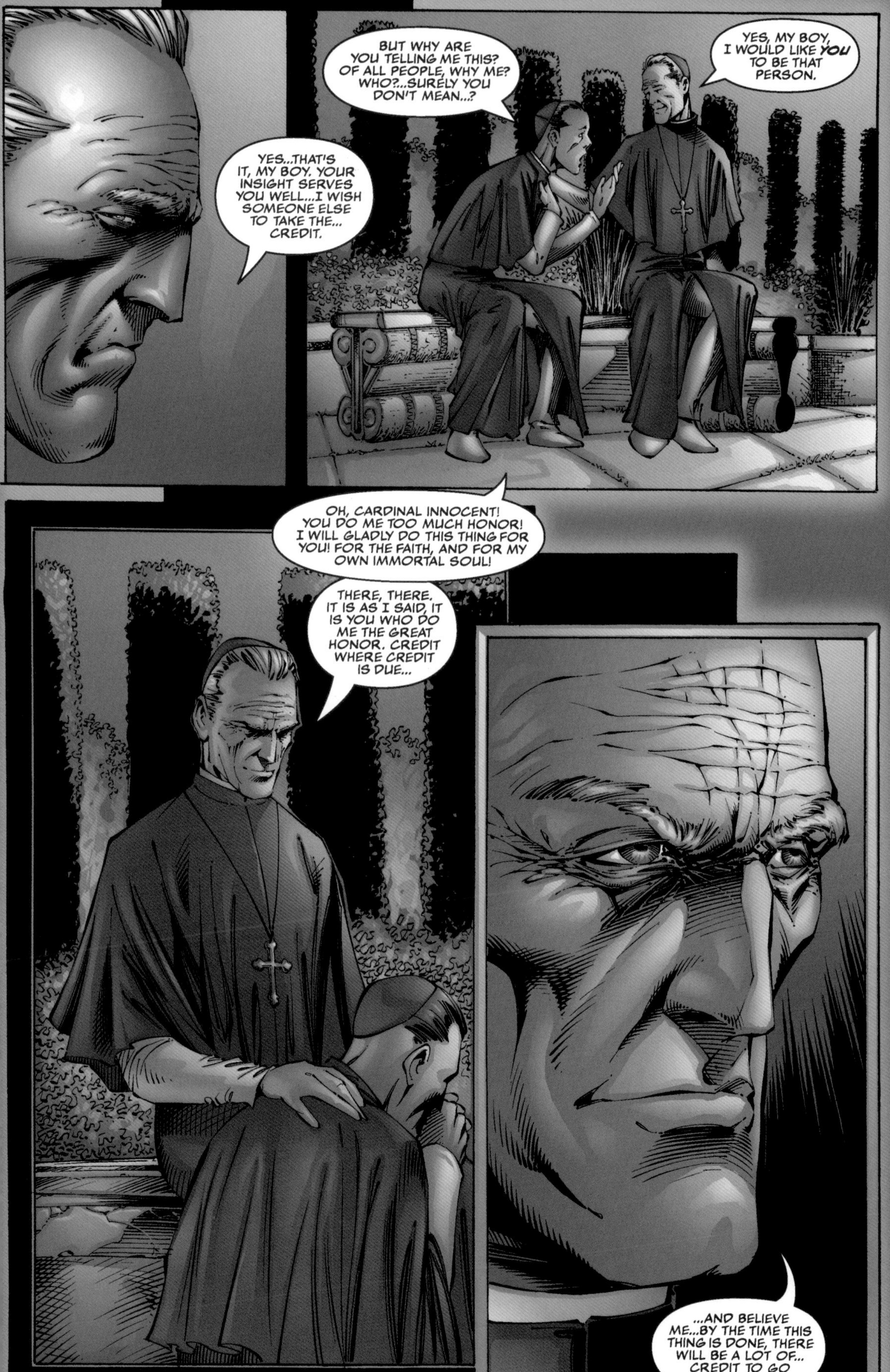
YES...THAT'S IT, MY BOY. YOUR INSIGHT SERVES YOU WELL...I WISH SOMEONE ELSE TO TAKE THE... CREDIT.
BUT WHY ARE YOU TELLING ME THIS? OF ALL PEOPLE, WHY ME? WHO?...SURELY YOU DON'T MEAN...?
YES, MY BOY, I WOULD LIKE YOU TO BE THAT PERSON.
OH, CARDINAL INNOCENT! YOU DO ME TOO MUCH HONOR! I WILL GLADLY DO THIS THING FOR YOU! FOR THE FAITH, AND FOR MY OWN IMMORTAL SOUL!
THERE, THERE. IT IS AS I SAID, IT IS YOU WHO DO ME THE GREAT HONOR. CREDIT WHERE CREDIT IS DUE...
...AND BELIEVE ME...BY THE TIME THIS THING IS DONE, THERE WILL BE A LOT OF... CREDIT TO GO AROUND.

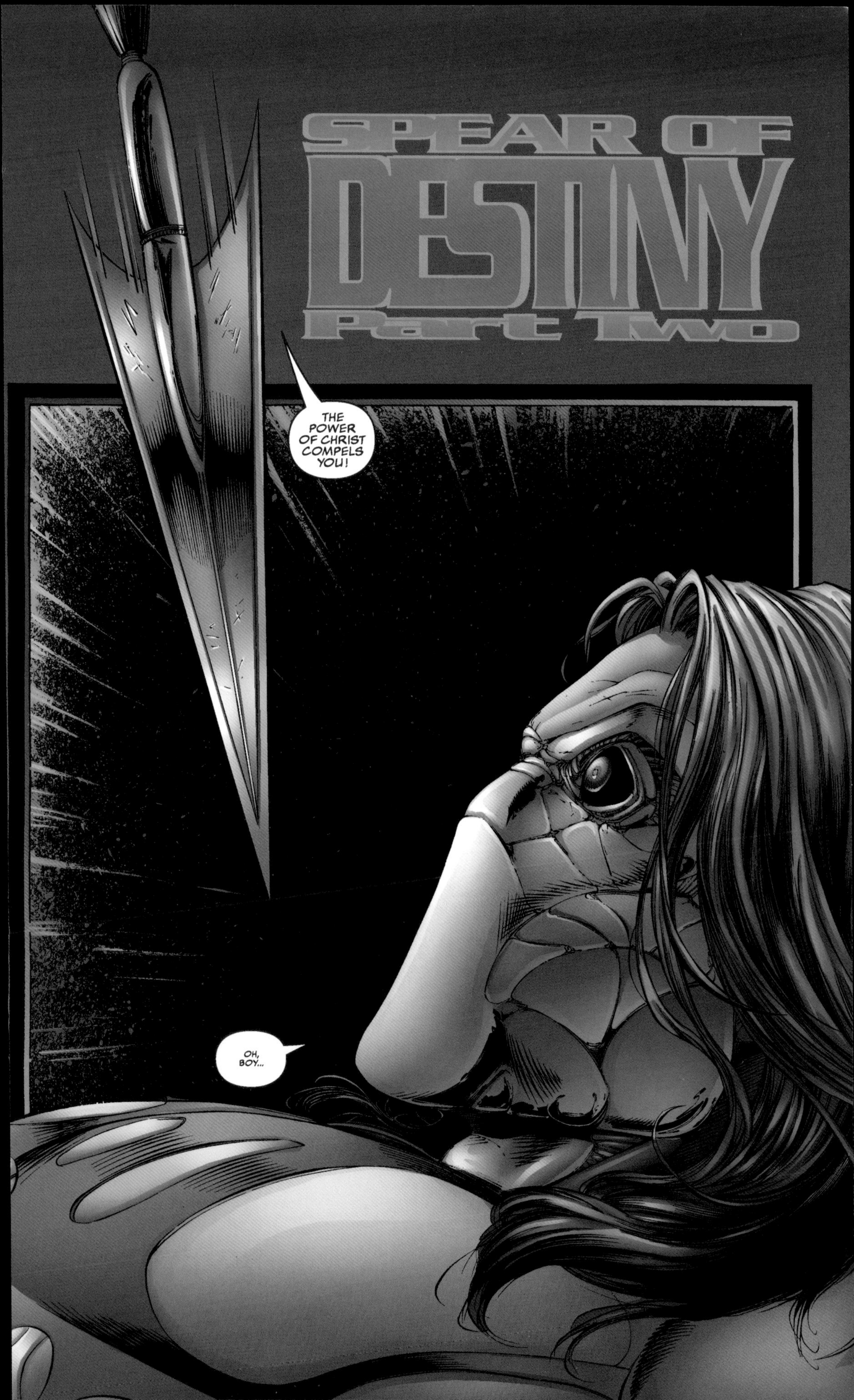
SPEAR OF DESTINY
Part Two
THE POWER OF CHRIST COMPELS YOU!
OH, BOY...

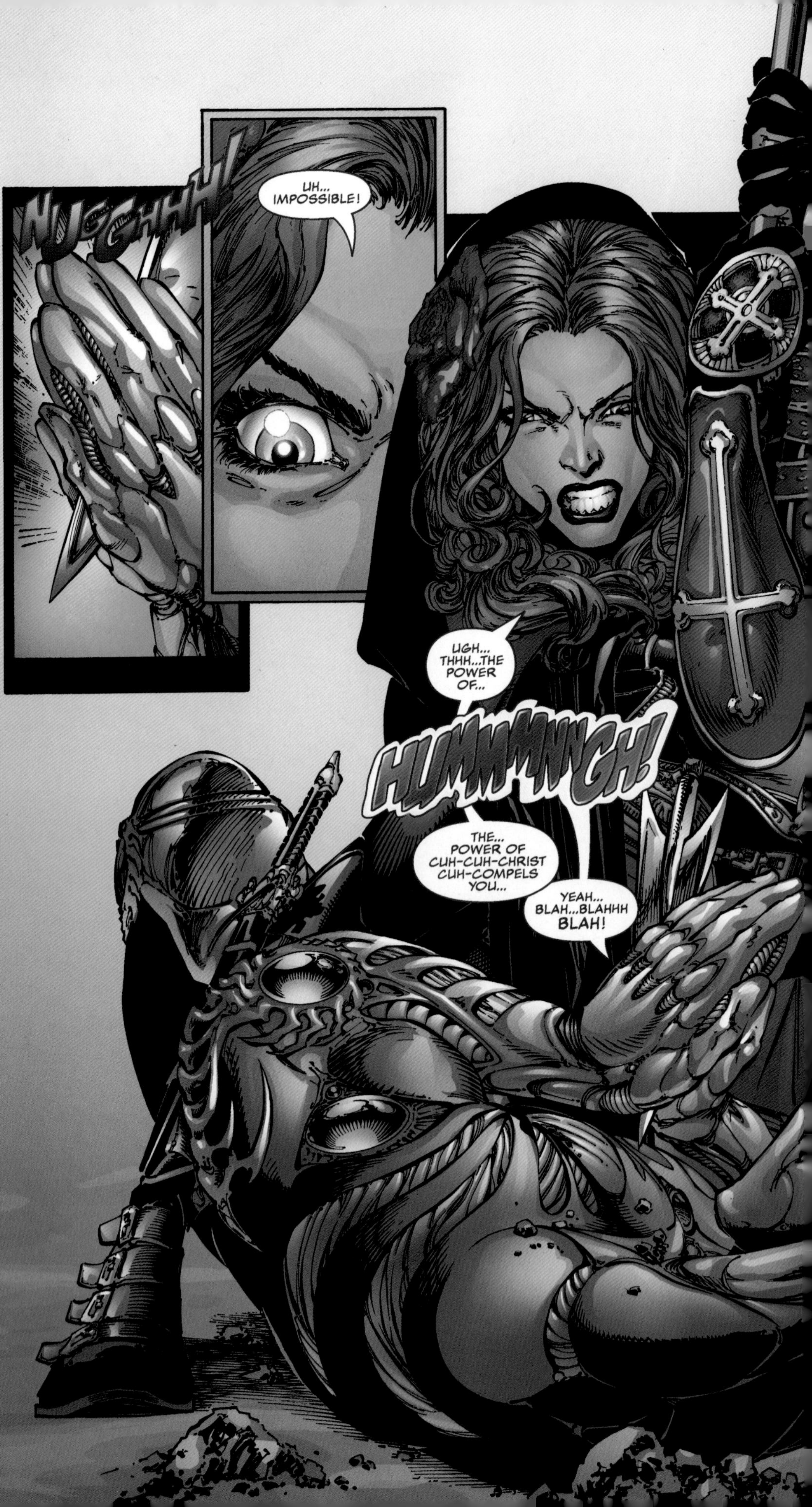
NUGHHH!
UH... IMPOSSIBLE!
UGH... THHH...THE POWER OF...
HUMMMNNGH!
THE... POWER OF CUH-CUH-CHRIST CUH-COMPELS YOU...
YEAH... BLAH...BLAHHH BLAH!

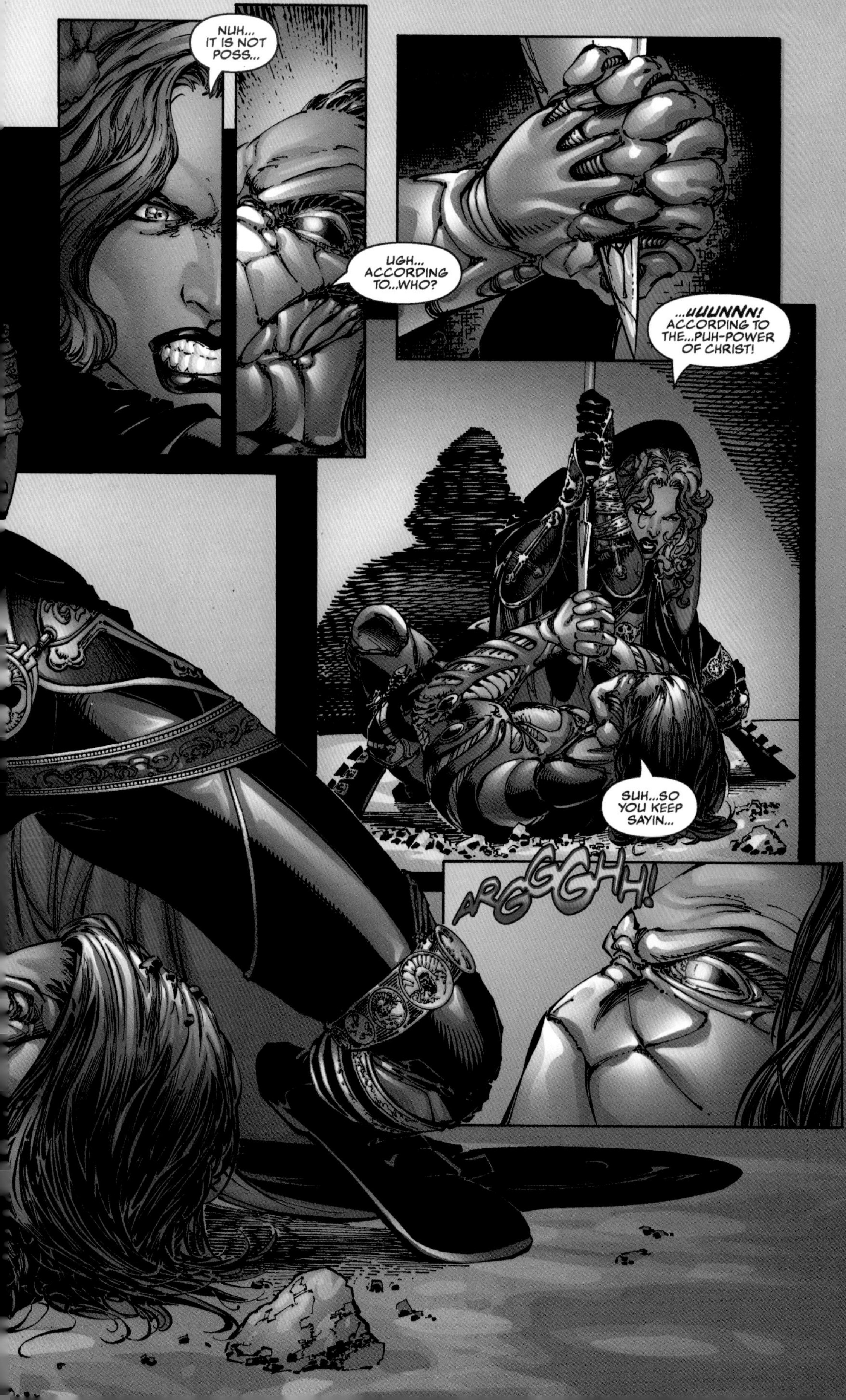
NUH... IT IS NOT POSS...
UGH... ACCORDING TO...WHO?
...UUUNNN! ACCORDING TO THE...PUH-POWER OF CHRIST!
SUH...SO YOU KEEP SAYIN...
ARGGGGHH!

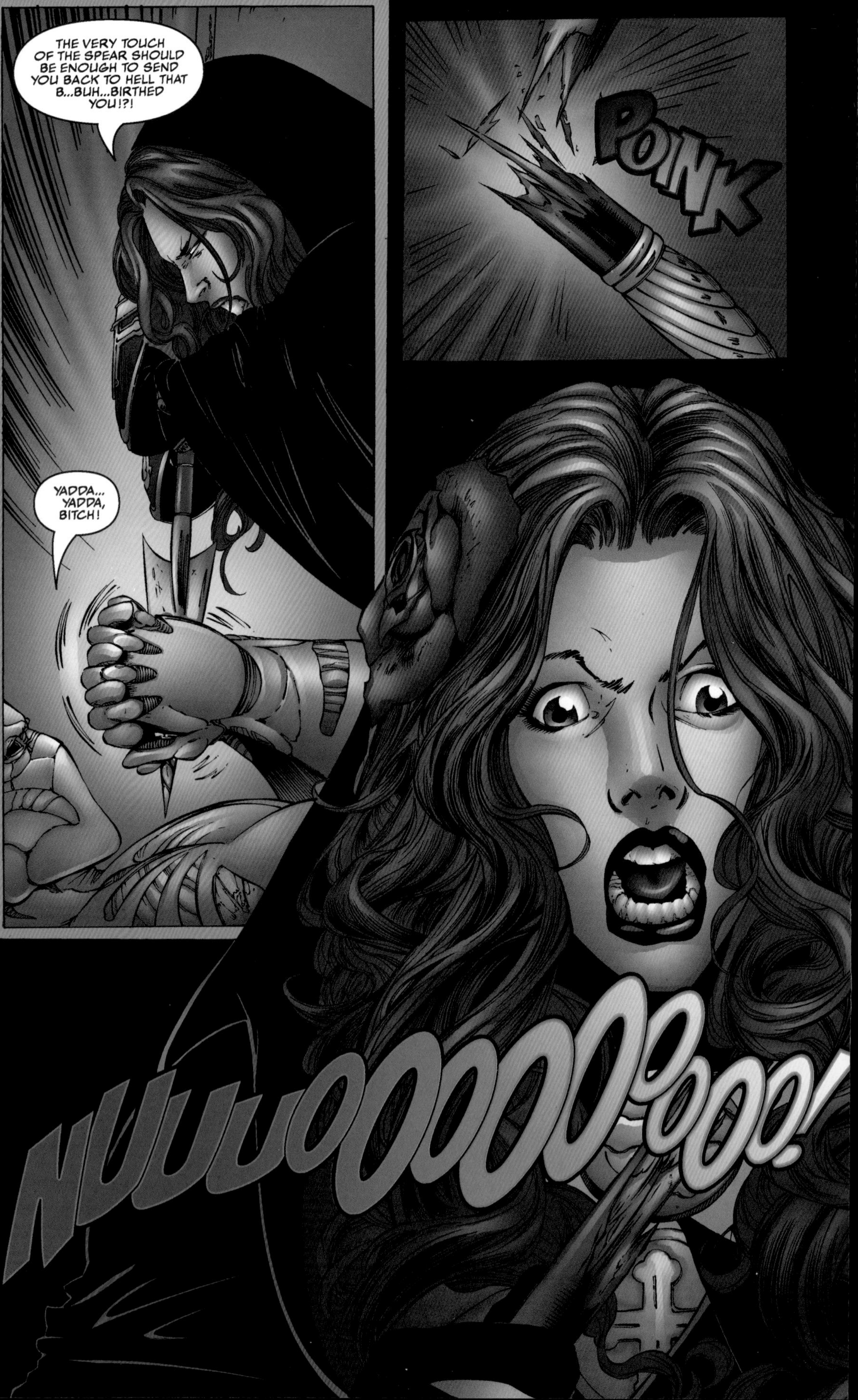
THE VERY TOUCH OF THE SPEAR SHOULD BE ENOUGH TO SEND YOU BACK TO HELL THAT B...BUH...BIRTHED YOU!?!
YADDA... YADDA, BITCH!
POINK
NUUUOOOOOOOOOO!

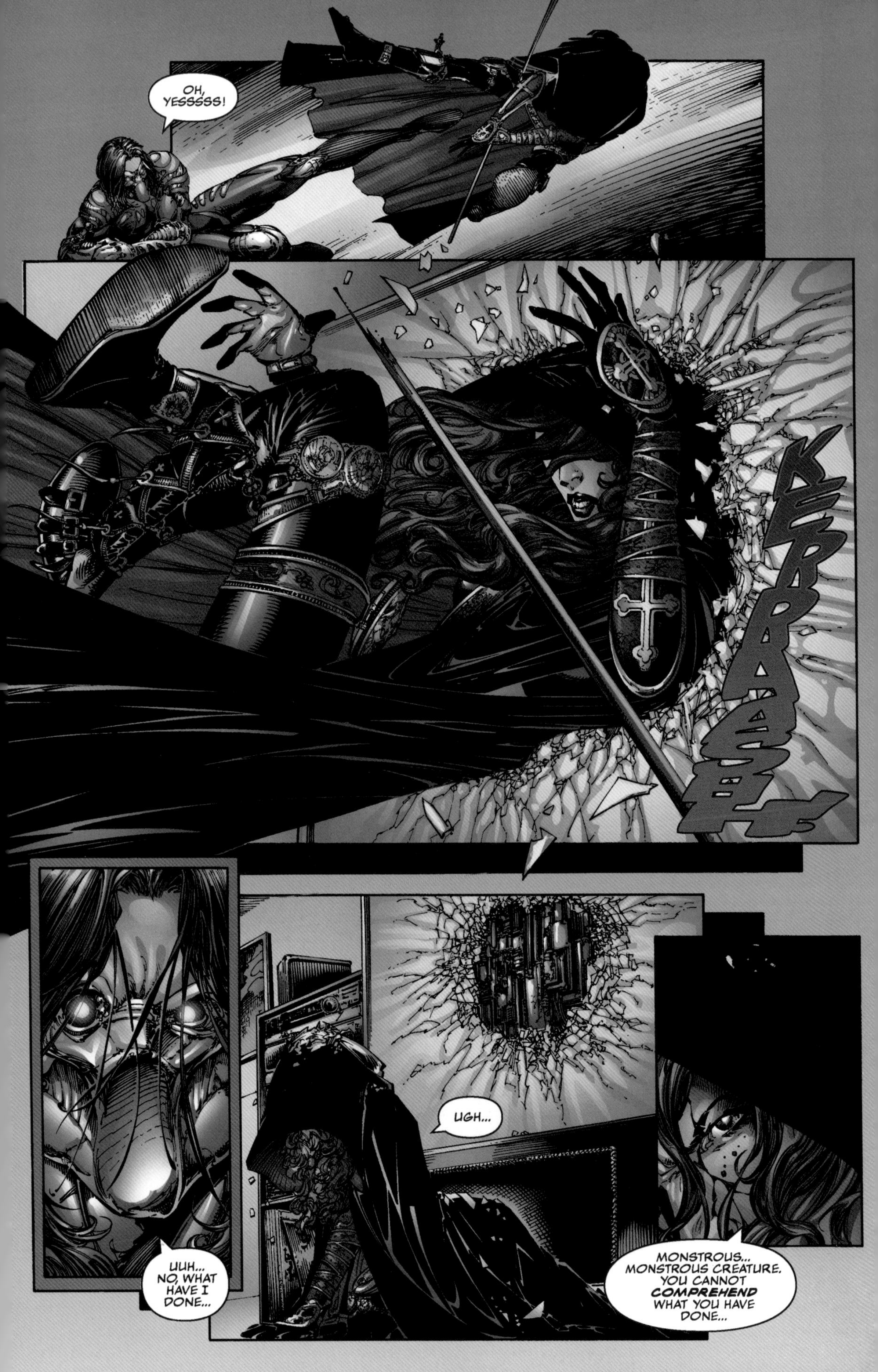

OH, YESSSSS!
KERRAASSH
UUH... NO, WHAT HAVE I DONE...
UGH...
MONSTROUS... MONSTROUS CREATURE. YOU CANNOT COMPREHEND WHAT YOU HAVE DONE...

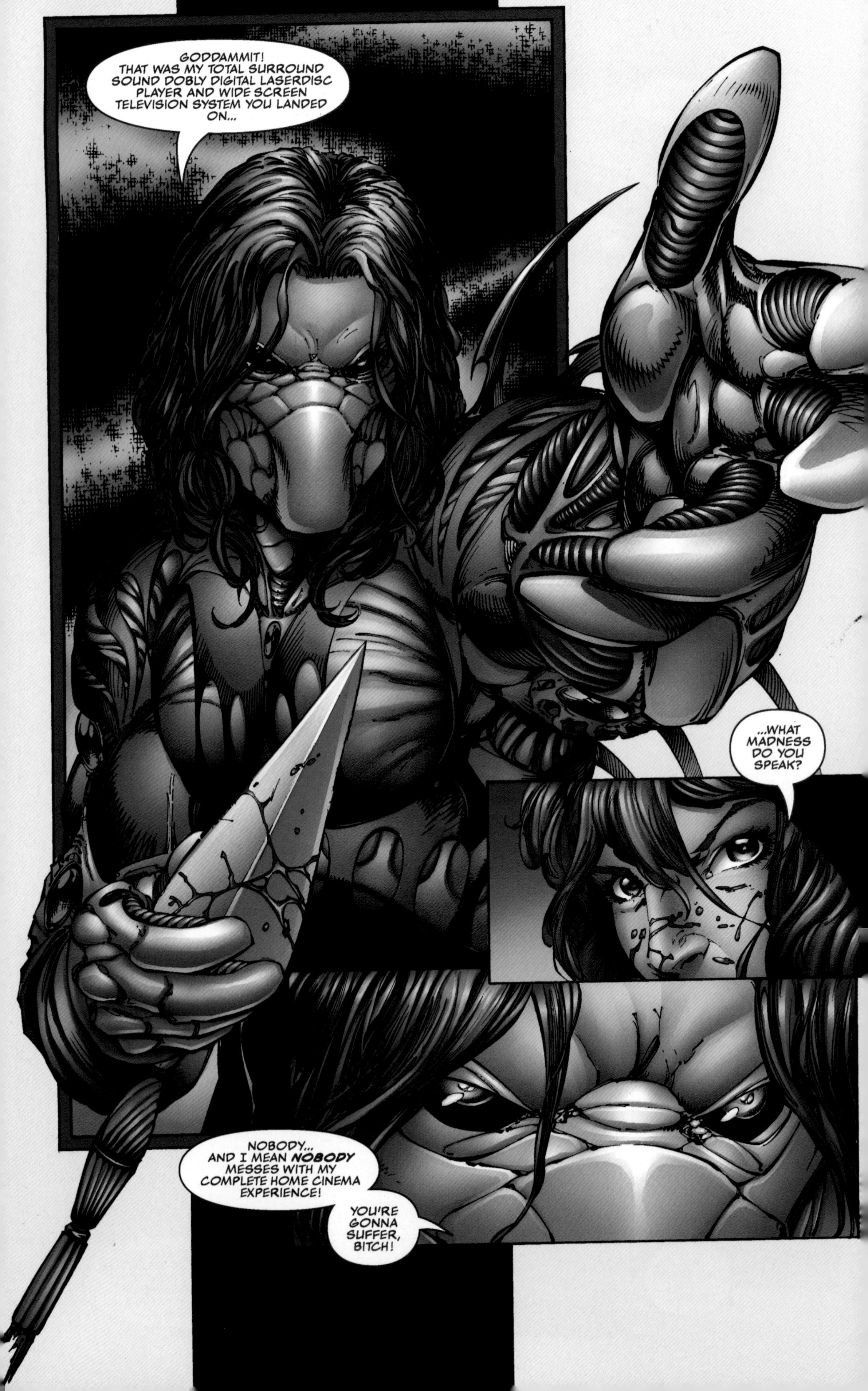
GODDAMMIT! THAT WAS MY TOTAL SURROUND SOUND DOBLY DIGITAL LASERDISC PLAYER AND WIDE SCREEN TELEVISION SYSTEM YOU LANDED ON...
...WHAT MADNESS DO YOU SPEAK?
NOBODY... AND I MEAN NOBODY MESSES WITH MY COMPLETE HOME CINEMA EXPERIENCE!
YOU'RE GONNA SUFFER, BITCH!

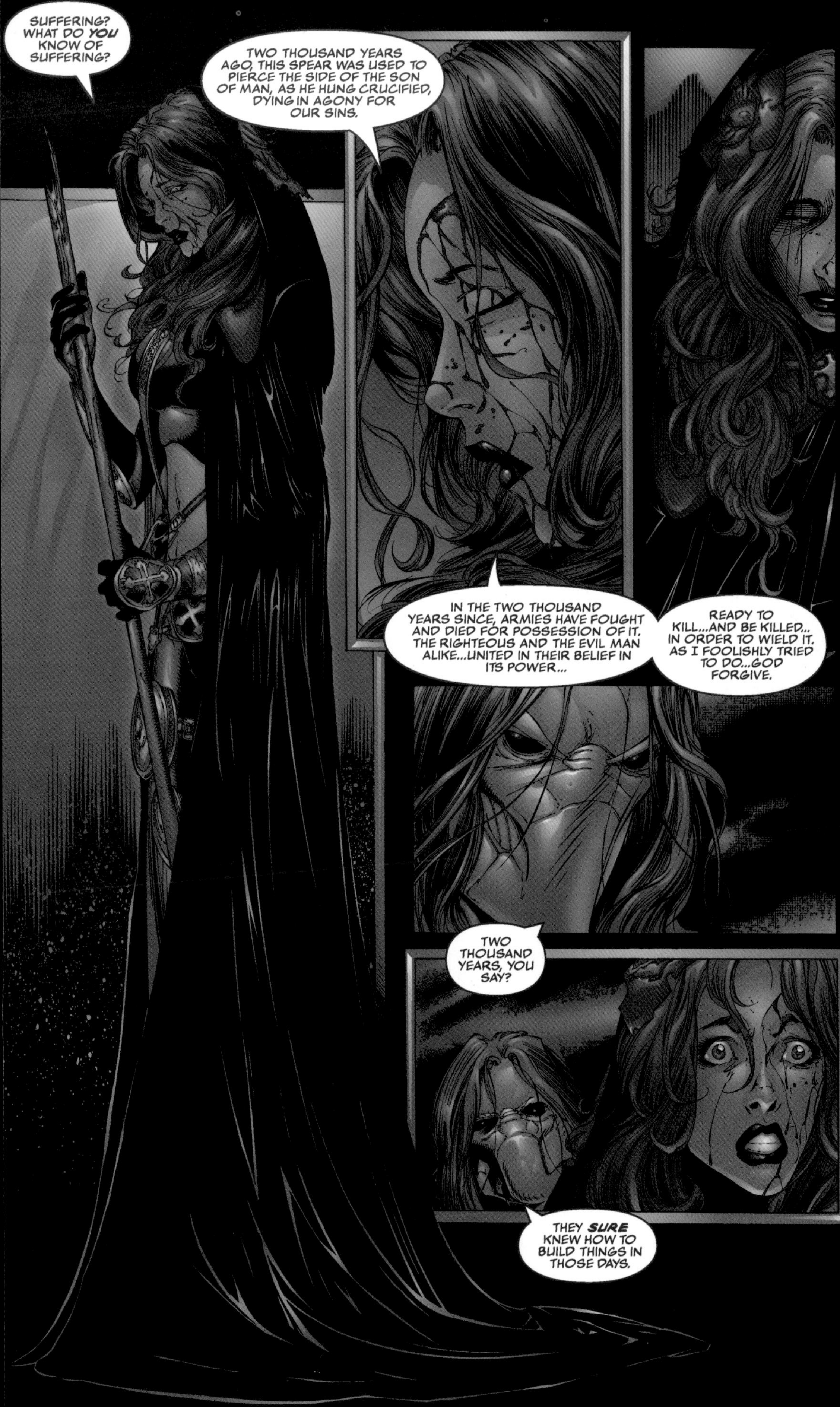
SUFFERING? WHAT DO *YOU* KNOW OF SUFFERING?
TWO THOUSAND YEARS AGO, THIS SPEAR WAS USED TO PIERCE THE SIDE OF THE SON OF MAN, AS HE HUNG CRUCIFIED, DYING IN AGONY FOR OUR SINS.
IN THE TWO THOUSAND YEARS SINCE, ARMIES HAVE FOUGHT AND DIED FOR POSSESSION OF IT. THE RIGHTEOUS AND THE EVIL MAN ALIKE...UNITED IN THEIR BELIEF IN ITS POWER...
READY TO KILL...AND BE KILLED... IN ORDER TO WIELD IT. AS I FOOLISHLY TRIED TO DO...GOD FORGIVE.
TWO THOUSAND YEARS, YOU SAY?
THEY *SURE* KNEW HOW TO BUILD THINGS IN THOSE DAYS.

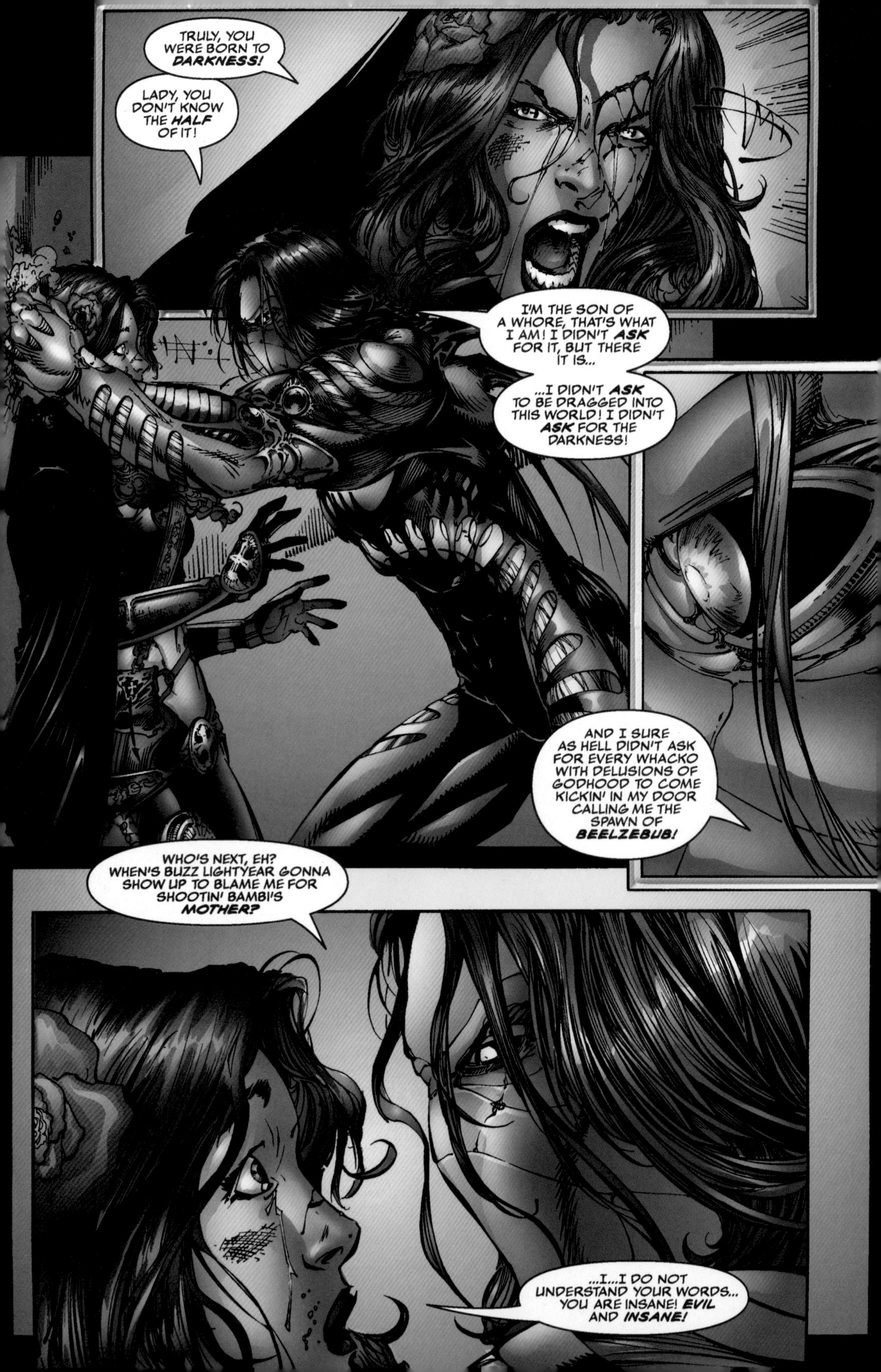
TRULY, YOU WERE BORN TO DARKNESS!
LADY, YOU DON'T KNOW THE HALF OF IT!
I'M THE SON OF A WHORE, THAT'S WHAT I AM! I DIDN'T ASK FOR IT, BUT THERE IT IS...
...I DIDN'T ASK TO BE DRAGGED INTO THIS WORLD! I DIDN'T ASK FOR THE DARKNESS!
AND I SURE AS HELL DIDN'T ASK FOR EVERY WHACKO WITH DELUSIONS OF GODHOOD TO COME KICKIN' IN MY DOOR CALLING ME THE SPAWN OF BEELZEBUB!
WHO'S NEXT, EH? WHEN'S BUZZ LIGHTYEAR GONNA SHOW UP TO BLAME ME FOR SHOOTIN' BAMBI'S MOTHER?
...I...I DO NOT UNDERSTAND YOUR WORDS... YOU ARE INSANE! EVIL AND INSANE!

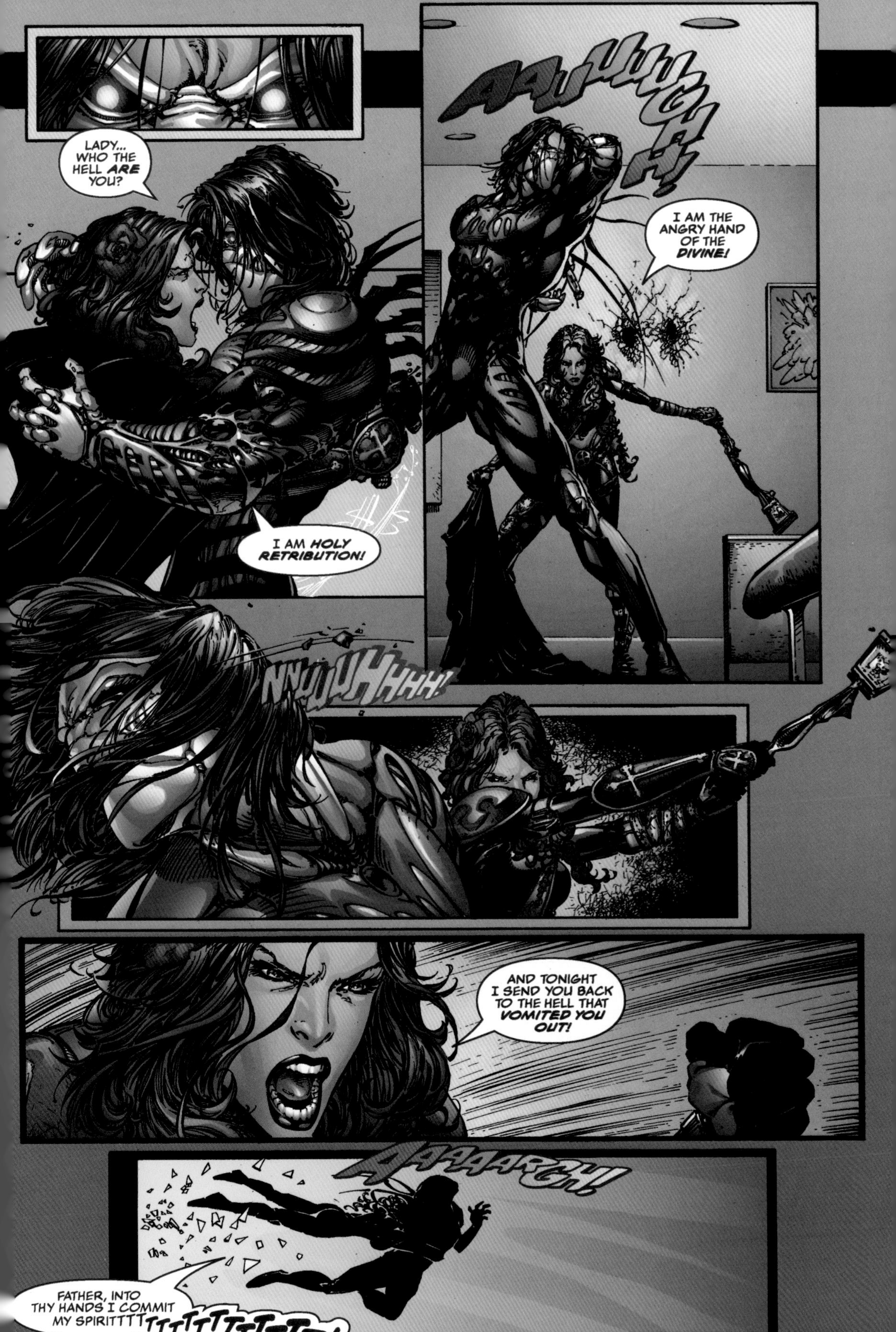
AAUUUUGHH!
LADY... WHO THE HELL *ARE* YOU?
I AM THE ANGRY HAND OF THE *DIVINE!*
I AM *HOLY RETRIBUTION!*
NNUUUHHHH!
AND TONIGHT I SEND YOU BACK TO THE HELL THAT *VOMITED YOU OUT!*
AAAAARGH!
FATHER, INTO THY HANDS I COMMIT MY SPIRITTTTTTTTTTTTTTTT!

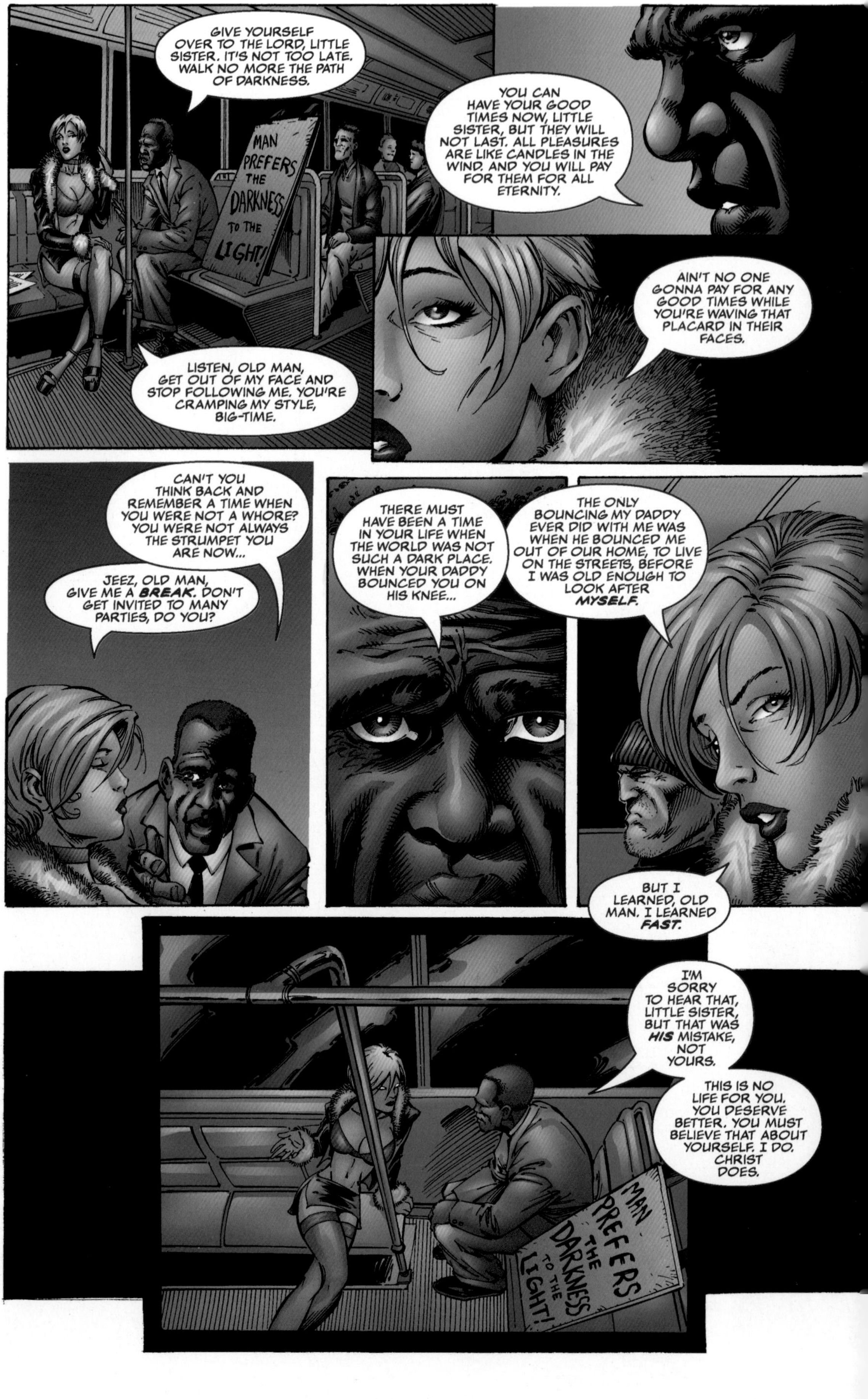
GIVE YOURSELF OVER TO THE LORD, LITTLE SISTER. IT'S NOT TOO LATE. WALK NO MORE THE PATH OF DARKNESS.
MAN PREFERS THE DARKNESS TO THE LIGHT!
YOU CAN HAVE YOUR GOOD TIMES NOW, LITTLE SISTER, BUT THEY WILL NOT LAST. ALL PLEASURES ARE LIKE CANDLES IN THE WIND. AND YOU WILL PAY FOR THEM FOR ALL ETERNITY.
LISTEN, OLD MAN, GET OUT OF MY FACE AND STOP FOLLOWING ME. YOU'RE CRAMPING MY STYLE, BIG-TIME.
AIN'T NO ONE GONNA PAY FOR ANY GOOD TIMES WHILE YOU'RE WAVING THAT PLACARD IN THEIR FACES.
CAN'T YOU THINK BACK AND REMEMBER A TIME WHEN YOU WERE NOT A WHORE? YOU WERE NOT ALWAYS THE STRUMPET YOU ARE NOW...
JEEZ, OLD MAN, GIVE ME A **BREAK.** DON'T GET INVITED TO MANY PARTIES, DO YOU?
THERE MUST HAVE BEEN A TIME IN YOUR LIFE WHEN THE WORLD WAS NOT SUCH A DARK PLACE. WHEN YOUR DADDY BOUNCED YOU ON HIS KNEE...
THE ONLY BOUNCING MY DADDY EVER DID WITH ME WAS WHEN HE BOUNCED ME OUT OF OUR HOME, TO LIVE ON THE STREETS, BEFORE I WAS OLD ENOUGH TO LOOK AFTER ***MYSELF.***
BUT I LEARNED, OLD MAN. I LEARNED ***FAST.***
I'M SORRY TO HEAR THAT, LITTLE SISTER, BUT THAT WAS ***HIS*** MISTAKE, NOT YOURS.
THIS IS NO LIFE FOR YOU. YOU DESERVE BETTER. YOU MUST BELIEVE THAT ABOUT YOURSELF. I DO. CHRIST DOES.
MAN PREFERS THE DARKNESS TO THE LIGHT!

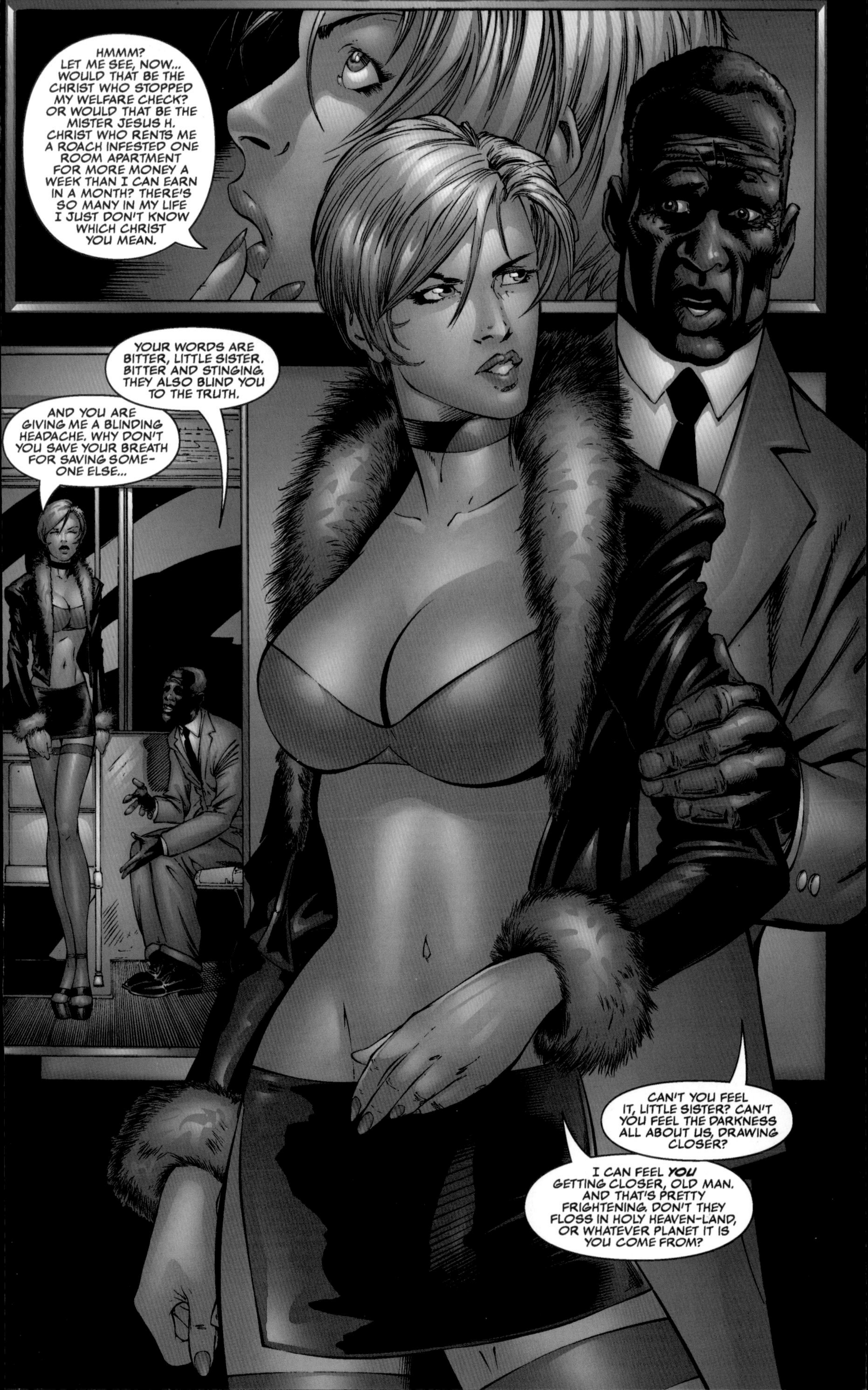
HMMM? LET ME SEE, NOW... WOULD THAT BE THE CHRIST WHO STOPPED MY WELFARE CHECK? OR WOULD THAT BE THE MISTER JESUS H. CHRIST WHO RENTS ME A ROACH INFESTED ONE ROOM APARTMENT FOR MORE MONEY A WEEK THAN I CAN EARN IN A MONTH? THERE'S SO MANY IN MY LIFE I JUST DON'T KNOW WHICH CHRIST YOU MEAN.
YOUR WORDS ARE BITTER, LITTLE SISTER. BITTER AND STINGING. THEY ALSO BLIND YOU TO THE TRUTH.
AND YOU ARE GIVING ME A BLINDING HEADACHE. WHY DON'T YOU SAVE YOUR BREATH FOR SAVING SOME-ONE ELSE...
CAN'T YOU FEEL IT, LITTLE SISTER? CAN'T YOU FEEL THE DARKNESS ALL ABOUT US, DRAWING CLOSER?
I CAN FEEL ***YOU*** GETTING CLOSER, OLD MAN. AND THAT'S PRETTY FRIGHTENING. DON'T THEY FLOSS IN HOLY HEAVEN-LAND, OR WHATEVER PLANET IT IS YOU COME FROM?

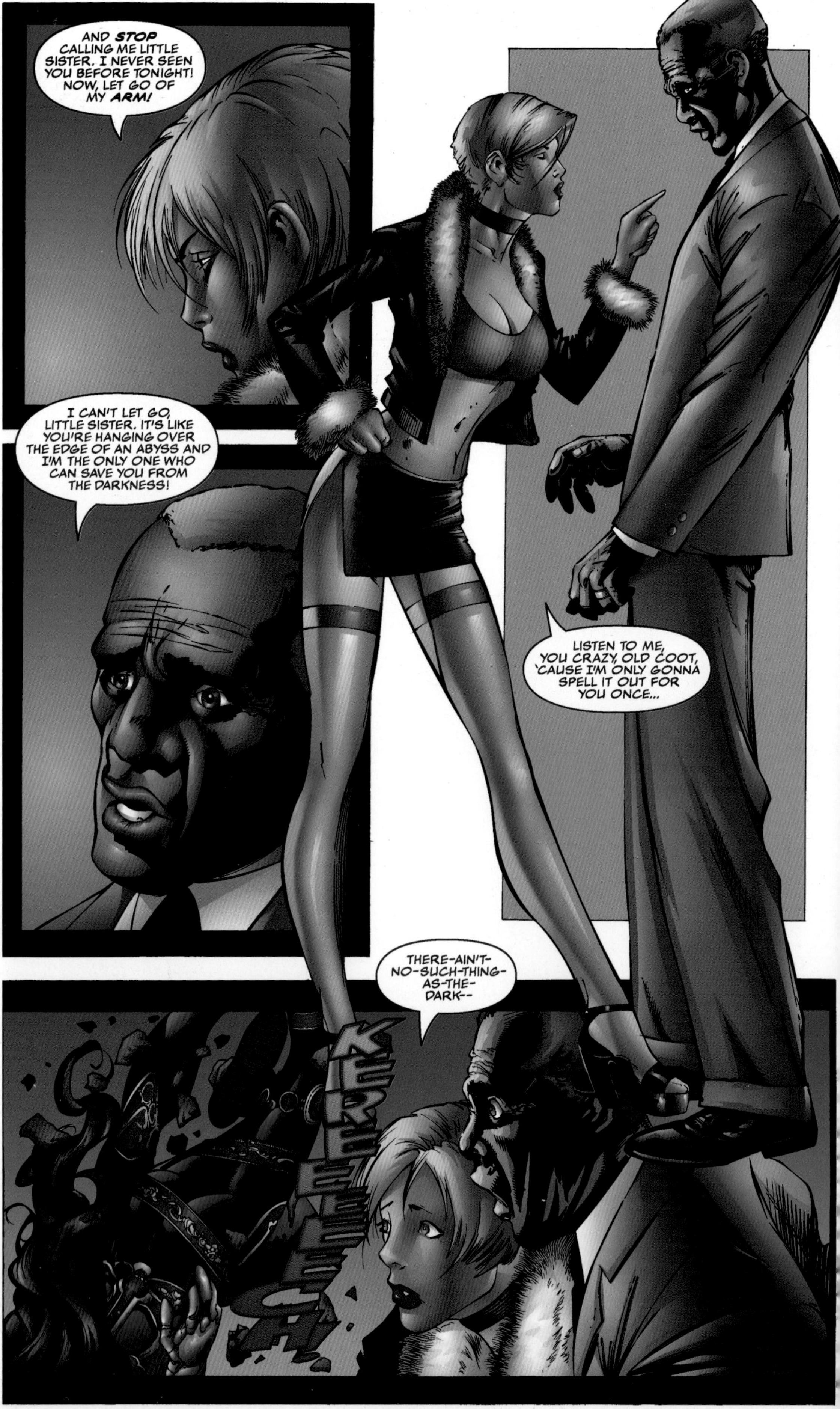
AND STOP CALLING ME LITTLE SISTER. I NEVER SEEN YOU BEFORE TONIGHT! NOW, LET GO OF MY ARM!
I CAN'T LET GO, LITTLE SISTER. IT'S LIKE YOU'RE HANGING OVER THE EDGE OF AN ABYSS AND I'M THE ONLY ONE WHO CAN SAVE YOU FROM THE DARKNESS!
LISTEN TO ME, YOU CRAZY, OLD COOT, 'CAUSE I'M ONLY GONNA SPELL IT OUT FOR YOU ONCE...
THERE-AIN'T-NO-SUCH-THING-AS-THE-DARK--

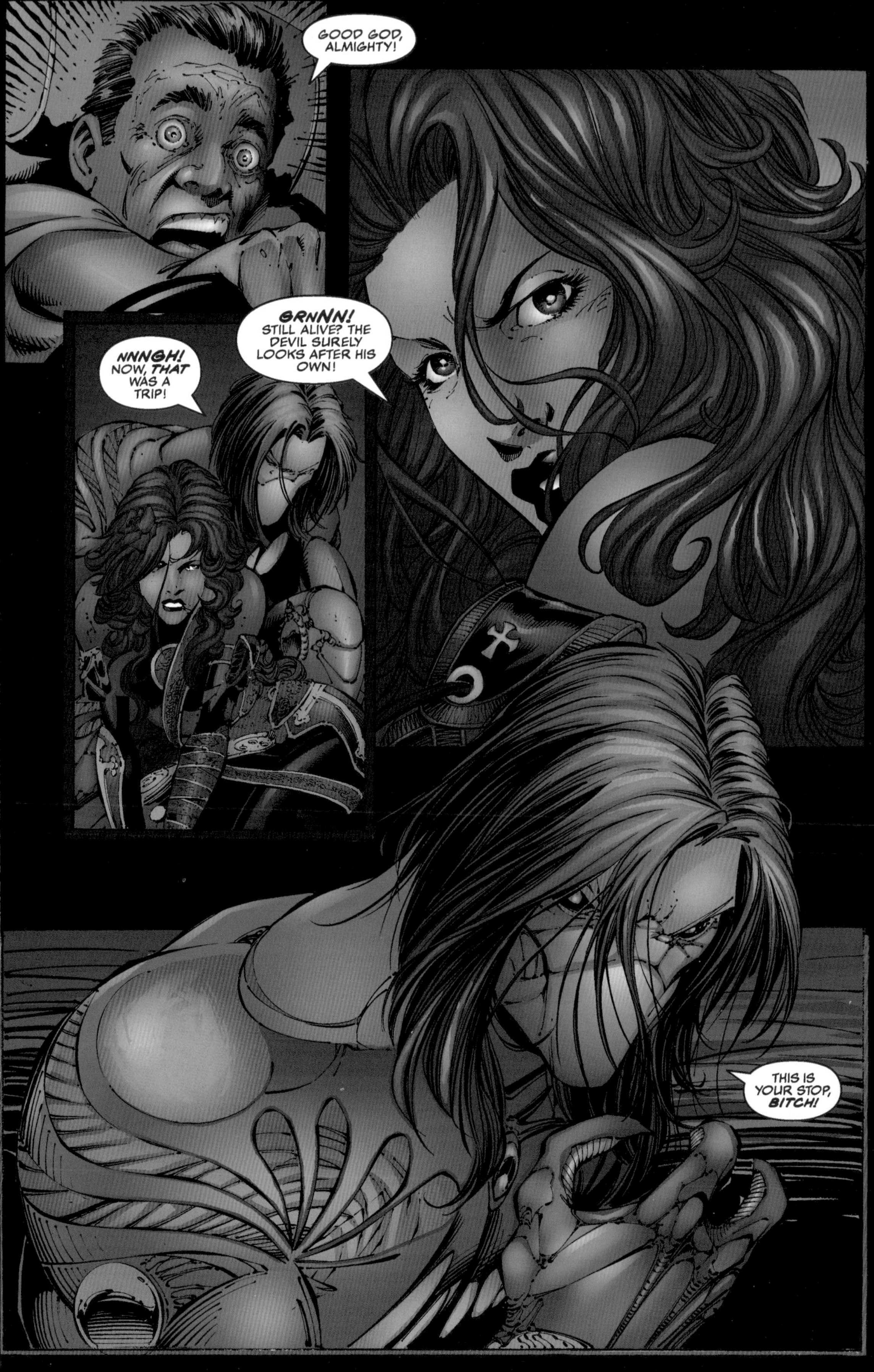
GOOD GOD, ALMIGHTY!
NNNGH! NOW, THAT WAS A TRIP!
GRNNN! STILL ALIVE? THE DEVIL SURELY LOOKS AFTER HIS OWN!
THIS IS YOUR STOP, BITCH!

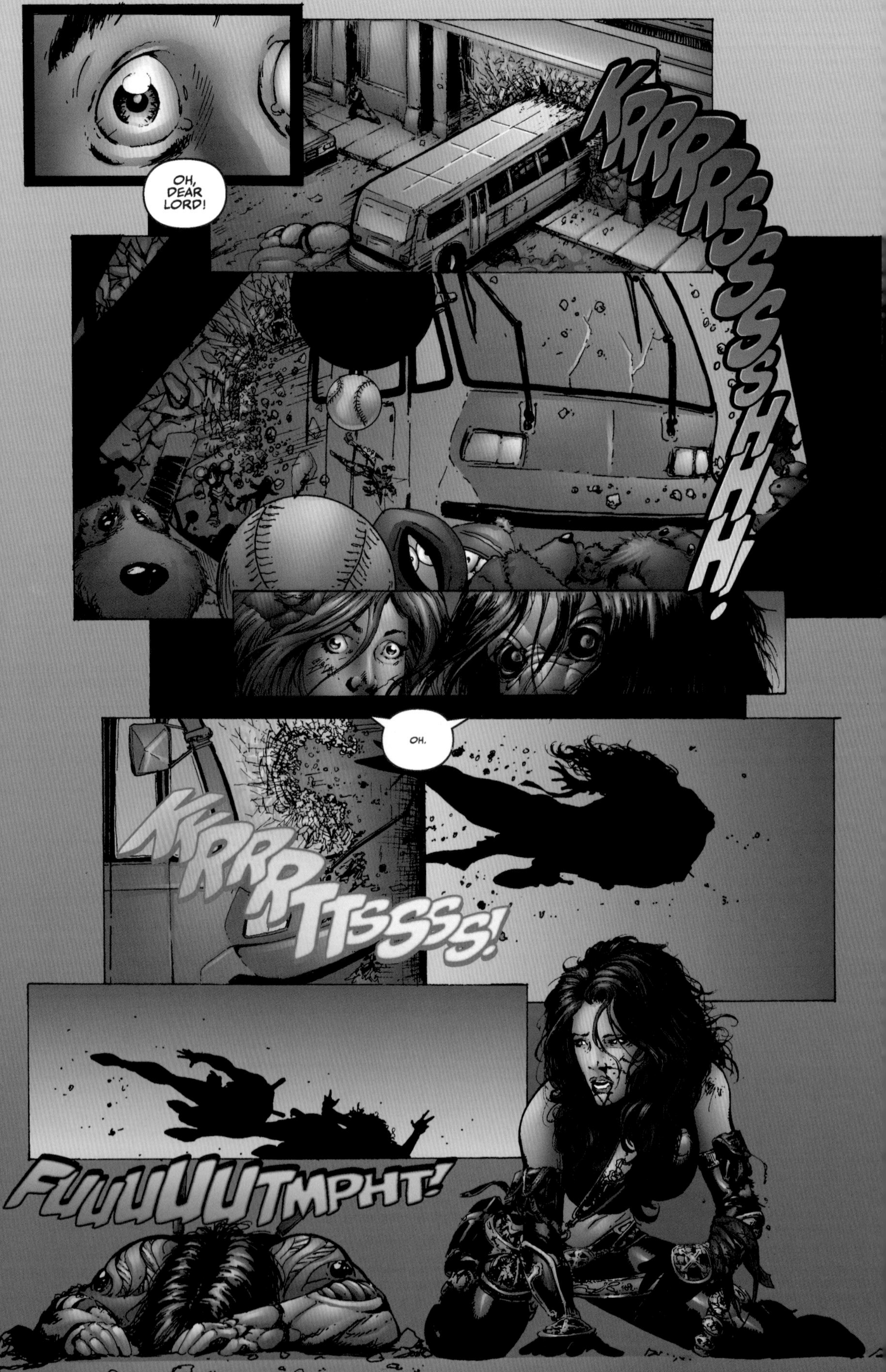
OH, DEAR LORD!
KRRRRSSSSHHHH!
OH.
KRRRRTTSSSSS!
FUUUUUTMPHT!

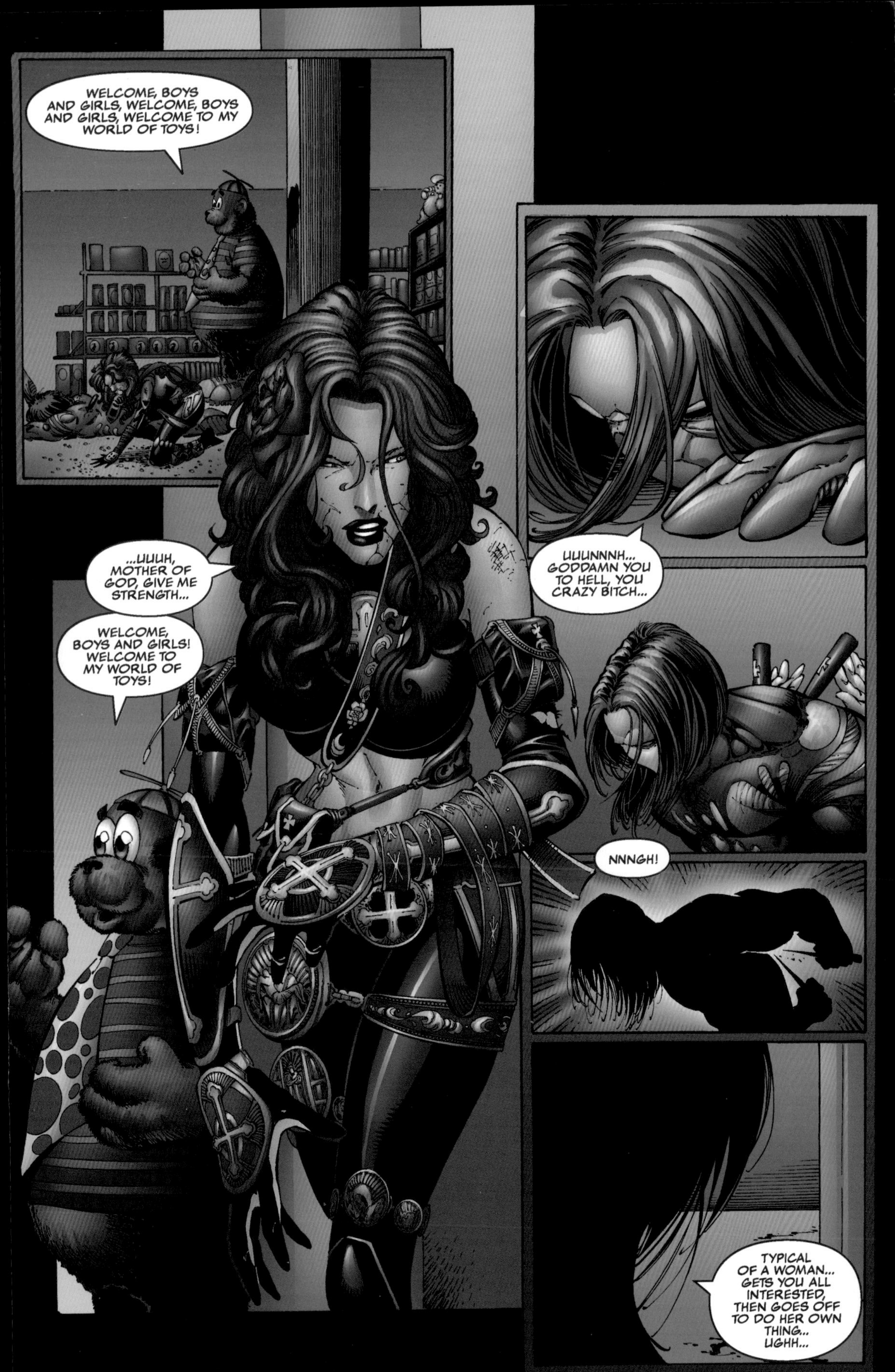
WELCOME, BOYS AND GIRLS, WELCOME, BOYS AND GIRLS, WELCOME TO MY WORLD OF TOYS!
...UUUH, MOTHER OF GOD, GIVE ME STRENGTH...
WELCOME, BOYS AND GIRLS! WELCOME TO MY WORLD OF TOYS!
UUUNNNH... GODDAMN YOU TO HELL, YOU CRAZY BITCH...
NNNGH!
TYPICAL OF A WOMAN... GETS YOU ALL INTERESTED, THEN GOES OFF TO DO HER OWN THING... UGHH...

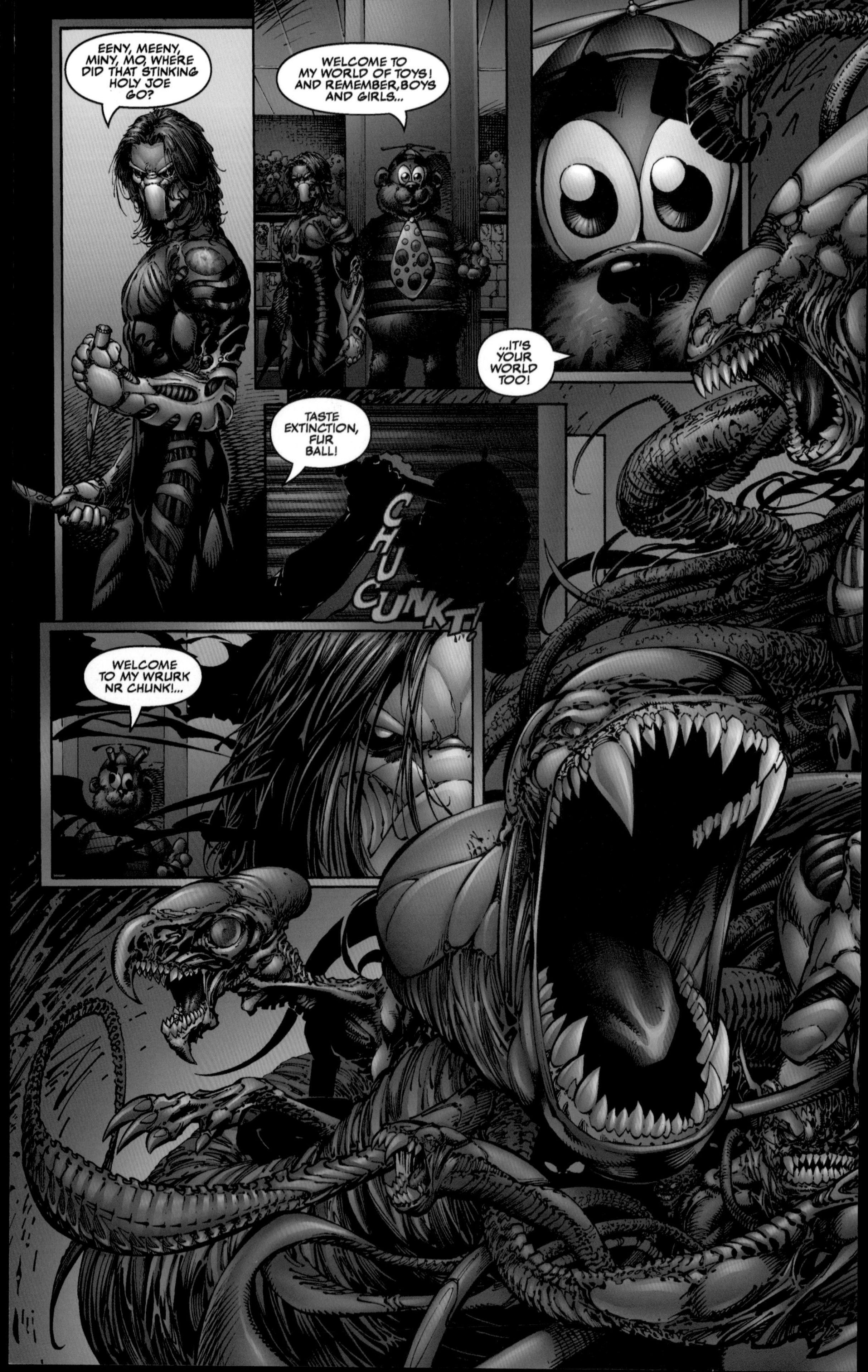
EENY, MEENY, MINY, MO, WHERE DID THAT STINKING HOLY JOE GO?
WELCOME TO MY WORLD OF TOYS! AND REMEMBER, BOYS AND GIRLS...
...IT'S YOUR WORLD TOO!
TASTE EXTINCTION, FUR BALL!
CHUCUNKT!
WELCOME TO MY WRURK NR CHUNK!...

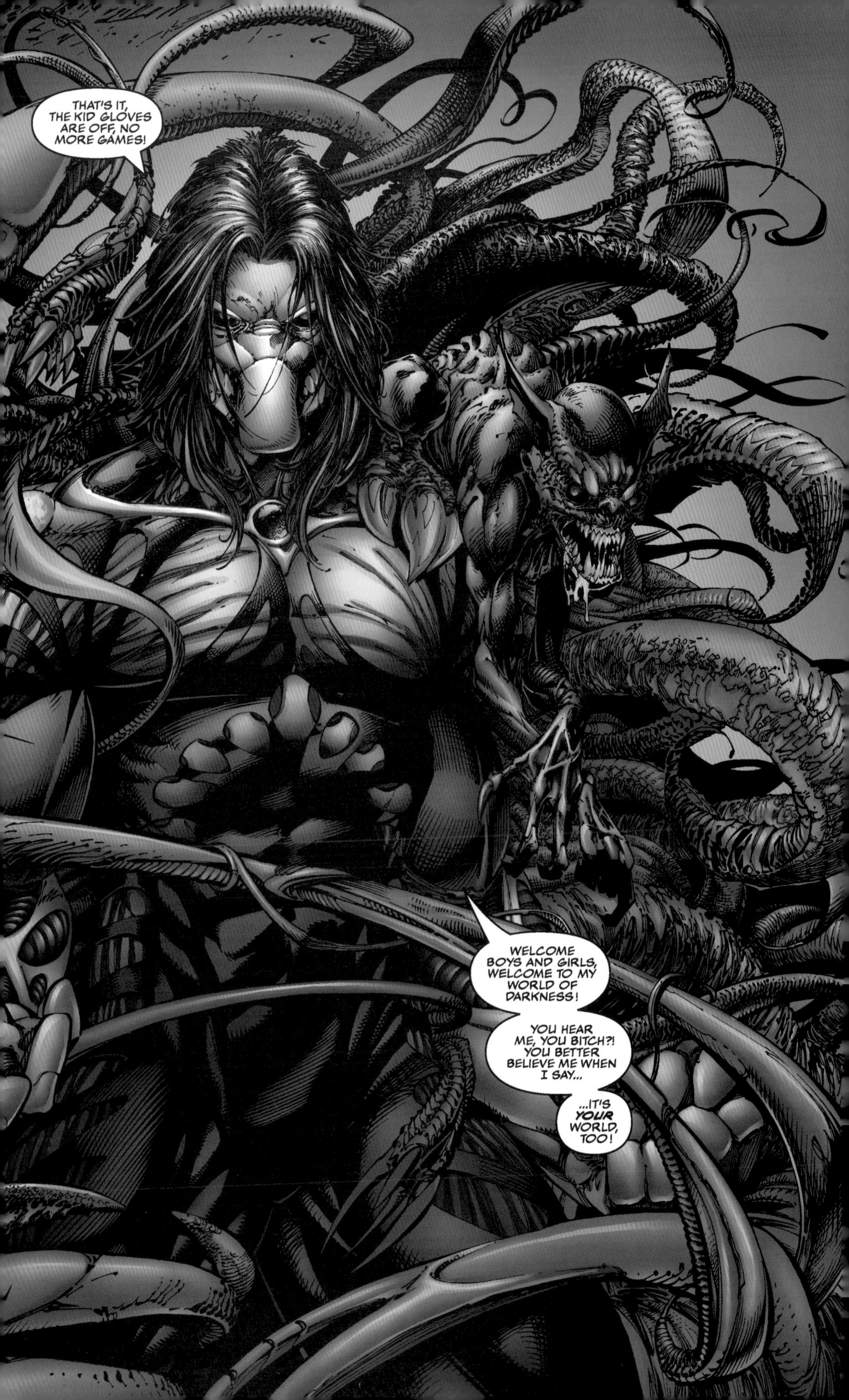
THAT'S IT, THE KID GLOVES ARE OFF, NO MORE GAMES!
WELCOME BOYS AND GIRLS, WELCOME TO MY WORLD OF DARKNESS!
YOU HEAR ME, YOU BITCH?! YOU BETTER BELIEVE ME WHEN I SAY...
...IT'S YOUR WORLD, TOO!

The Darkness
ISSUE #17

story by: Malachy Coney
pencils by: Joe Benitez, Dave Finch,
Clarence Lansang, Cedric Nocon
inks by: Joe Weems V, Victor Llamas,
Jonathan Livesay, Joe Benitez
colors by: Tyson Wengler, Matt Nelson,
Liquid!, Quantum Color FX, Richard and Tanya Horie
letters by: Dennis Heisler

inks assists by: Marco "Madman" Galli
Victor Llamas, Whitney McFarland, Dave Wagner

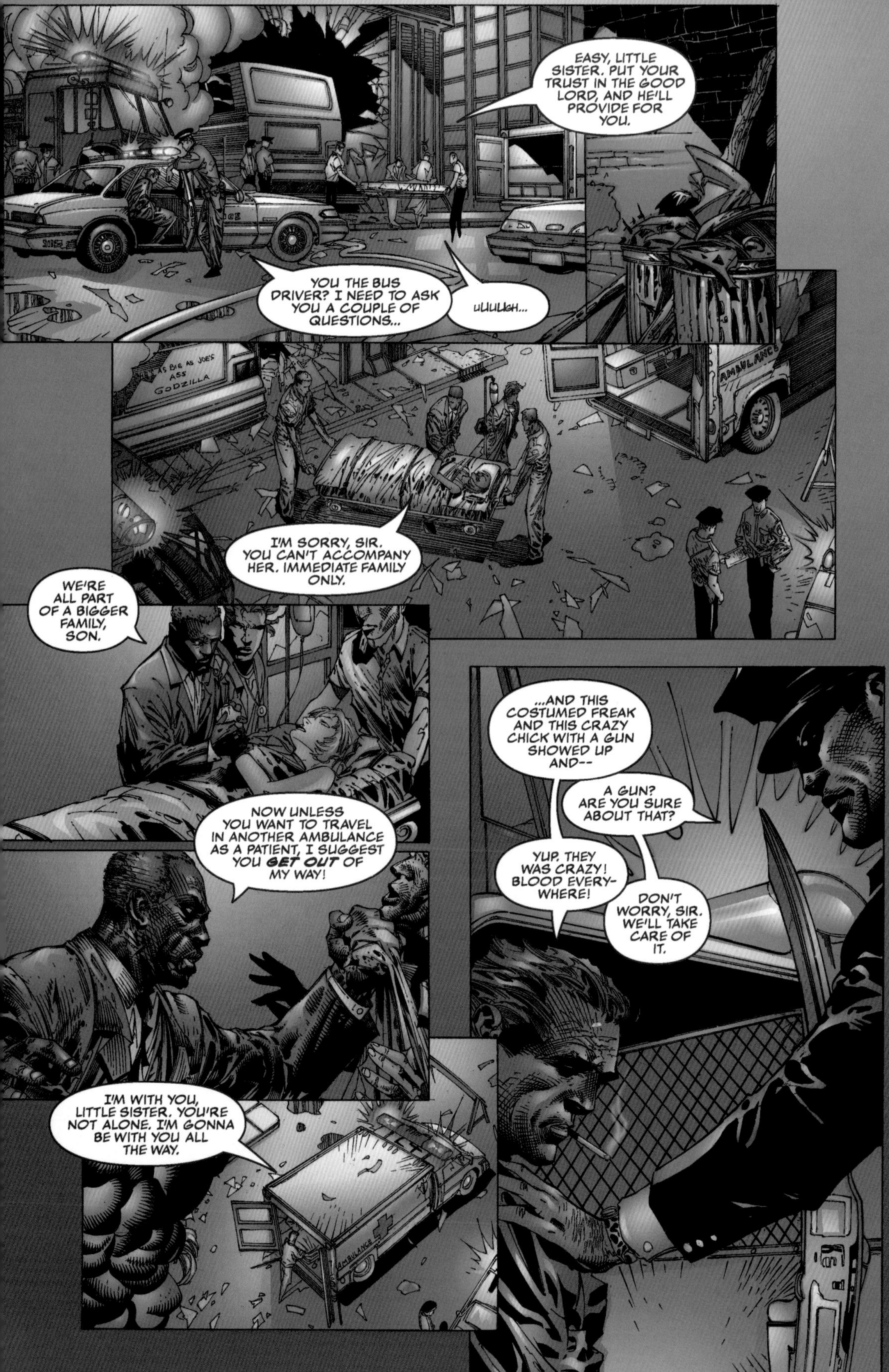
EASY, LITTLE SISTER. PUT YOUR TRUST IN THE GOOD LORD, AND HE'LL PROVIDE FOR YOU.
YOU THE BUS DRIVER? I NEED TO ASK YOU A COUPLE OF QUESTIONS...
UUULGH...
I'M SORRY, SIR. YOU CAN'T ACCOMPANY HER. IMMEDIATE FAMILY ONLY.
WE'RE ALL PART OF A BIGGER FAMILY, SON.
NOW UNLESS YOU WANT TO TRAVEL IN ANOTHER AMBULANCE AS A PATIENT, I SUGGEST YOU GET OUT OF MY WAY!
...AND THIS COSTUMED FREAK AND THIS CRAZY CHICK WITH A GUN SHOWED UP AND--
A GUN? ARE YOU SURE ABOUT THAT?
YUP. THEY WAS CRAZY! BLOOD EVERY-WHERE!
DON'T WORRY, SIR. WE'LL TAKE CARE OF IT.
I'M WITH YOU, LITTLE SISTER. YOU'RE NOT ALONE. I'M GONNA BE WITH YOU ALL THE WAY.

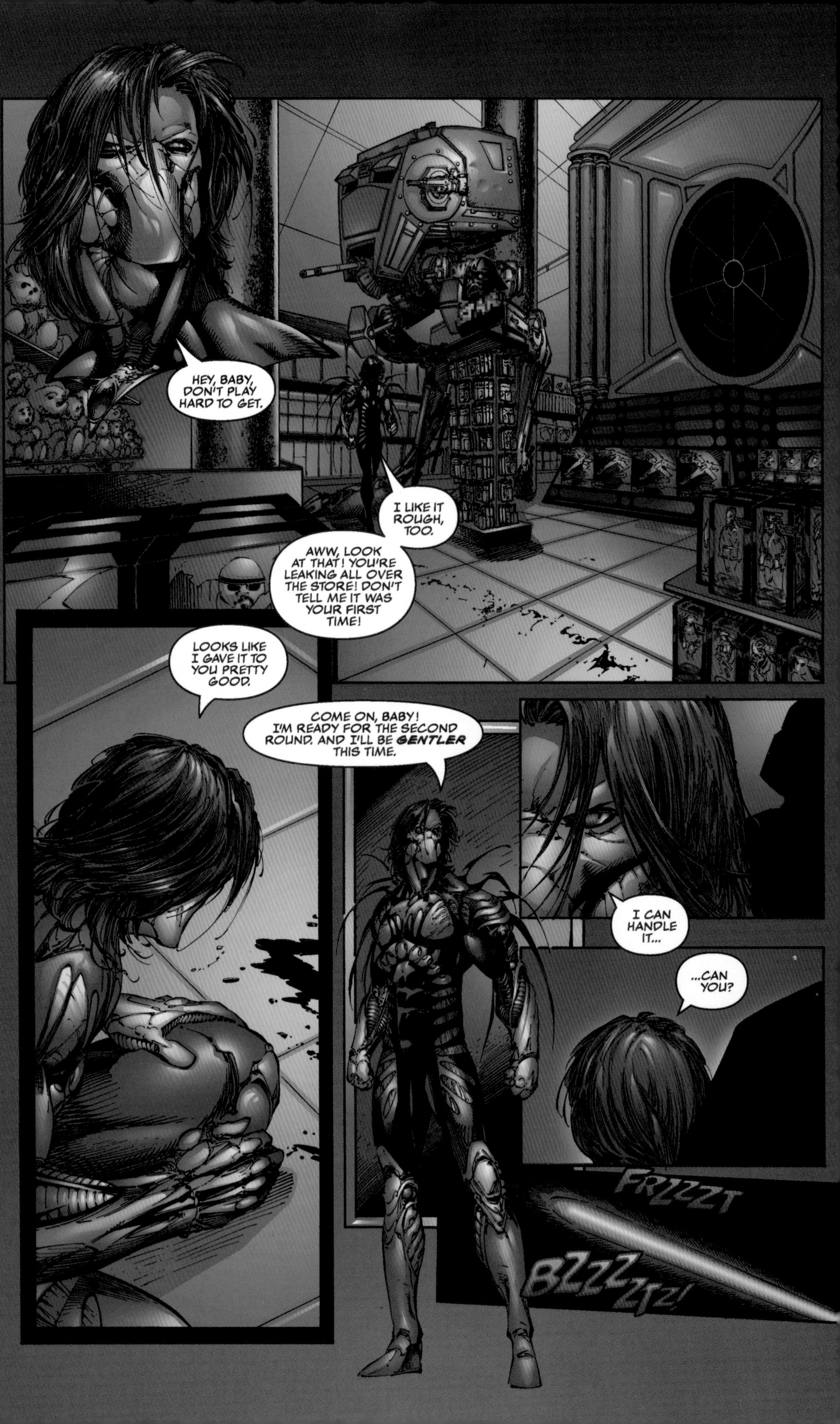
HEY, BABY, DON'T PLAY HARD TO GET.
I LIKE IT ROUGH, TOO.
AWW, LOOK AT THAT! YOU'RE LEAKING ALL OVER THE STORE! DON'T TELL ME IT WAS YOUR FIRST TIME!
LOOKS LIKE I GAVE IT TO YOU PRETTY GOOD.
COME ON, BABY! I'M READY FOR THE SECOND ROUND. AND I'LL BE GENTLER THIS TIME.
I CAN HANDLE IT...
...CAN YOU?
FRZZZT
BZZZZTZ!

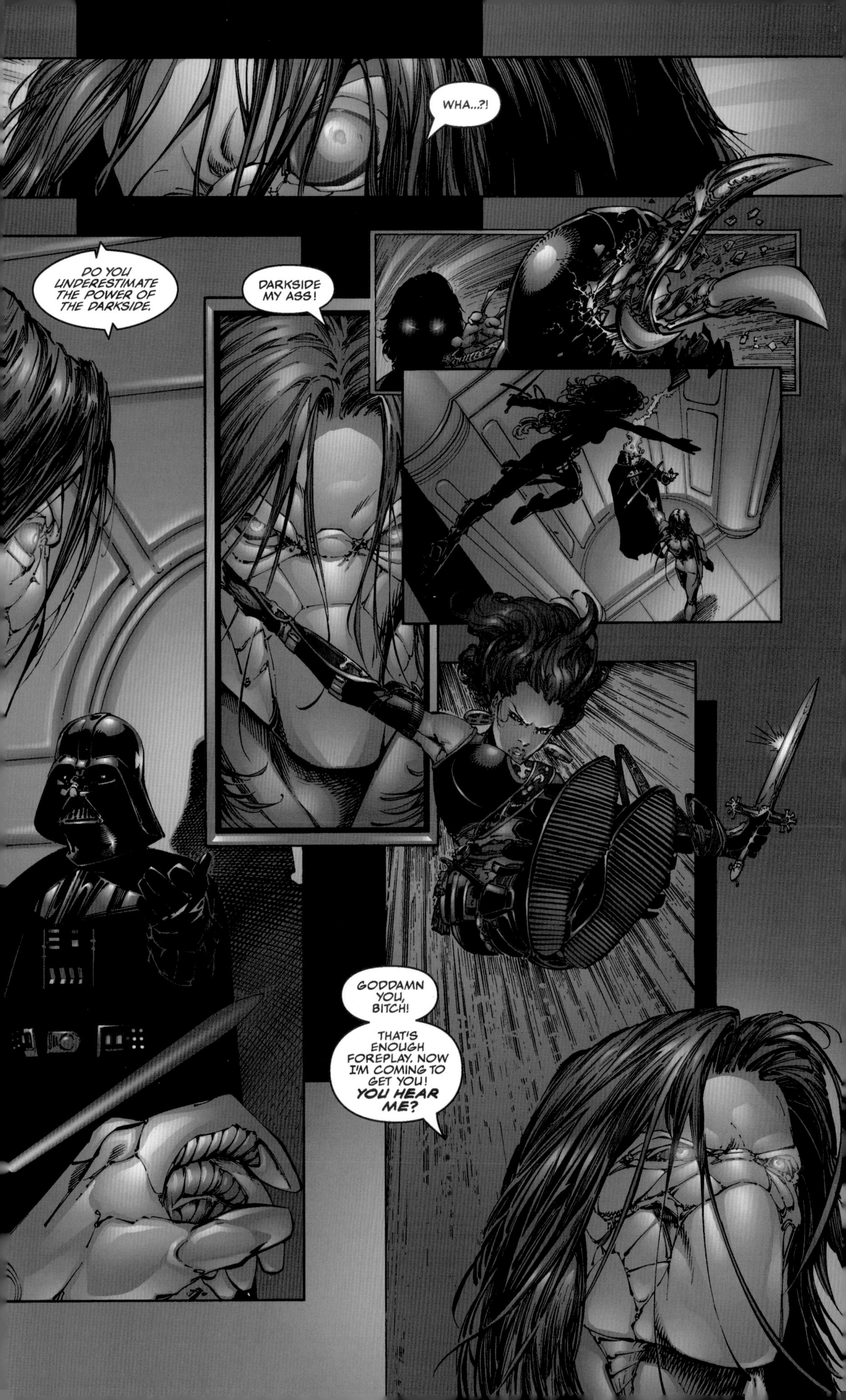
WHA...?!
DO YOU UNDERESTIMATE THE POWER OF THE DARKSIDE.
DARKSIDE MY ASS!
GODDAMN YOU, BITCH!
THAT'S ENOUGH FOREPLAY. NOW I'M COMING TO GET YOU! YOU HEAR ME?

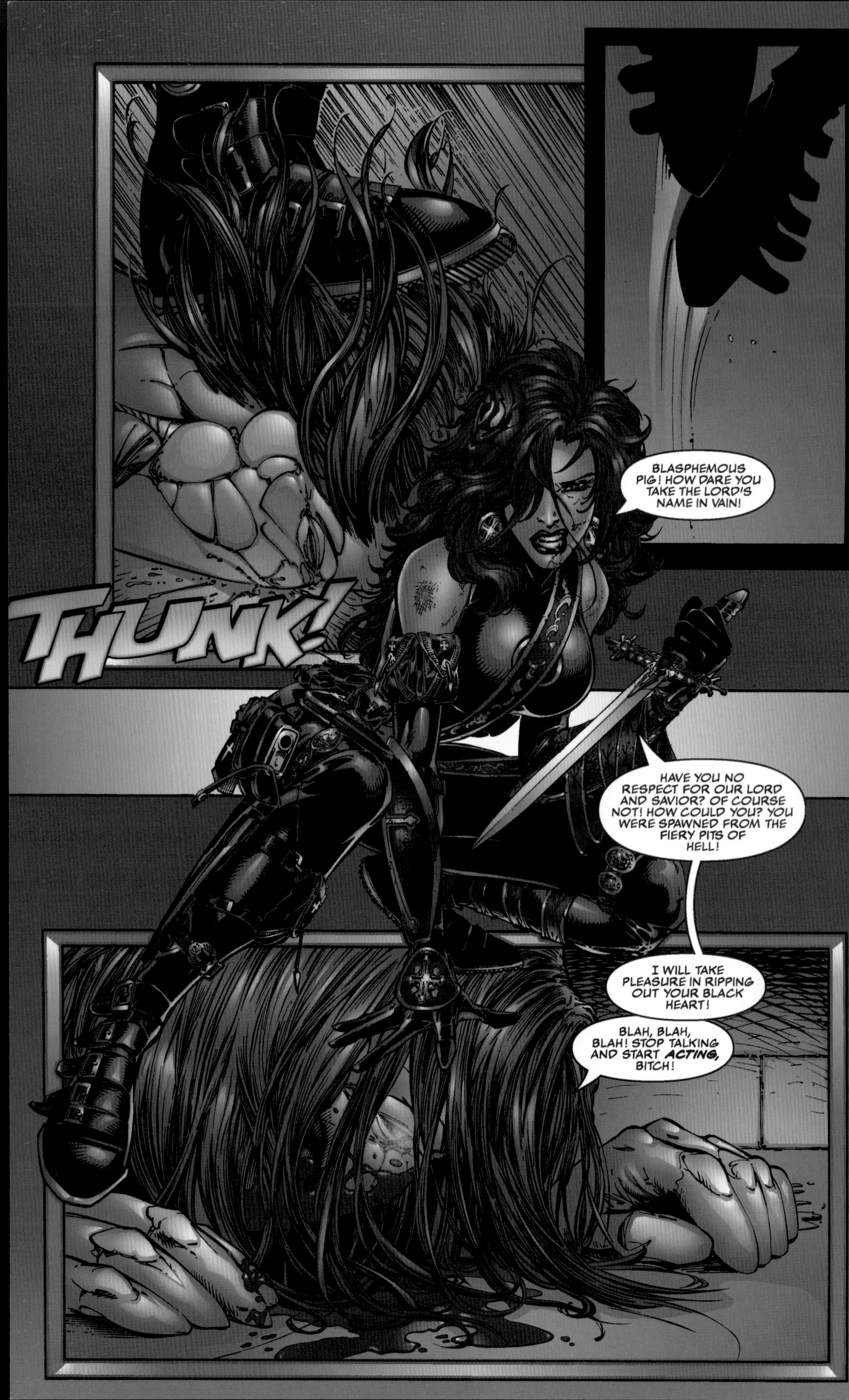

THUNK!
BLASPHEMOUS PIG! HOW DARE YOU TAKE THE LORD'S NAME IN VAIN!
HAVE YOU NO RESPECT FOR OUR LORD AND SAVIOR? OF COURSE NOT! HOW COULD YOU? YOU WERE SPAWNED FROM THE FIERY PITS OF HELL!
I WILL TAKE PLEASURE IN RIPPING OUT YOUR BLACK HEART!
BLAH, BLAH, BLAH! STOP TALKING AND START ACTING, BITCH!

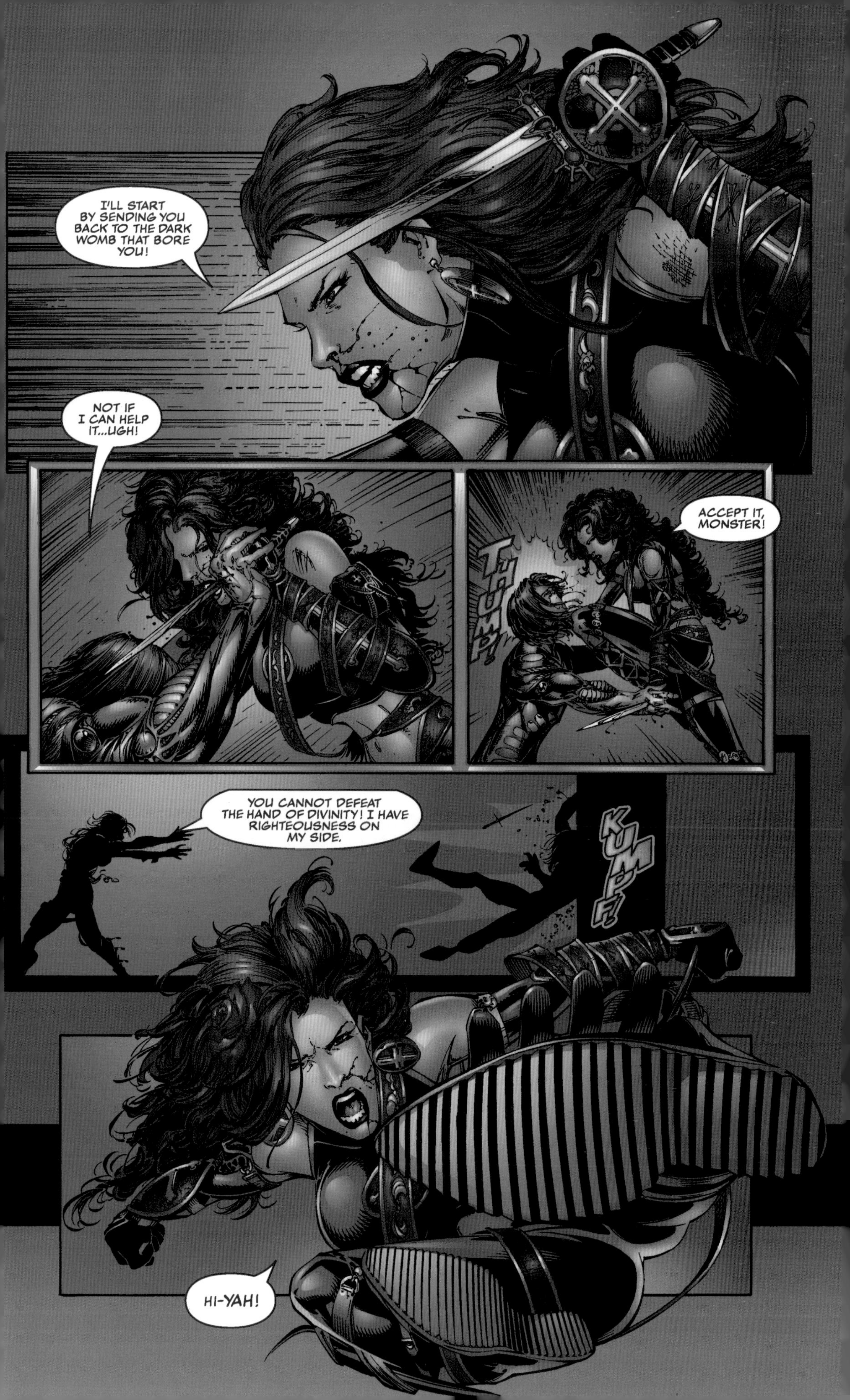
I'LL START BY SENDING YOU BACK TO THE DARK WOMB THAT BORE YOU!
NOT IF I CAN HELP IT...UGH!
THUMP!
ACCEPT IT, MONSTER!
YOU CANNOT DEFEAT THE HAND OF DIVINITY! I HAVE RIGHTEOUSNESS ON MY SIDE.
KUMPF!
HI-YAH!

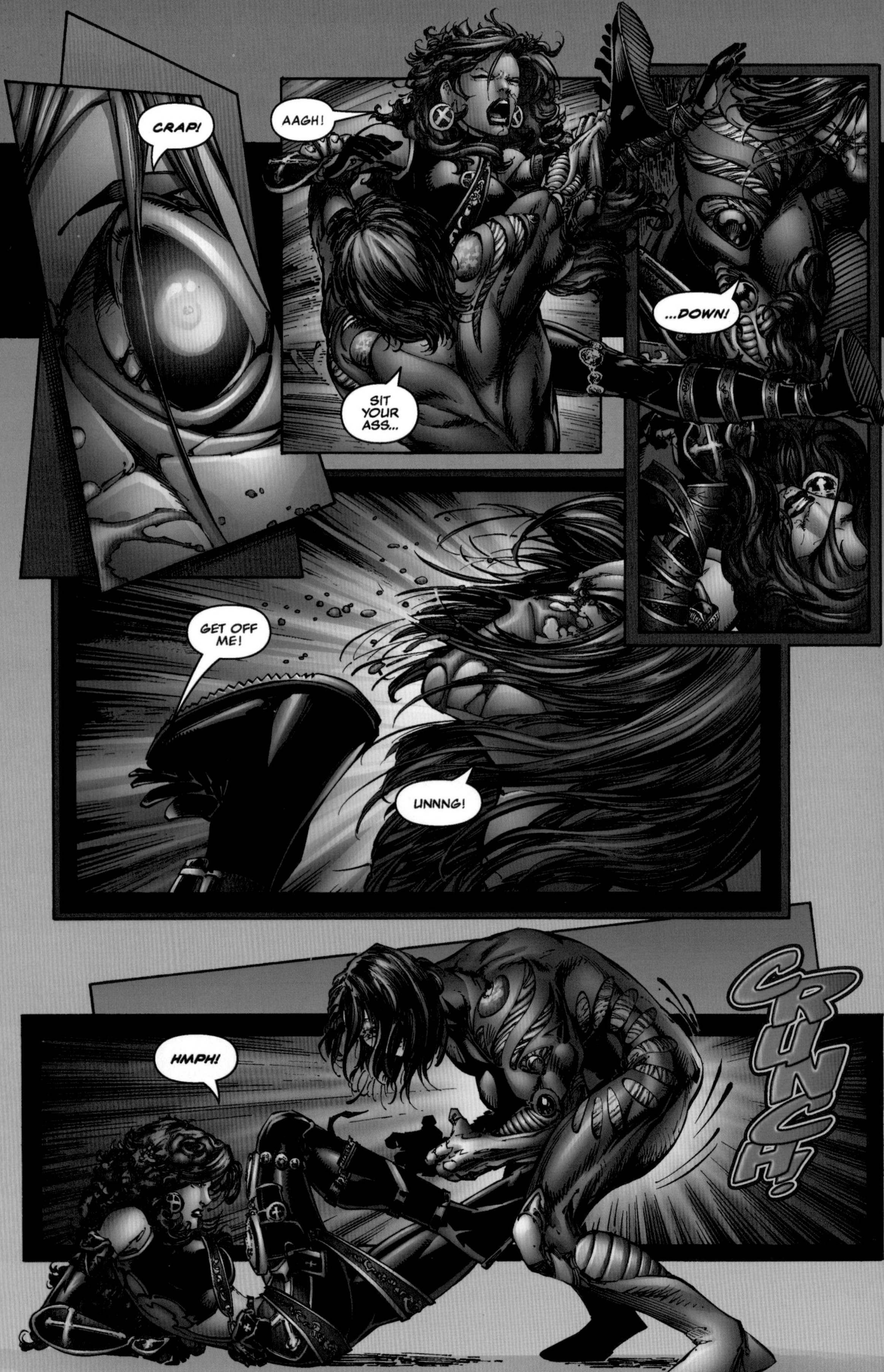
CRAP!
AAGH!
SIT YOUR ASS...
...DOWN!
GET OFF ME!
UNNNG!
HMPH!
CRUNCH!

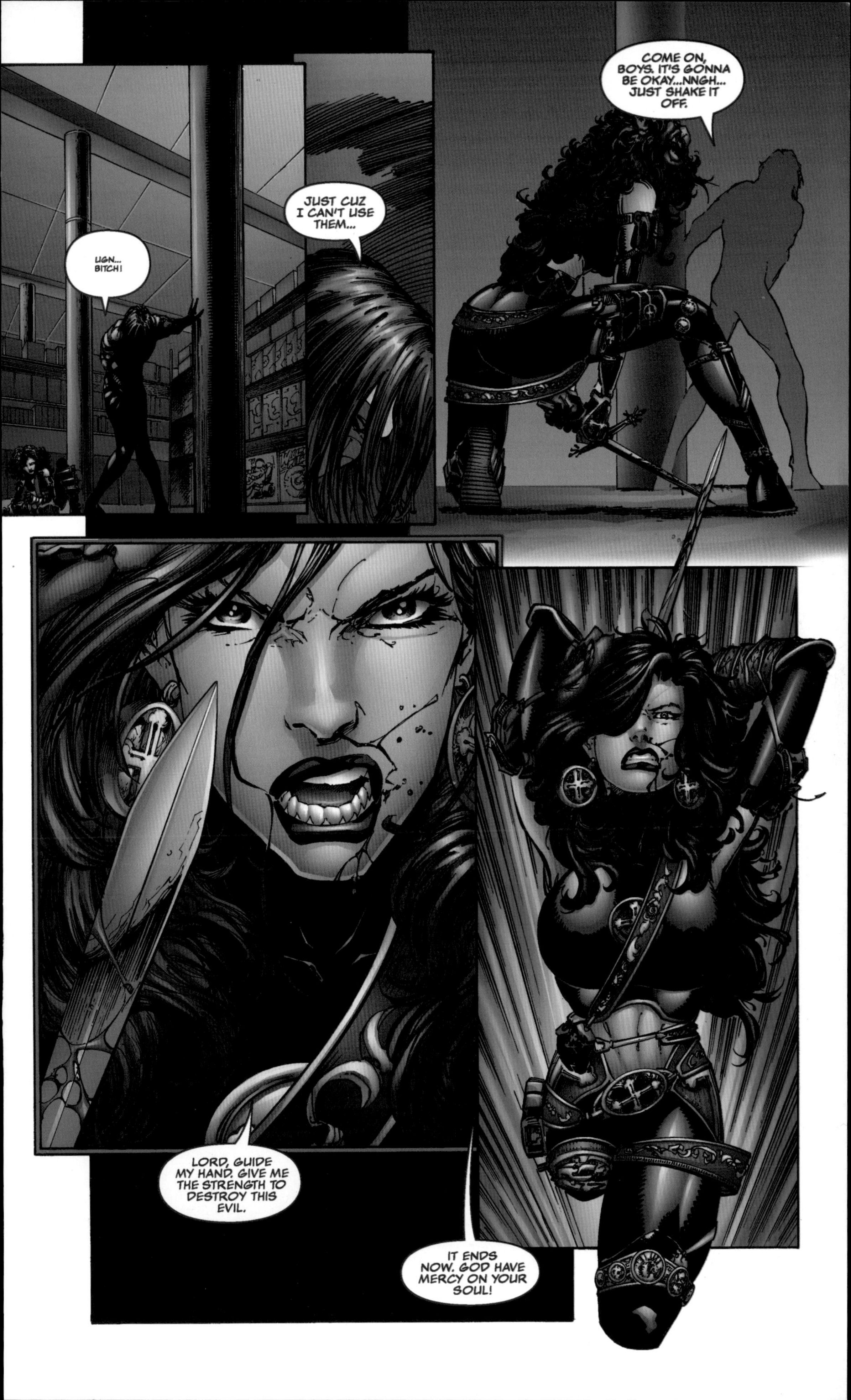
UGN... BITCH!
JUST CUZ I CAN'T USE THEM...
COME ON, BOYS. IT'S GONNA BE OKAY...NNGH... JUST SHAKE IT OFF.
LORD, GUIDE MY HAND. GIVE ME THE STRENGTH TO DESTROY THIS EVIL.
IT ENDS NOW. GOD HAVE MERCY ON YOUR SOUL!

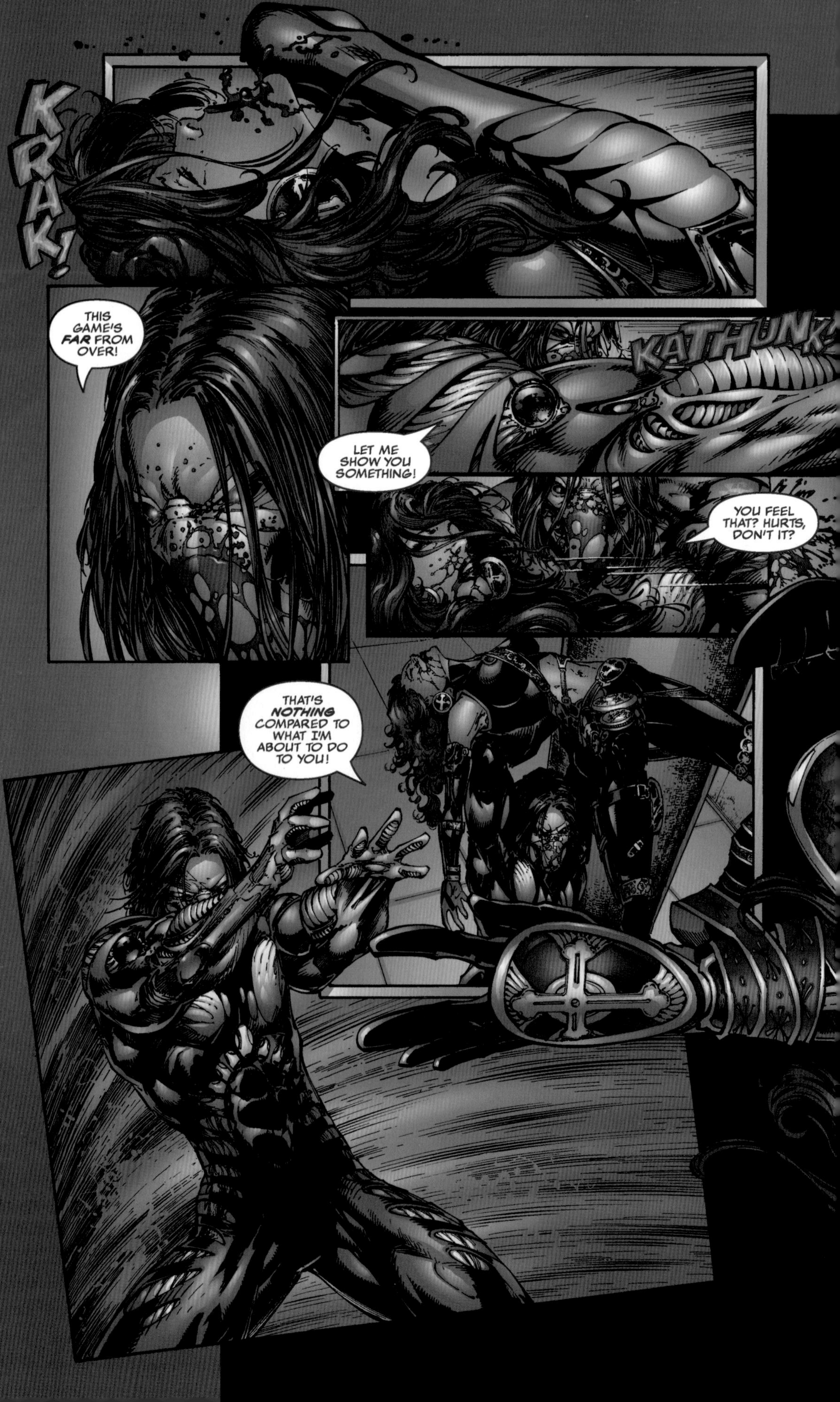
KRAK!
THIS GAME'S FAR FROM OVER!
KATHUNK!
LET ME SHOW YOU SOMETHING!
YOU FEEL THAT? HURTS, DON'T IT?
THAT'S NOTHING COMPARED TO WHAT I'M ABOUT TO DO TO YOU!

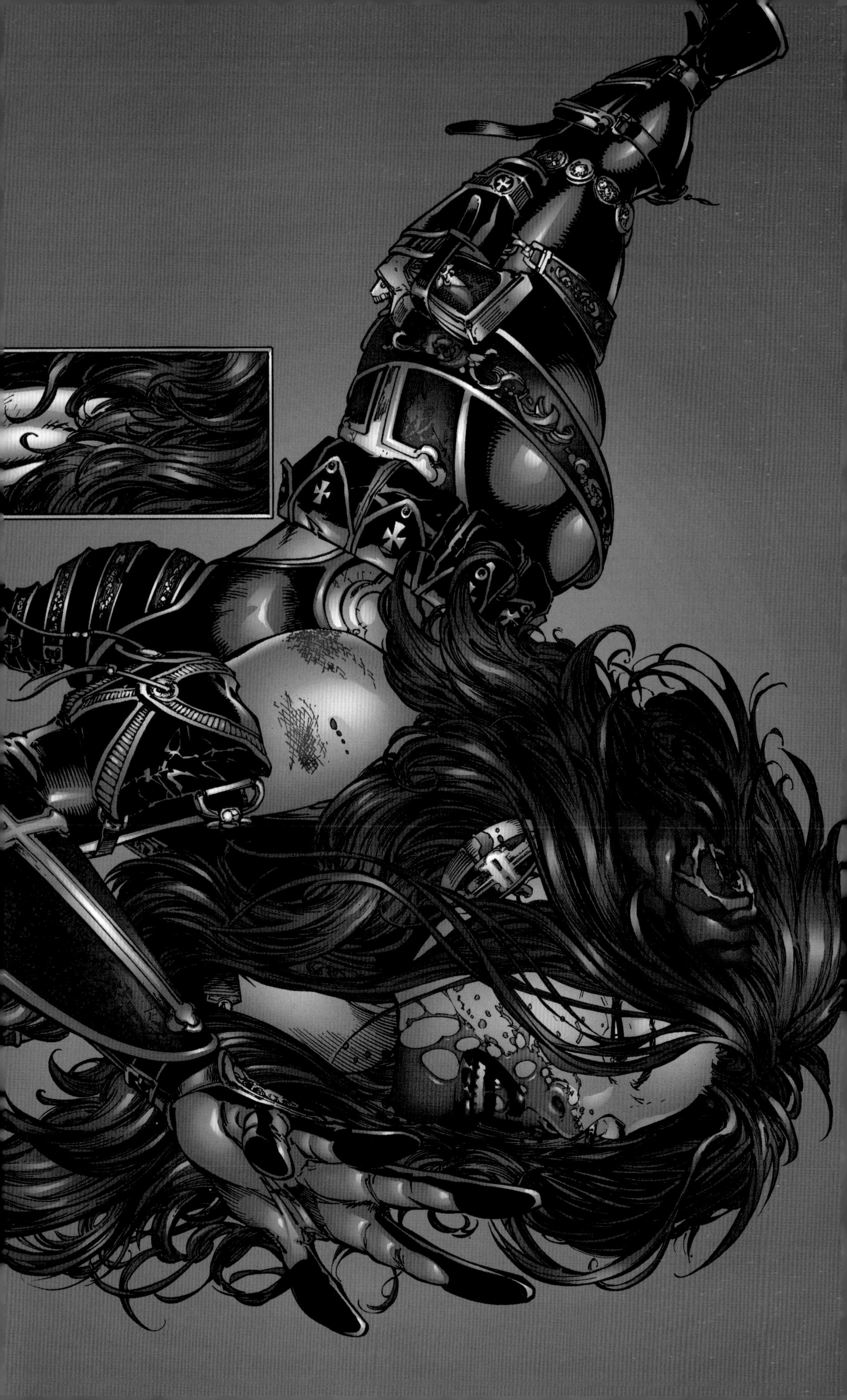

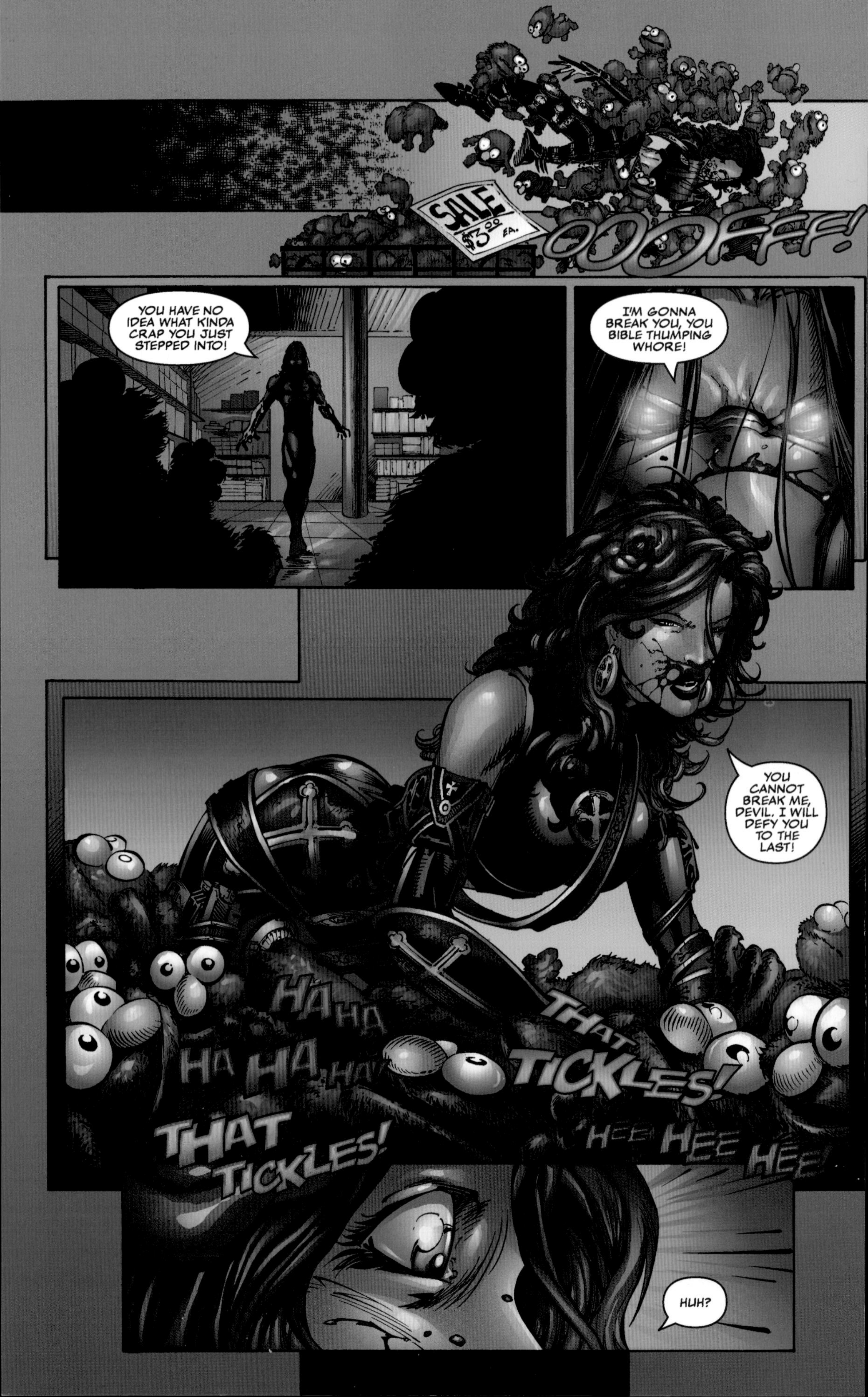
SALE $3.00 EA.
OOOFFF!
YOU HAVE NO IDEA WHAT KINDA CRAP YOU JUST STEPPED INTO!
I'M GONNA BREAK YOU, YOU BIBLE THUMPING WHORE!
YOU CANNOT BREAK ME, DEVIL. I WILL DEFY YOU TO THE LAST!
HA HA HA HA HA
THAT TICKLES!
THAT TICKLES!
HEE HEE HEE
HUH?

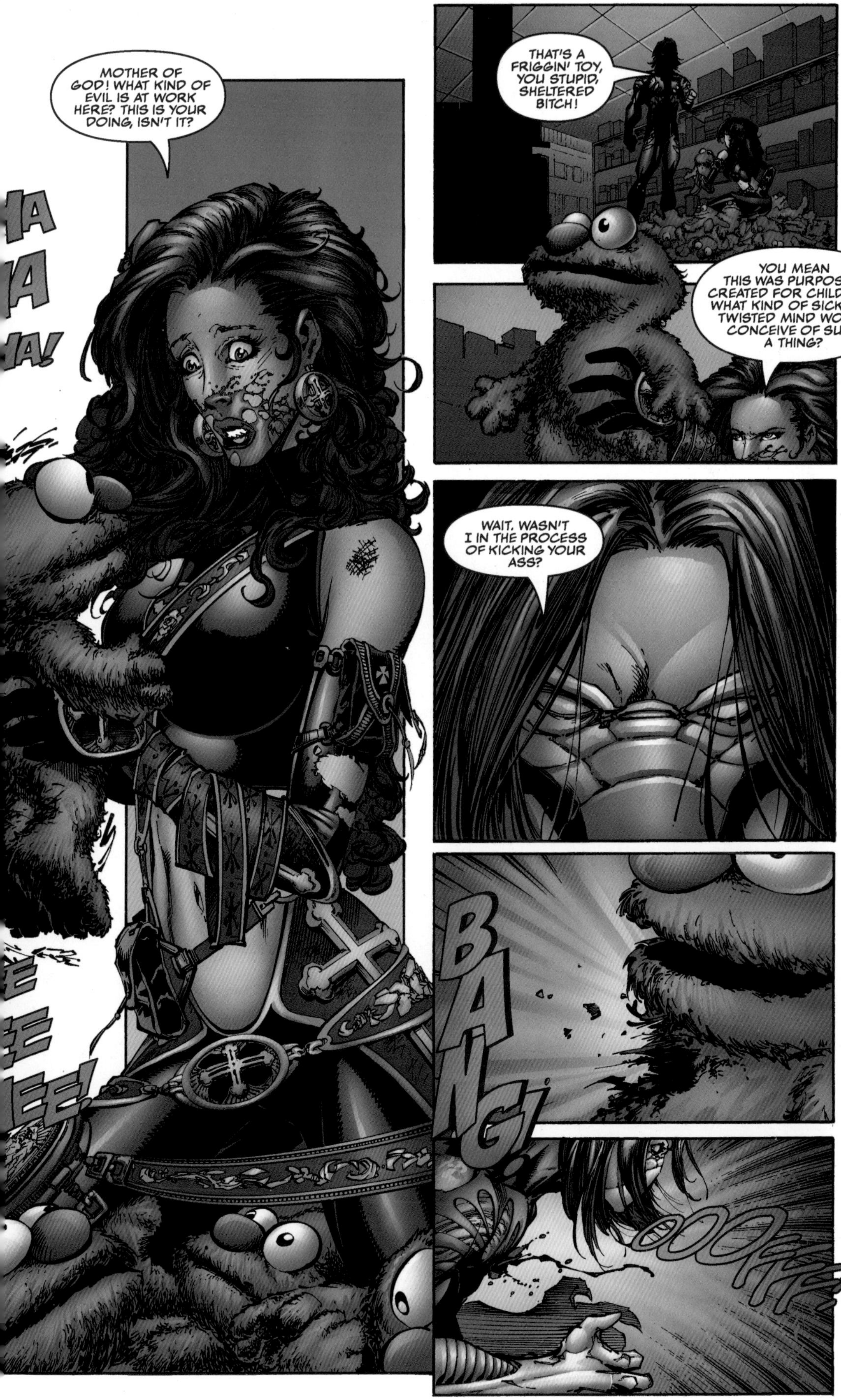
MOTHER OF GOD! WHAT KIND OF EVIL IS AT WORK HERE? THIS IS YOUR DOING, ISN'T IT?
THAT'S A FRIGGIN' TOY, YOU STUPID, SHELTERED BITCH!
YOU MEAN THIS WAS PURPOSELY CREATED FOR CHILDREN? WHAT KIND OF SICK AND TWISTED MIND WOULD CONCEIVE OF SUCH A THING?
WAIT. WASN'T I IN THE PROCESS OF KICKING YOUR ASS?
BANG!
OOOFFF!

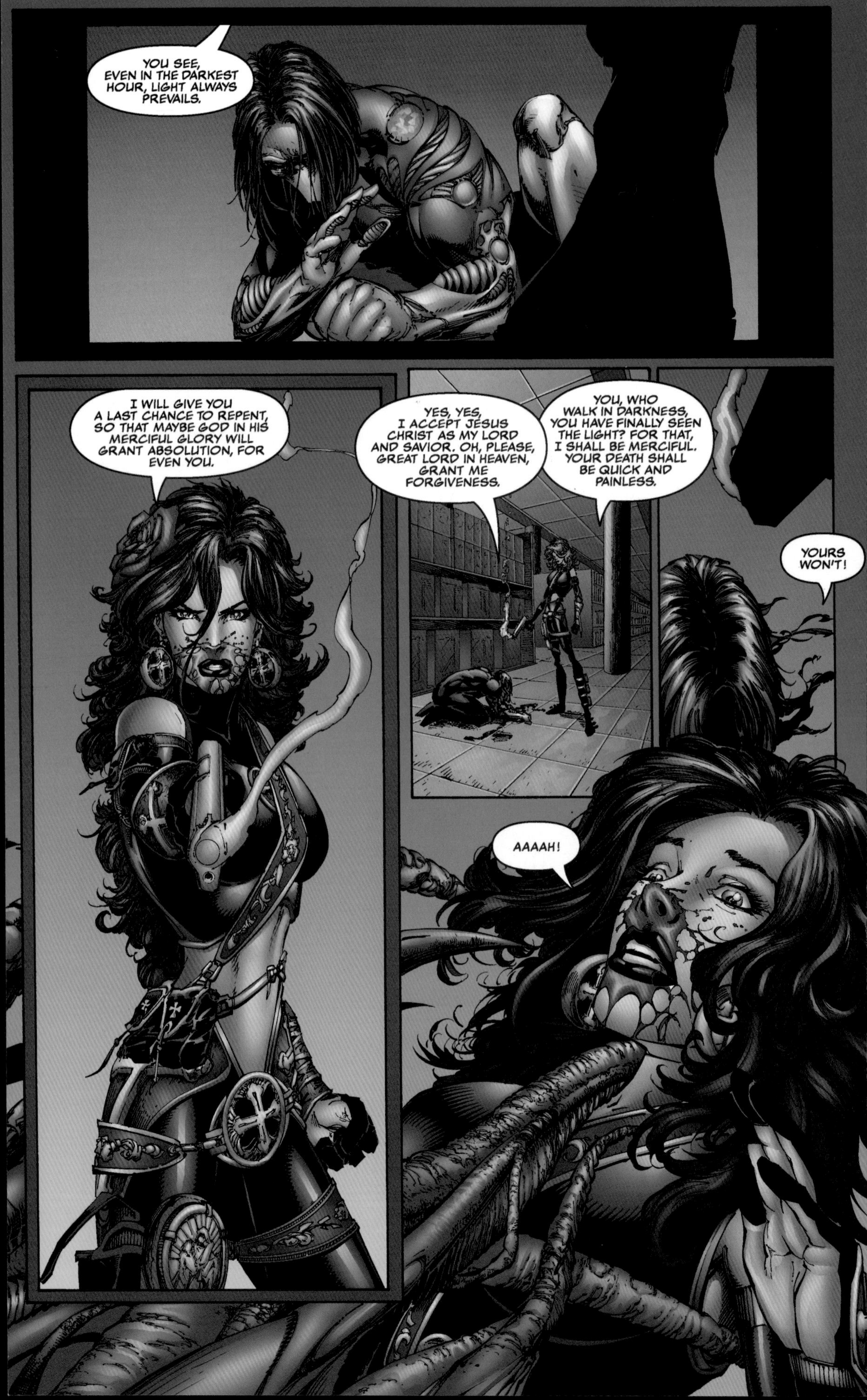
YOU SEE, EVEN IN THE DARKEST HOUR, LIGHT ALWAYS PREVAILS.
I WILL GIVE YOU A LAST CHANCE TO REPENT, SO THAT MAYBE GOD IN HIS MERCIFUL GLORY WILL GRANT ABSOLUTION, FOR EVEN YOU.
YES, YES, I ACCEPT JESUS CHRIST AS MY LORD AND SAVIOR. OH, PLEASE, GREAT LORD IN HEAVEN, GRANT ME FORGIVENESS.
YOU, WHO WALK IN DARKNESS, YOU HAVE FINALLY SEEN THE LIGHT? FOR THAT, I SHALL BE MERCIFUL. YOUR DEATH SHALL BE QUICK AND PAINLESS.
YOURS WON'T!
AAAAH!

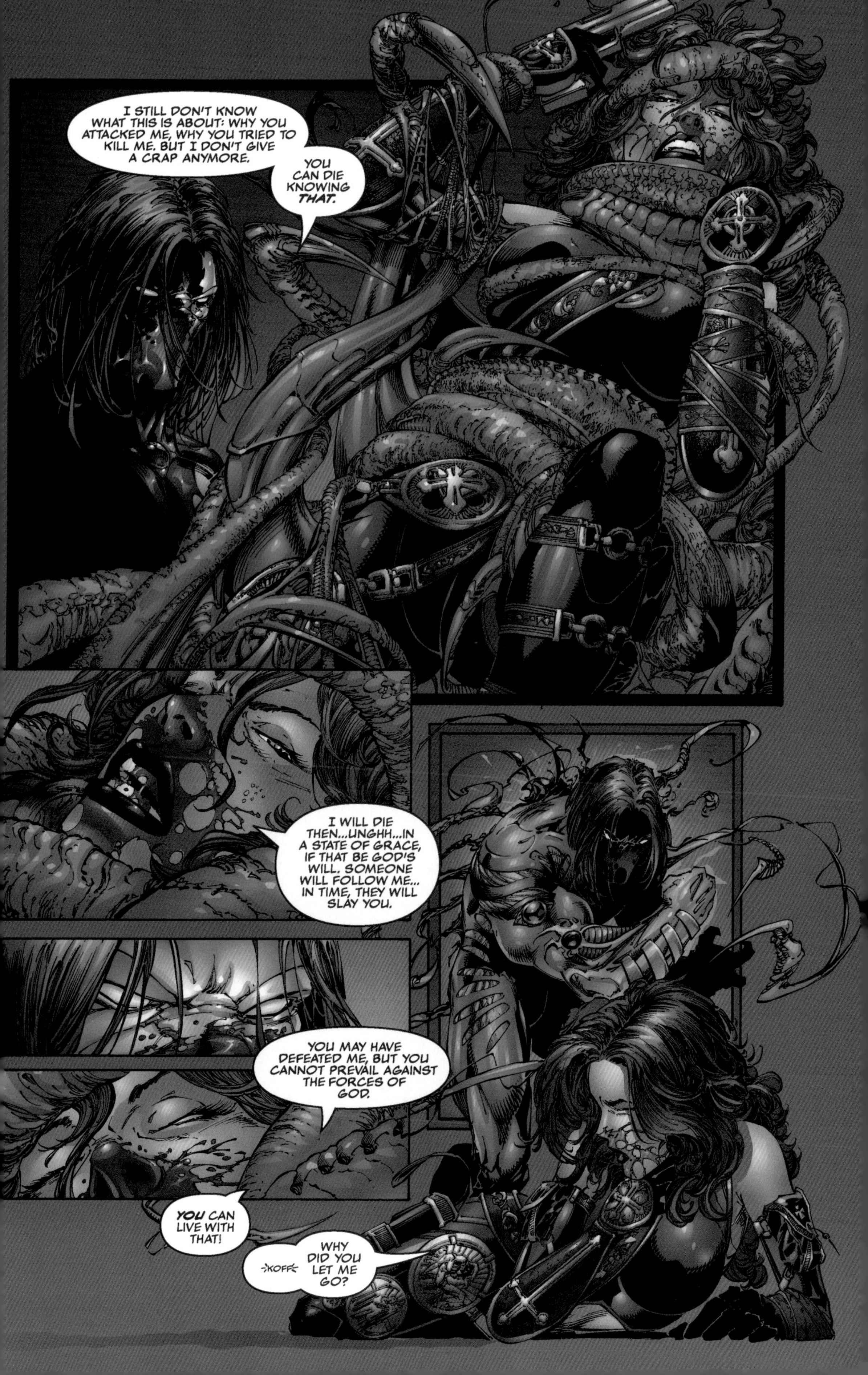
I STILL DON'T KNOW WHAT THIS IS ABOUT: WHY YOU ATTACKED ME, WHY YOU TRIED TO KILL ME. BUT I DON'T GIVE A CRAP ANYMORE.
YOU CAN DIE KNOWING *THAT.*
I WILL DIE THEN...UNGHH...IN A STATE OF GRACE, IF THAT BE GOD'S WILL. SOMEONE WILL FOLLOW ME... IN TIME, THEY WILL SLAY YOU.
YOU MAY HAVE DEFEATED ME, BUT YOU CANNOT PREVAIL AGAINST THE FORCES OF GOD.
YOU CAN LIVE WITH THAT!
KOFF
WHY DID YOU LET ME GO?

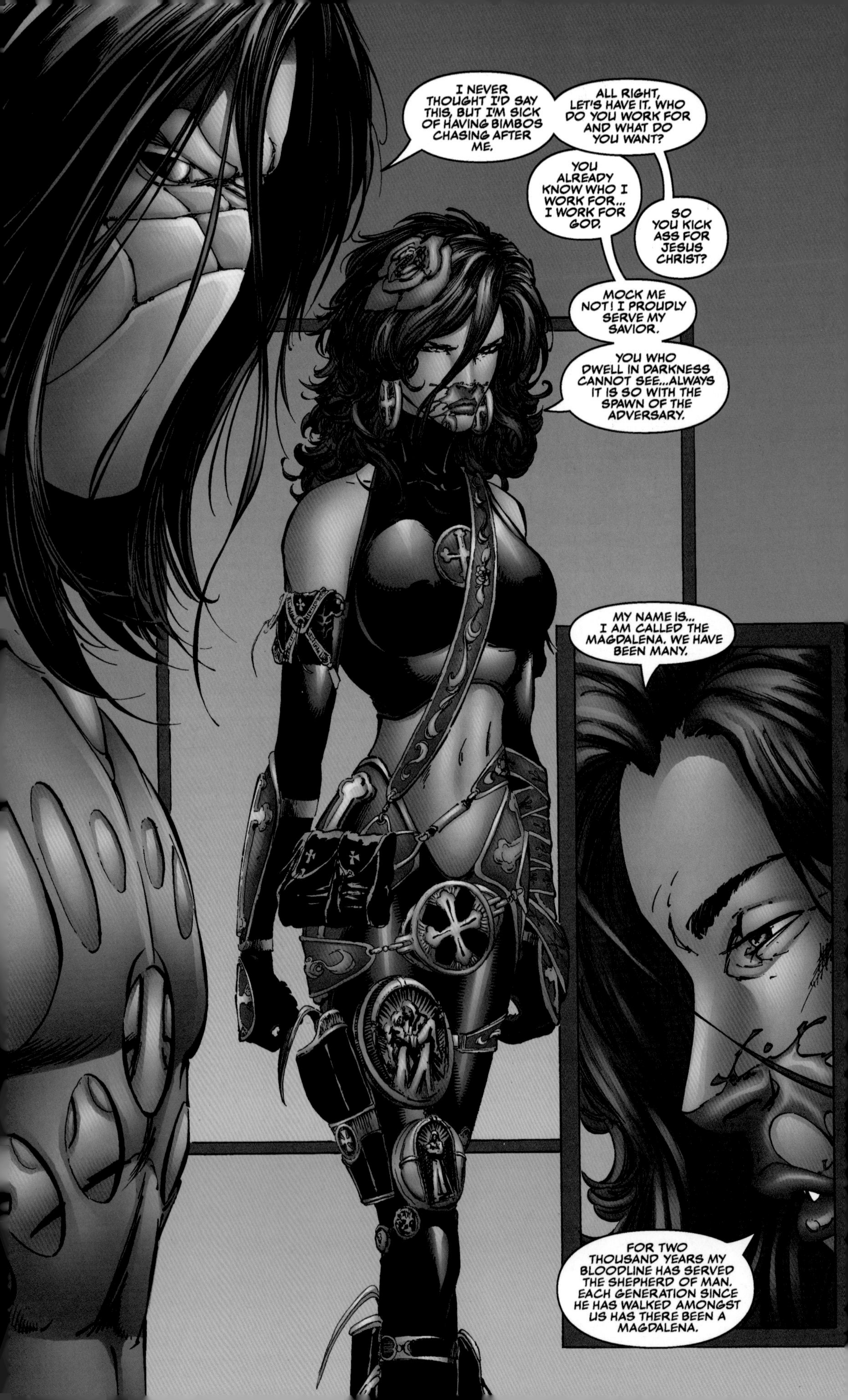
I NEVER THOUGHT I'D SAY THIS, BUT I'M SICK OF HAVING BIMBOS CHASING AFTER ME.
ALL RIGHT, LET'S HAVE IT. WHO DO YOU WORK FOR AND WHAT DO YOU WANT?
YOU ALREADY KNOW WHO I WORK FOR... I WORK FOR GOD.
SO YOU KICK ASS FOR JESUS CHRIST?
MOCK ME NOT! I PROUDLY SERVE MY SAVIOR.
YOU WHO DWELL IN DARKNESS CANNOT SEE...ALWAYS IT IS SO WITH THE SPAWN OF THE ADVERSARY.
MY NAME IS... I AM CALLED THE MAGDALENA. WE HAVE BEEN MANY.
FOR TWO THOUSAND YEARS MY BLOODLINE HAS SERVED THE SHEPHERD OF MAN. EACH GENERATION SINCE HE HAS WALKED AMONGST US HAS THERE BEEN A MAGDALENA.

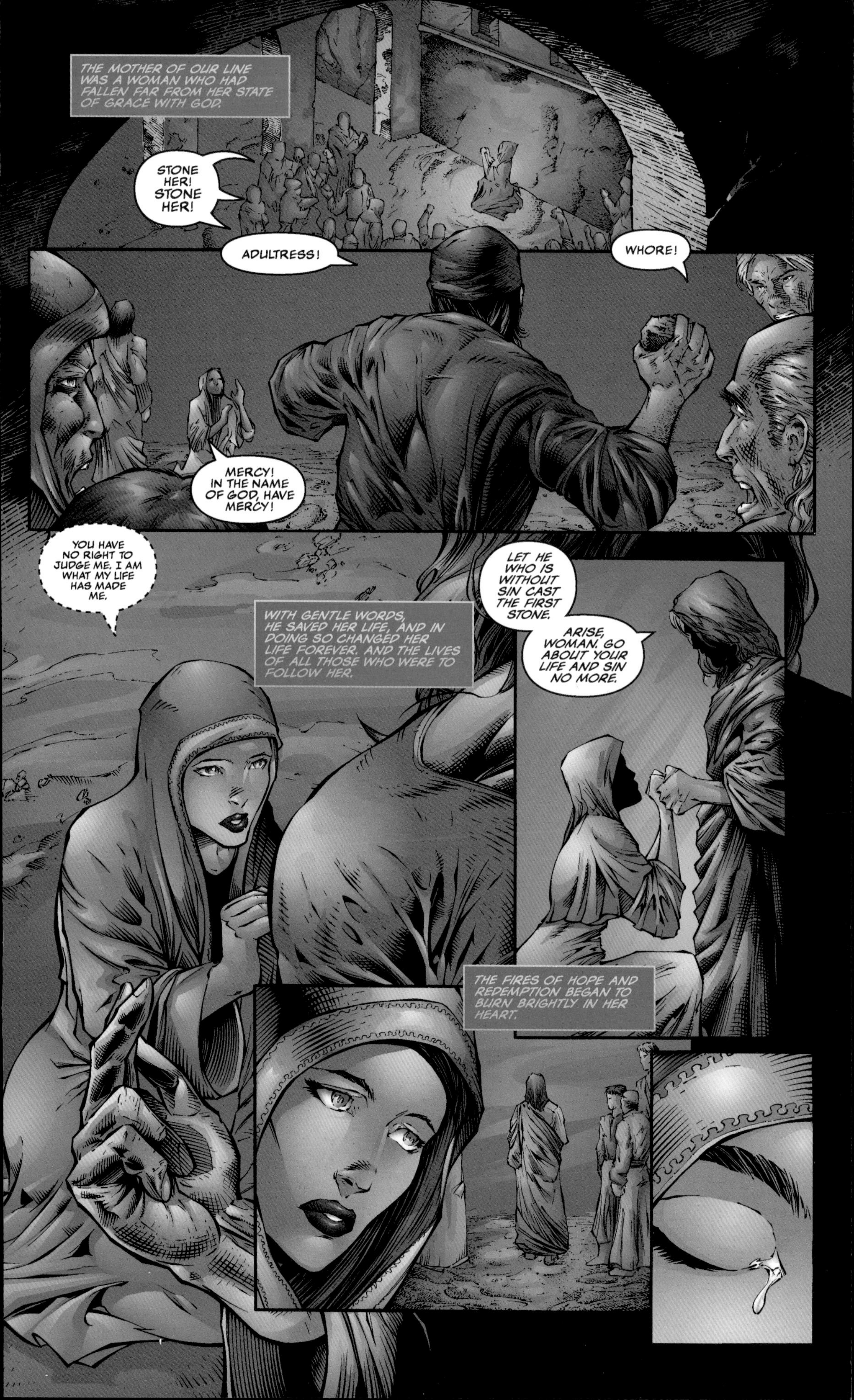
THE MOTHER OF OUR LINE WAS A WOMAN WHO HAD FALLEN FAR FROM HER STATE OF GRACE WITH GOD.
STONE HER! STONE HER!
ADULTRESS!
WHORE!
MERCY! IN THE NAME OF GOD, HAVE MERCY!
YOU HAVE NO RIGHT TO JUDGE ME. I AM WHAT MY LIFE HAS MADE ME.
WITH GENTLE WORDS, HE SAVED HER LIFE, AND IN DOING SO CHANGED HER LIFE FOREVER. AND THE LIVES OF ALL THOSE WHO WERE TO FOLLOW HER.
LET HE WHO IS WITHOUT SIN CAST THE FIRST STONE.
ARISE, WOMAN. GO ABOUT YOUR LIFE AND SIN NO MORE.
THE FIRES OF HOPE AND REDEMPTION BEGAN TO BURN BRIGHTLY IN HER HEART.

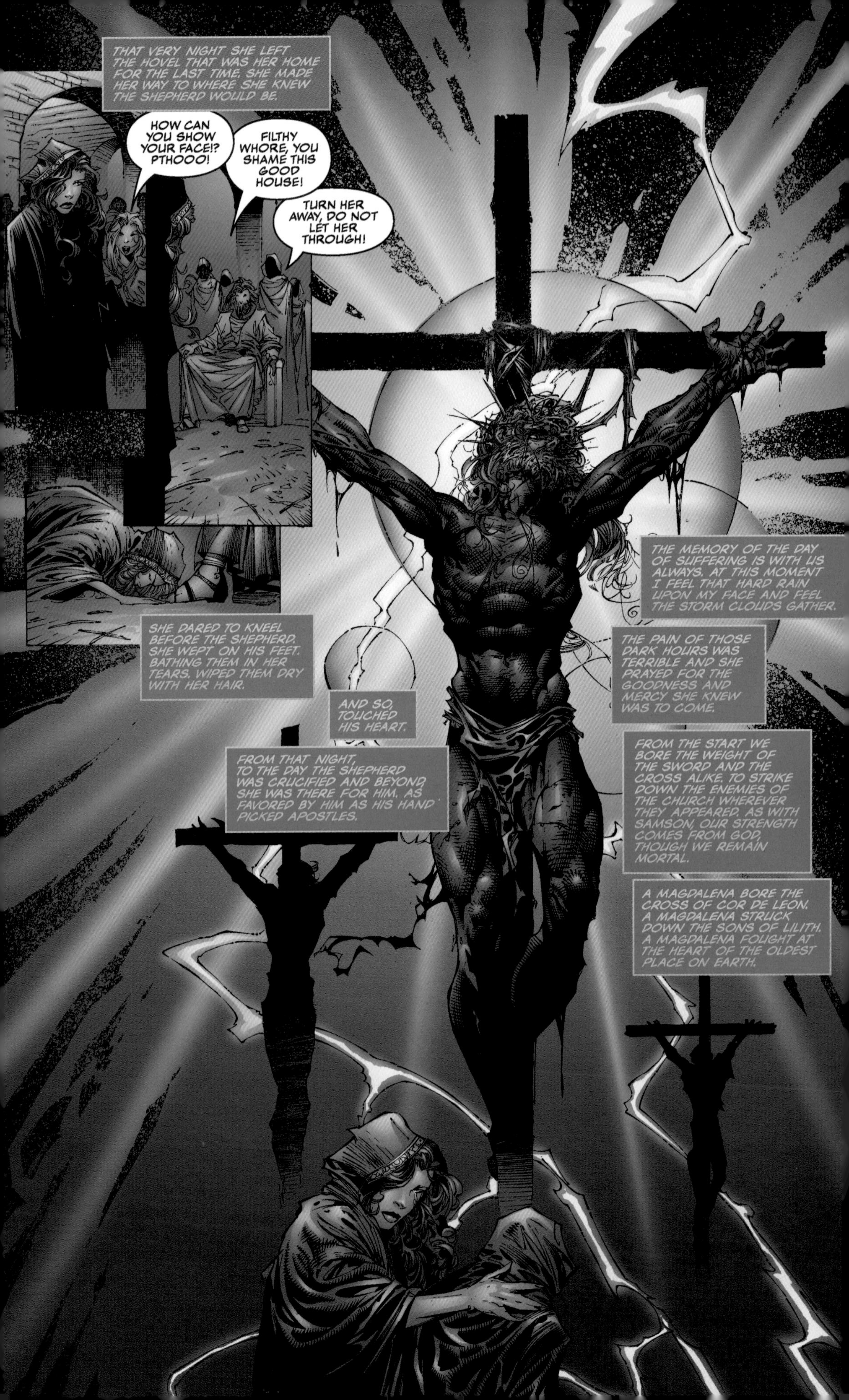
THAT VERY NIGHT SHE LEFT THE HOVEL THAT WAS HER HOME FOR THE LAST TIME. SHE MADE HER WAY TO WHERE SHE KNEW THE SHEPHERD WOULD BE.
HOW CAN YOU SHOW YOUR FACE!? PTHOOO!
FILTHY WHORE, YOU SHAME THIS GOOD HOUSE!
TURN HER AWAY, DO NOT LET HER THROUGH!
SHE DARED TO KNEEL BEFORE THE SHEPHERD. SHE WEPT ON HIS FEET. BATHING THEM IN HER TEARS. WIPED THEM DRY WITH HER HAIR.
AND SO, TOUCHED HIS HEART.
FROM THAT NIGHT, TO THE DAY THE SHEPHERD WAS CRUCIFIED AND BEYOND SHE WAS THERE FOR HIM. AS FAVORED BY HIM AS HIS HAND PICKED APOSTLES.
THE MEMORY OF THE DAY OF SUFFERING IS WITH US ALWAYS. AT THIS MOMENT I FEEL THAT HARD RAIN UPON MY FACE AND FEEL THE STORM CLOUDS GATHER.
THE PAIN OF THOSE DARK HOURS WAS TERRIBLE AND SHE PRAYED FOR THE GOODNESS AND MERCY SHE KNEW WAS TO COME.
FROM THE START WE BORE THE WEIGHT OF THE SWORD AND THE CROSS ALIKE. TO STRIKE DOWN THE ENEMIES OF THE CHURCH WHEREVER THEY APPEARED. AS WITH SAMSON, OUR STRENGTH COMES FROM GOD, THOUGH WE REMAIN MORTAL.
A MAGDALENA BORE THE CROSS OF COR DE LEON. A MAGDALENA STRUCK DOWN THE SONS OF LILITH. A MAGDALENA FOUGHT AT THE HEART OF THE OLDEST PLACE ON EARTH.

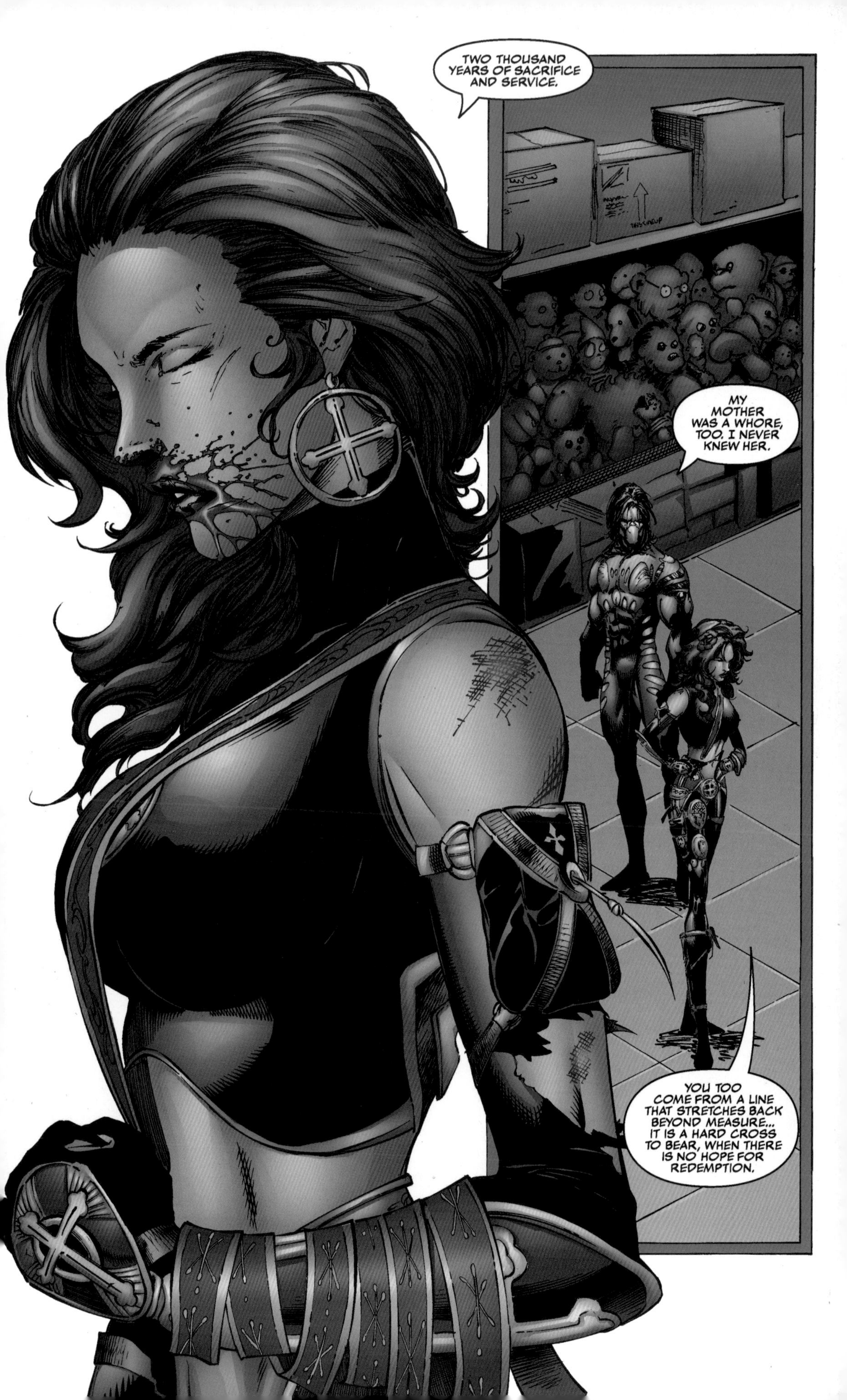
TWO THOUSAND YEARS OF SACRIFICE AND SERVICE.
MY MOTHER WAS A WHORE, TOO. I NEVER KNEW HER.
YOU TOO COME FROM A LINE THAT STRETCHES BACK BEYOND MEASURE... IT IS A HARD CROSS TO BEAR, WHEN THERE IS NO HOPE FOR REDEMPTION.

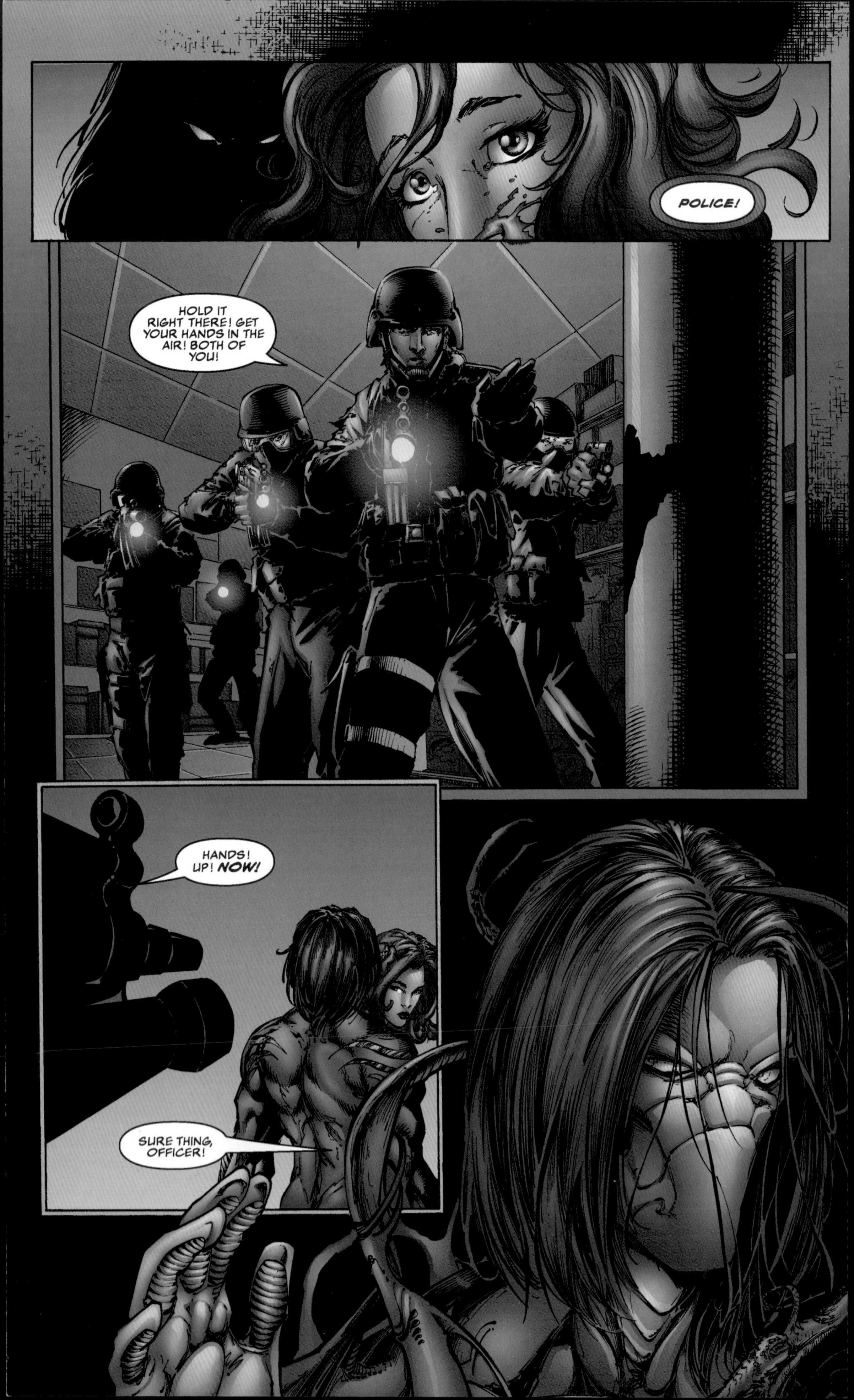
POLICE!
HOLD IT RIGHT THERE! GET YOUR HANDS IN THE AIR! BOTH OF YOU!
HANDS! UP! **NOW!**
SURE THING, OFFICER!

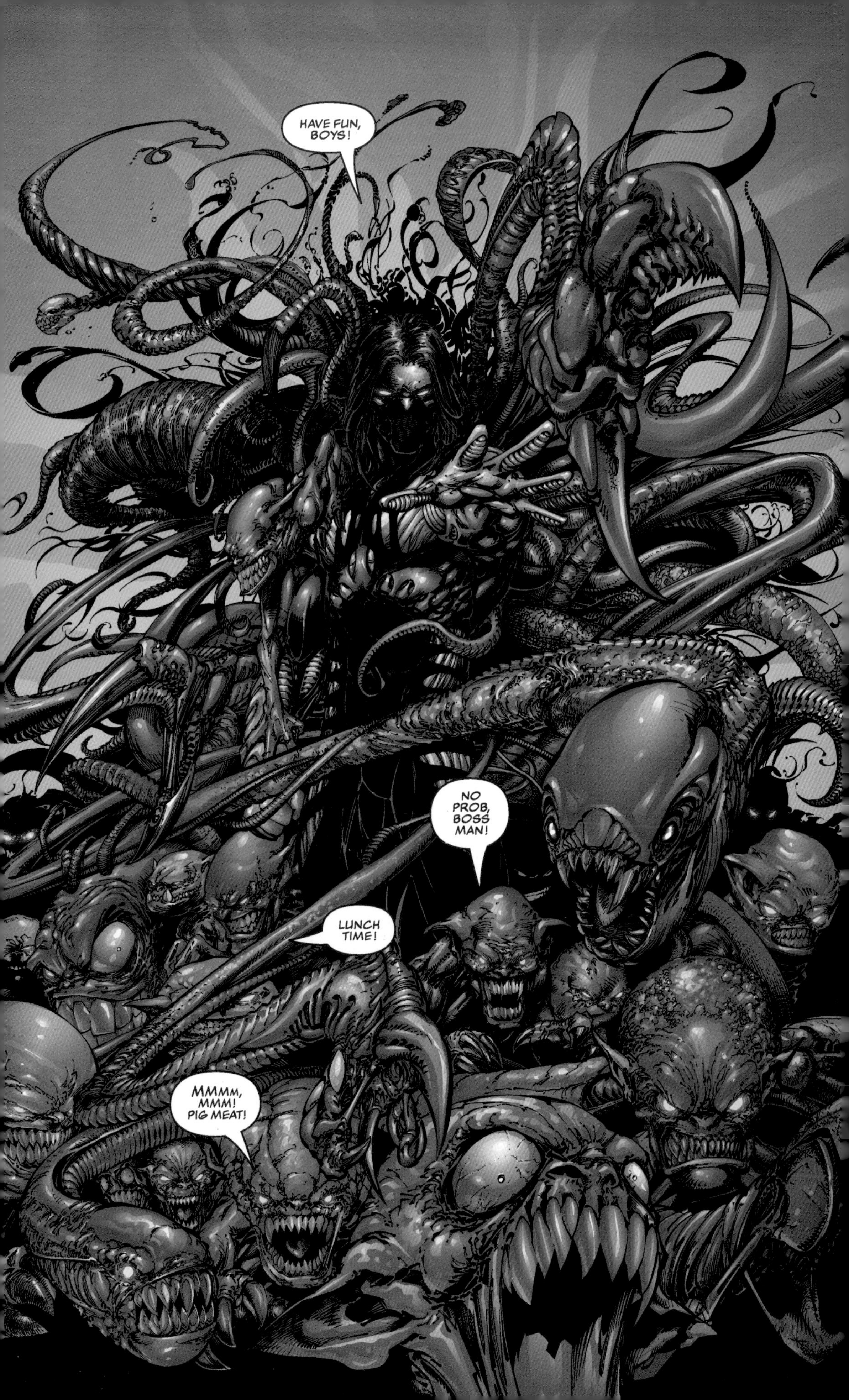
HAVE FUN, BOYS!
NO PROB, BOSS MAN!
LUNCH TIME!
MMMM, MMM! PIG MEAT!

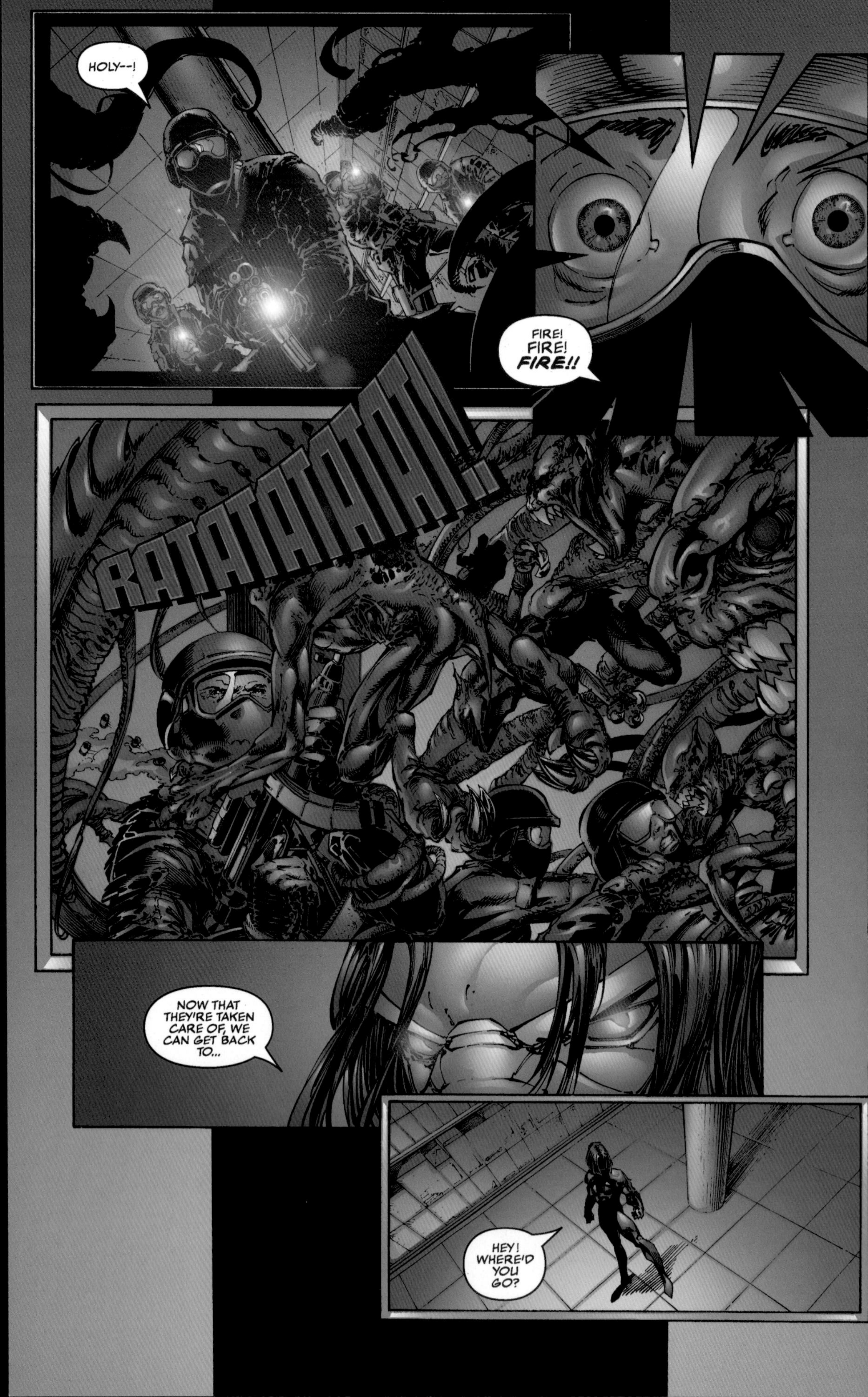

HOLY--!
FIRE! FIRE! FIRE!!
RATATATATAT!!
NOW THAT THEY'RE TAKEN CARE OF, WE CAN GET BACK TO...
HEY! WHERE'D YOU GO?

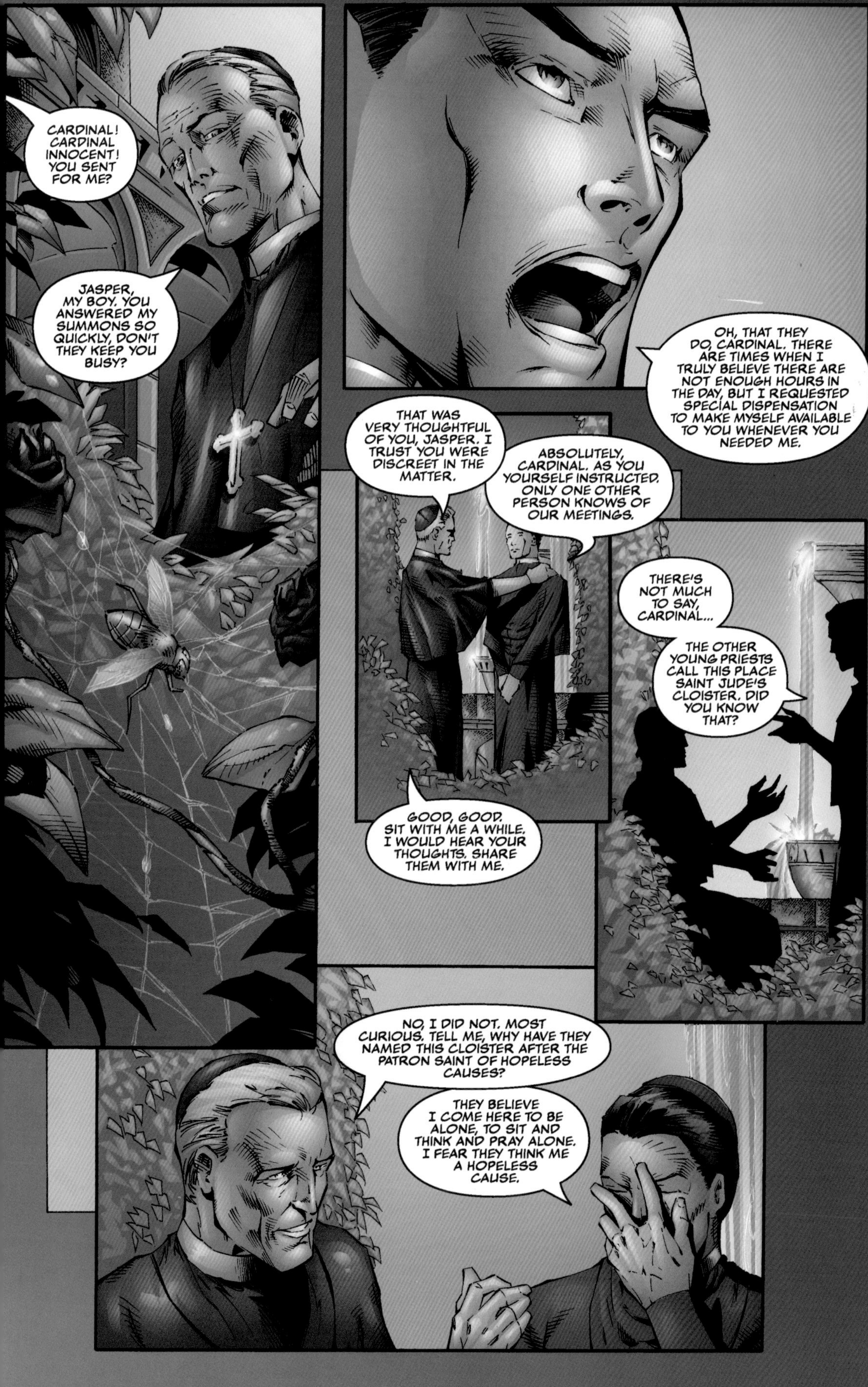
CARDINAL! CARDINAL INNOCENT! YOU SENT FOR ME?
JASPER, MY BOY. YOU ANSWERED MY SUMMONS SO QUICKLY, DON'T THEY KEEP YOU BUSY?
OH, THAT THEY DO, CARDINAL. THERE ARE TIMES WHEN I TRULY BELIEVE THERE ARE NOT ENOUGH HOURS IN THE DAY, BUT I REQUESTED SPECIAL DISPENSATION TO MAKE MYSELF AVAILABLE TO YOU WHENEVER YOU NEEDED ME.
THAT WAS VERY THOUGHTFUL OF YOU, JASPER. I TRUST YOU WERE DISCREET IN THE MATTER.
ABSOLUTELY, CARDINAL. AS YOU YOURSELF INSTRUCTED. ONLY ONE OTHER PERSON KNOWS OF OUR MEETINGS.
GOOD, GOOD. SIT WITH ME A WHILE. I WOULD HEAR YOUR THOUGHTS. SHARE THEM WITH ME.
THERE'S NOT MUCH TO SAY, CARDINAL...
THE OTHER YOUNG PRIESTS CALL THIS PLACE SAINT JUDE'S CLOISTER. DID YOU KNOW THAT?
NO, I DID NOT. MOST CURIOUS. TELL ME, WHY HAVE THEY NAMED THIS CLOISTER AFTER THE PATRON SAINT OF HOPELESS CAUSES?
THEY BELIEVE I COME HERE TO BE ALONE, TO SIT AND THINK AND PRAY ALONE. I FEAR THEY THINK ME A HOPELESS CAUSE.

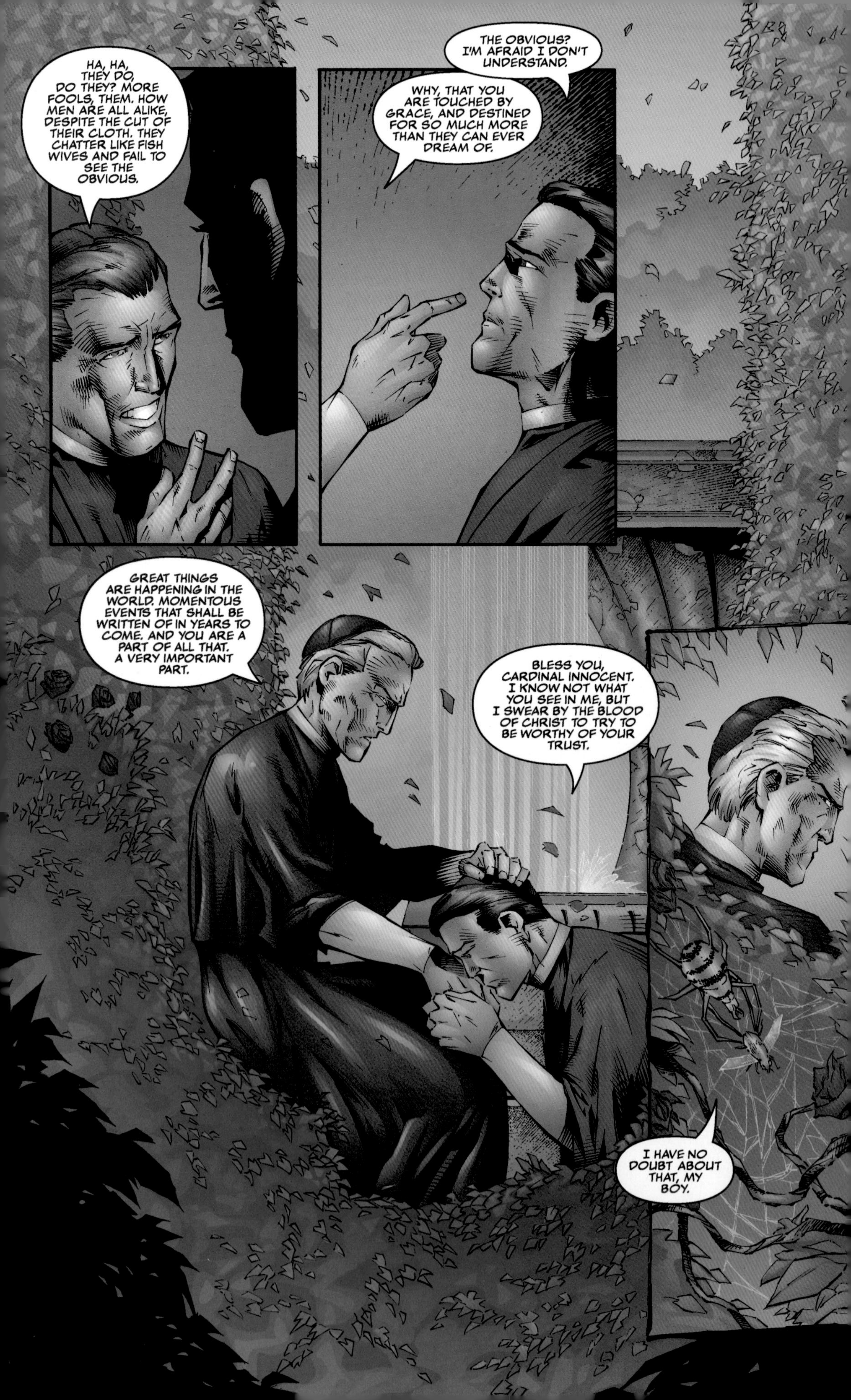
HA, HA, THEY DO, DO THEY? MORE FOOLS, THEM. HOW MEN ARE ALL ALIKE, DESPITE THE CUT OF THEIR CLOTH. THEY CHATTER LIKE FISH WIVES AND FAIL TO SEE THE OBVIOUS.
THE OBVIOUS? I'M AFRAID I DON'T UNDERSTAND.
WHY, THAT YOU ARE TOUCHED BY GRACE, AND DESTINED FOR SO MUCH MORE THAN THEY CAN EVER DREAM OF.
GREAT THINGS ARE HAPPENING IN THE WORLD. MOMENTOUS EVENTS THAT SHALL BE WRITTEN OF IN YEARS TO COME. AND YOU ARE A PART OF ALL THAT. A VERY IMPORTANT PART.
BLESS YOU, CARDINAL INNOCENT. I KNOW NOT WHAT YOU SEE IN ME, BUT I SWEAR BY THE BLOOD OF CHRIST TO TRY TO BE WORTHY OF YOUR TRUST.
I HAVE NO DOUBT ABOUT THAT, MY BOY.

The Darkness
#18
ISSUE

story by: Malachy Coney
pencils by: Joe Benitez
inks by: Joe Weems V, Jonathan Livesay, Marlo Alquiza
colors by: Matt Nelson, Richard Isanove,
Tyson Wengler, Richard and Tanya Horie, Jonathan D. Smith
letters by: Dennis Heisler

writing assists by: Joe Benitez, Marcia Chen
pencil assists by: Brian Ching, Keu Cha
inks assists by: Marco "Madman" Galli

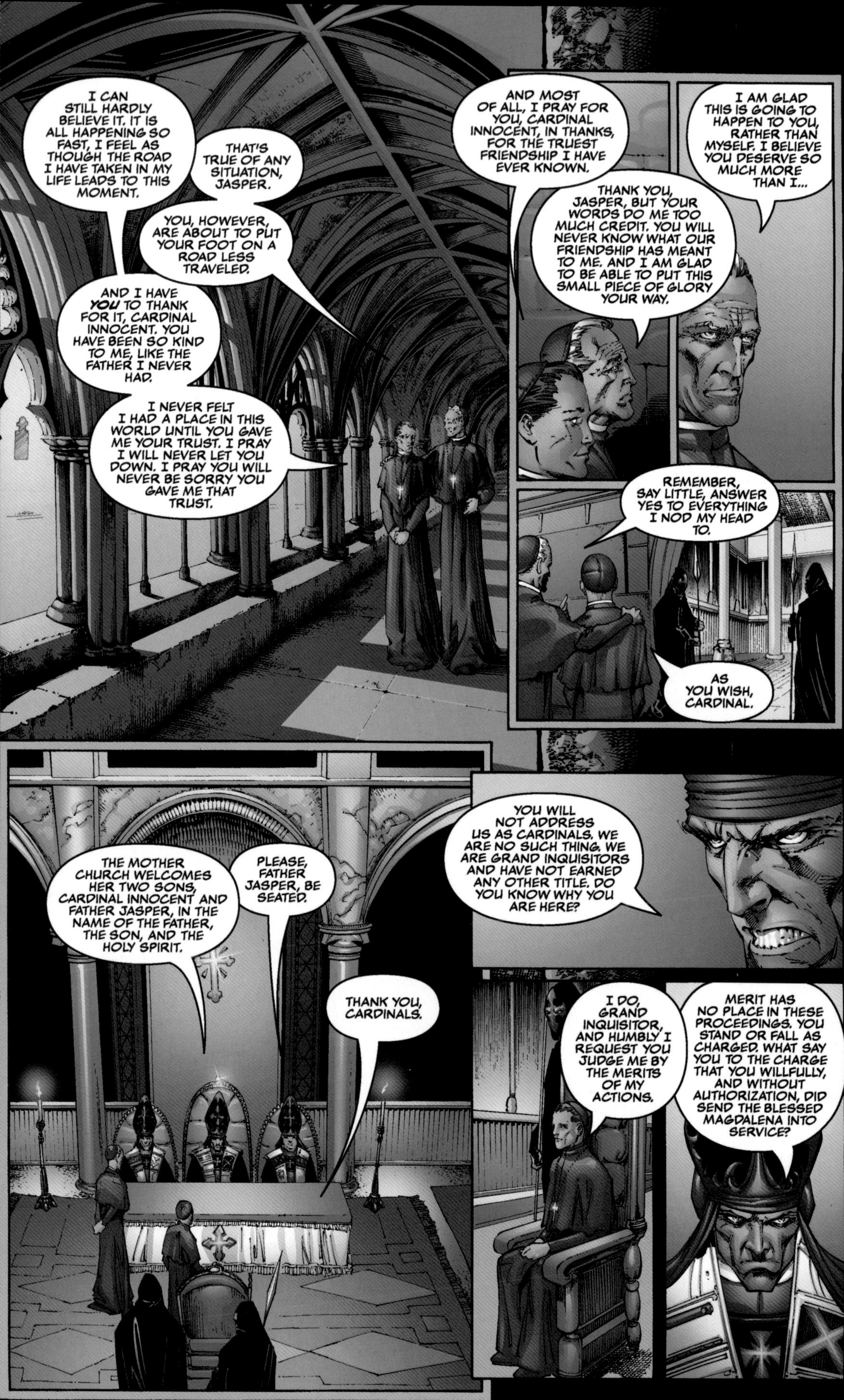

I CAN STILL HARDLY BELIEVE IT. IT IS ALL HAPPENING SO FAST, I FEEL AS THOUGH THE ROAD I HAVE TAKEN IN MY LIFE LEADS TO THIS MOMENT.
THAT'S TRUE OF ANY SITUATION, JASPER.
YOU, HOWEVER, ARE ABOUT TO PUT YOUR FOOT ON A ROAD LESS TRAVELED.
AND I HAVE YOU TO THANK FOR IT, CARDINAL INNOCENT. YOU HAVE BEEN SO KIND TO ME, LIKE THE FATHER I NEVER HAD.
I NEVER FELT I HAD A PLACE IN THIS WORLD UNTIL YOU GAVE ME YOUR TRUST. I PRAY I WILL NEVER LET YOU DOWN. I PRAY YOU WILL NEVER BE SORRY YOU GAVE ME THAT TRUST.
AND MOST OF ALL, I PRAY FOR YOU, CARDINAL INNOCENT, IN THANKS, FOR THE TRUEST FRIENDSHIP I HAVE EVER KNOWN.
THANK YOU, JASPER, BUT YOUR WORDS DO ME TOO MUCH CREDIT. YOU WILL NEVER KNOW WHAT OUR FRIENDSHIP HAS MEANT TO ME. AND I AM GLAD TO BE ABLE TO PUT THIS SMALL PIECE OF GLORY YOUR WAY.
I AM GLAD THIS IS GOING TO HAPPEN TO YOU, RATHER THAN MYSELF. I BELIEVE YOU DESERVE SO MUCH MORE THAN I...
REMEMBER, SAY LITTLE, ANSWER YES TO EVERYTHING I NOD MY HEAD TO.
AS YOU WISH, CARDINAL.
THE MOTHER CHURCH WELCOMES HER TWO SONS, CARDINAL INNOCENT AND FATHER JASPER, IN THE NAME OF THE FATHER, THE SON, AND THE HOLY SPIRIT.
PLEASE, FATHER JASPER, BE SEATED.
THANK YOU, CARDINALS.
YOU WILL NOT ADDRESS US AS CARDINALS. WE ARE NO SUCH THING. WE ARE GRAND INQUISITORS AND HAVE NOT EARNED ANY OTHER TITLE. DO YOU KNOW WHY YOU ARE HERE?
I DO, GRAND INQUISITOR, AND HUMBLY I REQUEST YOU JUDGE ME BY THE MERITS OF MY ACTIONS.
MERIT HAS NO PLACE IN THESE PROCEEDINGS. YOU STAND OR FALL AS CHARGED. WHAT SAY YOU TO THE CHARGE THAT YOU WILLFULLY, AND WITHOUT AUTHORIZATION, DID SEND THE BLESSED MAGDALENA INTO SERVICE?

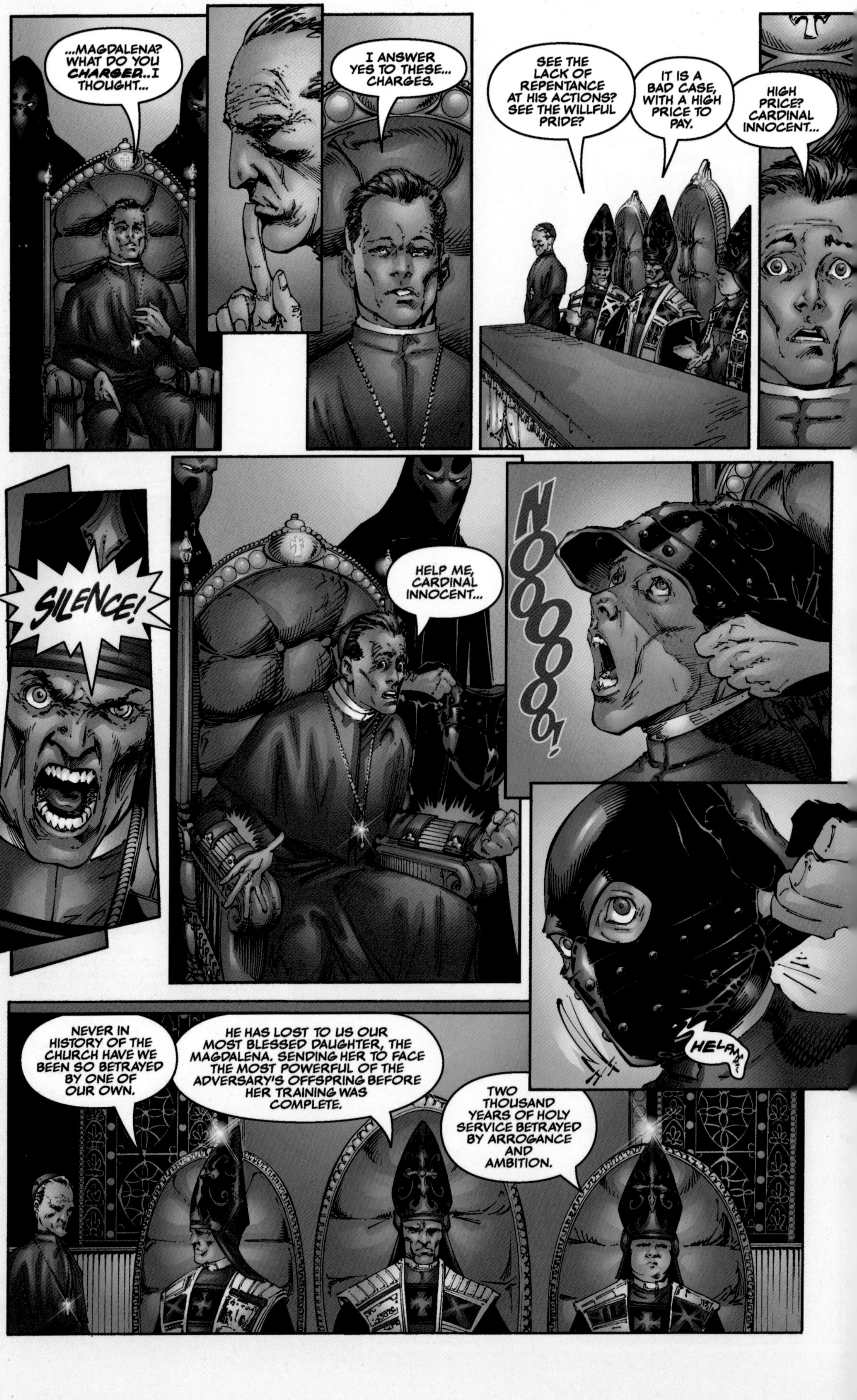

...MAGDALENA? WHAT DO YOU CHARGED...I THOUGHT...
I ANSWER YES TO THESE... CHARGES.
SEE THE LACK OF REPENTANCE AT HIS ACTIONS? SEE THE WILLFUL PRIDE?
IT IS A BAD CASE, WITH A HIGH PRICE TO PAY.
HIGH PRICE? CARDINAL INNOCENT...
SILENCE!
HELP ME, CARDINAL INNOCENT...
NOOOOOO!
HELP...
NEVER IN HISTORY OF THE CHURCH HAVE WE BEEN SO BETRAYED BY ONE OF OUR OWN.
HE HAS LOST TO US OUR MOST BLESSED DAUGHTER, THE MAGDALENA. SENDING HER TO FACE THE MOST POWERFUL OF THE ADVERSARY'S OFFSPRING BEFORE HER TRAINING WAS COMPLETE.
TWO THOUSAND YEARS OF HOLY SERVICE BETRAYED BY ARROGANCE AND AMBITION.

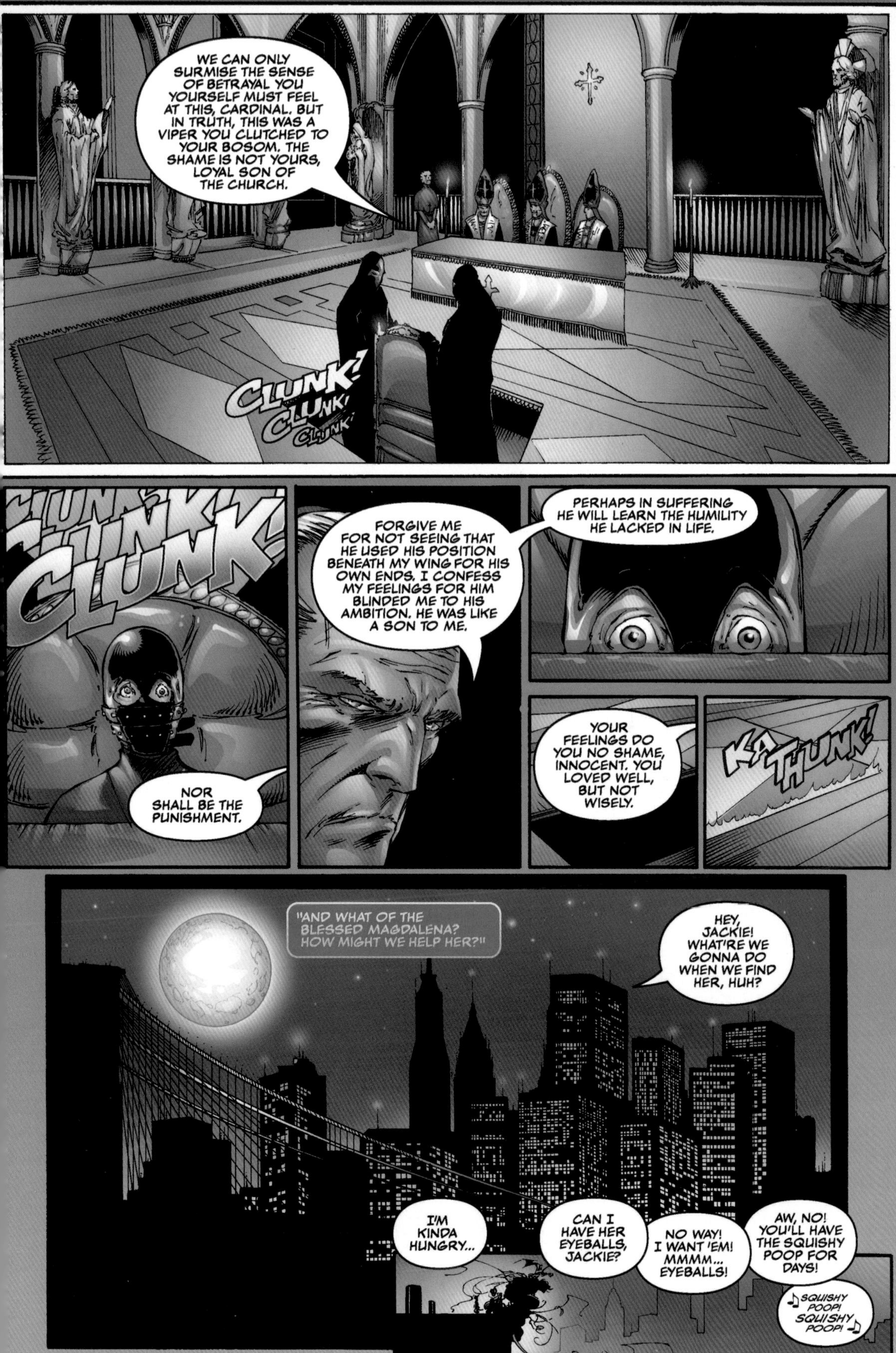
WE CAN ONLY SURMISE THE SENSE OF BETRAYAL YOU YOURSELF MUST FEEL AT THIS, CARDINAL. BUT IN TRUTH, THIS WAS A VIPER YOU CLUTCHED TO YOUR BOSOM. THE SHAME IS NOT YOURS, LOYAL SON OF THE CHURCH.
CLUNK! CLUNK! CLUNK!
CLUNK!
NOR SHALL BE THE PUNISHMENT.
FORGIVE ME FOR NOT SEEING THAT HE USED HIS POSITION BENEATH MY WING FOR HIS OWN ENDS. I CONFESS MY FEELINGS FOR HIM BLINDED ME TO HIS AMBITION. HE WAS LIKE A SON TO ME.
PERHAPS IN SUFFERING HE WILL LEARN THE HUMILITY HE LACKED IN LIFE.
YOUR FEELINGS DO YOU NO SHAME, INNOCENT. YOU LOVED WELL, BUT NOT WISELY.
KA THUNK!
"AND WHAT OF THE BLESSED MAGDALENA? HOW MIGHT WE HELP HER?"
HEY, JACKIE! WHAT'RE WE GONNA DO WHEN WE FIND HER, HUH?
I'M KINDA HUNGRY...
CAN I HAVE HER EYEBALLS, JACKIE?
NO WAY! I WANT 'EM! MMMM... EYEBALLS!
AW, NO! YOU'LL HAVE THE SQUISHY POOP FOR DAYS!
♪ SQUISHY POOP! SQUISHY POOP! ♪

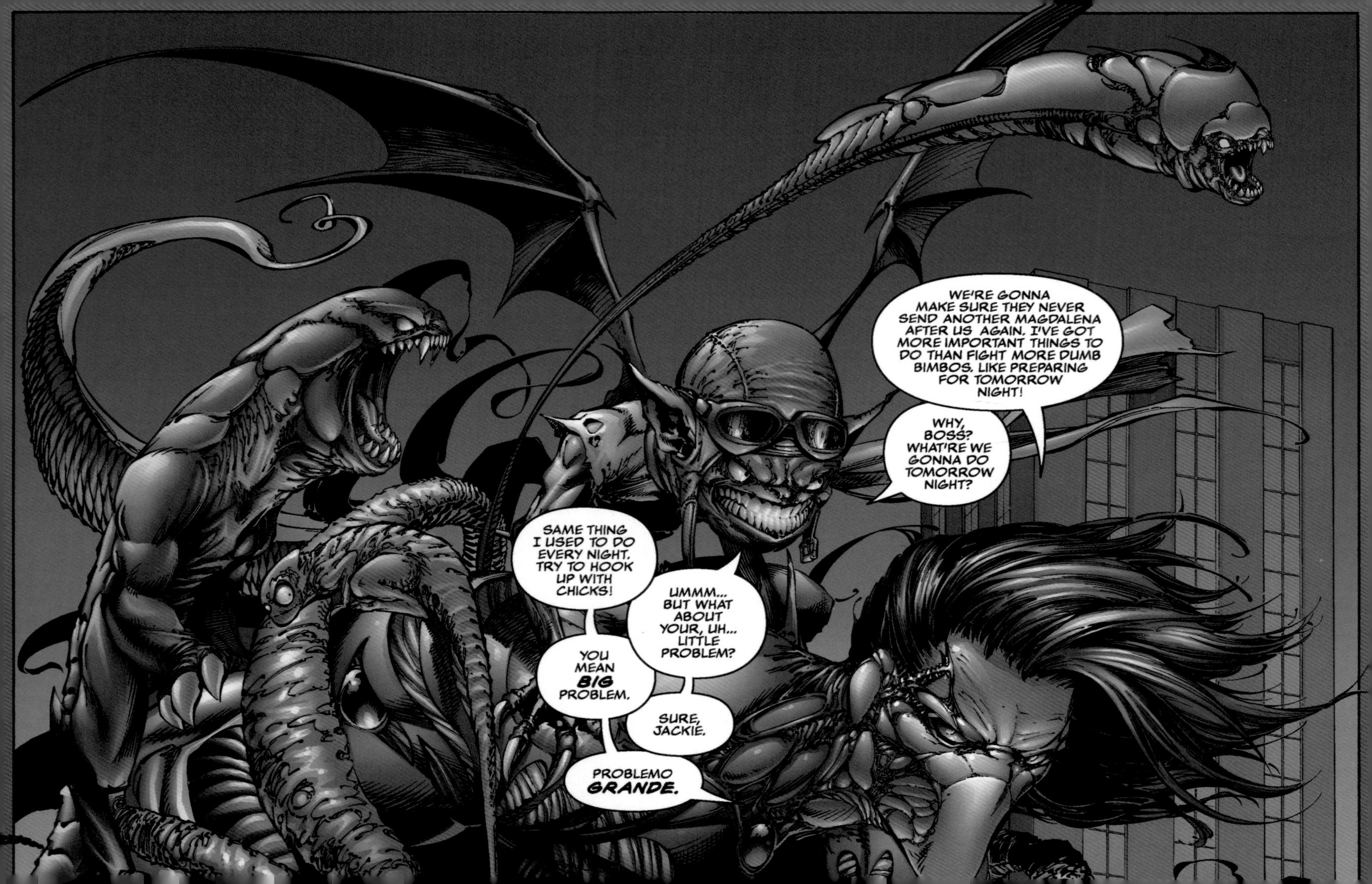
WE'RE GONNA MAKE SURE THEY NEVER SEND ANOTHER MAGDALENA AFTER US AGAIN. I'VE GOT MORE IMPORTANT THINGS TO DO THAN FIGHT MORE DUMB BIMBOS. LIKE PREPARING FOR TOMORROW NIGHT!
WHY, BOSS? WHAT'RE WE GONNA DO TOMORROW NIGHT?
SAME THING I USED TO DO EVERY NIGHT. TRY TO HOOK UP WITH CHICKS!
UMMM... BUT WHAT ABOUT YOUR, UH... LITTLE PROBLEM?
YOU MEAN BIG PROBLEM.
SURE, JACKIE.
PROBLEMO GRANDE.

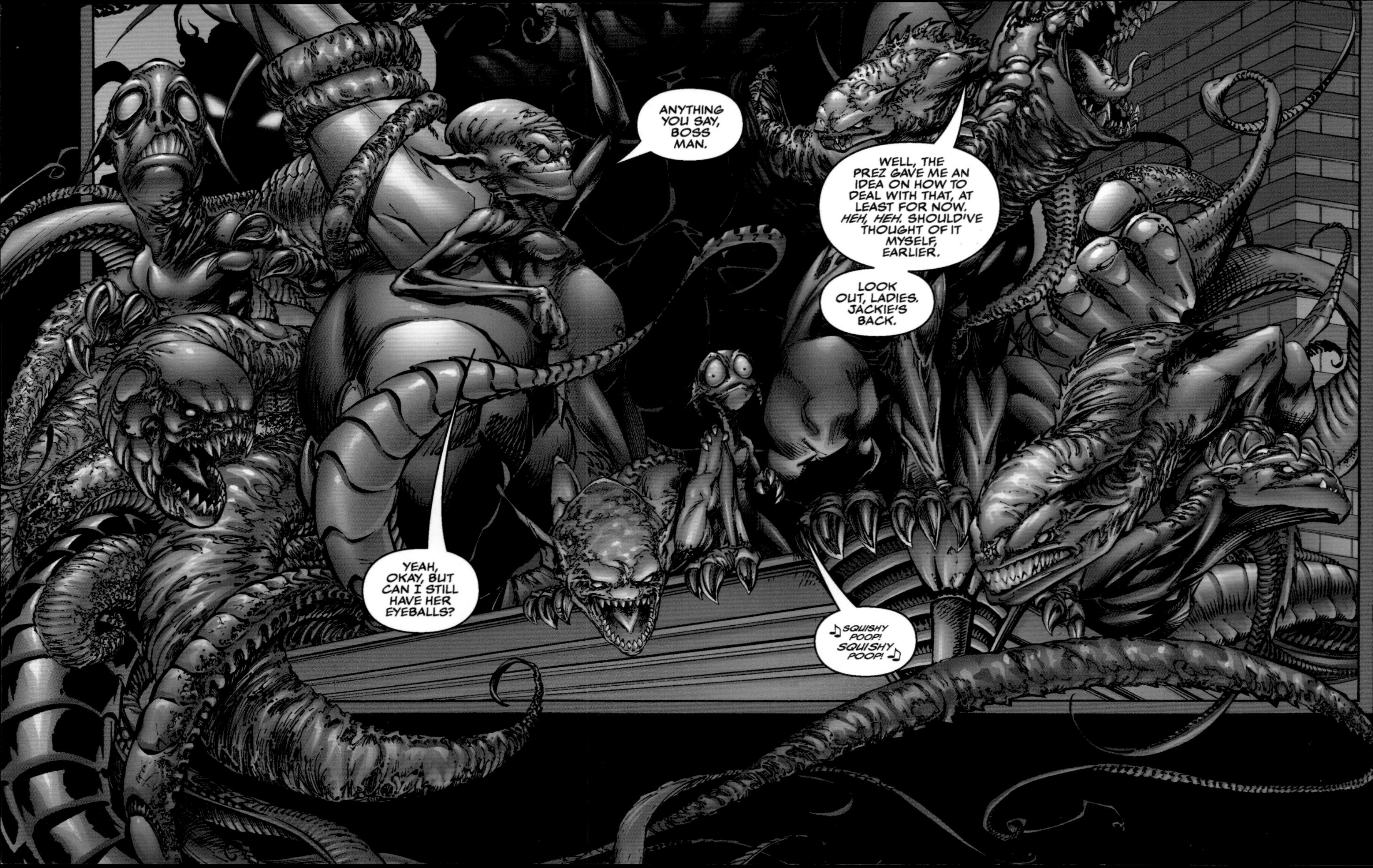
ANYTHING YOU SAY, BOSS MAN.
WELL, THE PREZ GAVE ME AN IDEA ON HOW TO DEAL WITH THAT, AT LEAST FOR NOW. *HEH, HEH.* SHOULD'VE THOUGHT OF IT MYSELF, EARLIER.
LOOK OUT, LADIES. JACKIE'S BACK.
YEAH, OKAY, BUT CAN I STILL HAVE HER EYEBALLS?
♪ SQUISHY POOP! SQUISHY POOP! ♪

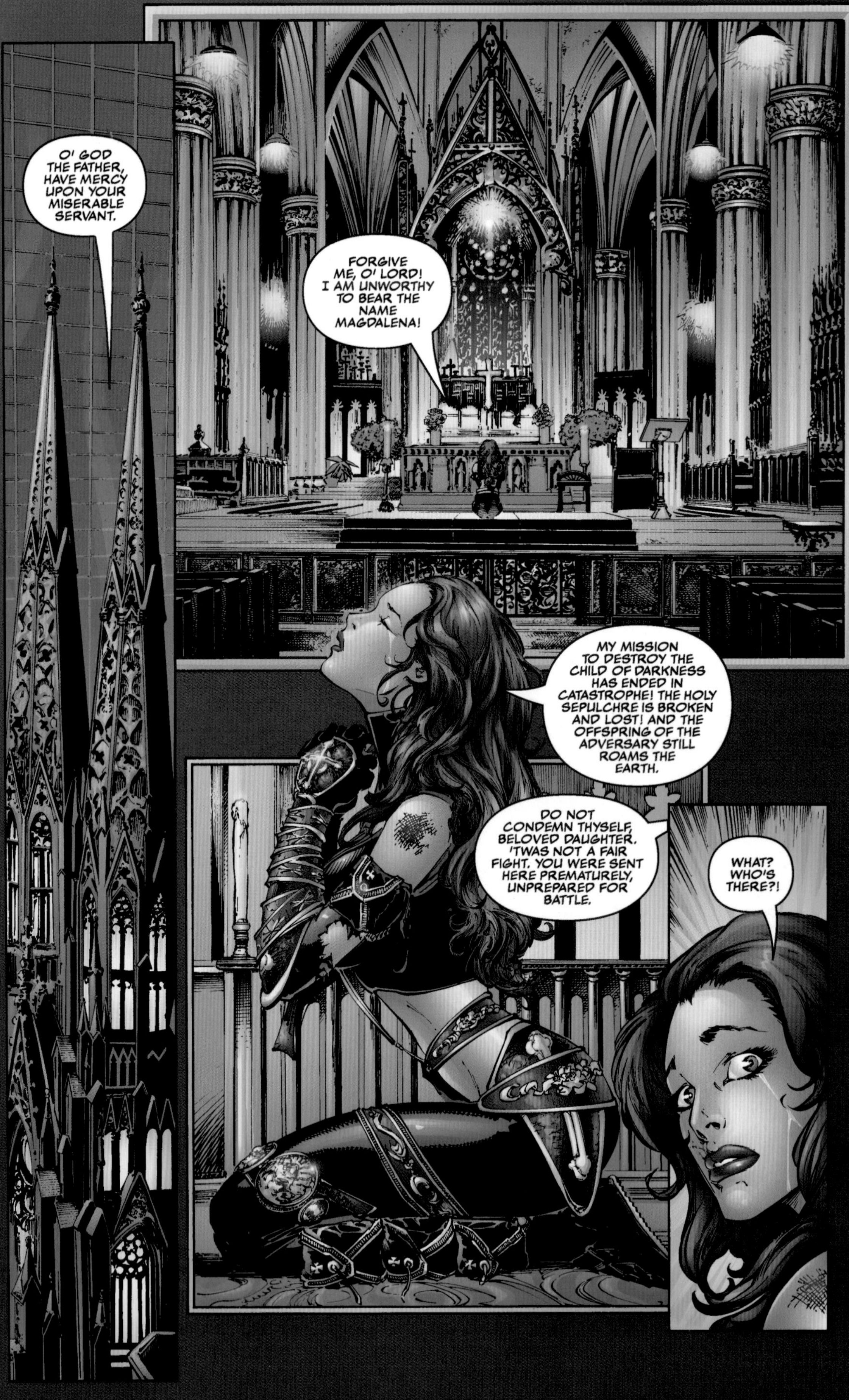
O' GOD THE FATHER, HAVE MERCY UPON YOUR MISERABLE SERVANT.
FORGIVE ME, O' LORD! I AM UNWORTHY TO BEAR THE NAME MAGDALENA!
MY MISSION TO DESTROY THE CHILD OF DARKNESS HAS ENDED IN CATASTROPHE! THE HOLY SEPULCHRE IS BROKEN AND LOST! AND THE OFFSPRING OF THE ADVERSARY STILL ROAMS THE EARTH.
DO NOT CONDEMN THYSELF, BELOVED DAUGHTER. 'TWAS NOT A FAIR FIGHT. YOU WERE SENT HERE PREMATURELY, UNPREPARED FOR BATTLE.
WHAT? WHO'S THERE?!

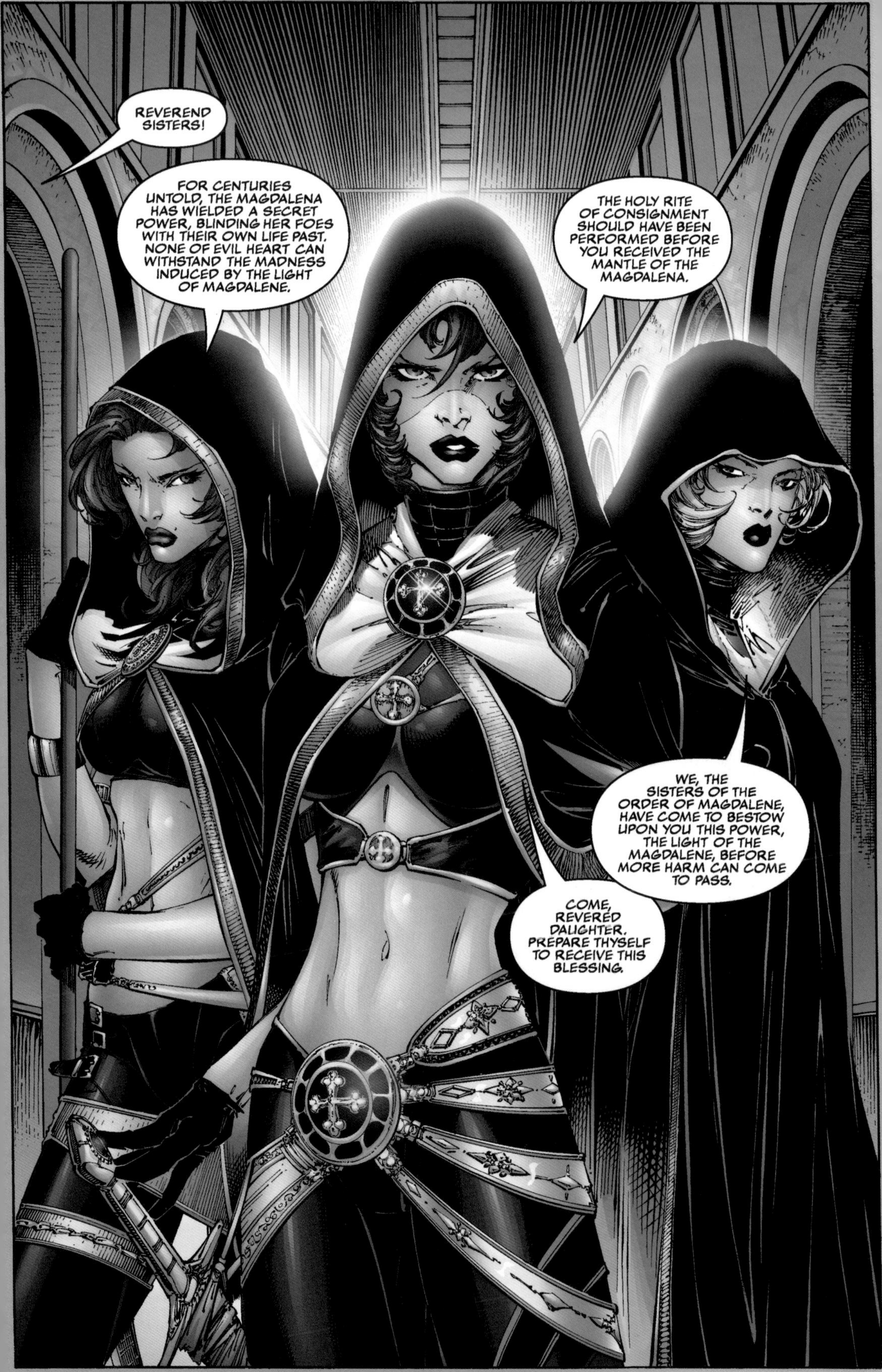
REVEREND SISTERS!
FOR CENTURIES UNTOLD, THE MAGDALENA HAS WIELDED A SECRET POWER, BLINDING HER FOES WITH THEIR OWN LIFE PAST. NONE OF EVIL HEART CAN WITHSTAND THE MADNESS INDUCED BY THE LIGHT OF MAGDALENE.
THE HOLY RITE OF CONSIGNMENT SHOULD HAVE BEEN PERFORMED BEFORE YOU RECEIVED THE MANTLE OF THE MAGDALENA.
WE, THE SISTERS OF THE ORDER OF MAGDALENE, HAVE COME TO BESTOW UPON YOU THIS POWER, THE LIGHT OF THE MAGDALENE, BEFORE MORE HARM CAN COME TO PASS.
COME, REVERED DAUGHTER. PREPARE THYSELF TO RECEIVE THIS BLESSING.

NEARLY ALL WOUNDS WERE SUPERFICIAL, SO YOU CAN LEAVE TONIGHT, IF YOU WISH. YOU DO HAVE SOME INTERESTING SCAR TISSUE THOUGH. YOU MUST LEAD AN INTERESTING LIFE.

NICE OF YOU TO SAY SO. DON'T GO TOO FAR AWAY NOW. I MIGHT NEED A BEDPAN SOON, WOULDN'T WANT YOU TO MISS THAT.

THANK YOU, NURSE.

YOU SHOULDN'T OUGHTA SAY THINGS LIKE THAT. SHE'S JUST DOING HER JOB.

SO WAS I, OLD MAN. SO WAS I.

IT MAY BE THE OLDEST PROFESSION, SISTER, BUT IT'S AS OLD AS SIN. YOU DON'T HAVE TO SELL YOUR BODY TO THE NIGHT...

HA, HA, HA, HALILIH, THAT HURTS...

SORRY, OLD MAN. I'M NOT LAUGHING AT YOU, BUT YOU JUST QUOTED A LINE FROM MY FAVORITE POLICE SONG. DAMN SONG'S THE STORY OF MY LIFE.

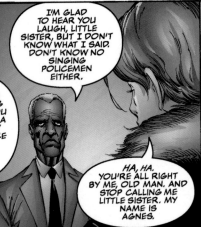

I'M GLAD TO HEAR YOU LAUGH, LITTLE SISTER, BUT I DON'T KNOW WHAT I SAID. DON'T KNOW NO SINGING POLICEMEN EITHER.

HA, HA. YOU'RE ALL RIGHT BY ME, OLD MAN. AND STOP CALLING ME LITTLE SISTER. MY NAME IS AGNES.

HELLO, AGNES. MY NAME IS ISAAC. COME ON, LET'S GET YOU OUT OF HERE.

WELL, ISAAC...HAVE YOU GOT A BIG PACKAGE INSIDE YOUR COAT, OR ARE YOU JUST GLAD TO SEE ME?

OH, YES, MY GOOD LUCK CHARM. THIS, I BELIEVE, IS WHAT SAVED US DURING ALL THE COMMOTION.

IS IT JUST ME, OR IS IT GLOWING?

IT IS A SIGN FROM OUR LORD. WHEN THE BUS CRASHED, I GRABBED IT, AND I PRAYED, AND THE LORD HEARD MY PRAYERS AND ANSWERED THEM, AND WE MADE IT THROUGH SAFELY.

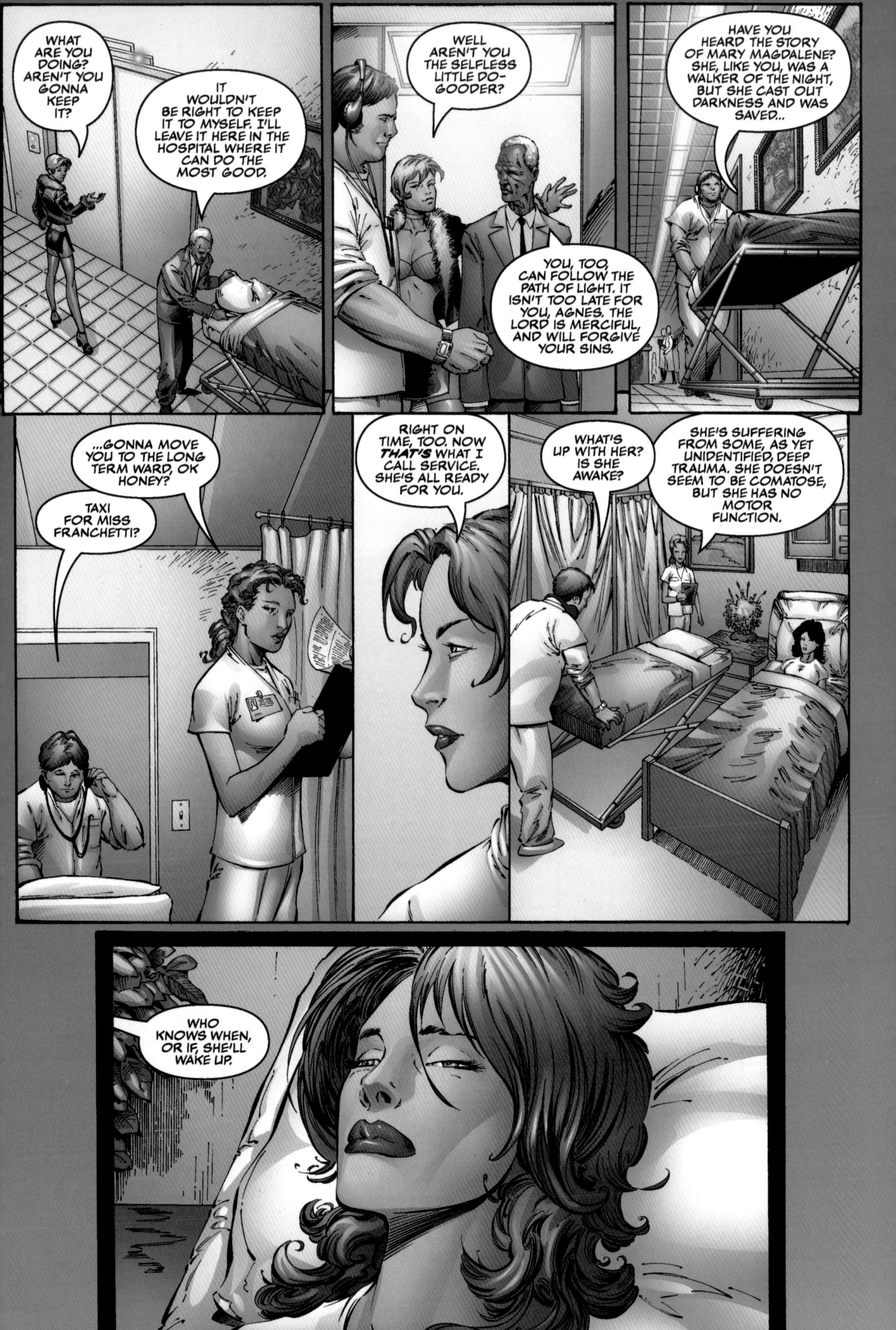
WHAT ARE YOU DOING? AREN'T YOU GONNA KEEP IT?
IT WOULDN'T BE RIGHT TO KEEP IT TO MYSELF. I'LL LEAVE IT HERE IN THE HOSPITAL WHERE IT CAN DO THE MOST GOOD.
WELL AREN'T YOU THE SELFLESS LITTLE DO-GOODER?
YOU, TOO, CAN FOLLOW THE PATH OF LIGHT. IT ISN'T TOO LATE FOR YOU, AGNES. THE LORD IS MERCIFUL, AND WILL FORGIVE YOUR SINS.
HAVE YOU HEARD THE STORY OF MARY MAGDALENE? SHE, LIKE YOU, WAS A WALKER OF THE NIGHT, BUT SHE CAST OUT DARKNESS AND WAS SAVED...
...GONNA MOVE YOU TO THE LONG TERM WARD, OK HONEY?
TAXI FOR MISS FRANCHETTI?
RIGHT ON TIME, TOO. NOW *THAT'S* WHAT I CALL SERVICE. SHE'S ALL READY FOR YOU.
WHAT'S UP WITH HER? IS SHE AWAKE?
SHE'S SUFFERING FROM SOME, AS YET UNIDENTIFIED, DEEP TRAUMA. SHE DOESN'T SEEM TO BE COMATOSE, BUT SHE HAS NO MOTOR FUNCTION.
WHO KNOWS WHEN, OR IF, SHE'LL WAKE UP.

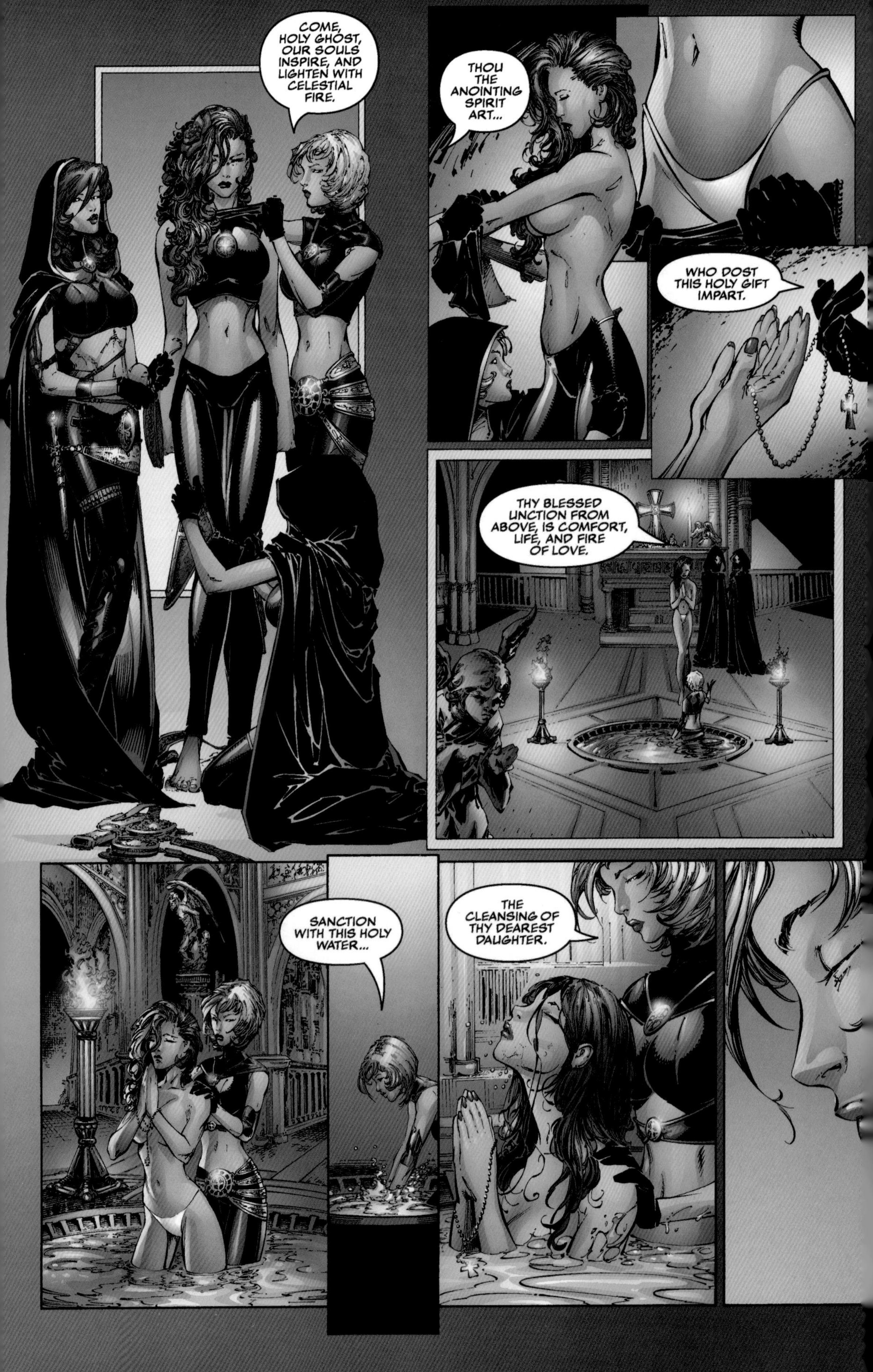
COME, HOLY GHOST, OUR SOULS INSPIRE, AND LIGHTEN WITH CELESTIAL FIRE.
THOU THE ANOINTING SPIRIT ART...
WHO DOST THIS HOLY GIFT IMPART.
THY BLESSED UNCTION FROM ABOVE, IS COMFORT, LIFE, AND FIRE OF LOVE.
SANCTION WITH THIS HOLY WATER...
THE CLEANSING OF THY DEAREST DAUGHTER.

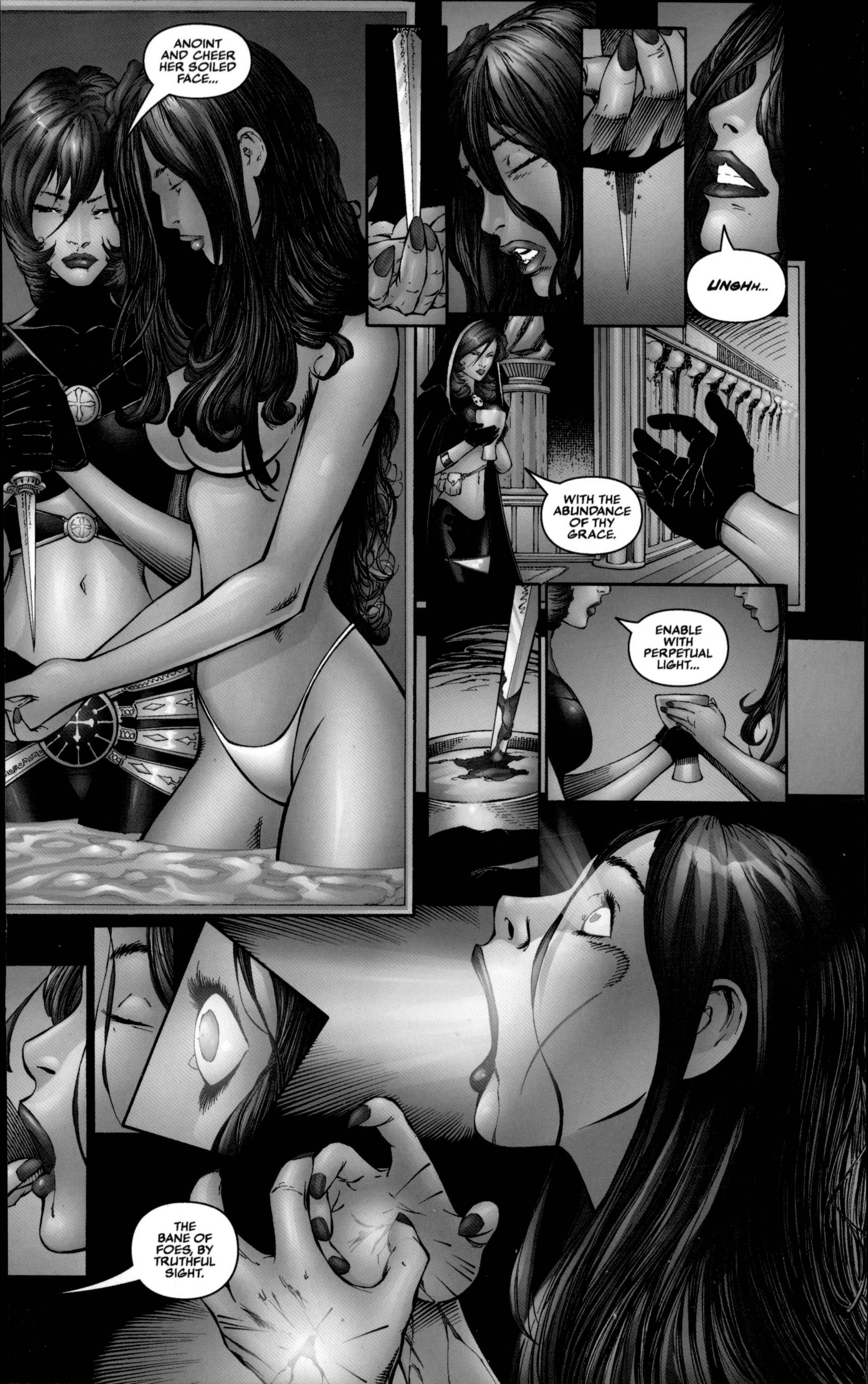
ANOINT AND CHEER HER SOILED FACE...
UNGHH...
WITH THE ABUNDANCE OF THY GRACE.
ENABLE WITH PERPETUAL LIGHT...
THE BANE OF FOES, BY TRUTHFUL SIGHT.

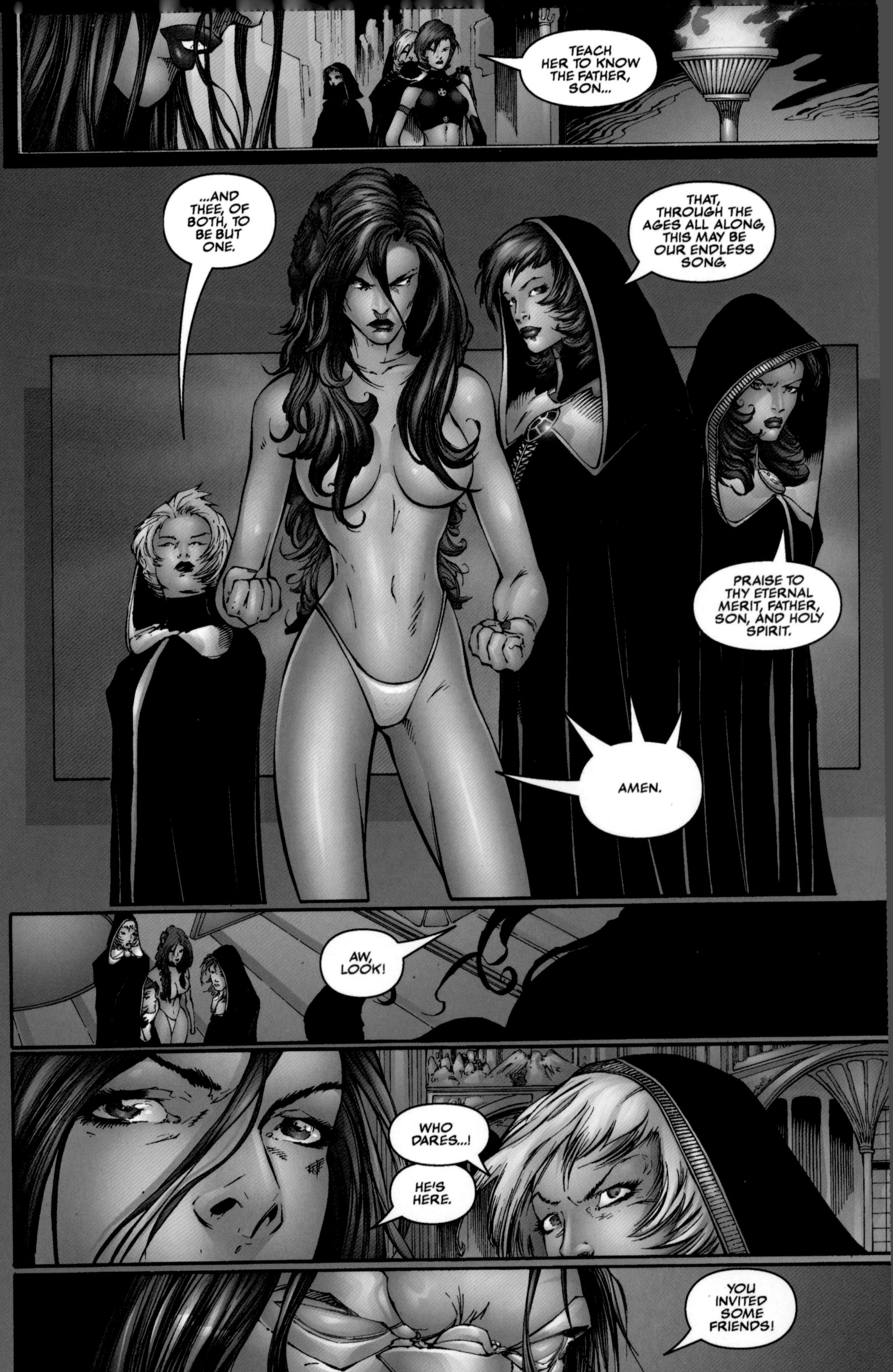
TEACH HER TO KNOW THE FATHER, SON...
...AND THEE, OF BOTH, TO BE BUT ONE.
THAT, THROUGH THE AGES ALL ALONG, THIS MAY BE OUR ENDLESS SONG.
PRAISE TO THY ETERNAL MERIT, FATHER, SON, AND HOLY SPIRIT.
AMEN.
AW, LOOK!
WHO DARES...!
HE'S HERE.
YOU INVITED SOME FRIENDS!

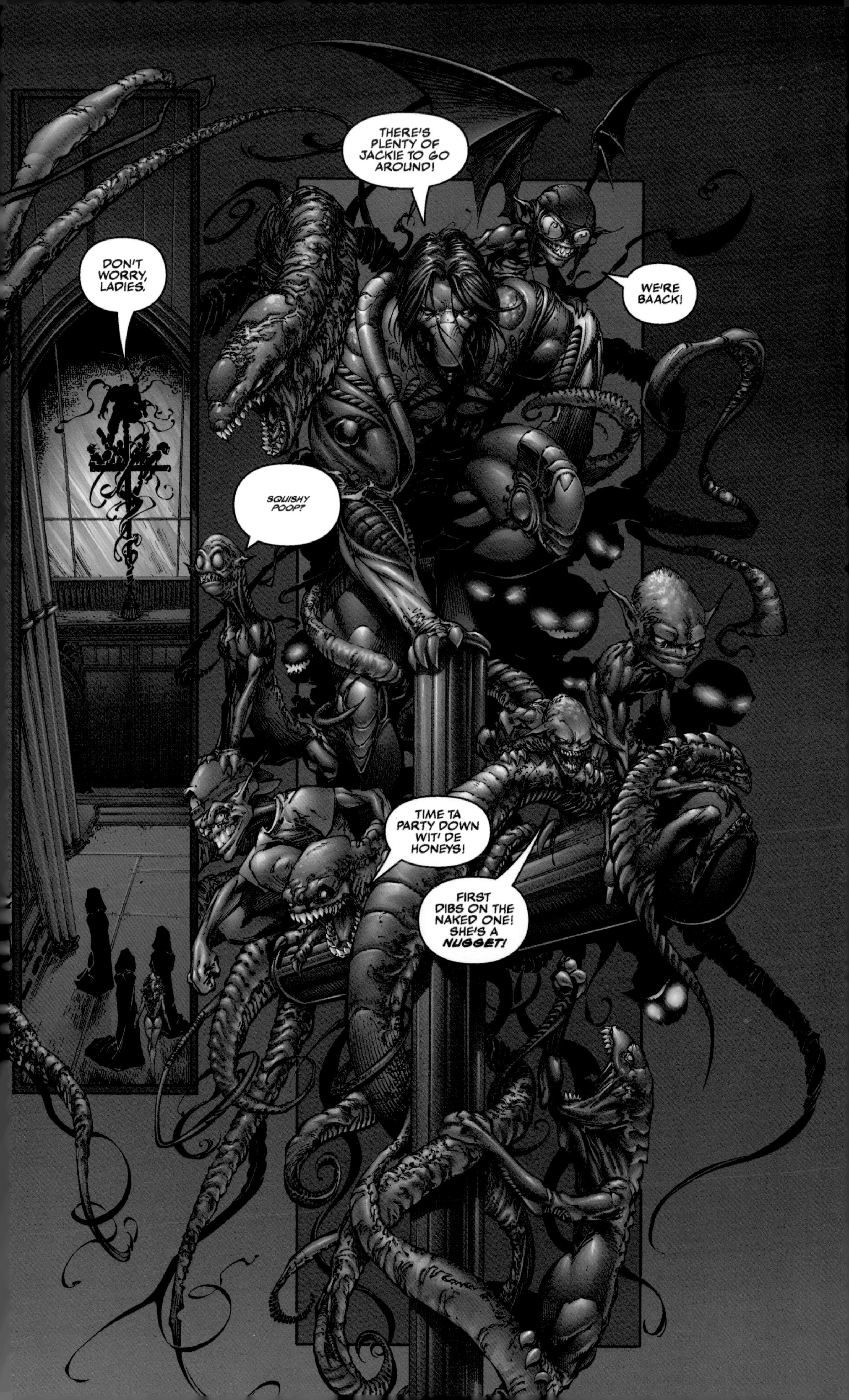
DON'T WORRY, LADIES.
THERE'S PLENTY OF JACKIE TO GO AROUND!
WE'RE BAACK!
SQUISHY POOP?
TIME TA PARTY DOWN WIT' DE HONEYS!
FIRST DIBS ON THE NAKED ONE! SHE'S A *NUGGET!*

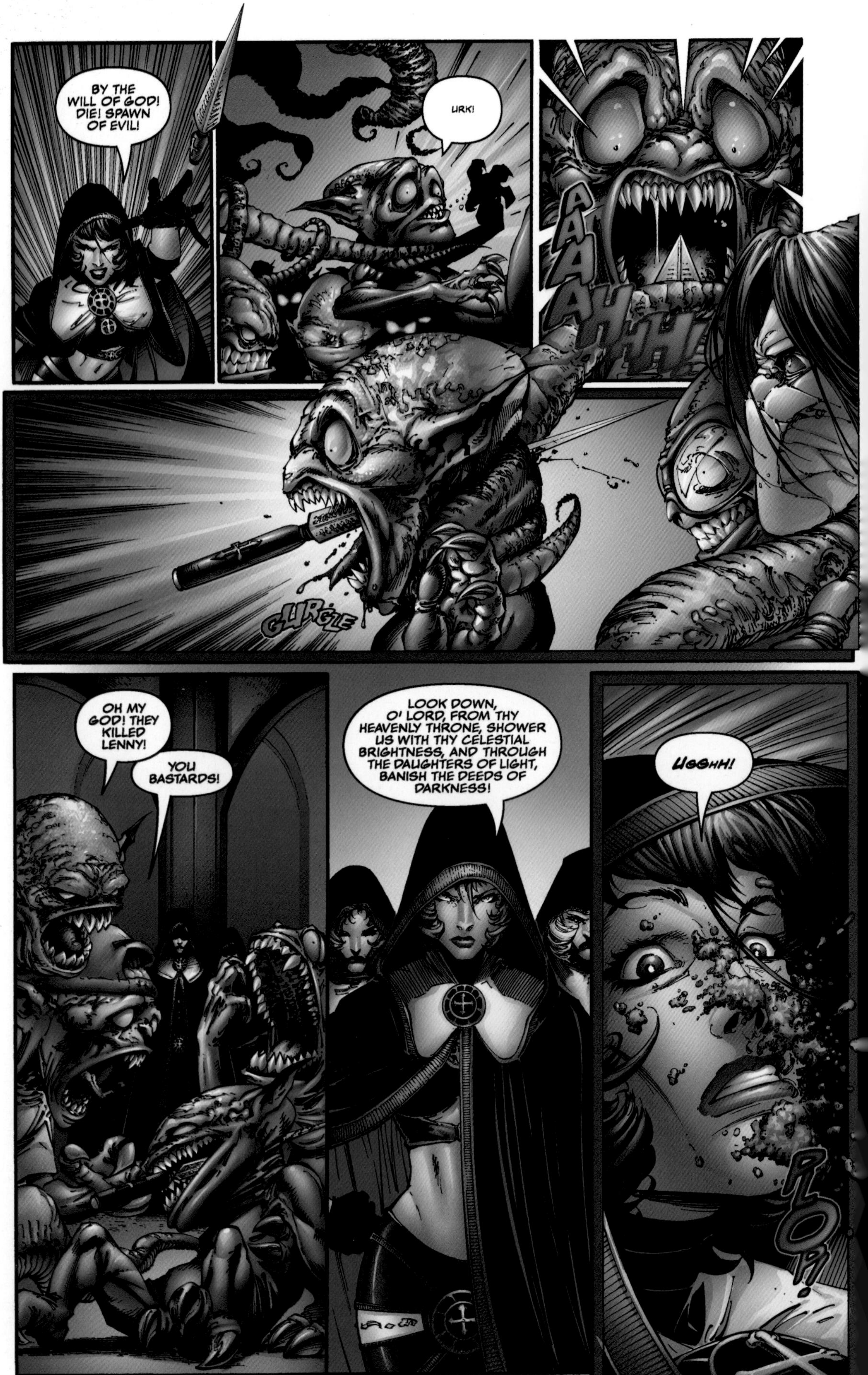
BY THE WILL OF GOD! DIE! SPAWN OF EVIL!
URK!
AAAAHHHH!
GURGLE
OH MY GOD! THEY KILLED LENNY!
YOU BASTARDS!
LOOK DOWN, O' LORD, FROM THY HEAVENLY THRONE, SHOWER US WITH THY CELESTIAL BRIGHTNESS, AND THROUGH THE DAUGHTERS OF LIGHT, BANISH THE DEEDS OF DARKNESS!
UGGHH!
PLOP!

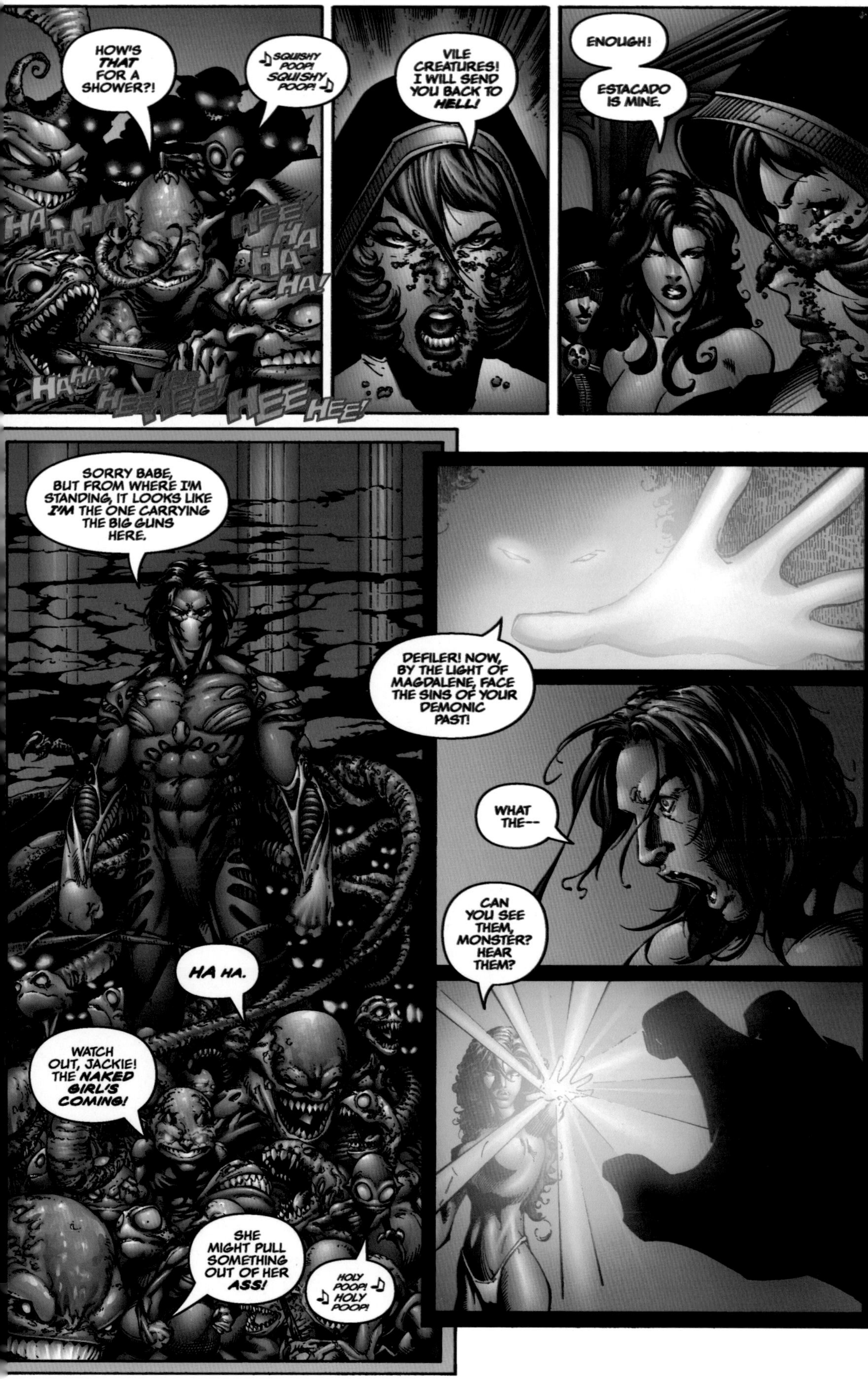
HOW'S THAT FOR A SHOWER?!
♪ SQUISHY POOP! SQUISHY POOP! ♪
HA HA HA
HEE HA HA HA!
HA HA! HEE HEE! HEE HEE!
VILE CREATURES! I WILL SEND YOU BACK TO HELL!
ENOUGH!
ESTACADO IS MINE.
SORRY BABE, BUT FROM WHERE I'M STANDING, IT LOOKS LIKE I'M THE ONE CARRYING THE BIG GUNS HERE.
HA HA.
WATCH OUT, JACKIE! THE NAKED GIRL'S COMING!
SHE MIGHT PULL SOMETHING OUT OF HER ASS!
HOLY POOP! ♪ ♪ HOLY POOP!
DEFILER! NOW, BY THE LIGHT OF MAGDALENE, FACE THE SINS OF YOUR DEMONIC PAST!
WHAT THE--
CAN YOU SEE THEM, MONSTER? HEAR THEM?

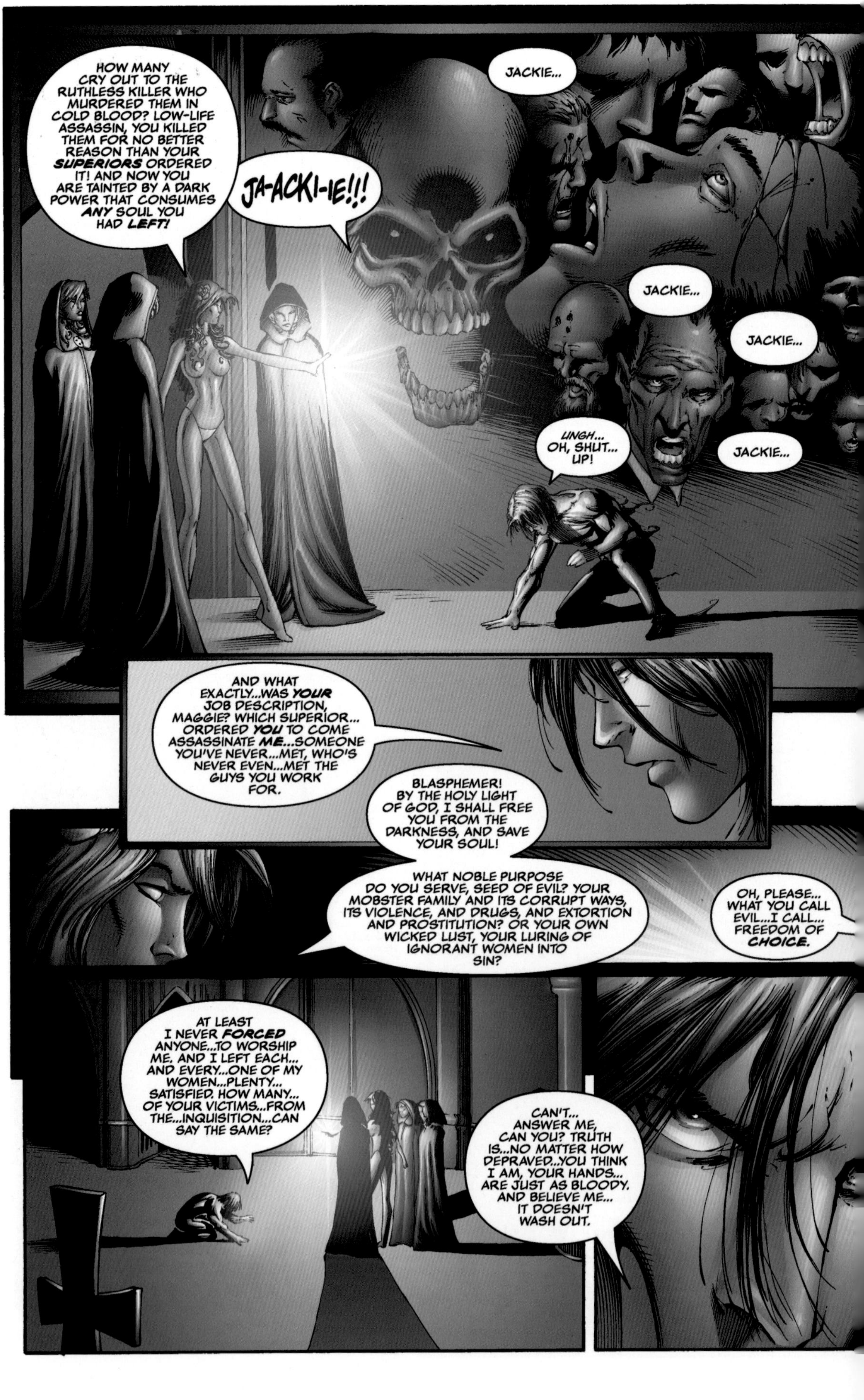
HOW MANY CRY OUT TO THE RUTHLESS KILLER WHO MURDERED THEM IN COLD BLOOD? LOW-LIFE ASSASSIN, YOU KILLED THEM FOR NO BETTER REASON THAN YOUR SUPERIORS ORDERED IT! AND NOW YOU ARE TAINTED BY A DARK POWER THAT CONSUMES ANY SOUL YOU HAD LEFT!
JA-ACKI-IE!!!
JACKIE...
JACKIE...
JACKIE...
UNGH... OH, SHUT... UP!
JACKIE...
AND WHAT EXACTLY...WAS YOUR JOB DESCRIPTION, MAGGIE? WHICH SUPERIOR... ORDERED YOU TO COME ASSASSINATE ME...SOMEONE YOU'VE NEVER...MET, WHO'S NEVER EVEN...MET THE GUYS YOU WORK FOR.
BLASPHEMER! BY THE HOLY LIGHT OF GOD, I SHALL FREE YOU FROM THE DARKNESS, AND SAVE YOUR SOUL!
WHAT NOBLE PURPOSE DO YOU SERVE, SEED OF EVIL? YOUR MOBSTER FAMILY AND ITS CORRUPT WAYS, ITS VIOLENCE, AND DRUGS, AND EXTORTION AND PROSTITUTION? OR YOUR OWN WICKED LUST, YOUR LURING OF IGNORANT WOMEN INTO SIN?
OH, PLEASE... WHAT YOU CALL EVIL...I CALL... FREEDOM OF CHOICE.
AT LEAST I NEVER FORCED ANYONE...TO WORSHIP ME. AND I LEFT EACH... AND EVERY...ONE OF MY WOMEN...PLENTY... SATISFIED. HOW MANY... OF YOUR VICTIMS...FROM THE...INQUISITION...CAN SAY THE SAME?
CAN'T... ANSWER ME, CAN YOU? TRUTH IS...NO MATTER HOW DEPRAVED...YOU THINK I AM, YOUR HANDS... ARE JUST AS BLOODY. AND BELIEVE ME... IT DOESN'T WASH OUT.

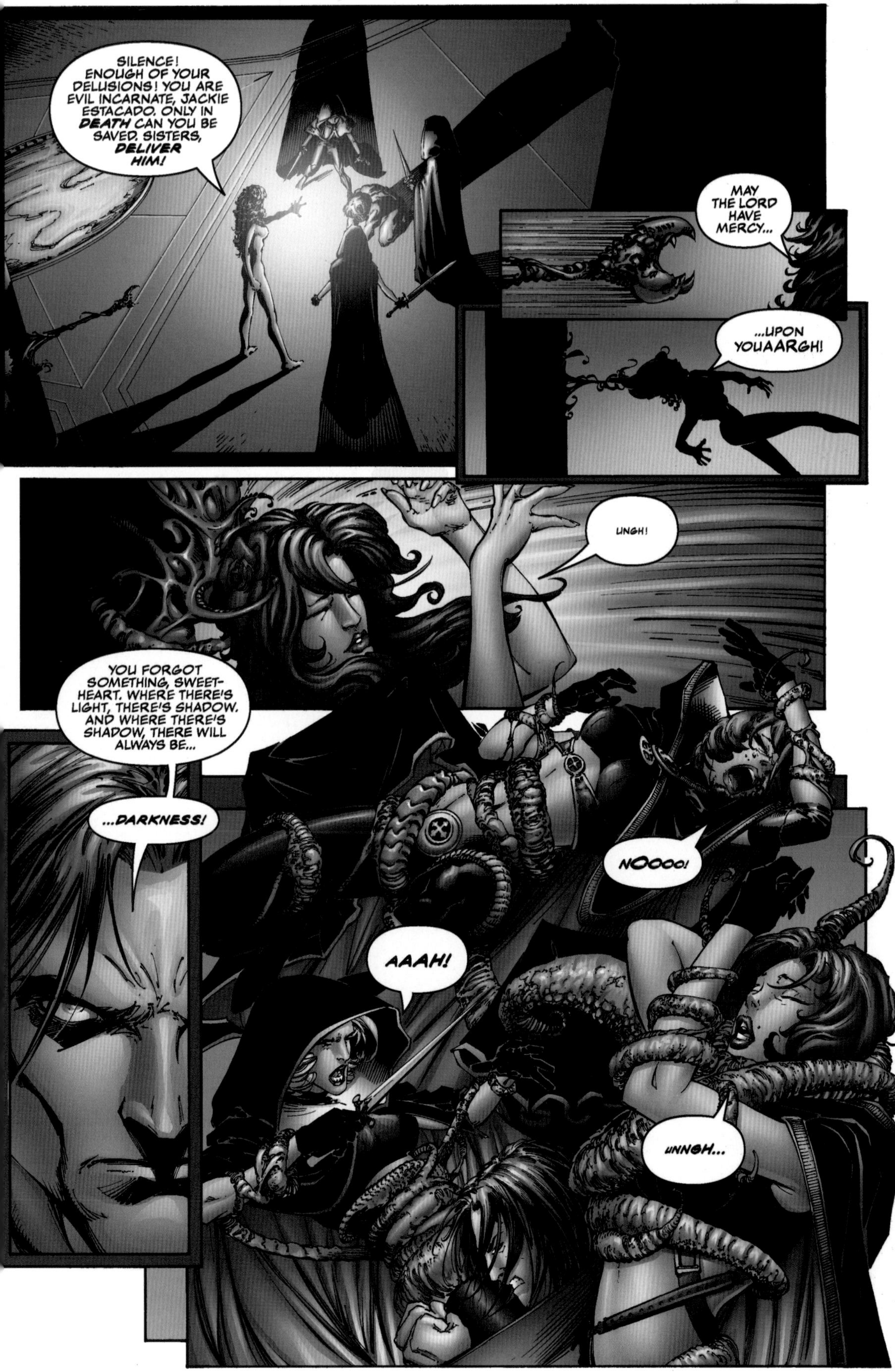
SILENCE! ENOUGH OF YOUR DELUSIONS! YOU ARE EVIL INCARNATE, JACKIE ESTACADO. ONLY IN DEATH CAN YOU BE SAVED. SISTERS, DELIVER HIM!
MAY THE LORD HAVE MERCY...
...UPON YOUAARGH!
UNGH!
YOU FORGOT SOMETHING, SWEET-HEART. WHERE THERE'S LIGHT, THERE'S SHADOW. AND WHERE THERE'S SHADOW, THERE WILL ALWAYS BE...
...DARKNESS!
NOOOO!
AAAH!
UNNGH...

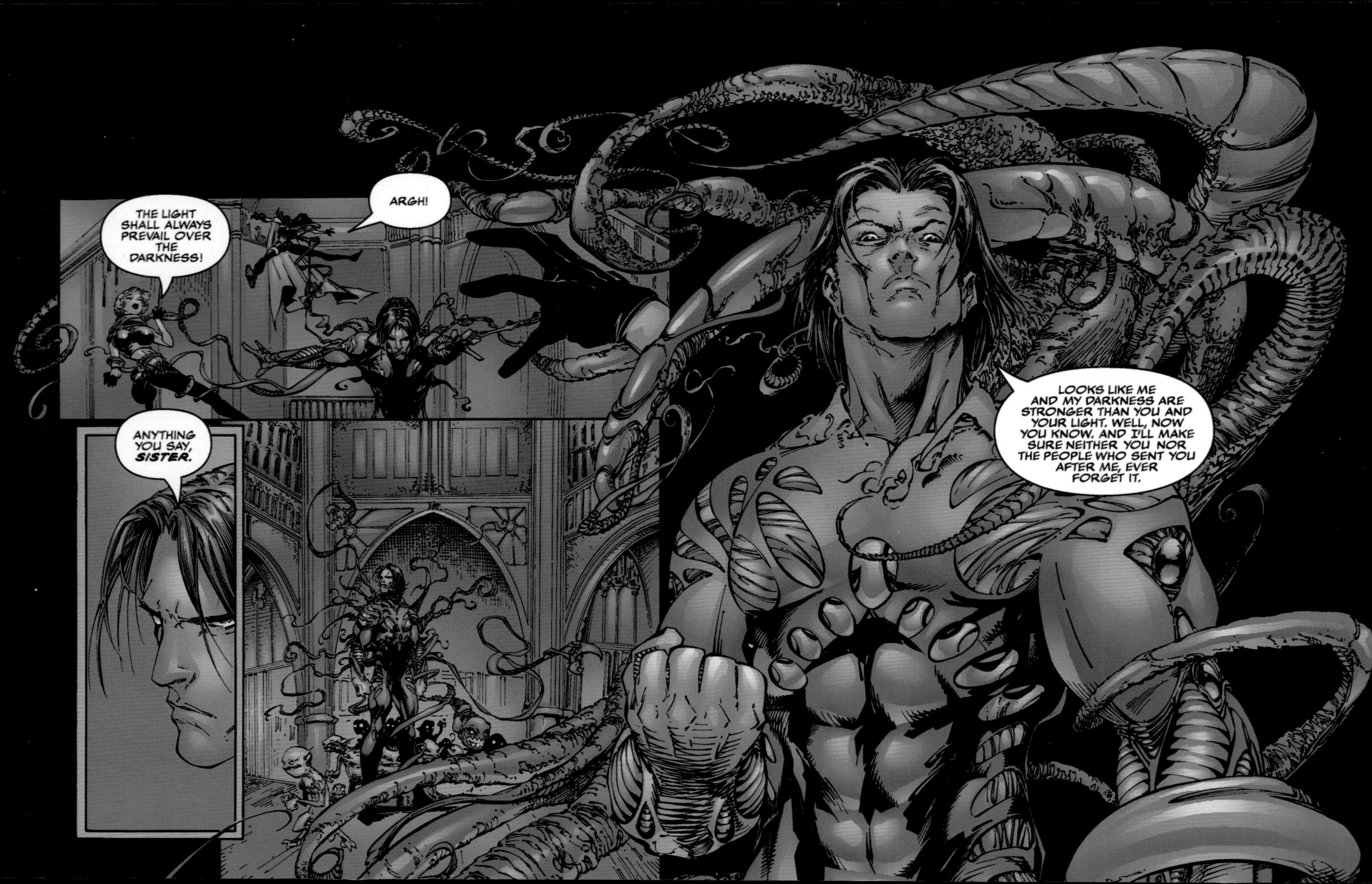
THE LIGHT SHALL ALWAYS PREVAIL OVER THE DARKNESS!
ARGH!
ANYTHING YOU SAY, *SISTER.*
LOOKS LIKE ME AND MY DARKNESS ARE STRONGER THAN YOU AND YOUR LIGHT. WELL, NOW YOU KNOW. AND I'LL MAKE SURE NEITHER YOU NOR THE PEOPLE WHO SENT YOU AFTER ME, EVER FORGET IT.

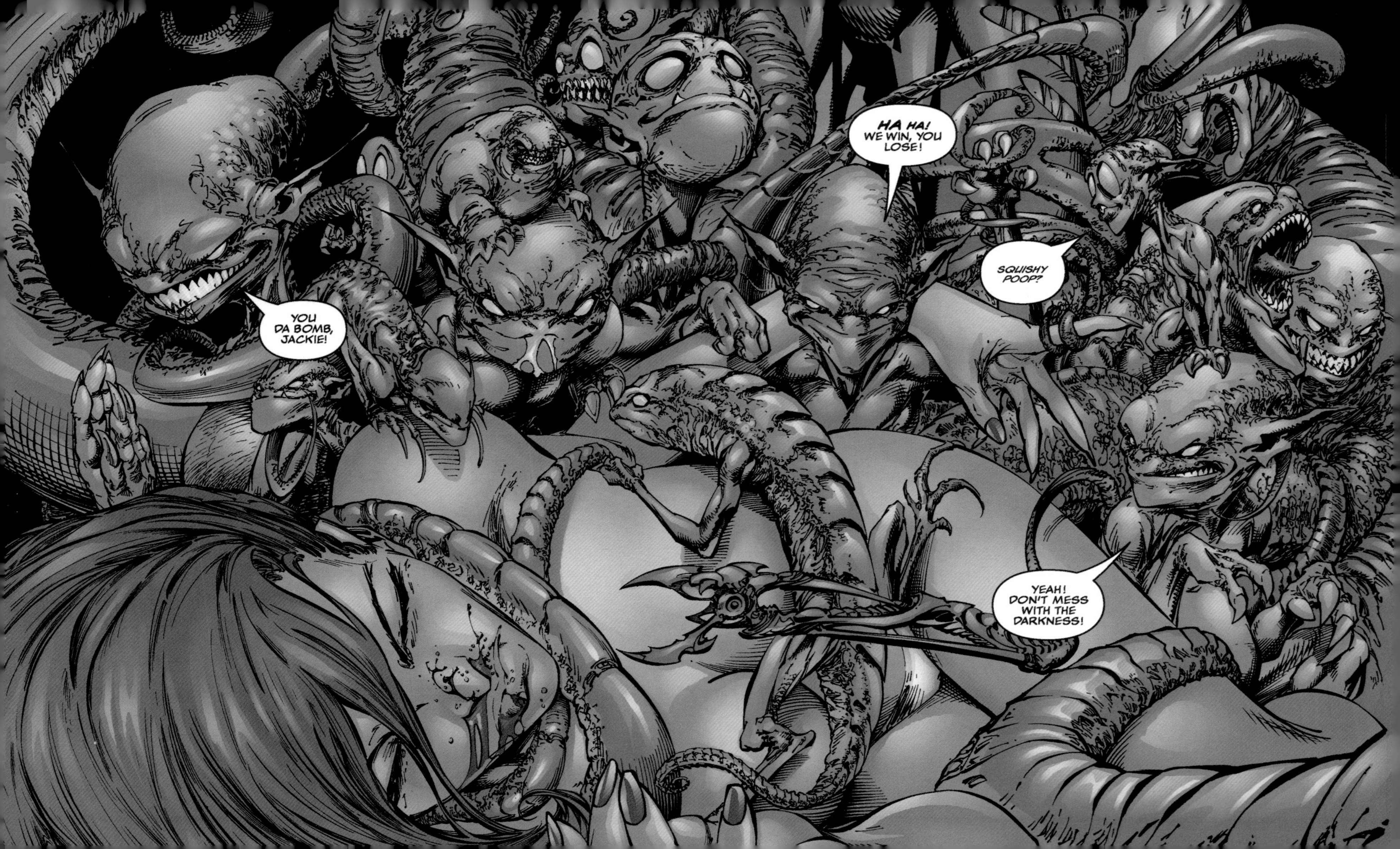
YOU DA BOMB, JACKIE!
HA HA! WE WIN, YOU LOSE!
SQUISHY POOP?
YEAH! DON'T MESS WITH THE DARKNESS!

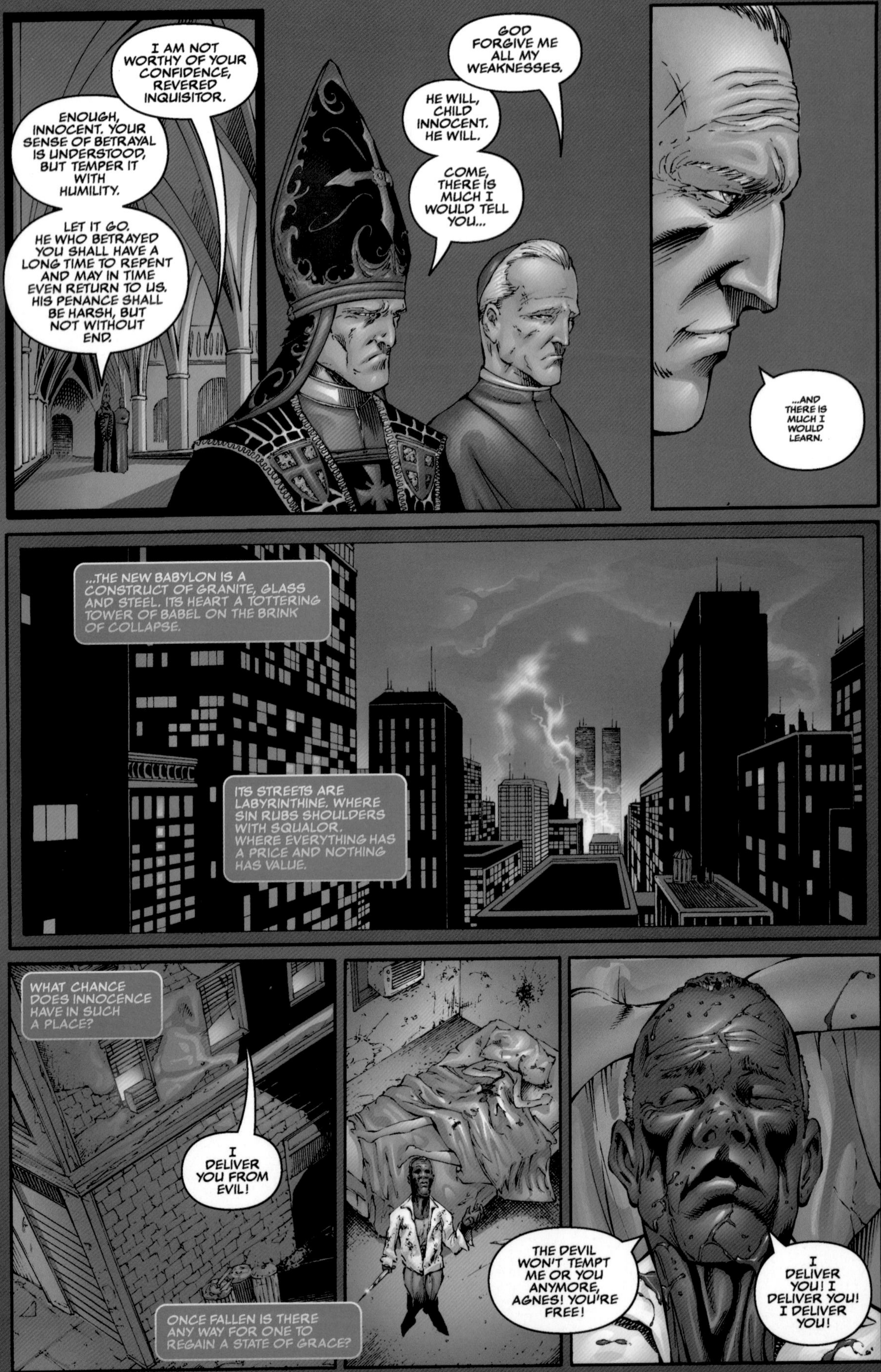
I AM NOT WORTHY OF YOUR CONFIDENCE, REVERED INQUISITOR.
ENOUGH, INNOCENT. YOUR SENSE OF BETRAYAL IS UNDERSTOOD, BUT TEMPER IT WITH HUMILITY.
LET IT GO. HE WHO BETRAYED YOU SHALL HAVE A LONG TIME TO REPENT AND MAY IN TIME EVEN RETURN TO US. HIS PENANCE SHALL BE HARSH, BUT NOT WITHOUT END.
GOD FORGIVE ME ALL MY WEAKNESSES.
HE WILL, CHILD INNOCENT. HE WILL.
COME, THERE IS MUCH I WOULD TELL YOU...
...AND THERE IS MUCH I WOULD LEARN.
...THE NEW BABYLON IS A CONSTRUCT OF GRANITE, GLASS AND STEEL. ITS HEART A TOTTERING TOWER OF BABEL ON THE BRINK OF COLLAPSE.
ITS STREETS ARE LABYRINTHINE. WHERE SIN RUBS SHOULDERS WITH SQUALOR. WHERE EVERYTHING HAS A PRICE AND NOTHING HAS VALUE.
WHAT CHANCE DOES INNOCENCE HAVE IN SUCH A PLACE?
I DELIVER YOU FROM EVIL!
ONCE FALLEN IS THERE ANY WAY FOR ONE TO REGAIN A STATE OF GRACE?
THE DEVIL WON'T TEMPT ME OR YOU ANYMORE, AGNES! YOU'RE FREE!
I DELIVER YOU! I DELIVER YOU! I DELIVER YOU!

...SO WHAT OF THE SPEAR OF DESTINY, THE HOLY SEPULCHRE, GRAND INQUISITOR?

WE MUST DO ALL WE CAN TO REGAIN POSSESSION OF THE SPEAR. IT IS VITAL TO OUR STRUGGLE IF WE ARE TO PREVAIL AGAINST THE POWER OF THE ADVERSARY.

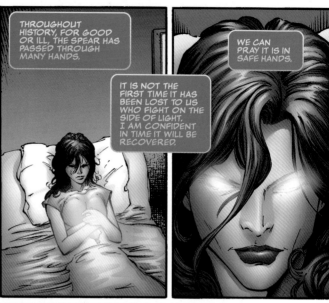

THROUGHOUT HISTORY, FOR GOOD OR ILL, THE SPEAR HAS PASSED THROUGH MANY HANDS.

IT IS NOT THE FIRST TIME IT HAS BEEN LOST TO US WHO FIGHT ON THE SIDE OF LIGHT. I AM CONFIDENT IN TIME IT WILL BE RECOVERED.

WE CAN PRAY IT IS IN SAFE HANDS.

...AND OUR BELOVED DAUGHTER, MAGDALENA?

WE HAVE SENT AGENTS TO RECOVER WHAT THEY CAN FROM THE SITUATION.

OUR PRAYERS AND THOUGHTS ARE WITH THEM, AND THE MAGDALENA.

HOLY SHIT...

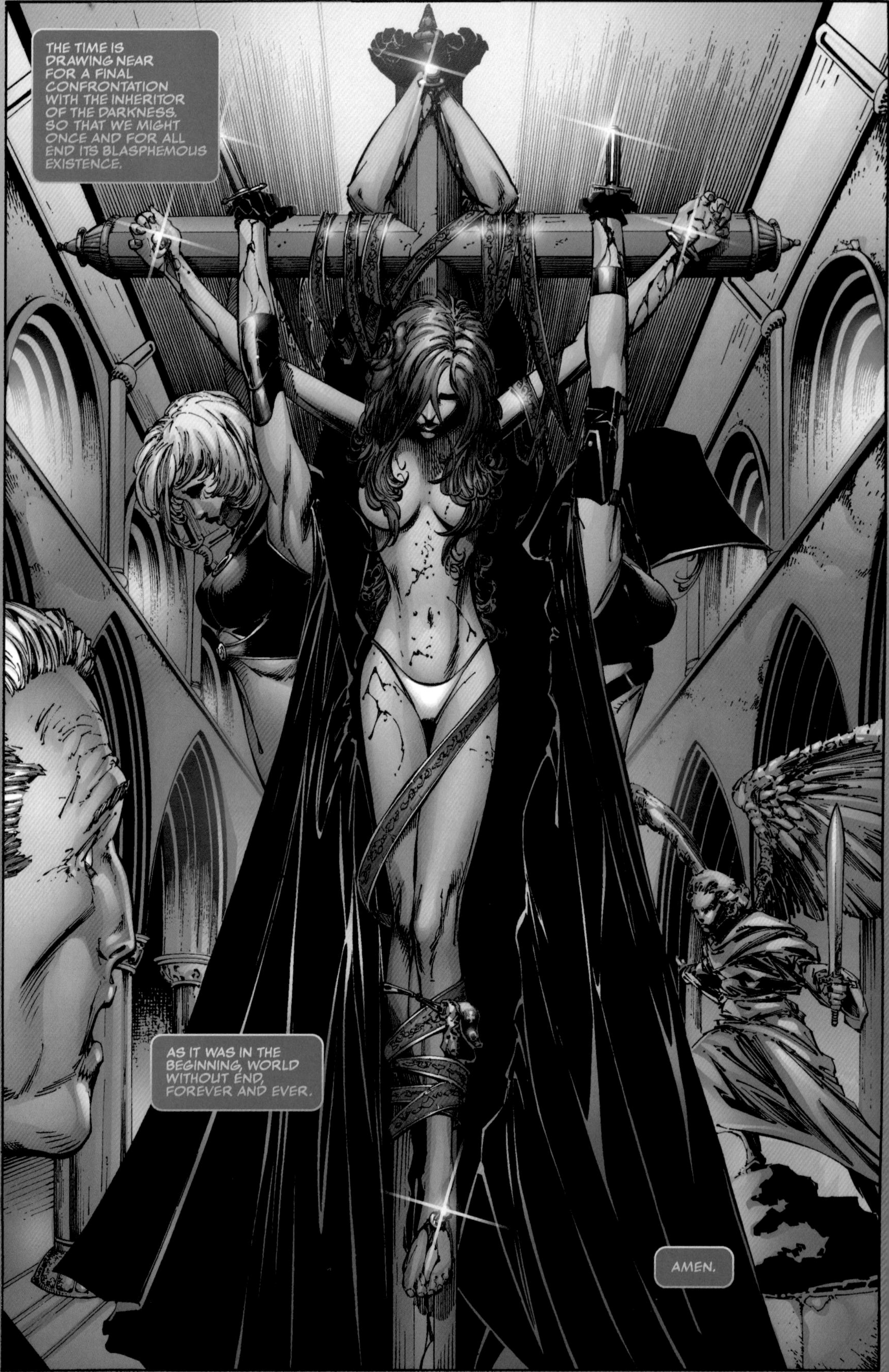
THE TIME IS DRAWING NEAR FOR A FINAL CONFRONTATION WITH THE INHERITOR OF THE DARKNESS. SO THAT WE MIGHT ONCE AND FOR ALL END ITS BLASPHEMOUS EXISTENCE.
AS IT WAS IN THE BEGINNING, WORLD WITHOUT END, FOREVER AND EVER.
AMEN.

VOLUME I, ISSUE #1

story by: **Marcia Chen**
pencils by: **Joe Benitez**
inks by: **Joe Weems V, Victor Llamas,
Matt "Batt" Banning**
colors by: **Tyson Wengler**
letters by: **Robin Spehar** and **Dennis Heisler**

inks assists by: **Marco "Madman" Galli,
Chris Lui**

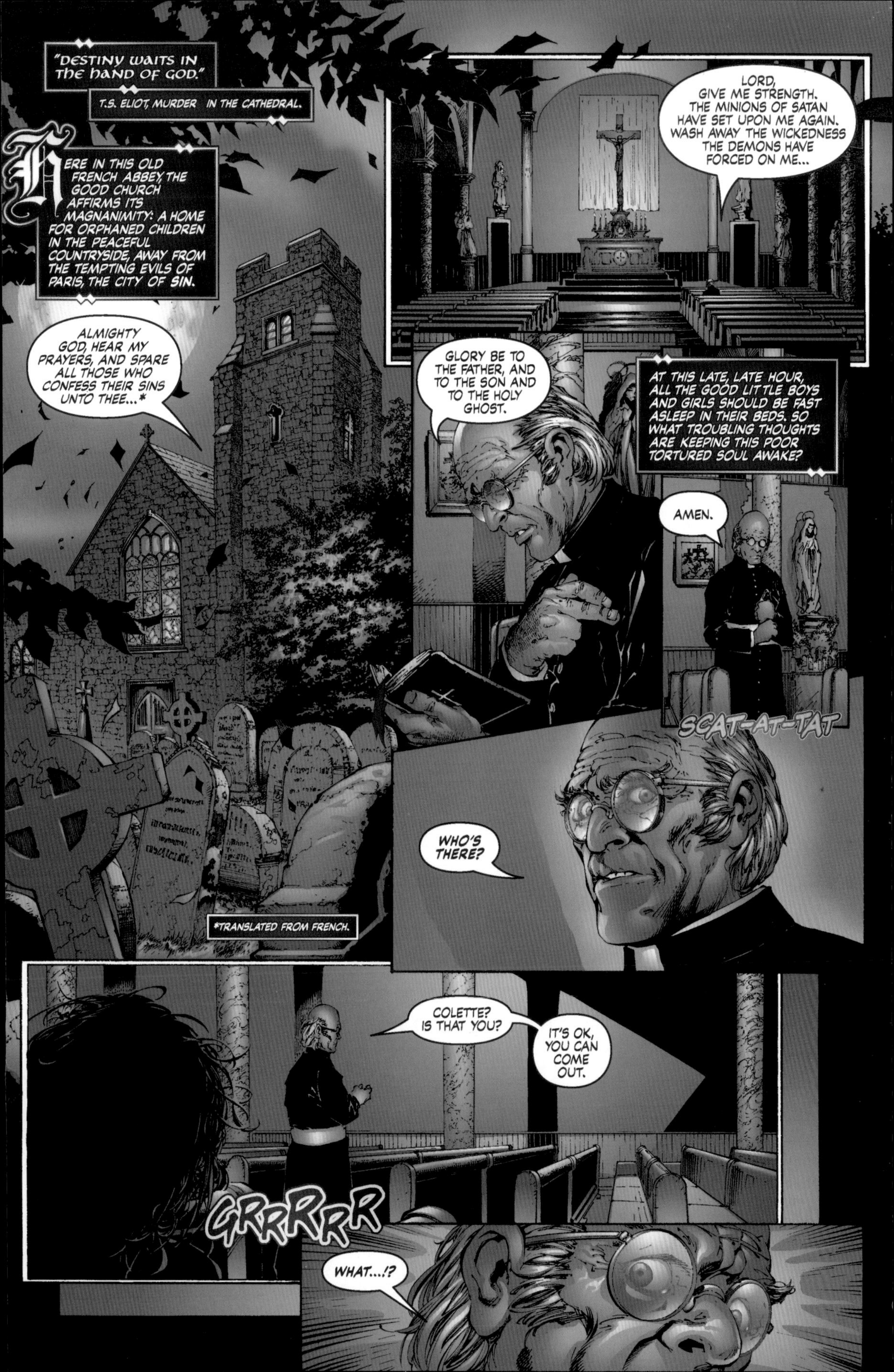
"Destiny waits in the hand of God."
T.S. ELIOT, MURDER IN THE CATHEDRAL.
HERE IN THIS OLD FRENCH ABBEY, THE GOOD CHURCH AFFIRMS ITS MAGNANIMITY: A HOME FOR ORPHANED CHILDREN IN THE PEACEFUL COUNTRYSIDE, AWAY FROM THE TEMPTING EVILS OF PARIS, THE CITY OF SIN.
ALMIGHTY GOD, HEAR MY PRAYERS, AND SPARE ALL THOSE WHO CONFESS THEIR SINS UNTO THEE...*
*TRANSLATED FROM FRENCH.
LORD, GIVE ME STRENGTH. THE MINIONS OF SATAN HAVE SET UPON ME AGAIN. WASH AWAY THE WICKEDNESS THE DEMONS HAVE FORCED ON ME...
GLORY BE TO THE FATHER, AND TO THE SON AND TO THE HOLY GHOST.
AT THIS LATE, LATE HOUR, ALL THE GOOD LITTLE BOYS AND GIRLS SHOULD BE FAST ASLEEP IN THEIR BEDS. SO WHAT TROUBLING THOUGHTS ARE KEEPING THIS POOR TORTURED SOUL AWAKE?
AMEN.
SCAT-AT-TAT
WHO'S THERE?
COLETTE? IS THAT YOU?
IT'S OK, YOU CAN COME OUT.
GRRRRR
WHAT...!?

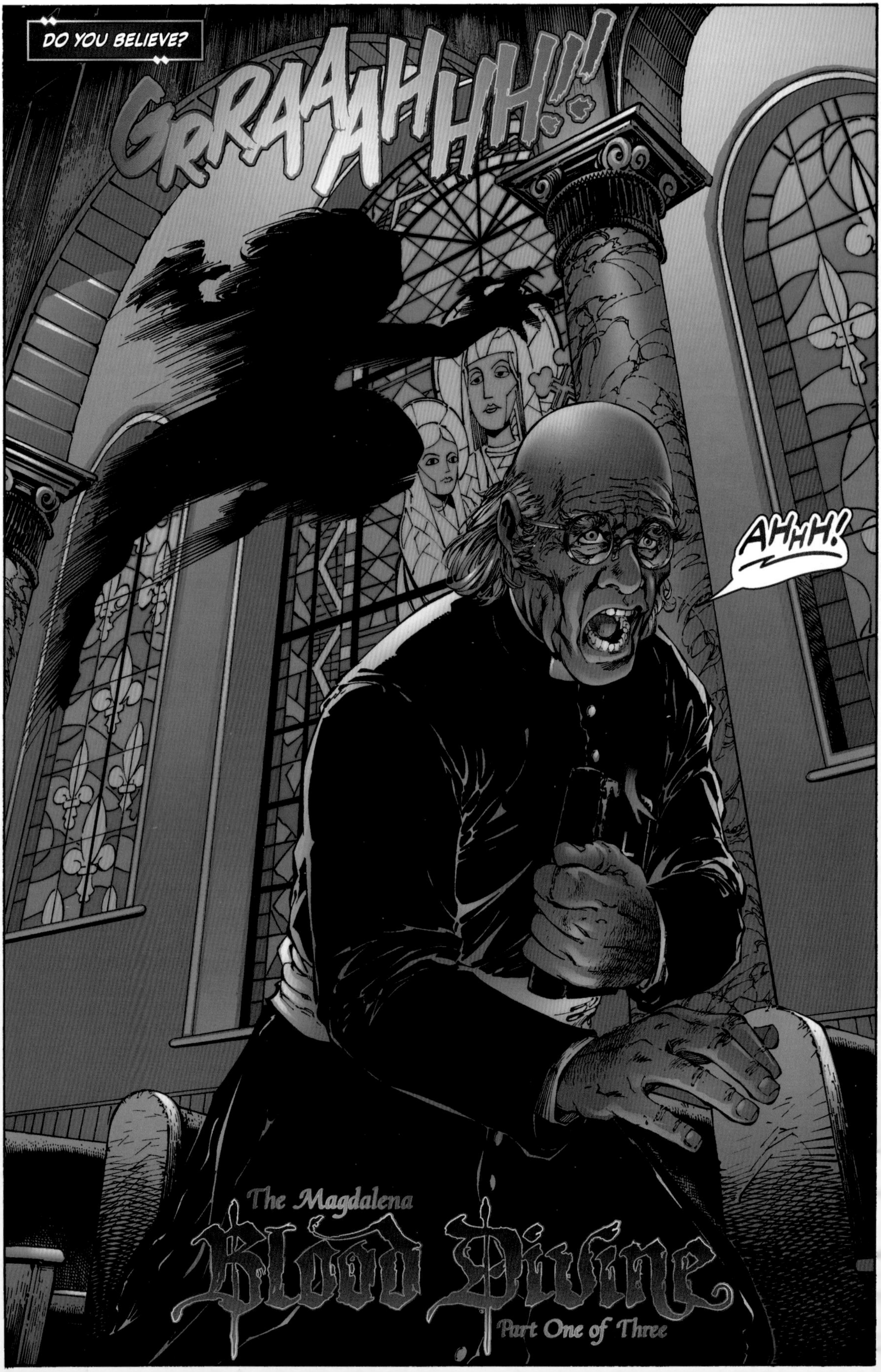
DO YOU BELIEVE?
GRRAAAHHH!!
AHHH!
The Magdalena
Blood Divine
Part One of Three

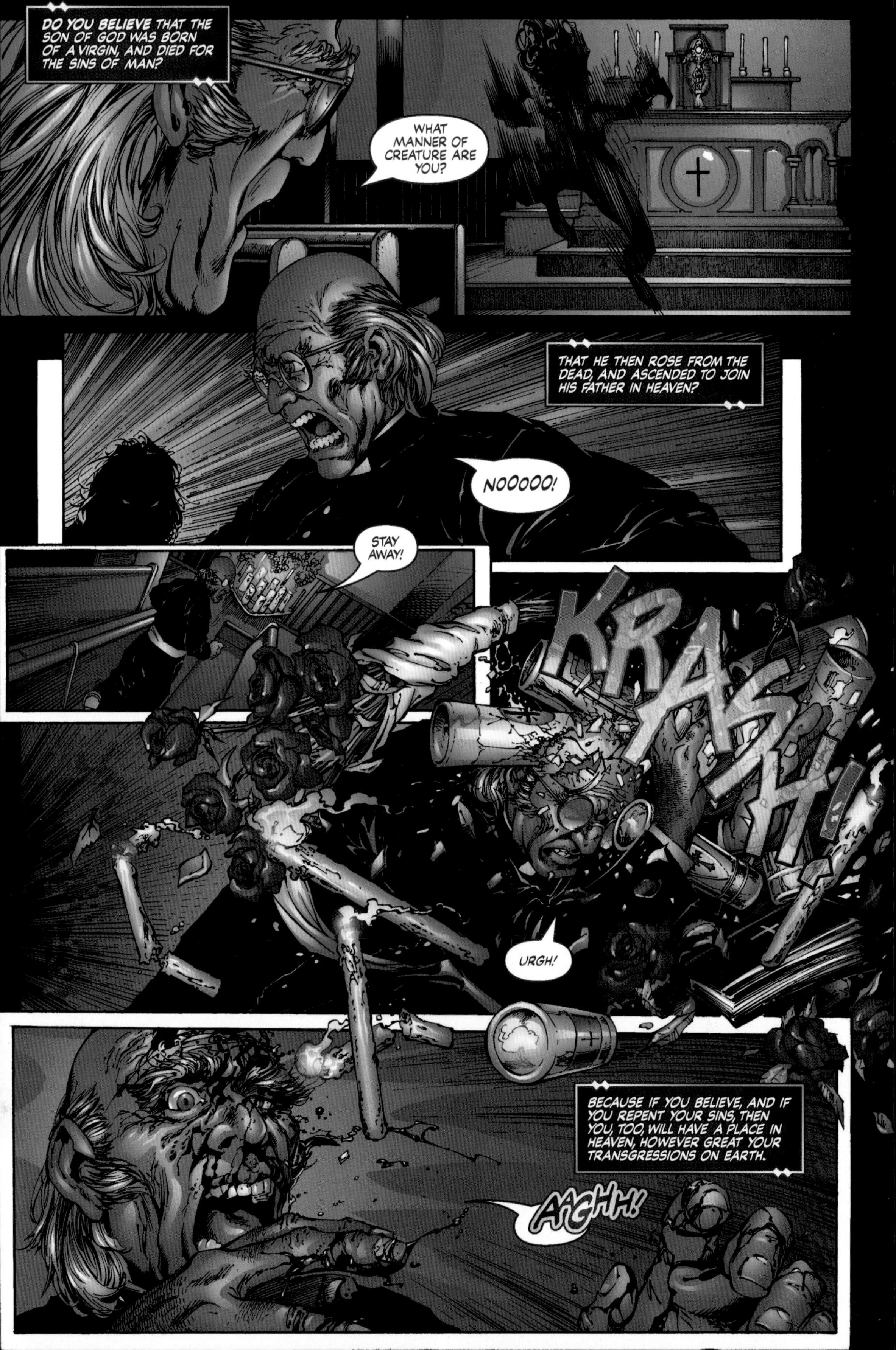
DO YOU BELIEVE THAT THE SON OF GOD WAS BORN OF A VIRGIN, AND DIED FOR THE SINS OF MAN?
WHAT MANNER OF CREATURE ARE YOU?
THAT HE THEN ROSE FROM THE DEAD, AND ASCENDED TO JOIN HIS FATHER IN HEAVEN?
NOOOOO!
STAY AWAY!
KRASSH!
URGH!
BECAUSE IF YOU BELIEVE, AND IF YOU REPENT YOUR SINS, THEN YOU, TOO, WILL HAVE A PLACE IN HEAVEN, HOWEVER GREAT YOUR TRANSGRESSIONS ON EARTH.
AAGHH!

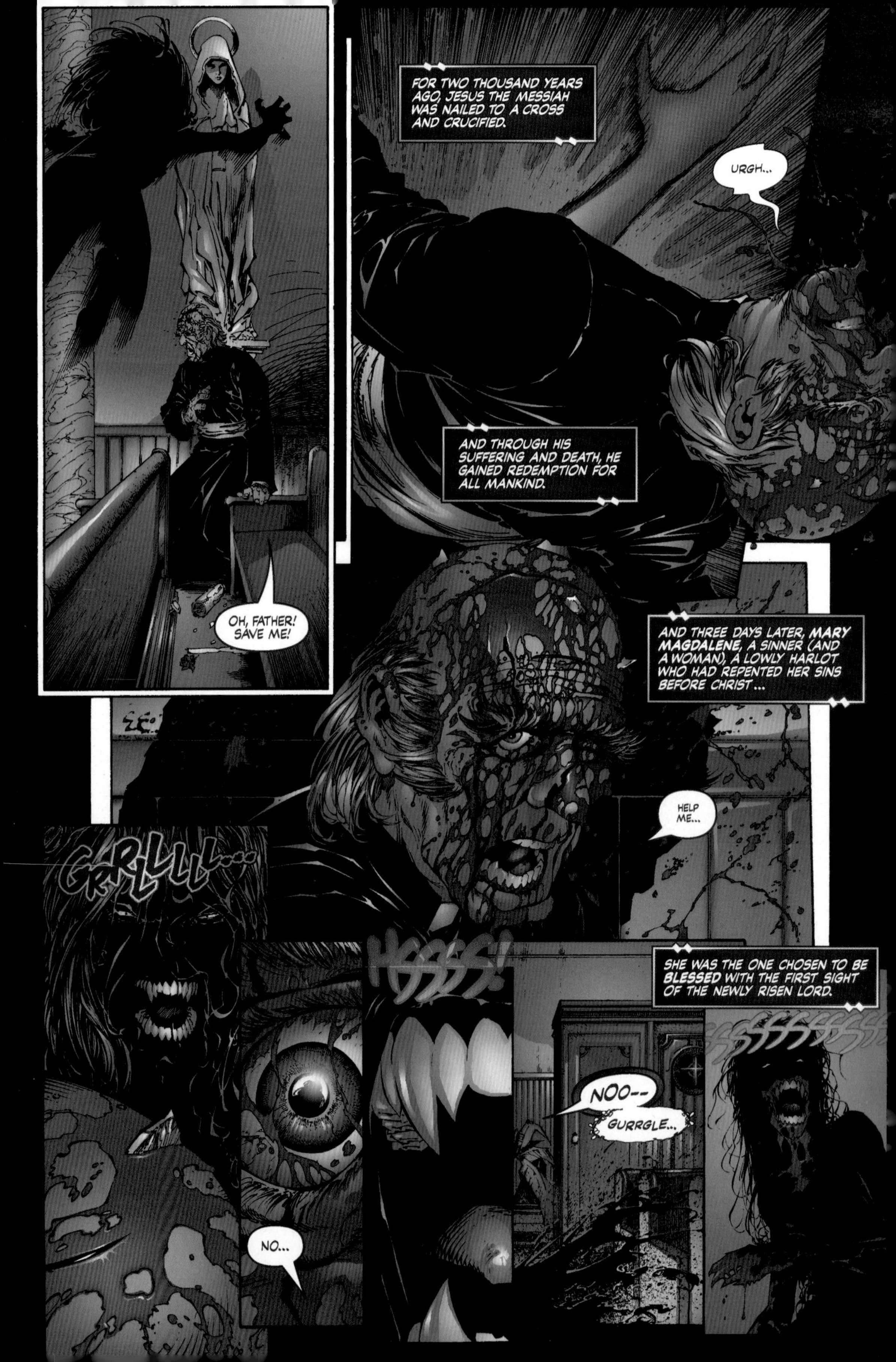

OH, FATHER! SAVE ME!
FOR TWO THOUSAND YEARS AGO, JESUS THE MESSIAH WAS NAILED TO A CROSS AND CRUCIFIED.
URGH...
AND THROUGH HIS SUFFERING AND DEATH, HE GAINED REDEMPTION FOR ALL MANKIND.
AND THREE DAYS LATER, MARY MAGDALENE, A SINNER (AND A WOMAN), A LOWLY HARLOT WHO HAD REPENTED HER SINS BEFORE CHRIST...
HELP ME...
GRRLLLL...
NO...
HSSSS!
SHE WAS THE ONE CHOSEN TO BE BLESSED WITH THE FIRST SIGHT OF THE NEWLY RISEN LORD.
NOO--
GURRGLE...
SSSSSSSSS

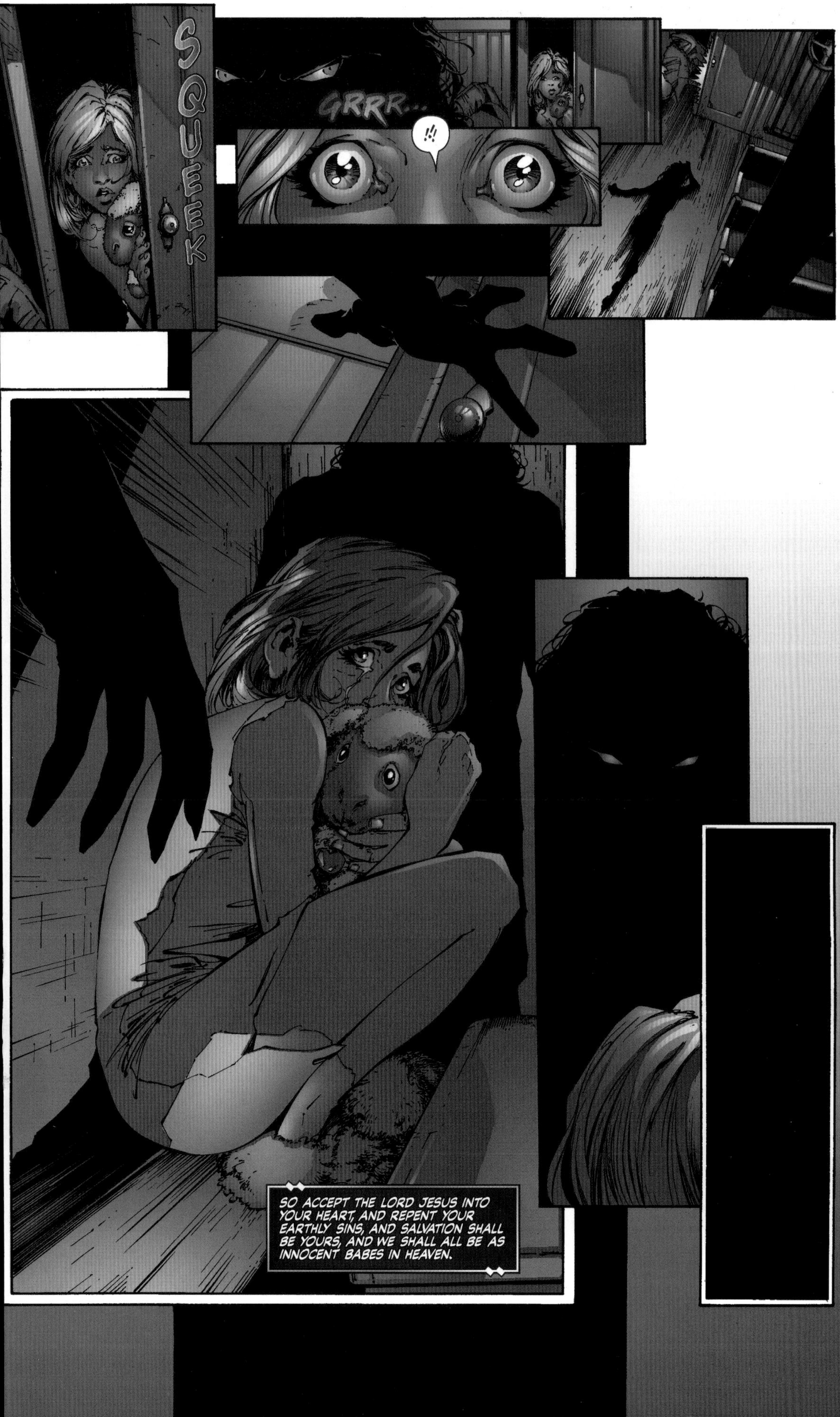
SQUEEK
GRRR...
!!!
SO ACCEPT THE LORD JESUS INTO YOUR HEART, AND REPENT YOUR EARTHLY SINS, AND SALVATION SHALL BE YOURS, AND WE SHALL ALL BE AS INNOCENT BABES IN HEAVEN.

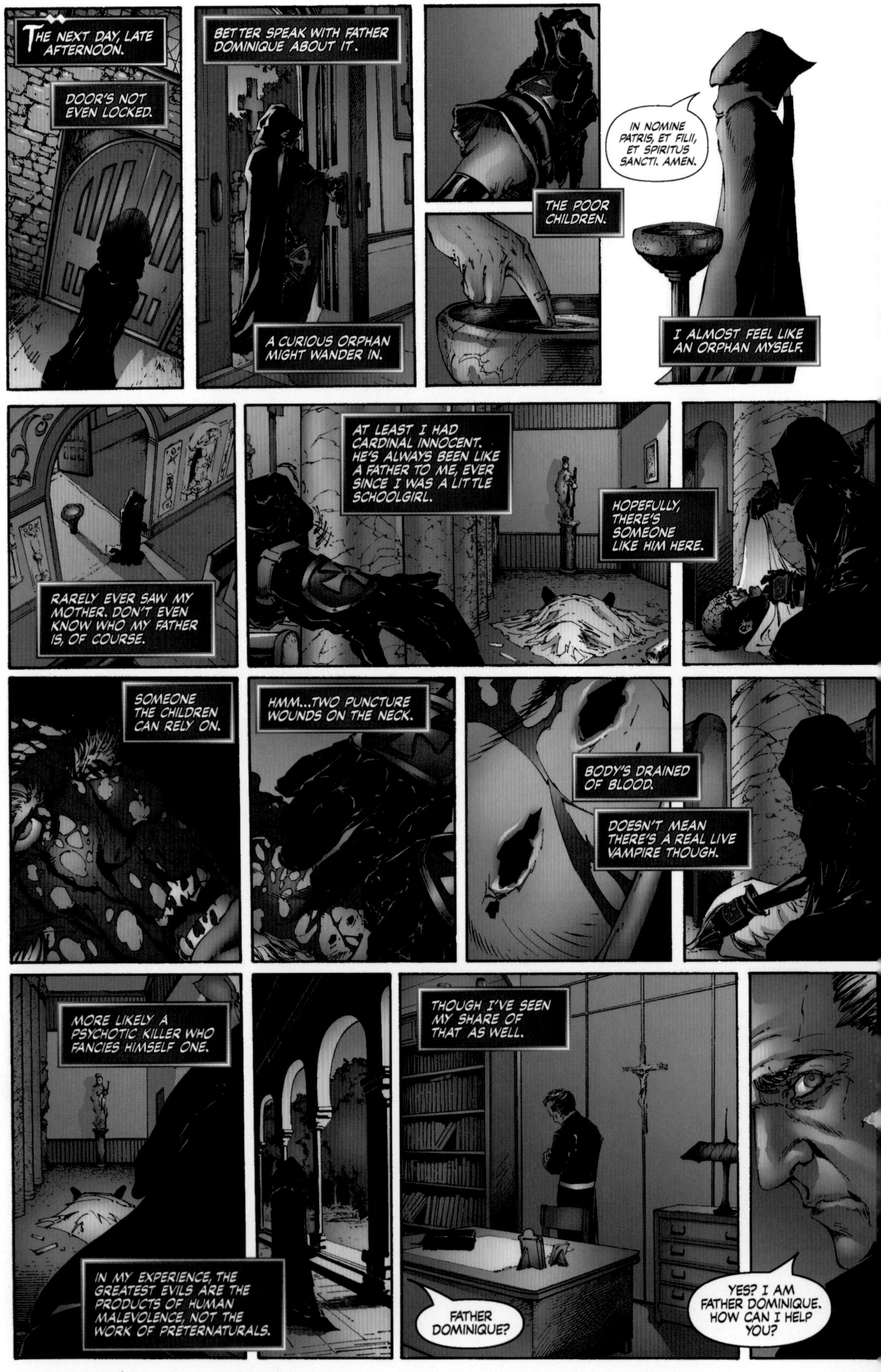
THE NEXT DAY, LATE AFTERNOON.
DOOR'S NOT EVEN LOCKED.
BETTER SPEAK WITH FATHER DOMINIQUE ABOUT IT.
A CURIOUS ORPHAN MIGHT WANDER IN.
THE POOR CHILDREN.
IN NOMINE PATRIS, ET FILII, ET SPIRITUS SANCTI. AMEN.
I ALMOST FEEL LIKE AN ORPHAN MYSELF.
RARELY EVER SAW MY MOTHER. DON'T EVEN KNOW WHO MY FATHER IS, OF COURSE.
AT LEAST I HAD CARDINAL INNOCENT. HE'S ALWAYS BEEN LIKE A FATHER TO ME, EVER SINCE I WAS A LITTLE SCHOOLGIRL.
HOPEFULLY, THERE'S SOMEONE LIKE HIM HERE.
SOMEONE THE CHILDREN CAN RELY ON.
HMM...TWO PUNCTURE WOUNDS ON THE NECK.
BODY'S DRAINED OF BLOOD.
DOESN'T MEAN THERE'S A REAL LIVE VAMPIRE THOUGH.
MORE LIKELY A PSYCHOTIC KILLER WHO FANCIES HIMSELF ONE.
IN MY EXPERIENCE, THE GREATEST EVILS ARE THE PRODUCTS OF HUMAN MALEVOLENCE, NOT THE WORK OF PRETERNATURALS.
THOUGH I'VE SEEN MY SHARE OF THAT AS WELL.
FATHER DOMINIQUE?
YES? I AM FATHER DOMINIQUE. HOW CAN I HELP YOU?

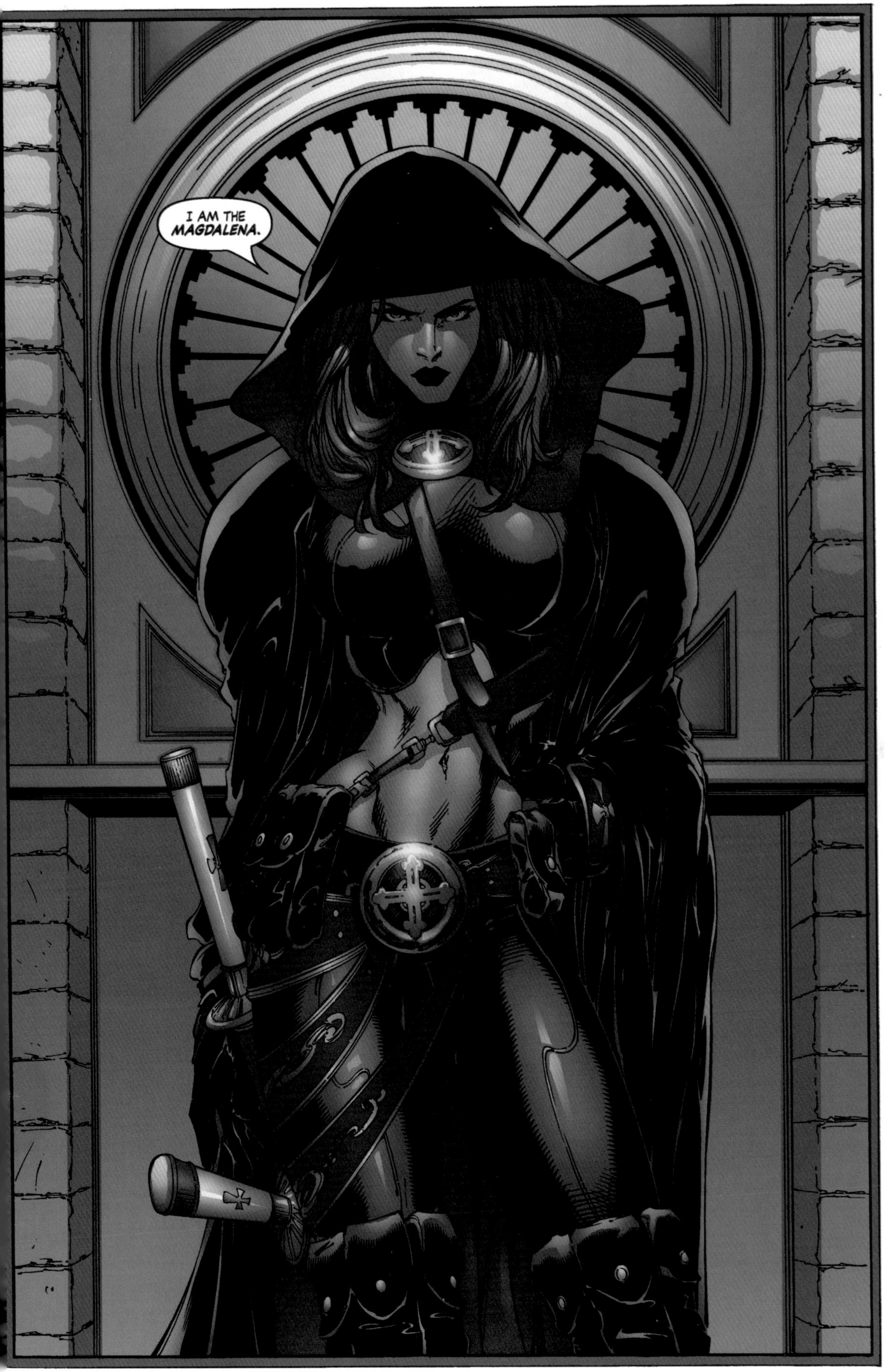
I AM THE MAGDALENA.

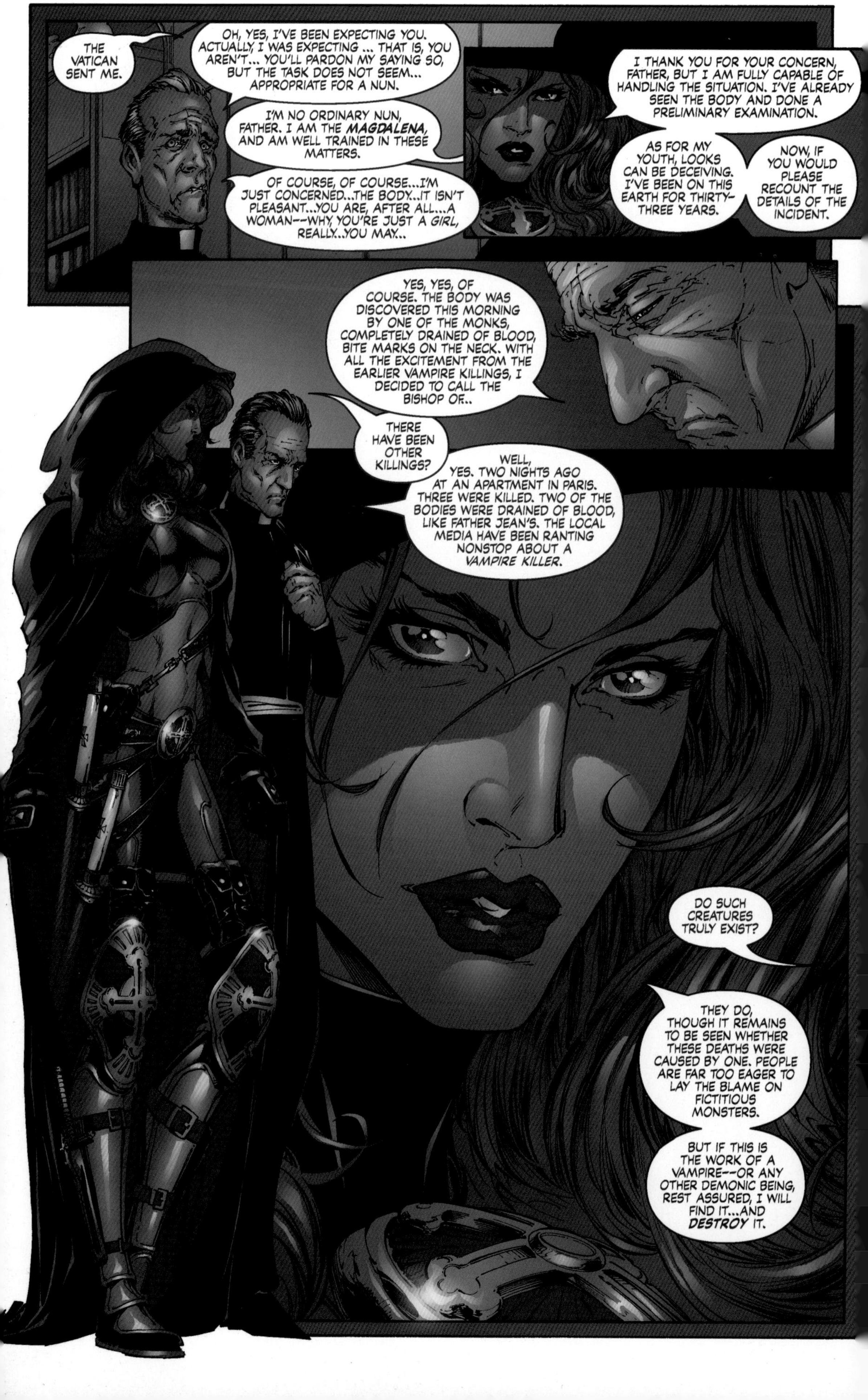
THE VATICAN SENT ME.
OH, YES, I'VE BEEN EXPECTING YOU. ACTUALLY, I WAS EXPECTING ... THAT IS, YOU AREN'T... YOU'LL PARDON MY SAYING SO, BUT THE TASK DOES NOT SEEM... APPROPRIATE FOR A NUN.
I'M NO ORDINARY NUN, FATHER. I AM THE *MAGDALENA*, AND AM WELL TRAINED IN THESE MATTERS.
OF COURSE, OF COURSE...I'M JUST CONCERNED...THE BODY...IT ISN'T PLEASANT...YOU ARE, AFTER ALL...A WOMAN--WHY, YOU'RE JUST A *GIRL*, REALLY...YOU MAY...
I THANK YOU FOR YOUR CONCERN, FATHER, BUT I AM FULLY CAPABLE OF HANDLING THE SITUATION. I'VE ALREADY SEEN THE BODY AND DONE A PRELIMINARY EXAMINATION.
AS FOR MY YOUTH, LOOKS CAN BE DECEIVING. I'VE BEEN ON THIS EARTH FOR THIRTY-THREE YEARS.
NOW, IF YOU WOULD PLEASE RECOUNT THE DETAILS OF THE INCIDENT.
YES, YES, OF COURSE. THE BODY WAS DISCOVERED THIS MORNING BY ONE OF THE MONKS, COMPLETELY DRAINED OF BLOOD, BITE MARKS ON THE NECK. WITH ALL THE EXCITEMENT FROM THE EARLIER VAMPIRE KILLINGS, I DECIDED TO CALL THE BISHOP OF..
THERE HAVE BEEN OTHER KILLINGS?
WELL, YES. TWO NIGHTS AGO AT AN APARTMENT IN PARIS. THREE WERE KILLED. TWO OF THE BODIES WERE DRAINED OF BLOOD, LIKE FATHER JEAN'S. THE LOCAL MEDIA HAVE BEEN RANTING NONSTOP ABOUT A *VAMPIRE KILLER*.
DO SUCH CREATURES TRULY EXIST?
THEY DO, THOUGH IT REMAINS TO BE SEEN WHETHER THESE DEATHS WERE CAUSED BY ONE. PEOPLE ARE FAR TOO EAGER TO LAY THE BLAME ON FICTITIOUS MONSTERS.
BUT IF THIS IS THE WORK OF A VAMPIRE--OR ANY OTHER DEMONIC BEING, REST ASSURED, I WILL FIND IT...AND **DESTROY** IT.

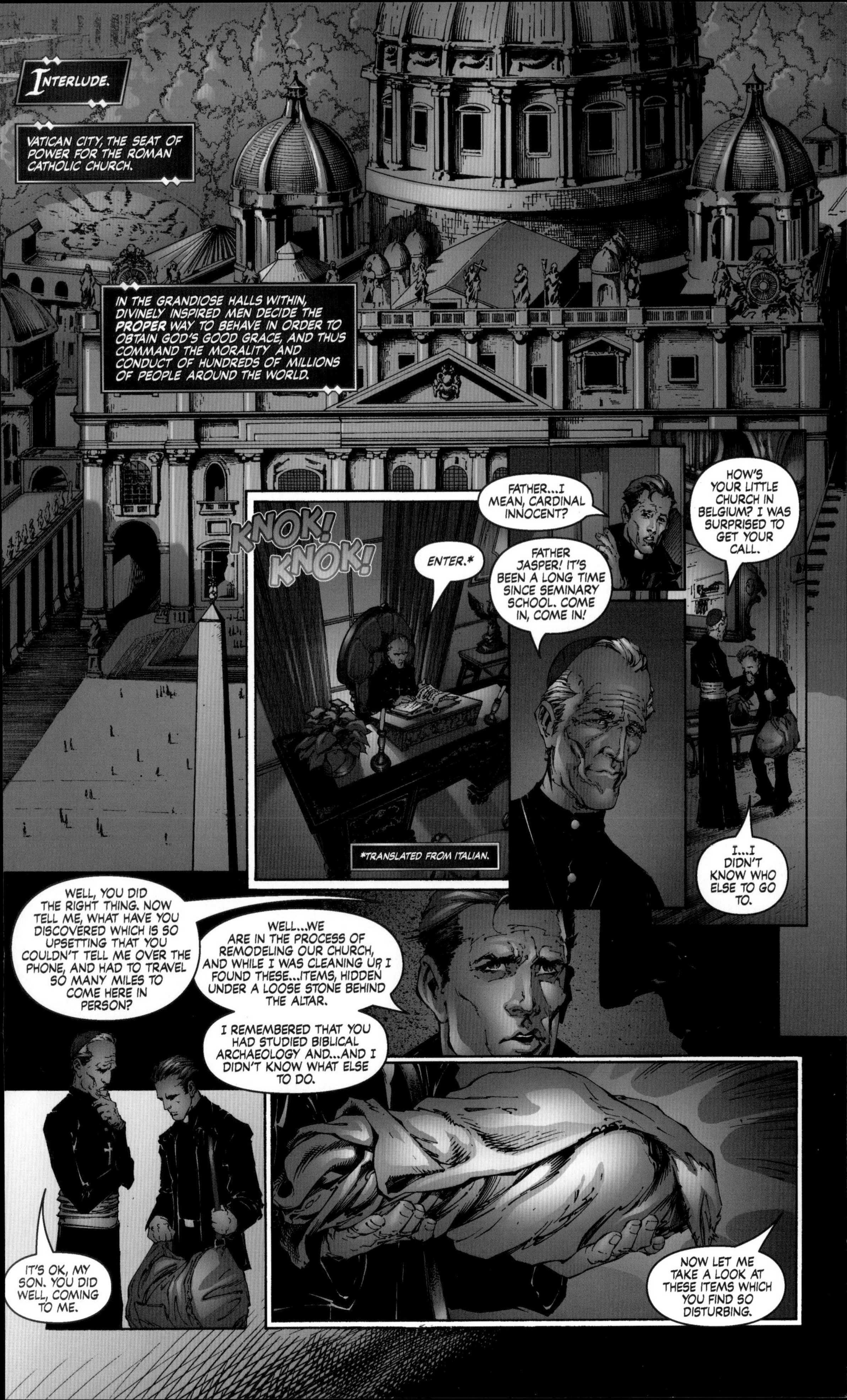

INTERLUDE.
VATICAN CITY, THE SEAT OF POWER FOR THE ROMAN CATHOLIC CHURCH.
IN THE GRANDIOSE HALLS WITHIN, DIVINELY INSPIRED MEN DECIDE THE PROPER WAY TO BEHAVE IN ORDER TO OBTAIN GOD'S GOOD GRACE, AND THUS COMMAND THE MORALITY AND CONDUCT OF HUNDREDS OF MILLIONS OF PEOPLE AROUND THE WORLD.
KNOK! KNOK!
ENTER.*
*TRANSLATED FROM ITALIAN.
FATHER...I MEAN, CARDINAL INNOCENT?
FATHER JASPER! IT'S BEEN A LONG TIME SINCE SEMINARY SCHOOL. COME IN, COME IN!
HOW'S YOUR LITTLE CHURCH IN BELGIUM? I WAS SURPRISED TO GET YOUR CALL.
I...I DIDN'T KNOW WHO ELSE TO GO TO.
WELL, YOU DID THE RIGHT THING. NOW TELL ME, WHAT HAVE YOU DISCOVERED WHICH IS SO UPSETTING THAT YOU COULDN'T TELL ME OVER THE PHONE, AND HAD TO TRAVEL SO MANY MILES TO COME HERE IN PERSON?
WELL...WE ARE IN THE PROCESS OF REMODELING OUR CHURCH, AND WHILE I WAS CLEANING UP, I FOUND THESE...ITEMS, HIDDEN UNDER A LOOSE STONE BEHIND THE ALTAR.
I REMEMBERED THAT YOU HAD STUDIED BIBLICAL ARCHAEOLOGY AND...AND I DIDN'T KNOW WHAT ELSE TO DO.
IT'S OK, MY SON. YOU DID WELL, COMING TO ME.
NOW LET ME TAKE A LOOK AT THESE ITEMS WHICH YOU FIND SO DISTURBING.

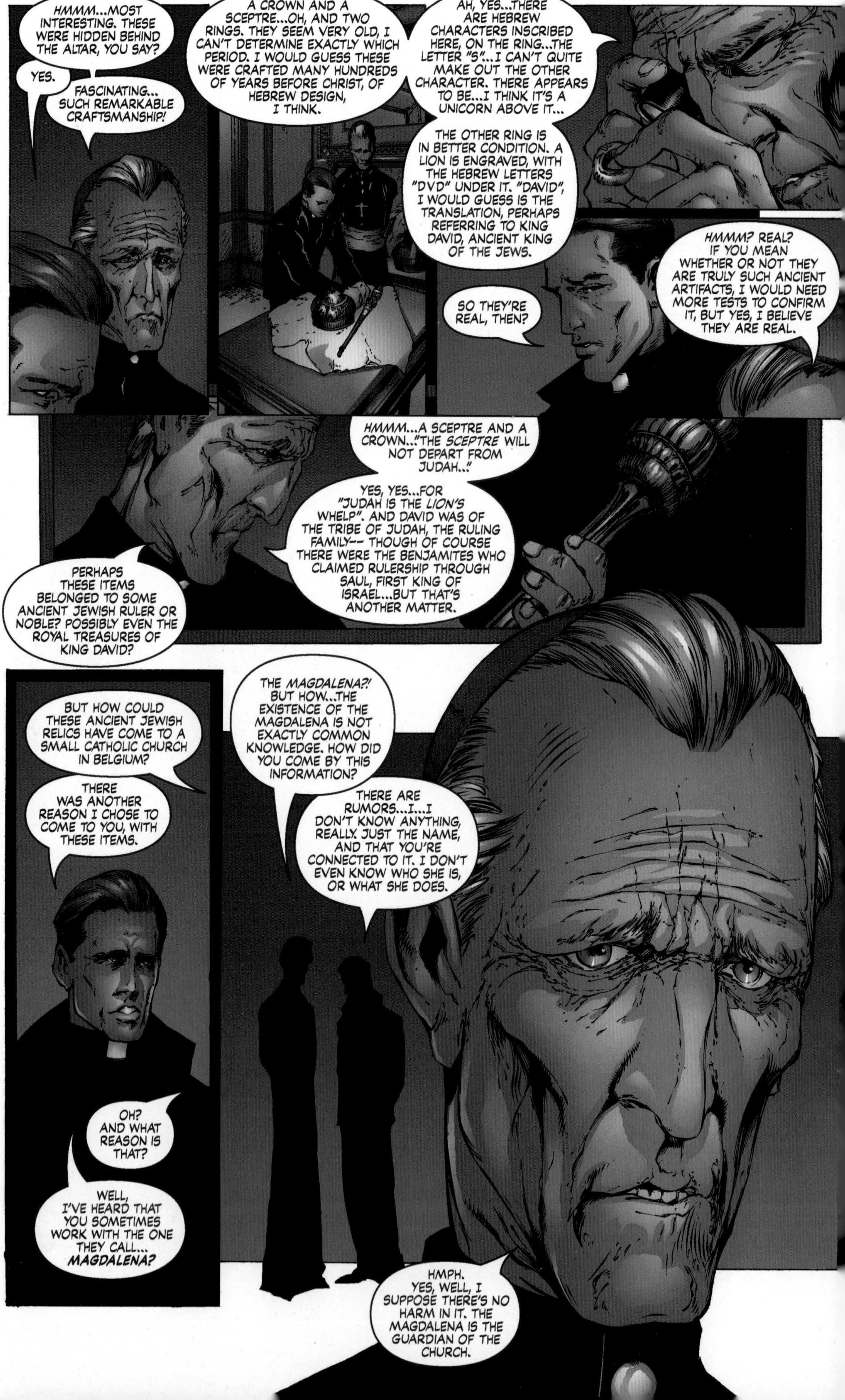
HMMM...MOST INTERESTING. THESE WERE HIDDEN BEHIND THE ALTAR, YOU SAY?
YES.
FASCINATING... SUCH REMARKABLE CRAFTSMANSHIP!
A CROWN AND A SCEPTRE...OH, AND TWO RINGS. THEY SEEM VERY OLD, I CAN'T DETERMINE EXACTLY WHICH PERIOD. I WOULD GUESS THESE WERE CRAFTED MANY HUNDREDS OF YEARS BEFORE CHRIST, OF HEBREW DESIGN, I THINK.
AH, YES...THERE ARE HEBREW CHARACTERS INSCRIBED HERE, ON THE RING...THE LETTER "S"...I CAN'T QUITE MAKE OUT THE OTHER CHARACTER. THERE APPEARS TO BE...I THINK IT'S A UNICORN ABOVE IT...
THE OTHER RING IS IN BETTER CONDITION. A LION IS ENGRAVED, WITH THE HEBREW LETTERS "DVD" UNDER IT. "DAVID", I WOULD GUESS IS THE TRANSLATION, PERHAPS REFERRING TO KING DAVID, ANCIENT KING OF THE JEWS.
SO THEY'RE REAL, THEN?
HMMM? REAL? IF YOU MEAN WHETHER OR NOT THEY ARE TRULY SUCH ANCIENT ARTIFACTS, I WOULD NEED MORE TESTS TO CONFIRM IT, BUT YES, I BELIEVE THEY ARE REAL.
HMMM...A SCEPTRE AND A CROWN..."THE SCEPTRE WILL NOT DEPART FROM JUDAH..."
YES, YES...FOR "JUDAH IS THE LION'S WHELP". AND DAVID WAS OF THE TRIBE OF JUDAH, THE RULING FAMILY-- THOUGH OF COURSE THERE WERE THE BENJAMITES WHO CLAIMED RULERSHIP THROUGH SAUL, FIRST KING OF ISRAEL...BUT THAT'S ANOTHER MATTER.
PERHAPS THESE ITEMS BELONGED TO SOME ANCIENT JEWISH RULER OR NOBLE? POSSIBLY EVEN THE ROYAL TREASURES OF KING DAVID?
BUT HOW COULD THESE ANCIENT JEWISH RELICS HAVE COME TO A SMALL CATHOLIC CHURCH IN BELGIUM?
THERE WAS ANOTHER REASON I CHOSE TO COME TO YOU, WITH THESE ITEMS.
OH? AND WHAT REASON IS THAT?
WELL, I'VE HEARD THAT YOU SOMETIMES WORK WITH THE ONE THEY CALL... MAGDALENA?
THE MAGDALENA?! BUT HOW...THE EXISTENCE OF THE MAGDALENA IS NOT EXACTLY COMMON KNOWLEDGE. HOW DID YOU COME BY THIS INFORMATION?
THERE ARE RUMORS...I...I DON'T KNOW ANYTHING, REALLY. JUST THE NAME, AND THAT YOU'RE CONNECTED TO IT. I DON'T EVEN KNOW WHO SHE IS, OR WHAT SHE DOES.
HMPH. YES, WELL, I SUPPOSE THERE'S NO HARM IN IT. THE MAGDALENA IS THE GUARDIAN OF THE CHURCH.

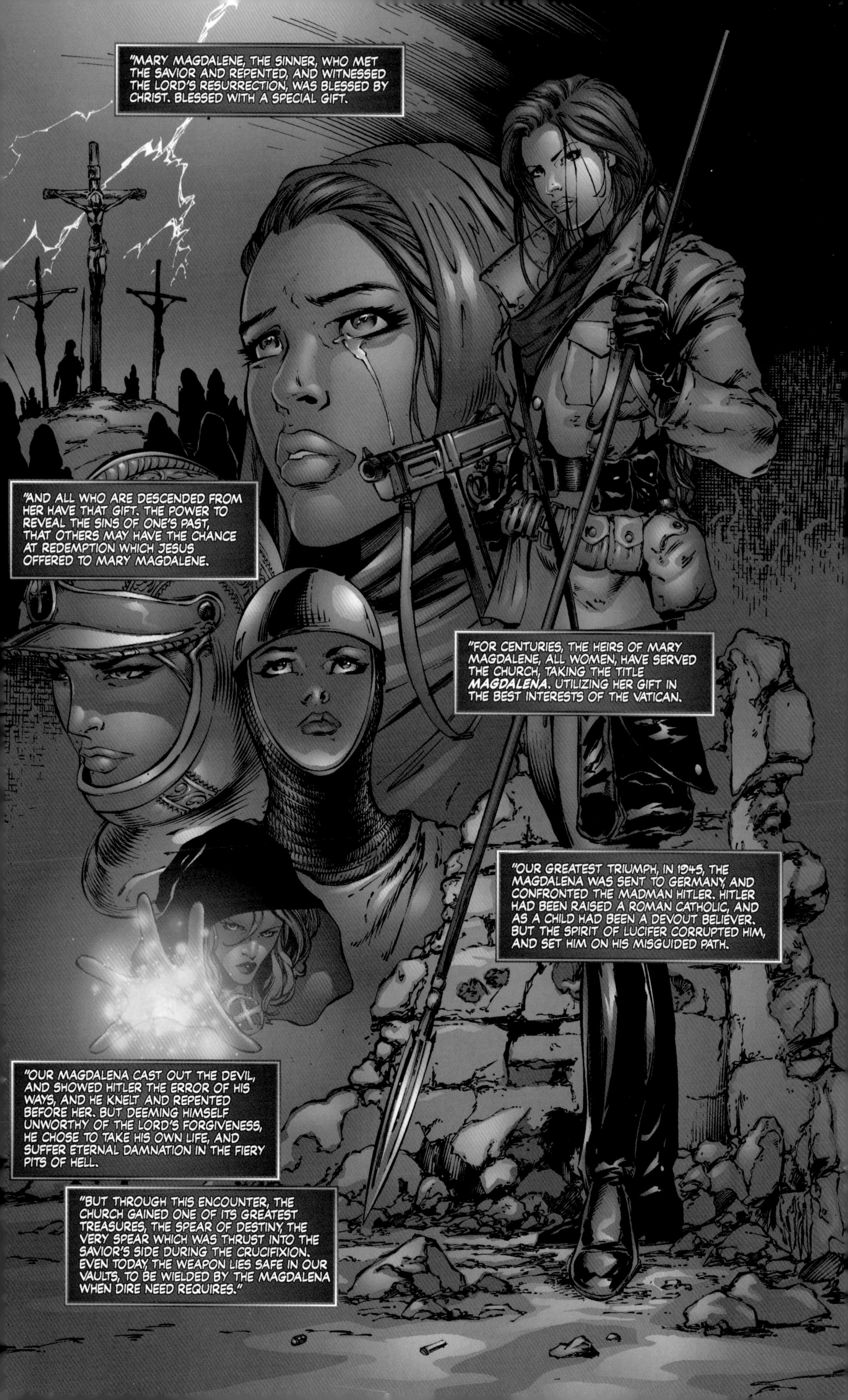
"MARY MAGDALENE, THE SINNER, WHO MET THE SAVIOR AND REPENTED, AND WITNESSED THE LORD'S RESURRECTION, WAS BLESSED BY CHRIST. BLESSED WITH A SPECIAL GIFT.
"AND ALL WHO ARE DESCENDED FROM HER HAVE THAT GIFT. THE POWER TO REVEAL THE SINS OF ONE'S PAST, THAT OTHERS MAY HAVE THE CHANCE AT REDEMPTION WHICH JESUS OFFERED TO MARY MAGDALENE.
"FOR CENTURIES, THE HEIRS OF MARY MAGDALENE, ALL WOMEN, HAVE SERVED THE CHURCH, TAKING THE TITLE MAGDALENA. UTILIZING HER GIFT IN THE BEST INTERESTS OF THE VATICAN.
"OUR GREATEST TRIUMPH, IN 1945, THE MAGDALENA WAS SENT TO GERMANY, AND CONFRONTED THE MADMAN HITLER. HITLER HAD BEEN RAISED A ROMAN CATHOLIC, AND AS A CHILD HAD BEEN A DEVOUT BELIEVER. BUT THE SPIRIT OF LUCIFER CORRUPTED HIM, AND SET HIM ON HIS MISGUIDED PATH.
"OUR MAGDALENA CAST OUT THE DEVIL, AND SHOWED HITLER THE ERROR OF HIS WAYS, AND HE KNELT AND REPENTED BEFORE HER. BUT DEEMING HIMSELF UNWORTHY OF THE LORD'S FORGIVENESS, HE CHOSE TO TAKE HIS OWN LIFE, AND SUFFER ETERNAL DAMNATION IN THE FIERY PITS OF HELL.
"BUT THROUGH THIS ENCOUNTER, THE CHURCH GAINED ONE OF ITS GREATEST TREASURES, THE SPEAR OF DESTINY, THE VERY SPEAR WHICH WAS THRUST INTO THE SAVIOR'S SIDE DURING THE CRUCIFIXION. EVEN TODAY, THE WEAPON LIES SAFE IN OUR VAULTS, TO BE WIELDED BY THE MAGDALENA WHEN DIRE NEED REQUIRES."

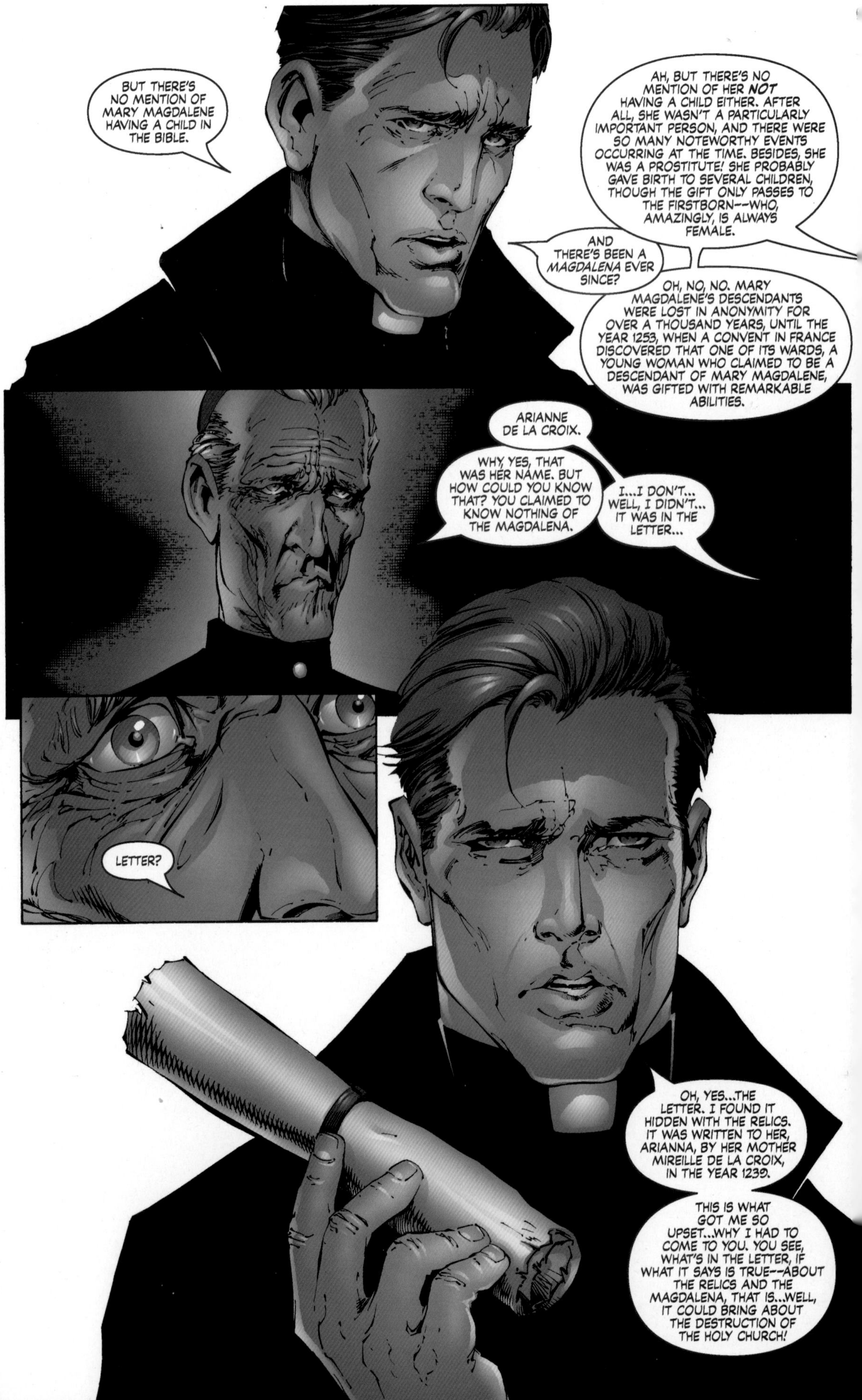
BUT THERE'S NO MENTION OF MARY MAGDALENE HAVING A CHILD IN THE BIBLE.
AH, BUT THERE'S NO MENTION OF HER NOT HAVING A CHILD EITHER. AFTER ALL, SHE WASN'T A PARTICULARLY IMPORTANT PERSON, AND THERE WERE SO MANY NOTEWORTHY EVENTS OCCURRING AT THE TIME. BESIDES, SHE WAS A PROSTITUTE! SHE PROBABLY GAVE BIRTH TO SEVERAL CHILDREN, THOUGH THE GIFT ONLY PASSES TO THE FIRSTBORN--WHO, AMAZINGLY, IS ALWAYS FEMALE.
AND THERE'S BEEN A MAGDALENA EVER SINCE?
OH, NO, NO. MARY MAGDALENE'S DESCENDANTS WERE LOST IN ANONYMITY FOR OVER A THOUSAND YEARS, UNTIL THE YEAR 1253, WHEN A CONVENT IN FRANCE DISCOVERED THAT ONE OF ITS WARDS, A YOUNG WOMAN WHO CLAIMED TO BE A DESCENDANT OF MARY MAGDALENE, WAS GIFTED WITH REMARKABLE ABILITIES.
ARIANNE DE LA CROIX.
WHY, YES, THAT WAS HER NAME. BUT HOW COULD YOU KNOW THAT? YOU CLAIMED TO KNOW NOTHING OF THE MAGDALENA.
I...I DON'T... WELL, I DIDN'T... IT WAS IN THE LETTER...
LETTER?
OH, YES...THE LETTER. I FOUND IT HIDDEN WITH THE RELICS. IT WAS WRITTEN TO HER, ARIANNA, BY HER MOTHER MIREILLE DE LA CROIX, IN THE YEAR 1239.
THIS IS WHAT GOT ME SO UPSET...WHY I HAD TO COME TO YOU. YOU SEE, WHAT'S IN THE LETTER, IF WHAT IT SAYS IS TRUE--ABOUT THE RELICS AND THE MAGDALENA, THAT IS...WELL, IT COULD BRING ABOUT THE DESTRUCTION OF THE HOLY CHURCH!

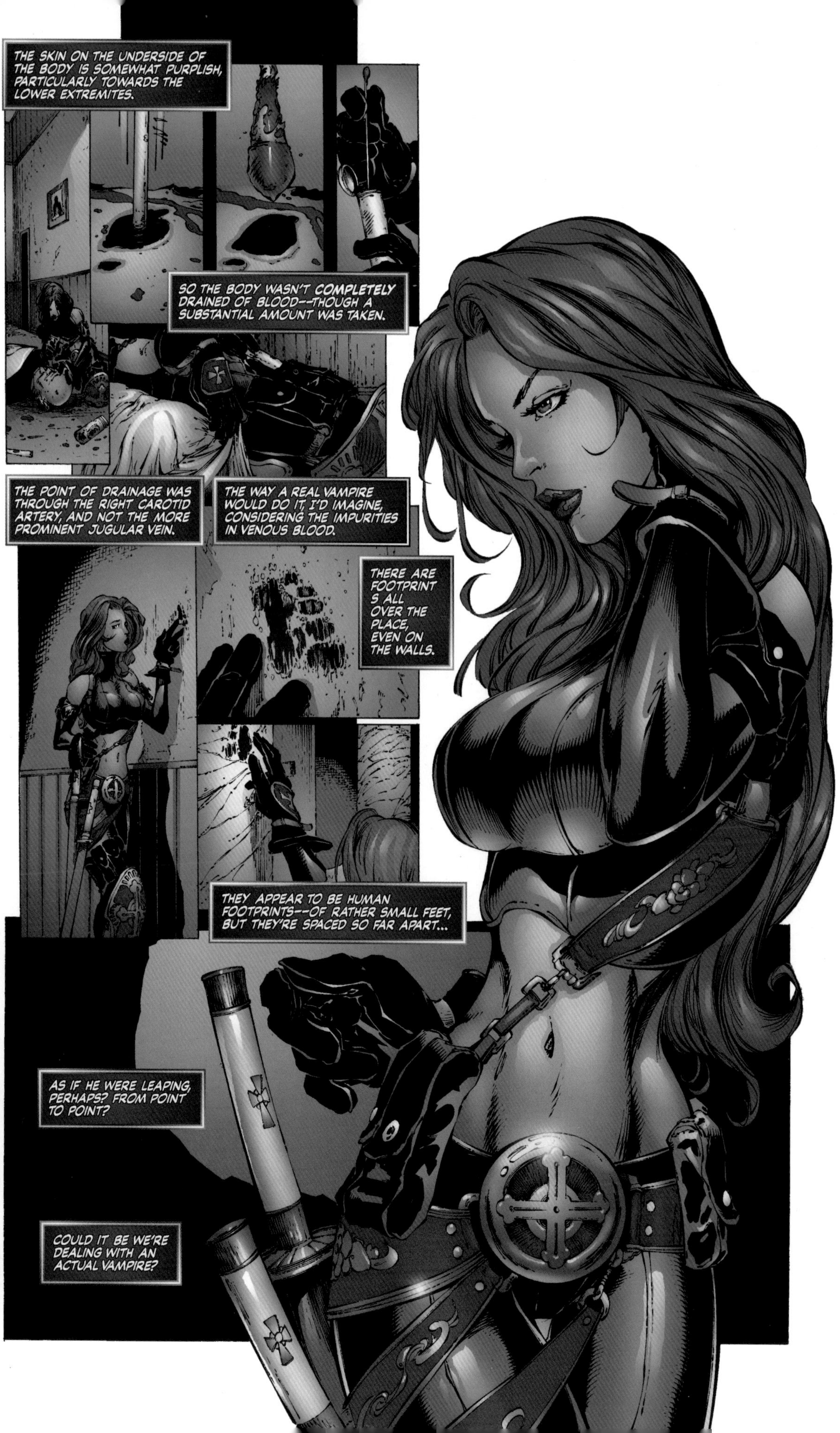
THE SKIN ON THE UNDERSIDE OF THE BODY IS SOMEWHAT PURPLISH, PARTICULARLY TOWARDS THE LOWER EXTREMITES.
SO THE BODY WASN'T COMPLETELY DRAINED OF BLOOD--THOUGH A SUBSTANTIAL AMOUNT WAS TAKEN.
THE POINT OF DRAINAGE WAS THROUGH THE RIGHT CAROTID ARTERY, AND NOT THE MORE PROMINENT JUGULAR VEIN.
THE WAY A REAL VAMPIRE WOULD DO IT, I'D IMAGINE, CONSIDERING THE IMPURITIES IN VENOUS BLOOD.
THERE ARE FOOTPRINT S ALL OVER THE PLACE, EVEN ON THE WALLS.
THEY APPEAR TO BE HUMAN FOOTPRINTS--OF RATHER SMALL FEET, BUT THEY'RE SPACED SO FAR APART...
AS IF HE WERE LEAPING, PERHAPS? FROM POINT TO POINT?
COULD IT BE WE'RE DEALING WITH AN ACTUAL VAMPIRE?

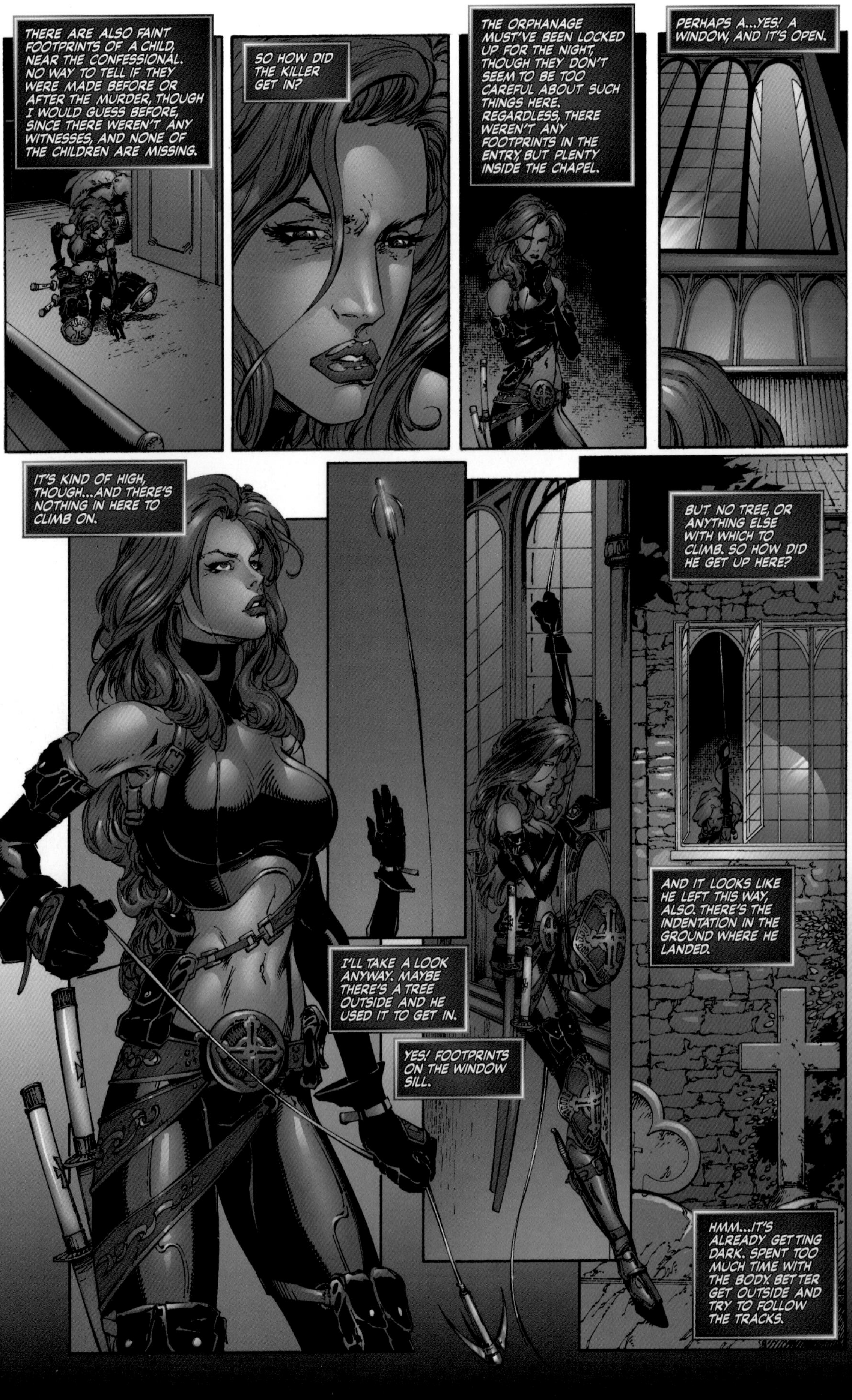
THERE ARE ALSO FAINT FOOTPRINTS OF A CHILD, NEAR THE CONFESSIONAL. NO WAY TO TELL IF THEY WERE MADE BEFORE OR AFTER THE MURDER, THOUGH I WOULD GUESS BEFORE, SINCE THERE WEREN'T ANY WITNESSES, AND NONE OF THE CHILDREN ARE MISSING.
SO HOW DID THE KILLER GET IN?
THE ORPHANAGE MUST'VE BEEN LOCKED UP FOR THE NIGHT, THOUGH THEY DON'T SEEM TO BE TOO CAREFUL ABOUT SUCH THINGS HERE. REGARDLESS, THERE WEREN'T ANY FOOTPRINTS IN THE ENTRY, BUT PLENTY INSIDE THE CHAPEL.
PERHAPS A...YES! A WINDOW, AND IT'S OPEN.
IT'S KIND OF HIGH, THOUGH...AND THERE'S NOTHING IN HERE TO CLIMB ON.
I'LL TAKE A LOOK ANYWAY. MAYBE THERE'S A TREE OUTSIDE AND HE USED IT TO GET IN.
YES! FOOTPRINTS ON THE WINDOW SILL.
BUT NO TREE, OR ANYTHING ELSE WITH WHICH TO CLIMB. SO HOW DID HE GET UP HERE?
AND IT LOOKS LIKE HE LEFT THIS WAY, ALSO. THERE'S THE INDENTATION IN THE GROUND WHERE HE LANDED.
HMM...IT'S ALREADY GETTING DARK. SPENT TOO MUCH TIME WITH THE BODY. BETTER GET OUTSIDE AND TRY TO FOLLOW THE TRACKS.

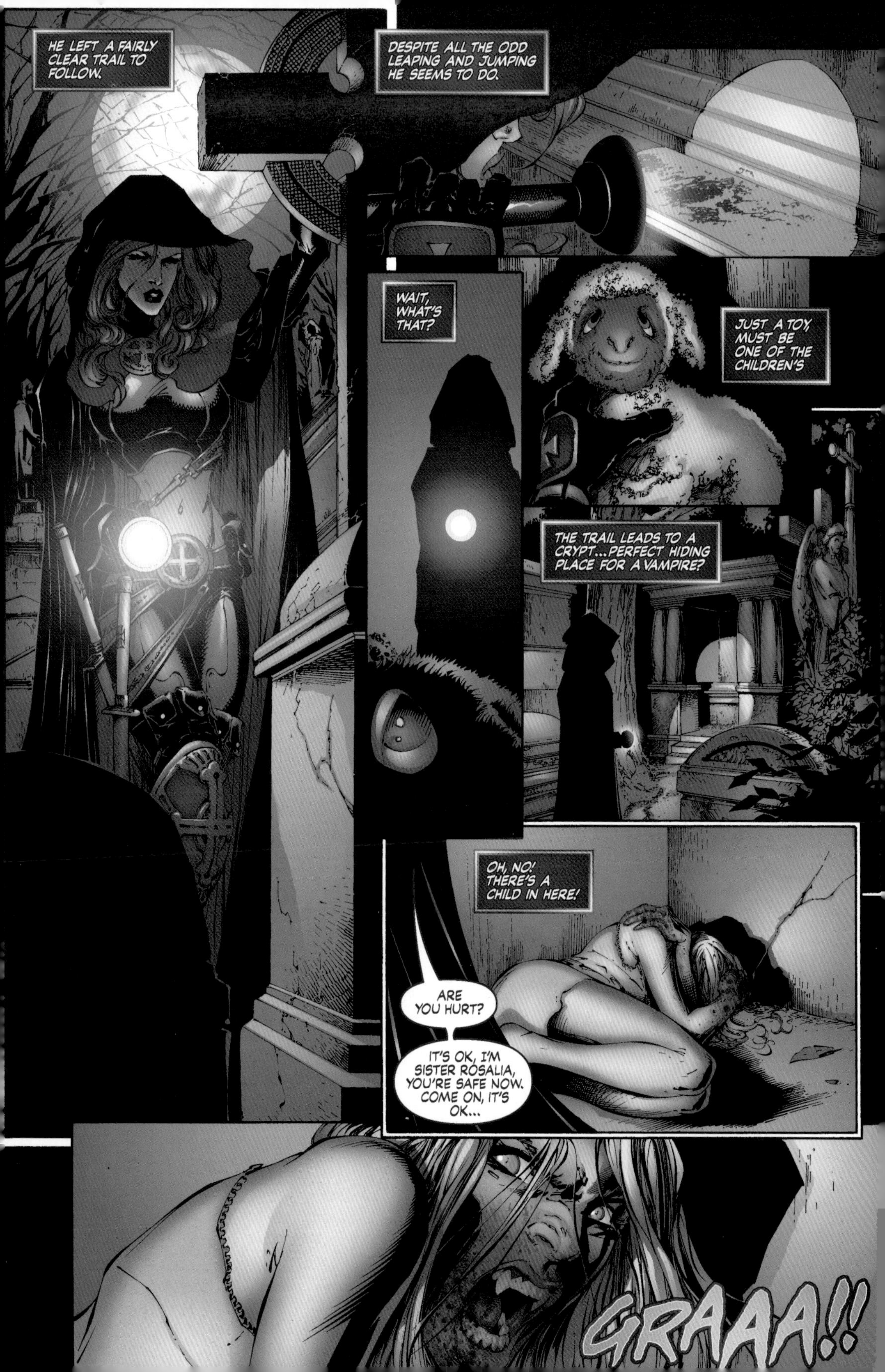

HE LEFT A FAIRLY CLEAR TRAIL TO FOLLOW.
DESPITE ALL THE ODD LEAPING AND JUMPING HE SEEMS TO DO.
WAIT, WHAT'S THAT?
JUST A TOY, MUST BE ONE OF THE CHILDREN'S
THE TRAIL LEADS TO A CRYPT...PERFECT HIDING PLACE FOR A VAMPIRE?
OH, NO! THERE'S A CHILD IN HERE!
ARE YOU HURT?
IT'S OK, I'M SISTER ROSALIA, YOU'RE SAFE NOW. COME ON, IT'S OK...
GRAAA!!

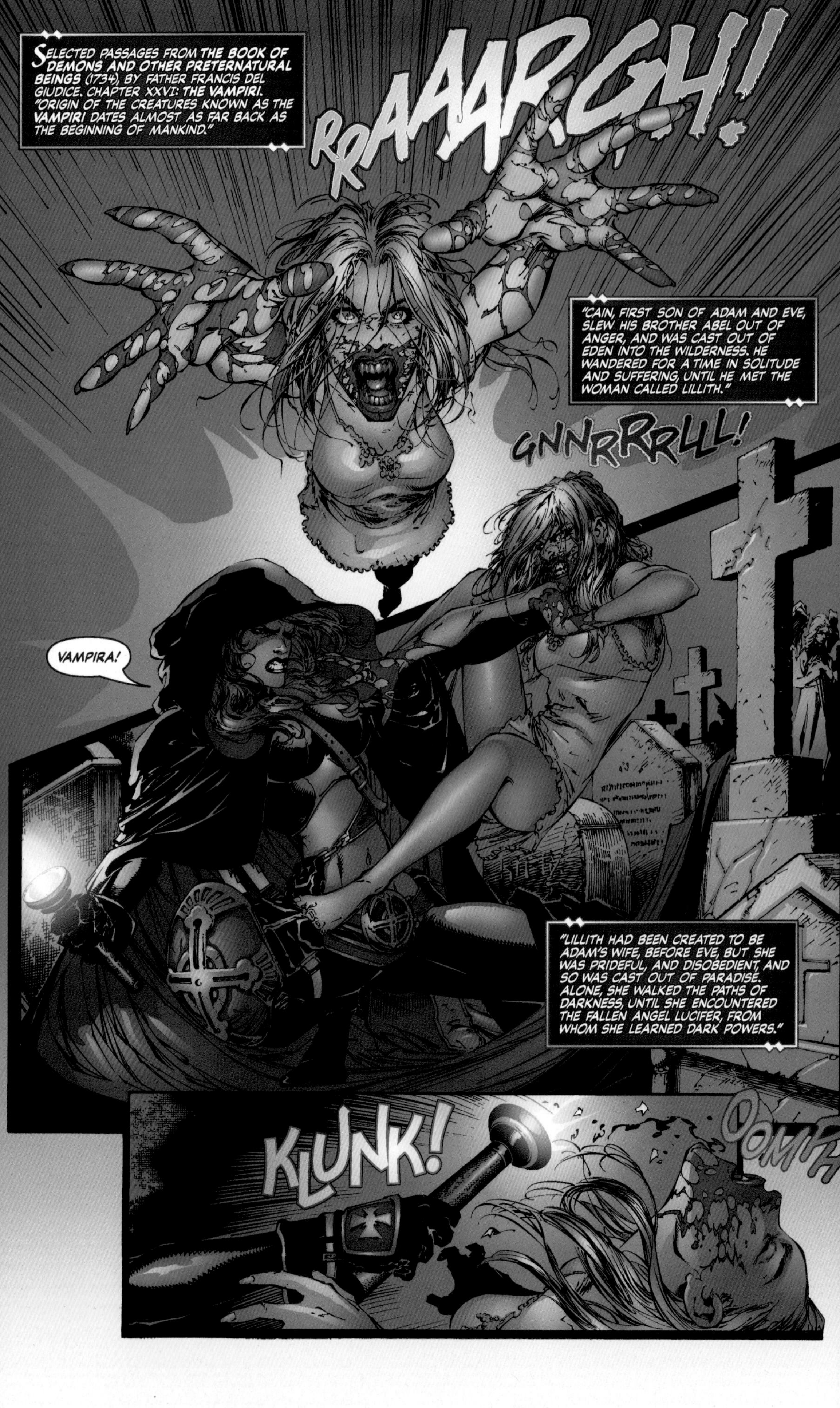
SELECTED PASSAGES FROM THE BOOK OF DEMONS AND OTHER PRETERNATURAL BEINGS (1734), BY FATHER FRANCIS DEL GIUDICE. CHAPTER XXVI: THE VAMPIRI.
"ORIGIN OF THE CREATURES KNOWN AS THE VAMPIRI DATES ALMOST AS FAR BACK AS THE BEGINNING OF MANKIND."
RRAAAARGH!
"CAIN, FIRST SON OF ADAM AND EVE, SLEW HIS BROTHER ABEL OUT OF ANGER, AND WAS CAST OUT OF EDEN INTO THE WILDERNESS. HE WANDERED FOR A TIME IN SOLITUDE AND SUFFERING, UNTIL HE MET THE WOMAN CALLED LILLITH."
GNNRRRLLL!
VAMPIRA!
"LILLITH HAD BEEN CREATED TO BE ADAM'S WIFE, BEFORE EVE, BUT SHE WAS PRIDEFUL, AND DISOBEDIENT, AND SO WAS CAST OUT OF PARADISE. ALONE, SHE WALKED THE PATHS OF DARKNESS, UNTIL SHE ENCOUNTERED THE FALLEN ANGEL LUCIFER, FROM WHOM SHE LEARNED DARK POWERS."
KLUNK!
OOMPH

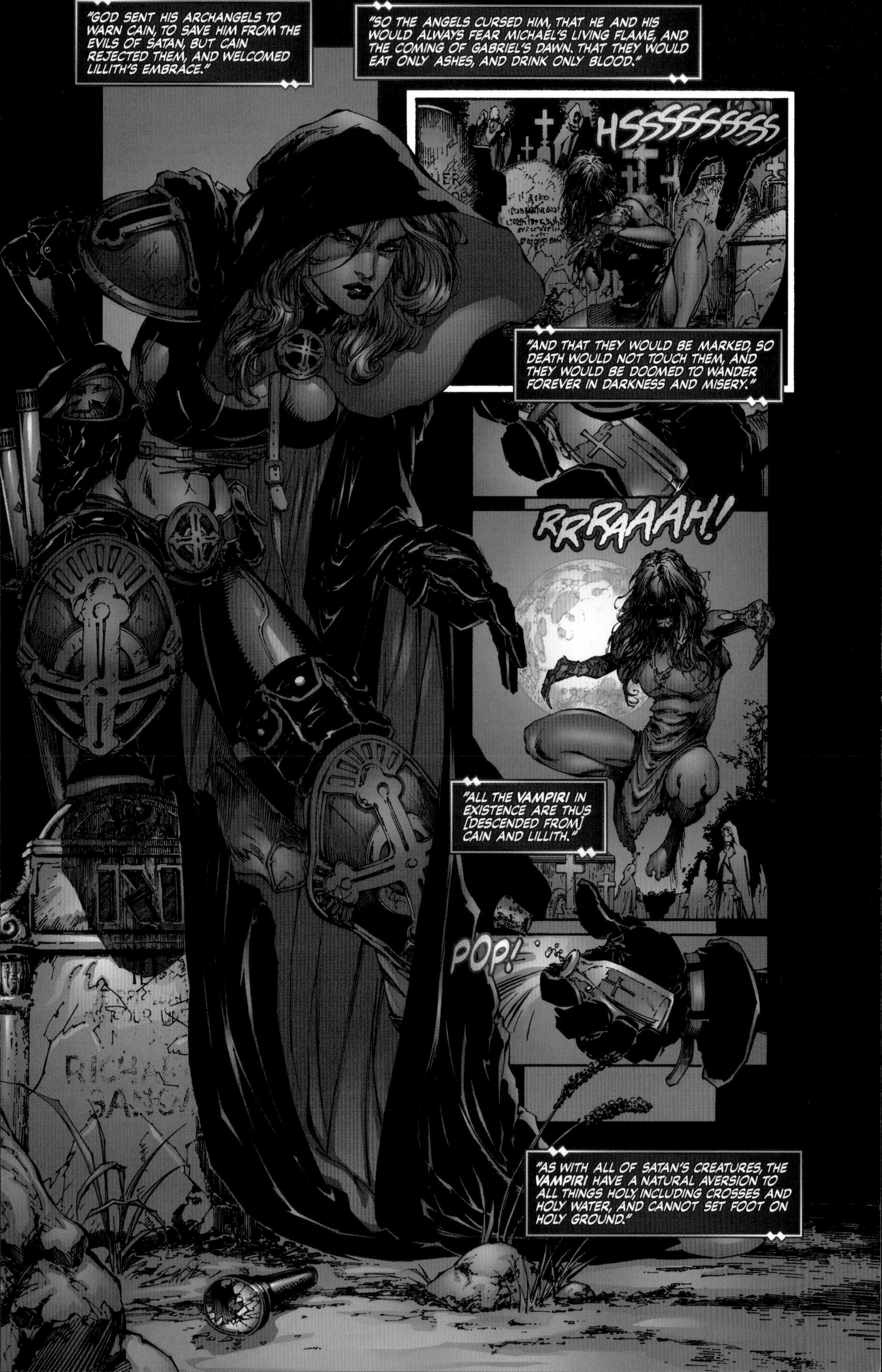
"GOD SENT HIS ARCHANGELS TO WARN CAIN, TO SAVE HIM FROM THE EVILS OF SATAN, BUT CAIN REJECTED THEM, AND WELCOMED LILLITH'S EMBRACE."
"SO THE ANGELS CURSED HIM, THAT HE AND HIS WOULD ALWAYS FEAR MICHAEL'S LIVING FLAME, AND THE COMING OF GABRIEL'S DAWN. THAT THEY WOULD EAT ONLY ASHES, AND DRINK ONLY BLOOD."
HSSSSSSSSS
"AND THAT THEY WOULD BE MARKED, SO DEATH WOULD NOT TOUCH THEM, AND THEY WOULD BE DOOMED TO WANDER FOREVER IN DARKNESS AND MISERY."
RRRAAAH!
"ALL THE VAMPIRI IN EXISTENCE ARE THUS [DESCENDED FROM] CAIN AND LILLITH."
POP!
"AS WITH ALL OF SATAN'S CREATURES, THE VAMPIRI HAVE A NATURAL AVERSION TO ALL THINGS HOLY, INCLUDING CROSSES AND HOLY WATER, AND CANNOT SET FOOT ON HOLY GROUND."

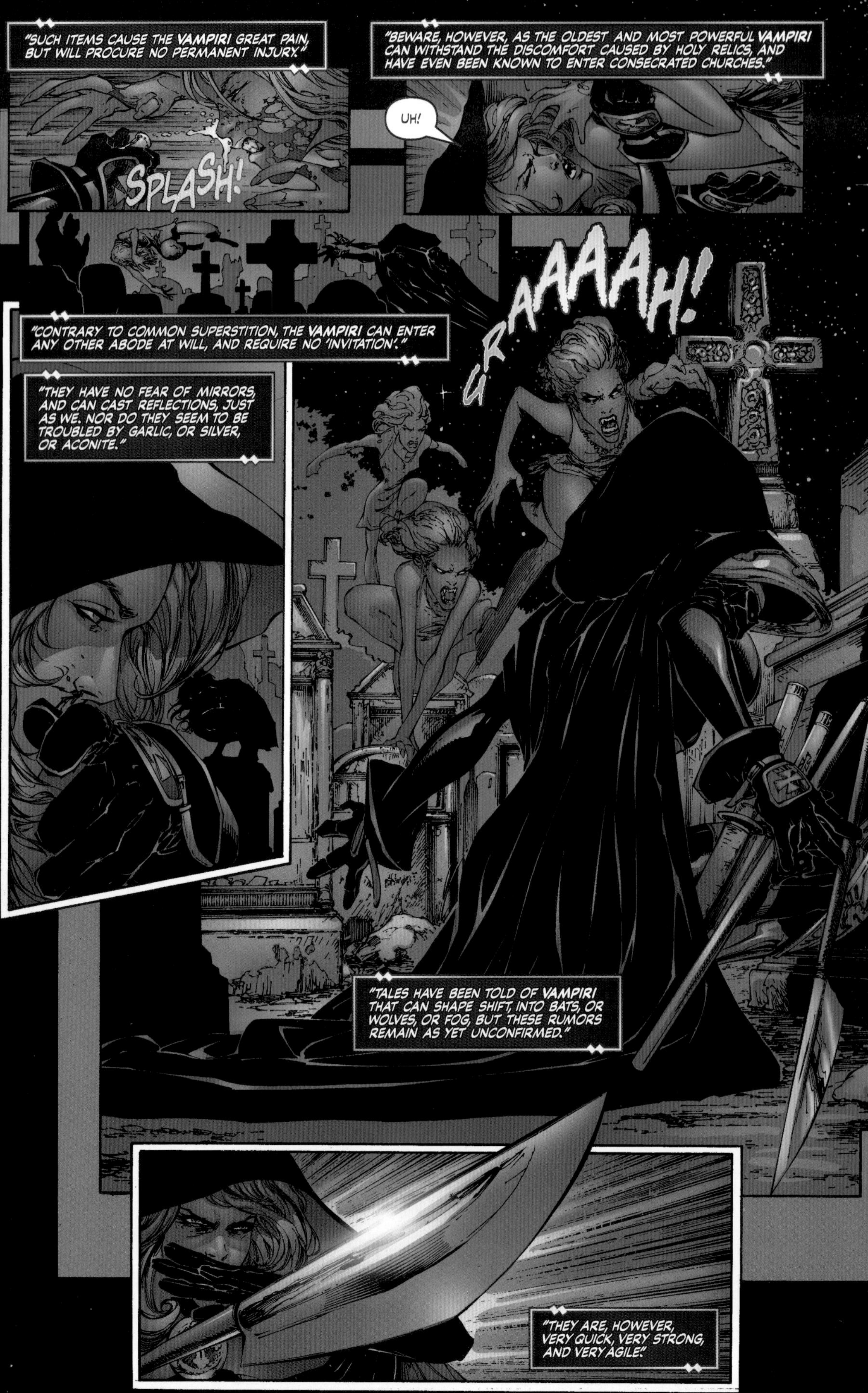
"SUCH ITEMS CAUSE THE VAMPIRI GREAT PAIN, BUT WILL PROCURE NO PERMANENT INJURY."
SPLASH!
"BEWARE, HOWEVER, AS THE OLDEST AND MOST POWERFUL VAMPIRI CAN WITHSTAND THE DISCOMFORT CAUSED BY HOLY RELICS, AND HAVE EVEN BEEN KNOWN TO ENTER CONSECRATED CHURCHES."
UH!
"CONTRARY TO COMMON SUPERSTITION, THE VAMPIRI CAN ENTER ANY OTHER ABODE AT WILL, AND REQUIRE NO 'INVITATION'."
"THEY HAVE NO FEAR OF MIRRORS, AND CAN CAST REFLECTIONS, JUST AS WE. NOR DO THEY SEEM TO BE TROUBLED BY GARLIC, OR SILVER, OR ACONITE."
GRAAAAH!
"TALES HAVE BEEN TOLD OF VAMPIRI THAT CAN SHAPE SHIFT, INTO BATS, OR WOLVES, OR FOG, BUT THESE RUMORS REMAIN AS YET UNCONFIRMED."
"THEY ARE, HOWEVER, VERY QUICK, VERY STRONG, AND VERY AGILE."

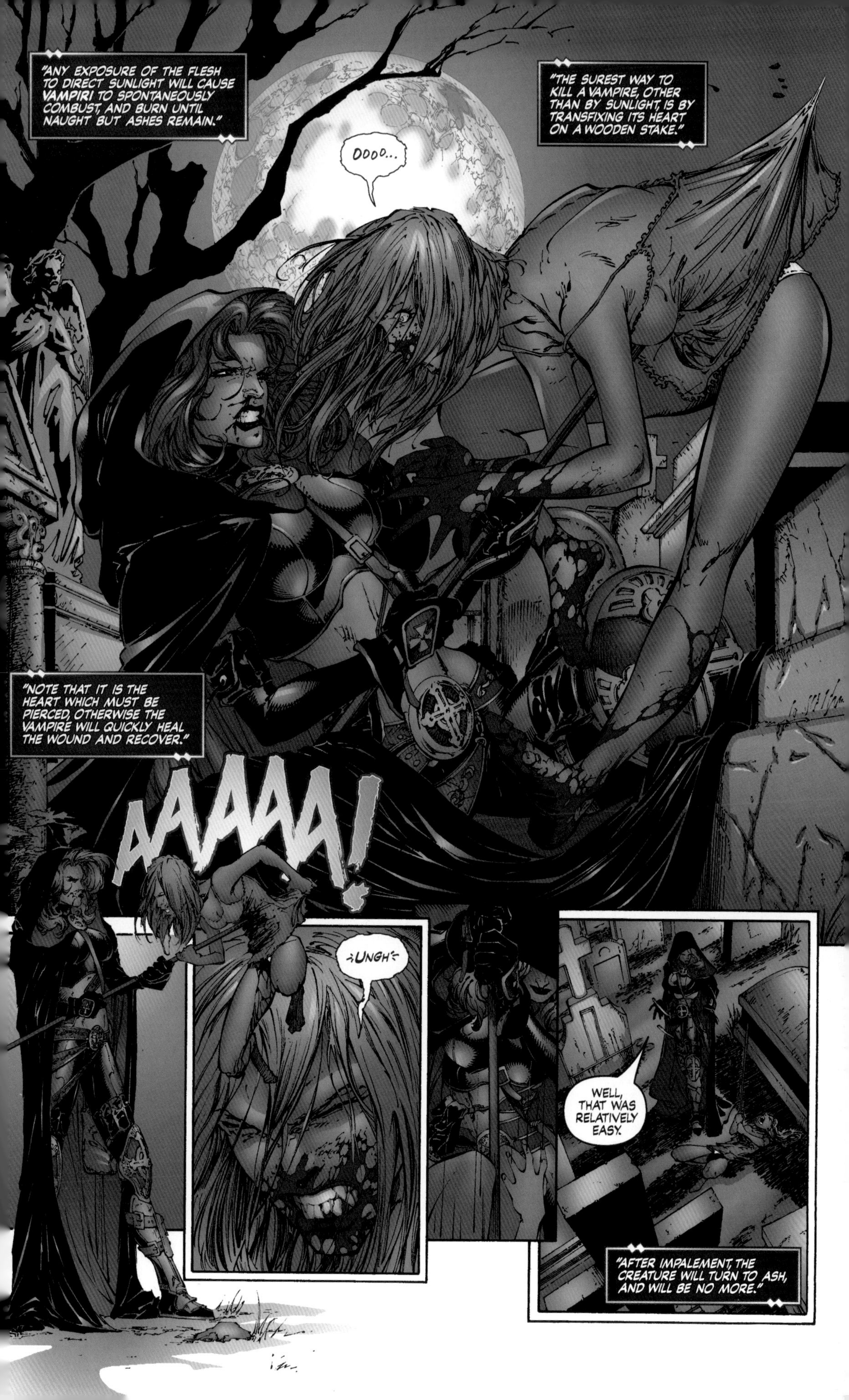
"ANY EXPOSURE OF THE FLESH TO DIRECT SUNLIGHT WILL CAUSE VAMPIRI TO SPONTANEOUSLY COMBUST, AND BURN UNTIL NAUGHT BUT ASHES REMAIN."
"THE SUREST WAY TO KILL A VAMPIRE, OTHER THAN BY SUNLIGHT, IS BY TRANSFIXING ITS HEART ON A WOODEN STAKE."
OOOO...
"NOTE THAT IT IS THE HEART WHICH MUST BE PIERCED, OTHERWISE THE VAMPIRE WILL QUICKLY HEAL THE WOUND AND RECOVER."
AAAAA!
UNGH
WELL, THAT WAS RELATIVELY EASY.
"AFTER IMPALEMENT, THE CREATURE WILL TURN TO ASH, AND WILL BE NO MORE."

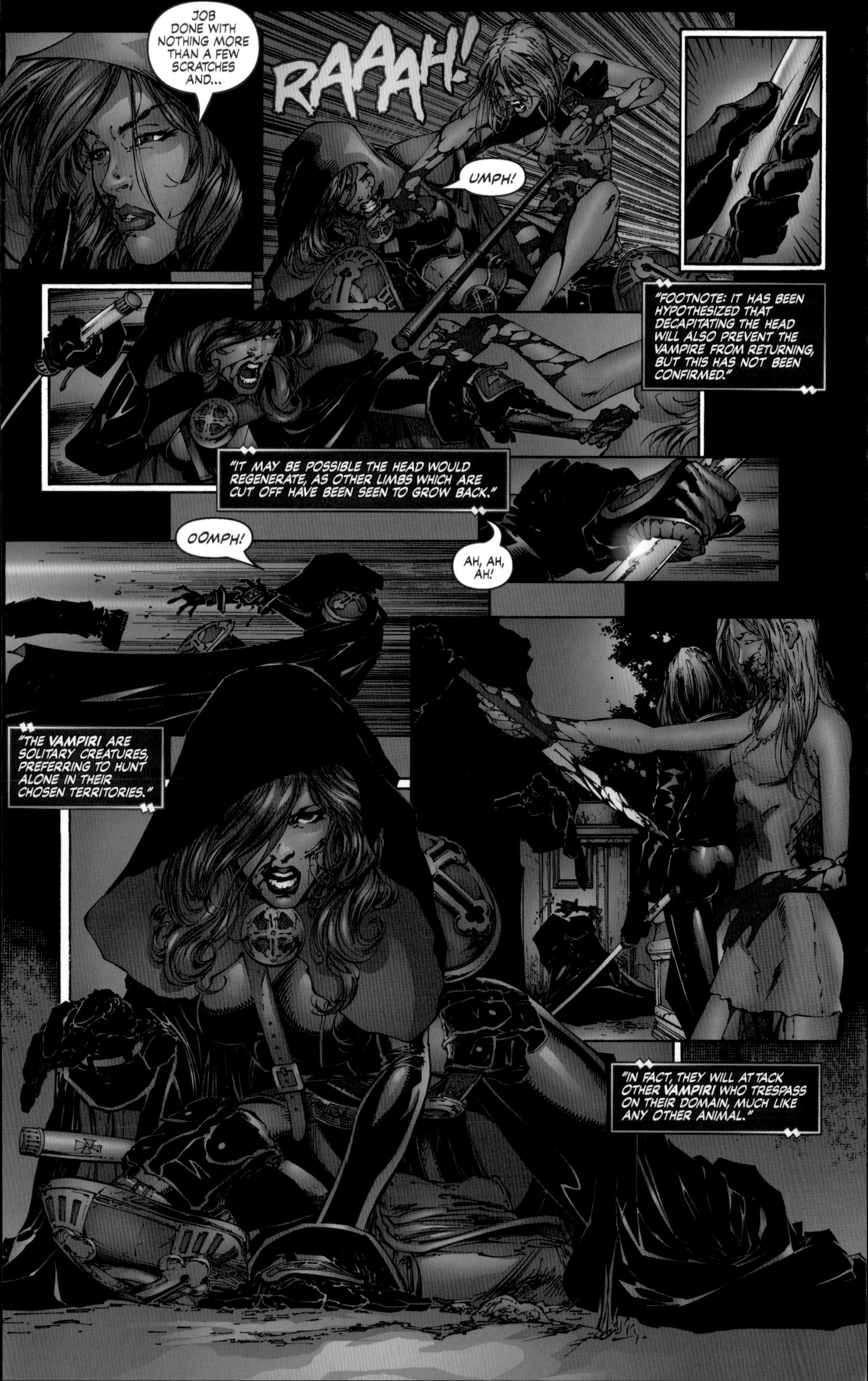
JOB DONE WITH NOTHING MORE THAN A FEW SCRATCHES AND...
RAAAH!
UMPH!
"FOOTNOTE: IT HAS BEEN HYPOTHESIZED THAT DECAPITATING THE HEAD WILL ALSO PREVENT THE VAMPIRE FROM RETURNING, BUT THIS HAS NOT BEEN CONFIRMED."
"IT MAY BE POSSIBLE THE HEAD WOULD REGENERATE, AS OTHER LIMBS WHICH ARE CUT OFF HAVE BEEN SEEN TO GROW BACK."
OOMPH!
AH, AH, AH!
"THE VAMPIRI ARE SOLITARY CREATURES, PREFERRING TO HUNT ALONE IN THEIR CHOSEN TERRITORIES."
"IN FACT, THEY WILL ATTACK OTHER VAMPIRI WHO TRESPASS ON THEIR DOMAIN, MUCH LIKE ANY OTHER ANIMAL."

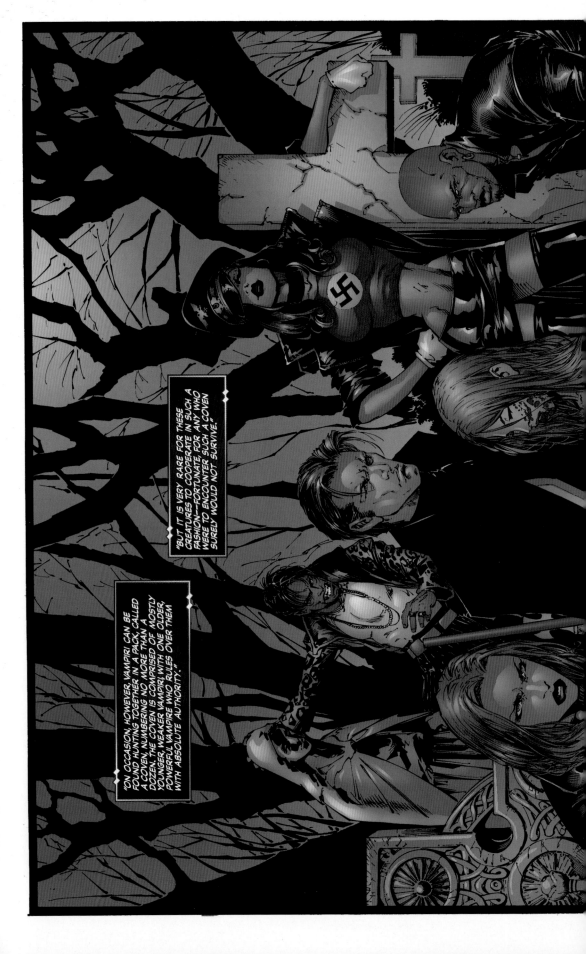

"ON OCCASION, HOWEVER, VAMPIRI CAN BE FOUND HUNTING TOGETHER IN A PACK, CALLED A COVEN, NUMBERING NO MORE THAN A DOZEN. THE COVEN IS COMPRISED OF MOSTLY YOUNGER, WEAKER VAMPIRI WITH ONE OLDER, POWERFUL VAMPIRE WHO RULES OVER THEM WITH ABSOLUTE AUTHORITY."

"BUT IT IS VERY RARE FOR THESE CREATURES TO COOPERATE IN SUCH A FASHION—FORTUNATE, FOR ANY WHO WERE TO ENCOUNTER SUCH A COVEN SURELY WOULD NOT SURVIVE."

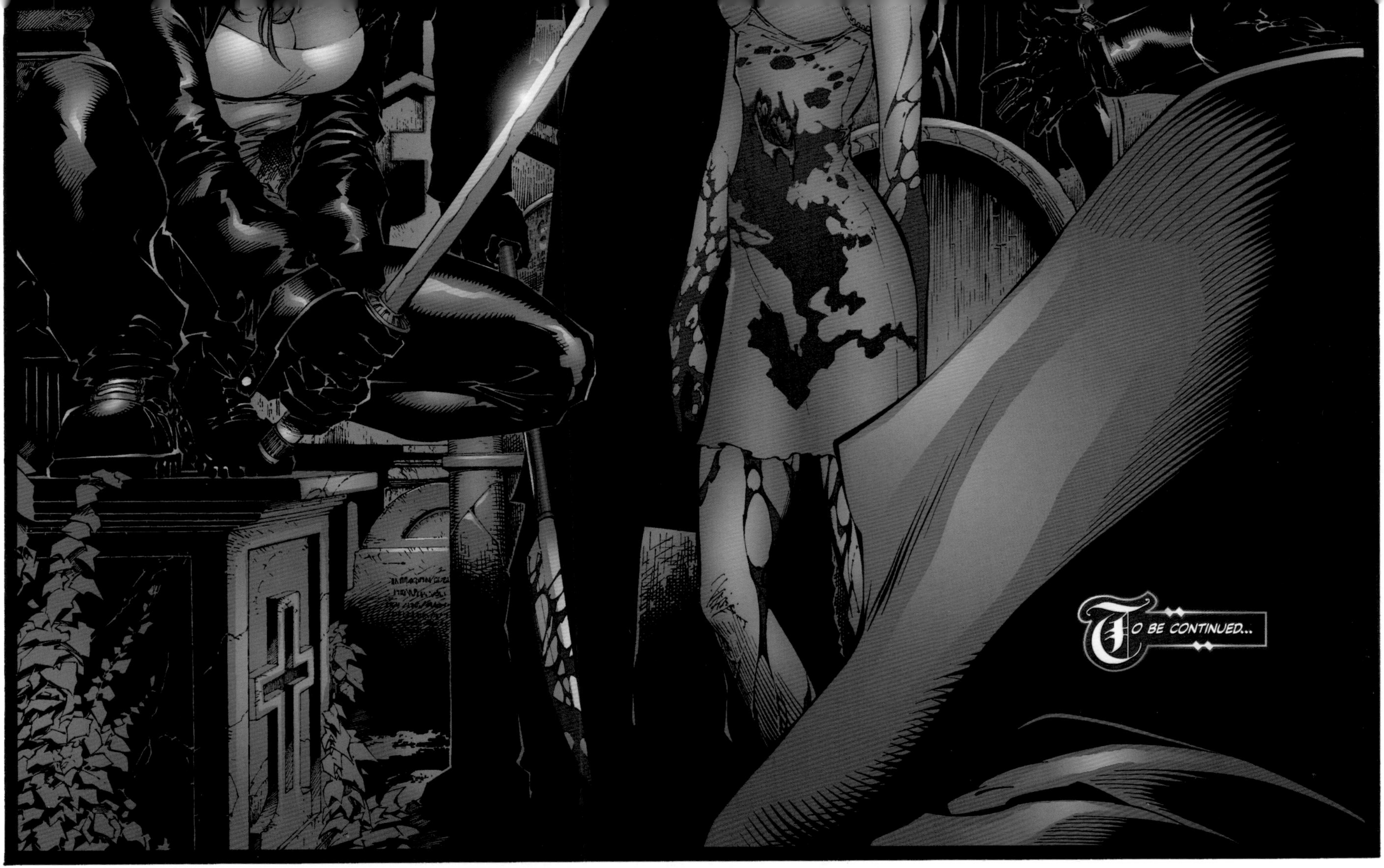
TO BE CONTINUED...

VOLUME I, ISSUE #2

story by: Marcia Chen
pencils by: Joe Benitez
inks by: Joe Weems V, Billy Tan,
Kevin Conrad
colors by: Jonathan D. Smith
letters by: Robin Spehar and Dennis Heisler

pencil assists by: Mun Kao
inks assists by: Marco "Madman" Galli

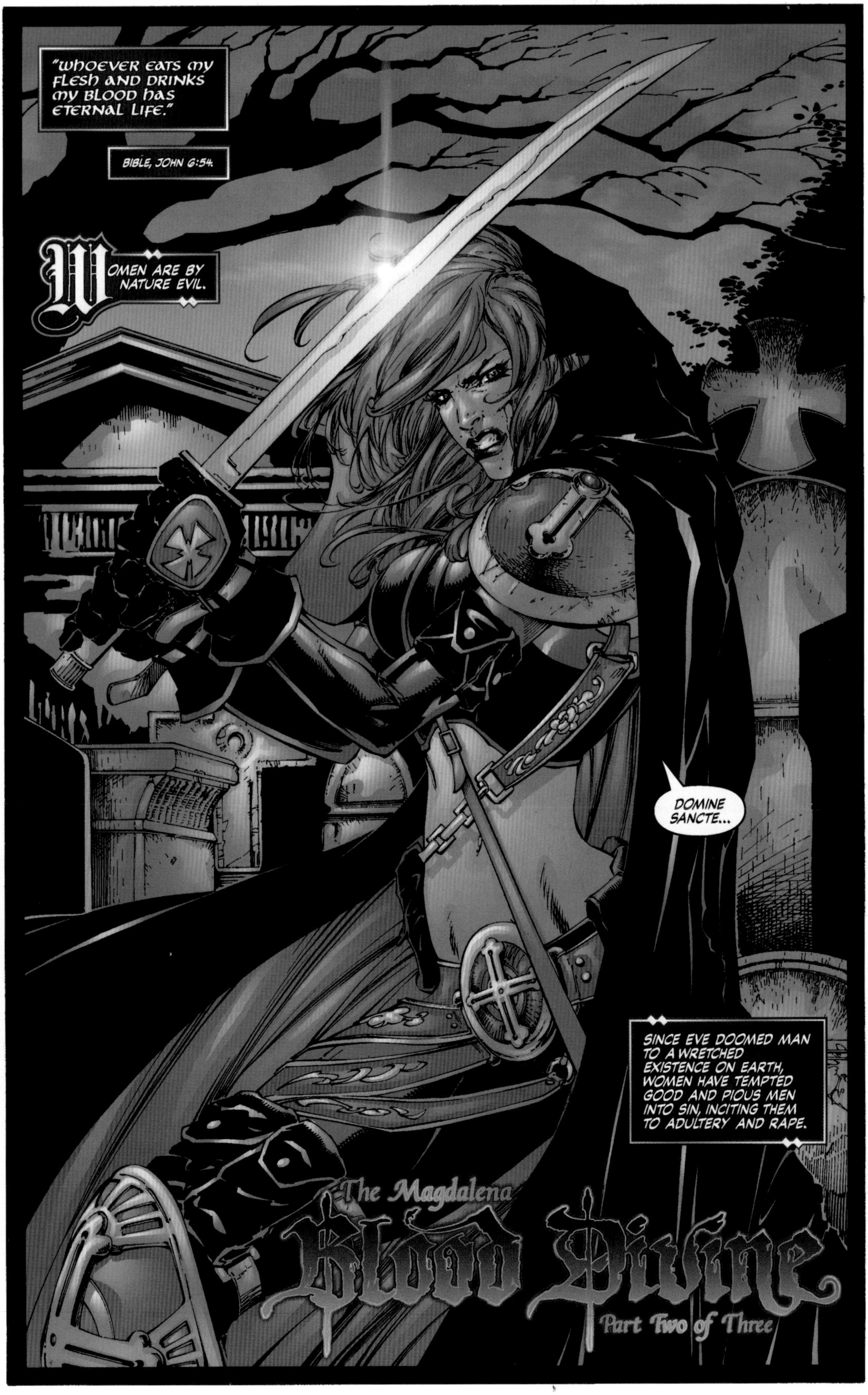
"WHOEVER EATS MY FLESH AND DRINKS MY BLOOD HAS ETERNAL LIFE."
BIBLE, JOHN 6:54.
WOMEN ARE BY NATURE EVIL.
DOMINE SANCTE...
SINCE EVE DOOMED MAN TO A WRETCHED EXISTENCE ON EARTH, WOMEN HAVE TEMPTED GOOD AND PIOUS MEN INTO SIN, INCITING THEM TO ADULTERY AND RAPE.
The Magdalena
Blood Divine
Part Two of Three

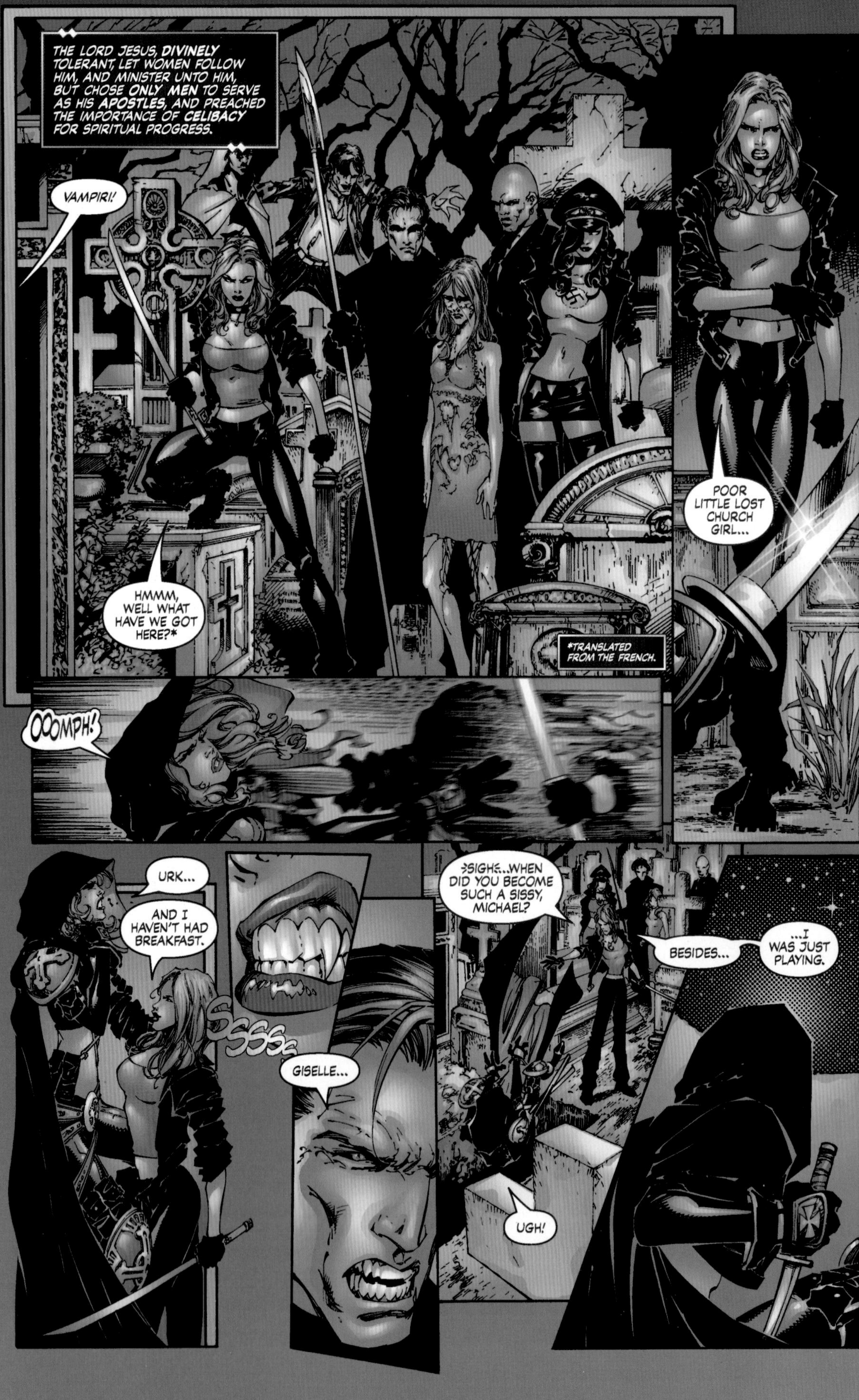
THE LORD JESUS, DIVINELY TOLERANT, LET WOMEN FOLLOW HIM, AND MINISTER UNTO HIM, BUT CHOSE ONLY MEN TO SERVE AS HIS APOSTLES, AND PREACHED THE IMPORTANCE OF CELIBACY FOR SPIRITUAL PROGRESS.
VAMPIRI!
HMMM, WELL WHAT HAVE WE GOT HERE?*
*TRANSLATED FROM THE FRENCH.
POOR LITTLE LOST CHURCH GIRL...
OOOMPH!
URK...
AND I HAVEN'T HAD BREAKFAST.
SSSSS
GISELLE...
>SIGH<...WHEN DID YOU BECOME SUCH A SISSY, MICHAEL?
UGH!
BESIDES...
...I WAS JUST PLAYING.

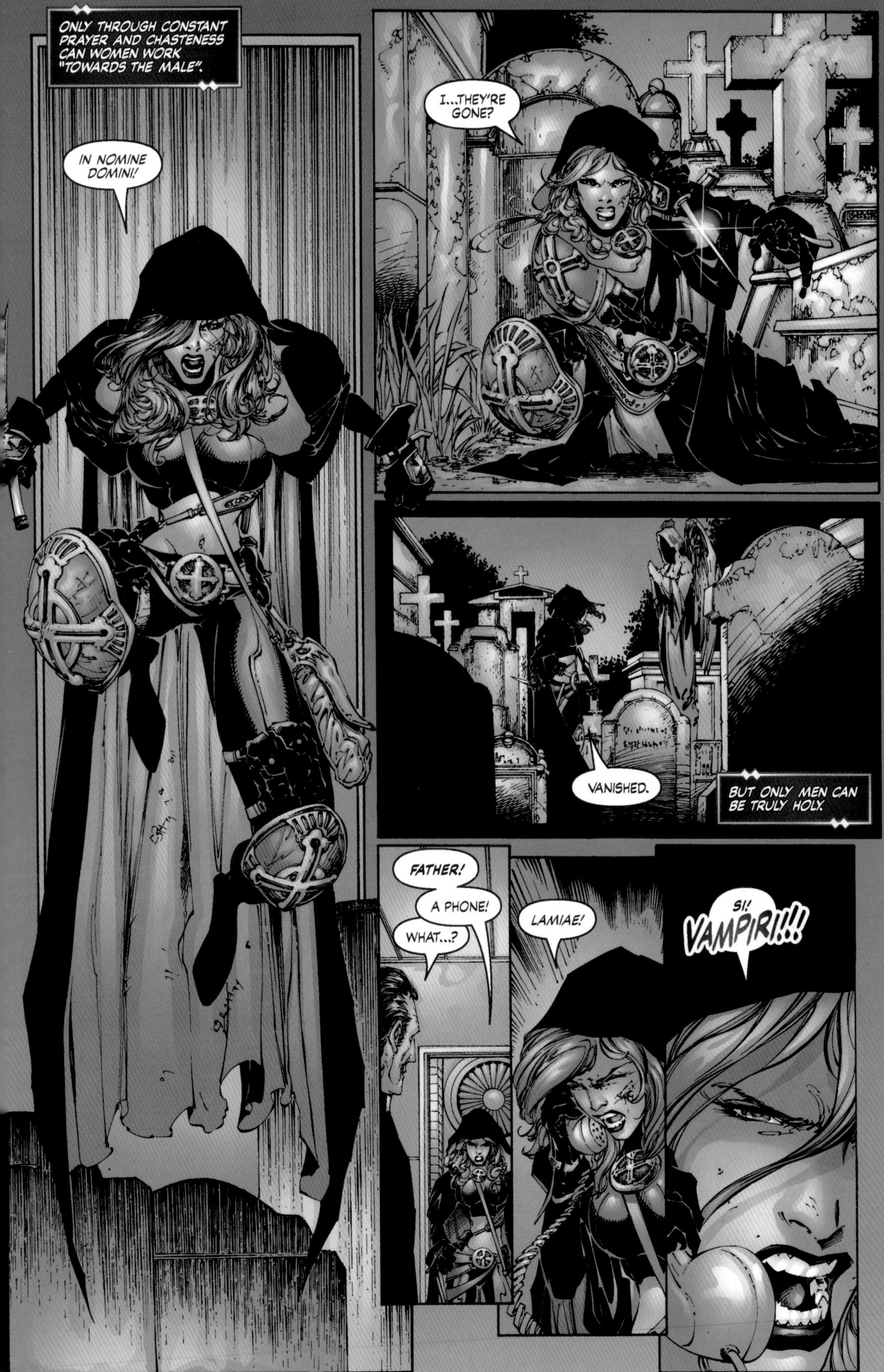

ONLY THROUGH CONSTANT PRAYER AND CHASTENESS CAN WOMEN WORK "TOWARDS THE MALE".
IN NOMINE DOMINI!
I...THEY'RE GONE?
VANISHED.
BUT ONLY MEN CAN BE TRULY HOLY.
FATHER!
A PHONE!
WHAT...?
LAMIAE!
SI!
VAMPIRI!!!

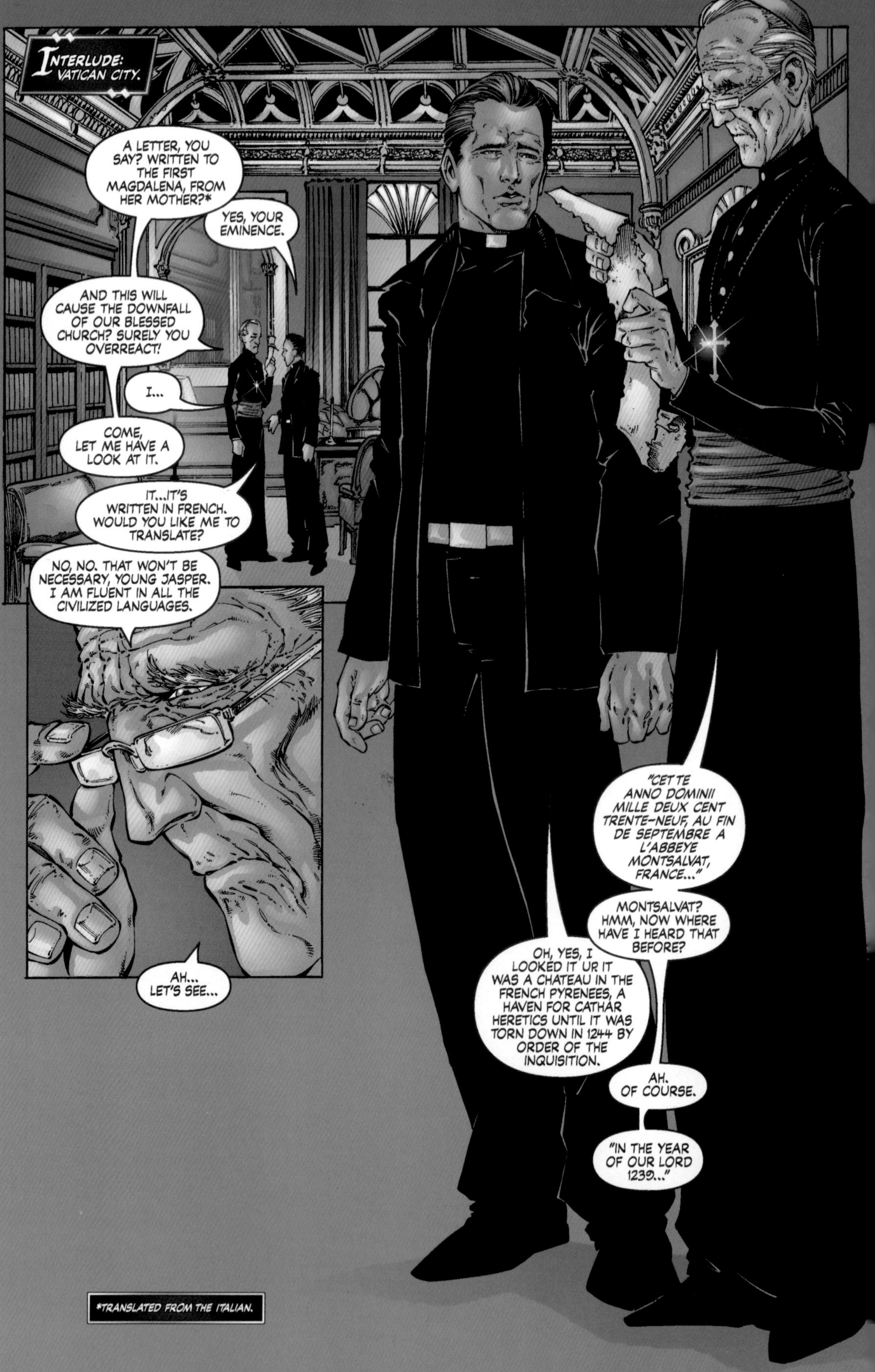

INTERLUDE: VATICAN CITY.
A LETTER, YOU SAY? WRITTEN TO THE FIRST MAGDALENA, FROM HER MOTHER?*
YES, YOUR EMINENCE.
AND THIS WILL CAUSE THE DOWNFALL OF OUR BLESSED CHURCH? SURELY YOU OVERREACT!
I...
COME, LET ME HAVE A LOOK AT IT.
IT...IT'S WRITTEN IN FRENCH. WOULD YOU LIKE ME TO TRANSLATE?
NO, NO. THAT WON'T BE NECESSARY, YOUNG JASPER. I AM FLUENT IN ALL THE CIVILIZED LANGUAGES.
AH... LET'S SEE...
"CETTE ANNO DOMINII MILLE DEUX CENT TRENTE-NEUF, AU FIN DE SEPTEMBRE A L'ABBEYE MONTSALVAT, FRANCE..."
MONTSALVAT? HMM, NOW WHERE HAVE I HEARD THAT BEFORE?
OH, YES, I LOOKED IT UP. IT WAS A CHATEAU IN THE FRENCH PYRENEES, A HAVEN FOR CATHAR HERETICS UNTIL IT WAS TORN DOWN IN 1244 BY ORDER OF THE INQUISITION.
AH. OF COURSE.
"IN THE YEAR OF OUR LORD 1239..."
*TRANSLATED FROM THE ITALIAN.

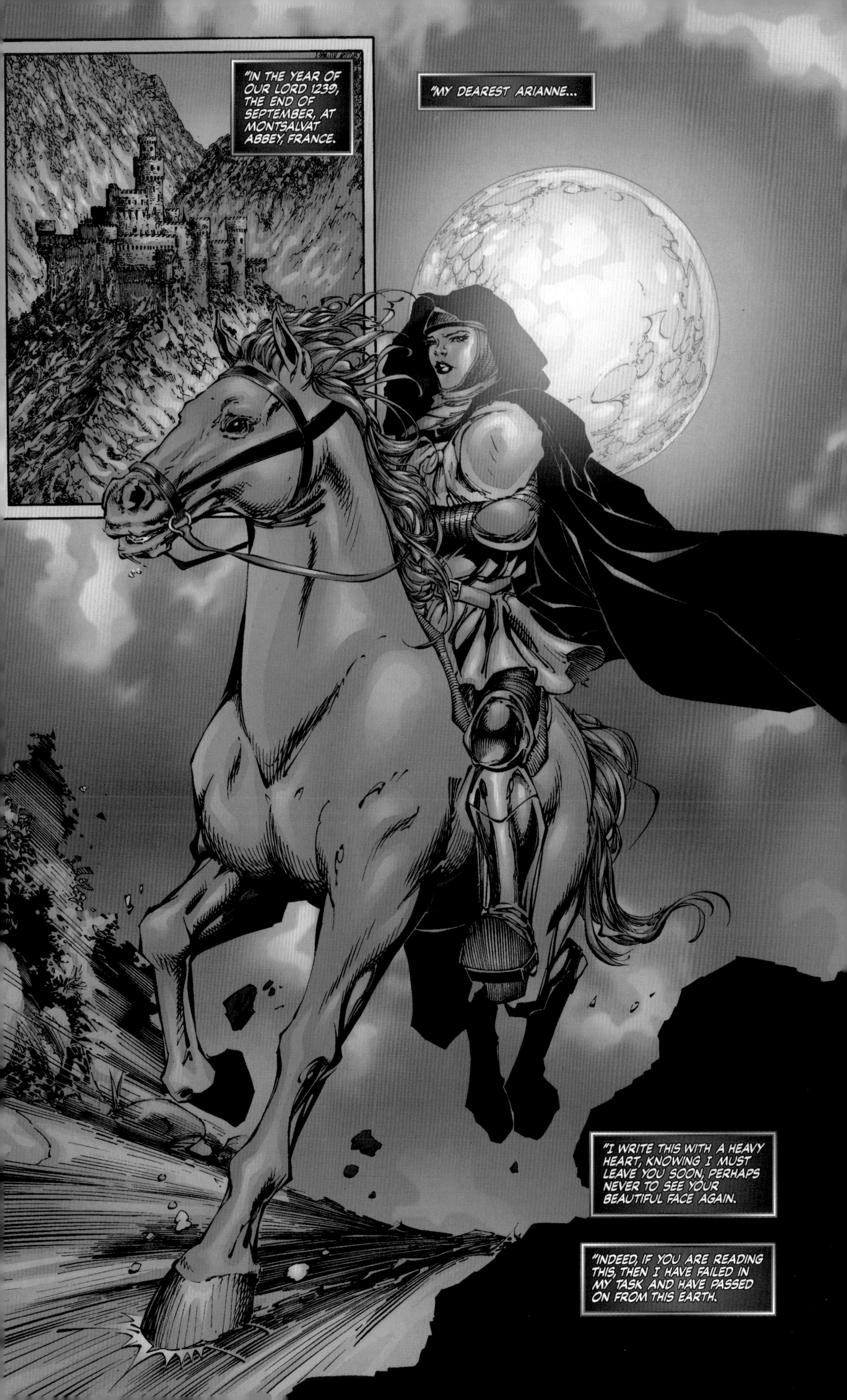
"IN THE YEAR OF OUR LORD 1239, THE END OF SEPTEMBER, AT MONTSALVAT ABBEY, FRANCE.
"MY DEAREST ARIANNE...
"I WRITE THIS WITH A HEAVY HEART, KNOWING I MUST LEAVE YOU SOON, PERHAPS NEVER TO SEE YOUR BEAUTIFUL FACE AGAIN.
"INDEED, IF YOU ARE READING THIS, THEN I HAVE FAILED IN MY TASK AND HAVE PASSED ON FROM THIS EARTH.

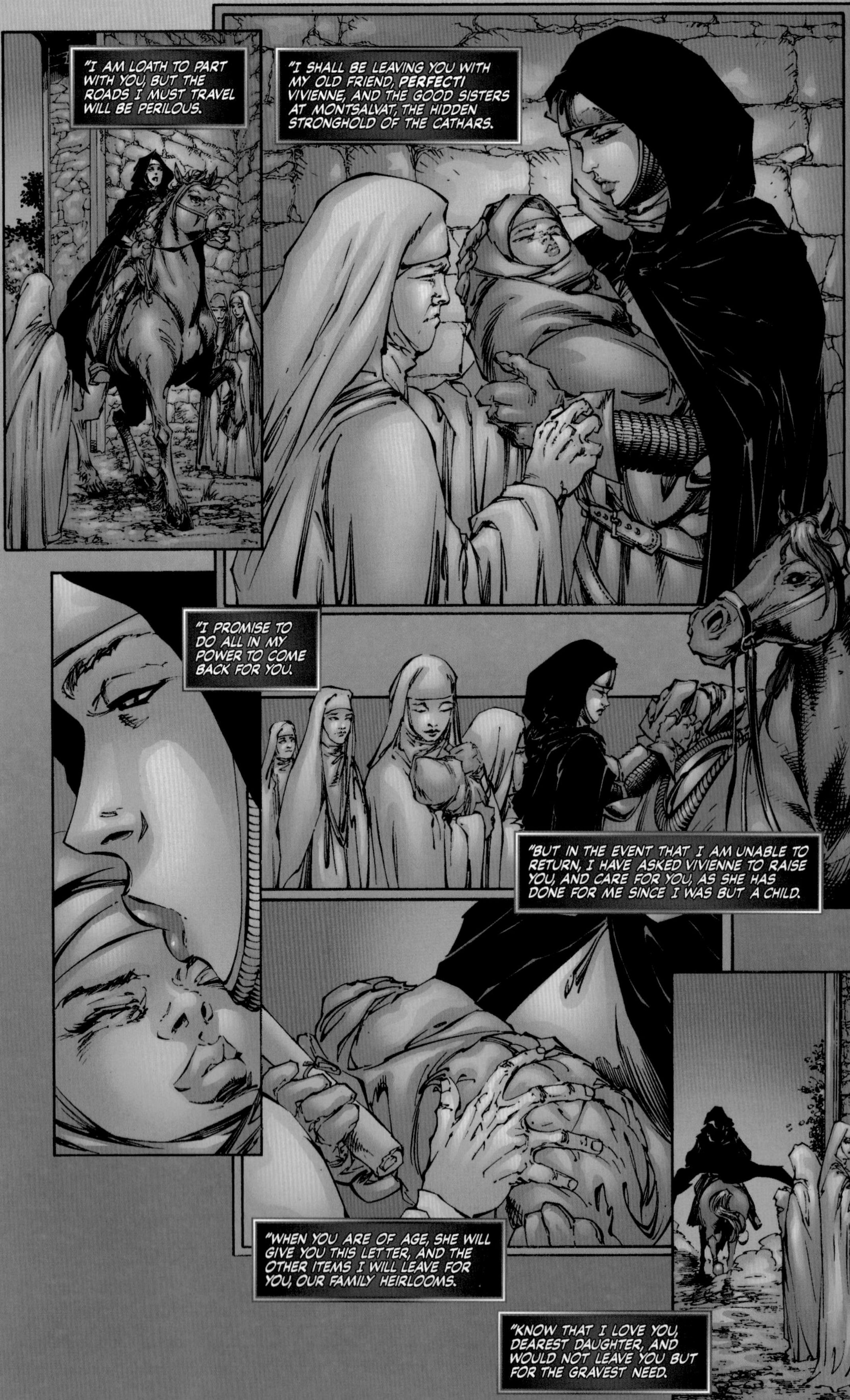
"I AM LOATH TO PART WITH YOU, BUT THE ROADS I MUST TRAVEL WILL BE PERILOUS.
"I SHALL BE LEAVING YOU WITH MY OLD FRIEND, PERFECTI VIVIENNE, AND THE GOOD SISTERS AT MONTSALVAT, THE HIDDEN STRONGHOLD OF THE CATHARS.
"I PROMISE TO DO ALL IN MY POWER TO COME BACK FOR YOU.
"BUT IN THE EVENT THAT I AM UNABLE TO RETURN, I HAVE ASKED VIVIENNE TO RAISE YOU, AND CARE FOR YOU, AS SHE HAS DONE FOR ME SINCE I WAS BUT A CHILD.
"WHEN YOU ARE OF AGE, SHE WILL GIVE YOU THIS LETTER, AND THE OTHER ITEMS I WILL LEAVE FOR YOU, OUR FAMILY HEIRLOOMS.
"KNOW THAT I LOVE YOU, DEAREST DAUGHTER, AND WOULD NOT LEAVE YOU BUT FOR THE GRAVEST NEED.

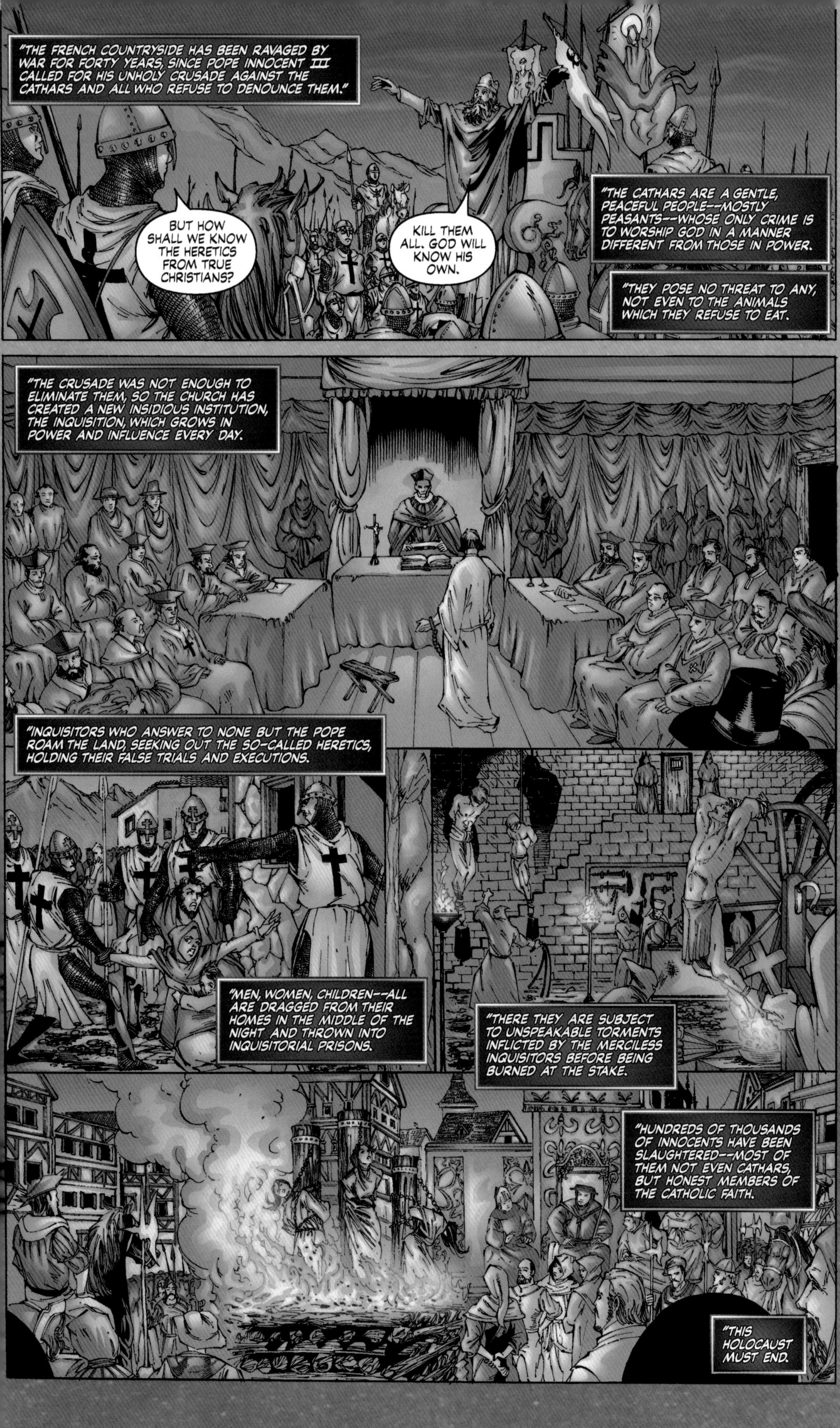
"THE FRENCH COUNTRYSIDE HAS BEEN RAVAGED BY WAR FOR FORTY YEARS, SINCE POPE INNOCENT III CALLED FOR HIS UNHOLY CRUSADE AGAINST THE CATHARS AND ALL WHO REFUSE TO DENOUNCE THEM."
BUT HOW SHALL WE KNOW THE HERETICS FROM TRUE CHRISTIANS?
KILL THEM ALL. GOD WILL KNOW HIS OWN.
"THE CATHARS ARE A GENTLE, PEACEFUL PEOPLE--MOSTLY PEASANTS--WHOSE ONLY CRIME IS TO WORSHIP GOD IN A MANNER DIFFERENT FROM THOSE IN POWER.
"THEY POSE NO THREAT TO ANY, NOT EVEN TO THE ANIMALS WHICH THEY REFUSE TO EAT.
"THE CRUSADE WAS NOT ENOUGH TO ELIMINATE THEM, SO THE CHURCH HAS CREATED A NEW INSIDIOUS INSTITUTION, THE INQUISITION, WHICH GROWS IN POWER AND INFLUENCE EVERY DAY.
"INQUISITORS WHO ANSWER TO NONE BUT THE POPE ROAM THE LAND, SEEKING OUT THE SO-CALLED HERETICS, HOLDING THEIR FALSE TRIALS AND EXECUTIONS.
"MEN, WOMEN, CHILDREN--ALL ARE DRAGGED FROM THEIR HOMES IN THE MIDDLE OF THE NIGHT AND THROWN INTO INQUISITORIAL PRISONS.
"THERE THEY ARE SUBJECT TO UNSPEAKABLE TORMENTS INFLICTED BY THE MERCILESS INQUISITORS BEFORE BEING BURNED AT THE STAKE.
"HUNDREDS OF THOUSANDS OF INNOCENTS HAVE BEEN SLAUGHTERED--MOST OF THEM NOT EVEN CATHARS, BUT HONEST MEMBERS OF THE CATHOLIC FAITH.
"THIS HOLOCAUST MUST END.

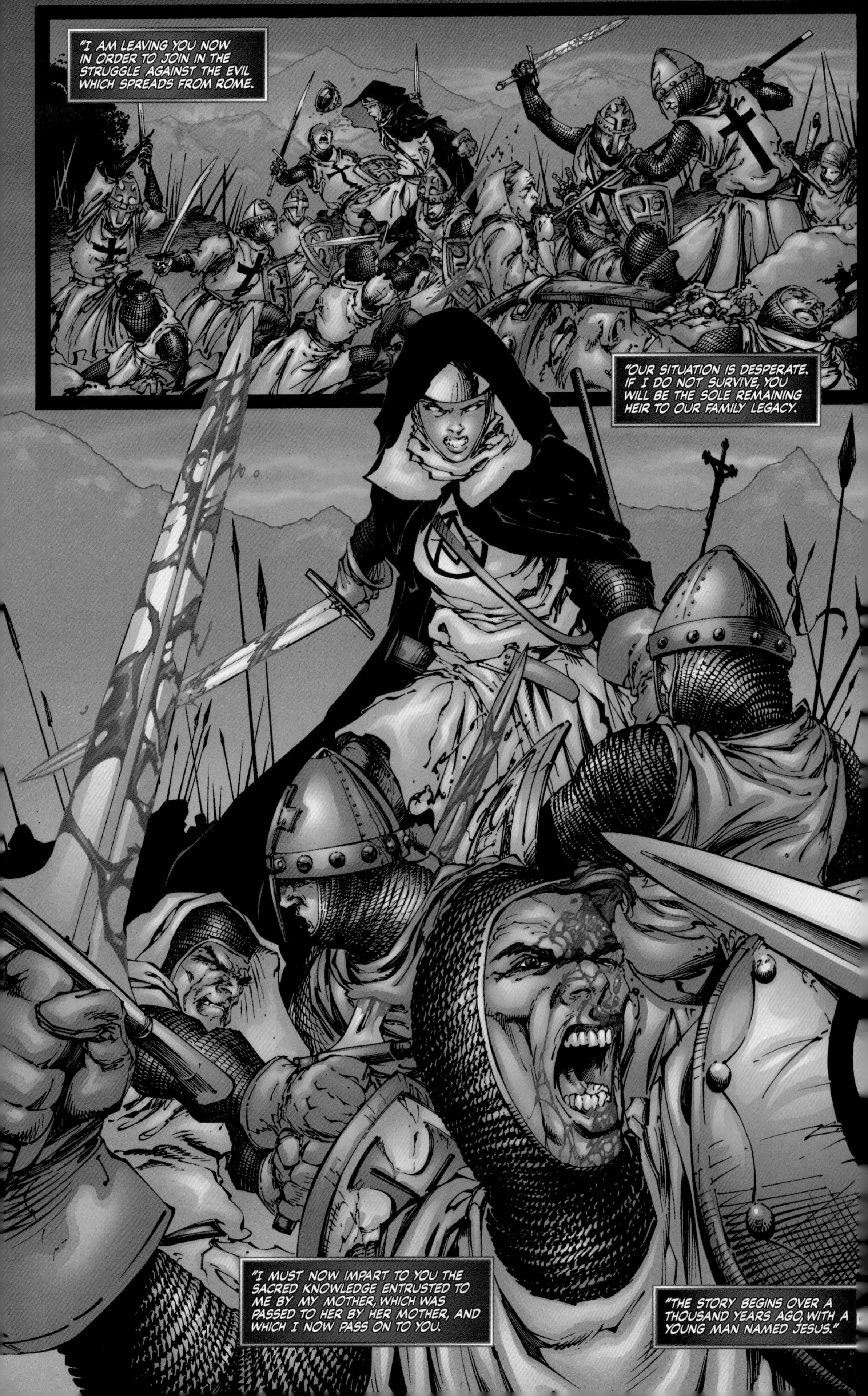
"I AM LEAVING YOU NOW IN ORDER TO JOIN IN THE STRUGGLE AGAINST THE EVIL WHICH SPREADS FROM ROME.
"OUR SITUATION IS DESPERATE. IF I DO NOT SURVIVE, YOU WILL BE THE SOLE REMAINING HEIR TO OUR FAMILY LEGACY.
"I MUST NOW IMPART TO YOU THE SACRED KNOWLEDGE ENTRUSTED TO ME BY MY MOTHER, WHICH WAS PASSED TO HER BY HER MOTHER, AND WHICH I NOW PASS ON TO YOU.
"THE STORY BEGINS OVER A THOUSAND YEARS AGO, WITH A YOUNG MAN NAMED JESUS."

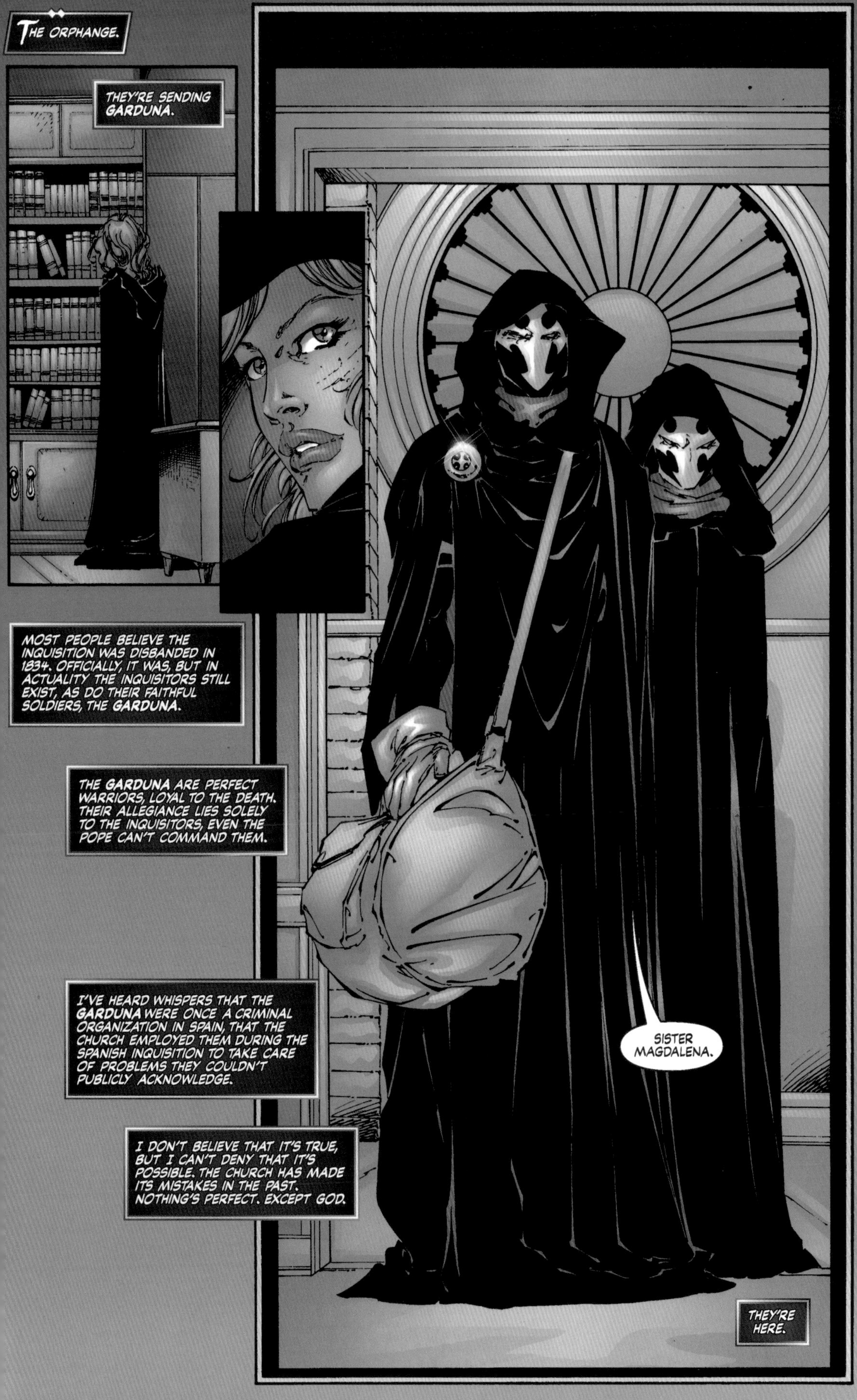
THE ORPHANGE.
THEY'RE SENDING GARDUNA.
MOST PEOPLE BELIEVE THE INQUISITION WAS DISBANDED IN 1834. OFFICIALLY, IT WAS, BUT IN ACTUALITY THE INQUISITORS STILL EXIST, AS DO THEIR FAITHFUL SOLDIERS, THE GARDUNA.
THE GARDUNA ARE PERFECT WARRIORS, LOYAL TO THE DEATH. THEIR ALLEGIANCE LIES SOLELY TO THE INQUISITORS, EVEN THE POPE CAN'T COMMAND THEM.
I'VE HEARD WHISPERS THAT THE GARDUNA WERE ONCE A CRIMINAL ORGANIZATION IN SPAIN, THAT THE CHURCH EMPLOYED THEM DURING THE SPANISH INQUISITION TO TAKE CARE OF PROBLEMS THEY COULDN'T PUBLICLY ACKNOWLEDGE.
I DON'T BELIEVE THAT IT'S TRUE, BUT I CAN'T DENY THAT IT'S POSSIBLE. THE CHURCH HAS MADE ITS MISTAKES IN THE PAST. NOTHING'S PERFECT. EXCEPT GOD.
SISTER MAGDALENA.
THEY'RE HERE.

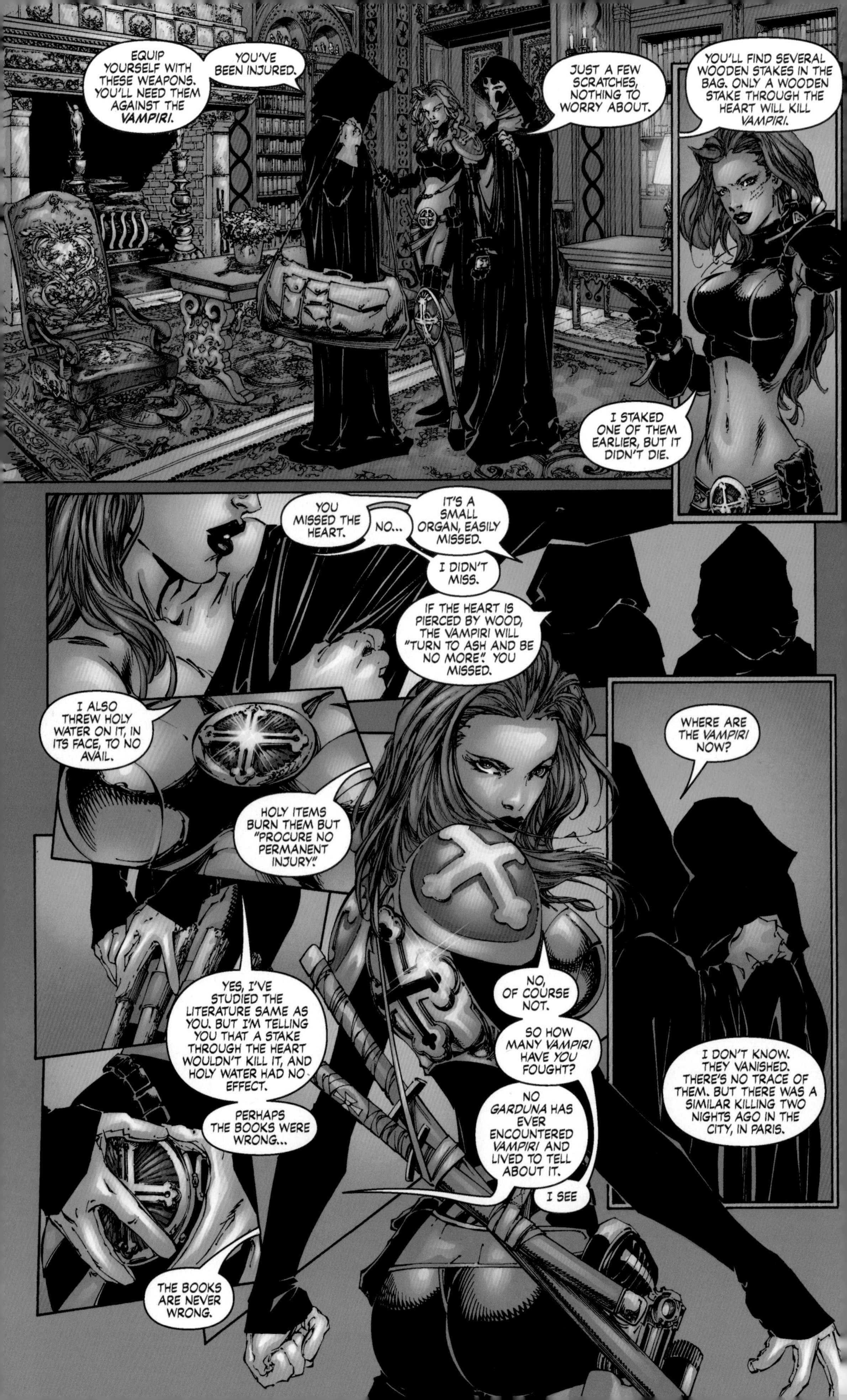

EQUIP YOURSELF WITH THESE WEAPONS. YOU'LL NEED THEM AGAINST THE VAMPIRI.
YOU'VE BEEN INJURED.
JUST A FEW SCRATCHES, NOTHING TO WORRY ABOUT.
YOU'LL FIND SEVERAL WOODEN STAKES IN THE BAG. ONLY A WOODEN STAKE THROUGH THE HEART WILL KILL VAMPIRI.
I STAKED ONE OF THEM EARLIER, BUT IT DIDN'T DIE.
YOU MISSED THE HEART.
NO...
IT'S A SMALL ORGAN, EASILY MISSED.
I DIDN'T MISS.
IF THE HEART IS PIERCED BY WOOD, THE VAMPIRI WILL "TURN TO ASH AND BE NO MORE." YOU MISSED.
I ALSO THREW HOLY WATER ON IT, IN ITS FACE, TO NO AVAIL.
HOLY ITEMS BURN THEM BUT "PROCURE NO PERMANENT INJURY."
YES, I'VE STUDIED THE LITERATURE SAME AS YOU. BUT I'M TELLING YOU THAT A STAKE THROUGH THE HEART WOULDN'T KILL IT, AND HOLY WATER HAD NO EFFECT.
PERHAPS THE BOOKS WERE WRONG...
THE BOOKS ARE NEVER WRONG.
NO, OF COURSE NOT.
SO HOW MANY VAMPIRI HAVE YOU FOUGHT?
NO GARDUNA HAS EVER ENCOUNTERED VAMPIRI AND LIVED TO TELL ABOUT IT.
I SEE
WHERE ARE THE VAMPIRI NOW?
I DON'T KNOW. THEY VANISHED. THERE'S NO TRACE OF THEM. BUT THERE WAS A SIMILAR KILLING TWO NIGHTS AGO IN THE CITY, IN PARIS.

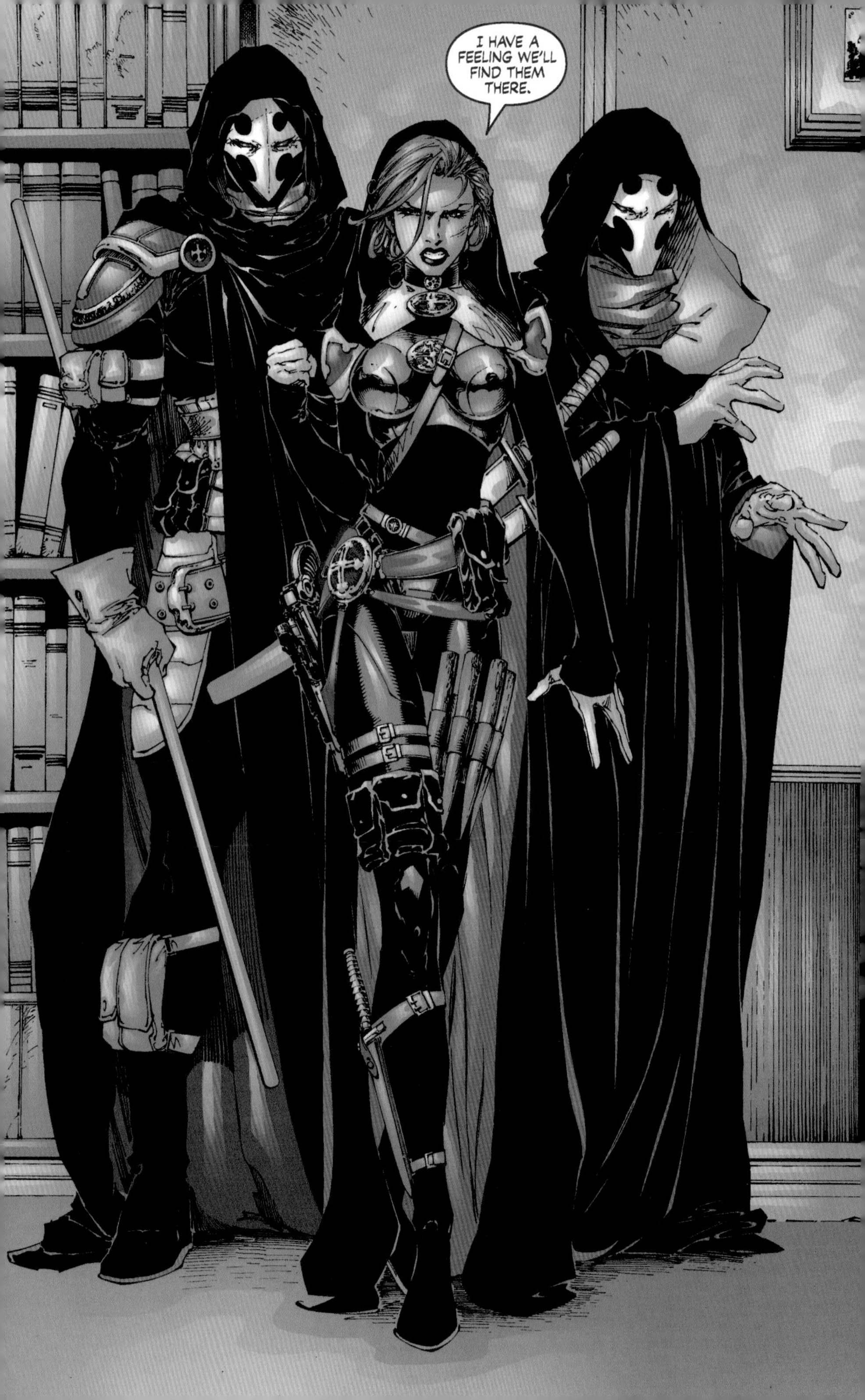
I HAVE A FEELING WE'LL FIND THEM THERE.

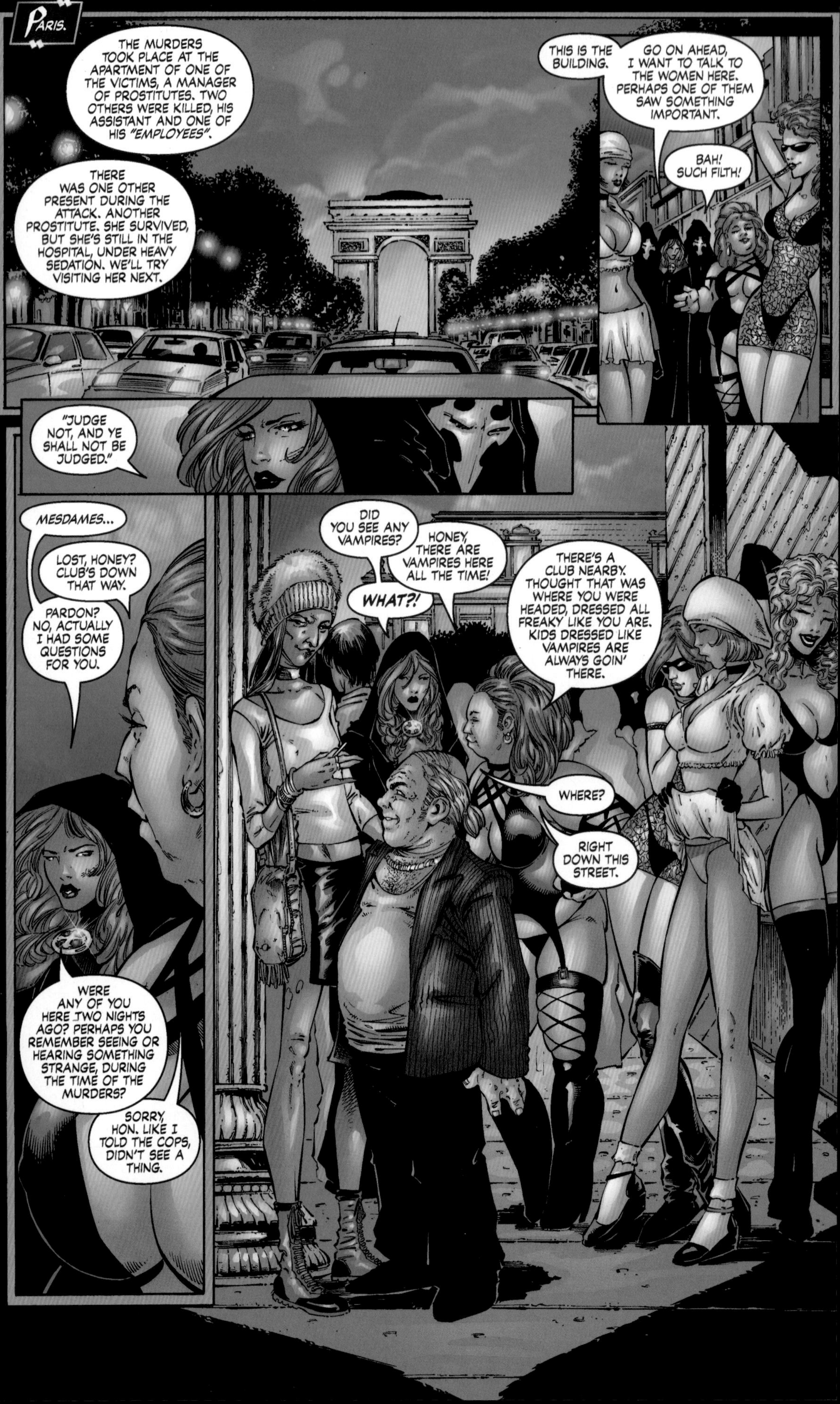

PARIS.
THE MURDERS TOOK PLACE AT THE APARTMENT OF ONE OF THE VICTIMS, A MANAGER OF PROSTITUTES. TWO OTHERS WERE KILLED, HIS ASSISTANT AND ONE OF HIS "EMPLOYEES".
THERE WAS ONE OTHER PRESENT DURING THE ATTACK. ANOTHER PROSTITUTE. SHE SURVIVED, BUT SHE'S STILL IN THE HOSPITAL, UNDER HEAVY SEDATION. WE'LL TRY VISITING HER NEXT.
THIS IS THE BUILDING.
GO ON AHEAD, I WANT TO TALK TO THE WOMEN HERE. PERHAPS ONE OF THEM SAW SOMETHING IMPORTANT.
BAH! SUCH FILTH!
"JUDGE NOT, AND YE SHALL NOT BE JUDGED."
MESDAMES...
LOST, HONEY? CLUB'S DOWN THAT WAY.
PARDON? NO, ACTUALLY I HAD SOME QUESTIONS FOR YOU.
WERE ANY OF YOU HERE TWO NIGHTS AGO? PERHAPS YOU REMEMBER SEEING OR HEARING SOMETHING STRANGE, DURING THE TIME OF THE MURDERS?
SORRY, HON. LIKE I TOLD THE COPS, DIDN'T SEE A THING.
DID YOU SEE ANY VAMPIRES?
HONEY, THERE ARE VAMPIRES HERE ALL THE TIME!
WHAT?!
THERE'S A CLUB NEARBY. THOUGHT THAT WAS WHERE YOU WERE HEADED, DRESSED ALL FREAKY LIKE YOU ARE. KIDS DRESSED LIKE VAMPIRES ARE ALWAYS GOIN' THERE.
WHERE?
RIGHT DOWN THIS STREET.

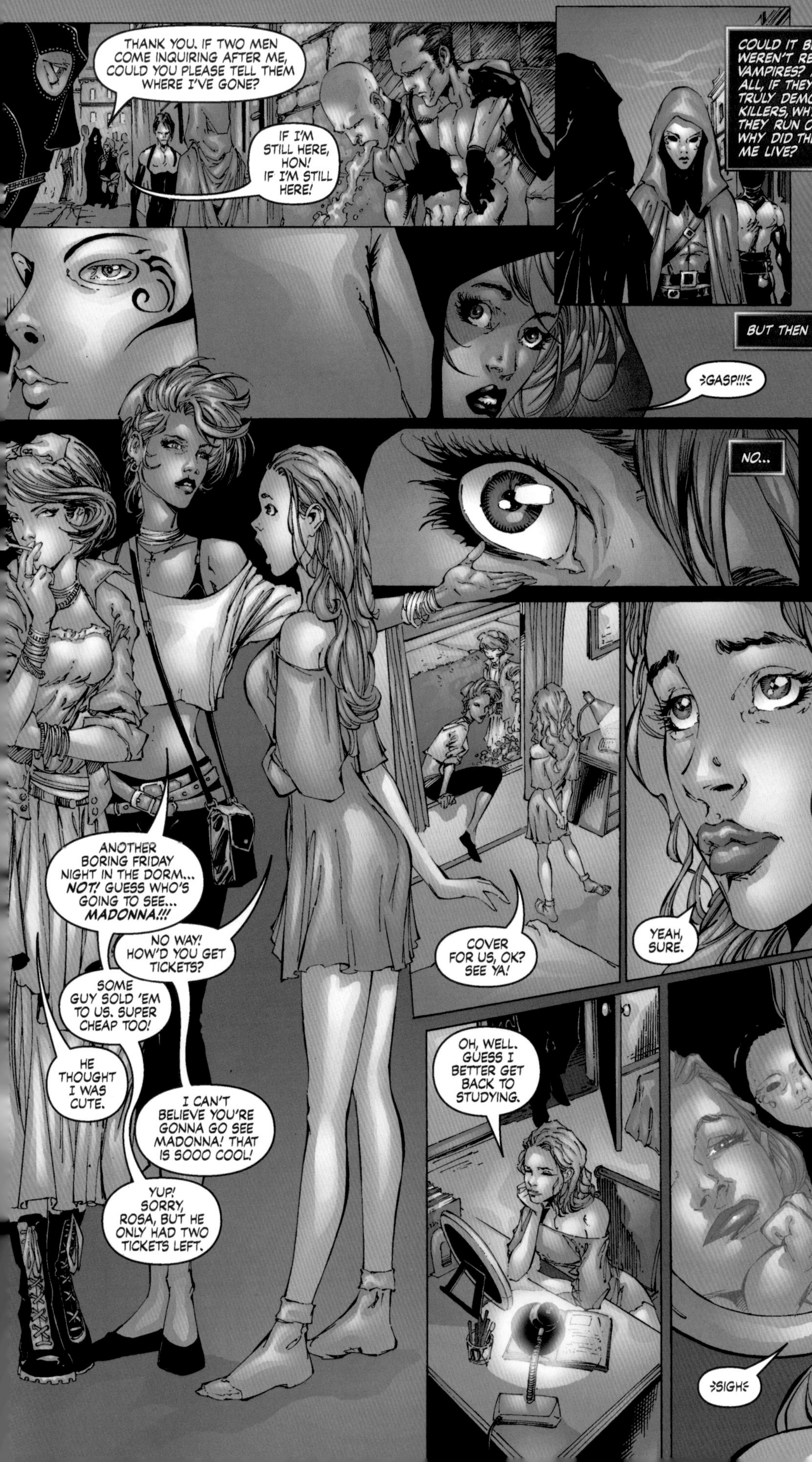
THANK YOU. IF TWO MEN COME INQUIRING AFTER ME, COULD YOU PLEASE TELL THEM WHERE I'VE GONE?
IF I'M STILL HERE, HON! IF I'M STILL HERE!
COULD IT BE THEY WEREN'T REAL VAMPIRES? AFTER ALL, IF THEY WERE TRULY DEMONIC KILLERS, WHY DID THEY RUN OFF? WHY DID THEY LET ME LIVE?
BUT THEN HOW...
GASP!!!
NO...
ANOTHER BORING FRIDAY NIGHT IN THE DORM... NOT! GUESS WHO'S GOING TO SEE... MADONNA!!!
NO WAY! HOW'D YOU GET TICKETS?
SOME GUY SOLD 'EM TO US. SUPER CHEAP TOO!
HE THOUGHT I WAS CUTE.
I CAN'T BELIEVE YOU'RE GONNA GO SEE MADONNA! THAT IS SOOO COOL!
YUP! SORRY, ROSA, BUT HE ONLY HAD TWO TICKETS LEFT.
COVER FOR US, OK? SEE YA!
YEAH, SURE.
OH, WELL. GUESS I BETTER GET BACK TO STUDYING.
SIGH

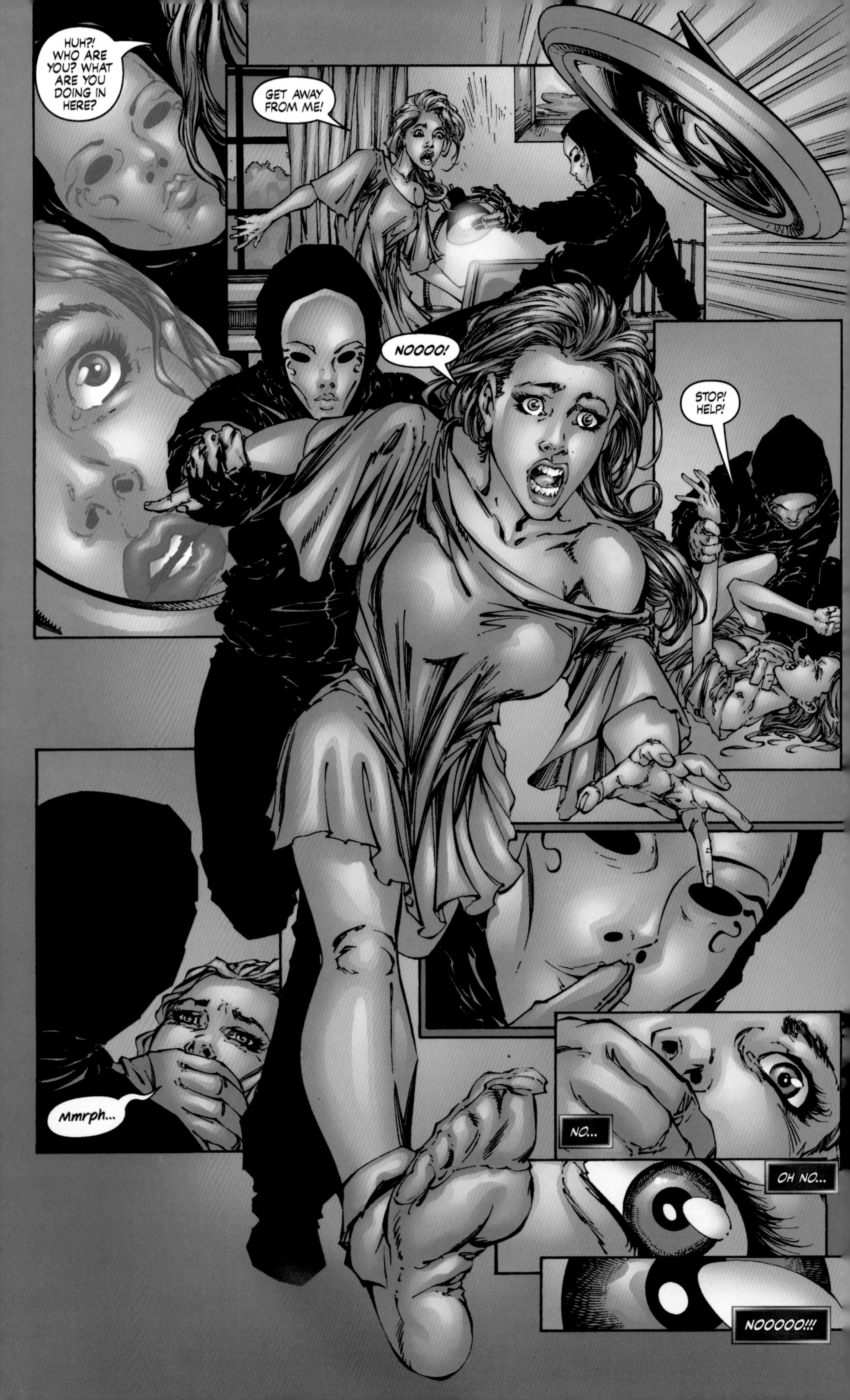
HUH?! WHO ARE YOU? WHAT ARE YOU DOING IN HERE?
GET AWAY FROM ME!
NOOOO!
STOP! HELP!
Mmrph...
NO...
OH NO...
NOOOOO!!!

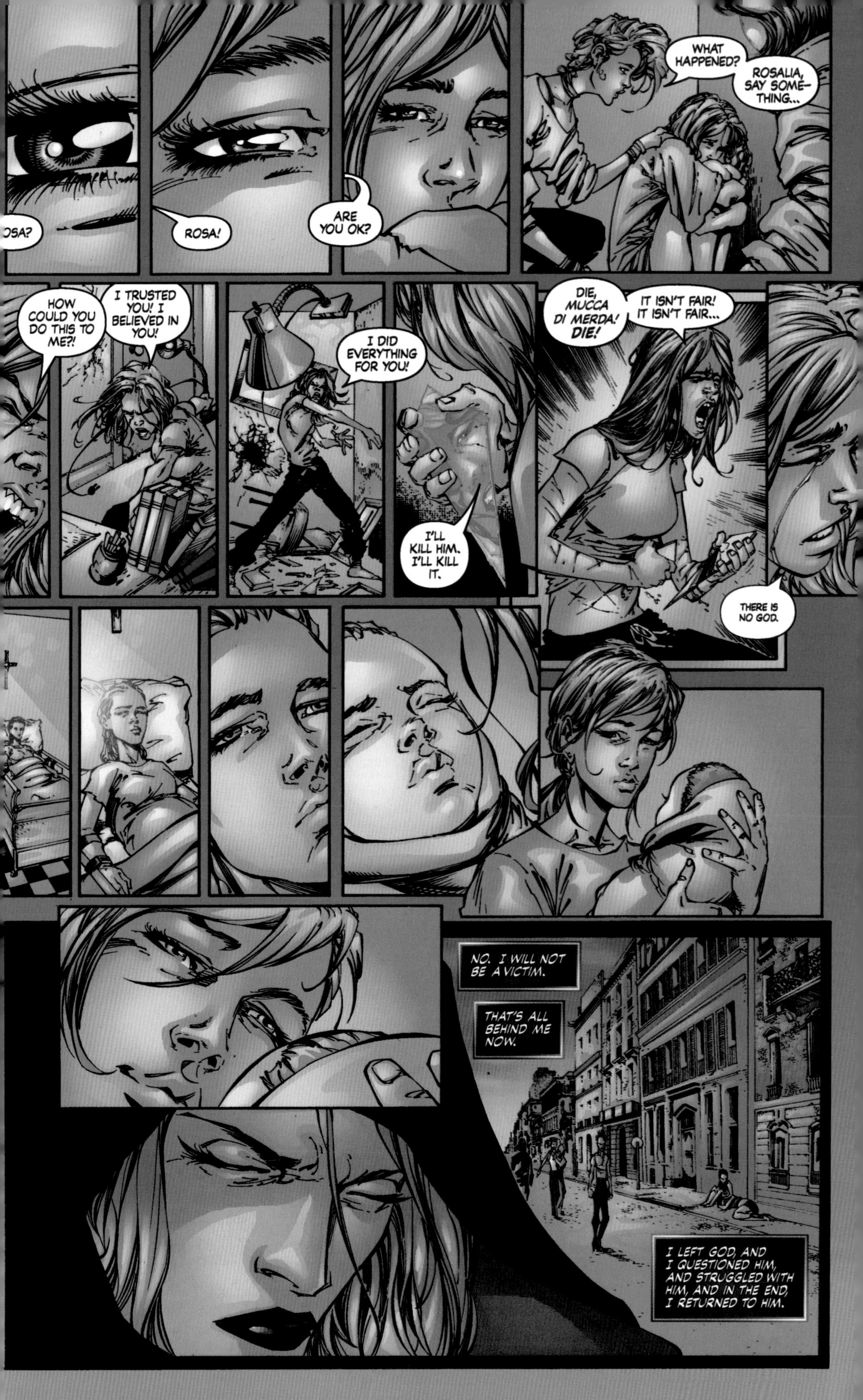
OSA?
ROSA!
ARE YOU OK?
WHAT HAPPENED?
ROSALIA, SAY SOME-THING...
HOW COULD YOU DO THIS TO ME?!
I TRUSTED YOU! I BELIEVED IN YOU!
I DID EVERYTHING FOR YOU!
I'LL KILL HIM. I'LL KILL IT.
DIE, MUCCA DI MERDA! DIE!
IT ISN'T FAIR! IT ISN'T FAIR...
THERE IS NO GOD.
NO. I WILL NOT BE A VICTIM.
THAT'S ALL BEHIND ME NOW.
I LEFT GOD, AND I QUESTIONED HIM, AND STRUGGLED WITH HIM, AND IN THE END, I RETURNED TO HIM.

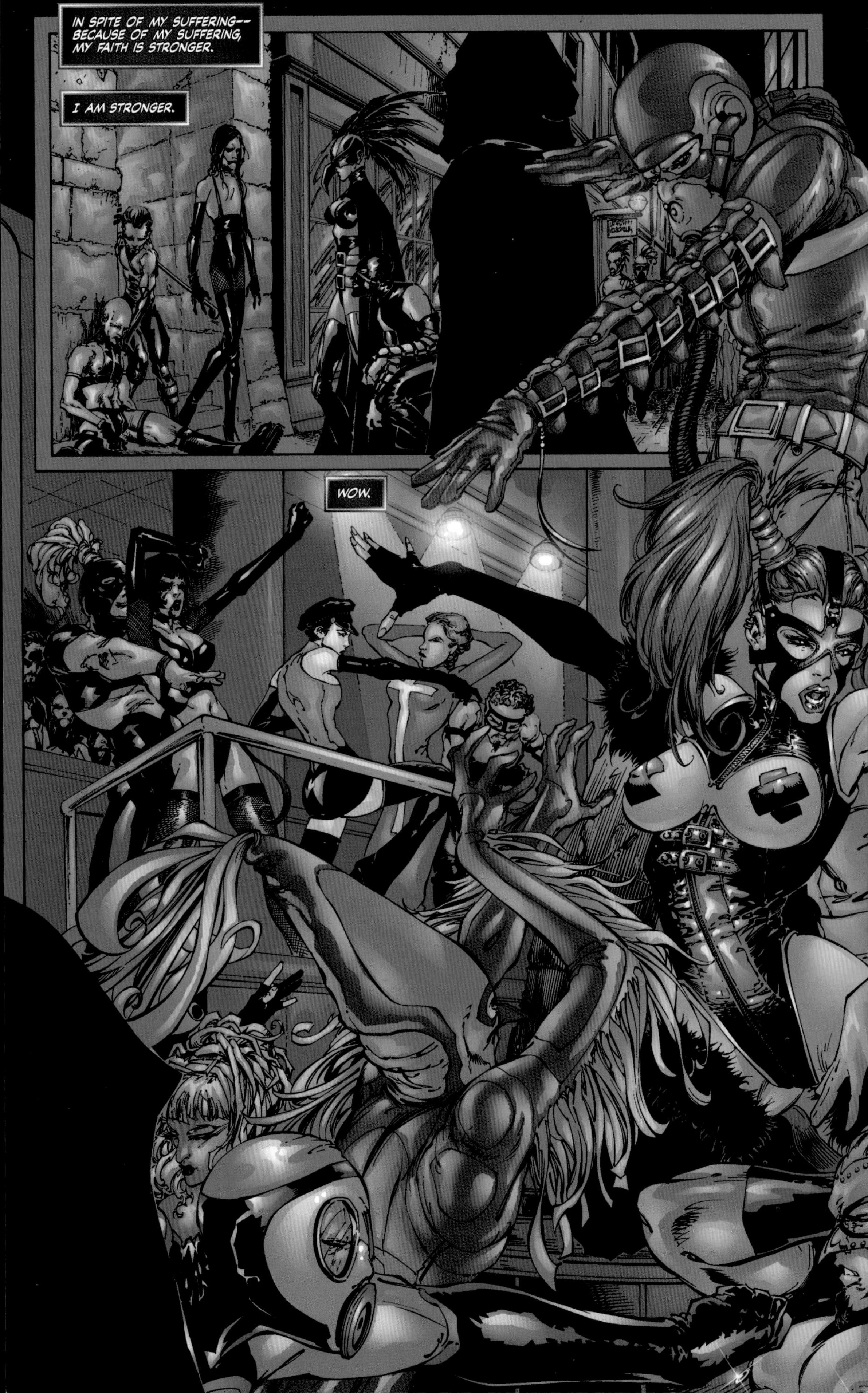
IN SPITE OF MY SUFFERING-- BECAUSE OF MY SUFFERING, MY FAITH IS STRONGER.
I AM STRONGER.
WOW.

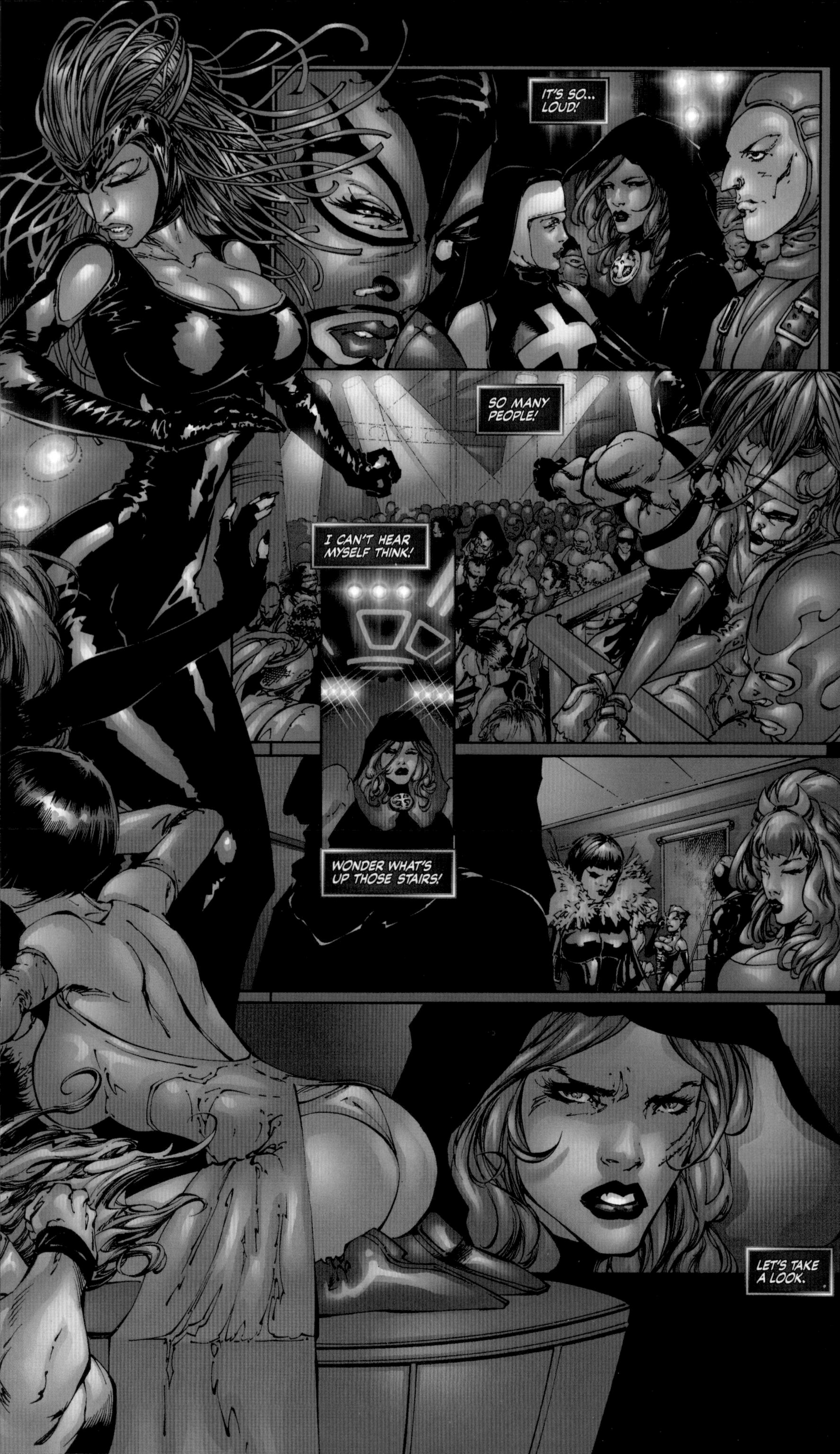
IT'S SO... LOUD!
SO MANY PEOPLE!
I CAN'T HEAR MYSELF THINK!
WONDER WHAT'S UP THOSE STAIRS!
LET'S TAKE A LOOK.

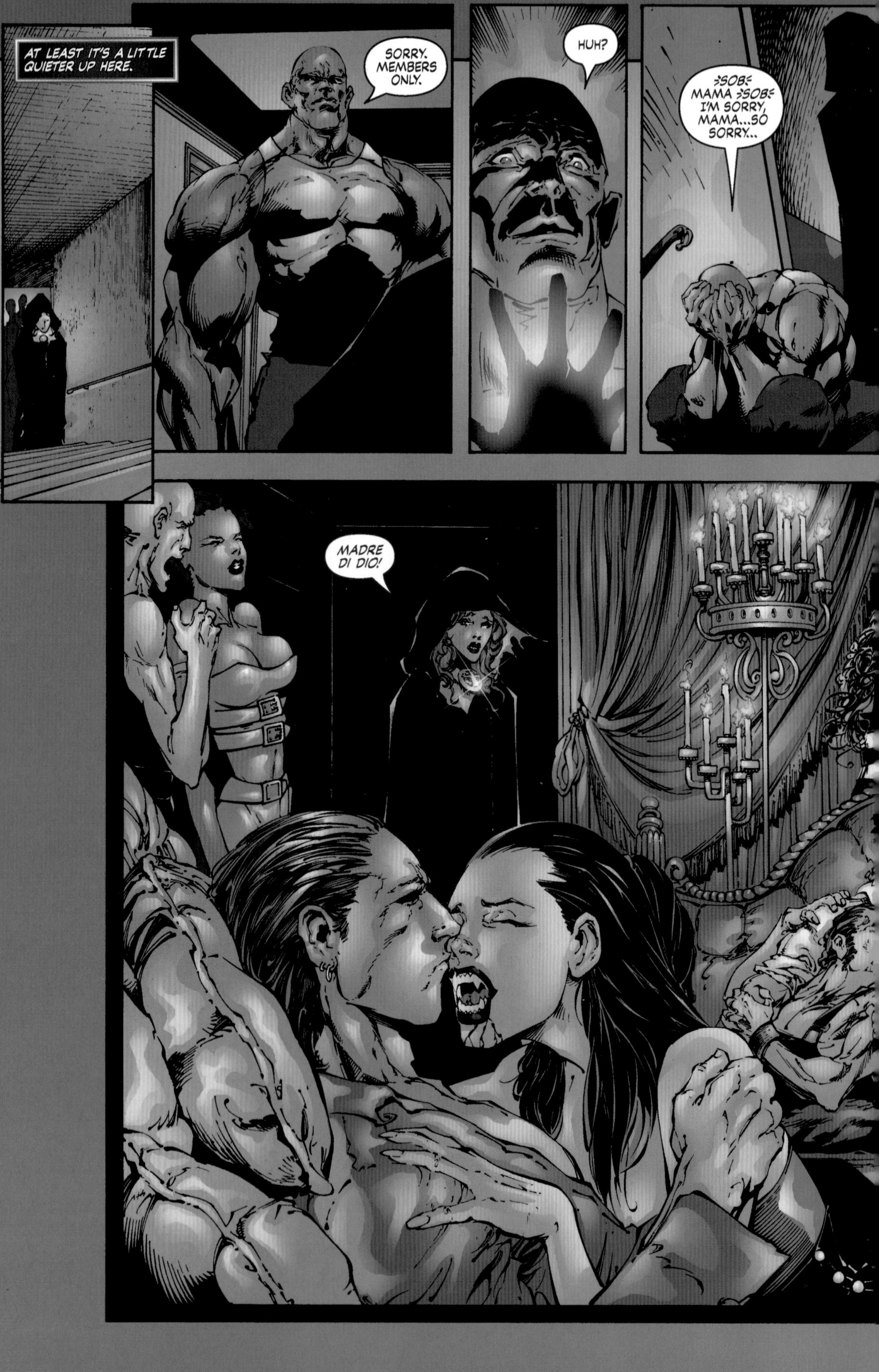
AT LEAST IT'S A LITTLE QUIETER UP HERE.
SORRY. MEMBERS ONLY.
HUH?
>SOB< MAMA >SOB< I'M SORRY, MAMA...SO SORRY...
MADRE DI DIO!

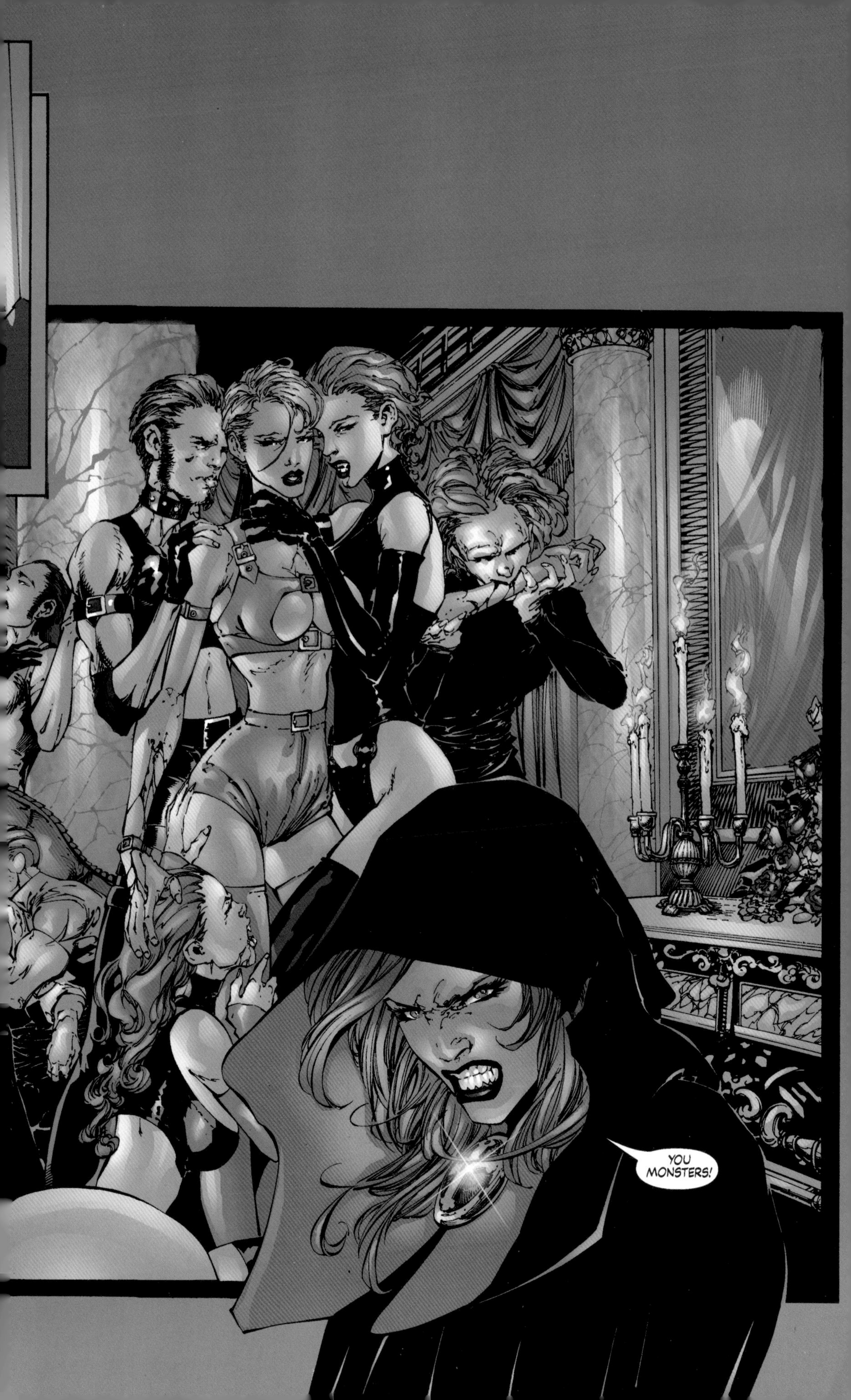
YOU MONSTERS!

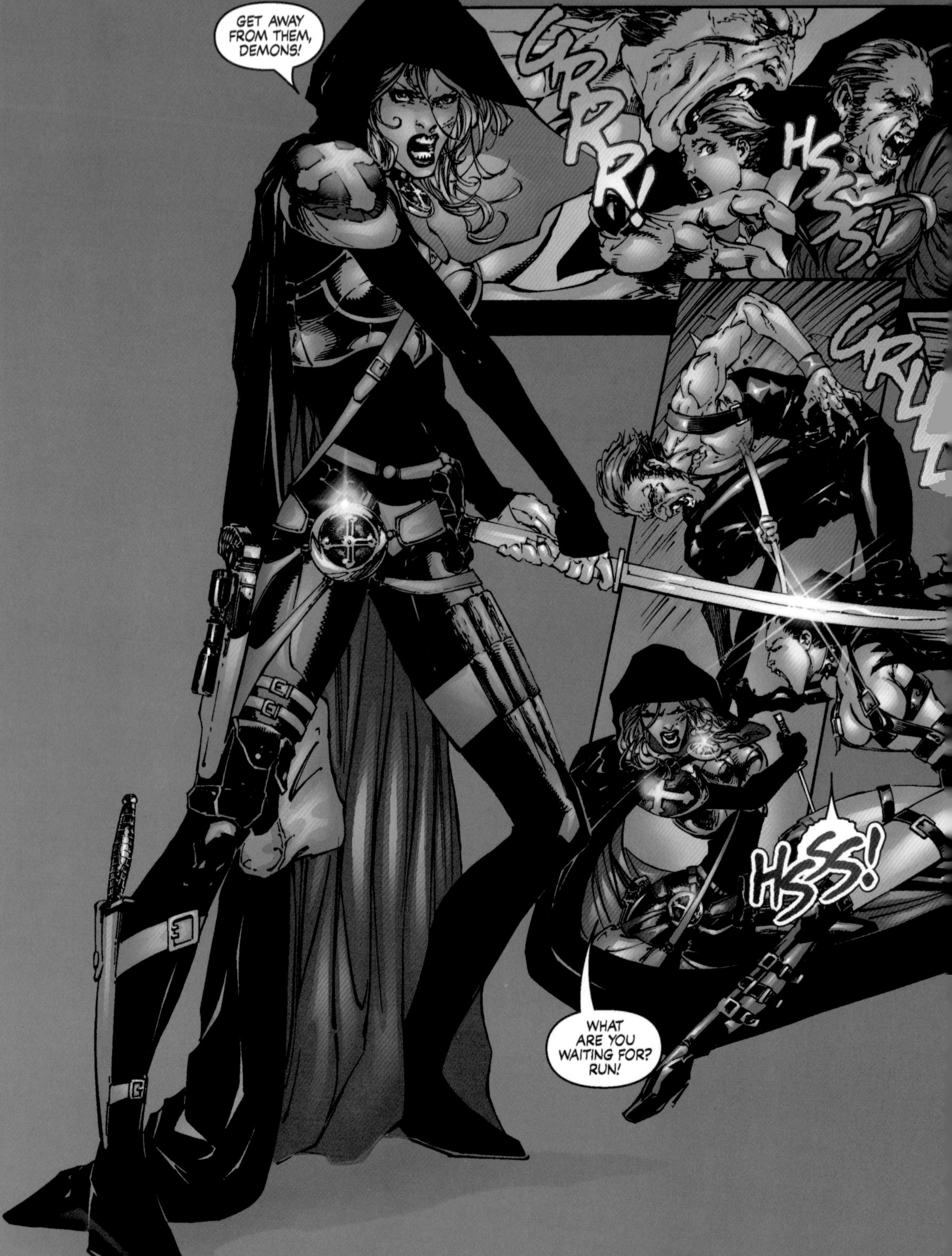
GET AWAY FROM THEM, DEMONS!
GRRR!
HSSS!
HSSS!
WHAT ARE YOU WAITING FOR? RUN!

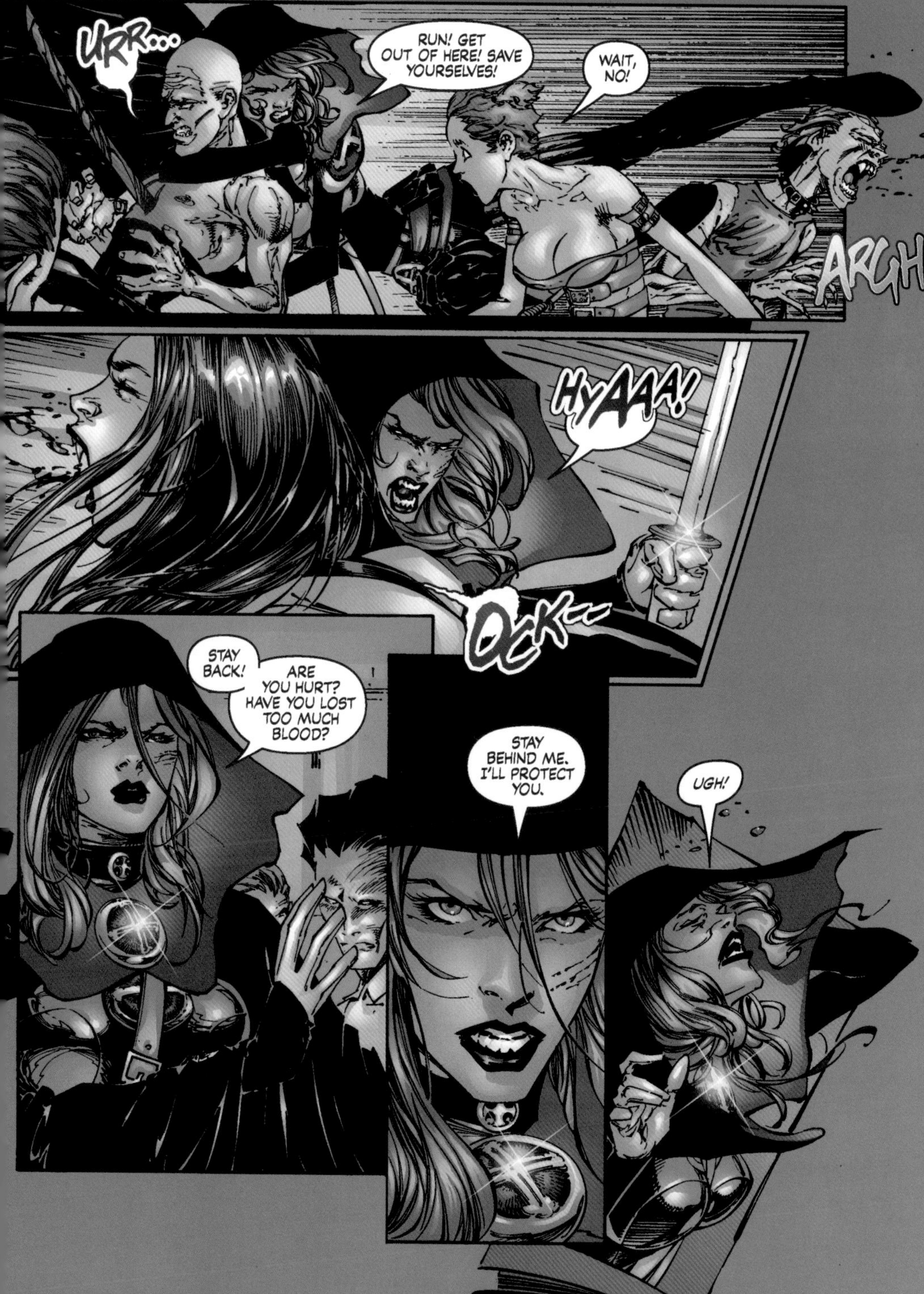
URR...
RUN! GET OUT OF HERE! SAVE YOURSELVES!
WAIT, NO!
ARGH!
HYAAA!
OCK--
STAY BACK!
ARE YOU HURT? HAVE YOU LOST TOO MUCH BLOOD?
STAY BEHIND ME. I'LL PROTECT YOU.
UGH!

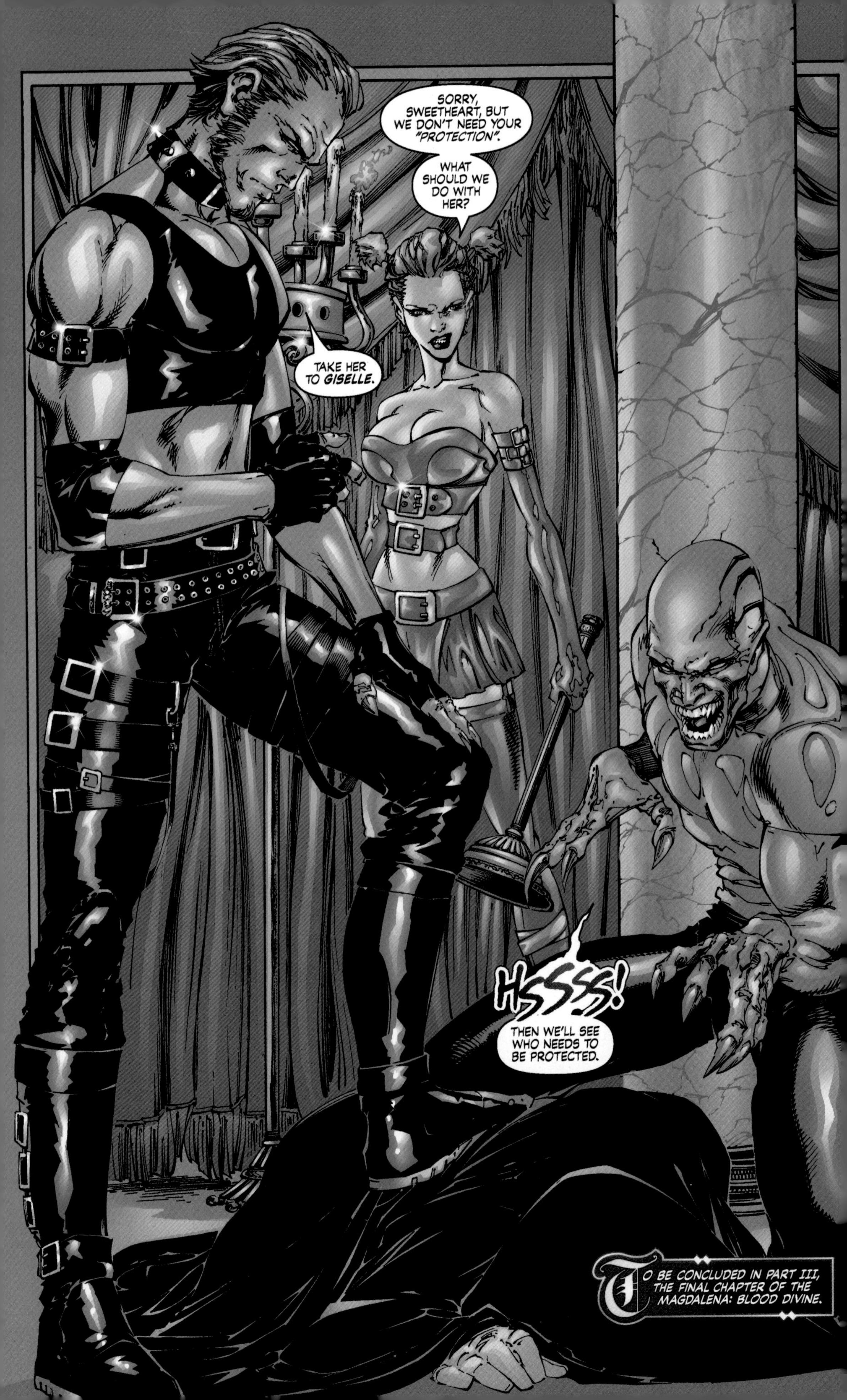
SORRY, SWEETHEART, BUT WE DON'T NEED YOUR "PROTECTION".
WHAT SHOULD WE DO WITH HER?
TAKE HER TO GISELLE.
HSSSS!
THEN WE'LL SEE WHO NEEDS TO BE PROTECTED.
TO BE CONCLUDED IN PART III, THE FINAL CHAPTER OF THE MAGDALENA: BLOOD DIVINE.

volume I, issue #3

story by: Marcia Chen
pencils by: Joe Benitez
inks by: Joe Weems V, Victor Llamas,
Matt "Batt" Banning
colors by: Jonathan D. Smith
letters by: Robin Spehar and Dennis Heisler

pencil assists by: Mun Kao and Brian Ching
inks assists by: Marco "Madman" Galli,
Jason Metcalfe, Jay Leisten, Steve Liang
and Annie Skiles

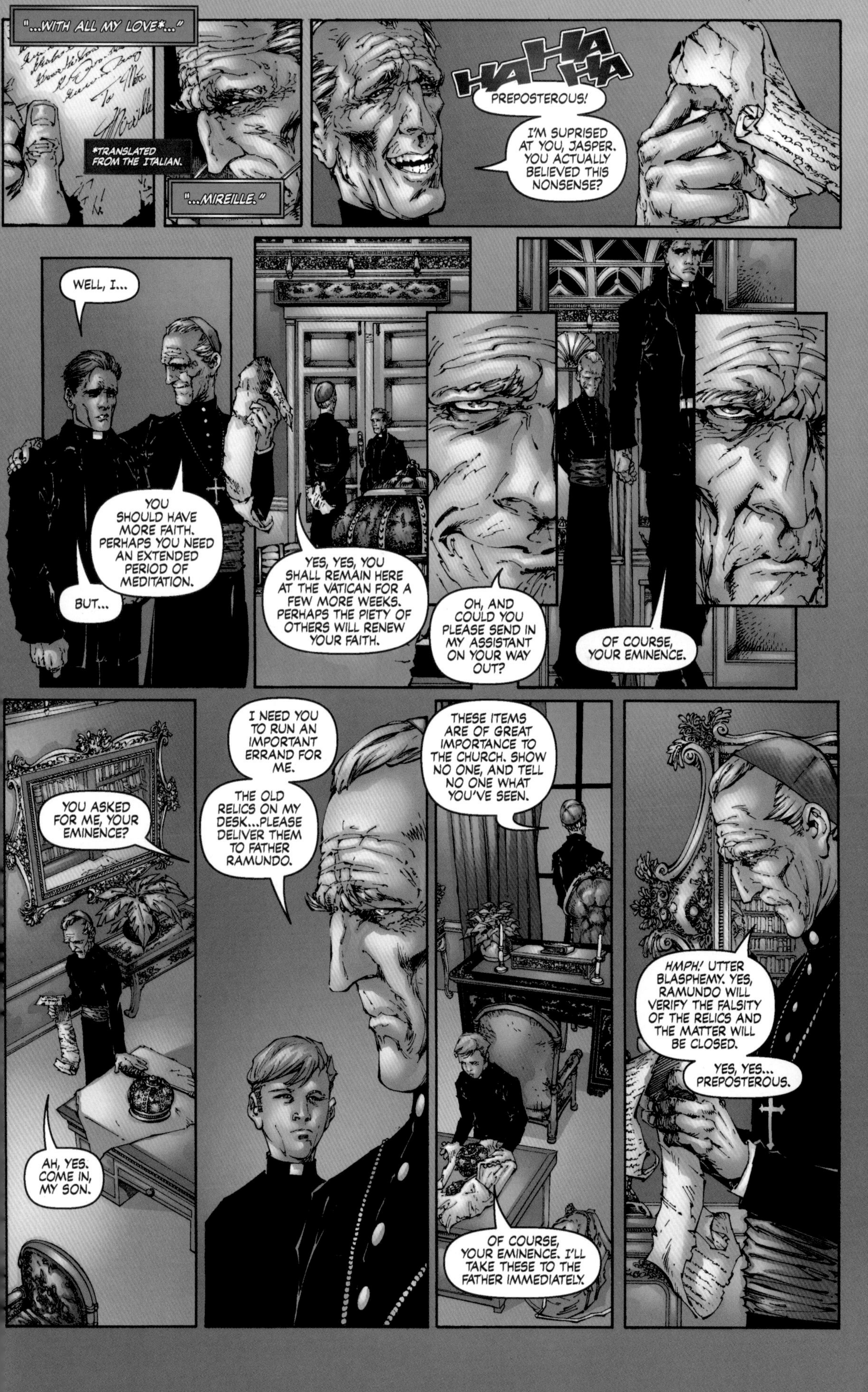
"...WITH ALL MY LOVE*..."
*TRANSLATED FROM THE ITALIAN.
"...MIREILLE."
HA HA HA HA
PREPOSTEROUS!
I'M SUPRISED AT YOU, JASPER. YOU ACTUALLY BELIEVED THIS NONSENSE?
WELL, I...
YOU SHOULD HAVE MORE FAITH. PERHAPS YOU NEED AN EXTENDED PERIOD OF MEDITATION.
BUT...
YES, YES, YOU SHALL REMAIN HERE AT THE VATICAN FOR A FEW MORE WEEKS. PERHAPS THE PIETY OF OTHERS WILL RENEW YOUR FAITH.
OH, AND COULD YOU PLEASE SEND IN MY ASSISTANT ON YOUR WAY OUT?
OF COURSE, YOUR EMINENCE.
YOU ASKED FOR ME, YOUR EMINENCE?
AH, YES. COME IN, MY SON.
I NEED YOU TO RUN AN IMPORTANT ERRAND FOR ME.
THE OLD RELICS ON MY DESK...PLEASE DELIVER THEM TO FATHER RAMUNDO.
THESE ITEMS ARE OF GREAT IMPORTANCE TO THE CHURCH. SHOW NO ONE, AND TELL NO ONE WHAT YOU'VE SEEN.
OF COURSE, YOUR EMINENCE. I'LL TAKE THESE TO THE FATHER IMMEDIATELY.
HMPH! UTTER BLASPHEMY. YES, RAMUNDO WILL VERIFY THE FALSITY OF THE RELICS AND THE MATTER WILL BE CLOSED.
YES, YES... PREPOSTEROUS.

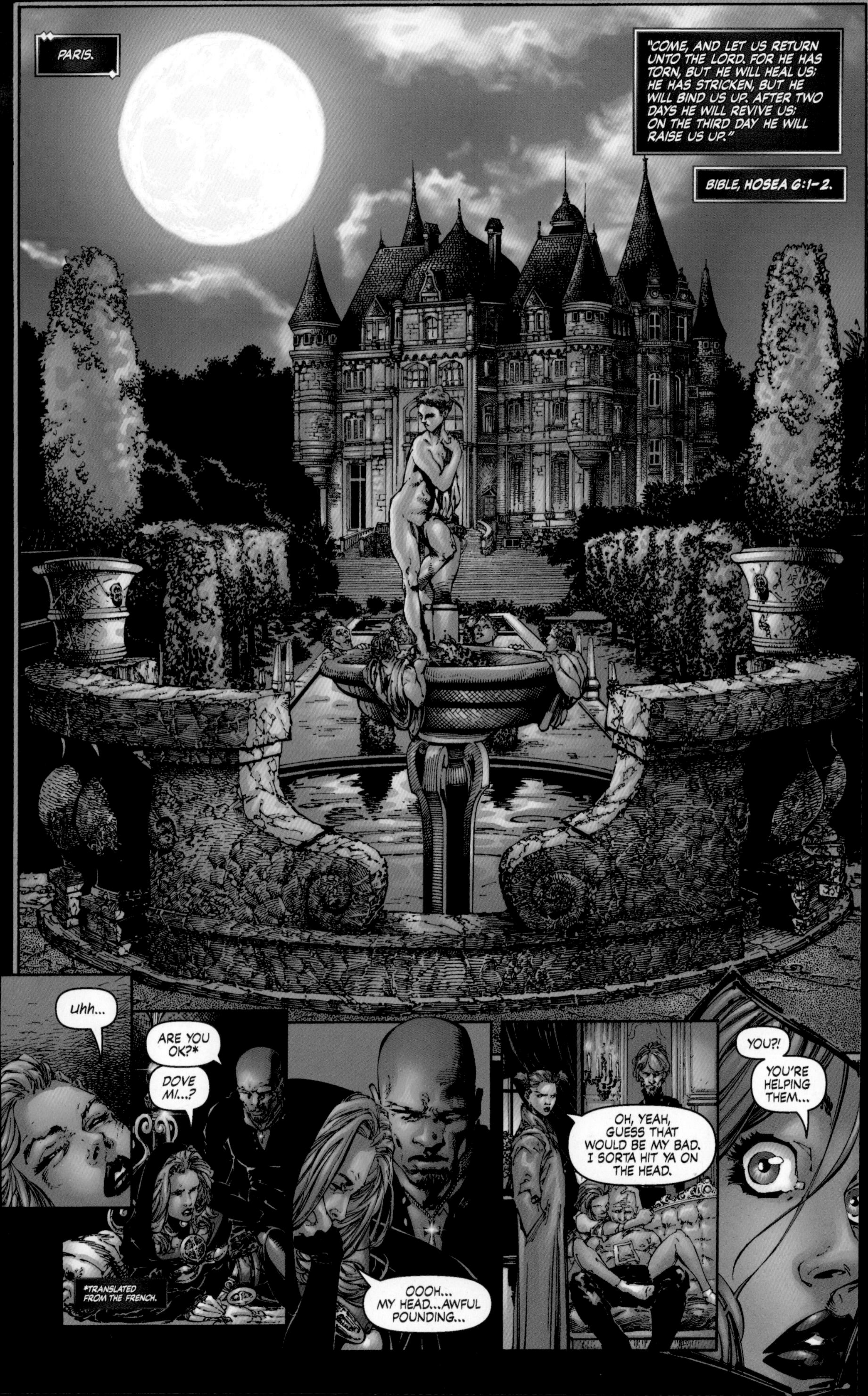
PARIS.
"COME, AND LET US RETURN UNTO THE LORD. FOR HE HAS TORN, BUT HE WILL HEAL US; HE HAS STRICKEN, BUT HE WILL BIND US UP. AFTER TWO DAYS HE WILL REVIVE US; ON THE THIRD DAY HE WILL RAISE US UP."
BIBLE, HOSEA 6:1-2.
uhh...
ARE YOU OK?*
DOVE MI...?
*TRANSLATED FROM THE FRENCH.
OOOH... MY HEAD...AWFUL POUNDING...
OH, YEAH, GUESS THAT WOULD BE MY BAD. I SORTA HIT YA ON THE HEAD.
YOU?!
YOU'RE HELPING THEM...

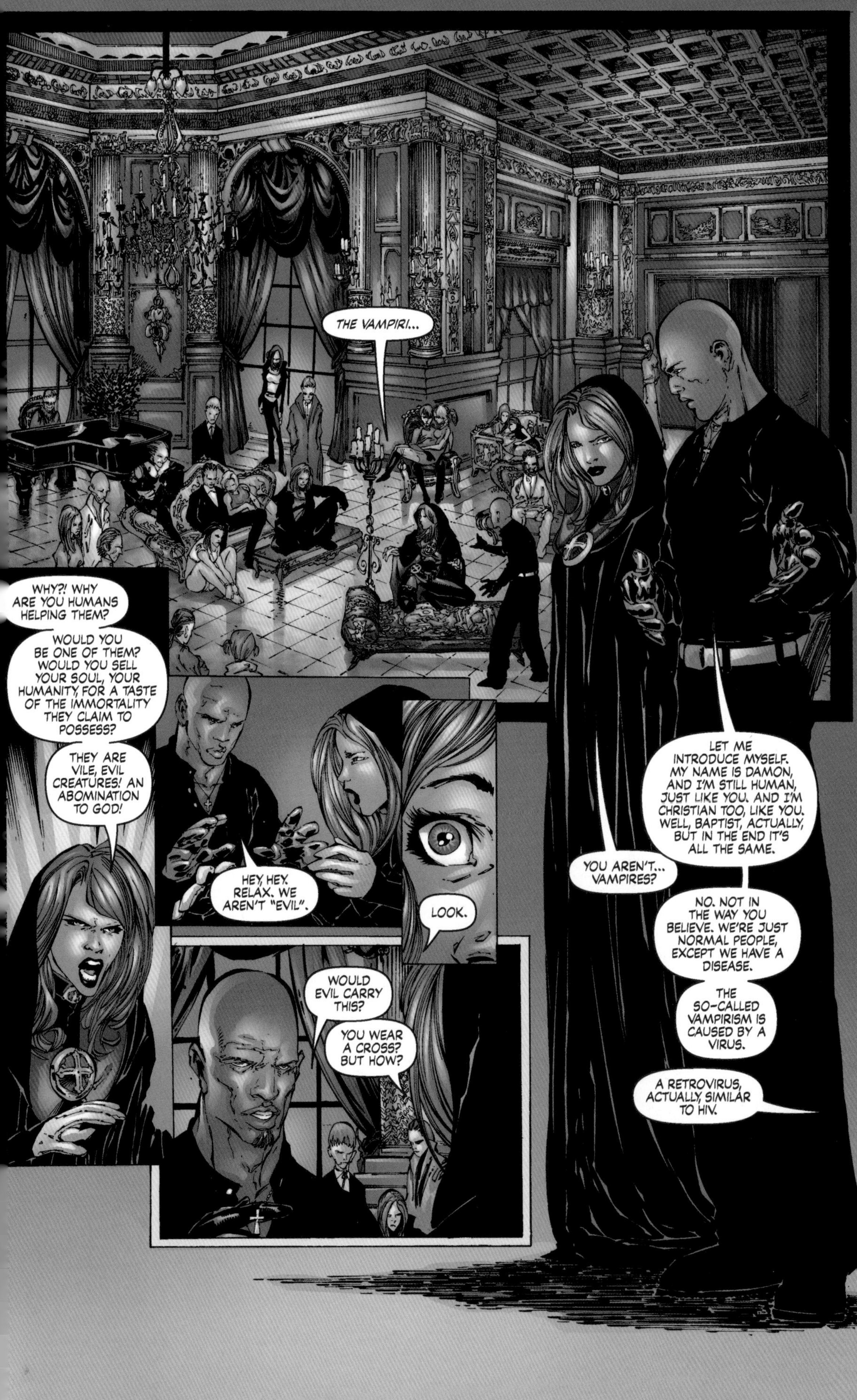
THE VAMPIRI...
WHY?! WHY ARE YOU HUMANS HELPING THEM?
WOULD YOU BE ONE OF THEM? WOULD YOU SELL YOUR SOUL, YOUR HUMANITY, FOR A TASTE OF THE IMMORTALITY THEY CLAIM TO POSSESS?
THEY ARE VILE, EVIL CREATURES! AN ABOMINATION TO GOD!
HEY, HEY. RELAX. WE AREN'T "EVIL".
LOOK.
WOULD EVIL CARRY THIS?
YOU WEAR A CROSS? BUT HOW?
LET ME INTRODUCE MYSELF. MY NAME IS DAMON, AND I'M STILL HUMAN, JUST LIKE YOU. AND I'M CHRISTIAN TOO, LIKE YOU. WELL, BAPTIST, ACTUALLY, BUT IN THE END IT'S ALL THE SAME.
YOU AREN'T... VAMPIRES?
NO. NOT IN THE WAY YOU BELIEVE. WE'RE JUST NORMAL PEOPLE, EXCEPT WE HAVE A DISEASE.
THE SO-CALLED VAMPIRISM IS CAUSED BY A VIRUS.
A RETROVIRUS, ACTUALLY, SIMILAR TO HIV.

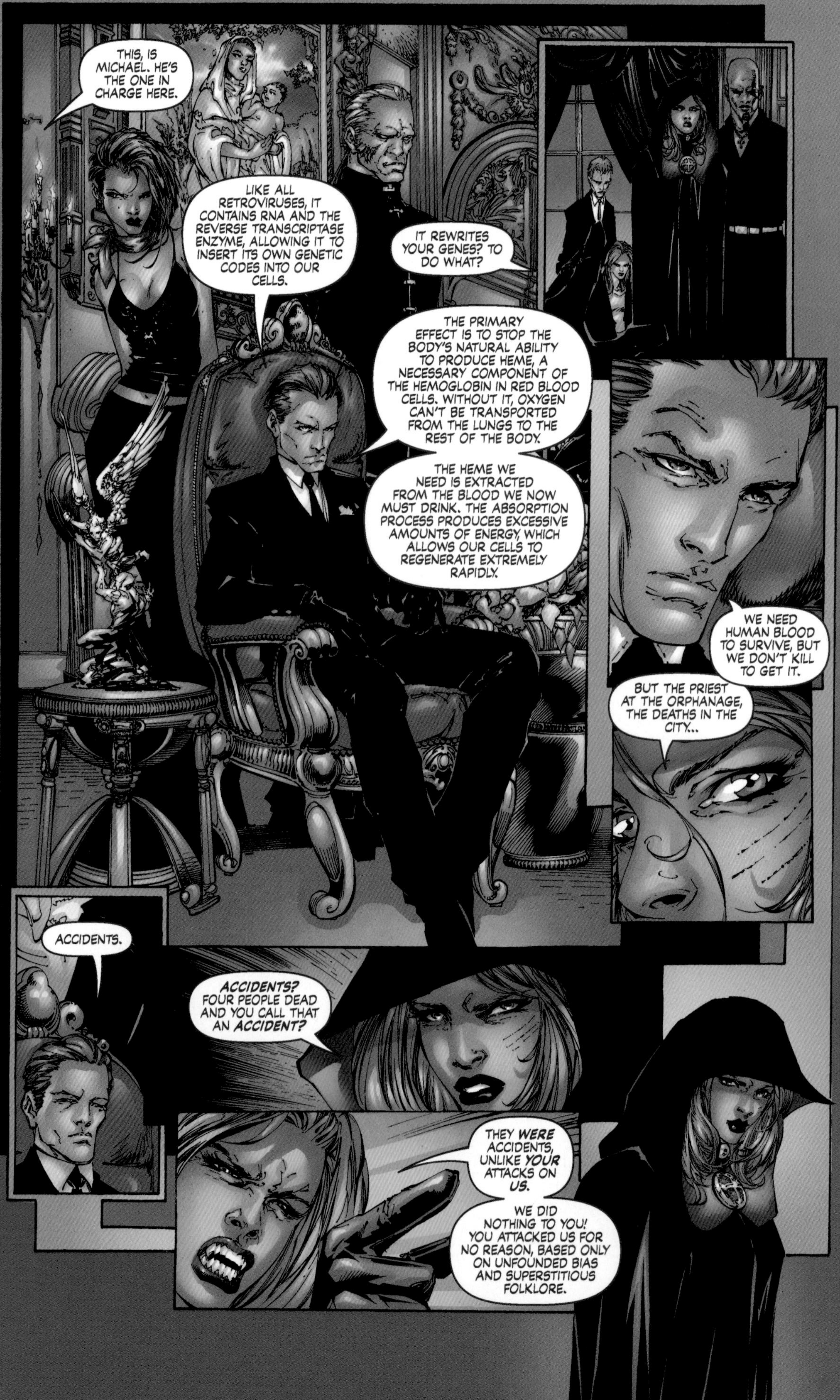
THIS, IS MICHAEL. HE'S THE ONE IN CHARGE HERE.
LIKE ALL RETROVIRUSES, IT CONTAINS RNA AND THE REVERSE TRANSCRIPTASE ENZYME, ALLOWING IT TO INSERT ITS OWN GENETIC CODES INTO OUR CELLS.
IT REWRITES YOUR GENES? TO DO WHAT?
THE PRIMARY EFFECT IS TO STOP THE BODY'S NATURAL ABILITY TO PRODUCE HEME, A NECESSARY COMPONENT OF THE HEMOGLOBIN IN RED BLOOD CELLS. WITHOUT IT, OXYGEN CAN'T BE TRANSPORTED FROM THE LUNGS TO THE REST OF THE BODY.
THE HEME WE NEED IS EXTRACTED FROM THE BLOOD WE NOW MUST DRINK. THE ABSORPTION PROCESS PRODUCES EXCESSIVE AMOUNTS OF ENERGY, WHICH ALLOWS OUR CELLS TO REGENERATE EXTREMELY RAPIDLY.
WE NEED HUMAN BLOOD TO SURVIVE, BUT WE DON'T KILL TO GET IT.
BUT THE PRIEST AT THE ORPHANAGE, THE DEATHS IN THE CITY...
ACCIDENTS.
ACCIDENTS? FOUR PEOPLE DEAD AND YOU CALL THAT AN ACCIDENT?
THEY WERE ACCIDENTS, UNLIKE YOUR ATTACKS ON US.
WE DID NOTHING TO YOU! YOU ATTACKED US FOR NO REASON, BASED ONLY ON UNFOUNDED BIAS AND SUPERSTITIOUS FOLKLORE.

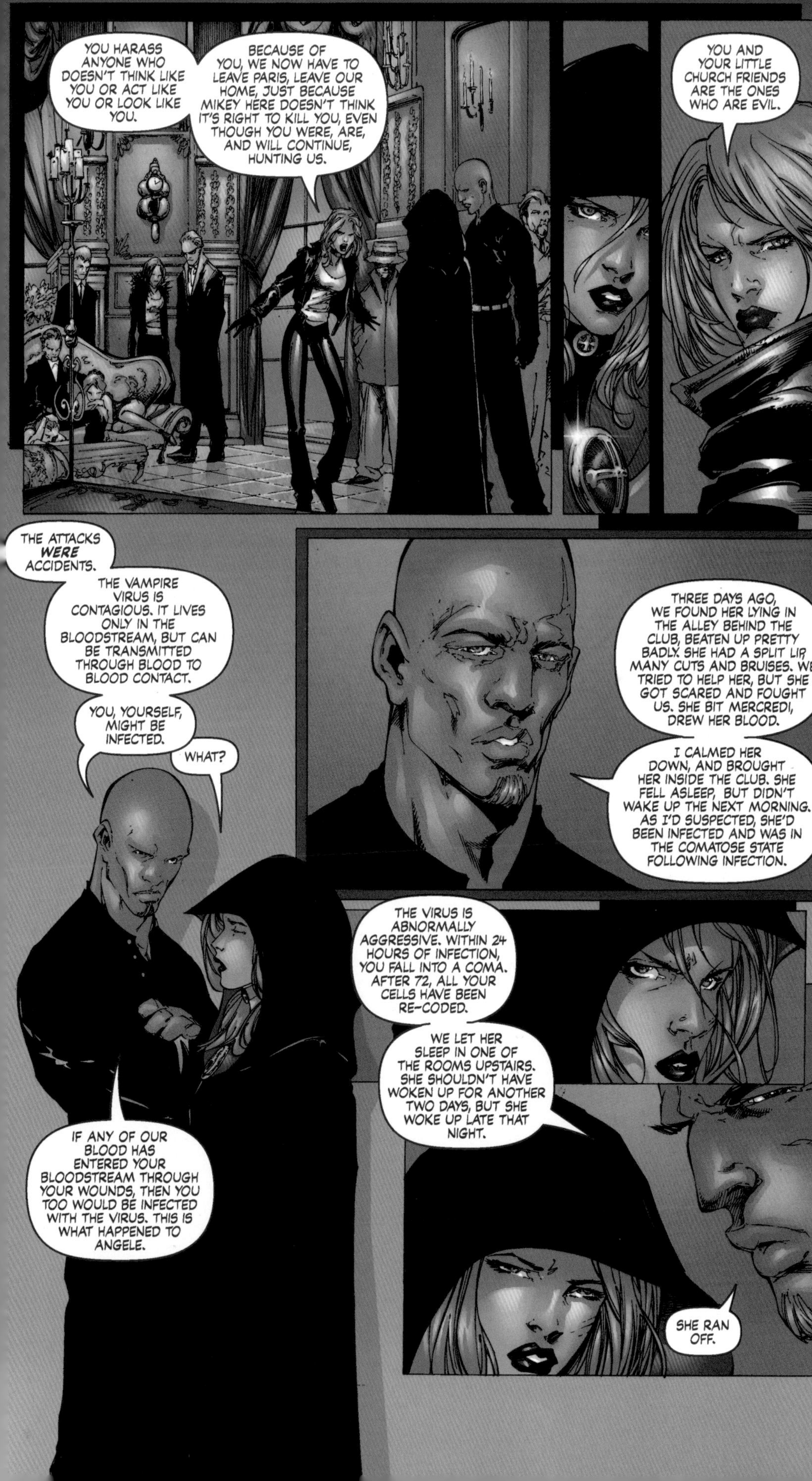
YOU HARASS ANYONE WHO DOESN'T THINK LIKE YOU OR ACT LIKE YOU OR LOOK LIKE YOU.
BECAUSE OF YOU, WE NOW HAVE TO LEAVE PARIS, LEAVE OUR HOME, JUST BECAUSE MIKEY HERE DOESN'T THINK IT'S RIGHT TO KILL YOU, EVEN THOUGH YOU WERE, ARE, AND WILL CONTINUE, HUNTING US.
YOU AND YOUR LITTLE CHURCH FRIENDS ARE THE ONES WHO ARE EVIL.
THE ATTACKS *WERE* ACCIDENTS.
THE VAMPIRE VIRUS IS CONTAGIOUS. IT LIVES ONLY IN THE BLOODSTREAM, BUT CAN BE TRANSMITTED THROUGH BLOOD TO BLOOD CONTACT.
YOU, YOURSELF, MIGHT BE INFECTED.
WHAT?
IF ANY OF OUR BLOOD HAS ENTERED YOUR BLOODSTREAM THROUGH YOUR WOUNDS, THEN YOU TOO WOULD BE INFECTED WITH THE VIRUS. THIS IS WHAT HAPPENED TO ANGELE.
THREE DAYS AGO, WE FOUND HER LYING IN THE ALLEY BEHIND THE CLUB, BEATEN UP PRETTY BADLY. SHE HAD A SPLIT LIP, MANY CUTS AND BRUISES. WE TRIED TO HELP HER, BUT SHE GOT SCARED AND FOUGHT US. SHE BIT MERCREDI, DREW HER BLOOD.
I CALMED HER DOWN, AND BROUGHT HER INSIDE THE CLUB. SHE FELL ASLEEP, BUT DIDN'T WAKE UP THE NEXT MORNING. AS I'D SUSPECTED, SHE'D BEEN INFECTED AND WAS IN THE COMATOSE STATE FOLLOWING INFECTION.
THE VIRUS IS ABNORMALLY AGGRESSIVE. WITHIN 24 HOURS OF INFECTION, YOU FALL INTO A COMA. AFTER 72, ALL YOUR CELLS HAVE BEEN RE-CODED.
WE LET HER SLEEP IN ONE OF THE ROOMS UPSTAIRS. SHE SHOULDN'T HAVE WOKEN UP FOR ANOTHER TWO DAYS, BUT SHE WOKE UP LATE THAT NIGHT.
SHE RAN OFF.

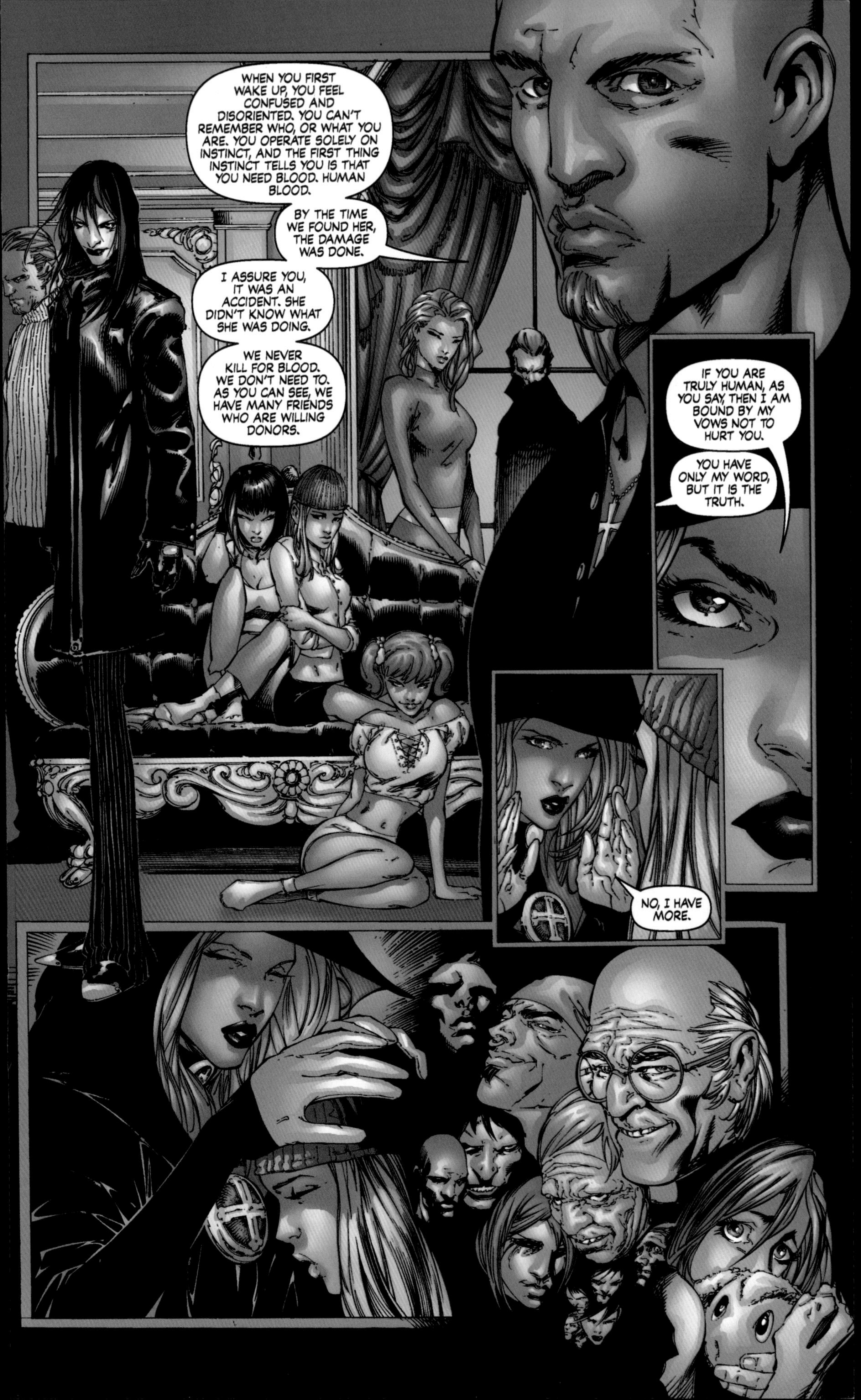
WHEN YOU FIRST WAKE UP, YOU FEEL CONFUSED AND DISORIENTED. YOU CAN'T REMEMBER WHO, OR WHAT YOU ARE. YOU OPERATE SOLELY ON INSTINCT, AND THE FIRST THING INSTINCT TELLS YOU IS THAT YOU NEED BLOOD. HUMAN BLOOD.
BY THE TIME WE FOUND HER, THE DAMAGE WAS DONE.
I ASSURE YOU, IT WAS AN ACCIDENT. SHE DIDN'T KNOW WHAT SHE WAS DOING.
WE NEVER KILL FOR BLOOD. WE DON'T NEED TO. AS YOU CAN SEE, WE HAVE MANY FRIENDS WHO ARE WILLING DONORS.
IF YOU ARE TRULY HUMAN, AS YOU SAY, THEN I AM BOUND BY MY VOWS NOT TO HURT YOU.
YOU HAVE ONLY MY WORD, BUT IT IS THE TRUTH.
NO, I HAVE MORE.

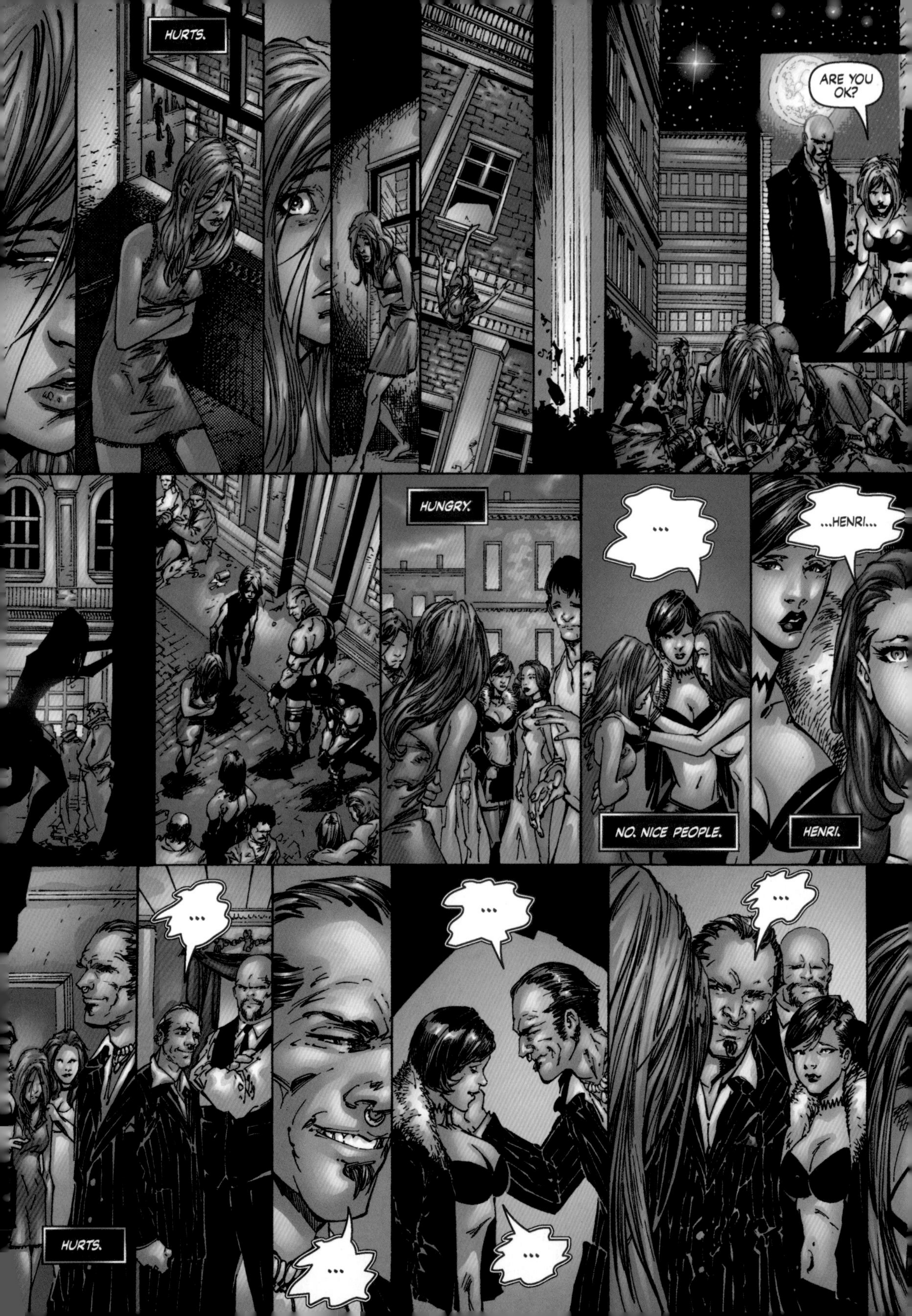
HURTS.
ARE YOU OK?
HUNGRY.
...
NO. NICE PEOPLE.
...HENRI...
HENRI.
HURTS.
...
...
...
...
...
...

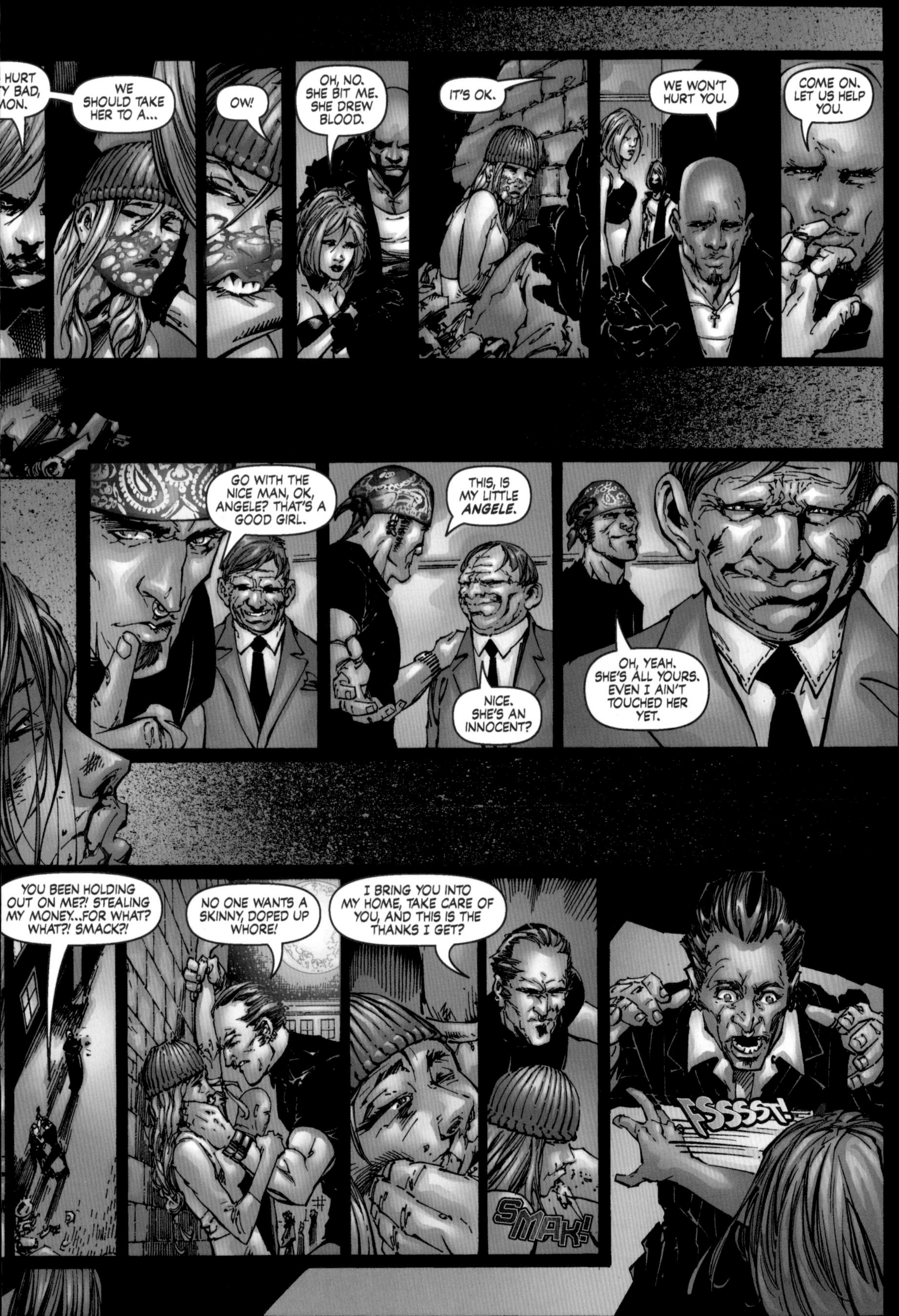
HURT
TY BAD,
MON.
WE SHOULD TAKE HER TO A...
OW!
OH, NO. SHE BIT ME. SHE DREW BLOOD.
IT'S OK.
WE WON'T HURT YOU.
COME ON. LET US HELP YOU.
GO WITH THE NICE MAN, OK, ANGELE? THAT'S A GOOD GIRL.
THIS, IS MY LITTLE *ANGELE*.
NICE. SHE'S AN INNOCENT?
OH, YEAH. SHE'S ALL YOURS. EVEN I AIN'T TOUCHED HER YET.
YOU BEEN HOLDING OUT ON ME?! STEALING MY MONEY...FOR WHAT? WHAT?! SMACK?!
NO ONE WANTS A SKINNY, DOPED UP WHORE!
I BRING YOU INTO MY HOME, TAKE CARE OF YOU, AND THIS IS THE THANKS I GET?
SMAK!
FSSSST!

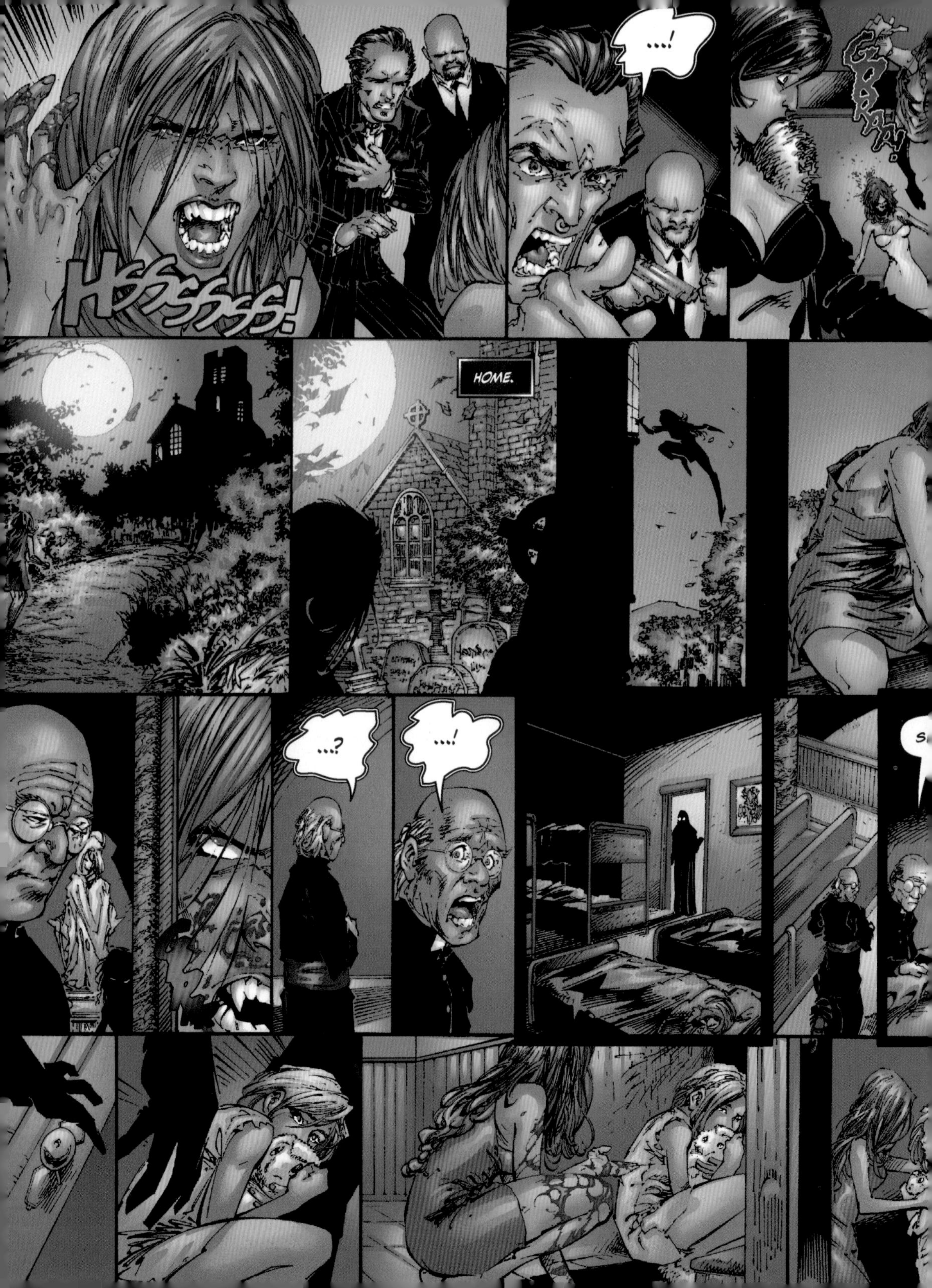

HSSSSSS!
...!
HOME.
...?
...!

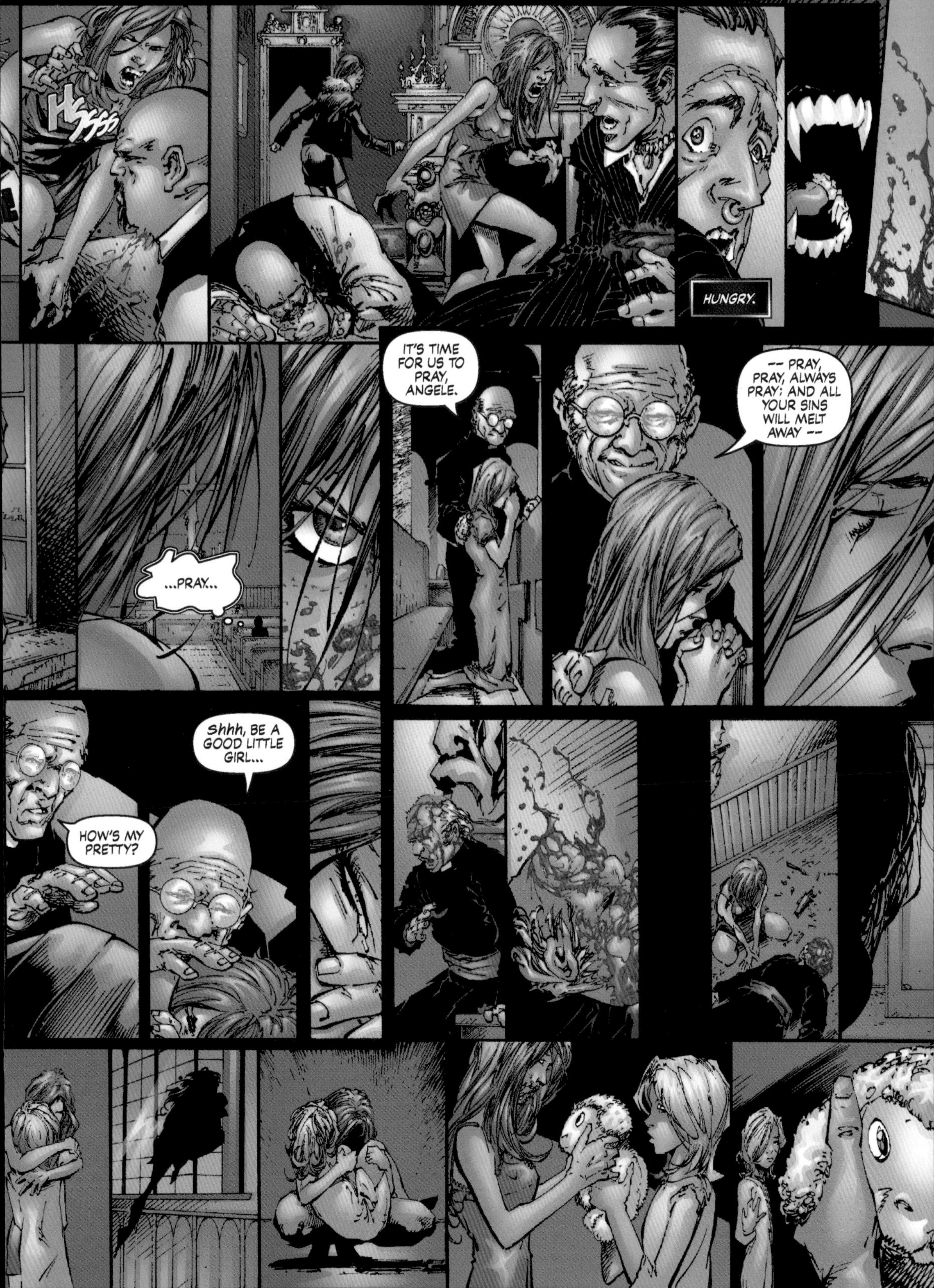
HSSSSS
HUNGRY.
...PRAY...
IT'S TIME FOR US TO PRAY, ANGELE.
-- PRAY, PRAY, ALWAYS PRAY; AND ALL YOUR SINS WILL MELT AWAY --
HOW'S MY PRETTY?
Shhh, BE A GOOD LITTLE GIRL...

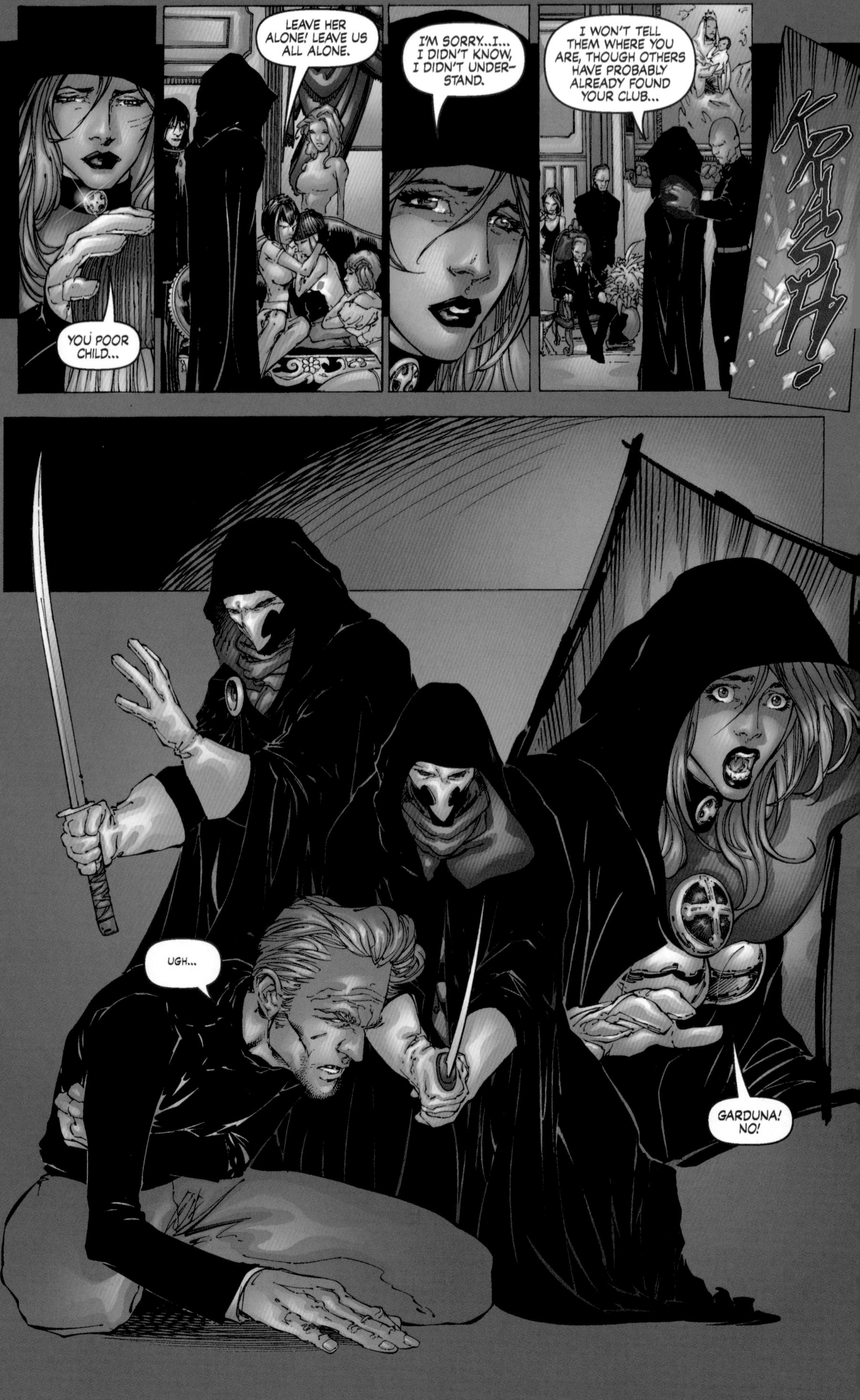
YOU POOR CHILD...
LEAVE HER ALONE! LEAVE US ALL ALONE.
I'M SORRY...I... I DIDN'T KNOW, I DIDN'T UNDERSTAND.
I WON'T TELL THEM WHERE YOU ARE, THOUGH OTHERS HAVE PROBABLY ALREADY FOUND YOUR CLUB...
KRASH!
UGH...
GARDUNA! NO!

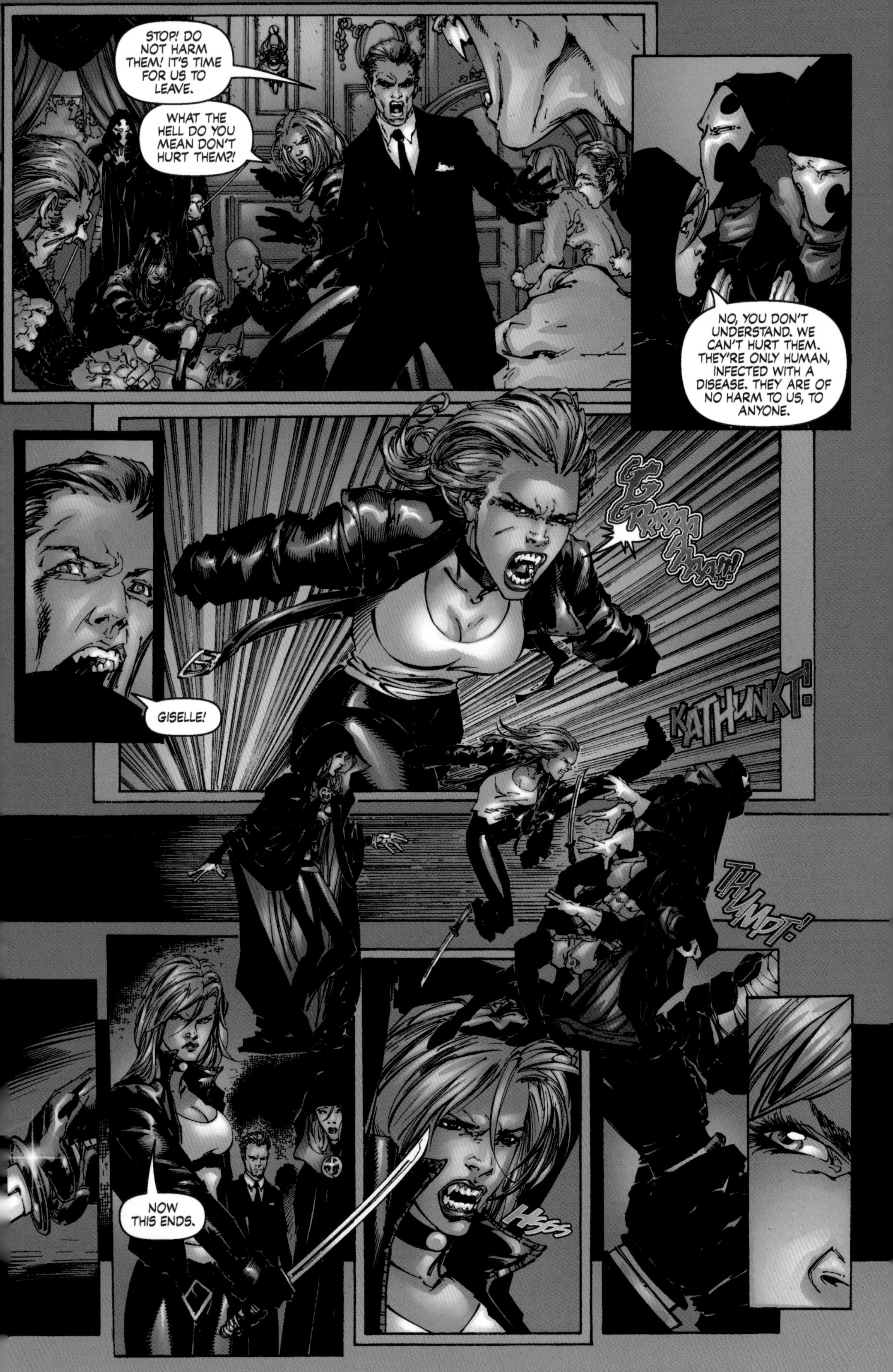
STOP! DO NOT HARM THEM! IT'S TIME FOR US TO LEAVE.
WHAT THE HELL DO YOU MEAN DON'T HURT THEM?!
NO, YOU DON'T UNDERSTAND. WE CAN'T HURT THEM. THEY'RE ONLY HUMAN, INFECTED WITH A DISEASE. THEY ARE OF NO HARM TO US, TO ANYONE.
GISELLE!
KATHUNKT!
THUMPT!
NOW THIS ENDS.
HSSS

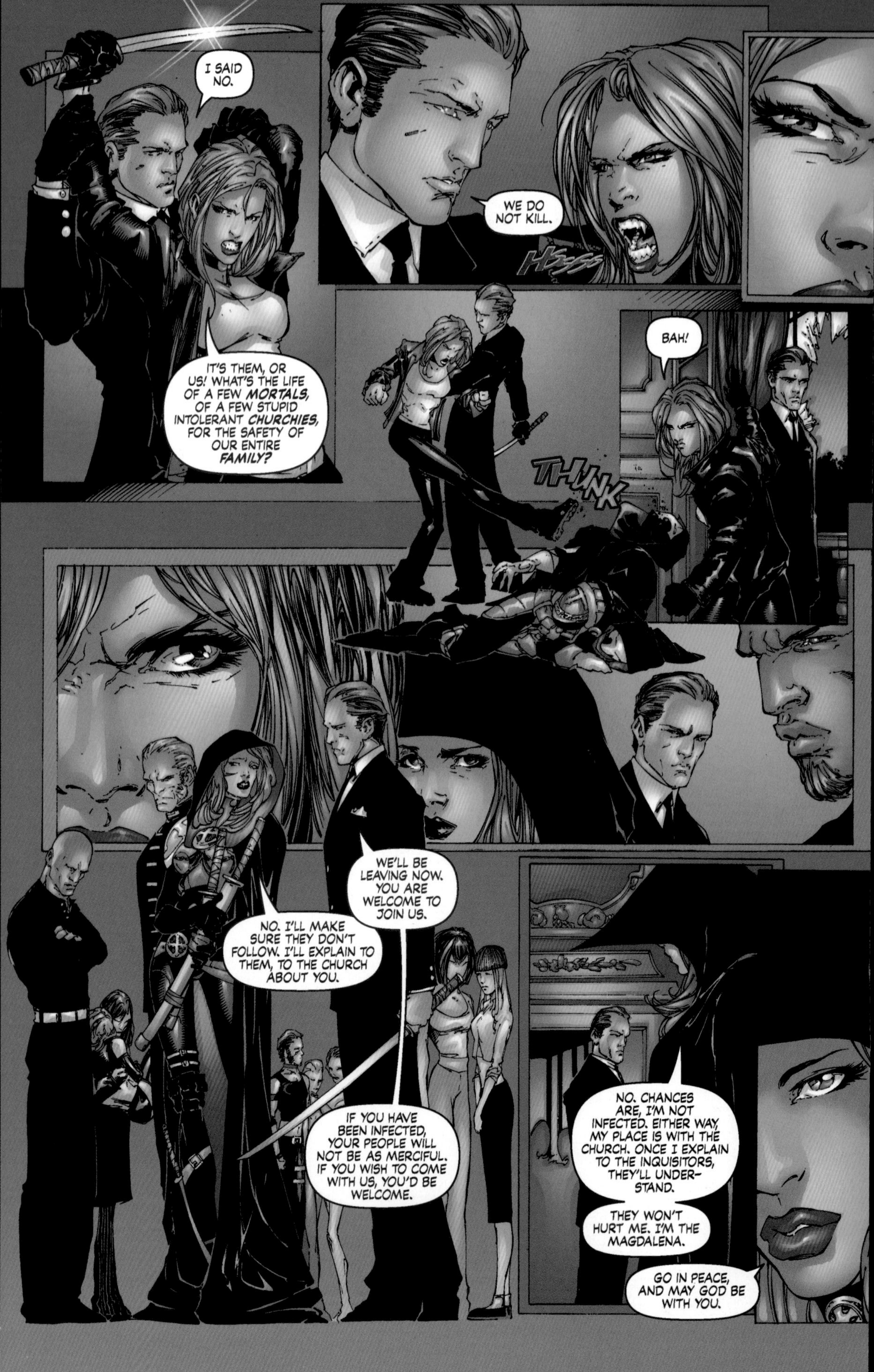

I SAID NO.
WE DO NOT KILL.
HSSSS
IT'S THEM, OR US! WHAT'S THE LIFE OF A FEW MORTALS, OF A FEW STUPID INTOLERANT CHURCHIES, FOR THE SAFETY OF OUR ENTIRE FAMILY?
BAH!
THUNK
WE'LL BE LEAVING NOW. YOU ARE WELCOME TO JOIN US.
NO. I'LL MAKE SURE THEY DON'T FOLLOW. I'LL EXPLAIN TO THEM, TO THE CHURCH ABOUT YOU.
IF YOU HAVE BEEN INFECTED, YOUR PEOPLE WILL NOT BE AS MERCIFUL. IF YOU WISH TO COME WITH US, YOU'D BE WELCOME.
NO. CHANCES ARE, I'M NOT INFECTED. EITHER WAY, MY PLACE IS WITH THE CHURCH. ONCE I EXPLAIN TO THE INQUISITORS, THEY'LL UNDER-STAND.
THEY WON'T HURT ME. I'M THE MAGDALENA.
GO IN PEACE, AND MAY GOD BE WITH YOU.

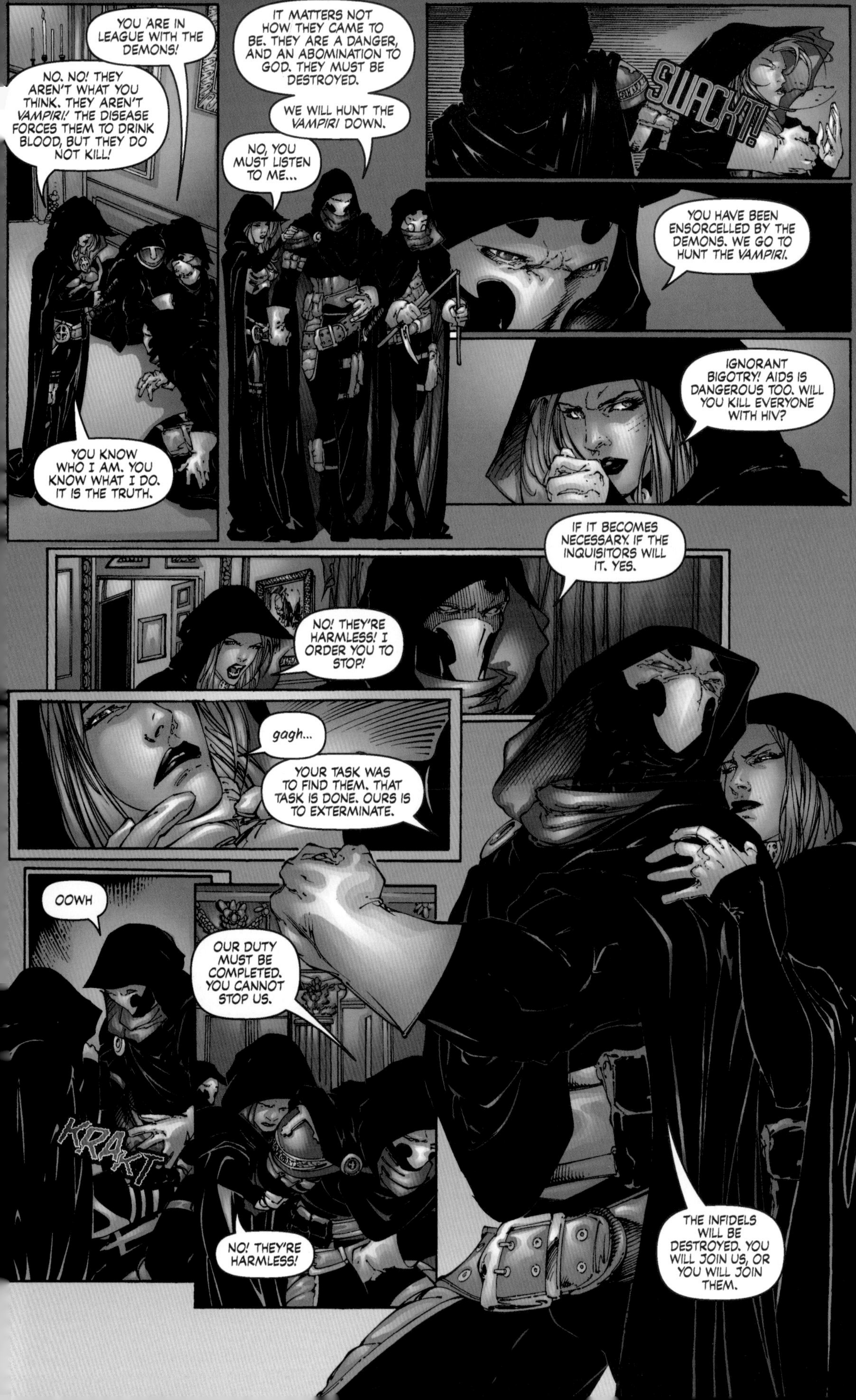
YOU ARE IN LEAGUE WITH THE DEMONS!
NO. NO! THEY AREN'T WHAT YOU THINK. THEY AREN'T VAMPIRI! THE DISEASE FORCES THEM TO DRINK BLOOD, BUT THEY DO NOT KILL!
YOU KNOW WHO I AM. YOU KNOW WHAT I DO. IT IS THE TRUTH.
IT MATTERS NOT HOW THEY CAME TO BE. THEY ARE A DANGER, AND AN ABOMINATION TO GOD. THEY MUST BE DESTROYED.
WE WILL HUNT THE VAMPIRI DOWN.
NO, YOU MUST LISTEN TO ME...
SWACK!!
YOU HAVE BEEN ENSORCELLED BY THE DEMONS. WE GO TO HUNT THE VAMPIRI.
IGNORANT BIGOTRY! AIDS IS DANGEROUS TOO. WILL YOU KILL EVERYONE WITH HIV?
IF IT BECOMES NECESSARY. IF THE INQUISITORS WILL IT. YES.
NO! THEY'RE HARMLESS! I ORDER YOU TO STOP!
gagh...
YOUR TASK WAS TO FIND THEM. THAT TASK IS DONE. OURS IS TO EXTERMINATE.
OOWH
OUR DUTY MUST BE COMPLETED. YOU CANNOT STOP US.
KRAKT
NO! THEY'RE HARMLESS!
THE INFIDELS WILL BE DESTROYED. YOU WILL JOIN US, OR YOU WILL JOIN THEM.

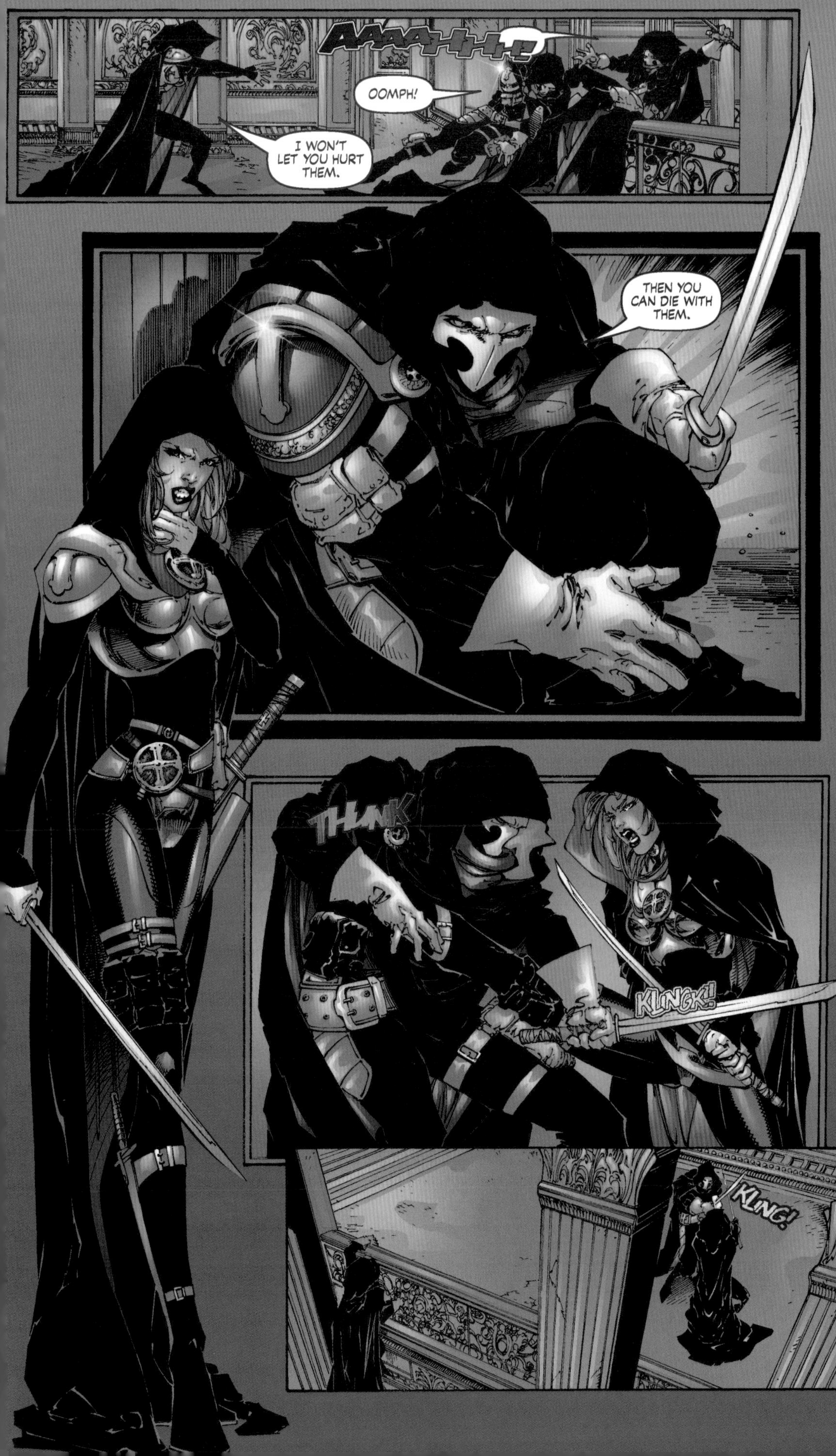
AAAAHHH!
OOMPH!
I WON'T LET YOU HURT THEM.
THEN YOU CAN DIE WITH THEM.
THUNK
KLINGK!
KLING!

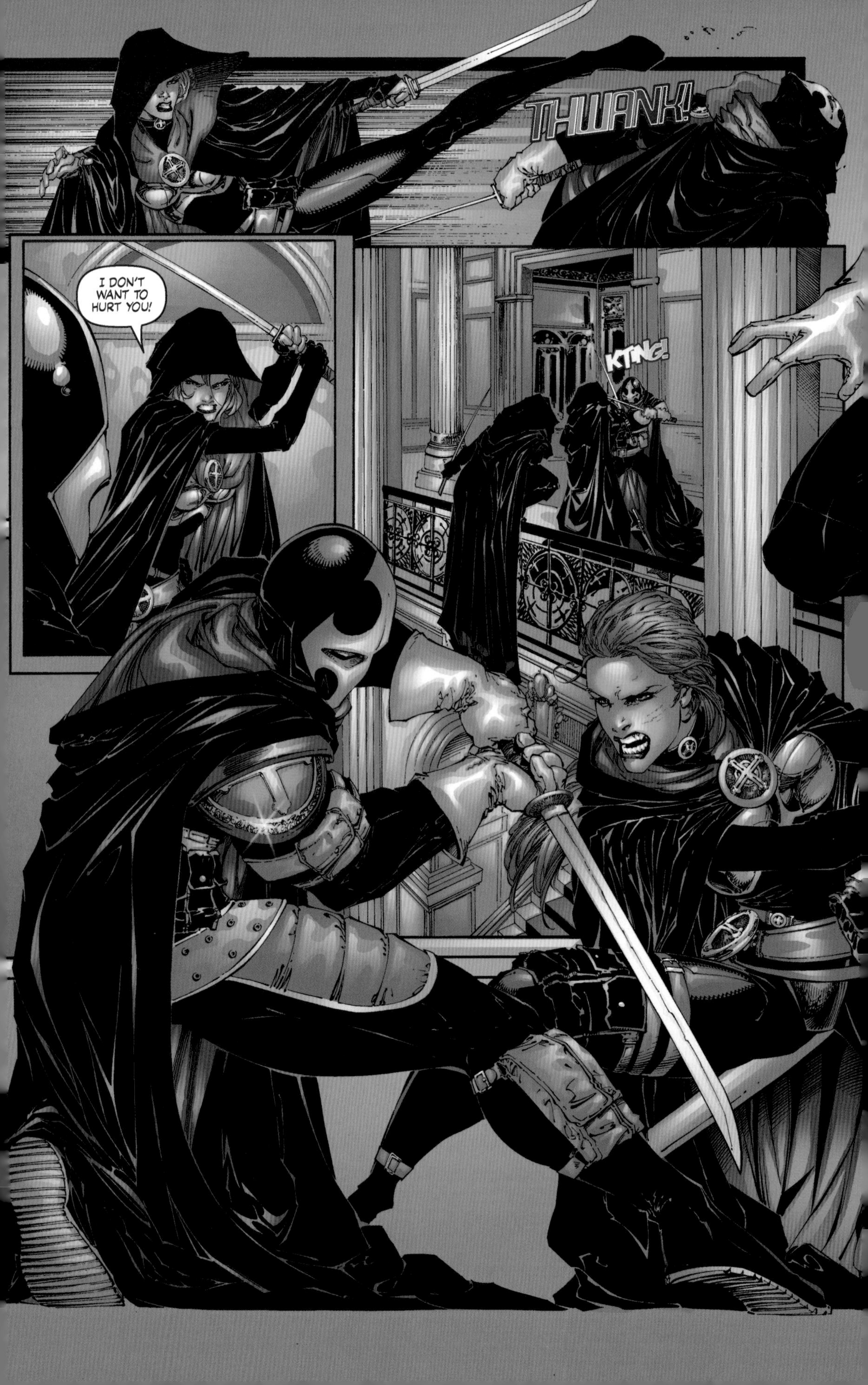
THWANK!
I DON'T WANT TO HURT YOU!
KTING!

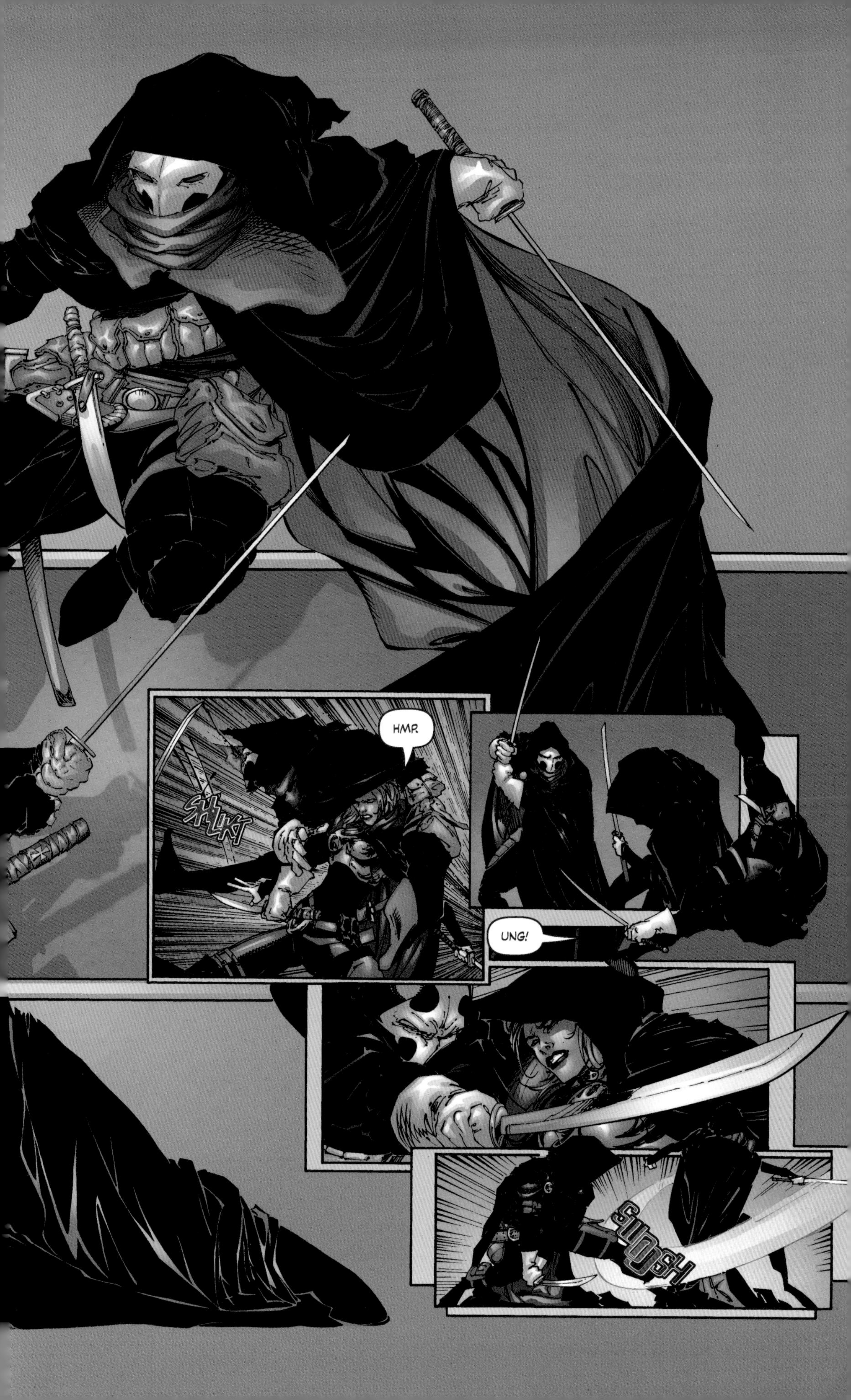
HMP.
SHLUKT
UNG!
SWOOSH

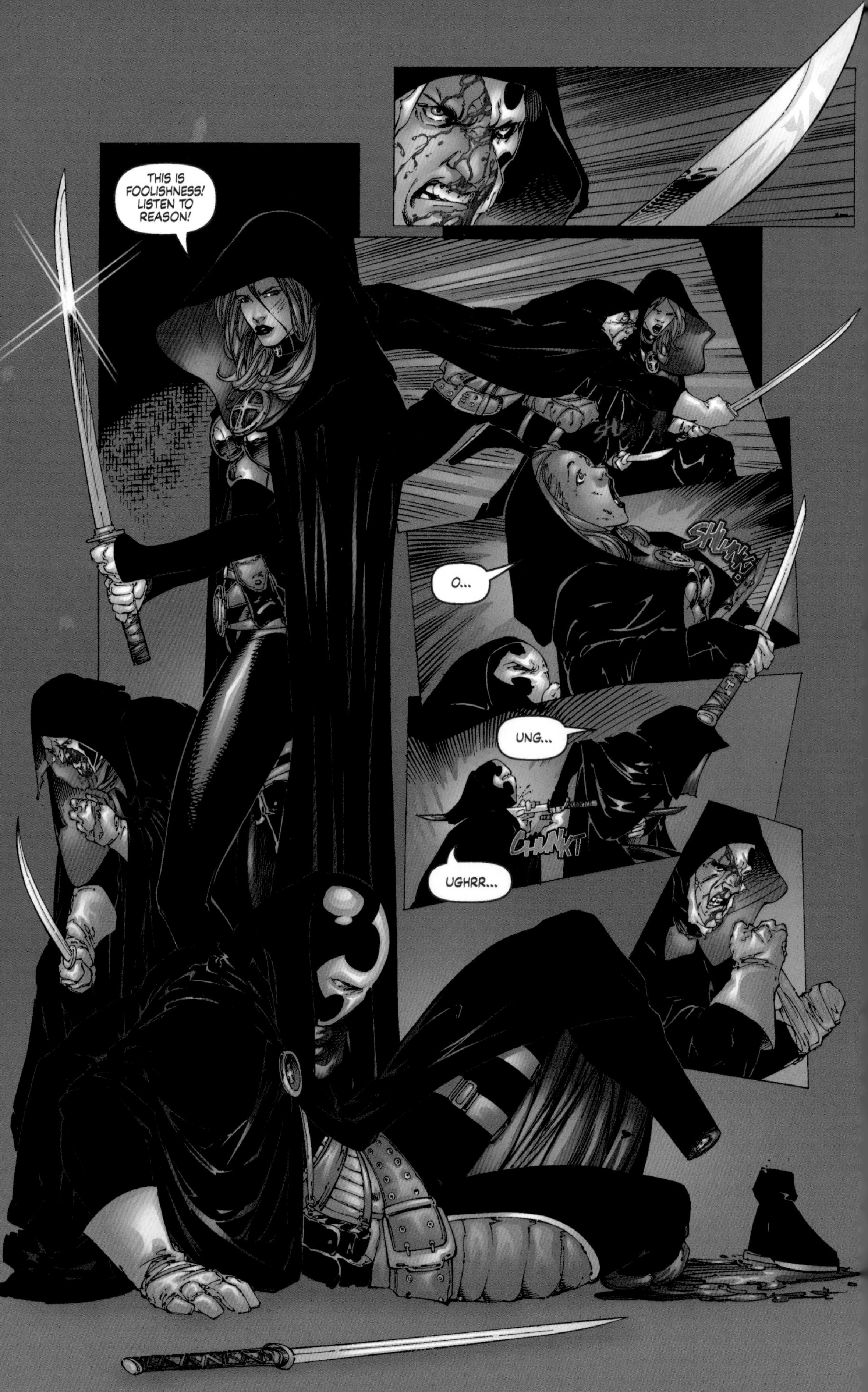

THIS IS FOOLISHNESS! LISTEN TO REASON!
O...
UNG...
CHUNKT
UGHRR...

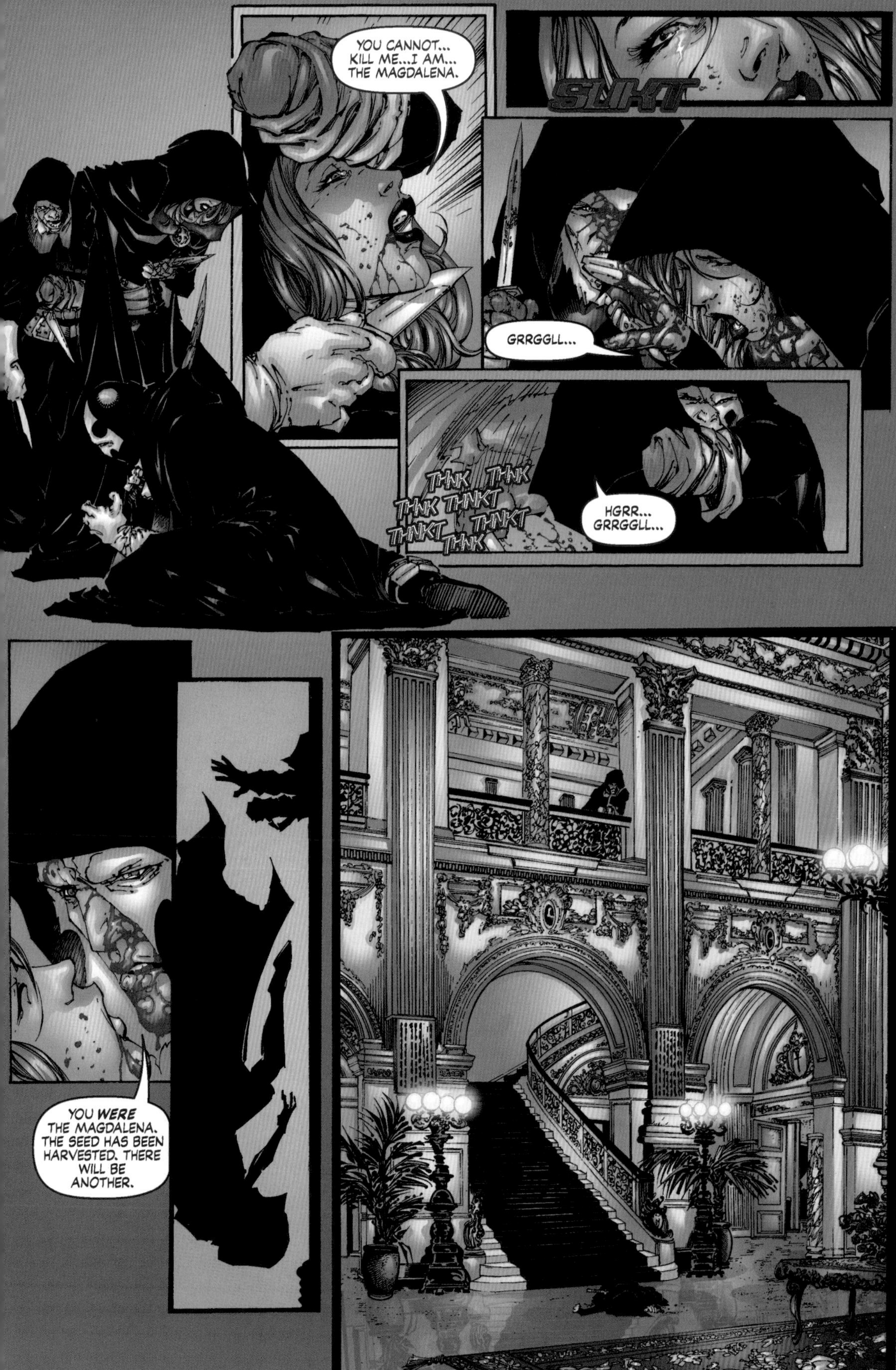
YOU CANNOT... KILL ME...I AM... THE MAGDALENA.
SLIKT
GRRGGLL...
THNK THNK THNK THNKT THNKT THNKT THNK
HGRR... GRRGGLL...
YOU *WERE* THE MAGDALENA. THE SEED HAS BEEN HARVESTED. THERE WILL BE ANOTHER.

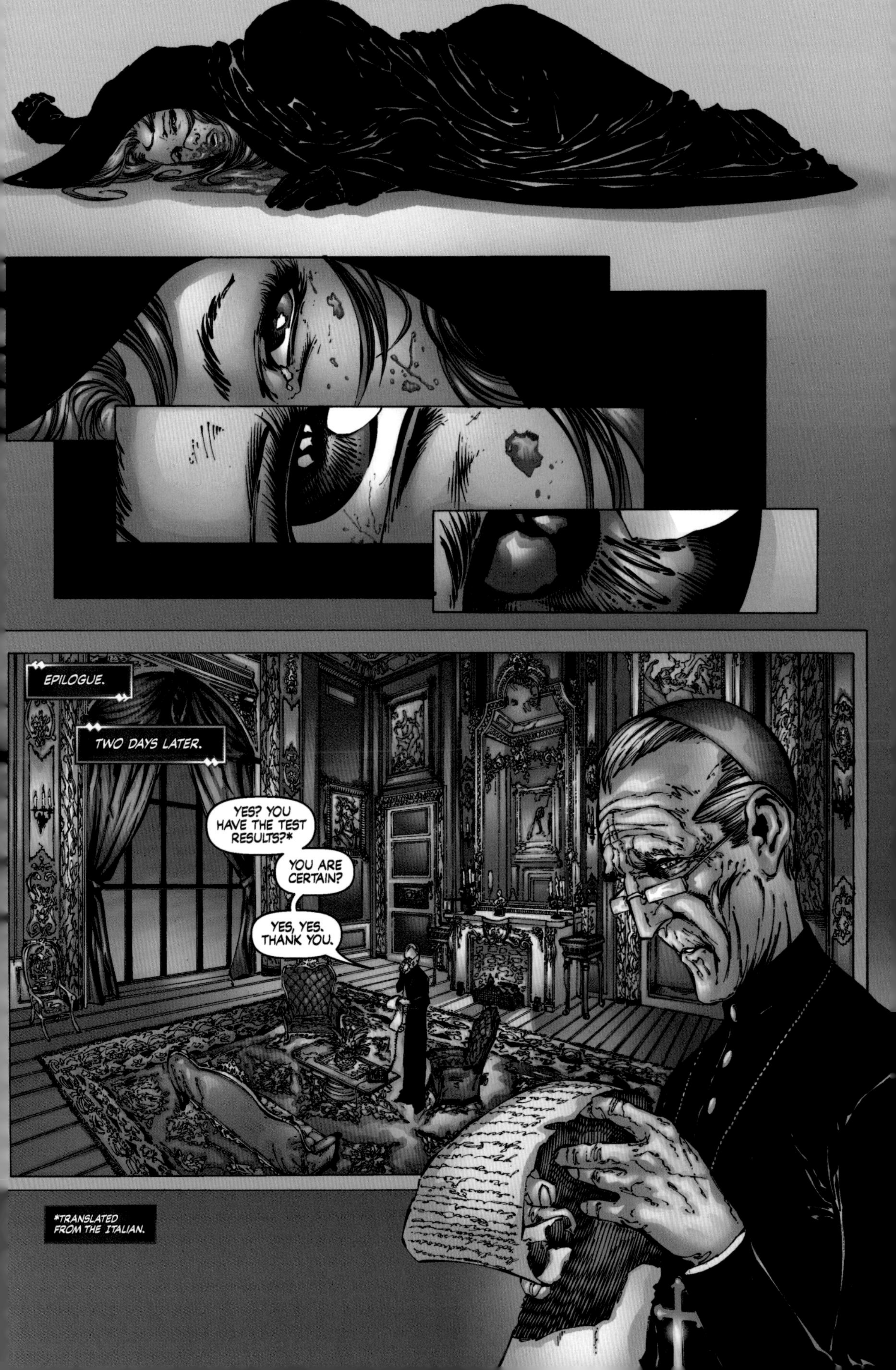
EPILOGUE.
TWO DAYS LATER.
YES? YOU HAVE THE TEST RESULTS?*
YOU ARE CERTAIN?
YES, YES. THANK YOU.
*TRANSLATED FROM THE ITALIAN.

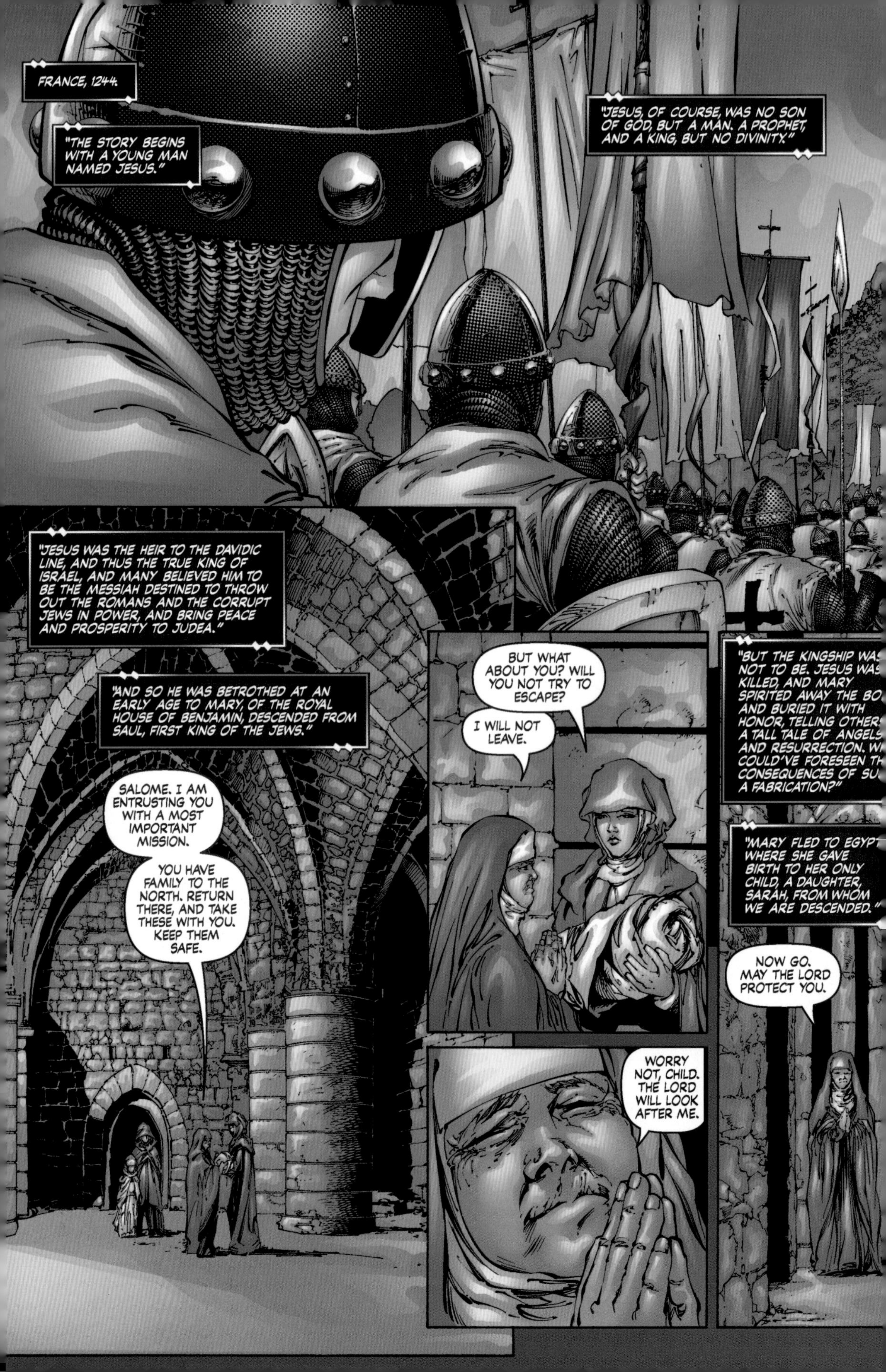
FRANCE, 1244.
"THE STORY BEGINS WITH A YOUNG MAN NAMED JESUS."
"JESUS, OF COURSE, WAS NO SON OF GOD, BUT A MAN. A PROPHET, AND A KING, BUT NO DIVINITY."
"JESUS WAS THE HEIR TO THE DAVIDIC LINE, AND THUS THE TRUE KING OF ISRAEL, AND MANY BELIEVED HIM TO BE THE MESSIAH DESTINED TO THROW OUT THE ROMANS AND THE CORRUPT JEWS IN POWER, AND BRING PEACE AND PROSPERITY TO JUDEA."
"AND SO HE WAS BETROTHED AT AN EARLY AGE TO MARY, OF THE ROYAL HOUSE OF BENJAMIN, DESCENDED FROM SAUL, FIRST KING OF THE JEWS."
SALOME. I AM ENTRUSTING YOU WITH A MOST IMPORTANT MISSION.
YOU HAVE FAMILY TO THE NORTH. RETURN THERE, AND TAKE THESE WITH YOU. KEEP THEM SAFE.
BUT WHAT ABOUT YOU? WILL YOU NOT TRY TO ESCAPE?
I WILL NOT LEAVE.
"BUT THE KINGSHIP WAS NOT TO BE. JESUS WAS KILLED, AND MARY SPIRITED AWAY THE BO AND BURIED IT WITH HONOR, TELLING OTHER A TALL TALE OF ANGELS AND RESURRECTION. W COULD'VE FORESEEN TH CONSEQUENCES OF SU A FABRICATION?"
"MARY FLED TO EGYPT WHERE SHE GAVE BIRTH TO HER ONLY CHILD, A DAUGHTER, SARAH, FROM WHOM WE ARE DESCENDED."
WORRY NOT, CHILD. THE LORD WILL LOOK AFTER ME.
NOW GO. MAY THE LORD PROTECT YOU.

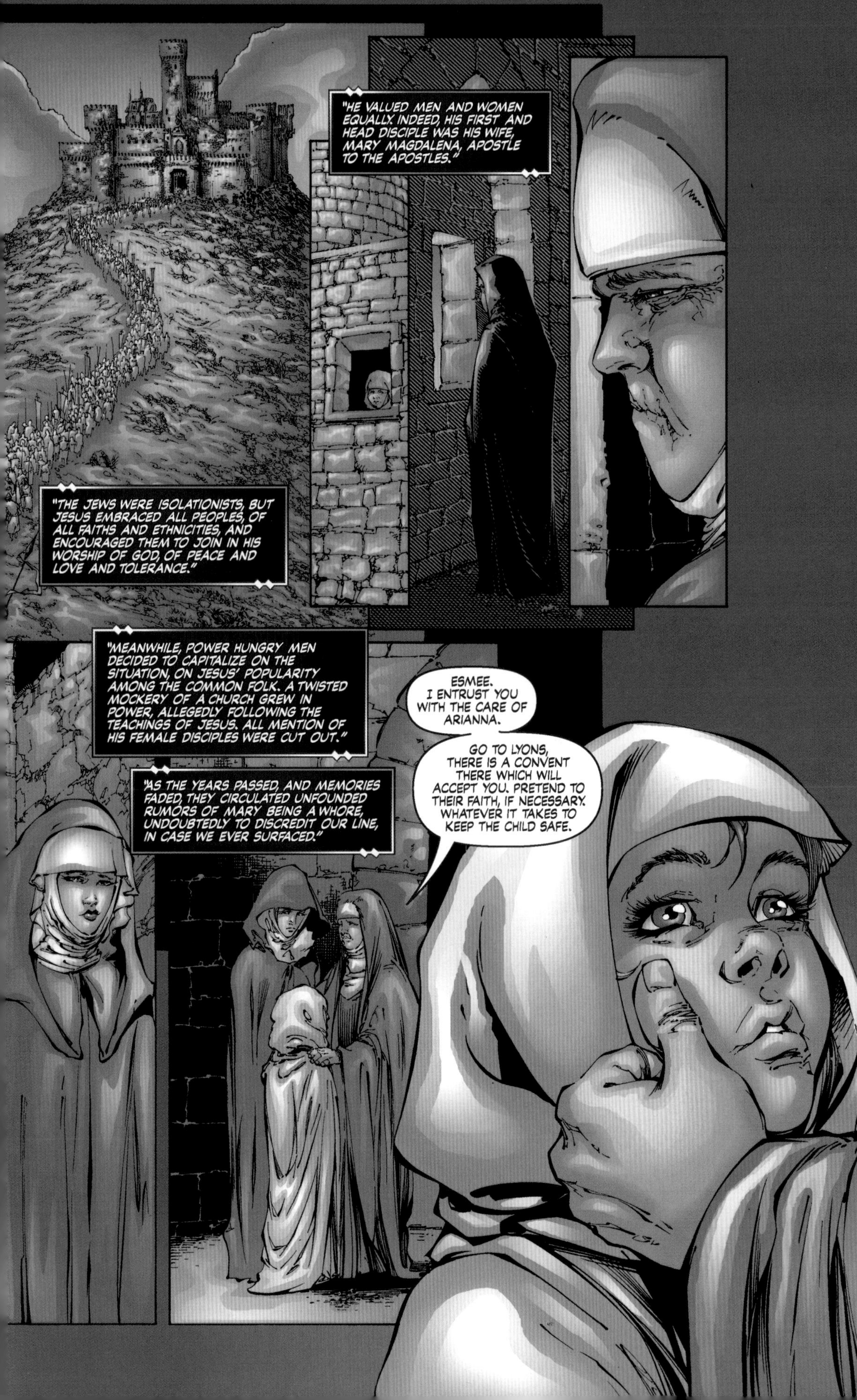
"THE JEWS WERE ISOLATIONISTS, BUT JESUS EMBRACED ALL PEOPLES, OF ALL FAITHS AND ETHNICITIES, AND ENCOURAGED THEM TO JOIN IN HIS WORSHIP OF GOD, OF PEACE AND LOVE AND TOLERANCE."
"HE VALUED MEN AND WOMEN EQUALLY. INDEED, HIS FIRST AND HEAD DISCIPLE WAS HIS WIFE, MARY MAGDALENA, APOSTLE TO THE APOSTLES."
"MEANWHILE, POWER HUNGRY MEN DECIDED TO CAPITALIZE ON THE SITUATION, ON JESUS' POPULARITY AMONG THE COMMON FOLK. A TWISTED MOCKERY OF A CHURCH GREW IN POWER, ALLEGEDLY FOLLOWING THE TEACHINGS OF JESUS. ALL MENTION OF HIS FEMALE DISCIPLES WERE CUT OUT."
"AS THE YEARS PASSED, AND MEMORIES FADED, THEY CIRCULATED UNFOUNDED RUMORS OF MARY BEING A WHORE, UNDOUBTEDLY TO DISCREDIT OUR LINE, IN CASE WE EVER SURFACED."
ESMEE. I ENTRUST YOU WITH THE CARE OF ARIANNA.
GO TO LYONS, THERE IS A CONVENT THERE WHICH WILL ACCEPT YOU. PRETEND TO THEIR FAITH, IF NECESSARY. WHATEVER IT TAKES TO KEEP THE CHILD SAFE.

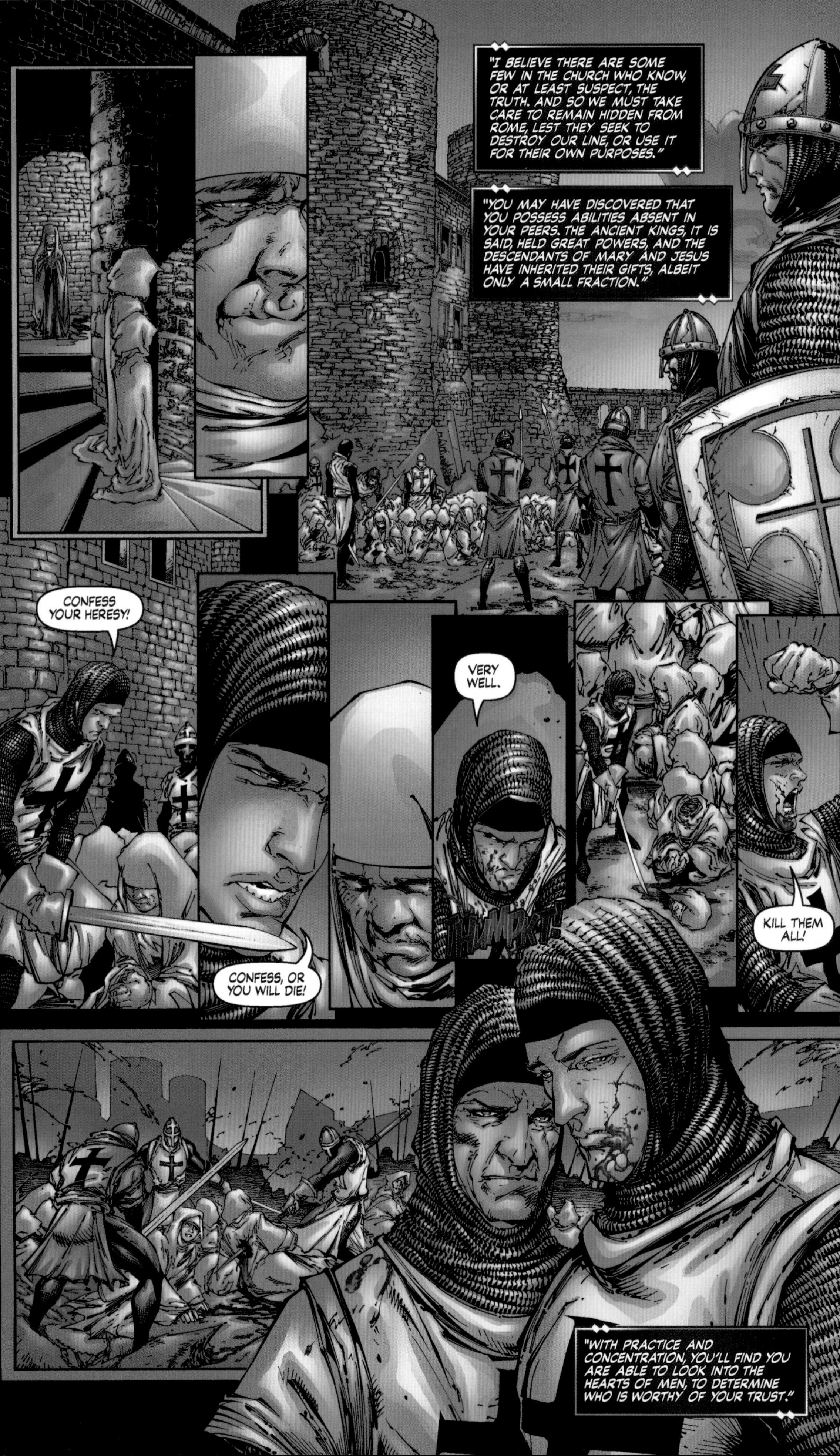
"I BELIEVE THERE ARE SOME FEW IN THE CHURCH WHO KNOW, OR AT LEAST SUSPECT, THE TRUTH. AND SO WE MUST TAKE CARE TO REMAIN HIDDEN FROM ROME, LEST THEY SEEK TO DESTROY OUR LINE, OR USE IT FOR THEIR OWN PURPOSES."
"YOU MAY HAVE DISCOVERED THAT YOU POSSESS ABILITIES ABSENT IN YOUR PEERS. THE ANCIENT KINGS, IT IS SAID, HELD GREAT POWERS, AND THE DESCENDANTS OF MARY AND JESUS HAVE INHERITED THEIR GIFTS, ALBEIT ONLY A SMALL FRACTION."
CONFESS YOUR HERESY!
CONFESS, OR YOU WILL DIE!
VERY WELL.
THUMPKT!
KILL THEM ALL!
"WITH PRACTICE AND CONCENTRATION, YOU'LL FIND YOU ARE ABLE TO LOOK INTO THE HEARTS OF MEN, TO DETERMINE WHO IS WORTHY OF YOUR TRUST."

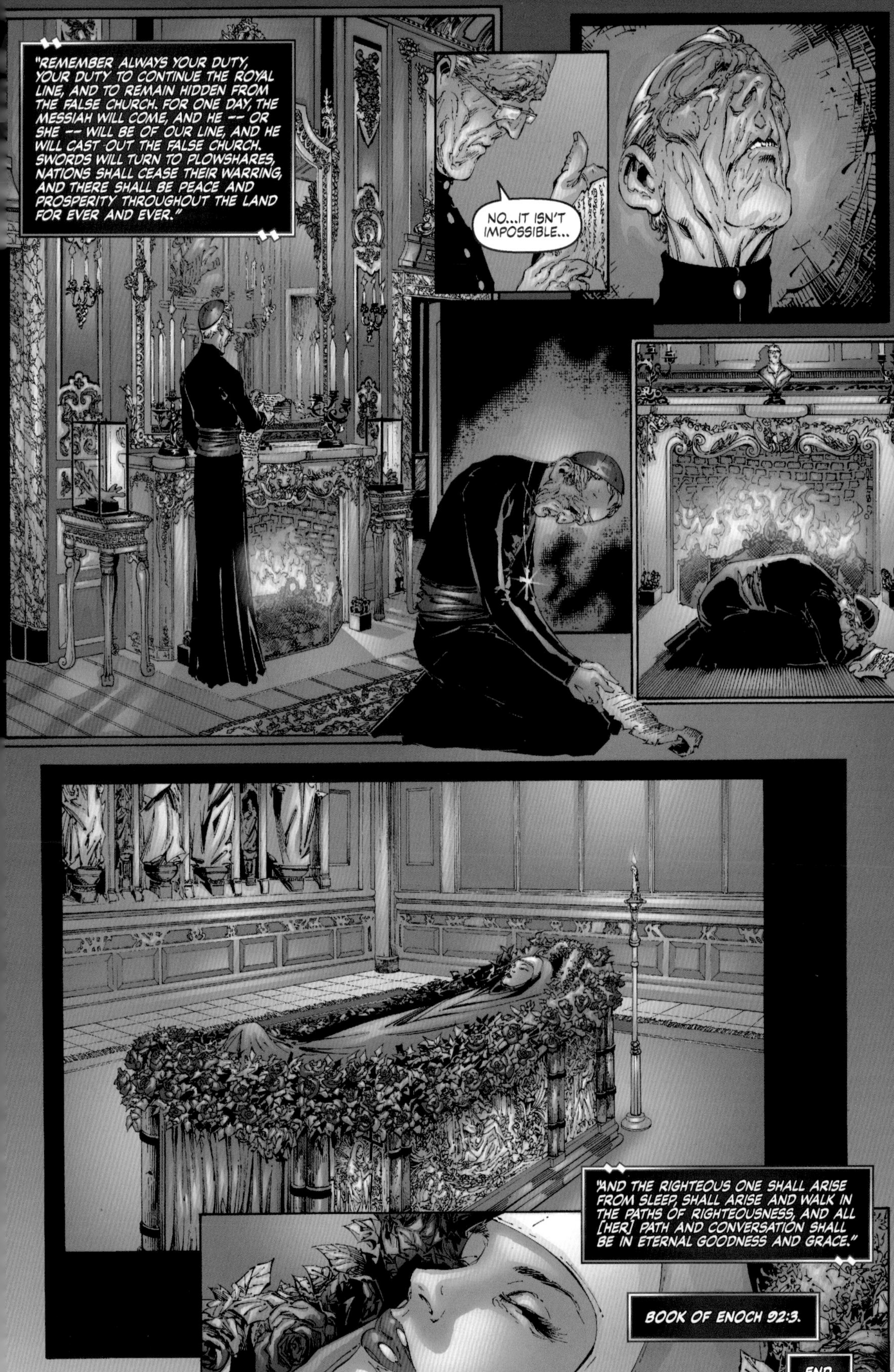
"REMEMBER ALWAYS YOUR DUTY, YOUR DUTY TO CONTINUE THE ROYAL LINE, AND TO REMAIN HIDDEN FROM THE FALSE CHURCH. FOR ONE DAY, THE MESSIAH WILL COME, AND HE -- OR SHE -- WILL BE OF OUR LINE, AND HE WILL CAST OUT THE FALSE CHURCH. SWORDS WILL TURN TO PLOWSHARES, NATIONS SHALL CEASE THEIR WARRING, AND THERE SHALL BE PEACE AND PROSPERITY THROUGHOUT THE LAND FOR EVER AND EVER."
NO...IT ISN'T IMPOSSIBLE...
"AND THE RIGHTEOUS ONE SHALL ARISE FROM SLEEP, SHALL ARISE AND WALK IN THE PATHS OF RIGHTEOUSNESS, AND ALL [HER] PATH AND CONVERSATION SHALL BE IN ETERNAL GOODNESS AND GRACE."
BOOK OF ENOCH 92:3.
END.

MAGDALENA: ORIGINS VOLUME 1

COVER GALLERY

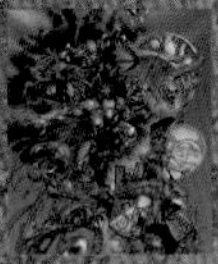

The Darkness issue #15
art by: **Joe Benitez, Joe Weems V** and **Tyson Wengler**

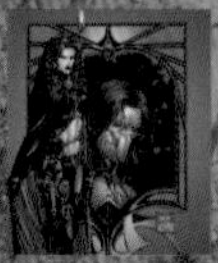

The Darkness issue #16
art by: **Joe Benitez, Joe Weems V** and **Tyson Wengler**

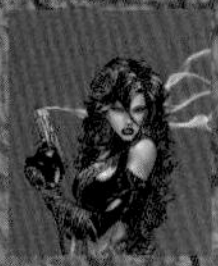

The Darkness issue #17
art by: **Joe Benitez, Joe Weems V** and **Peter Steigerwald**

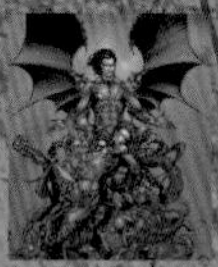

Witchblade issue #18
art by: **Joe Benitez, Joe Weems V** and **Liquid!**

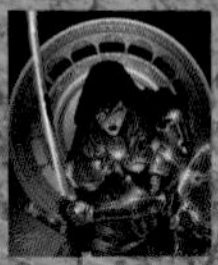

Magdalena vol. 1, issue #1
art by: **Joe Benitez, Joe Weems V** and **Peter Steigerwald**

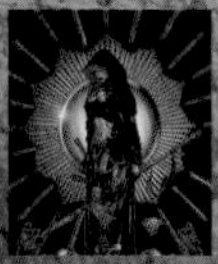

Magdalena vol. 1, issue #1
Alternate cover
art by: **Joe Benitez, Joe Weems V** and **Tyson Wengler**

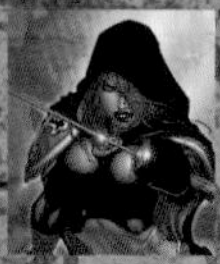

Magdalena vol. 1, issue #1 Alternate cover
art by: **Michael Turner, Jason Gorder** and **Steve Firchow**

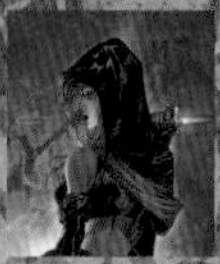

Magdalena vol. 1, issue #1 Alternate cover
art by: **Marc Silvestri, Joe Weems V** and **Steve Firchow**

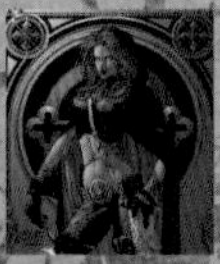

Magdalena vol. 1, issue #1 Alternate cover
art by: **Joe Benitez, Joe Weems V** and **Steve Firchow**

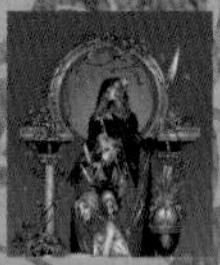

Magdalena vol. 1, issue #2
art by: **Joe Benitez, Joe Weems V** and **JD Smith**

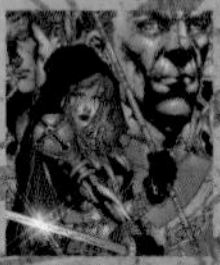

Magdalena vol. 1, issue #2 Alternate cover
art by: **Brian Ching, Victor Llamas** and **JD Smith**

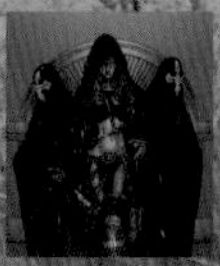

Magdalena vol. 1, issue #3
art by: **Joe Benitez, Joe Weems V** and **Tyson Wengler**

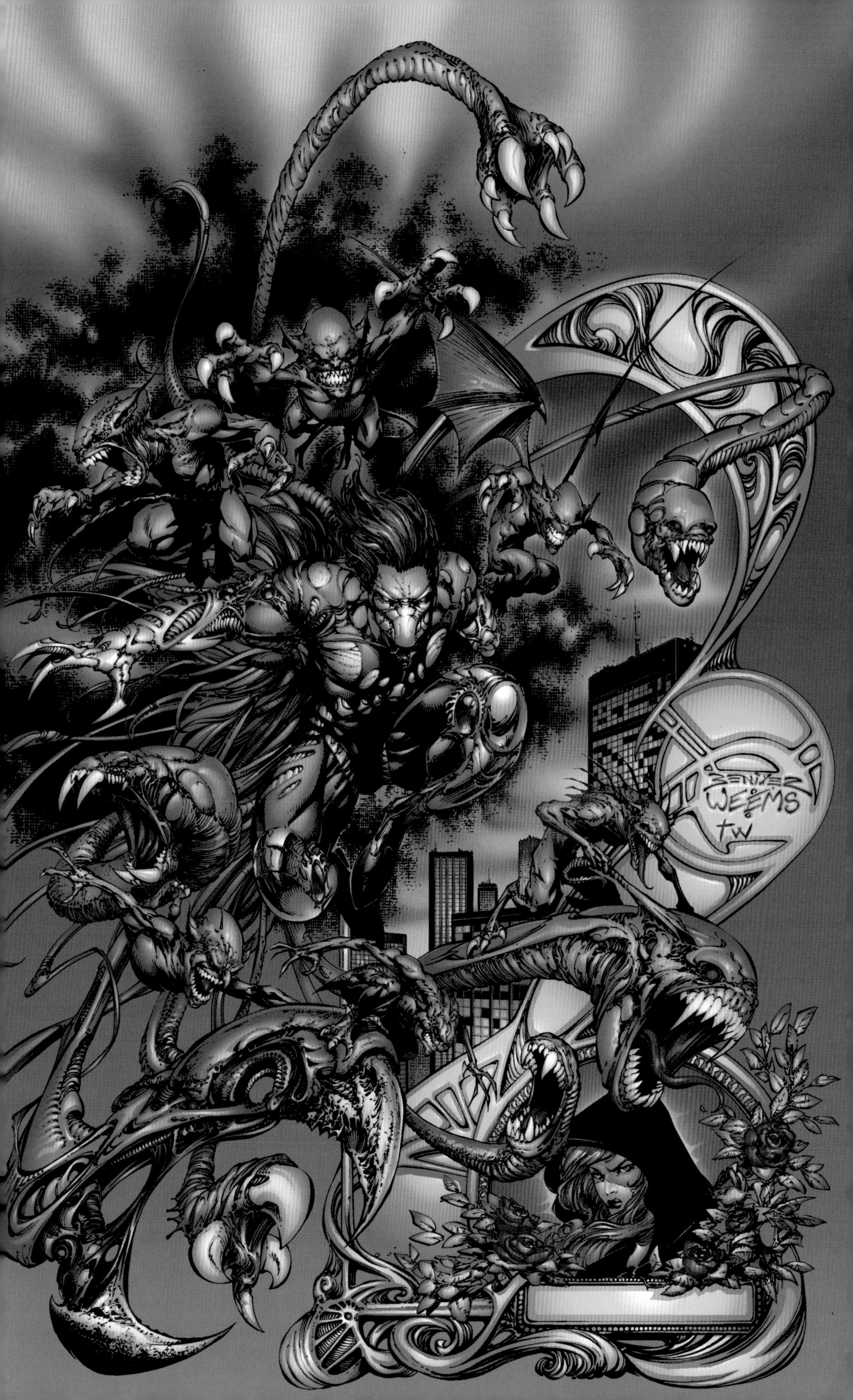
BENITEZ
WEEMS
tw

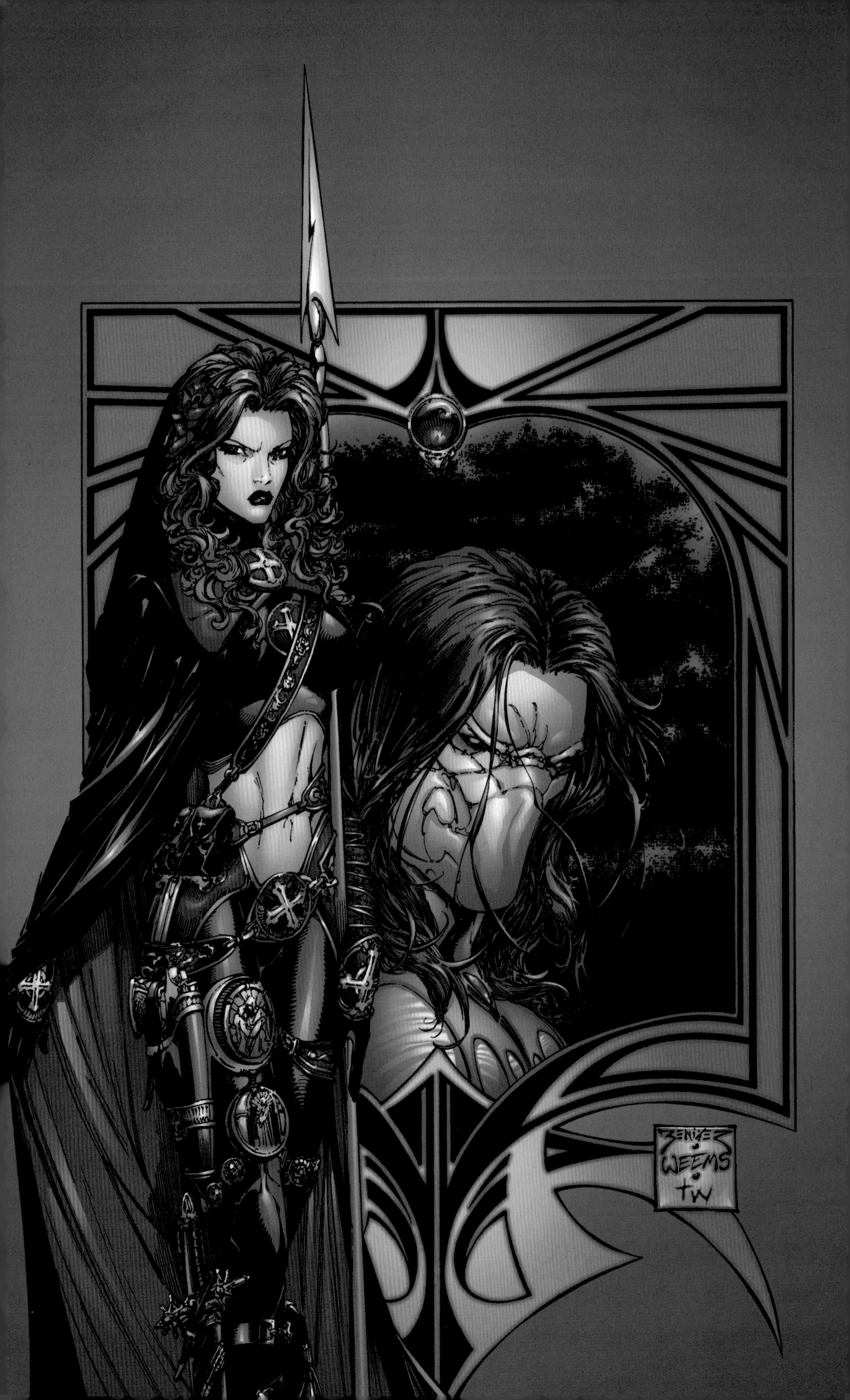
BENITEZ
WEEMS
TW

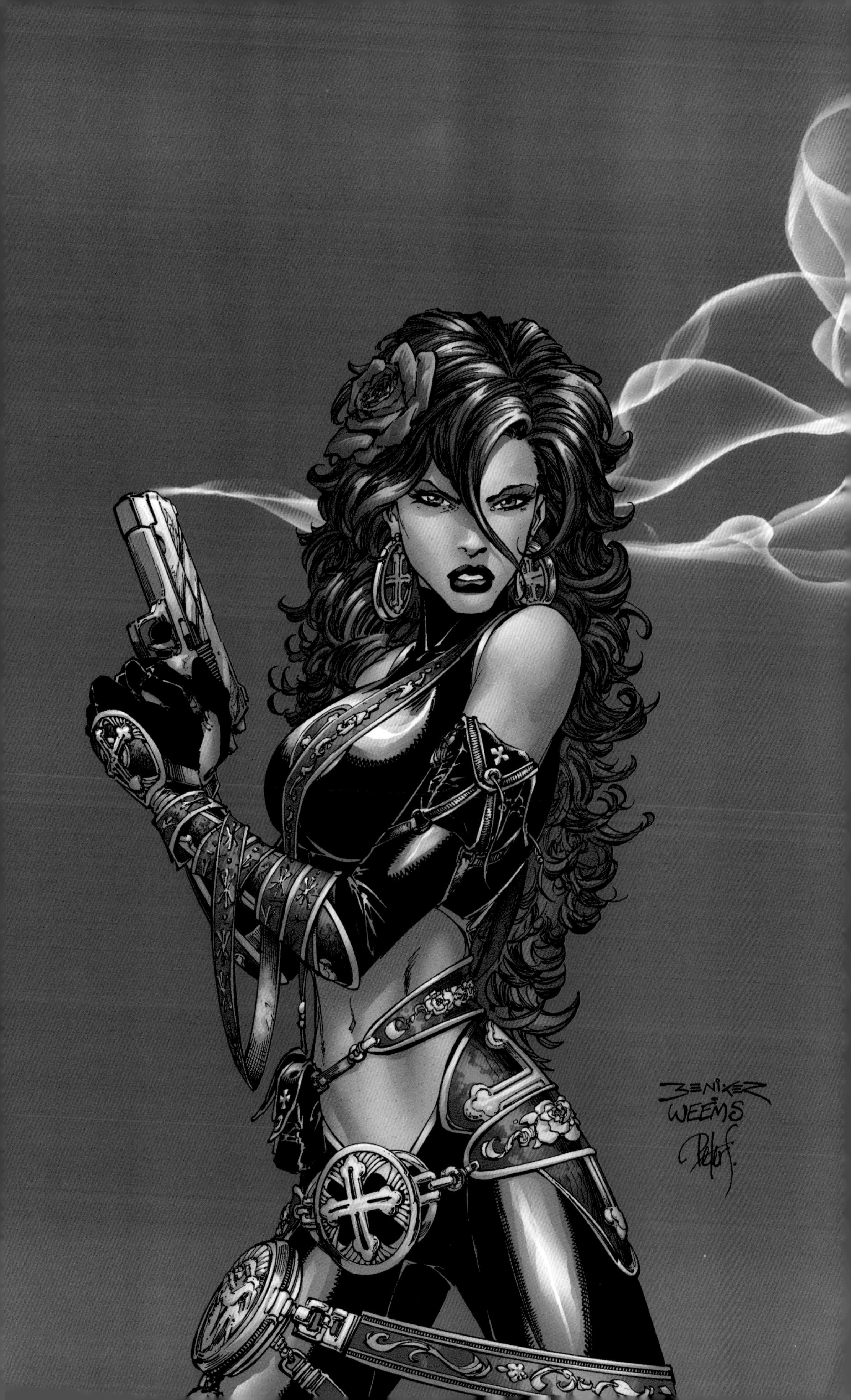
BENITEZ
WEEMS

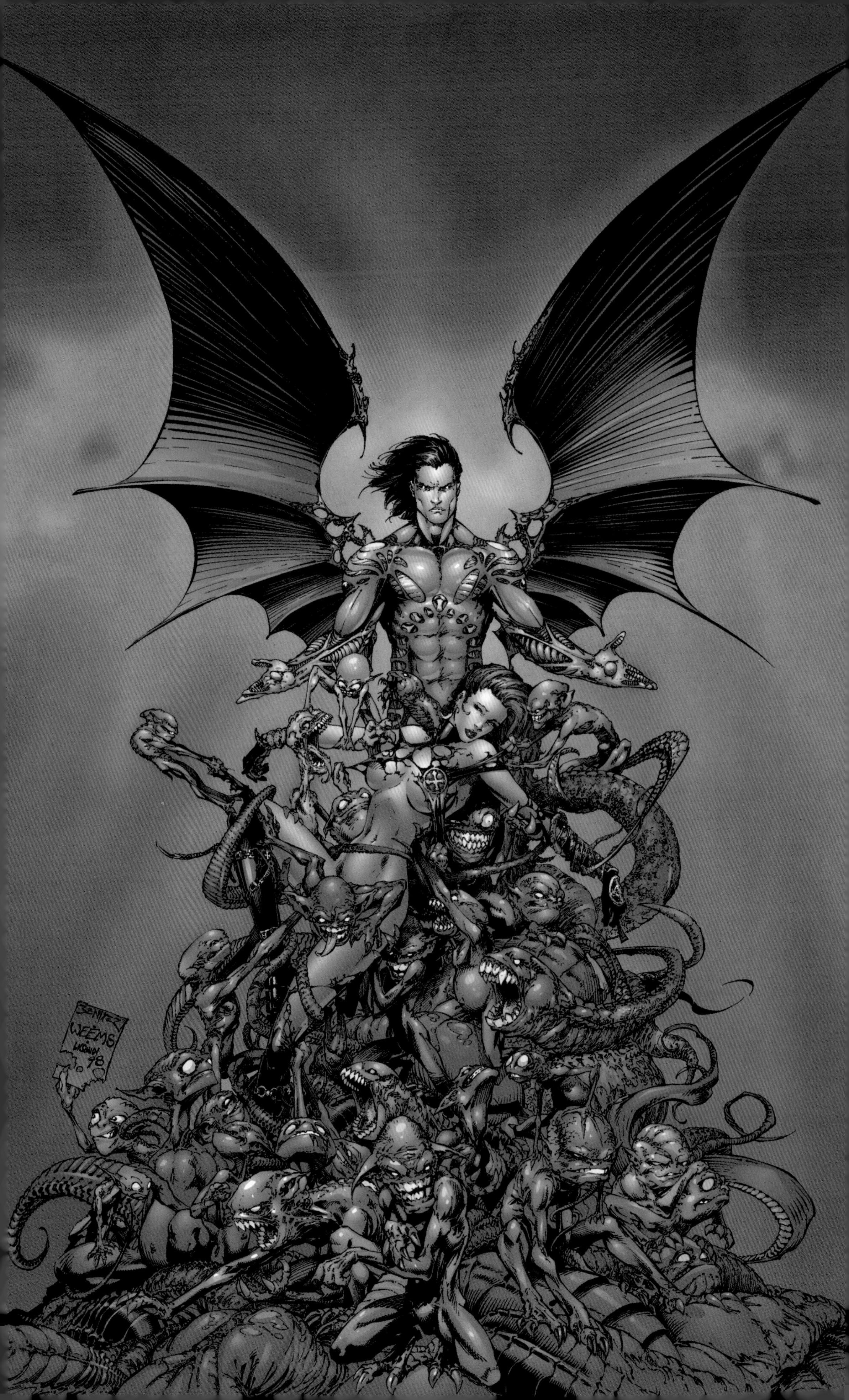
BENITEZ
WEEMS

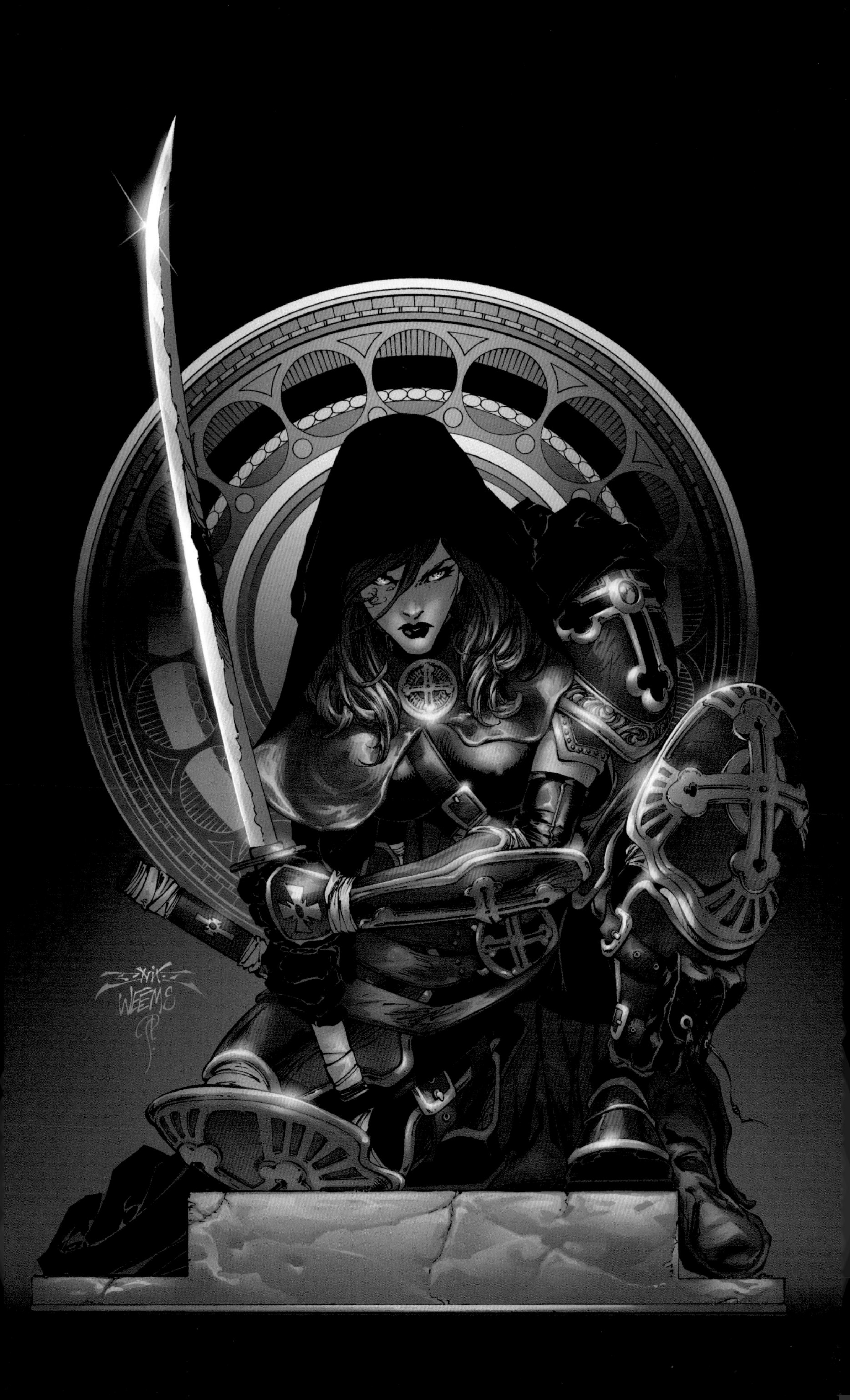
WEEMS

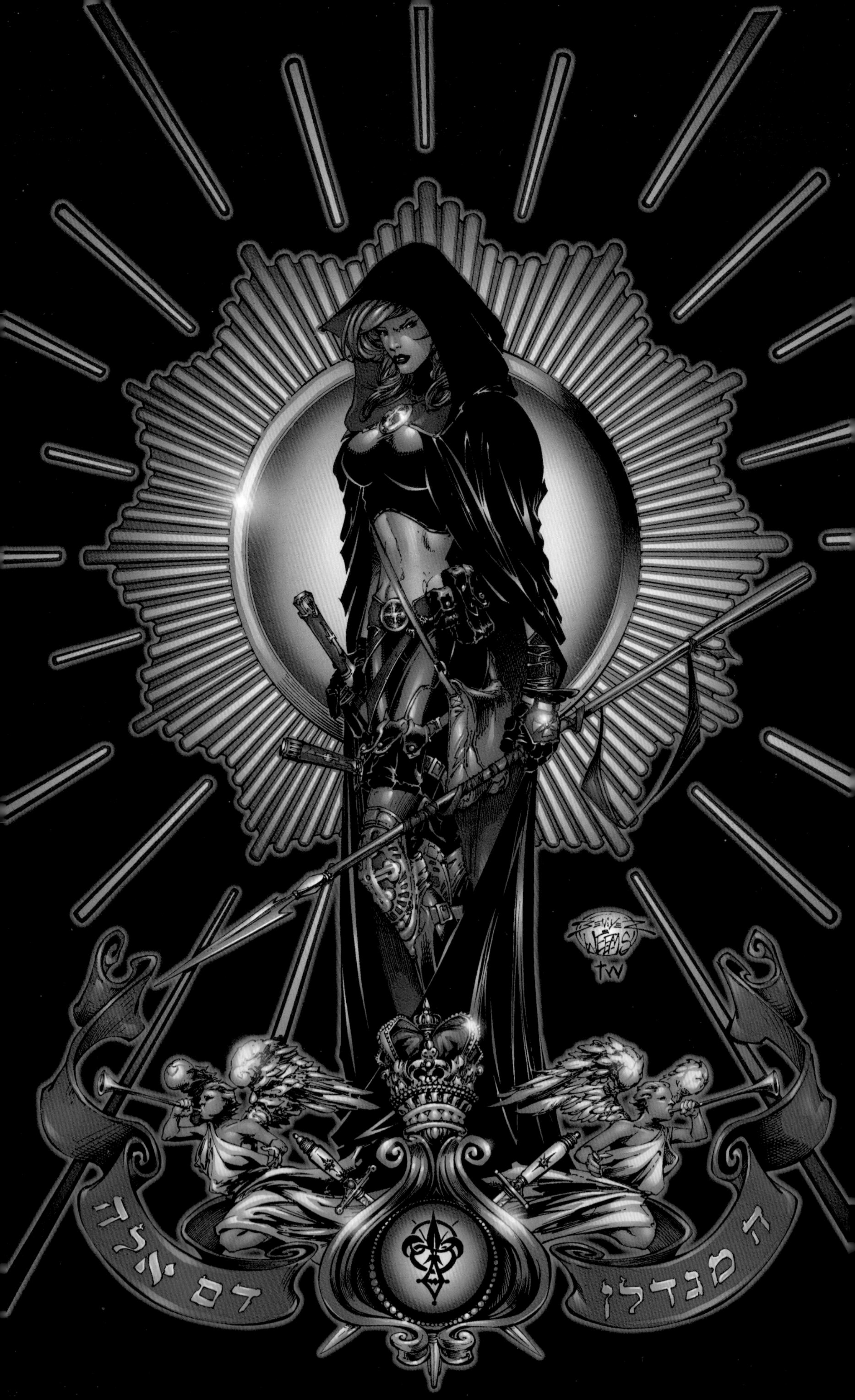
דם יאלה
ה מגדלן

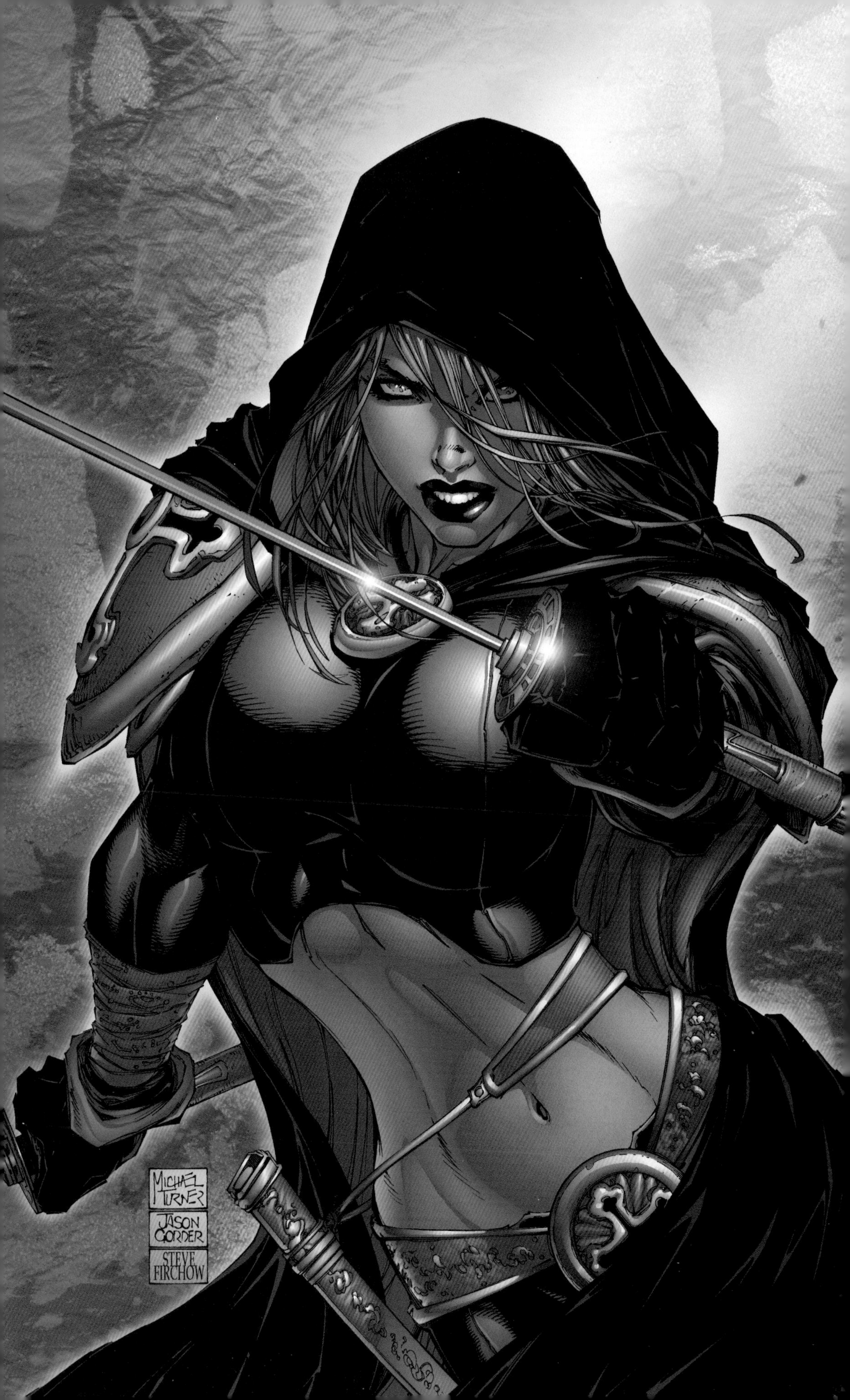
MICHAEL TURNER
JASON GORDER
STEVE FIRCHOW

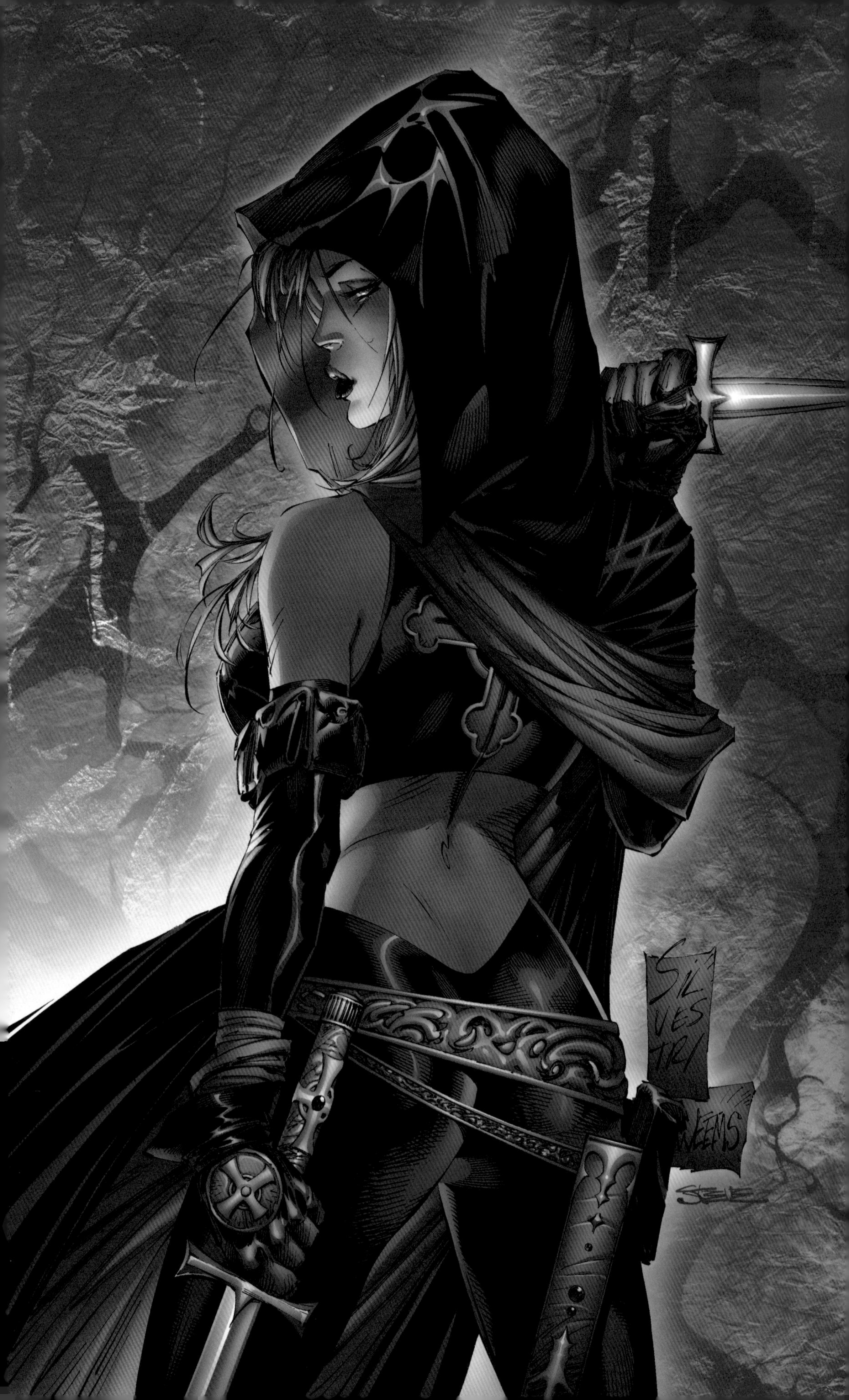
SIL VES TRI

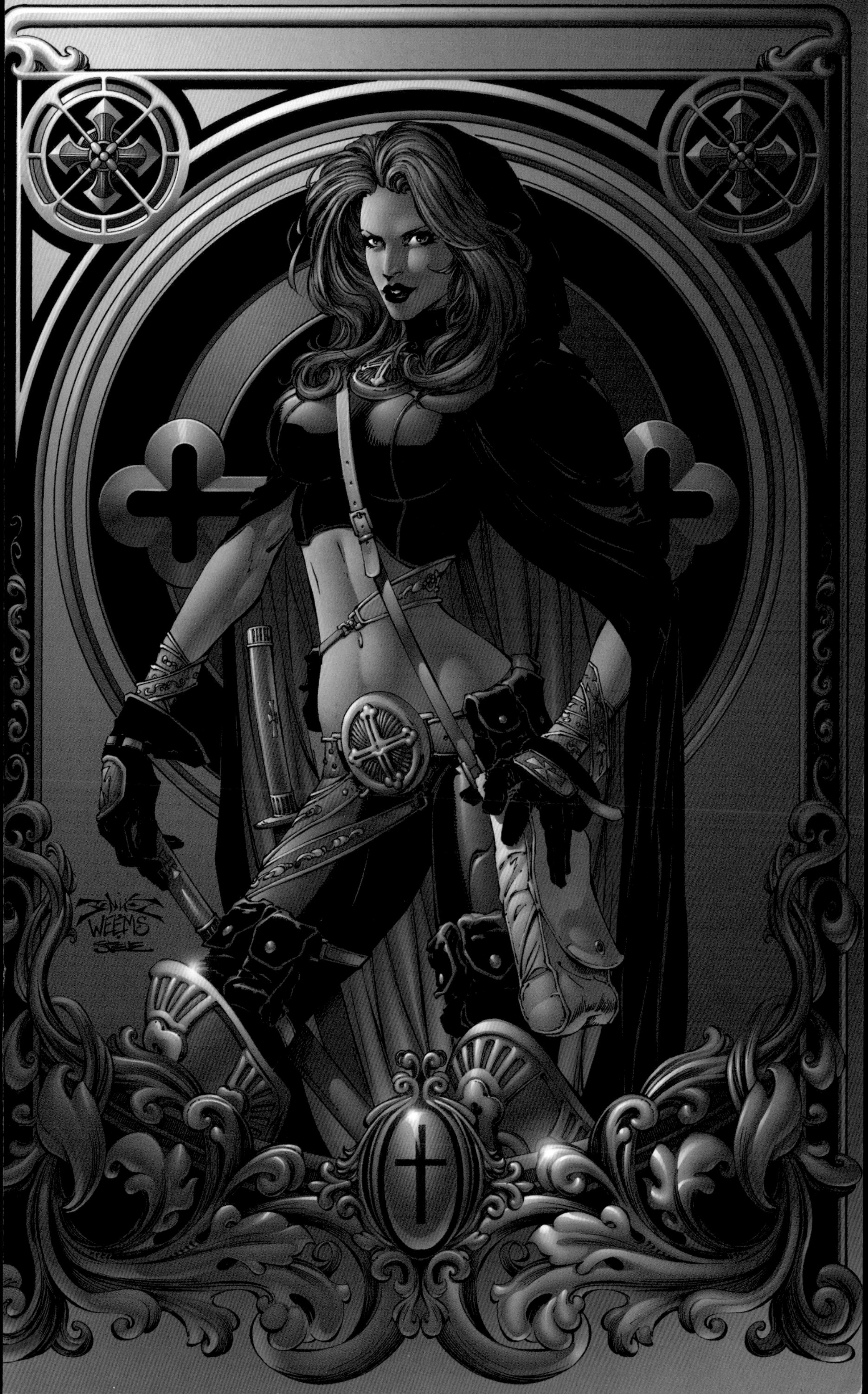
WEEMS

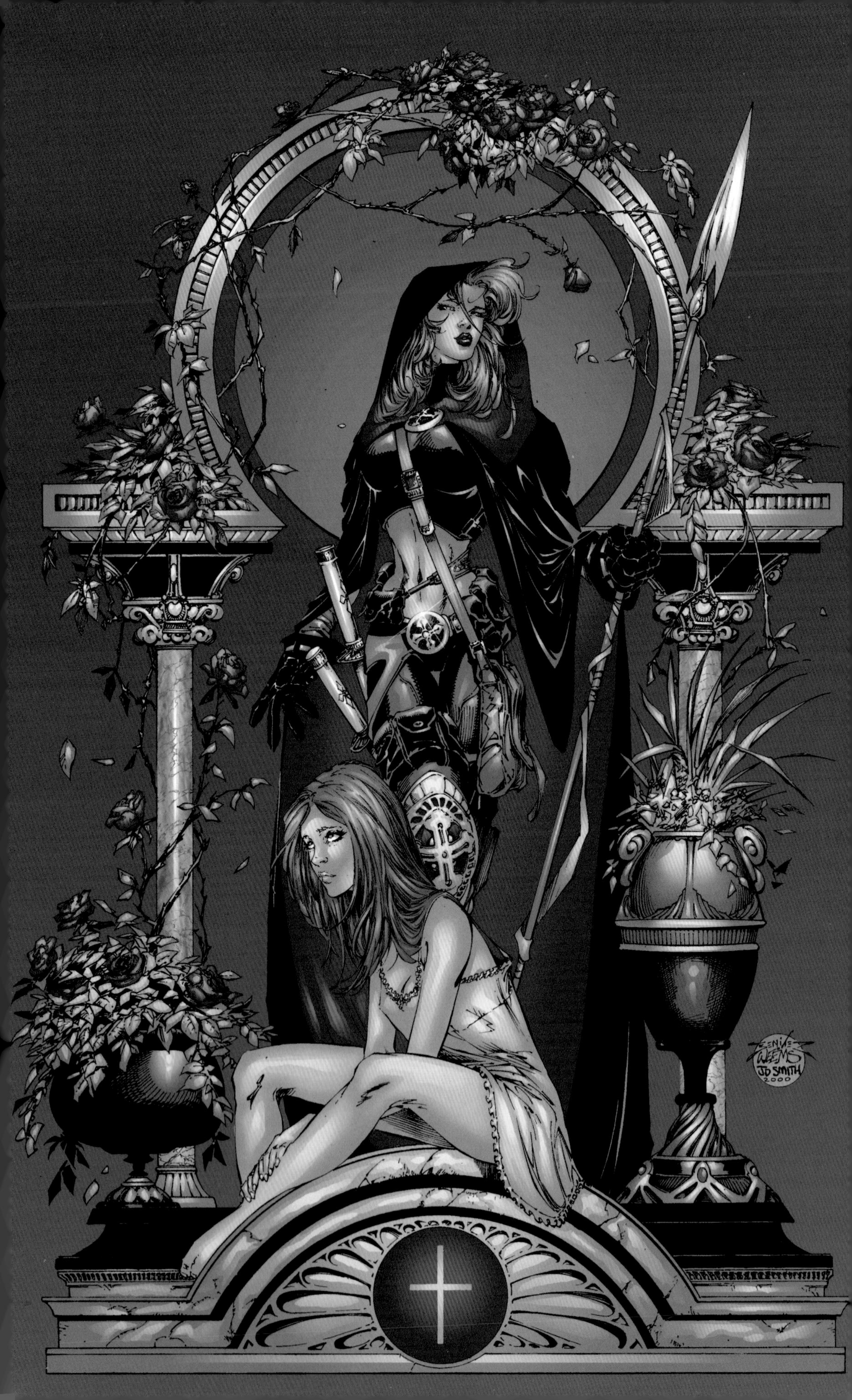
WEEMS
JD SMITH
2000

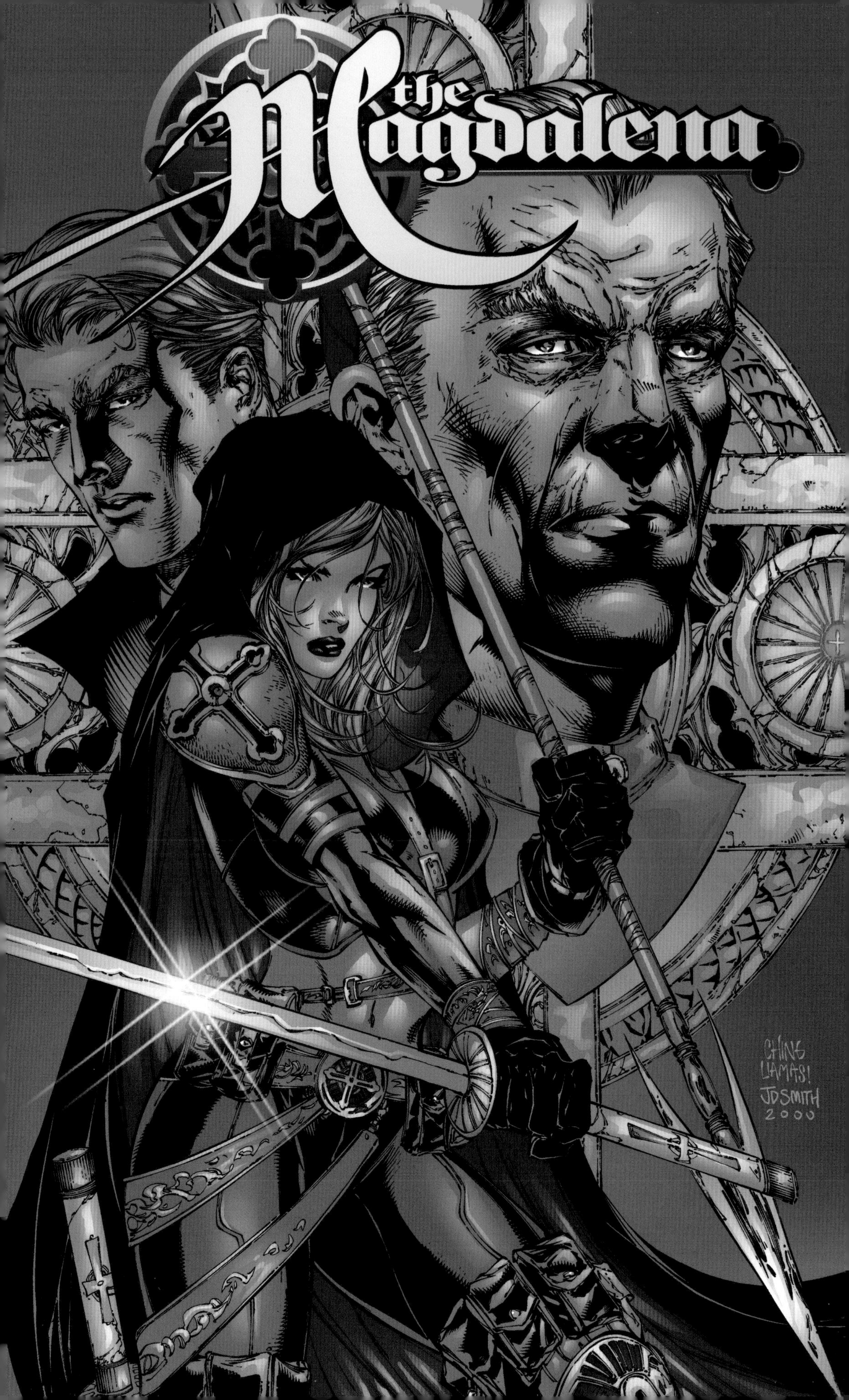
the Magdalena
CHING
LLAMAS!
JD SMITH
2000

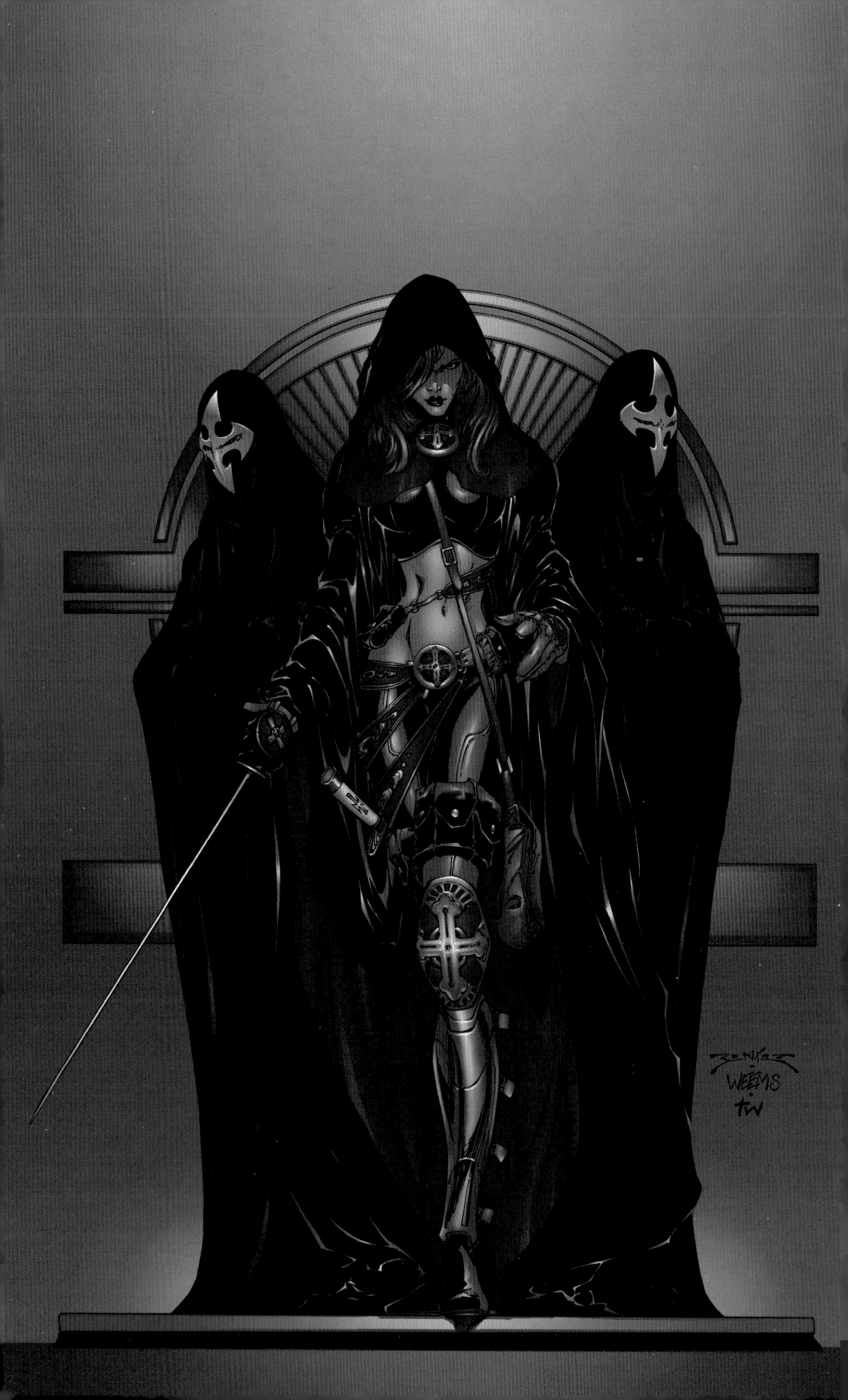
WEEMS
tw

Jump into the Top Cow Universe with The Darkness!

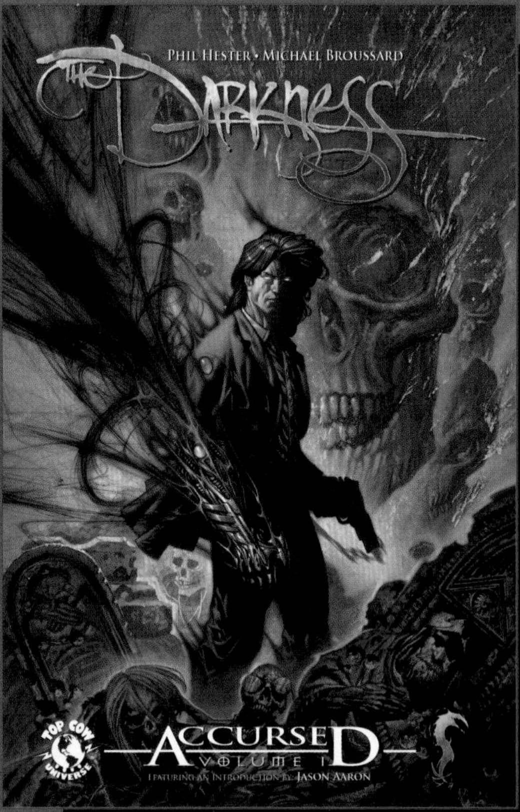

PHIL HESTER • MICHAEL BROUSSARD
THE DARKNESS
TOP COW UNIVERSE
ACCURSED
VOLUME I
FEATURING AN INTRODUCTION BY JASON AARON

The Darkness
Accursed vol.1

written by:
Phil Hester

pencils by:
Michael Broussard

Mafia hitman Jackie Estacado was both blessed and cursed on his 21st birthday when he became the bearer of The Darkness, an elemental force that allows those who wield it access to an otherwordly dimension and control over the demons who dwell there. Forces for good in the world rise up to face Jackie and the evil his gift represents, but there is one small problem. In this story...they are the bad guys.

Now's your chance to read "Empire," the first storyline by the new creative team of **Phil Hester** (*Firebreather, Green Arrow*) and **Michael Broussard** (*Unholy Union*) that marked the shocking return of *The Darkness* to the Top Cow Universe!

Book Market Edtion
(ISBN: 978-1-58240-958-0) $9.99

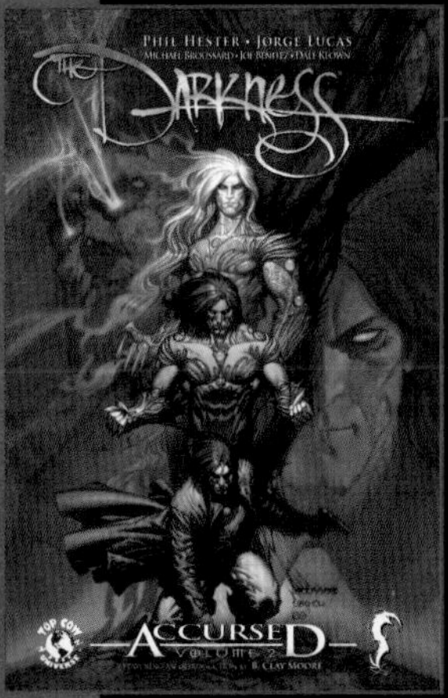

PHIL HESTER • JORGE LUCAS
MICHAEL BROUSSARD • JOE BENITEZ • DALE KEOWN
THE DARKNESS
ACCURSED

The Darkness
Accursed vol.2

written by: Phil Hester

pencils by: Jorge Lucas, Michael Broussard, Joe Benitez, Dale Keown and more!

Collects *The Darkness* volume 3 #7-10 and the double-sized *The Darkness* #75 (issue #11 before the Legacy Numbering took effect), plus a cover gallery and behind-the-scenes extras!

(ISBN: 978-1-58240-044-4) $9.99

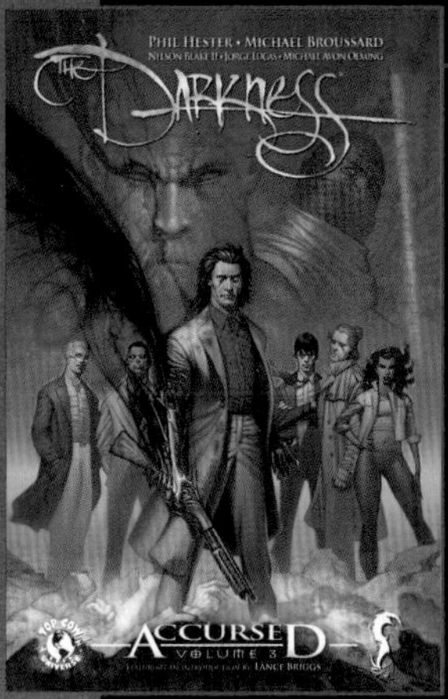

PHIL HESTER • MICHAEL BROUSSARD
THE DARKNESS
ACCURSED

The Darkness
Accursed vol.3

written by: Phil Hester

pencils by: Michael Broussard, Jorge Lucas, Nelson Blake II and Michael Avon Oeming.

Collects issues #76-79 plus the stand alone Tales of The Darkness story entitled "Lodbrok's Hand." Features art by regular series artist Michael Broussard (*Unholy Union, Artifacts*), Nelson Blake II (*Magdalena, Broken Trinity: Witchblade*), Jorge Lucas (*Broken Trinity: Aftermath, Wolverine*), and Michael Avon Oeming (*Mice Templar, Powers*).

(ISBN: 978-1-58240-100-7) $12.99

Ready for more? Learn more about the Top Cow Universe with *Witchblade!*

Witchblade
volume 1 - volume 8

written by:
Ron Marz
art by:
Mike Choi, Stephen Sadowski,
Keu Cha, Chris Bachalo,
Stjepan Sejic and more!

Get in on the ground floor of Top Cow's flagship title with these affordable trade paperback collections from Ron Marz's series-redefining run on Witchblade! Each volume collects a key story arc in the continuing adventures of Sara Pezzini and the Witchblade, culminating in the epic 'War of the Witchblades' storyline!

Book Market Edition, **volume 1**
collects issues #80-#85
(ISBN: 978-1-58240-906-1) $9.99

volume 2
collects issues #86-#92
(ISBN: 978-1-58240-886-6)
U.S.D. $14.99

volume 3
collects issues #93-#100
(ISBN: 978-1-58240-887-3)
U.S.D. $14.99

volume 4
collects issues #101-109
(ISBN: 978-1-58240-898-9)
U.S.D. $17.99

volume 5
collects issues #110-115
First Born issues #1-
(ISBN: 978-1-58240-899-6
U.S.D. $17.99

volume 6
collects issues #116-#120
(ISBN: 978-1-60706-041-3)
U.S.D. $14.99

volume 7
collects issues #121-#124 &
Witchblade Annual #1
(ISBN: 978-1-60706-058-1)
U.S.D. $14.99

volume 8
collects issues #125-#130
(ISBN: 978-1-60706-102-1)
U.S.D. $14.99